GHOST

The Rick Watkinson Story

TRISH FABER & JOHN COVENTRY

Wonder Voice Press
ISBN-13: 978-0-9877188-4-6

"I died inside at that moment.
I remember telling myself
'I am dead inside...I am a ghost'.
A sudden switch flipped, and I literally felt an empty coolness
inside my soul that brought comfort through absence.
It didn't take long over the next year to die
inside completely and 'train' myself not to feel.
I just stayed focused on the pain
and hatred spurned from that day, and reminded myself every time
that something happened that I should have feelings for that I couldn't...

Soon, I didn't even have to think about it
– it became completely natural for me to stay 'shut off'
and not feel anything about anything period.
I knew I hated my father for leaving and betraying us.
I hated God for letting it happen.
I hated the world for being so fucked up and cruel.
I knew the hate was there but I couldn't feel it.
All that was left was an utter apathy for everything in life.

Thus, Ghost was born."
-Rick Watkinson-

FORWARD

From Rick

My deepest thanks to my loving wife Brenda, whose loyalty and dedication made this work possible. This amazing woman has stood by my side for over two decades and made me the man I am today.

Also to John Coventry and Trish Faber – whose patience and compassion for me knew no bounds. My debt of gratitude for ensuring my story became known is truly everlasting.

And with deepest regrets to Amy. I'm sorry I let you down.

From Trish

I am deeply grateful to John Coventry for sending this project my way, and asking if I would like to write the true story of Rick Watkinson. It has been a long but incredibly wonderful journey. I am also deeply grateful to Rick for being so honest and forthright in his letters and our correspondence. I asked him to tell me everything, and he did – he opened his heart, and let it spill onto the pages of his handwritten letters, which made my job that much easier. I hope this process has given him the release and the peace he needs and deserves.

When writing this book, I did my best not to approach the story with any preconceived notions or opinions of Rick, or what he had done. He killed two people, those are the facts, and I recognized the horror of that. But I also realized that there had to be something more, there had to be reasons and mitigating factors for his actions. I'm a firm believer that children are not born with hate, are not born with vengeance, and are not born to kill. Something has to happen to set them on this course. Something had to happen to young Rick Watkinson.

And it did. Many, many things to be exact. My job was to tell that story. My job was to try and convey the 'why' behind his actions. I hope that I have, and I hope that after reading his story, we can all have a little more empathy for those children who face abuse of any kind, even if it's just once. That we, as a society, find a voice to speak up, and step in when we see a child in trouble, a child that's falling and can't seem to help themselves up. We must be the ones to help them up. Empower them. Show them that life and people don't have to be that way. Make a difference. Don't be afraid to be that person. Never be afraid to be that person.

Rick Watkinson is not a horrible person. He did a horrible thing for certain, and he will pay for that action for the rest of his life. All I ask is that you read his story with an open mind. Put yourself in his shoes and take a few steps. You probably won't like it. You'll probably feel uncomfortable. And you should.

We are all so good at judging the actions of others. Why? Because it's easy, judging is easier than actually sitting down and looking at the facts or the circumstances.

I am tremendously thankful for my family, my siblings, and friends, especially in a journey this long and emotional. They have always been nothing but supportive of me in my writing and creative pursuits, and I don't think they know how grateful I am for that – for always just letting me be me. Special thanks to my father, who always has the patience and love to put up with me, and to my sister, who is my best friend, my sounding board, and everything in between. You know what you mean to me. My readers for taking on this monumental task and giving honest feedback, and to "The Hurricane Girls" for always, well just being "The Hurricane Girls" and being there. I love you all!

And to my mom, I am forever grateful for the love and the life you instilled in me. For the wondrous spirit and imagination. Your stamp is all over me. I love you and miss you everyday. PS - sorry about all the swear words…

XI. Out

Pillars of light hold our dream on high, rising into the heavens from the sky,
Nothing but darkness holds me, sinking into the sadness of eternity.
I cry out for a healing rain, an escape from my everlasting pain
I hear an answer very far away, a soothing voice I hear say,

No way out
From the pain that covers you
No way out
From the Darkness into the blue
No way out
From under the blood red rain
No way out
From your everlasting pain

The storm that covers you will never die, because evil never listens to the cry
Your young life floats on a restless sea, never giving in to your hopes and dreams.
You cry out for a healing rain, trying to escape your everlasting pain
You hear an answer not too far away, the clouds race by as the thunder proclaims

No way out
From the pain that covers you
No way out
From the Darkness into the blue
No way out
From under the blood red rain
No way out
From your everlasting pain

-Rick Watkinson-
Song Lyrics 1993

CHAPTER ONE

Grabbing both his lock blades and Leatherman tool, the boy stuffed a handful of ammunition in his coat pocket before running back upstairs to the entryway. He didn't look at the carnage. He didn't feel their pain. He couldn't. He had nothing left. He was empty, a shell of a person, shattered and spent, just like the used shells that now littered the house he had once called home. The blast of frigid Alaskan air choked his lungs as he flew out the front door and tore down the driveway, his steel-toe boots crunching the hard-packed snow. He hadn't even thought to grab his gloves or a beanie for his head, and the thin winter jacket was no match for the plummeting November night. It didn't matter. He couldn't feel the cold anyway. Adrenalin surged through every ounce of his body, pushing him to run, to get the hell out of there as fast as he could. Man versus man. Man versus nature. Man versus himself. The first battle won, the second battle looming, and the third battle lingering.

With all trace of realistic reasoning abandoned, Rick squeezed the barrel of the Ruger .22 semi-automatic Long rifle and took off running north up Doggie Avenue. Even in the extreme cold, the barrel still felt slightly warm, still excited from the furious frenzy only moments before. His instincts sent him right on Shebanof Ave and up toward the Upper O'Malley Trail Head. The trail was off the road and shielded by a hill and some wooded shrubs, providing a semblance of cover from the police lights and sirens. The air was quiet for the moment, but he knew they would be coming.

Rick paused at the top of the hill, letting his pounding chest rest a beat. A right would take him into the deeply forested area towards Flattop Mountain and the lakes between Ptarmagin Peaks, where without shelter and supplies, he might escape capture for the time being, but would probably freeze to death in the mountains. A left would steer him back towards Anchorage, out-skirting around the back of Hillside East. He figured it was easier to get lost and hide in a highly populated area, so he took the left and set off down the trail. As the trail traversed the rising topography, Rick had a full view of Hillside, and the web of police cars screaming toward the neighbourhood. He crouched low in the snow and watched the myriad of flashing lights break the blackness of the still November night; all the while, his hands skillfully and mechanically looping his belt through the lock-blade cases and Leatherman pouch. Taking one last look at the commotion below, Rick picked the rifle up from the snowy ground and settled into a jog. He had no idea where he was going or how he was going to get there – he just knew he had to keep moving and stay off the roads.

There had never been a plan, despite what people would say. The day just happened. The pent up anger, hurt, and betrayal exploded, and it was more than his sixteen-year-old mind and heart could take, or even comprehend. Running through the minus ten-degree Fahrenheit wind chill, Rick still hadn't acknowledged exactly what he had done. He was in full survival mode, operating purely on animalistic instinct and adrenaline, his mind detached, his emotions locked in a windowless box. He kept his hands firmly around the wooden rifle-stock and maintained a good pace, following the trail as it snaked behind the upper-class neighbourhood he had come to loathe.

Keeping to the bike and power-line trails, Rick kept running; a void travelling through time and space, with few thoughts. He concentrated solely on the pounding of his heart, and the burning in his lungs, as the frigid air ripped down his internal passages. He had yet to utter a word, not even to himself, his voice silenced by the shock of his own horrific deeds. He could end it all, right then and there. He had a gun and a pocket full of ammunition. It would be easy to turn the gun on himself. One shot and all the misery of his life would be over. Done. Over. No more problems. It would be that simple. But he'd once made a promise to someone very special, and to break that promise would be a betrayal. And in his short life, Rick had had enough of betrayals. He would not take the easy way out.

He didn't break stride until he was above the Ski Area and could see the large spot-lights that usually illuminated Hillside Park. At 12:45 in the morning the park was dark. So still. Rick didn't trust the stillness or the darkness. Staying hidden in the icicle-laden woods, he carefully and quietly made his way past the Ski Office and the Ski Rental building, watching intently for any sign of movement. He couldn't remember whether the ski hill had dogs, but he knew with certainty they had guns. This was Alaska – everybody had guns. The last thing Rick needed was to have someone report someone 'sneaking' around the park. It wouldn't be too difficult for the police to figure out who was doing the sneaking.

Keeping out of sight, he crept along the west side of the access road until he finally caught a glimpse of Abbott Road. With the thick snow covered evergreens acting as cover, Rick felt somewhat safe from detection, although every set of headlights booming down Abbot Road sent him sprawling to the ground, his hand deftly on the trigger, instinctively ready to defend. The cold meant nothing. The numbness in his brain had spread throughout his entire body. He moved only because his adrenaline pushed, like an out of control train storming wildly through his veins. He had no strength to stop it. He went where it took him.

Conscience thought had yet to break free from its locked box. In a stupor and in a fog, he pressed on down the trail.

The snow-covered path led west away from Abbott Road and skirted the outer boundaries of Service High School. Rick somehow felt drawn to the school grounds; maybe since it had been the only place he felt he'd really ever fit in while in Alaska. Familiarity led him from the safety of the woods to the school's track, which he inexplicably crossed, right out in the open, on route to the parking lot. Elevated some twelve to fifteen inches feet than the track, Rick crept up the slight embankment, keeping his head below the guard rail, re-establishing his cover. Out of nowhere, Trooper Mike Marrs tore around the corner, ripping through the parking lot in his unmarked car. Safe behind the cover of the guard rail, Rick froze, his hand firmly gripping the rifle, his brown eyes never shifting focus from the trooper. Slowly, he raised the rifle to his shoulder and sighted-in the passenger side window with the gun scope. The dark night and the tinted windows blurred any type of distinctive picture. As he led the car in his sights, he processed the circumstances with lightning speed. Did the trooper see him? Had the ski resort reported a disturbance? Where was the trooper headed? Rick continued to watch the car from the gun-sight, as it turned another corner and sped back towards the road. He lowered the gun from his shoulder and lay down on the embankment. He could have fired a shot at the trooper but he didn't. It was the first rational decision he'd made all night.

Sure that Trooper Marrs was long gone, Rick headed back down towards the northwest corner of the track where a short trail led into his best friend's neighbourhood. Realizing that walking through a residential area in the middle of the night with a long-rifle in his hand was probably not the best idea, he found a large tree with low-lying branches near the end of the trail, and half buried, half camouflaged the rifle with pine branches, dirt and needles. There was no emotional attachment to the weapon. No feelings of relief that he no longer had to carry around the burden, or a sense of burying his sins along with the gun. His head wasn't there yet. Burying the gun was practical. Nothing more, nothing less.

Burrowing his freezing hands deep into the pockets of his jacket, he left the cover of the woods and ventured into the Abbott Loop neighbourhood like he done so many times in the last few months while walking his girlfriend home from school. Taking a right on Sahalee Drive, he walked slowly down the road to where it met Meridian. Still without a plan, the teenager was just sticking to what was familiar. He took another right on Jupiter, and thought for a moment about going to see his best friend Kristy, or maybe even stealing a car; but stolen cars get reported quickly, and he decided he was better off under the power of his own two feet. This boy wandering aimlessly through the neighbourhood was not the

Rick Watkinson that everyone knew. That Rick was methodical in his actions, someone who always had a well-thought out plan, weighing the pros and cons of his actions. Shock has a funny way of taking control of the senses.

A brief right on Elmore Road brought him to East 84th, where he immediately turned left. It was only about three miles from the high school to Crystal's house, less if you took the trails and short-cuts, and Rick covered the distance easily. He stood at the back of her house and paused, having no real idea what to do. Normally, he would climb up the side of the house and onto the roof that was level with her second story bedroom window. But after the events of this evening, normal was a distant memory. Did he wake her and tell her what happened? Should he even involve her? He had no idea what even possessed him go to her house in the first place. What was he thinking? Rick stood on the ground and stared at the window. Slowly, he turned and walked away. No point in involving anyone else in his mess of trouble. Besides, he was Ghost – and he would survive alone, or die alone.

Death wouldn't be far off if he didn't find some way to get warm. His ice cube toes were dead against the metal of his steel toed boots, his socks long since losing their ability to keep in any warmth. His fingers even worse. He tried to rub his hands together to create any sort of friction, but his fingers barely moved. All the surface capillaries on his hands were constricted, sending the blood coursing away from his skin and extremities, and deeper into his body, trying desperately to protect his vital organs. That's how hypothermia begins. Rick was already a few stages in. The sweat from his constant jogging had dampened his cotton shirt, and the wetness on his skin was dispelling any extra heat he had in his wiry teenage body. His core temperature dropping fast, he had to find shelter.

The residential side-roads of Crystal's neighbourhood brought him all the way to the corner of Abbott and Lake Otis Parkway, without seeing a soul. Crossing the intersection would be a challenge. Staying as hidden as possible in the dark, he waited and listened. One car, two cars. Silence. Ignoring the throbbing in his aching feet, he shot off across the road and into the parking lot of the Abbott Loop Community Church. Finding an alcove on the north-east side of the building, he ducked in and leaned against the wall, giving him a reprieve from the biting wind, which was better than nothing. With his adrenaline spent, fatigue quickly overtook his exhausted body, forcing his eyelids closed, and sending him into a deep sleep.

When he awoke two hours later, he hadn't even remembered falling asleep. The hours of not moving had drained every bit of heat he'd generated from running, and he could no longer feel his toes or his fingers. His whole body felt like it was frozen in his veins – like someone could take an ice chisel and shatter him with a few whacks. But while his body was frozen, his mind had thawed.

"What have I done?"

The images of the previous day came streaming back as if someone had hit the 'replay' button on a video. The cafeteria. His father stomping in red faced and pissed. Pulling him out of ROTC, the only place he finally felt he belonged and had a home. Another betrayal. Then home. All the yelling. The fucking yelling between his father and Rosemary. About him. Always about him. His father throwing him out in the Alaskan winter without even money for a ticket back to Oregon. Him choosing HER over him. Again. Just like when he was a ten-year-old boy. He had spent six full years hating his father for destroying his family, abandoning them, and then trying to have some say over his life. He had forfeited that right when he left.

And now six years later, his father was making the same choice again. Rick never wanted to move to Alaska with him. His father had forced that on him 'for his own good' – the same line he'd used the day he left. Bastard. Fucking bastard. He had taken him away from everything, ruined his life, and forced him to forge a new one. But none of that mattered to his father. He chose her. The spineless bastard chose her. Again. Rick was confused. He couldn't understand. And he hated his father for what he had done. Lying there on his bed. Just thinking. Just listening. Wanting it all to stop. For once and for all, wanting the pain to go away. Needing silence.

Then the dam broke. He couldn't control it, couldn't even really think or move. The years of hatred, pain, loss, depression, agony, apathy – all bottled up, swept under a rug. All the feelings of betrayal washed over him like glacier water, chilling him to the bone. This was the very reason he had 'died' six years ago; a family destroyed, loved ones abandoned, a son betrayed. It was why he had gone Ghost in the first place. He couldn't take the pain then. It was easier to 'die' and act like he didn't feel at all. Except the pain was still there; buried deep in a box he didn't even know existed. He had lied to himself about being 'dead' to his feelings. The emotions were all still there. Building. Waiting. Every friend he had lost, every defeat, every sorrow, every unfilled desire; he had trained himself as Ghost to feel nothing. None of it mattered. He had talked himself into believing that his emotions didn't exist. That he couldn't feel. But there, in that moment, lying on his bed listening to the incessant yelling, absorbing the second betrayal, his mind crazy with emotion, he couldn't deny the crashing waves of pain and heartache that exploded through his body. He was lost. Broken. Drowning. The tempest inside had completely taken control, and Ghost was replaced by a seething frenzy of feelings and memories.

He dimly remembered hearing the side door to the garage open and close, and the roar of a cold engine coming to life. He was going after her, leaving his crushed and shattered son alone, at a time when he needed the comfort and reassurance of a father; at a time when a son was screaming for an explanation, screaming for even just the slightest hint of love. Rick lay on the bed for another ten minutes or so, overwhelmed by memories and emotions, every minute past, a countdown to that moment when the soul is consumed, and all rational thought or consciousness is abandoned.

He suddenly found himself walking up the stairs and heading to his father and his step-mother's bedroom. He knew there were three guns in the house; a Ruger .22 Long-rifle, a small .22 Ruger pistol and a .38 caliber pistol. He told himself that he didn't want anyone to get hurt, scared that if things went too far between his father and Rosemary, they could use the guns on each other – or even him. Finding the long-rifle standing in its usual spot in the corner of the closet, he took it and the small carton of ammunition next to the box that contained the pistol, setting both on the floor. He took the pistol out of the box and removed both clips, checking to make sure there wasn't a round in the chamber. Removing all the clips and ammunition from the pistol served two purposes. If someone did grab it and try to use it, they couldn't. Second, if his father realized that it was unloaded, and the clips were missing, it would mean that he had gotten the pistol down, and more than likely had intended to use it on someone that night. Why else would he check?

He searched the closet for the .38 but it was nowhere to be found. Was it in the bathroom? The cupboards built into their bed? The garage? Rick had no idea where the .38 was but he knew if either his father or Rosemary came home and found him walking down the stairs with a rifle, hell would break loose. He ran back down the stairs to his bedroom, hoping that the .38 wasn't somewhere easily accessible. Without even checking to see if the gun was loaded or a round was chambered, Rick stuffed the long-rifle under the framework of his bed and emptied the box of ammunition in the bottom drawer of his nightstand. Laying back down on his bed, his troubled mind was overwhelmed. He had no idea where he'd be tomorrow. His father had told him to be gone by the morning, but where the hell was he supposed to go? All Rick knew was that Ghost couldn't save him now. The 'switch' had been thrown wide-open and he had no hope of shutting it off like he usually could.

Around 8:30 the ripping of tires up the driveway and into the garage told Rick that his father and step-mother had returned. The minute the car doors slammed shut, the arguing continued.

"What the fuck are they still arguing about," thought Rick. "He chose her, I have to leave, so what is the fucking problem?"

Still raging on full steam, the intensity of the screaming match hadn't changed from the moment Rosemary had stormed out the house and into her car a little earlier.

"Just shut the fuck up. Seriously. Shut the fuck up."

The actual words they were saying didn't even register with Rick anymore. It was like they were being spoken underwater or the soundtrack had gotten stuck on slow motion. The pressure in his head pounded against his skull, threatening to explode at any moment. The feeling reminded him of looking past the 'Veil'. There was a fluidity that permeated everything; a blurring of reality where one couldn't really tell where the world of spirits and demons stopped and the 'real' world began. The shadows, the shapes, the vile energy clinging to everything – like swimming through a dark ethereal matter that possessed a restrictive quality but no substance. And now this dark seething matter broiled deep within his core, threatening to suffocate him from the inside out.

"STOP IT!"

It could have been the door slam, it could have been Rosemary's blaring sobs, it could have been the mention of his name, again – he didn't know – but somewhere in the midst of all the noise and commotion the spark flew and his psyche exploded. The rage over the betrayal, the infinite sorrow over being cast away, forced back, only to be cast away again, was too much. Dropping to the side of the bed with his head in his hands, he just wanted to grab the rifle and shoot them both. Do anything to just SHUT THEM UP! Instead of reaching for the gun, he reached for his notepad, tore out a sheet and began to write extremely slow and methodically:

Operation Anarchy.

To commence at 0100hrs

On overdrive, his chaotic mind was a blur. Writing steps to his plan, all the while imagining what he would do to his father. He didn't actually see himself murdering them in his vision, nor did he see the aftermath, or freedom, or happiness afterward. It was a self-induced outburst focused on his hatred and the destruction of his father. He was so fucking angry that no punishment or harm could be enough for his old man. He deserved every torture the Nine Hells could give him.

Rick had no idea what he hoped to accomplish by writing the note, except to maybe dispel some of the anger by writing out, instead of acting out his rage. In that moment, the boy didn't care who lived or died, including himself. Anything would be better than the uncontrollable frenzy of pain that had overcome his entire being. Folding up the note, he slid the paper between the components of his stereo system, set his alarm for one A.M., then lay back down on his bed, staring at the ceiling with grey, empty eyes. He was there, but he wasn't there. His mind wasn't right. He felt more like an observer to the experience, neither conscious of his physical actions or the wanderings in his brain – like there was no more room in his head for thoughts, and all he could do was watch.

Then it stopped. The yelling. The only thing that was able to distract his mind, stopped. Had they gone to bed? Was his father banished to the couch for the night? The sudden silence was deadly. Almost unbearable. Without anything else to listen to, the reverberation in his skull amplified, a constant and unending 'whoomp', 'whoomp', 'whoomp' equivalent to slow moving helicopter blades slicing through the air, sending long, painful vibrations racing through his body. Time had ceased to have any meaning; all he could feel was the numbing howl of pent-up emotions screaming in his ears. He tried to breathe, to somehow slow the building rage. He tried to intercept his thoughts with others. He tried to wedge his conscious mind back somewhere into the present. He couldn't. The crushing weight of his angst was too much for the experience of his sixteen-year-old mind. His head felt heavy. The pressure built. His vision blurred. The pressure built. His muscles tensed. The pressure built. The betrayal. The betrayals. Not again. Never again. Then, like a single steel cable, brittle and taught – he snapped.

At five minutes to twelve, he removed the rifle from under his bed. All rational thought disbanded, Rick could only watch himself go through the motions, powerless to stop the monster that had risen from his teenage soul. Everything had taken on the hue of rust; an orangish blue colour like the reflection of a burning sunset off a crystal clear lake. He had seen that colour before. Fear. Unknown. The night of the betrayal. Quietly, he walked up the stairs. The couch was empty and the guest bedroom door was open. Rick figured they were both together in the master bedroom. With the muzzle of the rifle pointing towards the floor, he approached the door without a sound. He stood there listening for almost a minute. Silence. Slowly and carefully, he turned the door knob. As the door cracked, a soft light spilled out onto the hallway. He had been wrong. His father lay still under the covers on his side of the bed as if he were sleeping, while Rosemary was still sitting up, awake, and reading by a book light. From a far corner of his mind, Rick could hear his brain screaming for him to just turn around and not open the door. Chaos. Anger. Hurt. Betrayal. Jezebel.

Then Rosemary shifted, sensing something was off. She climbed out of bed and took two steps forward. Rick swung the door open, bringing the gleam of the rifle into full view. The metal clicked as he racked the bolt to chamber a round.

"Oh God, Bob!"

Everything happened at once. As Robert Watkinson started to get up from his side of the bed, Rick fired his first shot, center mass through the bed sheet and into his lower abdomen. He hadn't even raised the rifle to his shoulder yet. Instinct and madness took over. Accustomed to firing his single shot Springfield

Star .30-06 hunting rifle, Rick slid back the level of the .22 semi-automatic rifle, spitting out an unfired round on the bedroom floor. His father fell to his knees on the side of the bed. Rick raised the rifle to his shoulder and fired again, aiming point blank from ten feet. His father's body buckled as the shot hit him in the left shoulder, sending spurts of blood across the bed sheets. Rick ejected another live round from the magazine. Rosemary jumped from her side of the bed, grabbed Bob and flew into the bathroom, slamming the door shut behind them. Rick shifted position to the large wooden dresser standing to the left of the bathroom door. His mind jumped to the .38 pistol. Was it in the bathroom with them? Were they getting ready to fire back? With instinct and survival controlling his every move, Rick fired two rounds blindly through the bathroom door. He couldn't give him the opportunity to come after them with the .38. He ejected two more live rounds. Out of the nine shells, he had fired four and ejected five to the floor below. Hardly the model of planned efficiency.

Out of ammo, he raced back down the stairs and grabbed the shells from his nightstand. With no acknowledgement from his brain, he quickly reloaded the spent clip. Footsteps creaked the floorboards upstairs. On full 'op' mode, Rick crept slowly up the bottom level stairs and listened for movement. By the time he reached the mid-level entryway near the front door, he could hear his father on the telephone in the kitchen.

"I've been shot by my son."

Rick raised the gun between the wooden railing bordering the upstairs level, and locked his half-naked and bleeding father in the crosshairs of the low-powered scope. Forty-five degrees and two inches down to the left of his right ear.

"11481 Doggie Avenue…"

The crack of the shot rang clear to the 911 operator. With the bullet passing right below the bottom of his skull and cutting a tunnel through his cerebellum, Robert Watkinson fell forward from the chair onto the floor, right onto his forehead, almost in the fetal position, curled on top of the phone. A pink 'puff' of blood followed the bullet as it exited the other side of his neck. Rick slowly walked up the stairs, stopping at the edge of the kitchen, not four feet from where his father lay. He felt nothing. No sadness, no happiness. No anxiety, no relief. A deep-red pool of blood seeped out from under the body; the quiet disturbed only by the sound of blood trickling to the floor.

Rick turned from the kitchen. He imagined Rosemary hiding behind the door with the .38, ready to blow his brains out. With the rifle cocked and ready, he cautiously made his way back into the bathroom. Curled up in a ball, his step-mother lay shivering. Rick had no way of knowing that his first shot through the bathroom door had hit her square in the chest, piercing her lung, sending her sliding sideways into the bathtub as her chest cavity filled with blood. His second shot through the door went into the porcelain of the toilet bowl, spinning a full revolution before exploding out the side. Rick didn't even see the blood in the bathtub as he stood over her for just a brief moment. He thought she was just in shock from seeing her step-son kill his father. Her eyes didn't rise to meet his, her gaze locked straight forward into nothingness. There were no words. He raised the rifle barely two feet from her head and fired, hitting her exactly where he had hit his father mere seconds ago, putting her out of her misery. She'd been through so much like the rest of them, she didn't need to live through this trauma as well. It was over. Done.

Standing in the alcove of the church building, furious with cold, Rick was in his own shock and disbelief.

"What the fuck have I done?"

His mind ran. He knew he'd been angry at his father for many things but to kill him? And Rosemary? His body recoiled as the weight of the deed crashed down on his heart and his soul. On the run, he'd been too numb to even think of, let alone understand the ramifications of his actions. But no longer in that 'fight or flight' mode, with the tempest spent inside his head, rational thought returned. Over the years, he'd wished a lot of harm to his father, but standing in the cold December 1st morning, he just could not fathom what he had actually done.

There were no thoughts of running. Instantly, he knew his life was over. That irreversible line had been crossed.

"An eye for an eye, a tooth for a tooth. I need to die."

For Rick, that was the only acceptable outcome, the only outcome righteous and worthy enough for any thought at all. His life for theirs. He had taken two lives, and now his was forfeit. It was just a matter of how and when. He thought of the rifle buried in the pine branches. It wouldn't take him long to make it back out to the woods. But he had made a promise and he didn't want to violate that, not to her. There would be questions. Why did he do it? No, killing himself wouldn't bring anyone any peace. He needed people to know that it was his fault – that his father hadn't touched him that night and that he and Rosemary hadn't needed to die.

He could make them kill him. Engage the police in a shootout and die in the fight. The idea was quickly dismissed. What if his survival instincts kicked back in and he managed to injure or even kill someone else during the melee? As much as he thought he could, he knew he wouldn't go down without a fight. He just didn't trust his own mind yet. He'd completely lost control once, what was stopping him from completely losing control again? There had to be a better, non-hostile way.

The death penalty. He could turn himself in and be sentenced to death. If Oregon had the death penalty, then surely a frontier state like Alaska did? It would be poetic justice. He had killed with the gun; he would die by the gun. He would willingly turn himself in. But where? His mind raced. It had to be somewhere public, where the police wouldn't fire and hurt any innocent bystanders. The Mall? It wasn't open yet. The airport or the hospital? Both were far away and difficult to reach on foot, especially frozen foot. School. He would go to Service High School. The school was packed at seven thirty in the morning, and there was no way the police would make a scene or cause a confrontation. Besides, he wouldn't even take the rifle with him. He would just walk into the school counselor's office and tell her right away that he'd killed his parents last night.

Armed with his first real and cognizant plan of the past eight hours, he set off back into the cold, retracing the path that led him to the church only a couple of hours ago. His pace was deliberate. Not fast enough to be a jog, his frozen legs wouldn't allow it, but a walk with a purpose. As he stepped back onto Jupiter Drive, his mind shifted to Kristy and how lost he had been without her. To think that she might never see him again, or that he might be executed without so much as a 'goodbye' was something he didn't want either of them to live with.

He slowed his pace as he juggled the idea in his head. Him and Kristy hadn't been that close the past few months, and hadn't even really spoken since the mid-September party where she laughed in his face and told him that she didn't believe he could love her. But Rick knew they'd had a bond, and if anything, he at least wanted to apologize. She made him wear her rings to keep the violence with his father from escalating.

"Don't you get blood on my rings," she'd say.

Now, he'd done far worse than get blood on her rings, and after everything they'd been through together, she deserved an apology. He walked up to the front door of her house and knocked.

"Rick?" The middle-aged woman was somewhat surprised. "Come on in. What are you doing here?"

Kristy's mother Nora had always been an extremely sweet and compassionate woman, and Rick didn't want to alarm her.

"I was kicked out of the house last night and have been on the streets ever since."

"What are YOU doing here?" said a sleepy-eyed Kristy on her way down the steps.

"I was kicked out of the house last night and have been on the streets ever since."

"Oh," she said softly.

"Well you must be hungry Rick," said Nora. "I'm just making some pancakes for the kids. There's lots. Have a glass of orange juice.

Kristy sat across from Rick at the table, and he sensed right away that she knew something else was up. But she wouldn't press him in front of her mother. They never shared any of their secrets in front of anyone; that was saved for their quiet intimate moments alone.

"You look freezing Rick," said Kristy. "Take off your boots and let me warm up your feet."

He did what he was told, and they passed the time with small talk, none of it registering in his mind or memory. He was completely fixated on trying to find the right moment to apologize. But he knew he couldn't tell her why he was so sorry, especially not in front of her mother.

"You guys ready to go?" said Kristy's brother holding the car keys.

"We stopping to pick up your girlfriend?" said Kristy.

"Yep. So hurry up."

Kristy and Rick sat in the back of the car saying nothing. The girlfriend lived back up on the Hillside, and Rick half expected to see cop cars flashing their lights on the way. As they rode back down the hill towards Service Hill High School, Rick felt the desperate urge to hold her hand, to share one last intimate moment. Just as he was about to touch her, he stopped himself. She shouldn't have to live with that. There was blood on his hands now. How would she feel about holding his hand after she found out about what he'd done? He pulled his hand back, resting it uncomfortably on his knee.

Just then the song on the radio changed, and as Rick listened to the words of the chorus, the sealed box of emotions blew open once again, only this time, there was no anger or rage, just complete sadness and sorrow.

What if God was one of us?
Just a slob like one of us
Just a stranger on the bus
Tryin' to make his way home?

He became caught up in the words. What indeed if God was really one of us? Would he mourn all he had created when he witnessed horrific moments like this? If God could truly understand the desolate sorrow and unending regret in his heart right now, why did he make man so fallible? All the pain inflicted upon each other for the sake of immaturity and misapplied love? Why couldn't things have been different? And in the quiet of the moment, lost in the words and the memories, Rick had an epiphany. Amidst all that anger, all that hurt, all that bitterness, he should have walked upstairs and given his father a hug instead of a bullet. The thought pierced the very core of his soul, and it took every ounce of his ability to go Ghost at that moment and not sob uncontrollably. He had to keep his composure and not let Kristy see how far he had fallen. He couldn't, he wouldn't let things end that way. As the car pulled into the high school parking lot, Rick knew his time was slipping away.

"Kristy, I'm sorry."

News of the murders had travelled fast and Rick was completely unprepared for the onslaught of questions and distraught faces as he entered the school. The police had worked quickly, questioning at least half of his close friends by the time he'd even made it to school. The Troopers were careful, disclosing only that the Watkinson's had been murdered, not letting on that Rick was a suspect, only that they were concerned and looking for him.

"Are you okay man?"

"Yeah," Rick answered. "I don't know what happened. I got kicked out of the house and have been on the streets all night."

As soon as Rick saw Crystal with tears streaming down her face, he knew that she suspected what he had done. The police had been to see her hours ago. She knew the sort of violent, volatile relationship he had with his father. He couldn't bear to acknowledge the truth, not in the central hallway of the school, so he said nothing. Suddenly Rick felt a strong warm hand on the back of his right shoulder.

"Mr. McBroom."

The ex-Marine leaned in close to his ear. "You're in a whole lot of trouble son."

The second he felt the hand on his shoulder, Rick knew it was over; that it was time to come in from the cold. All the chaos and misery in his life had come to an end, and his path to atonement had just begun.

CHAPTER TWO

It hadn't always been this way. The pain and the anger. There were happier times, but they seemed so long ago, like a forgotten memory hovering on the wisps of reality. Born on May 20, 1979 in Red Bluff California, Rick was the first child of college sweethearts Bob and Brenda Watkinson. Brenda was 'First Chair' in the clarinet section of the college band, and didn't mind at all when the handsome Bob, with his thick dark hair slicked off to the side, took his assigned seat next to her. Simple conversation sparked the embers, and soon love blossomed. Weekends were spent amateur street car racing, although Bob's first love was flying. Starting out with single-prop small aircraft, Bob worked his way up, eventually getting certified to fly Lear jets. Standing in the backyard of the Red Bluff home, the young Rick would watch in awe as his Dad would fly by "rocking" the airplane wings, as if to wave hello. Rick wanted nothing more than to be up in the cockpit with him, soaring through the skies, sharing the adventure with the person he loved most in the world, his idol, his hero. A little shadow, Rick tagged along with his father every chance he could; to the airfield and to the hangers, breathing in the smells of Jet-A, and avionic fuel, oil and grease, like they were a sweet summertime nectar. Nothing fascinated the child more. He would stare at the pictures in his Dad's aviation magazines for hours upon hours, taking in every little detail of the planes, and marveling that his father could actually fly them. Other kids rifled through comic books to find their Superman, their hero, but Rick had his super-hero right at home.

When they weren't messing around with planes, father and son could often be found mucking about out in the garage with Bob's various electronics, radios, and gadgets. The huge shiny red industrial tool cabinet, with its multitude of packed drawers dwarfed the young boy as he kept in step with his father's every move.

"Daddy what does this do? Daddy can I help? I can't see what you're doing…"

With a wide grin, Bob would pick the petite sprite up and sit him on the long wooden work bench. He loved that his son shared his enthusiasm, and welcomed the occasion to teach and nurture him.

"You see Ricky, if you turn the radio dial here, and just move the antenna just a little, I think we just might be able to hear what they're saying."

His big brown eyes laughed with anticipation as his father placed a strong guiding hand over his, and together they moved the dial.

"Shhh Ricky. Now you have to be real quiet. Do you hear it?"

Little Ricky glued his ear to the speaker. "Not yet Daddy."

"Let's just give it another quarter turn here…"

"I hear it! I hear it! Daddy I hear it!"

Bob tussled his fingers through the five-year-old's coarse dark hair. "See what happens when you always try your best? When you try your best, you can accomplish anything you want. We put this radio together from a pile of parts on the floor. Remember what it looked like when we first started? Well look at it now! Works perfectly. And why? Because we never gave up, and we never stopped trying. You're a smart boy Ricky, but you'll go nowhere if you don't always give it your best. Promise me okay? Promise me you'll always try your hardest at whatever you do, no matter what."

"I promise Daddy."

"Don't let me down now Ricky. Daddy doesn't want you to ever let him down okay?"

"I won't Daddy. I won't ever let you down."

****

Placing his hand on the small of Rick's back, James "Top" McBroom led him out of the school hallway and into one of the Instructor's offices in the Navy Junior Reserve Officers' Training Corps (JROTC) classroom. He nodded at Crystal to follow along. Rick noticed the stern wrinkles on the older gentleman's battle worn brow. McBroom obviously knew Rick's parents were dead, and judging by the man's cautioned demeanour, he'd been made aware that Rick was a suspect or at least he suspected it himself. Rick took a seat across from the desk, while Crystal sat down in the empty chair beside him, clinging to her book bag, her cheeks glistening from the trail of tears. Soon the two were joined by John "Gunner" Goodwin, another of Rick's teachers in the Reserve Officers' Training Corps.

"Hi Rick," said Goodwin. "You look like you could use someone to talk to. Can I get you anything?" Rick stared right through him with vacant, lifeless eyes. "Tell them everything they need to know son," said Top. "Just be upfront. It's best that way."

Goodwin noted the boy's ragged, unkempt appearance. He wasn't used to seeing his normally sharp-looking student with such wrinkly, worn-looking clothes and messy hair. Kid looked like he'd been out all night, and was in some shock. An ex-Navy medic, Goodwin had seen his fair share of people in shock, and at that moment, Rick fit the profile. Rick had been an outstanding ROTC student, very involved in the program, always participating in community service and different activities, always willing to help. More of a quiet kid but he had his group of close-knit friends, but Goodwin never had an issue with him, never a problem. This kid sitting across from him was not the Rick Watkinson he knew. Goodwin didn't know what to feel. The kid's parents had been murdered, and the police were looking for him. They were waiting anxiously in the front office at this very moment. Goodwin looked through his office door and into the classroom, which was slowly starting to fill up with students ready for their first class.

Rick's bloodshot eyes stung as he sat slouched in the chair. Exhaustion wrecked his entire frame, and all he wanted to do was put his head down on the table and sleep. He fought the urge. He was numb. All his years of going 'Ghost' kicked in, and he shut down. Every last emotion buried deep, hidden away in his own Pandora's Box. Angels, demons, hurt, betrayal, abuse, violence, death. He was waiting for the troopers to come. Anticipating. He would confess everything. They would take him away and sentence him to die. His box of horrors would stay locked. The secrets of his life would stay hidden. He never wanted to hurt anyone. He had no idea how it had gotten this far. But he would make it better. He would protect them. All of them. He would die. Then it would be all be over.

And the troopers were waiting. Tired of waiting. Both Trooper Garrett and Trooper Baty had heard the All-Points Bulletin come over the police wire at precisely 2:07 am: "Stop and hold suspect in double homicide. Considered armed and dangerous." There was a warrant for this kid's arrest, and they wanted to bring him in now. They'd already wasted the night knocking on doors, talking to his friends, trying to track the little son of bitch down. The whole state was on the lookout. Alaska Border Control and every airport in Anchorage had a picture and a general description. There was no way the little murdering bastard was getting away. When they'd called Service High School principal, Marilyn Conaway early that morning before school even started, to set up a meeting in her office, they'd never really thought the kid would actually show up at school; they just wanted to make Miss Conaway aware of the situation with one of her students. But still, they were prepared for the possibility.

"We need to talk to you about Rick Watkinson," said Trooper Garrett. "His parents were murdered last night." The words shocked Marilyn Conaway. "We've been looking for Rick all night and want to be prepared in case he shows up for school this morning."

Miss Conaway checked Rick's timetable. "His first class is math. In the NB Hall. If his parents have just been killed, we can't have him going to class. Does he know?"

Garrett ignored her question. "We need to secure his locker. Right now."

The stern tone of Garrett's voice told her not to argue. "Of course. I'll have someone show you the way."

While Miss Conaway knew the troopers had to follow protocol, she found it rather odd that they were adamant about securing Rick's locker right away. The boy had just lost his parents. Shouldn't his welfare be their first concern?

"We need to interview the student," said one of the troopers.

Marilyn Conaway pushed back a strand of hair that had fallen over her worried brow. This was all so new to her. She knew the troopers were anxious to speak to Rick but she had her own concerns. If Rick happened to show up at the school, he was then her concern, and she wanted to make sure everything was done properly. The troopers had been vague with their information, so as far as she knew, someone had shot Rick's parents. Whatever the situation was, she had to put the safety and the concerns of her students at the top. If Rick did show up, she would make sure he was sequestered away from the prying eyes of other students. It was only fair.

"Mr. McBroom. Hello," she said picking up the telephone from her desk. "He is? In Mr. Goodwin's office?"

"Tell them to make sure he doesn't move!" interrupted Trooper Garrett.

The intensity of Garrett's command caught Miss Conaway off guard. "Okay. Keep him there. We'll be down to talk to him in a minute. Troopers Garrett and Baty are here in my office…" She nodded as Assistant Vice-Principal Dale Normandin entered her office. The troopers immediately pounced.

"We need to search Mr. Watkinson for weapons. There is a belief that he may be armed."

Miss Conaway hung up the phone. "Mr. Watkinson is with John Goodwin in his office in the NJROTC classroom."

"We need to search him."

"Is he a suspect?" asked Mr. Normandin.

Trooper Garrett just turned away, ignoring the question. The group made its way down to the NJROTC office, with Miss Conaway and Mr. Normandin in the lead. School security personnel Jeff Elkins and the plain clothed troopers followed behind. Two other security guards cordoned off the hallway outside the NJROTC classroom. The troopers waited across the hall in an empty band locker room.

Mr. Normandin opened the door to John Goodwin's office. He couldn't help but notice how emotionally drained the kid looked. His red, swollen eyes left no doubt that he'd been crying, and his whole demeanour had this withdrawn, subdued look. The last thing he wanted to do was upset the kid more than he already was, especially since he didn't know all the details himself.

"Hey Rick," he said softly. "I'm sorry to hear about your parents. We need to talk to you. Can you come with me? Crystal, I think it's best if you head to class now." Crystal looked at Rick once more and then was gone. Normandin led Rick the four or five steps across the hall to the empty band locker room. Troopers Garrett and Baty stood off to the side, their hands deep in the pockets of their long black trench coats, and their eyes never leaving their young suspect.

"It is okay if I grab your coat?" said Mr. Normandin. "The troopers here need to do a quick search."

"I'm Trooper Garrett and this here is Trooper Baty with the Alaska State Troopers." Baty briefly flashed his badge, making sure that Rick caught a glimpse of the handgun tucked at the side of his belt. "We need to speak to you regarding the incident at your home. Are you wounded?"

Rick shook his head no. It wouldn't have mattered if he'd said yes; his wounds ran too deep for the troopers to see or understand – that is if they even gave a shit.

"Please face the wall, lift your arms, and spread your legs." Trooper Baty began the pat-down. "Do you have any weapons on you?"

"A few knives."

"A few?" said Trooper Baty smirking. "Let's see, I've found a lock blade, a Leatherman tool, a pocket-knife, oh and whoops…here's another lock blade up here in your right-hand pocket. I'd say that's more than a few. Why so many?"

Rick didn't answer. The trooper put the weapons deep into the pocket of his coat, and nodded to Mr. Normandin.

"We're just going to take you upstairs now okay? To the activities office," said Mr. Normandin.

Rick nodded and said nothing.

"No hand cuffs though," said Miss Conaway to the troopers. "Let's just make this as quiet and normal as possible. I don't want a scene in the hallways.

Trooper Garrett nodded, then leaned in close to Rick's ear. "We don't have to worry about you trying to run from us now do we? I have to let you know that I am armed, and I would hate to have to shoot you."

They led him through the now empty halls, upstairs to another set of offices off the main office. The activities office had two parts, the Vice-Principal's office and the athletic director's area. Mr. Normandin led Rick to the large round table in his office.

"Have a seat Rick."

Both Mr. Normandin and Miss Conaway seemed slightly nervous, and a little uncomfortable with the whole situation, fiddling with the window blinds until they fell.

"Just leave them Dale," said Miss Conaway. "It's fairly private back here." She smiled warmly at her student, trying as best as she could to put him at ease and show him some support. "Rick, these gentlemen want to talk to you okay?" He looked so small sitting at the table, while Trooper Garrett stood nearby. She felt for the boy, and couldn't imagine what was running through his head at that very moment. It was obvious the police thought he'd killed his parents; not once had they even offered a sympathetic word to the boy. She didn't know the how's or the why's, but it broke her heart seeing one of her young students caught up in something so serious and tragic.

As soon as they were all sheltered in the back room, Trooper Garrett picked up the phone in the office. "Yes, we have him in custody…He's sitting right here…Four knives…No sir…we did not recover that."

Rick said nothing. He knew they knew, and he had nothing to hide. His life was over. He wanted to die.

"Miss Conaway" said Trooper Baty, "We need to have permission before we can speak to Mr. Watkinson."

"Well with his parents both…I guess…I guess…let me pull his file and check his emergency contact information. I'll be right back."

Still foggy and dazed, Rick sat completely silent in his chair. No expression. No emotion.

"Here we go," she said entering the room again. "You have a mother living in Oregon Rick? I didn't know that."

"Is there a number?" said Trooper Baty.

"Yes…I can…"

"Please call right now."

Keying the number into the phone pad, they all waited for a response from the other end. After four rings, the call transferred to the answering machine.

"Hello, this is Marilyn Conaway the Principal of Service High School in Anchorage Alaska. I'm calling in regards to your son Rick. It's quite an urgent matter, and I don't really want to give too many details over the phone like this, so if you could please call me back as soon as possible, that would be much appreciated." She hung up the phone and looked at Rick. It was just after eight A.M.

"She's probably at work. I can tell you where," said Rick.

"Is there any other number? Another contact?" Trooper Baty was impatient. There was no way they were waiting around for his mother to call them back. And even if she did, there was a good chance she'd tell him to keep his mouth shut until he spoke to a lawyer.

"A Jean Roth," said Miss Conaway. "It says here that she's a friend of Robert and Rosemary Watkinson."

"Might I have that number please?" Trooper Baty took out his notepad, scribbling furiously.

"Miss Conaway," said Trooper Baty pointing to the man just entering the office, "This is Sergeant Mike Marrs.

"Miss Conaway."

"Sergeant Marrs."

"I have the number of the emergency contact sir," said Trooper Baty.

"I left a message for his mother. Shouldn't we wait?" said Miss Conaway.

"This number will do," said Sergeant Marrs picking up the telephone and dialing. "Hello? Ms. Roth? This is Sergeant Mike Marrs from the Alaska State Troopers. You are the emergency contact for a one, Mr. Richard Watkinson? Okay. Fine. I'm wondering if we can have your permission to speak with him? His parents are dead. Yes, ma'am that's correct. No ma'am, not a car accident. There's been a homicide. I don't know if Rick knows what happened yet, but we need to speak with him. Thank you ma'am. I'm going to put school principal Conaway on the phone. She'd like to speak with you for a minute." The trooper handed the phone to Miss Conaway.

"Ms. Roth? Marilyn Conaway here. We have Rick here at the school and I'm very concerned about him. If he should need a place to go, would you be able to come and get him? Oh that's wonderful Ms. Roth. Thank you so much for your time."

Jean Roth had consented to allow the police to talk to Rick, Rosemary was a friend, and she just as much as anyone wanted to know what happened. Except, that consent wasn't Jean Roth's to give. She wasn't his parent, nor was she even his legal guardian. At that exact moment, Rick's real mother was going about her work day oblivious to the fact her ex-husband was dead, and her stunned, oldest son was in custody. All it took was a phone call. Rick knew where she worked, the number would be easy to find, yet the troopers didn't even bother to ask. The sixteen-year boy was truly on his own, nobody to talk to, nobody to lean on, nobody to advise him of his rights.

"Rick Watkinson? I'm Sergeant Marrs, and you've already met Trooper Garrett and Trooper Baty. I just want to ask you a few questions about last night. Trooper Garrett and Trooper Baty, would you mind if I spoke to Mr. Watkinson alone for a bit?"

A bear of a man, Sergeant Marrs smiled and sat down across from Rick.

"Listen Rick, I'm here because I want to help you." Rick stayed silent but watched as the man pulled out a tape recorder and placed it on the table. "I just want to get to the bottom of what happened last night. I just want to chat, but before we do I'm going to read you your Miranda rights. You have the right to remain silent. Anything you say can and will be used against you in a court of law.

You have a right to an attorney. If you cannot afford an attorney, one will be appointed for you." He paused and waited for Rick to respond. "You know son, this might be your only chance to tell the truth about what happened to your parents. So if you have something on your mind…something you want to say…now would be the best time. Do you understand?"

Supervisor of the major crime section of the Anchorage Criminal Investigation Bureau, Sergeant Marrs had probably interviewed thousands of suspects in his over twenty years on the force. He was a pro. He'd been there, done that. Seen this, heard that. He knew how to play the good cop. Hell, he had to do it all the time. It would be a piece of cake with this kid. He'd get Rick to trust him by being nice, make it seem like he truly wanted to help. But nothing this kid could say or do would make him change his opinion. Across the table sat a killer. A cold heartless killer. The fact Rick Watkinson was only sixteen was inconsequential. Sergeant Marrs was going to nail his sorry ass. It's one thing to kill a complete stranger, but to kill your own parents? That's just fucking cold.

"I will tell you whatever you want to know," said Rick. He didn't care. Didn't give a fuck anymore about anything or anyone. He was cold and tired. The adrenaline spike that had kept him functioning was waning. His strength was gone. There would be no fight. He had come to the school to turn himself in. He would tell the truth about last night, they would find him guilty, and then he would die. Simple. Easy. Done.

He confessed everything. Whatever Sergeant Marrs asked, he answered. No lies, no deceit. He had nothing to hide. There were no tears, no sobs, any emotion had dried up ages ago, and he was strictly on autopilot, running through the motions. With no food or water since well before the murders, his small frame was weak and he'd begun to feel somewhat nauseous, but he sat there and calmly answered every question Sergeant Marrs threw at him.

"Okay Rick, well here's what's going to happen. Because you just confessed to killing your father and your step-mother, and we have that on record, I'm going to have to place you under arrest. Do you understand?"

Rick nodded.

"Now about your mother. Do you want to call her now? Would you like to speak to her?"

"No." For Rick, it was already too late, and there was no sense in dragging his mother into this mess. She'd be inconsolable enough when she found out; he wanted to prolong that agony as long as he could. He couldn't stomach the idea of having to explain anything to his mother right now. She'd be devastated. Heartbroken. He'd always been the one to protect her, to look out for her. Her little 'warrior'. The 'man' of the house. The person she relied on when things got bad. He'd pulled her through those tough times, when it was just 'them'.

He'd been the one she had leaned on after the 'betrayal', when nothing seemed to make sense, and their life had fallen off track. He'd done his best, but he was so young, just a child, a child having to be a man, and he just couldn't handle it all. He didn't ever want to let her down, he never wanted to let anyone down. Yet, here he was. He'd not only let his father and his mother down, but himself. He should have been stronger.

"That's fine Rick. We'll take care of it." He motioned to Trooper Garrett through the glass partition window. "Can you have Principal Conaway come in here for a minute?" Nobody had even noticed Sergeant Marrs turning off the tape recorder.

"Principal Conaway, the situation has changed somewhat. Rick here has just admitted to killing his father and step-mother, and we've placed him under arrest for murder. We will be leaving shortly."

Her heart dropped. Murder? Rick seemed like such a sweet boy, and he'd always been so helpful, especially in dealing with other students. He'd never caused her or the school an ounce of trouble. What on earth happened in that house to cause such a horrific and shocking event? She'd certainly seen and dealt with some troubled kids over the years but nothing like this. Then again, some kids were so good at hiding what was going on in their lives beyond these school walls. Marilyn Conaway had no idea what Rick's life was like outside of Service High School, and she could only surmise what led this seemingly kind and caring teenager to commit murder.

"But his mother? She never called back?"

"Rick has informed me that he doesn't want his mother called."

"But as the school administrator, I have to call and speak to her…get her consent…"

"Thank you Principal Conaway," interjected Sergeant Marrs quickly. "That'll be all." He waited until both she and Trooper Garrett had left the room before he turned the tape recorder back on and turned his attention back to Rick.

"Well I don't know what to say Rick. You seem like a very bright and well-mannered young man. I feel like we could be out talking over a cup of coffee…like I wouldn't even mind you dating my daughter." His thick fingers shuffled through the dog-eared pages of his leather-bound notepad. "After doing something like this…you know killing your parents, what do you think should happen to you?"

"I should be executed." His response was cold and deliberate. "I took two lives and mine should be forfeit. An eye for an eye, a tooth for a tooth, a life for a life."

"Well I hate to tell you, but up here in Alaska we don't have the death penalty anymore, and the most you'll get is two life sentences in prison."

A wave of shock shot through Rick's gut like a bolt of lightning, and it was all he could do not to vomit. Out there in the cold and on the run, he had resigned himself to dying for his crimes, that's why he came to school. He confessed because he wanted to die. That should be his punishment; the ultimate punishment for your sins is death. Isn't that what God said? Isn't that what the Bible had taught? Why should he live a life, even if it was in prison, while his father and Rosemary were dead? He just couldn't understand, and he just wanted the misery of his life to be over, once and for all.

"I think this about does it for now Rick," said Sergeant Marrs. "I'm going to get Trooper Garrett back in here, and you are going to go with him in the patrol car, and show them where you hid the rifle okay?" He waved Trooper Garrett back into the room. "Trooper Garrett, Rick has agreed to go with you and I will follow. We need to apprehend the murder weapon. Rick knows exactly where he put it, and he's promised to lead you right there, isn't that right Rick?"

"Yes sir."

"Now I think to avoid a scene we'll let you walk out of here without any hand cuffs. Is there going to be any issues on the way out Rick?"

"No sir."

"Okay good. I didn't think so."

Without so much as a wave goodbye, Rick walked with the officers through the front doors of Service High School, shattered and broken, his will spent, his fight drained. Time ceased to matter. In a single moment of uncontrollable angst, the iron-clad doors locking in the past sixteen years were blown wide open, and as much as he tried to slam those doors shut again, he couldn't. The vault had been breached, and one by one, the secrets of his youth would find their freedom.

CHAPTER THREE

"C'mon Ricky! Swim! You can do it! Just like I showed you"

Ricky flapped his tiny water-winged arms as fast as he could, sending a shower of pool water squirting in every direction.

"Like a dog Ricky! Paddle your hands like a dog! Like this!" Bob cupped his hands like paws and stroked through the water as he stood waist deep in the shallow end. "That's it! That's it!" Scooping the excited boy up into his arms, he brushed the mat of sopping hair from his son's eyes. "That's my boy!"

"Good job Ricky," echoed his mother, who was sitting off in the shade with Jimmy, the newest edition to the family.

Brenda wiggled the nipple of the bottle in an attempt to re-engage her sleepy son. She loved her sons dearly but something in her life was missing; a little girl. She'd prayed and prayed so hard after Rick was born that the next child God blessed her with would be a little girl. And he had answered her prayers. "Little Rosebud" appeared loud and clear on the ultrasound, and as far as Brenda and the doctors could tell, everything looked perfect. Except that it wasn't, and Brenda miscarried before she ever got to lay eyes on her little girl. Angry and confused, she turned to God for answers, for some sort of explanation. Brenda had always relied on her faith to get her through those tough times. God would provide. God would bless. God would give her everything she needed if she prayed hard enough and believed. A powerful entity, the Holy Spirit only came to those who were 'true' believers. Brenda was a true believer, and somehow, some way, God would make up for her loss. And he did, he sent Jimmie. True Jimmy wasn't a baby girl, but Brenda could mould him and shape him. He could be a substitute for that little girl. Bob had his little rugged boy with Ricky, and now she would have Jimmy.

"Pretty soon you're going to be out of the water wings," said Bob. "Then we'll have some real fun."

There was nothing better than seeing the huge grin on his father's face, and little Ricky lapped up the attention like a puppy. He'd do anything to please his dad.

Soon, he was out of the water wings, and Bob would swim the youngster out into the middle of the pool, then simply let go, challenging Ricky to swim back to the edge. Not wanting to disappoint, Ricky would swim his guts out and make it back every time. As his swimming became more proficient, the games increased in intensity. He loved diving in the deep-end to retrieve Bob's waterproof watch, and when his little brother was old enough, his father would make Ricky 'rescue' the toddler from the middle of the pool, dragging him with one arm, while he attempted to swim safely to the edge.

"Don't let his head go under water Ricky! Tuck him under like this…no, no, his head needs to be higher! Be careful! That's it…strong strokes."

Ricky was too young to understand that Bob was always testing his mettle, seeing what his young son was made of. He didn't really care, the games were fun, and a great way to expunge his boundless energy. More importantly, they gave him a chance to spend time with his father, and really, that's all he wanted. In the warm California sunshine, smiles and laughter hid the storm clouds gathering below the surface. Young and naïve, Ricky was oblivious, preferring to spend his days playing Hot Wheels, mucking about the neighbourhood, and generally getting into anything and everything that wasn't nailed to the ground.

Life was a giant playground, and little Ricky made a point of exercising his boyish curiosity at every opportunity. Whether it was crawling through the kitchen cupboards or discovering the magic of 'ready-mix' cement, he took full advantage of his adventurous surroundings, learning valuable 'life-lessons' like it's best not to touch an electric fence with your bare hands, nor poke sticks down holes which may or may not belong to a resident bull snake. When Jimmy got old enough, he would venture about with his big brother, but it was always Ricky leading the pack. He was a natural leader, even at such a young age. Jimmy looked up to his brother, and often envied the way their father seemed to prefer Rick over him, but Jimmy just didn't like doing the sorts of things they did. He didn't like cars, or wrestling, and he never really felt comfortable around his father, like somehow his lack of boyhood aggression made him less of a man in his father's eyes. And being a 'man' was important to Bob, it was a sign of strength, a position in the family and society not to be taken lightly.

"I have to go away again for work Ricky. I'm going to be gone for a couple of days, and I'm leaving you in charge okay? You need to take care of your mother and Jimmy. Make sure nothing happens. You're the man in charge now. Don't let me down."

"I won't Daddy. I won't ever let you down."

Little Ricky took his responsibilities seriously, and from a very young age, felt an extreme sense of pride and obligation for both his mother and his brother. When his father wasn't around, he was their caretaker, he was the problem solver, and the one they both looked to for guidance. Ricky developed a sense of ownership over the house and the family, and in his eyes, he was the one charged with keeping it all together. His family, his little space in life was all he knew, and it's where he drew his strength and his comfort. Sure his parents argued, all parent's argued, but the night his father stormed out of the house, slamming the front door so hard it shook the walls, Ricky's perfect little world developed a crack. For a long time, he lay curled up in a ball on his bed, listening to the engine of his father's car idling in the driveway, his pillow silently soaking up his tears. Eventually, his father turned off the car and came back inside, but for Ricky, the incident awoke in him a constant fear - a terror that someday his father would actually put the car in reverse, and drive out of their lives forever.

****

"I'm going to have to cuff you now okay Rick?" Trooper Garret leaned across the front seat of his patrol car and snapped the cuffs around the teenager's wrists. The cold metal hardly registered against Rick's still frozen skin. "You said you stashed the gun where?"

"The dead end off Sahalee."

With Sergeant Marrs following behind in his own car, Trooper Garrett turned out of the school parking lot and headed down the street. It didn't take them long to reach their destination.

"It's just off the road a bit, up under a tree," said Rick. He led them a short way, and then stopped. "Under that tree there."

Trooper Garrett removed the large evidence bag from under his arm and began to search through the brush on the ground.

"Is it still loaded?" said Sergeant Marrs.

"I honestly have no idea," answered Rick. "I can't remember."

"Got it," said Trooper Garrett from under the tree. "A Ruger .22 semi-automatic Long rifle." Rick kept his eyes on the ground. He didn't want to see that rifle ever again. The trooper wrapped the gun in the evidence bag, as Sergeant Marrs led the way back to the cars. With the gun safely stowed in the trunk of the sergeant's car, Rick was shuffled back into the front seat beside Garrett. Without any sirens or fanfare, the car was back in motion and headed to the Alaska State Trooper headquarters in downtown Anchorage.

At the station, Trooper Garrett calmly led Rick through a series of different hallways and offices before arriving at Sergeant Marrs' office.

"Have a seat Rick. Sergeant Marrs will be here in a minute."

Rick sat on the hard wooden chair, his body and mind still frozen and numb. He had no idea how the rest of this day was going to play out, but he knew he was on a one-way ticket to hell, and he'd already lost his chance at jumping off the train. His brown eyes focused on the stainless steel wrapped around his wrists. He should have tried to run on the way to the car. Make them shoot him. He was dead already wasn't he? But he'd been dead for such a long time that nothing really mattered anymore. Everything that was once good in his life was gone. He should have run. He should have forced their hand. Made them do it. Maybe then, 'Ghost' could have finally found some peace.

"Okay Rick," said Sergeant Marrs closing the door behind him. "I want to go through what happened again but this time in a little more detail. I just want to make sure I understand everything that happened. Hold on one second…Just let me switch on this tape recorder…Okay…so let's start from the very beginning."

For the next hour or so, Rick repeatedly answered the Sergeant's questions. Completely exhausted, his tone was matter-of-fact and straight forward. Sergeant Marrs then moved Rick to one of the official interrogation rooms, and made him run through the entire event of the crime again, this time in front of a video camera. Three interrogations, three complete confessions, and still the teenager had not spoken to his mother or been given the opportunity to consult with a lawyer.

"Show me how you held the gun when you first fired into the bedroom," said Marrs uncuffing him and handing him the rifle. Mechanically, Rick took the gun and held it in front of him.

"What about when you shot through the bathroom door?"

Rick switched the gun position. He should have felt sick holding that gun in his hands again, cocking it into shooting position, but he didn't. He didn't feel anything. No smile, no frown, no grimace, no sneer. Nothing. The literal numbness of his body and soul had frozen out any type of emotional response, making him appear like an uncaring, calculated killer. The police would wonder about the teen's lack of tears, his lack of reaction when recalling the murders, and to them this only confirmed his guilt, and his premeditation. They just didn't understand. They couldn't. Assumptions were made and noted for the record; assumptions that would come back to taint the reality of Rick's situation that day. If Rick had truly been remorseful, he would have cried, he would have collapsed in anguish, he would have done anything except be the completely passive and compliant teen that they saw that day. It was all on tape, the evidence was clear. But they didn't know Rick, and they certainly didn't know Ghost.

For Rick, time felt so distorted, like the clock had been ticking in off-beats and his mind just couldn't register the hands ever moving. By the time the third interview ended, it was around 2:30 in the afternoon. At this time yesterday, he was happily chatting with his friends, waiting for classes to end so he could go to Drill practice. In less than twenty-four turns around the clock, less than a sunrise to a sunset to another sunrise, so much had happened, so much had changed. Time would never again be free.

"Where are you taking me now?"

"To the hospital for drug testing."

Sergeant Marrs had asked him a thousand times if he was drunk or high, and a thousand times Rick had honestly answered no, but they needed proof 'for the record'. Slipping in through a special back entrance, a handcuffed Rick waited on the chairs in the hallway with a now ever-present trooper by his side.

"Are you wounded at all," said the doctor as he did a quick over the clothes feel of Rick's body. "Your body still feels frigidly cold. You say you were out all night?" Rick nodded. "The wind chill went down to minus ten degrees Fahrenheit overnight. You're very lucky to be alive." He examined the tips of Rick's fingers. "Not even a trace of frostbite. That shocks me." He turned away and wrote something in his notes. "The only reason you're probably still alive right now is because you were in shock, full of adrenaline, and on the move most of the night. But the lack of frostbite is really quite extraordinary considering the sub-zero temperatures and the length of time you were exposed without the proper protection. I'm honestly surprised you're functioning as well as you are at the moment. We're just going to take some blood now and I need you to pee in this cup."

"I don't have to pee."

"Excuse me?"

"Sorry sir but I don't think I can pee. I haven't had anything to drink since…well…I can't even remember now."

The doctor shot an annoyed glance at the trooper. "Get the boy something to drink please, preferably something hot to help him warm up."

"What would you like?" said the trooper.

"An ott-shot Irish Cream coffee."

The trooper smiled. "An ott-shot?"

"It's eight shots of espresso in the Irish Cream." Rick figured this was probably his last chance at a real coffee for a very long time, maybe even the rest of his life. He was going big, and he was going to savour every last drop.

After finally being able to give a urine analysis, Rick was back in the car and headed to the 'welcoming' confines of the McLaughlin Youth Facility. The early winter snow hung heavy on the tree branches of the numerous evergreens alongside the entry driveway. Rick took a moment to admire the beauty, the peacefulness of the winter scene. He'd always loved the outdoors, and he was never happier than when he was out traipsing about in the snow, rain, or warm sunshine. Silently, he wondered if he'd ever get that chance again or feel that sort of soulful freedom. In a moment, the tranquil scene was gone as the car pulled into the entry garage, the big doors closing out the world behind.

The trooper passed his charge off to the Youth facility staff, and disappeared without so much as a passing glance. For the fourth time that day, the teen was sequestered in an office and asked a bunch of different questions but this time by a very concerned-looking staff. The staff had processed many youth offenders, but none could remember another case of parricide, especially a double parricide where a father and step-mother were killed. The crime itself was incredibly rare, not only in Alaska but in the entire United States, and by the looks of the kid sitting in front of them, he was in just as much shock as they were.

"Follow me please," said the guard cuffing Rick's hands behind his back. Rick didn't like that being cuffed from behind left him feeling so vulnerable and unable to protect himself. The lack of food and rest made his legs feel like iron casts, and it took all his remaining strength just to shuffle along the hall. The guard stopped him in front of an open cell.

"In you go." Rick just caught the letters "CTU" above the door before the guard gave him a slight nudge forward.

"What does the CTU stand for?" said Rick.

"Critical Treatment Unit."

Rick had no idea what that actually meant, but in his mind, it didn't sound all that comforting, and with a quick glance around, neither did the confines of his new home. A crummy little plastic covered 'Bob Barker' mattress on a single metal bed frame, a toilet, a sink, a slit window with frosted glass at the back of cell, and a tray-slot in the door. That was it. The slam of the door behind him, jolted his body forward.

"Put your arms through the slot and I'll uncuff you," said the guard. "Now take off all your clothes and hand them through the slot." Rick did as he was told. "Here you go." The guard handed him a pair of institutional boxer shorts and a wool blanket.

"That's it?" said Rick. "But I'm freezing. Seriously, can't I have a shirt or something?"

"Sorry, nope. That's it."

And there it was, the beginning of the rest of his new life. Cold, hungry, and half-naked in a concrete cell, he lost all consciousness of time and space. The ensuing days drifted into nights without so much as a whisper. The cement walls were no match for the raging Alaskan winter, and without any books, or anyone to talk to, young Rick spent the majority of his hours curled up on the bed, shivering under his thin blanket. Three times a day someone shoved some food through the slot in the door, but they never stayed to chat, or never asked if he needed anything. They never even let the kid have a hot shower to warm up or clean up. No one came to talk to him about the crimes he had committed, to even ask why, or even if he was okay. He just sat there alone, completely and utterly alone. He didn't cry, he didn't have any nightmares or any breakdowns. He couldn't. With the excruciating cold seeping into every pore of his body, his once fertile and active mind shut down, his body functioning only to keep the blood flowing to a dead and empty heart.

Rick had no idea that he'd initially been placed in the Critical Treatment Unit because the staff thought he might be suicidal, but who the fuck were they kidding? If he didn't want to kill himself before, he sure as hell must have had thoughts now. What a brilliant rehabilitation tactic, to put a 'potential mentally unstable' young person who'd just committed a very serious yet deeply personal crime, in a freezing isolated environment, with the absolute bare necessities of life, including human interaction, and expect him to come out mentally intact. No one was there to help. No one was there to offer any type of support. No one even gave a fuck.

"Watkinson. Get up and put this on." The guard threw a blue one-piece jumpsuit through the slot. "Make it quick."

"What's the date today?" said Rick picking up the clothes.

"December 8th, only a couple of weeks until Christmas."

"December 8th?" thought Rick. His mind drifted back and counted the days. He'd been in that God-damned cell for eight straight days! Time really had become meaningless.

"Come to the door. Time to cuff up."

This time the door opened, and two guards went to work, first cuffing Rick's hands at the front, then wrapping a rather heavy duty steel chain around his waist, pad-locked in the back. Finally, they secured a 'black box' to the chain which locked over the top of the handcuffs so the access to the keyholes was blocked.

"Step out of the cell and face the wall."

With his legs spread, they clamped leg-irons on each of Rick's ankles. Rick had no idea that this type of security was traditionally only reserved for escapees or the highest security risks. The boy had just spent a week in his underwear broken and alone, shivering just to stay alive. What the hell kind of strength did they think he had? But someone at the Youth Facility decided to make a point, probably politically motivated, and have Rick show up at his first court appearance secured like a little terrorist. The guard passed him off to a Department of Transportation officer, who then loaded him in the back of a car and drove him down to the 6th Avenue Jail where they hold the bail hearings.

The iron shackles weighed heavy. This was not the type of armour his mother would be proud of. From a very young age, she'd taught Rick to be 'God's little warrior', fighting the good fight against the demons who crept up from the underworld, engaging the believers in a fight to the spiritual death. Every morning Rick and Jimmy would don their 'spirit armour': the 'helmet of salvation', the 'girdle of truth', the 'breastplate of righteousness', the 'sandals of the gospel', the 'shield of faith' and the 'sword of the spirit'. And every night they recited an entire list of Bible verses centered on spiritual warfare, "For the weapons of our warfare are not carnal, but mighty in God for the pulling down of the strongholds, casting down imaginations and every high thing that exalts itself before the glory of the Lord".[1]

Rick closed his eyes, trying to block out the hundreds of verses flooding his teenage mind. He didn't want to go there right now. He couldn't. Fuck the Holy Spirit and his 'gifts' of sight and tongues. It hadn't help him. It'd only made things worse. Rick knew his mother was only trying to protect him, to make him stronger. There was no malice, no wrong intent, just an intense belief that took over her own existence, and forced itself upon her young, naïve and unwitting children. They were powerless to stop it, and it was the one secret that Daddy could never know.

"Have a seat," said the officer. "The judge will appear on the screen."

Feeling like an outcast, Rick glanced around at the other prisoners in the room. Most were simply cuffed at the front, and Rick could feel their curious eyes wondering what the fuck this scrawny kid must have done to end up in the irons. He turned away and concentrated on the screen. In a flash the screen came to life.

"I am Superior Court Judge Karl S. Johnstone. Time is twelve hundred hours on December 8th, 1995." One by one he went down the line of defendants, reading their charges and setting their bail. Most were misdemeanors with bail set at around $500, while a few felony charges netted a bail of $15,000. Rick sat quiet, patiently awaiting his fate.

"Mr. Watkinson." The judge was short and curt. "You are sixteen years of age and are being held for two counts of first degree murder." Every set of shocked eyes in the room turned their attention to Rick. "Due to the violent nature of the offences you will automatically be charged as an adult and be transferred to adult custody. Due to the severity of your crimes, I order your bail to be set at one million dollars, third party, cash only."

"Damn youngster!" said a voice to the left of Rick. "What the fuck did you do?"

Rick didn't answer. He just continued to stare at the television screen as it blinked off, trying to comprehend what had just happened. One minute a minor, next minute an adult. They weren't fucking around. There was no cake and ice cream at an adult jail, unless you were willing to have something shoved up your ass as payment. He would need to muster every single survival skill he had, both mentally and physically, not just to cope, but to survive. His father had been tough on him as a child, always testing, always pushing, seeing what he was made

[1] 2 Corinthians 10:4

of, and seeing how far he could push things before his son would crack. He would have to use those skills now.

Bob loved to wrestle, and was a wrestler in high school, as well as being a good general all-around athlete. One year, he even set the record for pole-vault height in the state of California. But wrestling was really his thing, and he loved to wrestle with little Ricky. Ricky knew his dad meant no harm, but it didn't change the fact he hated the trapped, powerless feeling he'd get when his dad pinned him down, and then, more often than not, taunted him to tears.

"What's wrong? Is the little Rickosaur all wrapped up? C'mon Ricky, try and get out of it!" Ricky would fight with all his might but his dad was just too big and strong for the youngster. "You can't do it can you? Maybe you're just not trying hard enough. Be a man Ricky. Fight."

Ricky was fighting. He was trying his best but a six-year-old is not a man.

"Maybe next time," laughed Bob, releasing his panicked son.

That feeling never left little Ricky; feeling trapped, powerless to control, like his life was a constant wrestling match. As he grew older, he pushed harder, trying to get out of the hold, trying to succeed and take some control, but Bob would push back, doing his best to hold his ground and his authority. Rick began to resent this authority, or any authority for that matter. He was always the little one, always the underdog, scratching and clawing, fighting until his little cheeks were flushed red, needing to get out from underneath the clutches. No one was going to mess with him. He would prove them all wrong, and he would succeed. This scenario played out time and time again in his young life, that trapped, hopeless feeling never far from the surface. Whether he was fighting demons, or play fighting soldiers in the back woods near his house, it was always survival of the fittest, always a battle, and always a constant need to break the 'wrestling pin' and come out on top.

For the next twenty-one months, Cook Inlet Pre-Trial Facility would serve as his new wrestling partner, testing him at every turn, a boy thrown into a man's world, where nothing was a joke, and the wrong tone of voice could serve you a shank to the gut. Rick stood in the booking room, sixteen years old, and a buck forty-five sopping wet. They put him through all the regular procedures; fingerprints, photo, strip search. As a sign of his graduation to adult jail, he had to turn in his 'juvenile' uniform and was given the navy steel blue pajamas that everyone in Cook Inlet wore. After another urinalysis, they threw him in a holding cell for hours and hours while the administration figured out what the hell to do with him.

Sixteen-year old's in an adult prison were a new thing for Cook, and there was great concern as to how Rick should be handled. It wasn't that they really gave a shit what happened to him personally, they were more concerned about their own legal liability should he get raped or beaten to an inch of his life. Always about the politics. Most juveniles went straight to the 'Hole' and were placed on 'A.S.' or Administrative Segregation Status', which is where they put all the people who were unfit for general population. People in Ad-Seg were either troublemakers or snitches, kept away from the general population for their own safety or the safety of others, at least that was the case for adults.

Like usual, Rick's journey would be different. He had the pleasure of being one of the first juveniles under Alaska's new Juvenile Waiver Law, which says that if a juvenile is charged and convicted of a violent felony, they are automatically waived to adult status and housed in the adult prison system. Toss them in the water and hope for the best.

"Hi Rick. My name is Bryan Brandenburg and I am the Mental Health Supervisor for Cook Inlet. Mind if I ask you a few questions?"

From first glance, Rick had an awful feeling about the man. There was just something in the way he kept looking at Rick, and the tone of his voice, condescending, and arrogant. The man ran through a gamut of questions alluding to Rick's mental stability and well-being.

"Are you suicidal?"

"No," said Rick looking the man straight in the eyes. "In fact, I made a promise to someone a long time ago that I would never kill myself, and it's a promise I plan to keep no matter what. I'm not someone who goes back on his word."

"What's that scar on your hand there? Did you purposely cut yourself and attempt suicide?"

"No," answered Rick. "I took a fall down the backside of Flattop and cut it on a jagged rock. I have a couple of friends who can verify the story."

"Really. That's a pretty big scar for a tumble. Look at it, it starts beneath your left thumb and goes all the way down your wrist."

"Yes," said Rick. "With a gap of about two inches where the rock hit my watch and not my arm."

Brandenburg scribbled something on his paper. "I see." He paused and scribbled some more. "Okay, I think we're done here."

Escorted back to the holding cell, Rick had no choice but to sit on the hard bench and wait.

"Okay Watkinson, let's go." The corrections officer handed him a bed-roll. "Your supplies." Rick followed him down to the very end of facility, stopping at a large solid door. "Welcome to Mike mod."

Cook Inlet had twelve 'mods' or housing units with about thirty-six cells on two tiers, eighteen stacked on top of eighteen. Some of the mods are large, some are small, but each one serves a purpose, from intake, to segregation, to workers, and three for those prisoners who were already sentenced. Each mod had a letter designation. At the time, Rick had no idea what any of this meant. The officer escorted him to one of the 'slider' cells on the bottom tier. With the tray-slot, it looked very similar to his cell at the youth facility except this one opened and closed electronically.

Rick turned around to face the officer and get uncuffed. "What exactly is Mike mod?"

The officer smiled. "The Psychiatric ward. You, know, where we house all the crazies. Welcome home kid."

The slam of the door pounded against his heart. The crazies? But he wasn't crazy? He'd told the guy the scar was from a fall and he was being honest. What the fuck was he doing in the Psych ward? Rick's brain spun out of control. He'd heard stories about prisoners being thrown in the crazy ward and just left there indefinitely. He could feel the demons lurking everywhere, hunting, waiting, and his third eye straining to open. He couldn't let it. He had to remain calm and collected, otherwise they really might think he was crazy. He unravelled the bed-roll; two sheets, two blankets, a pillowcase, and a paper bag with hand soap, a toothbrush, and some toothpaste. All the possessions he owned in the world, and they weren't even his, they were government property. All he had left was his sanity, his own thoughts, and even those, especially in Mike mod, would be subject to condemnation. He could show no feeling or emotion, nothing that anyone could pick up on and scrutinize. Every minute would be a new experience, a learning experience, and he would have to learn quickly, and on the fly, using all his wit and charm to con, coax, and persuade. The challenges would be great. He would have to step up, be a man – just like his father taught him.

CHAPTER FOUR

The summer of 1985 brought big changes for the Watkinson family. Ever onward and upward, Bob jumped at the opportunity to switch companies and start flying 747s instead of the smaller Lear jets. Part of the deal including relocating the family to a spot nearer a larger airport more suited for his routes and role. Bob and Brenda found a wonderful property in a little town called Federal Way, just south of Auburn in the Seattle, Washington area. Only a forty-five-minute drive to Sea-Tac airport in Seattle, the house was nestled in a secluded wooded area, a perfect playground for an adventurous boy with a vivid imagination. The new job also meant more time away from the home for Bob, sometimes three days, sometimes a week and a half, then he'd be home a few days, then gone again. With only mom in charge, Ricky and Jimmy had ample time to romp around the neighbourhood and get into all sorts of good old fashioned kid trouble.

While Brenda and Bob slept upstairs, the boys had their bedroom and play area on the bottom floor, accessible from the mid-level stairs or a sliding glass door that led out to the backyard. The best part of their room was the brand new bunk bed and dresser set. The beds made an upside down 'L' formation with the dresser neatly tucked underneath the open area of the top bunk, and the boys loved to drape the area with blankets, making the most ingenious forts, sleeping in sleeping bags, sometimes leaving the forts intact for days. While Rick liked playing in his room, he much preferred to be outside, running around, creating adventures.

The backyard itself was an awesome assortment of all things natural and wonderful. In the far right corner of the property stood a small thicket of low-lying tangled trees and brush, complete with a large moss-covered stump about five feet in diameter and about chest high on little Ricky. On the other side of the yard, a small steep hill rose and then blended into the thick, dense forest and ferns that ran along the back of the property. Every time it rained, which was often in Seattle, the huge dip in the ground near another large stump would fill with water and become a large inviting pond for a young, rambunctious boy. The huge property was pretty much perfect, and had everything a kid like Rick wanted, and it didn't take him long to become comfortable running through the wet, green mossy forests. Nature became his true friend and companion, and in its arms he felt free.

The woods around the neighbourhood had enough wildlife to keep Ricky on his toes, with plenty of snakes, frogs, spiders, yellow-jackets, slugs, ants, and even the occasional flying squirrel. The tree-tops were always filled with blue jays, woodpeckers, and a variety of other less interesting birds. About fifty yards behind the house at the bottom edge of the largest swath of forest sat a year-round bona-fide swamp. Because it bordered a gravel road, people often used it as a trash dump, tossing old rusted car frames, doors, scrap wood and lumber, and any other crap they deemed dispensable. Of course, this made it the perfect playpen for unsupervised boys.

The swamp itself was around sixty feet by fifty feet, and bled back into the woods, about three feet at its deepest. Parts of it were almost bog-like, especially around the edges with algae and moss so thick, it was nearly impossible to tell where dry land began. Under the direction of their fearless leader Ricky, the boys would use boards and trash to build bridges, delving them deeper into unexplored territory. Unfortunately, their engineering skills were lacking, and many times they'd arrive home soaking wet, stinking like muck. Many lazy summer afternoons were spent catching snakes and frogs, and storing them in an aquarium their mother had purchased for them. It was always a big score when they would find whole clusters of slimy eggs, which they would then transfer to the aquarium, where they could watch them hatch into tadpoles, feeding them fish food as they grew.

Rick genuinely came to love the forest and nature, and one of his favorite things were the animal biography cards from National Geographic. The simple cards contained a picture of the animal, its name, general location and habitat on the front, with a whole scholastic summary of its diet and characteristics on the back. His eager mind hungry for information, Rick became obsessed with collecting the cards, filling a huge two-foot box with the five inch square cards. He even got his hands on a 'Naturalist' kit, complete with a book of activities, binoculars, sample jars, and other tools. He respected nature and the preservation of it, but also strongly believed in the natural hierarchy of predator and prey, and survival of the fittest.

The more he romped along on his adventures, the more at one he became in the surroundings. Hide and seek and 'the hunt' became favorite games between him and his neighbourhood friends, sneaking up as close as possible to animals and hiding from each other. It didn't take long for Ricky to master the art of slinking silently through the forest, and camouflaging himself into the environment so well, that his friends just gave up looking. Jimmy didn't quite share Rick's enthusiasm for the outdoors, but he did on occasion come out to help Rick built forts, play games or run through the swamp. While Rick was outgoing, adventurous, and very much a reflection of his father, Brenda's desire to have a daughter affected her treatment of Jimmy, and he was timid and quiet, choosing My Little Ponies over G.I. Joe. Despite the differences in personality, the brothers were buddies putting on puppet shows or concerts for their mom. They'd set up a stage and rehearse for days, perfecting their performance before dragging their delighted mom in to watch.

For the most part, Rick was on his own, preferring the silence and solitude of the forest. He found peace with the birds, and peace when the heavy raindrops fell through the tall cedar and pine branches, tapping softly on the leaves and the ferns below. Rick would watch the rain from the seclusion and comfort of one of his many handmade forts spread throughout the forest. Like the animal cards, dwelling in the forest became an obsession for the boy, and he attempted to learn everything he could about survival and sustaining himself completely off the land. His pride and joy was the building of the forts and 'base camps' and then attempting to camp-out overnight, although the lure of a safe house and a soft warm bed was usually enough to send the eight-year-old scampering home.

One particular summer windstorm sent a number of old trees crashing down, creating wickedly fun cubby holes when the trees landed at all sorts of different angles. As soon as the storm subsided, Rick was out surveying the changes and seeing how he could manipulate the new environment into better forts and hiding spots. Taking a shovel and hacksaw to the remaining roots of one of the large felled trees, the boys dug further into the roots to make a sort of cave, then camouflaged the entire base with walls of pine boughs. This new masterpiece became the base of operations for many of the rest of the forest adventures. It also became a hang-out for older teenagers, and Rick would anger when he found cigarette butts, empty beer bottles, torn-up porn magazines, and even once a pair of panties. Fiercely territorial, the boy would clean up the mess, and then many times leave crude little booby-traps for the unwanted and disrespectful guests. But teenagers weren't the only unwanted guests that showed up in the Watkinson backyard.

One day while Ricky was out roaming around, not too far from the house, a dirty looking man with grey hair and shabby clothes approached him waving a small hunting knife and a chain.

"Do not try and run and do not scream," said the man in a dead calm voice.

"I don't know what you want but I don't have any money."

"Shut up! I don't care about money!" He pointed the knife at a mid-sized tree about twelve feet away. "Put your back up against that tree."

Ricky could feel his legs get weak and start to tremble. Should he run? He knew these woods better than anyone. But what if he had a gun? The youngster decided not to take any chances and backed up against the tree.

"I didn't do nothing to you mister."

The man jumped at Ricky, and quickly wrapped the twenty-foot chain around the boy's arms, waist, and legs. As much as he tried to be brave, the tears started streaming down Ricky's face.

"Shut up kid! Do you hear me? Shut the fuck up!"

Ricky did his best to stifle the tears but they kept coming. Terror ripped through his veins, and his tiny chest could barely contain his thumping heart. Nowhere in any of his survival manuals did it offer any suggestions on what to do if one was tied up to a tree by a crazy, creepy stranger. With his mother too far away to hear him scream, the kid was on his own. As the man clasp the chain around the tree and fastened it tightly, they heard the scraping of gravel and voices in the distance. Someone was walking along the road. The man glared at Rick, flashing the knife close to his throat. Rick knew the road wound close to where he was, and he only had to scream holy terror to get their attention but his voice stayed silent. The man studied the little boy then cocked his head towards the road. Five seconds later he was gone, walking off into the woods in the opposite direction.

Shocked Rick just stood there. Didn't yell. Didn't scream. He was too embarrassed that he'd been captured so easily, and on his own turf. The last thing he wanted was for anyone to see him chained to a tree crying like a baby. He was tougher than that. Listening for a good five minutes, until he was sure the neighbours had passed and his captor was gone, Rick began to wiggle around trying to loosen the chains. It took him another five minutes or so before he was able to squirm enough to reach and unhook the clasp, sending the chains to the forest floor. In a flash, he was off as fast as his scrawny legs could fly.

"Ricky what's wrong?" said his mother as he burst through the front door.

Shaking and quivering, Rick told her about the man and the chains.

"Oh my goodness Ricky! Are you all right?" She hugged him close. "Here let me wipe those tears. We're calling the police."

The police arrived shortly. "Can you describe the man son, and show us the tree with the chains?"

"He was real creepy. With grey hair and he was dirty. Like really dirty. He had a knife and kept just waving it at me."

"You were very brave Rick," said the officer picking up the chain. "This looks like it's a chain for a dog?"

"It is," said Rick. "It's the chain we use for Tramp, our dog. He must have come into the backyard to get it. I didn't see him though, and Tramp must have been in the house or he'd have been barking."

"Who is this man?" said Brenda.

"We don't know for sure," said the officer, "but we've had reports of a grey-haired man stalking between houses and trespassing on the local properties the past couple of weeks. Thanks for reporting this and we'll be sure to drive by more often and keep a look out. You'd best stay inside for the next little while son, just in case. You were lucky this time but you never know if or when he might show up again."

Ricky wasn't taking any chances. As soon as his father left for his next flight, Ricky stole off to the garage and found the large diving knife and calf sheath amongst his parent's full compliments of scuba gear. With its long serrated edge, the knife was much too big for Rick to carry around, but that didn't stop the youngster from hacking and stabbing trees, and trying to learn how to throw it like Crocodile Dundee. Knowing he couldn't keep the knife with him, Rick found a brilliant hiding place in the woods, and for a while, just knowing that the knife was there gave him a great sense of security in case the man ever returned to finish his business. Next time, if there was a next time, Rick wouldn't be so easily preyed upon.

Life continued; playing and acting out 'G.I. Joe' in the forest with his friend Ryan and generally just being a boy, wiping out on his bike, coming home with bloodied knees and scraped hands. His father indulged his sons' passion for all things combat and army by getting Rick an old authentic Army issued duffle bag, complete with a set of combat webbing, a canteen, a real helmet, and some other army gadgets like a compass. Rick put the bag up to his nose and inhaled the musty canvas. Definitely had that battle-worn smell. That shit was the real deal, probably belonged to some ex-Vietnam soldier. Rick couldn't have been happier, and took care of that gear as if Uncle Sam had issued it to him directly.

Still, the best times were those that took place with his father, either flying or sailing. Bob loved the water, loved the feeling of being on the open sea, battling the elements, and winning. The master. It didn't take long for little Ricky to share his father's enthusiasm. The boy came to love the ocean and the salt water byways, his fascination extending not only to boats and marinas, but to the innate danger of the water. The darkness, the deepness, and the lack of knowledge as to what really lurked beneath. The Watkinson's would pile the family onto their twenty-two foot Catalina and set out on adventures. While not huge, the boat was big enough for two adults, and two small children, with a small bathroom, a make-shift kitchen, and two couches that converted into beds, all onboard. A lover of gadgets, Bob had pimped the boat big time with all the latest gear and technology. Over time, he taught Rick how to read the instruments, and eventually let him handle the ropes and steer. Rick was in his glory, and nothing could change the glow that emanated from the boy's smile as he gazed at his father silhouetted against the sun – the pilot, the sea-captain, the hero.

When Bob developed an interest in sailboat racing, Rick was right by his side. Bob joined a formal league that held competitive races on Puget Sound, complete with rules, regulations, and a high class 'club house' to relax and grab some dinner and drinks. Tagging along, little Ricky would be assigned menial tasks like scrambling about the deck to grab this and that, or calling off numbers from the displays mounted in the cabin. On some of the races Bob let Brenda accompany him as his 'wingman' but mostly he brought along one of his sailing buddies. As Rick got older, he was able to handle the ropes, pull in the sail, and be smack dab in the middle of the action. Sometimes it would just be Rick and his Dad. A team, working together, just the two of them. Those were the best, and little Ricky cherished every moment. Dressed in their beanie hats and boating gloves, the two would work in sync, pulling and letting out the ropes, anticipating the winds, and reacting to each other's motions. Those were glorious times, the adrenaline billowing like the sails, the two relying on each other, just a father and a son together against the world.

The two raced many times, especially in the Pacific Northwest Annual Regatta's, even placing second a couple of times, which wasn't too bad considering Ricky's age, and the fact that he probably weighed less than a bucket of Pacific salmon. His little brown eyes beamed with pride as the man handed him and his father the trophy for second place.

Bob scuffed the boy's hair. "Nice job Ricky. I'm proud to have you as my wingman."

The trophy, engraved with both their names, found a home on the mantel of the fireplace, and every time the boy would walk by, he'd sneak a peek and smile. But the races weren't all fun and games, and Bob's competitive spirit was always alive. He wanted to win. One cloudy and windy race, they'd just rounded one of the buoy markers and had already set the new course for the next marker. The wind was lighter in their direction, and some of the other boats were trying to take a more curved and time-saving approach and over shoot the buoy to keep the wind in their sails. The mid-sized swells rose up from the sea about three or four feet, not seriously dangerous, but high enough to impede vision. One boat, not too far, and a little ahead of the Watkinson boat, decided it was time to tack, and they were so worried about making a smooth transition, they became totally oblivious to their surroundings. Their new angle and speed sent them careening right for Rick and Bob.

"Hold on Ricky!" said Bob leaning heavily on the tiller.

The boat glanced off the bow of Bob's boat; his quick thinking saving them from a full on broad-side crash. Shaken and scared, Rick had never seen his father so angry.

"Are you kidding me?" he yelled to the other boat. "What the hell were you thinking? Jesus!"

The bow of the other boat had given Bob's boat a good crack, and both boat crews had to push each other off and deploy deck buoys to assess the damage.

"I'm sorry man," said the other captain.

"You're damn fucking right you're sorry," screamed Bob. "Look at my fucking boat! Look at the fucking crack! She's got a nice sized tear in the hull. And of course yours is fine. You're lucky the tear is above the waterline. Jesus fucking Christ!"

"Like I said, I'm sorry. Not sure what happened."

"Oh you're sorry? What fucking good is that going to do me?" Ricky ducked behind the sail rigging. The red in Bob's face was about to explode out through his ears. "Is sorry going to repair this fucking hole?" Ricky thought for sure his father was going to jump ship and beat the shit out of the other guy.

"I'll call it in," said the other man.

"Damn fucking right you will," answered Bob. "Ricky, get that pail and get ready to bail. We're going to have to use the outboard motor to get back to the harbour." Bob stared down the other captain. "Fucking asshole."

They managed to slowly maneuver the wounded Catalina through the swells and back to the harbour with minimal bailing. Ricky knew enough to keep his mouth shut on the return trip, and just do what he was told. The anger in his father scared him. Sure it was justifiable, the guy did ram their boat, and the end result could have been much worse than it was, but still, he'd never seen his father act that way or use those types of words before. It wouldn't be the last.

When they weren't on the sea, father and son were in the air, or traipsing around the grounds of the Seattle-Tacoma airport. Bob drove past the expansive Boeing complex, and Ricky lost count of the number of hangars and office buildings. Even Evergreen, where Bob worked, had an impressive set-up, and a decent sized set of hangars and offices. The airport was like a little city unto its own, with all the nooks and crannies an adventurous kid liked to explore. One of his favorite spots was the aviation museum with its old 1950s quad-propeller passenger plane that they'd converted into a diner. The museum also had a deactivated F-14 Tomcat that you could climb into and sit in the cockpit. For a little kid, nothing was cooler than being a part of this world, and having his pilot father show him the ropes.

"Want to try the flight simulator?"

"Are you serious Dad?"

"Of course I'm serious," laughed Bob. "Get in and I'll coach you through."

Rick was in the simulator before his Dad even finished the sentence. "It's got hydraulics and everything!"

"Yes it does," said Bob. "Okay, let's see what kind of a pilot you are!"

They zipped through a few runs with Bob guiding his eager son.

"Left! Left! Hard left Ricky!" Ricky poured his entire weight on the stick.

"That's it! That's it! Now back to the right. Easy…easy…a little easier on the stick. Nice job."

But the best times were still when Bob took Ricky up in the air with him, both in the jets and in the smaller propeller planes that Bob would rent for a few hours. Bob would walk Ricky through the pre-flight inspection of the Cessna-152, and taught him how the flaps increased drag which slowed the airplane down, and how the foot pedals were really the rudders, which controlled which way the plane would turn. Rick learned the meaning of, and how to read all the gauges, what to do in a stall, when to pull up during take-off, and of course the basics of landing. The kid was in his glory. His father instilled in him a great respect for airplanes, and Ricky fell in love with the power and capability they represented.

Nervous and scared, Rick's first take-off was a disaster as he over-compensated while he tried to get the feel for the rudder pedals, almost driving the plane off the runway. Calm and collected, Bob coaxed him through, the boy's euphoria exploding as the wheels left the ground and they sailed into the sky. Once in the sky and over open land, Bob would let Rick have the stick and walk him through the basic maneuvers. Ricky was never so proud or honoured when his Dad let him sit in the left-hand pilot's seat. For a kid who could barely see over the cockpit dashboard, he relished the sense of power, control, and complete freedom.

"Wanna see what G-forces can do?" said Bob. Ricky grinned his approval as Bob set a pen on the dashboard. "Ready?"

With a great thrust, Bob pushed the yoke all the way forward, sending the plane into a nosedive. Holding on for dear life, Ricky watched the pen float up to touch the ceiling of the plane, before Bob leveled back out and the pen came back to earth.

"That was seriously cool."

"What about some yee-haw's? Want to do some of them?" Bob really didn't even need to ask. By the grin on his son's face, he knew the answer.

Bob drove the stick forward, increasing the throttle, picking up as much speed as possible for the Cessna. Then, all at once, he'd pull back on the steering, nosing up into a steep climb.

"We're going to stall!" yelled Ricky.

"Nah," said his dad laughing. "Here we go!"

The plane shot down at tremendous speed, like an air born roller coaster flying off the tracks.

"Yee Haw!" both screamed as the G-forces hit, and their stomachs attempted to make their way up through their throats with little concern for age or decorum.

"How was that?" Bob said laughing as soon as they leveled out again and they could breathe.

"Awesome Dad. Just awesome. I want to be just like you when I grow up. You can do everything. You're the best ever. Seriously. I want to be just like you. It's perfect."

****

Rick collapsed onto the shitty mattress, burying his head in his hands. "The Psych ward? What the fuck am I doing in the Psych ward? I'm not crazy." His mind ran amuck. He had no idea why he'd been sent to Mike mod. He'd told Brandenburg that he wasn't suicidal. Why didn't he believe him? He tried to lay down and rest but sleep was distant and his thoughts disturbed.

"So how are you doing tonight?" said a middle-aged woman dressed in medical clothing.

"How am I doing?" said Rick quietly. "I don't know how to answer that because I haven't yet figured out why I'm here…in Mike mod. I don't even know what prison I'm at or what the hell is going on."

"Ah," said the woman. "So no one's talked to you yet? Explained anything?" Rick shook his head. "Well, right now you're in a pre-trial facility, which means you'll stay here until your trial, and then, depending on the verdict, you'll either be set free or sent off to another more-long term prison facility. This section of this facility is known as 'Mike mod' but more formally it's the mental health unit. It's where we house all those prisoners who have confirmed or suspected mental health issues."

Rick wanted to puke. He could only imagine the types of deranged lunatics that surrounded his cell. He'd heard the stories, he watched television; he knew the types they kept here. The fucking crazy bastards. What he did was wrong, he admitted that, but he didn't belong here. Not with them, and especially not as a sixteen-year-old kid. Fuck.

"You'll be kept locked in your cell for twenty-three hours a day for the next week for observation purposes."

"Observation purposes? What does that even mean? I thought that already happened right after I was arrested? I don't understand?"

She could only offer Rick a non-committal smile. "If you need to talk to someone or you feel as though you want to hurt yourself, you need to let us know right away."

"I'm fine," Rick snapped. The last thing he needed was to open up to some shrink, say the wrong thing, and end up in a strait-jacket and padded cell for the rest of his life. He was prepared to pay for his crimes, but not like that. Not in that way. He'd never let them in. He'd do everything possible to convince them he wasn't crazy. But it was too late. Opinions had already been formed.

The newspaper headlines screamed about the ruthlessness of his 'execution style' crime, and how only someone cold-hearted and crazy, could have committed such horrendous acts. Nobody killed their parents. It was practically unheard of, especially from such a quiet, slender, compliant sixteen-year-old with no prior issues. What made him do it? And if he snapped once, there was a very good chance he might snap again, only this time taking his own life, which according to public opinion was too good an ending for the little self-serving bastard.

Breakfast, lunch, and dinner was served through the little slot in the door, and three times a day a nurse came around to ask if he was okay. He always answered yes. Very polite. Very forthright. His arraignment was held at two in the afternoon on December 11, but on the advice of his public defender, he didn't attend. The public defender entered the plea of 'not-guilty' on his behalf, not because he wasn't guilty, but because it was the only plea that would preserve his legal rights as a criminal defendant, and his defence team needed time to sort through the circumstances of his case. All this was new to Rick. He had no idea how the legal proceedings went, and he had to place all of his faith and trust in the legal team appointed to him by the state.

Did they even give a shit about him? Would they believe the events leading up to the murders? Were they really on his side or were they just saying that to fuck with him? Really, what did it matter to them? They were going to get paid one way or the other, and because he'd already confessed, it's not like they could proclaim his innocence. He just had to trust them and hope for the best. Hope for a little understanding. Hope that they'd look after his best interests, at least from a legal perspective. But they couldn't help him, especially not in Mike mod. He was on his own, trying to manoeuver through the unknown surroundings; uncertain, uncomprehending, and completely lost. For a boy used to roaming the forests, sailing the seas, and flying the open skies, Rick knew freedom, now, could only be a state of mind.

The first week in Mike mod gave Rick a chance to get settled and survey his surroundings. Because the front of his cell was a clear four by four foot Plexiglas window, he was afforded no privacy, which also meant he was privy to what was going on in many of the other cells in the mod. The first thing he noticed was that he seemed to be one of the only prisoners who didn't take some sort of medication. Some took a little, and some took a lot. The prisoners however weren't really what he expected in a stereo-typical 'crazy' sort of way. There was one older gentleman who sat in the corner under the stairs and talked to himself, and another tall balding, goofy-looking guy who staggered across the mod like a zombie, only to stare at the same bulletin board for the twentieth time that day. The little Buddha-like native guy just sat still for hours, with his chin resting in his hands, before breaking out into a fit of laughter for no apparent reason. They were weird, but none of them seemed all that psychotic to an unfamiliar Rick.

About one in the morning on his fourth night of residence, a huge banging jolted Rick from his sleep. Someone was kicking the snot out of their cell door, and getting pretty pissed because it wasn't breaking. From his vantage point, Rick could see everything. The cells were all locked so everyone was safe, but this bastard, a kid in his early twenties, just wouldn't shut up.

"You're all just fucking with me!" he screamed, mule kicking the door. "I'm going to kill you all!"

"Settle down," answered the mod-cop who'd rushed in to take control.

"Fuck you! Fuck all of you!" With hands and feet flailing, the guy threw his weight against the door. "I'm gonna get out of here and fucking kill all of you!"

Rick watched from the shadows of his cell, unsure of what to think, captivated by the action. It was obvious this guy was having some sort of mental breakdown. His strength was deceiving. In a flash, a sergeant and three more corrections officers bolted into the area. The sergeant quickly took control, sent the nurses out of the area, and told one of the COs to ready the hand-held video camera. Rick was about to witness his first cell extraction.

"Oh no you don't," screamed the guy, suddenly realizing they were coming in to get him. "You can fuck right off. I ain't going nowhere!" Quickly, he tried jamming his mattress against the door to block their view and their path, throwing his full weight against the mattress. Big mistake. Rick watched the Sergeant break into tactical mode, giving his troops hand signals and whispering instructions. With two officers to either side of the cell door, he slowly and quietly slid the key into the lock.

"Quit blocking the door!" screamed the Sergeant. "Quit blocking the door!"

The kid pressed every ounce of strength against the mattress, mounting his best defence against the impending intruders. Except, he didn't realize the door swung out and not into the cell. As soon as the Sergeant turned the key and flung the door open, both the kid and mattress plowed through with the force of a ram. In a blink, four guards were on his back. The kid did his best to fight back, even trying to bite one of the guards, but with four full grown men digging their knees into your kidneys and shoulder blades, it's pretty much game over.

They cuffed him behind his back, then with each officer grabbing a limb, they picked him up and carried him across the mod toward the exit. Out of his view now, Rick could only listen as they threw the kid into Mike 1, the 'full restraint room'. The ripping of what sounded like Velcro strips from their base, and the rattling of wood peaked Rick's curiosity, and he ventured to the very edge of his cell. Rick couldn't see them strapping the kid to the wooden board that was bolted securely to the concrete floor, and he couldn't see the nurses ready the 'rig' by inserting the syringe in one of the bottles from a drawer in the medical cart. All he could hear was the kids' frantic and desperate screams.

"Don't you put that shit in me! Don't fucking touch me bitch!" He just kept repeating the words over and over. Then there were tears. Sobs actually. Great big sobs, followed by more sobs. Rick figured the kid must have cried his eyes out for more than ten minutes. Then silence. Rick stood there just staring out from his cell, not uttering a sound, too stunned to even breathe.

"Nothing to see Watkinson," said one of the CO's as he walked by Rick's cell. "Get back to bed. Show's over."

But the show wasn't over, and every day there'd be something, someone screaming their guts out, someone laughing like a fucking hyena, or someone just walking, back and forth, and back and forth, going nowhere, but arriving late when he got there. Rick tried to shut it out, tried to keep his mind clear and focused. He couldn't succumb to the madness; he couldn't let the underworld take control. He had to be strong. He had to fight, and the only way to fight was to turn the emotion off. The only way to survive was to go Ghost.

CHAPTER FIVE

Rick had witnessed firsthand the effects of the 'devil juice' and he wanted nothing to do with it. The incident with the kid had scared the shit out of him, one minute he's got the strength of Zeus, the next minute he's crying like a baby for his momma, then he's silent, dead to all the senses except maybe the beating of his own heart. All because of the syringe. No fucking thanks. From that moment on, Rick vowed to never let them get him, and he would never give them the excuse to use it. Never. It wasn't for lack of trying on behalf of the medical staff though.

"What is that?" Rick asked as the nurse slid a small cup filled with a clear thick liquid.

"Oh just something to help you calm down if you're feeling stressed."

"Well I'm not, but what is it?"

Her voice sounded a little nervous. "Just a low dose of Thorazine".

"Thorazine?" Rick's blood began to boil at the mere thought of them offering him an anti-psychotic drug. He stood as tall as his small frame would allow, and looked the nurse dead in the eye. This time, he wasn't backing down.

"Check this out, I have been perfectly behaved and haven't acted out towards any of your staff. I don't need any medication. I'm not going to take any medication, and if you force me to, I will sue the fuck out of this place!" He spun on his heels and sat back down at the desk, refusing to acknowledge her response. It wasn't until she was completely out of sight that he finally realized how lucky he'd been.

"Jesus, Rick," he thought. "She could have called the CO's on you, you stupid prick! And then there might have been some serious trouble. You have to be more careful. Do not let them get control. Don't give them a reason."

Already, after just three weeks in prison, Rick was in full survival mode, and he hadn't even made it into the general prison population yet. Every word out of his mouth had to be calculated, nothing rash, nothing hasty. He didn't deny that he'd become a mouthy kid over the past few years, especially with his father and Rosemary, but he'd have to keep that impulsivity in check, and harness the bitterness of his situation. This was prison, this was Mike mod, and no matter what, he'd never have the upper hand. It was just something he'd have to deal with.

Later that evening, one of the other nurses stopped by, one that Rick liked and for the most part trusted, and he told her what had happened.

"I heard they tried to give you meds," she sighed. "You did right by saying no."

"I was scared," said Rick. "I was only supposed to be in 'observation' for a week, but it's been like three, and I have no idea what's going on, or what the hell is going to happen to me."

The nurse flipped her blonde hair to the side and motioned for Rick to come closer. "Brandenburg has ordered us to keep you here until at least the end of the month, and if you don't act up, or cause any trouble, then you should be out of Mike mod and placed in general population. But there's a catch. You are supposed to participate in the programs the prison offers. You know, like twice a week they have Narcotics Anonymous and once a week there's Alcoholics Anonymous. And the 'Wellness Checks'. You need to do those."

"Is that where everyone sits around and just talks about how they feel?"

"More or less," she answered. "But even if you keep quiet and to yourself like you are now, going to the groups is going to get you out of here faster. Do you have a GED or high school diploma?"

"Not yet. I'm only sixteen. I didn't get a chance to finish high school."

"Okay, well I can get in touch with the Education supervisor for you. I think it's a good idea to start working on your GED. Something to keep you busy at least."

"I'd like that, thanks."

"Oh, and one other thing. Be careful of some of the other inmates…even the ones who appear all friendly. There are some serious sicko's in here Rick, in a real sexual predatory way, and you need to steer clear."

"Thanks for your help and the advice. I really appreciate it. You didn't have to be so nice to me but you were, so thanks."

"Well I like you Rick, and despite what you did, I think you're a reasonably good kid. I'm not sure what happened, and really it's none of my business, but you're young, and you're small, and I'm not saying you couldn't defend yourself because I don't know you all that well, I'm just saying be careful."

Rick's first day out of isolation came on December 16. The morning nurses had stopped by the cell to tell him that he'd be let out for lunch, and if he behaved, he'd be allowed to stay out of his cell the rest of the day. When lunch rolled around, his cell door slid open and he was 'free' for the first time since his incarceration. Keeping to himself, he picked a tray of food from the mobile cart and found a seat at the edge of the mod. It wasn't that he didn't want to mingle or get to know anyone, but with so much unknown about his surrounding mod mates, playing it safe and cool seemed like the best option. Rick sat at the four by four steel table, and began to eat. He tried to ignore the short, fat man who sat down in the chair directly across from him, his eyes bearing down on Rick like a tiger.

"Hey youngster. Let me get that tray." The man's tone wasn't overly aggressive but it was harsh enough to prick the ears of both the nurse and the CO sitting at their desks about fifteen feet away.

"I'm eating this dude," said Rick passively, shoving more food into his mouth. He didn't want a confrontation. Not on his first day out.

"I'm not asking. I'm telling you to give me the tray you little punk."

"Hey!" yelled the nurse to the man. "Knock it off."

All those years of being the underdog, playing hunt or be hunted, and honing his fighting skills percolated in Rick's rising blood. The adrenaline was kicking in. Survive. This man wasn't his father, he could fight back, he could defend himself, take a stand. He stopped eating and looked the man dead in the eyes.

"And I told you, I'm eating this food, now get lost."

The man half-smiled. "You can get lost when you give me your food."

Before the man's smile had a chance to creep full out to the corners of his mouth, Rick was across the table, his hand finding the back of the man's head, thrusting it downward, slamming him face first into Rick's own tray of food. The man bounced back off the table, falling ass first on the hard concrete floor, bits of food dangling from his chest and forehead.

"Have it then you stupid mother fucker." Rick turned from the table and headed back across the mod towards his cell.

"Watkinson go lockdown!" screamed the CO in the midst of the stunned and silent room.

"Jesus!" said the nurse making her way to check on the guy.

Rick calmly entered his cell, sat on his desk, and put his feet up on the bolted stool. He'd made his point. No one was going to fuck with him.

"Control! Close Mike 7!"

Rick's cell door slammed shut. He didn't care. He had no idea what was going to happen to him for assaulting another prisoner, the only thing that mattered was that everyone had seen how he didn't back down. He didn't back down from anyone when he was a kid on the streets, and he sure as hell wasn't going to start in prison. Rick wasn't going to be the prison bitch. No fucking way. He may be young, and he may be scrawny, but life had taught him to be scrappy. After all, he was a warrior. God's Little Warrior.

****

On the surface, Ricky's childhood seemed idyllic; planes, boats, running free in the woods, hanging with his little brother. But for some the surface isn't really what it appears to be, and that surface can just be a mask for the many layers that lie underneath. While the sun shines, and the rain, rains, the world spins, and nobody seems to notice the forces that drive the heavens and the earth. But the forces are there, hidden, yet lurking in the shadows, visible to only those who have 'the gift'. For those that believe, the world is in a constant state of warfare between the forces of good and evil, and the only way to win the war, was to arm yourself and those you love with the proper tools. Spiritual warfare is not fought with bullets or spears, it's fought with fire and brimstone, and prayer. Lots and lots of prayer. And those that have 'the gift' are relied upon to take the reins, and lead the charge as God's warriors on earth, fighting the demons, and ridding the world of Satan's mischief.

Religion had always been a part of little Ricky's life. His father was raised in a conservative Christian atmosphere, while his mother began to embrace a more experimental progressive form of Christianity. The two didn't mix, and soon became a source of anxiety in the marriage and the family. The Watkinson house was a solid Christian stronghold, with church every Sunday, and Bible stories and verses for the children to memorize. Like a good Christian boy, Rick could easily convey the story of Abraham and Isaac, Moses and the Red Sea, or Joseph and his coat of many colours. Over time, the learning of these stories and verses all became much more structured and almost rigorous, taking a distinct turn from simply learning about the Bible to applying the lessons and the Word. For Brenda, religion quit being about just going to church and having a belief in God. It became the focus of her entire life; God and His Will.

For hours and hours, she'd sit in her recliner, Bible in one hand, a highlighter in the other, with various other religious books tucked down the side of the chair or on her knees. Ricky and Jimmy knew not to bother her, so they'd go outside to run wild in the forest, or bike down the old country road. They never strayed all that far, and they knew no matter what, that God would protect them and keep them safe. Ricky loved the sense of freedom, being out on his own, with no one to answer to, and no one to tell him what to do. Who doesn't want the freedom to roam unsupervised when you're an eight-year-old kid? The time Brenda spent reading would only intensify when Bob was away. He believed, but he didn't believe that much, and he scoffed at Brenda's diligence and devotion.

They tried to find a happy medium; a church that held true to both their values, but what worked for Bob wasn't strict or progressive enough for Brenda, and what worked for Brenda was unacceptable to Bob. At one point, they thought they'd found the perfect compromise, that is until the pastor covertly suggests 'wife-swapping' as a way for the congregation (and himself) to get to know each other a little better. Bob just couldn't understand where Brenda was heading or what her mind was thinking. He didn't believe in 'speaking in tongues' or demon possession or some of the 'weird' and 'stranger' practices of this new form of Christianity. He wanted to go to church on Sunday's, then come home and crack a beer before saying grace at dinner. Simple religion. You believe, and when you die, you go to heaven. But for Brenda, religion was so much more. It wasn't something you just practiced on Sunday's, it was something you lived each and every hour of the day.

The training started in earnest when Ricky was about seven or eight, when Brenda would sneak him and Jimmy off to services at one of her new 'non-denominational' churches.

"You have to promise me boys," said Brenda fixing their little dress jackets. "You can't ever tell your father."

"Why?" said Rick. "Doesn't Daddy know Christ?

"Daddy just doesn't understand things like I do. He just isn't ready yet. But you and Jimmy should pray for him. Pray that he will open his eyes so that he too might be saved before it's too late. In the meantime, you can't tell him about our little trips? Promise me. In the name of God."

"We promise. In the name of God," echoed both boys.

Ricky didn't really understand why they couldn't tell their Dad about the church, but he figured if it stopped them from fighting, he'd agree and get Jimmy to agree as well. His parents had been arguing a lot lately, especially about church, and he hated listening to them argue. They loved each other, and if they loved each other, that meant they shouldn't argue. So if Ricky had to keep a secret, well then, he had to keep a secret. That's just the way things worked. At least that seemed to be good reasoning for a kid still shy of his ninth birthday.

Ricky didn't necessarily hate going to these new churches, in fact, the people babbling on in some incoherent language fascinated him.

"Why do the people talk like that Mommy?" he asked one day as they were driving home.

"They're speaking in tongues Ricky, which means that God is speaking to them directly, telling them his prophecies, and His Word."

"But I couldn't understand what that guy was saying?"

"Well that's why someone else is there to translate the words into English. That person understands God's language, and you must always remember Ricky that God's language is the most powerful thing on earth."

"Oh." He still didn't truly understand but the explanation sounded reasonable to his young ears. "Will I ever be able to speak like that?"

"If you pray hard enough and believe, Ricky. Just pray, pray, pray.

Ricky learned all about the power of the Word, and how sometimes the sheer strength of hearing the Word caused people to fall on their hands and knees and roar like lions or faint and fall over backwards from being so completely filled with the Holy Spirit.

"You see boys," said Brenda. "Demons are very real. They are all around us, in people, in places, and we must cast them out. It's our duty as God's Warrior's."

"But I don't see any demons Mommy."

"Being able to actually see the demons is a true gift from God Ricky, and only a chosen few have that gift. But you just have to trust me…demons are everywhere and you must be very careful."

Terrified, Ricky quickly peeked over his shoulder, just to make sure there wasn't a demon sitting in the back seat. He had no idea what they might look like, but he could only imagine that they must be the most terrible, horrifying creatures ever. He'd start carrying his Swiss Army knife at all times now, just in case.

Brenda began to hold Bible study meetings at the house, training the boys in the Holy Spirit, teaching them about demons, spiritual warfare, and what one was capable of when God was channelled through them. And learn they did.

Ricky stood off to the side of the room, with five-year-old Jimmy huddled closely under his protective arm.

"Heal her Jesus!" The group formed a circle around the screaming woman; her wild hair flapping as her demon-possessed soul flayed against the circle of warriors.

"Cast thy demon out!"

A wolf-like howl ripped from the depths of the woman's bowels, her teeth set now like fangs, trying to bite and gnaw, thrashing about. To a feverish pitch, the passion rose, then rose some more. As the heat in the room touched the fires of hell, Ricky pulled Jimmy closer, burying his little brother's head in his own chest. Every ounce of his conscience was begging him to look away, but he couldn't. The whole group was chanting, screaming, and praying, the language of God at the forefront of every tongue.

"Ricky," sobbed Jimmy. "Make it stop!"

"Shh Jimmy. It'll be okay, I'll protect you."

Ricky caught a glimpse of his mother, right in the thick of the circle, her eyes closed in a haze of fervour, praying for the soul of the damned, praying to cast the demon out. He felt himself drawn to the action, and more importantly, he felt the power of God filling every ounce of the room. With a final tortuous scream, the possessed woman dropped to the ground, her body wracking and shaking as the demon took his final stand. Screams were replaced by sobs; the power of God had triumphed. The warriors victorious.

Over the next while the boys witnessed many such events, and eventually both gained the ability to speak in tongues. It wasn't quite what Ricky thought it would be. He was praying and praying about something when suddenly he felt himself open up to God, and then these random sounds just sort of exited through his mouth. God didn't actually whisper any words in his ears, and Ricky had no idea what he was saying, but he sure as hell knew that some sort of babble was spewing out of his eight-year-old mouth.

"Ricky!" said his mother. "You did it! You're speaking in the language of the angels!"

"But what does it mean Mommy? I don't feel any different. Do I look different?"

"No son. But you are glowing with the word of God. You are now armed, even stronger in the battle Ricky. God bless you. One day, the Holy Spirit will reveal itself to you. I just know it."

"How will I know when that happens?"

"Oh Ricky, you'll be able to feel it with every ounce of your soul."

Ricky still had no clue what it all meant, nor did he understand why he'd been able to talk that way. Was he just caught up in the moment? Or had God really spoken to him? For a young boy, the enormity and the chaos of the situation was overwhelming and confusing. He desperately wanted to tell his father about his new-found gift but his mother's words echoed through his head.

"You must never tell your father. You must never tell your father."

"I'm so proud of you Ricky," she'd say. "My sweet little warrior."

Life continued in the Watkinson household. The boys kept their secret, and when Bob was home there was no mention of demons or the devil. Ricky began to look at the world differently, his mind consumed with what lay in the shadows and haunted the night. While still his safe place, the forest took on new meaning, and the rustles in the leaves might not always represent a slithering snake or a scampering racoon. He thought too much, and spent too much time alone, wondering and wandering. His head should have been filled with love and laughter, thoughts of ponies and frogs, instead, he dwelled somewhere in the in between, never sure what was of this world or the other. He desperately wanted to please his mother. She was only looking out for her boys because she loved them. But he also loved his father, more than he could ever describe, and the secrets and lies began to push those worlds in different directions.

"Are you ready to receive the gift of the Holy Spirit?" The man looked intently into Ricky's brown eyes. The boys were with their mother in a small hotel room in Seattle. Bob was gone, so Brenda took the opportunity to take the boys to a prayer meeting. Had Bob known, he would have exploded with rage.

"Um, yes?" Rick answered.

"People. Gather around young Ricky."

Rick stood terrified in the middle of the circle as those surrounding him began to speak in tongues and lay their hands on him.

The man cupped his hand on the boy's forehead. "Dear Lord, I call on you to bless this boy and fill him with all the blessings of the Lord. Fill him with the Holy Spirit." The chant like tone of his voice lulled Rick away. "Lord, come down and bless this boy. Fill him with the Holy Spirit. Help him seek the light that draws the chosen few to your service. Lord, we ask of you. Fill his soul with the Holy Spirit."

As the words continued, Rick closed his eyes and gave into the power of the circle, his voice over-taken by the language of the angels. As he prayed, a hot tingling sensation drifted through his little body, rendering him powerless and powerful all at the same time. The Holy Spirit. The room blanked white and his knees collapsed, sprawling him to the floor. Distorted choruses of "Praise the Lord!" and "Hallelujah!" rang through the air, reaching Rick's ears in a muffled state of consciousness. He was there, but he wasn't. Slowly the room came back into focus, and the boy was like a drunk picking himself up off the carpet, blurred and dizzy. A tight vise-grip clawed his iron hot forehead, and Rick thought for sure his head was going to explode. That was it. It was over.

They said he'd received the Holy Spirit, but there were no miraculous visions or divine messages. As he moved to his feet, he did notice that he felt strange, like somehow, he was floating outside of his body, seeing things, but not really aware of what they were or what he was doing. Being in the hotel room, yet floating high above the streetlights, passing cars, and the Seattle nightlife. At the time, he didn't understand that at that precise moment he'd been given 'the gift', not just of the Holy Spirit, but of 'the sight', and he was way too young to comprehend the profound effect this experience would have on his life.

Brenda and the boys kept attending the strange churches behind Bob's back, continuing their training in spiritual warfare and preparing themselves for 'God's Will'. Of course, Brenda was always on the lookout, knowing evil lurked everywhere, almost a religious paranoia, that she could no longer control. Her senses sharpened when a woman in her late fifties just sort of appeared on the scene. She lived directly behind the Watkinson house but no one had really seen or noticed her before. She came by one day for coffee with Brenda, and Ricky thought nothing of the woman's visit. She didn't seem strange or crazy, just an old woman with short grey hair and an ugly sweater. A few days after that initial get together the woman showed up at the house again, just as Brenda was trying to get the car started.

"What seems to be the problem Brenda?"

"Oh this dumb car! I don't know what's wrong with it!"

"Mind if I have a look under the hood?"

Brenda shrugged her shoulders. "Sure. I guess it can't hurt."

The lady stuck her head under the hood, and fiddled with something. "Try it now."

Brenda turned the ignition and the car jumped to life, purring like a cat. "What was wrong?"

"Oh just a little loose wire."

As the lady walked back out of sight, Brenda turned the car off. Something wasn't right.

"Can we go get ice cream now Mommy?" said Jimmy. "The car works."

"No Jimmy," she answered. "No ice cream tonight."

"But you said!"

"Jimmy I said no! That's it. End of story."

The car sat in the driveway until Bob got home from his business trip a few days later.

"You were right not to drive it Brenda," he said closing the hood. "The brake fluid is almost completely empty. Who knows what would have happened if you got driving and ran out. Loss of brakes for sure. You and the kids were lucky."

But Brenda didn't see anything as luck. She had a feeling. The minute Bob was back on the road, she pulled the boys aside.

"I think that creepy lady had something to do with the car. In fact, I'm quite sure of it."

"All she did was look under the hood," said Rick.

"And while she was looking, she cursed it. She put a curse on the car and made it unsafe to drive. We need to lay hands on it, pray in tongues, and ask God to cleanse it and remove any wickedness."

For the next thirty minutes, Brenda and the boys 'cleansed' the car with words and prayers. But still that wasn't enough.

"Ricky, I need you to do something for me…for all of us. We need to be safe."

"What Mommy? I'll do it."

"That woman. I just don't trust her. She has this evilness about her. I could sense it. Couldn't you?"

All Ricky had sensed was that maybe the woman might want to consider taking a shower every so often, but he wasn't about to disagree with his mother, especially when it came to demons. "I guess so Mommy."

"When she leaves, I want you to sneak into her house and look around."

"You want me to break into her house?"

"Yes. Look around and tell me what you see. Pay special attention to any books, statues, or strange symbols. You have to be my eyes Ricky. Don't let me down. The arms of the devil are nearer than we think."

Ricky just shrugged his shoulders. The fact he had his mother's permission to sneak into someone else's house and snoop around was pretty cool. It's a good thing he'd had so much practice slinking through the woods unnoticed, and blending in with the surroundings. The chance to be able to do it for real was exhilarating. They waited until they were sure the woman had driven away. Brenda kept a look out from the cover of the woods behind the house, cupping her hand above her eyes to keep the blazing sun out.

"Okay now Ricky! Go! Be careful." she whispered.

Light on his feet, Rick dashed across the back lawn, his shoes barely making an imprint in the soft grass. The closer he got the house, the more his anxiousness rose. What if they were wrong and she hadn't left the house? Or what if she had other people living there? In all of his eight years he'd never been so nervous or scared, his pounding heart ready to bust through his chest. Gulping hard, he opened the magnetic box under the front porch lantern and retrieved the key. With a quick look back over his shoulder and the safety of the woods, he stuck the key in the door and turned the lock. Fully expecting to be stabbed through the head by a waiting axe-murderer or shot point blank, the boy took a deep breath and said a quick prayer. Isn't that what all warriors did before going into battle?

Silent but unsure, Rick crept through each of the rooms, keeping a watchful eye for anything 'Satan-like'. He really had no idea what he was looking for but supposed he'd know it if he saw it. He picked up one of the books from the large bookshelf.

"This has a moon symbol and it says Goddess," he thought. "Maybe that means something."

The exotic jackal headed art work on the wall scared the shit out of him but it looked more like something he saw in the books about Egypt and the Great Pyramids, than anything about Satan. And he really regretted opening the dresser drawer that stored her seemingly gigantic bras and panties. That was an image he could definitely live without. The house did have sort of a creepy vibe to it, nothing that made Rick really scared for his soul, just more of an 'I'm snooping around some old lady's house all by myself and I'm sure as hell something is going to jump out and get me' sort of creepiness.

"Well," said Brenda as soon as Rick was back in the safety of the woods. "What did you see?" Rick told her everything he saw, which was really nothing all that important. "I knew it! She's a witch! Oh Ricky, the evil that lurks in that house." Her body quivered ever so slightly. "We must go back."

"Now?" said Rick.

"No. Tonight. We'll go back tonight and rid that house of the evil."

Rick wasn't at all sure he wanted to return to the house, and especially not at night, when real evil was out prowling around. At least the daylight afforded them some protection, in the dark of night, Satan always had the upper hand.

After dinner, Brenda, Ricky, and little Jimmy waited at the edge of the forest. The woman hadn't yet returned and Brenda was taking a huge risk. If they got caught, it would mean the police and probably charges. Bob would find out and there'd be hell to pay.

"The Lord will protect us. Put all your trust in him boys."

"Yes Mommy," they answered.

As soon as the sun set behind the trees, they set off on their mission. Rick found the key and once again unlocked the door.

"I'm scared Mommy," said Jimmy.

Rick squeezed his little brother's hand and whispered. "Be brave Jimmy. We're warriors. God will protect us."

Rick led them into the main room, and showed Brenda the book.

"Jesus, Lord, help us to cleanse this house of the inherent evil that dwells. Boys, pray with me."

All three of them began to pray with all their might that the Lord cleanse the house and send the woman, the 'emissary of the Devil' away for good.

"Send her away from this place oh Lord. Let her move and bring her evil somewhere else. Turn the evil that she wished upon us, back unto herself oh Lord."

They continued praying until Ricky thought that he just couldn't pray any more, yet still they stayed.

"Pray harder boys. God will hear our prayers."

Finally, Brenda said they were finished, it was in the Lord's hand now. They'd done all they could. Ricky and Jimmy were happy. They just wanted to get the hell out of there and go back home and play in their bedroom fort.

"I'm proud of you tonight boys. You did God's bidding, and you're both very special warriors. Be strong because there is so much more work to be done. This is just the beginning. And remember, whatever you do, do not tell your father what happened here tonight. His eyes are still shut to the power and the necessity of our work."

His mom didn't have to worry. Ricky had no plans of telling his father that'd he'd broken into the witch neighbour's house, not once but twice in the same day, and that they'd all prayed their guts out for either her salvation or her quick yet painful death. Bob would have flipped a lid on both he and his mother, and there would have been serious consequences. Ricky wasn't that stupid. His parents already fought like crazy over religion, he'd heard them many times. Sometimes, they'd slam some doors or whack something against a table. He'd seen his father's temper. He wasn't going to say a bloody thing to make things worse. Instead, he'd pray for him. Mommy said the best thing to do for Daddy was to pray for him. So he did.

CHAPTER SIX

Rick laid back down on his bed and waited for the authorities to come get him. He had no idea what sort of punishment slamming a guy's head into a tray of food yielded, but he figured he was in for some sort of disciplinary action. He didn't give a shit. He'd stuck up for himself, and at this point, that's all that mattered. If it bought him some respect, all the better. He wasn't there to cause trouble, but he also wasn't about to let himself get taken advantage of. He wasn't a punk, never had been, and never would be, and if copping an attitude meant he'd be afforded some peace, then so be it.

"So you ready to try again?" said the morning nurse poking her head in front of the cell window. "It's a new day and a fresh start?"

Rick eyed her cheerful smile with a hint of suspicion, then shrugged his shoulders. "Sure." Grabbing a tray of food from the trolley, he deliberately made his way to a back table, and this time, no one bothered him. His first prison triumph; a small yet satisfying feat.

Although the common area wasn't all that large, it gave the active teen a chance to burn off some of the pent up energy pulsing through his legs. It felt like a lifetime since he'd been able to roam at will, and his mind wondered if he'd ever feel the crunch of the forest or the breeze on his face again. Would he ever see or hear from anyone again? His Mother? His friends? Would they even want to talk to him? He couldn't go there. As far as he was concerned, all his dreams were dead. They had to be. Dreaming of the future was even more pointless then dwelling in the past. Too many memories, too many mistakes, too much pain and anguish. He couldn't go back, yet he couldn't move forward; life was a constant state of inertia, a treadmill going nowhere, no matter how fast he ran. Hope was gone, bottled up and thrown down the river with its counterparts, optimism, anticipation, and faith. Faith, such a loaded word. Faith in God, faith in himself. All had failed. He had failed God, and in a very real way, God had failed him, hung him out to dry, left him alone and confused, overwhelmed and unprepared to handle the demons raging in his own head. He'd gone to war for Christ, but when he needed God to step up and snap him out of that incredible moment of despair, and to keep him from making a horrible mistake, the Saviour was absent. Faith. Redeemer. Believer. Sometimes words are just words, and sometimes it's all just plain bullshit.

It didn't take long for Rick to fall into the routine of life in Mike Mod, especially since every minute of that routine stayed the same, day after day after day. He'd grab a few tattered books from the bookshelf to occupy his time, but they were always a shitty read, and he much preferred the newspaper when he could get his hands on it. When he wasn't reading, he was watching; watching his back, watching his meager belongings, and watching just what being crazy was all about. He'd never felt so alone.

"Watkinson. These are for you." The guard handed him a stack of envelopes.

"What's this?"

"It's your mail."

"Mail?"

"Yes mail," said the guard with a half-hearted smirk. "You're in prison, you're not dead."

"Jesus. I never knew we could get mail?"

"Have fun reading."

Rick took the stack of letters and settled at the desk in his cell, his brown eyes wide with wonderment. He had no idea that he'd still be able to communicate with people from his 'old life'. Why he thought that was beyond his own comprehension at that moment, but spending the first sixteen days of your 'new life' in complete isolation had a way of skewering perceptions.

"They're still out there. And they care. They probably hate my fucking guts but at least they took the time to write. Jesus." His voice hardly reverberated above the pounding in his chest. His hands traced over the handwritten return addresses. "Kristy. Crystal. Natalie. Kayleen. Mom. Oh my God. Mom." He set that letter aside, his courage of heart waning.

"Kristy. My dear sweet Kristy." Apprehension guided his shaking fingers as he dug his forefinger under the small gap where the fold meets the glue. Things hadn't ended well between them. Things were said, and shit happened, dumb, stupid shit, that in the scheme of life, didn't mean a God damn thing. He'd wanted so bad to take her hand and to explain everything the morning after the murders. They'd been there for each other so many times, yet in this instance, he had to protect her, he had to keep her as far away from this fucking mess as possible. She was going to hate him for what he did, and really, Rick wouldn't blame her if she did.

Dear Rick,

I still can't believe what happened and I'll never really understand why you did what you did. I knew it was bad at home but Jesus. You should have said something. I could have helped you. I'm not going to tell you that I'm not angry as fuck for what you did. It was stupid.

So, so fucking stupid! But I feel bad for you, and I'm sorry that we drifted apart over the last few months. Something was different though, like you weren't the same, like you weren't really there. And I take some responsibility for that because I should have known something was really wrong, and I should have been there to help you. I'm sorry. I'll never forgive myself for being such a shitty friend…

"Fuck Kristy, none of this was your fault! How can I make you see that and understand? I'm the one who snapped! You had nothing to do with it. Fuck. Please don't take even an ounce of blame for this."

With each letter, the guilt coursed, the pressure building on his already incapacitated heart. Crystal professing her undying love, saying she was going to stand by him no matter what. Sweet Natalie, totally blaming herself for what happened. Saying she spent hours kicking the wall outside her house, wondering where it all went wrong, and how she couldn't have seen how distraught he was. How did she not see? How could she have been so blind? They all blamed themselves. They blamed themselves for his fucked up mess. His eyes wandered about the confines of his existence, the air in the cell hot and thick against his heaving chest. Every word from every letter etched itself deep in his soul. Despair. Despondency. Utter fucking guilt. For the first time, he truly understood the magnitude of his crime, and how wide the profound circle of hurt radiated. Friends, family, acquaintances. All had been touched. All had somehow been affected, some more than others, but nevertheless, Rick felt their pain, and absorbed their own guilty feelings into the swell of his own.

He stared at the letter from his mother. He knew at some point he'd have to read it. He wasn't there yet. So much had happened between himself and his mom. There were reasons he'd been sent to Alaska to live with his father. So many mistakes. So many quarrels. Neither side absolved from any blame. Rick certainly hadn't been a model teenager, and many times he'd pushed the buzzer and ignited the fires with both his mother and his father. With his dad dead, his mom was all he had left. Would she too reject him? Would she choose to cast him aside, just like his father had done? As he stared at the letter, the ground beef he'd eaten at lunch began jumping around his stomach like it still had legs. He needed to just calm down and read the letter. Get it over with. If she wanted nothing more to do with him, then at least he'd know and he could move on, or at least try to move on. He picked up the envelope and tore open the back.

My Dearest Rick,

There are so many things I want to say right now but can't seem to find the words. I can't even imagine what you are going through. My poor, poor son. Please try to remain calm and hopeful. We still love you bird. We're all praying for you and God will make sure this isn't the end of your life. You won't die in prison. Be strong. You have to be strong! We're all here for you and support you. I don't condone what you did, and I'm trying to understand how things with your father got so bad. I'm sorry you felt you had no other option. Remember, we love you, and I will try to get to visit you as soon as I can. Be strong with God Rick.

Love you always, Mom

The words hit hard. He wanted to cry. He knew he should cry, but the tears just wouldn't come. The emotional void 'Ghost' provided left him empty, even when he so desperately wanted to feel. Reading the letters should have negated the nothingness, instead it just made him more aware of how deep his desolation ran, and how powerless he was to control it. The past six years he'd made a conscious effort not to feel, to turn it all off, and bury it deep within his soul. At every turn, he'd programmed himself, made himself believe that he couldn't feel, and now when he truly wanted to feel, to experience that release, he couldn't. So far, the psychological barriers he'd put up to protect himself from all the pain, and now, the reality of his crime, held strong against the natural physical reactions that would have afforded him some relief. Something, anything, even just a tiny droplet, would have at least let him know that he was still capable of catharsis, still capable of experiencing human emotion. Despite what the world thought of him, he wasn't a cold-hearted monster. The emotions were there, and the tears were there, but they were buried under years of hate, and years of trying not to give a shit about anyone or anything. 'Ghost' was just an apparition shrouding the truth. The night of the murders blew the dam wide open, and eventually the river of sorrow would come crashing through. It had to, before it drowned his soul for good.

Over the next couple of weeks, Rick settled into the Mike Mod routine. There were Narcotics Anonymous and Alcoholics Anonymous meetings to attend, although he was neither an addict nor an alcoholic. Attending the meetings showed a willingness to co-operate, and Rick figured anything he could do to pump up his 'prison resume' for good behaviour was a plus. For the most part, he stayed quiet during the meetings, choosing more to observe rather than share his own story. It's not like he was itching to talk about it anyway, and especially not in an open forum of crazy-asses. The quietness fit his perceived 'prison profile' and that was fine with him. The more the staff and nurses saw him as a scared, relatively harmless little sixteen-year-old, the better. And while to a certain extent they were right, they also had no idea how much violence and fighting that 'scared' little kid had encountered in his lifetime. No stranger to being the underdog, Rick figured out rather quickly that using the 'victim' stance to his advantage afforded him the safest way to exist in this new environment.

Mike Mod wasn't like roaming the streets in the middle of the night, running into the odd fucked up crack ball, who was too drunk to take two steps, let alone chase your ass down. This shit was real. There was nowhere to run, and certainly no place to hide. He had to be smart and use every life lesson living on the streets taught him; always be aware of your surroundings, and always have a way out, some sort of escape route. Never let yourself get trapped in a situation you can't handle, and if at all possible, keep your damn mouth shut.

"I can never let them think I'm even the slightest bit crazy," he thought. "Everyone in this fucking place is on some sort of meds whether they need it or not, and there's no way I'm going to let them dope me up. Never going to let it happen. That poor old man. They fucked him up pretty good, and for no reason."

Rick didn't know all the details but apparently, the elder man had been admitted to the Mod because he was distraught over losing his wife. The guy seemed stable, and at first interacted and spoke with everyone just fine. Then staff gave him some sort of psychotropic medication to 'calm his nerves'. In less than forty-eight hours, he completely spun out and trashed his room, destroying everything he could, including his personal property. Rick could hear him screaming; didn't know what the hell he was saying, but the anger and rage flailing from his lungs disturbed even the most battle worn troop.

"Get a hold of him!"

"Calm down sir, calm down now!"

"Bring the med tray!"

As soon as the needle full of Thorazine pierced the elderly man's skin, the screaming stopped, and in turn, so did his waking existence. Like so many others in the Mod, the man joined the walking dead, those who just shuffled along, slow and deliberate, with vacant glazed eyes looking off into the nothingness.

"That is not going to be me," said Rick.

Some of the prisoners needed a hell of lot more than a dose or two of magic juice in their arms to keep their stability in check. Rick dreaded the late night droning mantra coming from the slider across the room.

"God is shit. God is shit. God is shit."

Over and over and over. He didn't know whether to laugh or cringe as the man spread his own shit all over himself and everything in his reach. If it was just a onetime thing, maybe he could understand, but it wasn't just a onetime thing, and watching the scene unfold time and time again, really gave new meaning to the word disturbing. This guy was 'bad' crazy. Nothing redeeming about him. There was a difference between 'good' crazy and 'bad' crazy. Some people have their quirks, like fast-talking or playing gin rummy with some guy no one else can see. That shit makes them funny and interesting, although sometimes volatile in an almost hyper but not dangerous way. Those were the types of guys he'd encountered on the streets, nothing too dangerous, but strange enough that you wanted to keep your distance. The 'bad' crazy were those types who were just barely holding themselves together; the guys you didn't even want to make eye contact with because you had no idea what they would do or how they might attempt to fuck you over. If his mother had been there, she'd have been horrified at the plethora of evil lurking behind every shadowed leer and every comely glance. There was nothing Jesus could do to save these souls, no matter how hard anyone prayed; salvation had long slipped out of reach, greased by the contemptuous wail of minds unhinged.

Rick did everything he could to steer clear and not ruffle the feathers of those whose feathers had already clearly been ruffled.

"You know you can go to Rec if you want?" said the nurse.

"What's Rec?"

"Recreation. It's not much but it'll give you a chance to get outside."

The frigid Alaskan air blasted against his thinly clothed body. No hat, no coat, no mitts. He didn't care. The cold air sunk deep into every pocket of his lungs, shocking his muscles into movement. Not that there was much room to move. More of a cement courtyard, than a recreation area, solid cement walls stretched around twelve feet into the sky on all sides of the triangular shaped enclosure. The fifteen-foot grated fence shouldered by the cement walls made sure the only recreation taking place was on the ground. No matter, at least the chain-link fence roof allowed in the sun, affording a much more pleasing aesthetic natural light than the fluorescence of his cell.

"I guess I just walk?" said Rick looking around at the lack of available play things. "One, two, three…thirty."

He'd already reached the tip of the triangle. He desperately wanted to run back and forth, just to feel the muscles in his legs again, to see if they even still worked. His mind shifted back to all those times his breath ran ragged from sprinting through the forest, hopping and leaping over fallen trees, being the complete master of his domain. Total freedom. Doing as he pleased. Or the nights he'd slip out his bedroom window and roam the streets like an urchin, befriending those who lived in the shadows of anonymity, doing what he had to, to fit in, to be accepted, living a double life. Living a lie. But he wasn't the only one living a lie.

****

Not long after Rick's tenth birthday, the family made the move to the small town of McMinnville, Oregon. Evergreen International had promoted Bob to 'Chief Pilot', which meant he was now in charge of Evergreen International's entire fleet of 727s. While a promotion usually seems like a good thing, for Bob it meant his beloved cockpit was replaced with a chipped wooden desk loaded with flight schedules and timesheets; not ideal for a man who thrived on adventure and pushing the limits. The only thing he was pushing now was papers.

The family purchased a two-storey house on Johnson Street, with a workshop, and a decent property, although Rick was sad to leave his forest behind. But new surroundings meant new exploration, and Ricky was keen to map out the area, and plot his territory. With an apple tree, a huge maple, and a couple of large evergreens, the boys were set for things to climb, and for things to throw at each other. The main intrigue became the shopping center, just a quick climb up the maple tree, and a drop down the other side of the fence to the uninhabited grassy corner of the block, then a quick scoot across the road. Freedom. Loaded with stores like The Gap, Payless, Safeway, McDonalds, and a Pizza Hut, the area was a treasure chest for a kid like Rick, so much to explore. Behind the shopping center, a long, paved stretch of loading docks bordered an apartment complex and some more dwellings. For a kid used to running free and unseen in a forest, this concrete jungle became a new challenge to maneuver, with the numerous streets, homes and stores providing a maze of get-away routes. Lying on the far side of the shopping complex was Highway 99, the final frontier, a raging river of cars, and at the time, the apex of his explorations.

With the bustle of the move and the pre-occupation with his new environment, the kid was in his glory, completely happy and carefree, unaware of the trouble brewing, and completely unprepared for the emotional explosion lurking in the shadows.

"Daddy's home!"

Bob shut the front door and brushed past his oldest son. "Can I speak to you boys in your room?"

"Maybe he brought us something Jimmy?"

Jimmy burst into a huge grin and followed his big brother like a little puppy. Both boys took a seat on the hardwood floor, while Bob took a seat on Ricky's bed. Curious about all the commotion, Brenda leaned inside the doorway. Although still day, the beaming sun against the partially closed yellowish blinds cast an eerie orangish-glow, an almost rusty blood-red, throughout the room as if the sky outside was on fire.

"I'm leaving your Mom. We're getting a divorce. I won't be living at home anymore."

Ricky didn't understand. What did he mean he wouldn't be living there anymore? He had to live there, he was their Dad. That's how families worked. Ricky looked to his mother for reassurance but she was a white sheet, the wall barely supporting her defeated frame. It would have been nice if Bob had at least given her the courtesy of divulging his divorce plans before he told the boys. She'd known it'd been a possibility for a while now, but to do this to her and the boys in this way, without even giving her a chance to prepare them was unforgivable. Fucking bastard. She could feel the weight of Rick's stare but she was helpless, and turned her eyes away.

"But you can't leave!"

"Mom and I aren't getting along Ricky. I'm leaving." He rose from the bed, and walked out of the bedroom towards the front door.

Little Ricky was a blur. Everything and everyone in the room had blended into the orange glow, distorting the lines of reality. Was this really happening? Was his father, the person he loved and cherished most in the world, leaving? Life without his father, his mentor, his hero - incomprehensible. As if he'd stuck his finger in an electrical socket, his little body jolted with pain and anguish. The rusty glow intensified as he tried to make sense of the situation. His head pounding. His heart booming. His lungs ready to explode.

"NO! DADDY NO! YOU CAN'T LEAVE! PLEASE DON'T LEAVE! DADDY WE NEED YOU!"

He clung to his father's leg, the tears uncontrollable, the high-pitched fervour of his cries wounding the air. Bob dug his hands into the little boy's shoulders and pushed him away like he was flicking a fly on a hot summer's night.

"This is best for everybody!"

Without another word or even a glance at his quivering son, Bob walked out the front door and out of their lives. Shattered. Helpless. Abandoned. Betrayed. Destroyed. Ricky couldn't move. His entire body frozen in shock, stifled in pain. How could this possibly be what was best for everyone? Ricky refused to believe that. He couldn't understand, too young to comprehend the trials of adulthood, and especially relationships. All he knew in that moment, all his ten-year-old brain could grasp was that he was no longer important to his father. He couldn't see his father's own unhappiness in the marriage, and he couldn't see that he could still be a part of his father's life. All he knew was fury, and all he felt was deception.

Jimmy and Brenda collapsed onto the floor, and the three of them huddled together, crying until there were no more tears to be cried, burying their own pain in the pain of each other.

"Don't worry," said Brenda. "God will protect us. God will take care of us now."

That's all the comfort she had to offer, all that her own broken heart could muster. But it wasn't nearly enough to comfort the aching in the hearts of her two boys. They needed some understanding, they needed to know that their father still loved them, and that this had nothing to do with them; that sometimes adults fall out of love, and need to live apart. They needed assurance. They needed answers. They got nothing – not from their mother, and certainly not from their father. Without responsible answers or direction, Ricky would be forced to surmise his own truths, truths, whether right or wrong, that would shape his understanding of the event for the rest of his life. He needed some space, some time alone to digest the sickening feeling retching in his gut.

His limbs weighted with stress, Ricky slowly and deliberately climbed the maple tree, coming to rest in his favorite branch spilt. The leaves had just begun their colourful descent to death, spraying the hue with shades of yellow, orange, and faded red. Yesterday, Ricky would have noticed the colours, he would have examined the patterns and took glory in the beauty of the changing landscape. Today, his red, swollen eyes saw nothing but anger, his mind a tangled mess of unanswered questions and wailing thoughts.

"How could he do this? Why would he leave? Does he not love us enough to stay? To try and work things out? What was life going to be without him? Why would he abandon us like that? Am I really not that good of a son?"

The last question stung the boy hard. He took it personally. Bob leaving was a direct betrayal of the relationship between father and son. As much as he tried, the boy didn't understand, and the more he tried to understand, the more his mind entombed his sadness into rage.

"What's so wrong with our family that he had to leave? That he had to walk away? How dare he abandon us and destroy our family! How dare he hurt us like this and walk away!"

Rage begat rage. His troubled ten-year-old mind making assumptions and coming to conclusions, sitting all alone in a tree, as the twilight descended, both on the day, and on the life he once knew, and the happiness he once felt. By walking out of his life, Bob had lost the privilege to be Rick's father. Simple as that. For the first time, Rick tasted the bitterness of hate. It tore through every ounce of his body, pushing out the innocence of childhood, and settled deep into his heart, slamming the door to forgiveness on the way by. The anger boiled, and the rage seethed. He had betrayed them, the very family he had raised, he had discarded like a random piece of trash. Ricked hated him for it. He hated the way his father made him love him, only to throw it all away, like it meant nothing at all. Everything in the past was examined through Rick's muddled lenses. Had his father ever really loved him? Had all those times together just been for show? He had no way of knowing, and there was no one brave enough to be honest about their feelings to help guide his tormented soul. He hated the power his father had over him – to break him like this and shatter him. No control. He could never let it happen again. He could never allow himself to feel again. Ever. Fueled with rage, the engine of hatred mounted and spun at a delirious pace. Thoughts and emotions became jumbled, twisted and tortured under the immense pressure, his young head and his young heart unable to process the array fast enough. The pressure building. Deeper. Crushing. Hate. Overload. Explosion. Darkness. Death.

In that moment, in that tree, the world stopped. Something happened. He could feel it. Like a red-hot fire burning through every part of his brain snapping every bridge that connected emotions to rational thoughts. Instantly. Done. Severed. His mind went numb and an eerie, icy, calm eviscerated his entire soul. No sound. No wind. Just a cold empty blackness within. He had died inside. Fully. Completely. He had lost his soul. His flesh, now just a mere cover for the empty shell underneath, his body working only to keep him physically alive. The uncontrollable fire storm of rage and betrayal left his heart a boiling pot of molten lava, seething and bubbling, a volcano building deep within, protected for now by a cold vacuum of empty space.

He told himself that no one would ever be able to hurt him like that again; he'd never give anyone that kind of power. He told himself that he was dead inside, convinced himself that he could never feel again, that he could control everything that happened to him. He gave himself the power. He took that power away from his father and gave it to himself. It's all he could think of to do. The hate for his father was as real as the deadness he felt inside. There was no forgiveness, there would be no escape. He would never hurt or shed a tear again. Nothing could phase him. He told himself he was invincible, in control of everything. He had to find his way to cope. He had to find his way to survive – and he did, in the most simple and straightforward way a child could cope. He'd just turn off the switch that made anything matter. He truly believed he had the strength and capabilities to do such a thing. At ten years old. Just turn everything off, like you'd turn off the lights.

When the soul is in darkness it doesn't have to recognize or deal with the pain. It doesn't mean the pain disappears or new pain doesn't occur, it's just easier to shove it all down deep and convince yourself that it doesn't exist. For a ten-year old, this shit was real, and his belief that he could pull it off, and grow up without it boiling over was also real. From now on, he would live two separate lives, manoeuvering between the light and the dark like a ghost. He became 'Ghost', living as a shadow, a mere apparition that slid seamlessly through both worlds, just trying his best to survive the challenges, and constantly trying to understand what went wrong. But whatever he did, he would not feel. He would not feel pain; he would not feel sorrow. He would not spend another minute mourning the loss of his father. The bastard could go fuck himself. Rick didn't care. Bob had betrayed them all. He had ruined their lives. Fuck him.

CHAPTER SEVEN

Gloom and sadness descended over the household. Rick not wanting to feel, and Brenda feeling too much, especially in front of her young and impressionable children.

"He left us for a whore you know! Some flight attendant living in Boise. A flight attendant! Can you believe it? The spirit of Jezebel she is!" Her rage only fed the fires. "Another woman. Been seeing her for who knows how long. Right under our noses. He abandoned us for someone else. How dare he? He's an adulterer and he's going to Hell for what he did…mark my words."

But her words only enforced the hate and anger brewing in Little Ricky. He had no escape, no one to turn to, no one to calm the increasing insanity. If his father had even just sat him and Jimmy down and said, "Look boys, I love you to death, and that's never going to change. You'll always be my sons and I'll always be proud of you, no matter what. But things just aren't working out with your Mom and I, and I have to leave. I've found someone new that I want to have a life with, and I want this new life to include you. I love you boys – that will never change. Remember that." But there was nothing. For Bob and Brenda, words were daggers, thrown with conscious precision, ripping a nasty path through every heart in their wake.

"That whore. That Jezebel. He chose her over us. Her. That woman."

Rick heard everything. The betrayal was deliberate. Bob had never cared about them, and he certainly didn't care about them now, especially now that he had her. Rosemary. Fucking bitch. He hated her. Bob had been in his life for ten years, and this woman for a few months, yet he chose her. His family meant nothing. It couldn't have. The little heart hardened.

"You're the man of the house now Rick. It's your job to take care of us. God's little warrior. My strong son."

Ten years old and now the man of the house. How was he supposed to calm his mother's anger and rage, when he couldn't deal with his own? He may have been equipped to fight demons but there was a definite chink in Christ's armour that left him ill-equipped to deal with his mother's grief. Sometimes she would be in near hysterics, and inconsolable, while other times she would just sit in her recliner crying, her hands resting atop the worn Bible in her lap. What possible words could Little Ricky muster to help ease his mother's pain, and knock her out of her stupor? He was ten years old! All he could do was sit by, quietly watch her cry, assure her that he loved her, and that everything was going to be okay.

Of course, nothing would ever be all right again. Ever. Not for him, not for his mother, and not for Jimmy. Jimmy simply withdrew, his spirit broken. He didn't get angry, he didn't rage against the world, he simply ceased to engage, except when he was crying or attempting to console his mother. Like a menacing shadow, sadness crept into every crevice of the family's existence. They all felt it. The depression. The despair. The hopelessness. Someone had to step up. Someone had to take charge, be the adult. Keep the family moving. Ricky didn't know how he was going to do it; he just knew he had to. Bouts of depression filled his veins with ice but the anger and burning rage in his heart kept him focused. His father fucked them over, and now it was his job to fuck his father over every chance he got.

"Your father will be here in a few minutes to pick you and Jimmy up," said Brenda. "He wants you to meet Rosemary. You can go if you want, but you don't have to meet that Jezebel. Right now it's your choice. The courts may force you to later, but right now, if you want to stay home it's your choice."

"I want to stay home," said Ricky.

"Me too," said Jimmy.

"Then it's settled. You'll stay here." Rick could sense the satisfaction in his mother's voice. Like she was keeping score. Brenda 1 – Bob 0.

Bob pulled the Wagoneer into the driveway. Rick could see the bitch calmly sitting in the passenger side, watching Bob walk towards the front door. Why was she here? He didn't want to fucking see her. Not now. Not ever. Bob rung the bell.

"I'll handle this boys," said Brenda turning the handle.

"Are they ready?"

"They don't want to go with you Bob. I'm sorry."

"Excuse me?"

"They don't want to go with you. I asked them and they said no."

Bob ran one hand through his thick black hair, the veins in his neck pulsing.

"Really? They don't want to go with me? Is that so?" Rick shivered at the tone in his father's voice. He needed to stay strong.

"Bob, don't make a big deal about it. I asked and they said no."

"Fine. But I want to hear it for myself. I didn't raise shit ass children. They can think and speak for themselves, so let them tell me."

Ignoring the shaking in his wobbly legs, Ricky stepped out from behind his mother to face his father. He was the man now. His father looked bigger standing at the bottom of the front porch steps with his hands on his hips, like somehow the last couple of days had distorted the boy's reality, as the demonization of his father had taken hold. He waited for his father to say hello or even crack a warm, friendly "gee I'm happy to see you kid" smile. Nothing. With a hard gulp, Ricky swallowed his fear.

"We're not going with you. Period."

A flash of seething anger coloured Bob's face and he exploded.

"Oh yeah? Is that what you think? Then maybe I should just fucking move to Madrid!" he screamed as he stormed back around the car, slamming the door behind him.

Like red hot lasers, Ricky focused his angry eyes on the car as it flew out of the driveway, and peeled off down the road. For the first time in the last five minutes, he allowed himself to breathe. And smile, if ever so slightly. It wasn't a huge victory but it was a victory nonetheless. For the first time in his life he had openly defied his father. He was the man of the house now. Ricky 1 – Dad 0. Fuck him. It felt good to win, to have the power. His dad came to the house looking for a fight, and that's what he got. Not once did his father soften his voice and say, "Hey guys, I've been missing you and I'd really like to spend some time with you." Nothing. The bastard came demanding. Demanding that the boys do what he said, never once taking their feelings into consideration. Jimmy was too young and too scared, cowering behind his mother's leg, but Ricky, Ricky wasn't about to back down and give into his father's demands. After what he'd done to them? Not a fat fucking chance that was going to happen. And on that day, a precedent was set. Man versus man. Father versus son. The battle lines drawn, neither side ready nor willing to give an inch.

The euphoria of the victory was short-lived as the tension snapped and the mother and brothers collapsed in tears.

"I'm so proud of you Ricky," said Brenda cradling her eldest boy. "You did a good job standing up to your father like that…showing him who's boss."

Ricky had no reply. He didn't know how he felt. On one hand, he was proud of himself, but seeing his dad again reinforced how much he really missed him. He could pretend all he wanted that it wasn't the case but his ten-year-old heart ached for his father and the life they once had. And there was nothing wrong with the way he was feeling. If he wasn't missing him, then he wouldn't have been so depressed, so distraught. Unfortunately, Ricky never had any direction on how to deal with those feelings. The last thing Brenda wanted to hear from her boys was that they missed their father. It would be almost sin-like to even entertain the thought. Nobody ever told him it was okay. So Ricky pushed those feelings aside, and the hurt metastasized into hate, spreading viciously though his soul.

A few weeks later Bob returned, alone.

"Can I talk to you a minute Rick?" said Bob with a smile.

"Now he wants to talk?" thought Rick. "Now he wants to explain? What the hell. It was way too late for this sort of shit."

"Come and have a seat." He pointed to the two lawn chairs he'd set up at the side of the house. "How are you? I've missed you."

"I'm fine."

"Yeah? Things are going okay?"

"They're fine." The boy showed no emotion. He'd already cried his tears and died inside. And now every day, he had to watch his little brother and his mother struggle. Struggle to breathe, struggle to even take a baby step forward. The brown-eyed man looking at him wasn't his father, he was a stranger, a stranger who betrayed and abandoned them. A stranger whom he hated. A stranger who broke his heart.

"So do you think you'll want to come and hang out with me someday soon?"

"I hate you."

The twitch in Bob's left eye sparked but he kept control.

"I don't think you really hate me. You're just saying that because you're upset and you're confused, and I know you've been hurt by everything that's gone on…but trust me, you don't really hate me. I'm your father."

"Trust him?" thought Rick. "How the hell am I supposed to trust him ever again after what he did to us? You can't trust a cheater." The boy turned to his father.

"No. I hate you," said Rick. "I'm always going to hate you and you're not my father anymore."

That was it. Bob exploded. "Listen here! I am your father and there is nothing you can do about it! You will have to come and see me. It's the law! Until you turn twelve years old you have no choice. Do you hear me? You have no choice. You'll come and see me when I say so! Is that clear?"

Ricky wasn't going to stand for this shit.

"I'm not doing shit! I don't care if it's the law or not! I don't want anything to do with you!"

With every word, Bob raged with anger. How could this little shit defy him like that? He would do as he was told!

"If you keep refusing to visit and spend time with me, you're only hurting yourself and your mother."

"What are you talking about?"

"The courts wouldn't see too kindly on a parent who's influencing their children to stay away from their father."

"She's not doing that, you liar! I don't want to go because I hate you!"

"Well sorry kid, but the court doesn't care whether you hate me or not. They'd see me as a father who just wants to see his kids but keeps getting refused. They'd probably even award me custody."

"I ain't going to live with you ever! We're not leaving Mom, especially not to go live with you and her!"

"Like I said, for two more years, it's not your decision to make. You have no say."

YOU HAVE NO SAY. The words smacked Ricky in the face like an open hand. Pure hypocrisy.

"I'll do what I have to Ricky. You and Jimmy are my children and you WILL be a part of my life whether you like it or not."

I'LL DO WHAT I HAVE TO. Rick wasn't quite sure what that all entailed but the thought of what it could mean sent a blast of fear through his young brain. Could the courts take them away from their mom and force them to live with their father? How far would his father use his legal power against them? What would happen to their mother? If she lost custody of the boys? Rick couldn't even begin to think of her reaction. She could barely function now, and he was the one holding their shit together. Without him around, Rick was certain she would collapse. So much pressure, so much stress for a boy too young to understand, and not yet possessing the maturity to perceive and deal with the situation.

"I don't care what you do," said Rick. "I hate you. And I'll hate you forever."

"Have it your way," said Bob almost knocking over the chair as he got up. He'd heard enough. This hadn't gone well. Certainly not as planned. If his son wasn't going to listen to reason, then he'd use his parental force and make him do as he was told. He was the father wasn't he? Still the man of the family, even though he no longer lived under the same roof. Rick would just have to understand that. And surely the kid didn't hate him? That was just a hurt little boy talking. He'd get over it. He'd meet Rosemary, see how wonderful she is and fall in love with her just like he had. He'd come around. Couldn't he see how miserable he'd been at home? Brenda and her fucking religious bullshit? Rosemary was uncomplicated. She liked fine things. She liked sports. He felt comfortable and wanted. He felt those pangs of love again. He'd forgotten what that felt like. He'd felt that way about Brenda once but things change. Rick would just have to understand. He'd come around, and once he did, they could just resume their life. Go flying, go sailing, do all the things they loved to do with each other. He's only ten years old – he'll get over it.

Where Rick lacked the maturity, Bob lacked the vision to see how truly damaged the relationship with his son had become. There would be no just "getting over it". The hurt ran far too deep for the youngster. But Bob couldn't see it. Or maybe he just didn't want to acknowledge it because to acknowledge it would mean he would have to admit some blame, some responsibility for what happened, and that he wouldn't do. He'd been right to leave. Eventually things would calm down and everyone would see that he was right.

Bob's blindness only intensified the slow downward spiral. Rick needed help. He needed someone to talk to, someone he trusted, someone that didn't have a vested interest in either side. But no one saw it. Not his mother, and certainly not his father. They were too wrapped up in themselves. Thinking about themselves. Their needs. Their situation. No one even attempted to look at the big picture or to see how tortured both Rick and Jimmy had become. They became the carry-on bags throughout the divorce proceedings; tossed around, and more often than not, forgotten and left behind in a closed off compartment of some former happiness.

"You boys wait out here in the lobby, and play with your toys. I shouldn't be that long. Be good." said Brenda.

But she was always long when she had a meeting at the lawyer's office. Sometimes the boys had to sit there for hours while their parents hashed it out in the conference room. You didn't have to have an ear to the door to hear the raised voices, and acrimonious tone. And what they didn't hear, Brenda kindly filled them in on during the ride home.

"I just feel so bullied by your father. He knows what to say and how to get to me. I feel so inadequate."

In her pain, frustration, and tears, Brenda unwittingly used her boys, and especially Rick as a sounding board. Rick never knew what to say but he knew how her words made him feel. His father was a bully. He was treating them unfairly. He didn't love them anymore, if he ever even did. Embittered. Hurt. Rage.

"That asshole doesn't want to give us any child-support." Brenda quickly shot a glance at her horrified oldest son sitting in the passenger sit. "I'm sorry I shouldn't have said that but…"

"What do you mean he doesn't want to pay any child support? I don't understand?"

Brenda could only shrug her shoulders. "I don't know son."

"Seriously?" thought Rick. "He doesn't even want to pay any money to help take care of us? What the fuck? I know he's not rich but he certainly has more than enough money kicking around." Nothing his father could ever say would explain this bullshit. "Why would he not want to pay any money to take care of his children and at least make sure they were okay?" The questions steamrolled the young boy's brain. He was confused. Hurt. Distraught. His mother had always just been his mother. As far as Rick knew, she'd never worked outside of the house since she'd been married, and at forty-three years old, with no experience and no post-secondary education to fall back on, she was looking at flipping burgers or taking the change at the local gas station, and that certainly wouldn't be enough income to raise two kids. No wonder she was crying, and felt so defeated. Rick couldn't stand that his father put them in this situation. Not when he had the means. Without an income, Rick figured they'd be out in the streets in no time. Maybe that was his father's plan? To force them out onto the streets, so he'd look like the better parent and the courts would award him custody?

Rick's assumptions weren't all that far from the truth. Bob was so against giving Brenda anything in the divorce settlement, that he would rather have his children go without than to award her with a reasonable child-support sum. Like she was the one who had fucked around? Like she was the one who went and got herself a boyfriend, left, and destroyed the family. Bob had it all wrong, and in Rick's young mind, this deceitful tactic only cemented his feelings of rage, hate, and abandonment. It was the killing blow. Any smidgen of love that might have hidden itself away in his heart was gone; washed away in a tsunami of disgust. The transformation was complete. At ten years old, Rick hated his father. Hated everything about him, and everything he stood for. Every time Bob bought something new or even worse, something for Rosemary, they would all be reminded of how he loved her and himself, more than his boys.

Rick came to loath anything and anyone who had money, not because he was jealous per se, but because to him, they represented selfishness, and the idea that people can and do choose to put money over family and morals. Morals like doing the right thing, like providing for your children. Rick became a champion for the underdog, for the little guy, the scrappy kid who would fight for what he believed in. The kid who would stand up and protect those who needed protecting. A kid with unwavering loyalty, especially to his mother, and to all those he perceived as victims. This seed fostered roots that dug deep and hard into the young boy's mind, and from then on, anything remotely associated with being 'rich', like having a nice car, became a symbol and a projection of everything he despised. Society became his father, and his father became society. The lines blurred, and there was no separating the two, and this idealistic hatred posed a dangerous threat in a mind so young and impressionable. Any move, well-intentioned or not, by Bob or Rosemary now would be a threat. He didn't need them. He didn't want them. And he sure as hell wasn't going to listen to them. The chance for peace had been lost. The time of clandestine warfare had begun.

After many long and stressful months, the courts finally awarded full custody of the boys to Brenda, with mandatory visitation for Bob. The kids had to go, they had no choice. Brenda kept the house, and most everything in it, as well as a vehicle. While Bob was forced to pay a meagre sum for child support, barely enough to pay the bills, he walked away with the rest of the finances and assets, leaving his ex-wife and kids with a roof over their heads but nearly destitute.

Realizing the severity of their financial situation, Brenda immediately enrolled at Chemeketa, the local community college, and while this was a very positive step for her, it increased her time away from home, and gave Rick an overwhelming sense of freedom and independence.

Afraid of what the courts might do to their mother, the boys had relented and begun to visit their father while the divorce proceedings had been going on. The visits were hell, and both boys loathed being there. Bob had sold the old Catalina sailboat and purchased an RV, which he then plopped at a local trailer park, at least giving the courts the appearance that he was living on his own and not with Rosemary. It was always about keeping up appearances. In happier times, Rick would have had a heyday playing with the cool tape player stereo system and mucking about in the various cubby holes and storage spaces, but these were not happy times, so the trailer and the whole trailer park held little interest. What conversation there was, was muted and sombre, a mere extra-curricular to the uncomfortable body language and oppressive fog that clouded the air.

"So boys," said Bob pulling out of the driveway. "I have a special treat for you today. We're not going back to the trailer. I want you to meet Rosemary. It's time." Silence ruled the car.

"You'll like her. I know you will, and she's been so anxious to meet you both." Bob snuck a sideways glance at his son. No reaction. No emotion. He was sure that the boys would get over the whole ordeal eventually, and all the negativity and anger would be forgotten. It would just take some time.

Rosemary welcomed them at the door of her small apartment with a smile. Rick cringed as he watched his father slide his hand around her fit and toned waist. He didn't need to see that. Jimmy stuck to his side like a piece of Velcro, his eyes following every move his older brother made.

"Boys," said Bob. "I'd like you to meet Rosemary." The boys looked up but said nothing. "Rick… Jimmy, say hello to Rosemary." Bob's tone sharpened.

"Hello," said Rick.

Jimmy just nodded.

"Well I'm happy to meet you boys. Please come in and make yourselves at home."

The collection of art hanging on the walls, and the ornate vase perfectly positioned on the simple yet elegant side table immediately fed the flames of Rick's malcontent. She was a snob. An uppity sort of bitch. He could tell just by the furniture and the smell in the air. The décor was simple but top notch. Everything had a place, a spot, and as Rick looked around, it was clear this spot was for adults and not children.

"Oh Jimmy," said Rosemary, "please put that down. Carefully. That's not something that's meant to be played with. It's a 'just for looking sort of thing' you know."

"Put it down Jimmy," said Bob.

Jimmy shrugged his shoulders and placed the pale coloured glass object back on the wooden table. Rick didn't know what the big deal was. Jimmy was just looking at it in his hands. Mom never would have given him shit for that. Snotty bitch, this whore. She ran through a whole list of things they could and couldn't touch, and could and couldn't do, and with each new rule, Rick hated her more. Sit up straight at the kitchen table and hold your fork this way, not like that. Bitch. No running around. Fucking bitch. Please don't touch the vases or anything on the tables. Fucking bitch whore who stole our father.

Rosemary was in a no-win situation. She knew she was the 'other woman'. She knew the boys didn't want to meet her, and she knew they definitely did not want to be having dinner at her apartment that evening. More than one dagger of disdain had met its mark. Bob said they were good kids but just needed some time. Their mother had filled them with nastiness and hate. They'd get over it. They'd get past it. All kids did. They just had to be patient. So Rosemary put on her best smile and tried to make the evening as pleasant as possible. She didn't take it personally when the boys lowered their eyes or turned away when she spoke, she just smiled and acted like nothing was wrong. It wasn't the boys fault. They weren't to blame. They were caught in the middle and were stuck living with their crazy ass mother. Although Rosemary had to admit, she was glad that Bob hadn't gained full custody. She'd already raised her children and didn't want to go through the whole process again, especially with someone else's children. That was the deal. Just because she loved Bob, didn't mean she had to love his children.

Rick couldn't wait for dinner to be over so they could get the hell out of there. He didn't like her. Didn't like what she stood for, and especially didn't like the way she had changed his father. He'd always been so outdoorsy, laid back and casual. His father had never been a snob. Until now. She did that. She made him this way. And she made him not love them anymore. He'd rather be with her. This uppity, preppy snob. She was a Jezebel. Meeting her for the first time only confirmed his suspicions. She stole the one thing in his life that had truly ever mattered, his hero, his idol, and here she was smiling and pretending like nothing had ever happened. Oh how's the chicken Rick? And the potatoes? He couldn't stand it. His jaded ten-year-old brain had no adult reasoning, and he couldn't see that Rosemary was nothing more than the instrument for all his pain – the object that his father had chosen over them. The person his father had chosen to love instead of him. He betrayed them for her. That whore. That Jezebel.

CHAPTER EIGHT

With nothing to do but stare at his four cell walls, Rick decided to take the nurse up on her offer and begin studying for his GED. There was no chance in hell he'd ever be returning to a regular school, so the next steps in his formal education were going to have to come from his own motivation and self-study. He'd always been a smart kid, and probably could have pulled off straight 'A's' if he'd ever really given a shit about school, and not that he really gave a shit now, but studying for the GEDs at least kept him occupied and out of trouble. That was part of his problem, everyone knew he was a smart kid, his teachers, his parents, and it frustrated the hell out of them to see him not trying, or even more, not even caring. But that had always been his pattern; giving one hundred percent to the things he felt were worthwhile, and minimal effort to anything else, especially those types of things society deemed worthwhile, like education. Ninety-six days after walking into prison, Rick passed all five of his GED tests and was given his high school diploma, actually ranking in the eighty-first percentile of U.S. scores nationwide. He hadn't just passed the tests, he'd aced them. Even he had to wonder what he might have accomplished in school had he'd put in even a half-assed effort.

Christmas came and went, and the New Year brought the promise and recommendation of finally leaving Mike Mod and getting transferred into general population. He just wanted out, to go somewhere normal where the people weren't fucked up on drugs or smearing shit all over themselves. He'd done his time there. He'd been a good inmate, and besides the one incident at lunch, a model prisoner. The Recommendation Board saw no reason he shouldn't be allowed to join 'General Population'.

"I'm so sorry Rick," said the nurse. "Mr. Brandenburg has ordered you be kept here for observation for at least another month."

"He can't do that!" said Rick. "They recommended I be sent to general population!"

"I know…and I'm sorry. But as the Administrator of this facility, he does have the power if he thinks the stay is warranted."

"That is bullshit!" The anger boiled. "What can I do? Is there anything I can do to change it? Jesus. I am not staying here for another month. Fuck that. They just want to keep me here long enough so I that I do actually become crazy and they can medicate me and fuck me up forever!"

"Well," she whispered. "Your only hope is to maybe write a letter to the Superintendent…he's Brandenburg's boss…and explain the situation and how you feel. But you can't rant and rave like you are now. It has to be formal letter. Otherwise, he'll just trash it. Oh, and don't mention my name either, or where you got the suggestion. I'd like to keep my job."

That night, Rick sat down at his desk and wrote his first 'cop-out', a standard Request form for prisoner/staff communication. You couldn't just walk up to the Superintendent's door and yell, 'Hey Dude, we need to talk!" Everything had to be formally requested and have a paper trail, which was probably a good thing because then with paper proof, no one could deny that the request had been asked. Rick laid it all on the line to the Superintendent. How Brandenburg had said that if he behaved and participated in the programs, that he would be moved out of Mike Mod by the end of December. He had behaved. Now Brandenburg arbitrarily decided to extend his stay another month. What's going to happen at the end of next month?

"I don't belong here," he wrote in his neat, small print. "I will do anything to get into normal population. Please sir."

Rick signed the letter and handed it to the guard who would send it along to the Superintendent. The very next day Brandenburg showed up at his cell door, unable to mask his angry scowl. He was losing his star inmate.

"The Superintendent has granted your request and you'll be moved to general population in a few days. You got your way."

"Thank you. Can I ask you why you sent me here, to Mike Mod in the first place?"

"I thought you were suicidal."

"I told you I wasn't. I looked you straight in the eye and told you that I wasn't. I wouldn't even consider it."

"I thought you were lying."

That was it. His final answer. It wouldn't have mattered what Rick had said during that intake meeting, his own honesty didn't mean a damn thing against the authority or opinion of a Brandenburg or anyone else. Rick's first taste of how arbitrary, unfair, and tyrannical the prison system could be, singed an acrid scar on his already fragile psyche, only deepening the schism in his societal 'us versus them' mentality. Brandenburg's 'expert' opinion thought putting a sixteen-year old in an adult mental health unit would be a good idea. Did he even consider how the experience might have affected the teen? Especially one who had just been through a traumatic experience of his own? Was there no other option? No other means of rehabilitation for an already confused and distressed kid? Apparently not.

For a person already prone to 'seeing' and feeling the underlying's of the underworld, the mental health unit was a nightmare of intense demonic pressure. They were everywhere, lurking and lying, just as possessed and bent as the humans they were attached to. The sense and reality of it all made Rick wish that he could end it all, just to free himself from the psycho-empathic stench permeating every inch of Mike Mod. He lived in constant fear that one day he would wake up and he too would be bat-shit crazy. Is that how it happened? One day you're fine and the next you wake up crazy? Or did these people all start out like him, a cold vacuum, unable to process or deal with their long tucked away emotions. Did those emotions bubble and brew until the conscious mind could no longer control their existence, instead shutting down like an overloaded circuit, leaving the subconscious to run the show. Rick had been there. On the night of the murders. His subconscious had taken control and it had made him do some horrible things. Regrettable things. He'd always believed he'd had complete control over his conscious mind but in a split second, it had vanished. Is that what had happened to these guys? Was it only a matter of time? Rick had enough on his plate without having to worry about his perceived 'craziness' in his eyes or anyone else's. He knew he wasn't crazy. Never had been, but the atmosphere in Mike Mod certainly wasn't conducive to any sort of rehabilitation, either mental or emotional, and he needed to get the hell out of there fast.

"Just sign here," said the Sergeant sliding a piece of paper across the interview table.

"What is it?" said Rick.

"It's a waiver. You need to sign it before you can go to general population. Read it for yourself but it just says that you won't hold the Department of Corrections responsible for any physical or sexual violence you may be subject to while in general population. I have a few suggestions on what to do if someone does beat you up or tries to rape you…"

Rick had already signed the waiver and tuned him out. He could deal with the violence, and God help the poor bastard that tried to rape him. He knew how to contend with the violence, he'd been doing it for a while now.

"I don't care," said Rick as politely as possible. "I can deal with it. I'll be dealing with this for the rest of my life, so I just want to get on with it."

"I understand," said the Sergeant picking up the form. "I'll take you back to your cell now. The transfer will be made in the next few days or so."

"Thank you sir."

That night, January 4th, 1996, an officer came into his cell and told him to 'roll-up'. Rick threw his measly possessions onto the bed and rolled them up in his blankets. The experience of Mike Mod was finally over, it was time to move on and get his first taste of general population. It wouldn't last that long, but it was his next initiation in becoming a 'convict' and really understanding the ins and outs of doing time.

****

The winds of change continued to blow for Ricky. First the divorce, now a new school. September 1989 began with Ricky's first foray into public school education. He and Jimmy had always gone to a private Christian school, but with the family break-up and the uncertainty of finances, the two were shuttled off on the bus to begin their experiences at Adam's Elementary School. Adam's Elementary could not have been more different than their previous school, Puyallup Valley, and the transition was tough on both boys. Disciplined, structured, and academically advanced, Puyallup Valley was more like a junior prep school, where there were just certain expectations and concrete consequences when those expectations were not met. Styled in the same structure as almost every other public school in America, Adam's Elementary was a large two story building with a covered outdoor basketball court, a junior-sized soccer field, and a junior-sized baseball diamond. Assigned to the affable Mr. Gentry's Grade 5 class, Rick enjoyed his teaching style but was bored with the material, since most of it he'd already covered in his grade 4 year at Puyallup. There wasn't even a school band or music program to keep him interested. Boredom begat boredom, and soon Ricky began looking for other sources of amusement.

He made himself a few friends, and while he was well-liked in his peer group, he began to withdraw, refusing to talk about himself or his home life. Other kids respected his athletic ability and while there were a few bullied jabs about his thin, wiry size, most of the kids sensed he could kick their ass if he really wanted to, so they left him alone. As the school year went on and the divorce played out, Rick became more and more depressed and remote. He quit caring about school and really about life in general, the sadness overwhelming any sort of happiness that even attempted to break through. Sure there were happy moments but these were isolated incidents, like tropical islands popping up through the raging stormy seas. His anger broadened. His father. Society. God. How could God let this happen? He was supposed to love us? He'd been the best little soldier and faithful follower he could be yet, still, God let this happen. His mother always assured him that even though it hurt like hell this was part of 'God's plan' and they just needed to have faith and follow it through. Not much solace for a ten-year-old who just wanted his dad. The idea was all too abstract for him to comprehend. But he did as he was told and while he 'didn't lose the faith' in God, he did lose his will to do whatever anyone else wanted him to do.

Midway through the school year, the call came home to his mother. The school wanted a meeting with both parents. Grades had dropped significantly and homework wasn't being done.

"He's had such a hard time dealing with the divorce," said his mother. "I'm afraid he's dealing with some depression."

"He'll get it done Mr. Gentry," said Bob. "I can assure you of that."

Of course, this only sparked an after meeting argument between the two in the parking lot.

"You have no idea what this has done to him Bob!"

"I don't care how he feels! He needs to get through school!"

A witness to the hostilities and uncomfortable situation, Mr. Gentry did his best to be understanding and work around the situation but he could only do so much. Rick passed Grade 5 by the skin of his ass, and even then there was no sense of relief or accomplishment. He'd have to actually care to feel that way.

Rick's problems at school were only compounded by the complications at home. With little money and no real source of income, Brenda was forced to go back to school, and try and get a decent job as soon as possible. This also meant she was often gone when the boys got home from school and into the evenings, necessitating the need for a babysitter. Brenda thought she'd hit the jackpot when she found Mike, the son of a preacher from the new church they'd just started attending. Only two and half years older than Rick, Mike quickly taught Rick plenty of things that neither Brenda nor Mike's preacher father would be too happy about. Almost every second word out of the boys' mouth was an F-bomb or something just as bad, and while Rick was already quite adept at throwing around swear words, he managed to learn a few new expressions from the older more experienced kid.

Games consisted of chasing each other around the house with sharp implements, trying to light a fire on the side of the house, or the good old wholesome 'match fights' with strike anywhere matches. If Brenda's intention had been to have a more mature person to ensure the boys safety and good conduct, she was sorely mistaken. Mike only sped up the boys' corruption. Half the time Jimmy was scared shitless during the games, and on occasion he even ratted the older boys out to Brenda. But for the most part, he was a good sport and played along. Mike's only rule was that homework had to be done first. He was wise enough to know that they'd all be in royal shit if it wasn't finished. Many times he'd help both boys while he was doing his own, but more often than not, he'd have them rush through it, or even just give them the answers to save time. And that didn't include the many times Rick just lied and said he didn't have any. Mike never bothered to check, it's not like he really cared whether or not the kid did his homework.

On the nights Mike was unavailable or had to leave early, Rick and Jimmy were home alone. Rick relished the freedom, even on the nights that Mike was there, they basically had free range to do whatever the hell they pleased. This sense of freedom took no time in corrupting his psyche. With each passing day, he began to see how life 'could be' without any parental influence and how unnecessary parents were. If you were hungry, you popped a 'hot pocket' in the microwave or had some cereal. If you were bored, you just chilled and watched whatever you wanted on television. Of course, his mind hadn't developed enough to realize that there wouldn't always be hot pockets in the freezer if no one was buying them or there would be no T.V. to watch if someone wasn't paying the bills. These aren't things a ten-year-old thinks of. All he knew was that when the adults were around, the ability to have fun or do whatever the hell he wanted was gone. He didn't like that. The concept only intensified over the years as the types of 'fun' became more daring and unauthorized. Combined with his hate for his father and for society, he developed a strong anti-authoritarian attitude, which guided many of his actions and decisions as he moved into his teenage years. Give a child, especially one as bright and mischievous as Rick, too much freedom, and they'll take every advantage they can possibly muster.

The circumstances were stacked in Rick's favour. Bob would have taken the boys had he even known how much they were home alone, but with all the anger and resentment, there was no way the boys would go, even if Brenda had suggested it. The idea would have probably been nixed by Rosemary anyways. So Brenda was stuck. What choice did she have? She'd done her best to find a sitter and well, there were times the boys would just have to be on their own for a short while. She had to go to school, to think of the future, and their own financial standing. They couldn't afford to live on child support forever. She had to make a choice. It wasn't a selfish choice by any means, but a smart choice for the family. But Rick was too young to see the nuances of their lives, and how their survival depended on Brenda going to school, and eventually getting a job to support them. Had he understood the choice his mother had to make, he may have reined in his adventurous spirit and kept his brat ass home. But he didn't. All he saw was the opportunity to do as he pleased, and roam where he wanted. He began to prefer when parents weren't around. It gave him a sense of power to make his own decisions based on his own needs and wants. The freedom consumed him.

Like many young kids, Rick got himself a paper route. So every morning at five am he'd crawl out of bed, chug outside to collect the two stacks of heavy papers, and begin the monotonous task of folding, rubber-banding, and depositing each paper into its own individual sleeve. When the couple hundred papers were all packed tightly in his shoulder slung double sided pouch, he'd hop on his bike and set off on his route. Sometimes when it was cold, Brenda would let him borrow her insulated leather driving gloves. He loved those things and desperately wanted a pair of his own. When he saw a pair just like them sitting on the shelf at the local 'Payless', he knew he just had to have them.

"These feel awesome," he thought sliding his little hand into the fur lined leather. He had some money from his paper route but it wasn't near enough to purchase the gloves.

"Shit. What do I do? I want them. I want them bad."

After a quick look over his shoulder, he ripped the tags off, shoved his gloved hands in his pockets and walked right out of the store. The gloves were his. Rick knew what he'd done was wrong but he also knew he was sick of freezing his hands off at five in the morning. And there it was. His first theft. It'd been so easy that it hardly even counted. At least in his mind. The whole 'who's to say it's wrong if you don't get caught' mantra played through his young mind and made stealing a very realistic alternative in the future. He was good at it. Nicked those gloves without even turning a head. He worked his ass off delivering those papers, getting up at the crack of dawn in the cold and rain. It sucked. This was easy. This was simple. This is the sort of thing he could get used to. Just the beginning really.

Not all of Rick's time outside of school was spent getting in trouble. He did all the things that regular ten-year-old boys did including exploring every nook and cranny of McMinnville on his bike, hanging out with a few of the neighbourhood kids, and playing in a soccer league. To most observers, he seemed like a well-adjusted witty kid, a little quiet maybe, but nothing out of the ordinary. He always tried his hardest, especially at sports, and was always sweet and polite to the adults. He'd show no inkling of the turmoil brewing underneath. That was part of his charm. He knew how to play people, to make them see what he wanted them to see, tell them what he wanted them to know, including his own family. He never told his mother how badly he was hurting. Never shared those secrets with his brother, and he certainly never said a thing to his father or Rosemary. Not that they would have cared anyway. The kid with the smile was dying inside. Hurting from the hatred and the depression. He'd even convinced himself that the pain wasn't even there, so there was nothing to concern himself about. But it was. And in this state of self-denial, where you can't even admit your feelings to yourself, it becomes impossible to express them or even admit them to anyone else. Especially when you're only ten-years-old.

Strapped with the inability to talk about his feelings, he found other ways to express himself. The drop in school, the sneaking out at night, his foray into smoking cigarettes. None of it on its own was all that concerning, but coupled together, with the addition of his strange spiritual and religious happenings, he began to experience a slow but deepening shadow in his personality. No one saw it, not even him, and no one stepped in to help. He was too good at hiding. Always had been. Whether it was stalking through the forests back in Washington or running the streets of McMinnville, Rick was well practised in the art of deception.

Not long after Bob left, Rick began sneaking out of the house late at night. The bedroom he shared with Jimmy was on the second floor of the house, and had a single, double-panel sliding window with a protective screen on the north wall.

"Please don't Rick," said Jimmy. "It scares me."

"Just shush and go back to sleep. I'll be fine." Rick positioned the flathead screwdriver to the side of the window and carefully popped out the screen.

"When are you coming back?"

"I dunno. When I feel like it."

"What if you get caught? Or killed!"

"I'm not going to get killed Jimmy. Quit being so God damn over-dramatic."

"I'll tell Mom."

"You tell Mom and I'll beat the living shit out of you. Now go back to bed."

Jimmy slinked down under the covers. He was too scared to even watch. Dressed in his black sweat pants and dark hoodie, Rick slipped out the window, and slid down the slightly slanted roof of the covered back patio. It was a perfect set-up. With an easy eight-foot drop to the ground, Rick was free. Free to explore the night and venture wherever he wanted, sight unseen. That was his philosophy. 'You can't kill or capture what you can't see.' The simple statement became a complete mode of thought for the youngster, born innocently from his G.I. Joe days, and games of endless hide and seek.

"Invisibility equals invincibility."

Heady ideas for a youngster. The invincibility felt by becoming invisible. By disappearing into the night. By closing off all his emotions. Going 'Ghost'. Void of any sort of physical or emotional presence. His way of coping. His way of taking control of his life. Feeling the incredible power in that specific moment when he is totally alone. Just him against the world.

As he darted down the side streets and through the back alleys, the thrill of the game was always to remain stealth, undetected. If a car came by, he dove for the bushes or a random parked car. If a light shone through a neighbour's window, he'd carefully duck under or skirt around. Always silent. He explored backyards, hopped fences, and somersaulted over hedges, running quickly across streets or the highway, his destination always somewhere where he wasn't supposed to be. He could have just walked down the sidewalk but that wasn't part of the mission, the game. The rules stated he couldn't afford to be anything but invisible. The game took him all over town, until eventually over the ensuing months, he'd explored most of the surrounding five square miles from his home. He had escape routes. Knew all the best places to hide; a shadow in the night.

"I wonder if this thing has power running through it," he thought as he stood by a large grounding wire leading from the roof of the bank to the ground. A little hesitant at first, he smacked his hand against the wire. No shock. He tested again. Nothing.

"Sweet shit!"

Rick didn't waste any time shimmying up the eighteen-foot wire to the bank roof top. The roof was flat with a palisade of about a foot and a half around the entire perimeter, a perfect little wall to hide behind. Carefully crouching at the front of the roof, Rick had a perfect view of Highway 99, and from his vantage point, he could see many of the businesses that bordered the highway itself.

"This is fucking incredible!"

It took everything in his power not to scream at the top of his lungs, and he knew in that moment, looking over his 'urban forest', that he had the ability go anywhere and do anything, as long as no one knew and there was no one to interfere. Freedom became his drug of choice. It soothed his soul, quieted his mind, and gave him the courage to do things not many other ten-year-boys would ever even think of doing.

He didn't sneak out every night, and nor was he always gone for long periods of time; sometimes only an hour, sometimes more. Friday and Saturday nights were the best. No school in the morning meant he could stay out as long as he liked, sometimes three or four hours depending on how far he travelled, or if anything caught his attention. Most of the time, he'd be home before one or two in the morning, but on occasion he was out until four or just before five. Those nights he'd purposely keep himself awake until it was time to go downstairs and start sorting his papers. Made for a very long school day. But he didn't care. Being exhausted and non-functional all day was a small price to pay for the freedom. His mother caught him a few times, but there was never any real punishment, and it certainly didn't deter him from venturing out again. No adults, no supervision, no rules or limitations – just him and his environment. He was living the dream - at ten-years-old.

The more Rick experienced his isolated freedom, the more closed off he became with others. It was his little secret. Jimmy knew but that was just Jimmy, he really didn't pose a threat. He certainly wasn't going to tell any adults, and didn't yet trust any of his school buddies enough, for fear they'd tell their parents. So he stuffed this secret with all the other secrets he'd been keeping; the demon hunting, his dad leaving for another woman, and the rage. Everything he said and did was measured carefully against those secrets, and the more he let the secrets run his life, the more withdrawn he became. Over time, the secrets themselves and the sense of separation and solitude became his friends; a place of solace that no one could reach or ever really disturb. He only trusted himself. And when the time was right to let someone else in, someone he could have complete confidence in, he would be the one to decide. Only then, and only if.

Like most kids his age, Rick loved to collect stuff. Random keys without a corresponding lock, trinkets, coins, miscellaneous tools and scraps, and of course things that your parents definitely didn't want you to have, like a broken saw blade or an extremely sharp knife. On his travels, Rick was always on the lookout for interesting shit to add to his collection, and once his collection became large enough, he had to find a good hiding place to stash it all, a place his mother would never find nor even think of looking.

"What are you doing?" said Jimmy eyeing his big brother.

"Nothing. Just looking at something."

"What?"

"I wonder where that cubby hole in the top of the closet goes. See it?"

Jimmy peered up. "I dunno."

"Betcha it leads to the attic. Get me that chair over there will ya?"

Jimmy handed Rick the chair. "What are you gonna do?"

"I'm gonna climb up there and see if it opens. Hold the chair."

With Jimmy holding tight to the back of the chair, Rick climbed onto the top shelf of the twelve by three-foot closet.

"Be careful."

Rick just smiled at his little brother. Always the worrier.

"If I need a hammer or something to get this open, you're going to have to run to the garage and get it okay?"

"Mom is not going to be happy Rick."

"She's not going to care. Besides, she's not even home."

Rick surveyed the situation. He didn't see a handle but there were hinges, so it had to open somehow. He wished he would have brought some tools with him.

"I wonder…if the hinges are facing that way…that means the door will open this way…"

"What?" said Jimmy.

"Nothing. I'm just thinking this through." He placed his left hand on the right side of the door and pressed. Like magic, the door popped open. "Hmmm…thought it might be spring loaded. Jimmy, throw me up my flashlight. It's on my dresser. See it?"

Jimmy retrieved the flashlight and tossed it up to his brother. "What's up there?"

Switching on the flashlight, Rick took a quick look around. Nothing all that menacing. Setting the flashlight on the attic floor, he propelled off the chair and up into the cubby hole with a thud. Jimmy shuddered and stole a glance to the door.

"Relax man, she's not home," he said poking his head out of the hole.

"This thing is cool! You coming up Jimmy?"

"Umm not yet. I'll let you look around first I think."

"Suit yourself bro."

Rick disappeared through the cubby door and up into the attic. The attic itself was around twenty-four feet by forty feet across, with the peak of the roof being high enough that Rick could stand stand-up. One look around told him he'd found his perfect hiding spot.

"No way Mom is climbing that ladder and coming up here!" He had to laugh at his genius. Totally on top of his game.

Part of the space under the center of the attic was covered with plywood nailed across two by four beams. A perfect spot to throw down some carpet, get some cardboard and make some kick ass play forts. The rest of the attic floor was open, save for the layer of six-inch insulation covering the drywall of the living and dining room ceilings below. Step on that and there'd be one less kid in the attic, and one more kid laying splat on the living room floor. Rick didn't hesitate to venture out into the middle of the insulation area, balancing along the wooden beams with ease.

"I wonder…" A huge smile unfolded across his lips.

"Right there."

He made his way back to where the insulation met the plywood and dropped to his knees.

"I could shove shit right under the insulation and there's no fucking way anyone would ever find it! No way Jimmy or Mom is ever going to touch this fiberglass shit."

He carefully lifted a corner to scope out his new hiding spot.

"Jesus, I'm good."

This hiding spot drove his thoughts to another perfect hiding spot, the attic in the shop, because every kid needs at least two good hiding spots for stuff. If the first one gets busted, then you always had the second for back-up. Rick loved hanging out in the shop, and especially climbing through the trap door in the plywood ceiling to get to the large attic space. All he had to do was pull the long cord and down popped a set of fold-out steep stairs, almost a slightly slanted ladder. Brenda rarely went up in the shop attic since the shop itself had more than enough space for storage.

One night, a medium-sized metal footlocker disappeared off of someone's back porch and mysteriously ended up in the attic of the shop. Immediately, Rick found a gold-plated lock and matching key that fit the footlocker clasp perfectly.

"Look at the size of this baby," he said staring at his new three foot by eighteen, by twelve-inch treasure chest. "This is gonna fit a tonne of cool shit! Now, where can I put this key so that no one will ever find it but me?" His laser-like eyes darted over the many wooden drawers, shelves, and cupboards in the shop. "A drawer or a cupboard is too easy. I need to make it a really good spot." He walked over and gave one of the lower cupboards a soft kick with his foot. The dust scattered then settled on the wooden floor. Shifting back a few steps, the same wooden floor boards creaked under his weight. The light bulb flashed. He'd found his spot. Giving a quick check out in the backyard to make sure no one was lurking, Rick carefully slid the key under the bulge in the floor, just under the far cupboard.

"I'll just use this old metal shim here to get it in there real good. Perfect." He spent the next five minutes putting the key in and out of the hiding spot, making sure he'd be able to retrieve it when the time came to add more treasures to his stash.

Some time after the mysterious appearance of the foot locker, Brenda happened to be up in the attic storing away some old dishes.

"Ricky. Where did this metal box come from?"

The kid just shrugged his shoulders. "Beats me."

"Really," she drawled. "You have no idea how this very large metal box came to reside in the shop attic?"

"Don't have a clue how it got here. Sorry."

"What about the lock? What's in the box?"

"Just some old junk and extra tools."

"Where's the key? Can I see what's in the box?"

"Well I'd love to show you Mom but I have no idea where the key is. It's been lost for like, forever. Seriously."

"So it's lost is it?" Brenda wasn't buying the shit her son was shooting. "No idea where it is?"

"Nope. Sucks I know. I was thinking of just breaking it open with a mallet or a hack saw or something but just hadn't gotten around to it."

Brenda took one last look at the box. "Have you seen that other cardboard box with the Christmas decorations in it? I have this Santa plate and mug and I want to put it in there so we don't forget to use it over the holidays this year."

The air silently exhaled from Rick's lungs. She'd lost interest in his treasure box. Finally. "Umm, I think it was down with the other boxes behind the shop door. Brenda made her way back down the ladder and began to rummage through the stack of boxes.

"You were right! Here it is." She placed the plate and mug in the box and refolded the cardboard flaps. "Dinner will be ready soon, about a half hour or so, so make sure you're in and washed up in time okay?"

"Yup, gotcha! Be in a bit." Rick listened as the shop door swung closed against the frame.

"That was fucking close," he laughed patting the top of the locker. "If she'd seen the shit I had in here, I'd a been grounded for the better part of the year!"

His secrets were safe. He'd held it together under some serious rapid fire questioning. Not that he'd ever doubted he would. He just wasn't the snitching type. Not on others, and certainly not on himself. When he knew a secret, he kept it. No matter what. Consequences be damned.

CHAPTER NINE

General population wasn't going to a picnic in the park. Rick knew that. But he also knew he couldn't stand another moment in the crazy ward. Mike Mod had been a major culture shock, surely G.P. couldn't be that much worse. Like any other kid, he'd heard stories about what it was like in prison, watched things on television and the movies, but as an outsider, it's hard to distinguish between fact and fiction, truth and downright lies. Still, from the moment he entered, he could sense the 'us versus them' mentality, and it wasn't far off from what he'd experienced his whole life. The only person you could really trust was yourself, and you never, ever, ratted someone out, especially to the cops. All of these societal rules and ideals were reproduced in a microcosmic sense in prison, a 'mini-state', with its own culture, politics, and bureaucracy. The whole 'good guys versus bad guys' concept is flipped, where the good guys are no longer the law enforcement officials, but the prisoners themselves, and how much of a criminal you actually are is really measured by how faithfully you hold this belief outside of prison.

A true criminal sees the police as the bad guys whether he's locked up or free. Anyone who's done time will reaffirm that there's actually a good amount of people in prison who are not actual criminals, either in their conduct or their mentality. This gives rise to the difference between 'convicts' and 'inmates'. An inmate is typically not really a criminal and nor does he think like one. An inmate will treat the guards like friends, follow the rules faithfully, and even turn to the guards for help when they're in trouble. A convict puts his faith in no one, trusts nothing more than his ability to keep his own mouth shut, and never gives the authorities an opportunity to interfere in his activities. The trick to surviving in prison is to be somewhere in between these two points. But the number one rule and the absolute worst thing you can do in prison is be a rat or a snitch. Once you cross that line and inform upon your fellow prison brother, life becomes hell, and you're pretty much fucked. Mistakes followed you in prison, there was no forgiveness. If you fucked up, you'd pay. Maybe not that exact day, but some day down the line, they'd find you, and exact their revenge.

Of course, when Rick walked into Intake, he didn't know all the details of the prison culture, but he was smart enough to know that keeping his cards close to his chest and his mouth shut, was probably going to be a good start. Emotionally, he wasn't ready to talk anyways. An officer escorted him to a cell on the far side of the bottom tier of the prison.

"Welcome home," said the guard slamming the door behind him.

"I didn't know I'd have a roommate," said Rick returning the stare of the kid sitting on the top bunk. "I'm Rick."

"Tommy," said the kid holding out his hand. "I didn't know I was getting a roommate either."

Rick threw his roll on the bed and began to make himself at home.

"Your box is the one on the bottom," said Tommy. "I didn't have much shit to put in mine. Only been here about a month."

"Yeah me too," said Rick. "First time in general pop though."

"Oh yeah? Where'd they have you?"

Rick wasn't about to tell the kid he'd been up on the psych ward; first impressions were important in prison. That much he knew.

"Some medical unit or whatever."

"Cool."

The two spent the evening just sort of sniffing each other out. No one wanted to say too much until they at least knew each a little better, but right away Rick sensed the kid was a good dude; had this goofy-like persona which helped put the more reserved Rick at ease.

"So how old are you?" said Rick.

"Sixteen."

"Yeah? Me too."

This common thread helped break the ice, and the two bonded shooting the shit about teenage life. It still took a couple of days for both teens to trust each enough to tell their stories.

"I shot my father," said Tommy. Suddenly Rick didn't feel so lonely.

"But he shot me first." Tommy held up his left forearm. "Right through there." The wound was fresh and still healing.

"Jesus man. That looks like it hurt."

"Hurt like a fucking son of a bitch."

"Why'd he shoot you?"

"We was both drunk and got into an argument about shit you know? He got so pissed at me that he pulled a .357 and fired. That's the shot that went through my arm. I went nuts thinking he was gonna shoot again, so I tackled him and wrestled the gun away from him. And I shot him. A bunch of times. Don't really know what happened but when the cops and the paramedics came I was just slumped up against the wall in the hallway. Fucking blood everywhere. I think it was from my arm. But I just couldn't stop pulling the trigger. All the bullets were gone so I was just shooting the air."

"I'm sorry man."

"Yeah me too. So what about you?"

"I shot my father and my stepmother. Lots of shit going on you know…so much history and just fucking shit to deal with. But long story short, there was an argument with my Dad. He said I had to leave. Just fucking kicked me out. Said I was causing problems with his wife. Just a bunch of shit going on. I don't know exactly what happened…but I just fucking snapped…"

"That's harsh bro."

"If I could take back that night. That fucking moment...I would."

"I hear ya."

They spent some more time comparing stories, but Rick was still very much guarded in his responses. He'd hardly processed the events of that night himself, and even just thinking about it tore him up inside.

"I know I'm in here for life," he said. "I turned myself in because I thought Alaska had the death penalty. If I'd have known they didn't, I would have run my ass off and made them shoot me. Would have been justice for my father and for Rosemary."

"Nah man, don't think that way. Like you said, there's so much shit that happened. The court will see that. You ain't dying in here dude!"

"Well from what you've told me about your father, you shouldn't even be here or spend a minute in jail. Jesus! What a prick!"

"Who knows…I guess we'll just have to wait and see. Not much else we can do at the moment can we?" He pointed to the cell doors. "Not like we can just walk out of here anytime we please!" He started to laugh. A slow sad laugh.

Rick smiled. "Fuck man. How the hell did this even all happen?"

"I dunno man," Tommy said shrugging his shoulders. "I dunno."

The two soon settled into life in G.P. and quickly became close friends and comrades. Tommy was Rick's first real 'prison brother'.

"Yo man," said Tommy swinging his legs across the desk. "You and me, we got to stick together."

"I agree. I've got your back man. Whatever happens, I'm there for you."

"Me too, man. Me too."

"And the first person that does try anything to either of us or test us you know," said Rick. "I say we beat him to a bloody pulp. Make an example out of them, so no one else tries anything."

"I agree, and have no problem doing that."

They didn't have to wait long. One day while they were out in the day room, a Mexican dude still locked up in his cell started waving his arms trying to get Rick's attention.

"Hey Holmes!"

Rick wandered over to see what he wanted.

"Are you the little sixteen-year-old punk who shot his parents?"

The question caught Rick off guard and he shrugged his shoulders ever so slightly.

"Don't look so puzzled," said the man glaring. "I'm going to slap the taste out of your mouth you little disrespectful punk! How dare you take the lives of the motherfuckers that raised you!"

Rick didn't say a word, shook his head and walked away, while the man continued to threaten and berate. Tommy was lying on his bed when Rick walked in.

"What's up man? You look weird. Something happen?"

Rick told him about the Mexican.

"Motherfucker had no right man," said Tommy. "We need to do something to teach him a lesson. Seriously."

"I agree," said Rick. "Let's jump him the first chance we get."

"Deal."

Tommy and Rick went on high alert, and for the next few weeks they made sure to sit across from each other so they could literally watch each other's backs. Anytime the cell door was open, they made sure they knew exactly where each other was, just in case someone tried something funny. They waited for the Mexican but he was never unlocked at the same time they were. Probably for the best. Youth and anxiety don't really mesh all that well, and who knows what might have happened in their exuberance to prove a point. They had no idea who the Mexican was connected to, or if he had a posse who would just love to sink their chops into a couple of teenagers.

The middle of January, both Tommy and Rick were finally moved from Intake to a normal general population mod. They went from a corner cell in Golf Mod to the bottom tier corner room in Charlie Mod.

"Damn! I didn't bring my suitcase," laughed Tommy rolling up his meagre belongings.

"No shit eh?"

As the boys walked through Charlie on the way to their cells, more than a few of the other inmates were enthused by their arrival.

"Did someone just fucking whistle at us?" said Tommy throwing his bed roll on the top bunk.

"I heard it too. We'd better be ready for anything."

Not sure what to expect, the boys wandered out into the middle of the mod to have a look around. It was a younger crowd, not something either of them expected. There were even another couple of minors. Rick had no idea what they'd done but figured it had to be pretty serious if they were here and not in juvy.

Over the next few days, the boys mingled and sniffed out their fellow inmates. Turns out they really weren't in that bad of company.

"You guys got nothing to worry about man," said the young guy with the black curly hair. "The older dudes are more scared of us than we are of them."

Rick soon learned that the older one was, and the longer he'd been in prison, the more tired he'd grown of the violence and the more hesitant he was to employ it. 'Youngsters' however, had the reputation of being 'young, dumb, and full of cum', too hyperactive, and too overaggressive. They hadn't yet suffered the consequences of their actions long enough to wake-up and understand that there are more mature ways to handle a situation. The curly-haired guy was right, the older guys in the Mod gave most of the juveniles and pretty much anyone under the age of twenty-four a fairly wide berth. This was the fighting age. The age where you still had to prove your worth and earn your respect. Those willing to fight and stand up for themselves were always more respected than the punks who refused to fight, and once you refused a fight, you were labelled a 'pussy' and anyone had free range to do what they pleased like humiliate, slap you around, disrespect, or rob you. Around the wrong predator, a punk could easily end up as someone's bitch, and used for all sorts of sexual satisfaction.

Rick had no intention of ever backing down or becoming anyone's bitch. He'd never backed down outside of prison, so there was no way in hell he was going to start now. The most important thing was respect. The quicker you earned it, the better off you'd be. Rick honestly didn't think he'd have any trouble gaining respect. His days on the streets had taught him many valuable lessons, and he knew how to keep his mouth shut. He may have been young but he certainly wasn't naïve. He'd already had far more life experiences than many of the dudes in Charlie, experiences that he never wanted to share with anyone. They wouldn't understand. They'd think he was a freak. He could never tell them he'd once been God's Little Warrior.

****

Despite the ongoing distraction of the divorce, Rick's spiritual training continued. Brenda turned to God even more as a way to cope, and for guidance on how to move forward. Everything in Brenda's life was spiritualized, seen through the lens of a different hue, an extreme hue. And this method of interpreting life became so ingrained and programmed, that it literally became the normality of her perception, making her unable to consider or even acknowledge other valid points of view. This made things even harder for Rick and Jimmy.

Bob wasn't someone who fell out of love with his wife and found someone else more suitable to his needs and lifestyle, he was an 'adulterer' who was going to Hell for his transgression. He would be punished and plagued by God in the most horrific Old Testament way. In her eyes, the divorce itself wasn't caused by an irreparable breakdown in their relationship, but because Bob had not fully embraced the blood of the Lamb and had allowed Satan to creep into his heart. The forces of Darkness had misled and deceived him. Had his heart been right with God, none of this would have happened and the family wouldn't be suffering so much.

'Hand of God'. 'God's Will'. These expressions permeated the daily conversations, and stuck in Rick's head. Everything in life, every occurrence, trial or tribulation, good or bad, was done at the 'Hand of God' and in accordance with 'God's Will'. They didn't necessarily have to like what God was dishing, but they had to accept it as part of the Divine Plan, and do their best to be dutiful and grateful children of God. Everything perceived through a one-dimensional lens, everything had a spiritual connotation or consequence they had to strive to understand. Black or white. Good or Evil. There were no in-betweens. Everything and everyone was either one or the other. Except for Rick. He lived in the day, and he lived in the night. He knew the word of God but he also experienced the darkness of temptation and sin. Confused and conflicted, he couldn't talk to his mom, she just wouldn't understand. And he couldn't talk to his father, he wouldn't understand either. He only had himself. And at ten-years-old, that just wouldn't cut it.

Every night before bed the boys would study with their mom. "God is my All'. "God is my strength." "God is my foundation." "God is my source of wisdom, with God I can do anything, and without Him I am nothing." This single-minded focus on God completely robs the individual of any motivation or reason to develop his own strength, wisdom, and capabilities. Why strive for anything when God will give you everything you need? Why try in school? Why do this? Why do that? God will provide. "Godaphilia" - subservience to His Will and His Power. Belief is one thing, extremism is quite another.

As Rick grew older, Brenda began to increase his knowledge in the true art of 'spiritual warfare'.

"You must see everything in life spiritually Ricky. Everything is connected to God, and there can be no other explanation for why something happened except that it was the Will of God. Do you understand?"

"I guess so."

"See, anything that is God's Will is good, and will be rewarded by Him. Everything working in opposition of God's Will is evil, the work of Satan. And those that are evil will perish in the same lake of fire as Satan himself when Christ returns."

"Okay…" All Rick really heard was that you were either a good guy or a bad guy. And if you fucked up and were a bad guy, then you were going to Hell in everlasting flames.

"Our job is to stay firmly planted with the good guys and oppose anything that we think is in opposition with God's Will. It is our responsibility Rick. Yours, mine, Jimmy's… As children of God we must join the 'War in the Heavens' and do or very best to actively fight and wage war against the Forces of Darkness. We can't just sit back and let the Devil take over. We must fight. Not just in our minds and in our hearts but we must be active on the ground. Search out the Forces of Darkness and destroy them before they destroy us!"

"But what if we can't?"

"We have to try Rick, we have to try! We are the persecuted ones. Evil is always after us, trying to turn us into one of Satan's minions…but we can't let him. Evil is everywhere, we're outnumbered for sure, which is why we have to be so strong. Like David and Goliath. We are David, fighting the giant Goliath. But we can do it because we have God on our side. You must always be on the lookout for evil."

For Brenda and other militant Christians, every broken home, every act of violence, every act of sex outside of marriage, are all just symptoms of a rotten society, and a proclamation that society is the playground of the Devil. If you are not 'saved' by the blood of the Lamb you are by default a willing and blindly ignorant pawn of Satan, therefore, you can be driven to commit further sins by manipulating your own dark wants and needs. It was that simple. Black and white. Good versus evil.

"Rick, you must understand that people who live in sin, like your father, actually become possessed by the Devil or his demons themselves, and can be pushed into the most destructive activities and lifestyles."

"Daddy is possessed?"

Brenda looked intently into her oldest son's terrified brown eyes. "It certainly is a possibility Rick. Wouldn't you say? Look what he's done to us? That is the work of the Devil. Daddy didn't believe enough and the Devil got him."

Rick shuddered to believe what his mother was suggesting. Was it true? It couldn't be. But he also didn't have any proof otherwise. Evil was everywhere, and his father certainly didn't believe in God as strongly as they did, he knew that much. What if he was? What if his father was possessed? Rick couldn't even comprehend the thought, or the consequences.

"We are persecuted and face overwhelming odds against the Forces of Darkness. We are powerless without God's divine strength…"

His head felt heavy. He just wanted to turn his ears off. He'd heard enough.

Why wouldn't she stop talking? Daddy is possessed?

"You have a gift Rick. A true gift from God. You can see the other side. This makes it even more important that you stay close to God and become a young soldier for Christ. It's your duty. Your obligation. You have the gift. Not many people do. You must use it."

He didn't want the gift. He didn't even really know what gift she was talking about. Yes, he could speak in tongues, and yes he'd received the Holy Spirit, and yes he sometimes saw things and felt things in the shadows that may or may not have been there. He didn't know why, and he certainly didn't see it as a gift. He saw things the way he saw them. He didn't know that other people didn't see things the same way he could. Didn't everyone see through the same lens as he did?

Rick retreated in horror to the shop. He needed some time and he needed some space. His whole body felt tired and heavy like someone had replaced his blood with cement. He needed to think things through. Just be alone, and the shop was the best place. His little sanctuary. He hadn't bothered pulling the cord to turn on the single bulb overhead light, since enough sunlight managed to squeeze its way through the clouds and in through the two small windows. He was so confused. And depressed. His mind on constant reply, enveloped by intense sadness.

"He can't be possessed. Why couldn't he just see the Light and come fully to the Lord? He had to. Then he could be saved. Why couldn't he be like us? Warriors? We'd all be together. A spiritual team of a family."

The thoughts steamrolled.

"Dad wasn't really that bad was he? He didn't do drugs. He hardly ever drank or even swore. There was the thing with Rosemary but other than that…"

Pounding.

"Was simply not giving yourself completely to God enough of a sin to warrant being possessed and driven by Satan to destroy your family?"

The boy was terrified. If it happened so easily to his father, what stopped it from happening to him? Was he on the same path? He certainly had unclean thoughts, swore like crazy, and enjoyed mucking about and being mischievous. It was way more fun being mischievous. Was that a sin? That he found it even more fun to be rebellious that to be 'Godly'? What would it even feel like to be possessed? Was it something you even felt?

"What would I do? Would I even know?"

It was in this train of thought that the chasm began to open. Slowly, the boy's senses heightened and he became aware of something else, something that wasn't really of this world. A shadow. Up in the corner and to the right. His eyes strained but saw nothing. Was it just a feeling? He thought for sure he'd felt something, not like someone reached out and touched him on the shoulder, but something more subversive.

"I'm just freaking myself out man. Seriously Rick, get a grip. Fuck." He sort of laughed, trying to brush it off. But he was powerless to let it go.

"But what if something was there?" What if it had heard his thoughts and had been drawn in by his doubt and vulnerability. The second-sight. The gift. Was this what his mother had been talking about?

"If I open myself up to the Holy Spirit, I should be able to see." He concentrated. Focused. Poured every thought and every effort into reaching out and trying to feel if something was there. Nothing.

"I knew I was just psyching myself out. Okay one last time. If there is something there, I should be able to sense it through the power of the Lord. Help me see Lord." He closed his eyes and concentrated. "Help me see Lord. I believe in your power." The room was still. Silent.

Then a rush of wind darted to the corner behind him, like a quick solid ripple and flap of a flag. Then again to the shadows of the corner to the upper left. His eyes flew open, terrified at what they might behold. A flicker in the shadow. Not like a light going on but a flicker that made the dark even darker. Blackness. Rapid and indiscernible. The boy began to shake. His eyes drawn to the dark, not wanting to look, but unable to look away. His legs bolted to the floor, unable to move. Was the darkness watching him? The air stifled. Unbreathable. Dense. Another dash across the floor. Another corner. Wide-eyed, Rick followed. He could see something, but was it with his eyes or with his mind? The flickering of the shadow and ripping of the wind intensified, mirroring the flickering of fear and doubt in the young boys' mind. Was he really experiencing this? Fear and confusion. He had to know. Two more dashes. Past his right shoulder, then his left. Then back in front of him. Rick focused even harder.

"Don't you run from me!" The silent words screamed from his brain. His mind was spinning out of control. Fear. Disbelief. Was this real? He had to know.

"Show yourself to me!" His voice shrieked through the fear, and echoed through the shop.

For a second or two longer, the shadow flickered in the upper left hand corner, just above the shop door. From nothingness, a thick black smoked rolled from above the door. All doubt and disbelief was suspended. This shit was real. He froze, stunned by the yellow orbs glaring from the half dog, half bat face. Black, dirty, dripping. The eyes. Dripping with puss, illuminated by an eerie light from within. The ears and nose were of a bat, and its rotten skin, hairless and grotesque, looked damp as if it had just been pulled from the womb.

"Motherfucker!"

Rick bolted for the door, flying right under the demon, slamming the shop door behind him as hard as he could. When he got to the middle of the lawn, he stopped and spun.

"Don't you come through that door you motherfucker! Don't you even think about it!"

His laboured breath heavy with fear, burned his throat, while the rest of his body went numb. There was no longer a shred of doubt in his soul that the world of demons was real, and that spiritual warfare and the War of the Heavens was just as prevalent as the air he breathed and the ground under his feet.

"What do I do? What do I do?" he said, his bulging eyes transfixed on the door.

Sensing that the creature wasn't going to follow him out into the daylight, he turned and ran into the front yard, getting as far away from the shop as possible. He didn't want to run in and tell his mom what had happened. She'd spoken of demons but she'd never actually told him if she ever seen one herself.

"I did this. I'm the one who drew it out. I shouldn't have thought those thoughts. It was sinful to do that. Wrong."

He was wracked with guilt, like for some reason he was responsible for what he saw. He had sinned. He had brought this horror upon himself and brought demons to their property. He wasn't ready to talk about it, but mainly he didn't want his mother knowing he was wondering what it was like to be possessed. He stayed outside in the front of the house for the rest of the day, making sure he never got a glimpse of the shop. As night descended, he went inside, making sure he turned on every light in every single room he went. No shadows. That was his new rule.

"There is no fucking way I'm falling asleep tonight," he said double checking that his closet doors were shut tight.

He turned on his desk lamp and grabbed a National Geographic. Eventually sleep overtook his terrified little soul, and he passed out on the bed.

For the next few days, he continuously checked out the shadows and left as many lights on as possible. The experience had shaken him to the core, causing a complete psychic shutdown in reaction to the terrifying realization that the stories of the Devil and his minions were not just tales from the Bible, or the rantings of the overzealous, or 'monsters under the bed', but real. In his mind, in his young consciousness, they had manifested themselves and come alive. The only reason people couldn't normally see them was because their minds and spirits were closed to its presence. That reality only pushed him closer to Christ's open and waiting arms. Now he knew he needed protection, and that he really was helpless without His power. From now on, he prayed a little harder, and took the donning of his spiritual armour a little more seriously. He didn't want to be possessed or be used as one of Satan's pawns – like his father.

"Demons and spiritual warfare can manifest in people's lives Rick," said Brenda, as the two of them talked one night about a week later.

"I know. I saw one."

"You what?" She almost sounded excited.

"In the shop, last week." He ran through the whole ordeal detail by detail. "I felt attacked…like Satan had sent a demon to harm me."

She hugged her boy. "Oh Rick!"

"It was awful and I didn't know what to do."

She pulled his little face close to hers. "All you have to do is call on the power of Christ and the blood of the Lamb, and no demon can harm or stand against you. If you imagine your spiritual armour and call upon the Holy Ghost itself, you will be an invincible child of God and the demon will flee."

Rick felt guilty for not having more faith, and weak for allowing the demon to frighten him. He also felt a degree of separation from his mother, like he had experienced something she never had.

"You have a gift son. You can see what others can't. You are blessed. God has blessed you. You were given this gift for a reason and eventually the Lord will have plans for its use."

He didn't feel blessed. In fact, he felt even more shut out from the world than before. No one would understand what the hell he was talking about, and there was no way he could even begin to explain it. Some fucker would think he's a lunatic and throw him in a straightjacket.

The next day the two of them went back out to the shop together.

"It's okay Rick. We'll turn on all the lights, and open all the doors and the windows, including the big front door. And we'll pray."

So they did. For the next hour, they prayed for the Holy Spirit to cleanse the shop. They called on Jesus to ward and protect it, and to drive away any Forces of Darkness. They prayed and prayed and prayed. Over and over and over. The same words, the same prayers. Rick prayed with all his might, and he secretly prayed for his own soul, that he never be possessed. And he prayed for his father. He may have hated his guts, but still, he didn't deserve a demon.

"It's safe now," said Brenda. "The shop is free. No evil can enter."

Despite that, he was still skittish going into the shop for the next while. But at least now he knew he could just call on God to protect him if the demon ever came back. It was a long time before he attempted to 'see' again, the reality of the horrors just too much to bear. But what he never understood was that the demons never went away, at least not the ones that dwelled in his heart. And God couldn't protect him from those, since God was one of the demons circling.

CHAPTER TEN

The afternoon in the shop haunted Rick. He wanted to believe it wasn't real, but he couldn't shake the sensations and visions that still tremored through his body. The mind can play tricks, he knew that, yet he had a sense that what he experienced was so profound and outside of his own existence that he could not have made it up. The demon was not a reflection of something he'd seen on television or in the movies; he was never allowed to watch those types of programs. Could his vivid imagination really delve that deep into the underworld? Or did he have to face the possibility that what he saw was real, and that horrific creatures did indeed lie in the world that was neither here nor there. And why him? He didn't want the gift. He didn't want to see what he saw or feel the way he felt. So many questions in his life with no discernable answers.

No longer able to keep a firm grip on the greased rope of his conscious, the boy slipped deeper and deeper into despair. Were demons always lingering around, only showing themselves to those who could 'see'? And really, how many people were infected or under their influence? Christian doctrine taught him that anyone who was a sinner was susceptible to being inhabited or influenced by a demon. Almost everybody sinned didn't they? Isn't that why Jesus died on the cross? Because everyone was sinners and needed to be saved? So if everyone was a sinner, then everybody was at risk. The only way to be protected was to be 'born again' and washed in the blood of the Lamb. His thoughts seesawed back to his father. He'd been 'misled' by the Devil into destroying his family, blinded to God's 'truth' by some foul spirit. He hadn't been a good enough Christian to fend off the demon. Didn't believe enough. Didn't devote his life and his love to Christ. He said he was a Christian, but was he really? If he was, then none of this would have ever happened. Rick thought his father would have been stronger, more able to defend himself against the possession, after all, his father could do anything, fly planes, sail boats, race cars, and if he was vulnerable, Lord help the rest of the population. How many people just walking around, doing their daily business and living their lives were susceptible? Or maybe even already possessed? The boy couldn't get the thought out of his head.

A trip to the mall or the grocery store was no longer just a trip to pick up food and supplies, it was an exercise in observation. Was that person possessed? What about the blond lady picking through the apples? Did she have a demon living inside of her? In his young reasoning he decided that most people had to be under the influence of the Devil in some way, and there had to be some sign or indication. But what was it? After his own encounter in the shop, he was too terrified to try and 'see' again, or even concentrate enough to pick up any psycho-spiritual signs. He desperately wanted to know, but he didn't really. And it bothered him that so many people, hundreds and hundreds of thousands of people passing by each other each day, oblivious to the 'war' being fought around them. People who had no idea how lost they already were or how vulnerable they were to the Forces of Evil. He debated the odds. One in ten? Three in ten? Six in ten? That's a whole hell of a lot of people who were in trouble and working for the Devil. The overwhelming odds were not easy to swallow for God's Little Warrior. How was he supposed to tackle all of this? His mother said he had the gift, and God would show him how to use it, but even with the gift, he was at a loss as to how he could make a difference. He had no control, no power to change anything. All he could do was pray for their souls and hope for the best.

While he prayed for others, his own soul churned. Yet, his fear and apprehension at the potential presence of demonic forces, didn't stop him from sneaking out at night. It just heightened the anxiety. Sometimes, as the hairs on the back of his neck would tingle, he'd wonder just how close 'they' were behind him. He'd run a little faster. Freeze in the shadows and wait for the feeling to pass. He was a sinner. He knew he was. He smoked. He snuck out at night. He stole things. He was God's Little Warrior, but he was also a sinner. He worried about his own susceptibility and opening the door of his spirit to the Devil. Sometimes areas would feel 'heavy' and Rick would race through them just a little quicker, saying a quick prayer to Christ for forgiveness and protection.

Sometimes though, he felt the threat so severe, that he would just turn around and go home. He knew that he should just stay home for good, but he couldn't. Too entwined in the dark part of his life, 'The Game' was simply something he just couldn't give up, cherishing the freedom and independence more than the consequences. He always knew that God would forgive him in the end anyways. It didn't matter what he did, God would always forgive. That's what he'd been taught, and that was his belief. Besides, if such a high percentage of people were susceptible to demonic influence or possession, and they seemed for the most part to live happy, productive lives, then it couldn't really be all that bad could it? Sure it wasn't what God wanted, and it would hurt him that someone deliberately turned from the light, but his love was boundless, and he would always forgive you and take you back. Always. No matter what.

And so Rick lived in a paradox. Knowing that what he was doing was bad, but knowing he had the protection and the forgiveness of God. He could push the limits, and he did, every chance he got. He could take risks, and he did, every chance he got. With Mike, the pastor's son, he played with a Ouija Board, inviting the spirits to awaken, even though he knew full well the malice they caused. Fascination versus extreme fear, so susceptible to anything and everything that peaked his curiosity. Ghost stories, folklore and forbidden places, like the mine shaft and the thick orchard on Dell Smith's property. All places he wasn't supposed to go, all places on his list of places to go. He could never walk away from a challenge, constantly having to test his mettle and his own worth to the other kids, but mainly to himself. Could he do it? Was he good enough? Where did it all come from? His nature? His father?

Running unabated, his mother fed his curiosity with books. Of course, the books she gave her son all related to spiritual warfare, prayer, and Christianity.

"I know it's not quite your eleventh birthday yet but I have a bit of a present for you. Well not really a present but a book you might like to read. It's by a man named Frank E. Peretti."

"This Present Darkness?" said Rick.

"There's a whole series if you like this one."

Rick took the book into his room and flopped on his bed. The cover looked interesting enough. He flipped to the inside flap to read the review.

This Present Darkness, by Frank Peretti, is among the classic novels of the Christian thriller genre. First published in 1986, Peretti's book set a suspenseful standard in spiritual warfare story-telling that has rarely been met by his contemporaries. Set in the apparently innocent small town of Ashton, This Present Darkness follows an intrepid born-again Christian preacher and newspaper reporter as they unearth a New Age plot to take over the local community and eventually the entire world. Nearly every page of the book describes sulfur-breathing, black-winged, slobbering demons battling with tall, handsome, angelic warriors on a level of reality that is just beyond the senses. However, Christian believers and New Age demon-worshippers are able to influence unseen clashes between good and evil by the power of prayer. Peretti's violent descriptions of exorcisms are especially vivid: "There were fifteen [demons], packed into Carmen's body like crawling, superimposed maggots, boiling, writhing, a tangle of hideous arms, legs, talons, and heads." This book is not for the squeamish. But for page-turning spiritual suspense, it's hard to beat.

As if the boy wasn't terrified already, and having trouble distinguishing between fiction and reality. What ever happened to a good old Hardy Boy mystery or Charlie and the Chocolate Factory? The kid wasn't even eleven yet. Rick couldn't put the book down. It magnified all the thoughts and feelings he'd been having about the forces around them, and confirmed everything his mother had been telling him over the years; the entire world was a battlefield between God's angels and the Forces of Darkness, with mankind caught in the middle, the medium through which they fought. Just like Rick, characters in the book could at times see these angels and demons. He didn't feel so alone. Or crazy.

It had arms and it had legs, but it seemed to move without them, crossing the street and mounting the front steps of the church. Its leering, bulbous eyes reflected the stark blue light of the full moon with their own jaundiced glow. The gnarled head protruded from hunched shoulders, and wisps of rancid red breath seethed in laboured hisses through rows of jagged fangs. It either laughed or it coughed- the wheezes puffing out from deep within its throat could have been either. From its crawling posture, it reared up on its legs and looked about the quiet neighbourhood, the black, leathery jowls pulling back into a hideous death-mask grin. It moved toward the front door. The black hand passed through the door like a spear through liquid; the body hobbled forward and penetrated the door, but only halfway.

Suddenly, as if colliding with a speeding wall, the creature was knocked backward and into a raging tumble down the steps, the glowing red breath tracing a corkscrew trail through the air. With an eerie cry of rage and indignation, it gathered itself up and off the sidewalk and stared at the strange door that would not let it pass through. Then the membranes on its back began to billow, enfolding great bodies of air, and it flew with a roar headlong at the door, through the door, into the foyer – and into a cloud of white hot light.

The creature screamed and covered its eye, then felt itself being grabbed by a huge powerful vise of a hand. In an instant it was hurling through space like a rag doll, outside again, forcefully ousted. The wings hummed in a blur as it banked sharply in a flying turn and headed for the door again, red vapors chugging in dashes and streaks from its nostrils, its talons bared and poised for attack, a ghostly siren of a scream rising in its throat. Like an arrow through a target, like a bullet through a board, it streaked through the door –

And instantly felt its insides tearing loose. There was an explosion of suffocating vapor, one final scream, and the flailing of withering arms and legs. Then there was nothing at all except the ebbing stench of sulfur and the two strangers, suddenly inside the church.[2]

Just a perfect, easy, non-nightmare inducing before bed read for an almost eleven-year-old. After tearing through the first and then second book in the series, Rick had no doubts as to the authenticity of the war going on around them. But new questions arose. Why had he been given the gift, and if he had truly been given the gift by God, how was he supposed to use it? It was all so overwhelming for him.

"The second sight that you have Ricky is a gift! A truly brilliant gift from God," said Brenda. "It's so very rare, and you have been so blessed to receive this gift. Most Christians, even the most spiritual believers go their whole lives without seeing the other side, but you…you are so young…and you've already experienced the glory."

"I wouldn't call it glory. It was terrifying!"

"Yes, but see how much clearer things are now? You see what others can't. You know the truth of what we face in the fight."

[2] Excerpt from "This Present Darkness" by Frank. E Peretti

Rick didn't really think his gift made him see anything clearer at all, in fact, it just muddled up an already muddled mind.

"God has given you the gifts for a reason Rick. The gifts of the Spirit are to be used for him. It's just another tool you have in your arsenal. Consider yourself lucky."

Rick still didn't understand how he was supposed to use this gift, and instead of it making him feel special, it made him feel even more like an outsider. No one wanted to be friends with the kid who saw demons and shit. It wasn't cool. It was just downright creepy.

"I have some new people that I want you to meet. They understand your gift."

"Another new church?" said Rick.

"This one is different. Jack and Jill…and yes don't laugh but those are really their names…they just moved here from Arizona. They have a ministry called Potter's House. They're like us Rick. They are comrades in arms. They have a daughter a couple of years older than you, Sarah is her name, and a boy, Paul…he's a bit younger than you, and a two-year-old named Andrew. Wonderful people…but more importantly, I finally feel like we may have found a church home."

Brenda didn't have many close friends, and almost no one shared her fervor or view of Christianity. Meeting Jack and Jill was not only a spiritual connection but a break from the social isolation she'd imposed on herself after the divorce. Considered non-denominational, 'Potter's House' preached itself as contemporary Christianity, 'growing with the times' and constantly evolving. Both Jack and Jill believed in praying in tongues, intercession and power of prayer. Neither were as informed or studied in the practice of spiritual warfare as Brenda, but their combined knowledge and dedication allowed them to feed off each other, producing a sometimes almost delirious atmosphere of praise and worship. They also believed that in order to be saved, you had to accept Christ and be cleansed by the blood of the Lamb. Minor sins and unclean thoughts just demonstrated how un-Christ-like the average person was, and how much God was needed.

"These so called small sins are still stains upon our souls. But they can be wiped clean with a simple prayer of forgiveness to the Lord. That's all it takes. You must pray to God to forgive you, and embrace his teachings. Give your life to him."

"Dear Lord," said Rick. "Please forgive my sneaking out at night, and all the other sins I do when I'm out."

There. He'd prayed and he was forgiven. No consequences. Not from his mother or from God. What better deal could you have? Total freedom and independence and when you fuck up, you just say a little prayer and all is good again. Perfect. And even when you were 'back-sliding', which meant you'd had a royal fuck-up or were constantly living in sin, it was still okay. You just had to return to God, get re-saved, and start fresh. The heavier your life was stained, the more susceptible you were to demonic influence and Satan's minions, and the more you needed Christ. The trick was to remain as Christ-like for as long as possible and not backslide, but even if you did, there was always forgiveness, as long as you asked for it. It was all just a big circle, an addiction of sorts, where you could fall off the wagon as many times as you wanted. As long as on the final journey of life you were back on the wagon, and not riding under the rails, the Pearly gates would open and you'd be admitted on into heaven. Those who refused to ever get back on the wagon or who's hearts had hardened against God were 'lost'. But even they could still hit the reset button for redemption.

'Potter's House' met two nights a week in a small rented office space just off Highway 99. The space didn't really have that church sort of feel with its fold-up chairs and old wooden stand for a pulpit but it suited the purposes of the congregation. If you could even call it a congregation. While the room could technically fit about twenty-five, there were usually only about eight people attending, Brenda, Rick and Jimmy, and Jack and Jill and their three kids including the little Andrew. Every once and a while a few stragglers would shuffle in but that didn't happen very often. The very first worship service involved a cleansing.

"Dear Jesus," said Jack. "Please cleanse this space with the blood of the Lamb and keep it safe from the forces of evil. Cleanse any stain, and banish any evil that lies within these walls."

Rick never realized that places as well as people could be possessed. This was new.

"Why did we have to cleanse the building?"

"Places that may or may not have been the site of constant sinful activity are contaminated Rick," explained Jack. "These are prime places for demons to lurk and dwell."

"But it's just an office building," said Rick.

"Do you know exactly what's gone on in this building?"

Rick felt stupid. "No."

"Well then, it's better to be safe than sorry isn't it?"

Rick thought about this for a while. If they needed to cleanse this simple little office building, then what the hell were they going to have to do to all the bars, adult stores, and street corners? He wasn't naïve to what went on in these sorts of places. Sin. And everyone inside were sinners.

"You see Rick," said Jack. "There are zones of good and evil everywhere. Churches and places of worship are good, they are protected, while the places where evil transpires are bad. You must never venture to those places. Places where they sell drugs or do other questionable things. Dancing, smoking, all those sorts of things. These are all sins Rick, and you must be aware of the evil that lurks in these places. I know you're young now but someday the temptation will arise from these dens of iniquity but you must resist the urge. Do you understand?"

Rick nodded. "Yes sir, I do."

"Those places that are not protected by the blood of the Lamb are doomed. As it says in Exodus chapter twelve verse seven, 'And they shall take of the blood, and strike it on the two side posts and on the upper door post of the houses, wherein they shall eat the lamb', and then Exodus twelve twenty-three, 'When the LORD goes through the land to strike down the Egyptians, he will see the blood on the top and sides of the doorframe and will pass over that doorway, and he will not permit the destroyer to enter your houses and strike you down.'. That is why we cleanse Rick. We are the protectors. God relies on us to mark the doors, so he knows which houses are holy and which must face his wrath."

The whole thing terrified the boy. Not only did he have to worry about 'seeing' the other side, and wonder if the person next in line at the McDonald's was possessed, now he had to worry if the McDonald's itself was possessed. Jesus Lord in heaven. It was all too much for him to handle. He couldn't feel the evil per se, at least he didn't think he could, but his mother and Jill could. They frequently got 'bad feelings' about certain people and places. Consequently, this made the whole world a rather problematic place to live, especially for a boy with an already troubled soul and tormented heart.

"We must be careful everywhere we go Rick," said his mother. "Everywhere is a hazard."

Rick had to let it all sink in. The person walking ahead of him in the aisle at the grocery store could have sinful thoughts, and if he wasn't careful or protected by God's armour, he could walk right through the lingering psychic impression of the stain, and be affected himself. Christ was the only way to fortify your own spirit and prevent the taint from attaching itself to you. The statement 'evil was everywhere' was a definite understatement. With the 'Potter House' congregation, 'zone warfare' and cleansing tainted areas became a ritual. The boundaries of the Lord's purity had to be reinforced and areas of evil cleansed and re-cleansed. It was their job. It was their duty.

Services would begin with Jack, Jill, and their daughter Sarah leading 'praise and worship' either with a guitar, synthesizer, or both. Then Jack would take to the pulpit to deliver the Lord's message for the evening, and they would end it all with prayer. Sometimes there would be more praise and worship at the end, and sometimes the prayer would go on late into the evening, especially if some wayward soul wandered in looking for redemption.

"Gather round everyone and lay your hands on this poor soul. Let us pray. Dear Jesus please cleanse the soul of our brother and help bring him to the light of Jesus…"

Sometimes they'd spend an hour or more laying hands and praying in tongues for the stain to be removed from their troubled soul. Emotionally exhausted, Rick would come home, flop on his bed and try to make sense of it all. Had they really helped? They'd been demon fighting for as long as he could remember yet none of it seemed to make a difference. The struggle was too great. There never seemed to be any real progress or marked victories. The same drunk that came in to be cleansed would show up on the street corner a couple of months later, booze in hand, sin smeared across his inebriated smile. But he had no choice. He had to keep fighting. They were underdogs against overwhelming odds, and all they could do was hang in there until Christ returned to Earth and led them all to victory.

Underneath it all, he was still just an eleven-year-old boy. A kid. A kid who saw demons, but nevertheless, still a kid. He hadn't even hit puberty yet. So even though Rick fully believed in what he saw, he never spoke about it to anyone but his mother and their church friends. He didn't dare mention it to his father. He'd have had a shitfit on his ex-wife and there'd be no telling what Bob might have done. And he didn't dare mention it to any of the neighborhood kids, especially the group of teenage boys that hung out in the garage of the house at the end of the street. Rick longed to hang out with them and loved watching them skateboard. They knew all the tricks, and at that time he was so lame he didn't even have his own board.

"Happy Birthday Rick!"

"No way! A skateboard? Are you serious?" He flew into his mother's arms. "Thank you!" The board was nothing special, made of cheap graphite but he didn't give a shit. He had his own board, and that's all he cared about. He practised on that thing for hours, first trying to master the basics, then trying out some of the moves he'd seen the older boys do.

"God damnit!" he said as his ass hit the curb for the thousandth time. "Why can't I pop a fucking Ollie? It can't be that difficult."

Wham! He'd be down again. As the frustration boiled, the temptation to toss the bloody board in the trash built.

"Stupid fucking thing."

His ego wouldn't let him give up. He'd master the hell out of that thing one way or another. The other boys were out grinding curbs and catching air as Rick wheeled his way down the street. He had to know how to do the tricks, even if it meant swallowing his pride.

"Hey," he said giving the boys a nod.

"What's up?" said Devon.

"I've been watching you guys ride and I was wondering if you'd…you know…show me how to do some tricks and shit."

"Hey Tim," said Devon waving over his buddy. "This kid wants us to teach him how to ride."

"Is that so?" Tim laughed. "How old are you kid?"

"Eleven."

"Eleven? Jesus Christ. You are just a kid," said Devon.

"What kind of music do you listen to?"

"I dunno," said Rick. "I like lots of different shit."

"Metallica? Slayer? Pantera?" said Tim.

Rick hadn't even heard of any of those bands. His credibility was shot to shit.

"Bet you've never even drank or fucked a chick have you?" laughed Devon.

"Jesus Devon," said Tim. "He is only eleven. Don't tell me you were fucking chicks at eleven because if you do, I'd say you're a fucking liar."

"What's your name kid?"

"Rick."

"I'm Tim, and that asshole is Devon."

"You smoke?" said Devon.

"Yeah of course. Who doesn't?" he lied. Credibility restored. "How old are you guys?"

"I'm sixteen and Tim is nineteen."

"So what do you do for fun Rick?" said Tim.

"Hang out I guess. Shoot the shit with whoever."

"That's your board?" said Devon laughing. "Dude. It's a piece of shit."

Rick's heart sank.

"I mean look at it? You can't ride with all that shit on the front. Those guards. Did you pick this out yourself?" said Tim.

"No. I just got it for my birthday."

"Well seriously dude, you need to lose all the non-essentials from your board. Like this fucking nose and tail guard…and what the fuck with these plastic side rails? I'm not teaching you shit until you at least have a proper board to ride."

There was hope.

"I can fix it. I'll make it better. I promise. I'll do whatever you tell me to. Please, I just want to learn and get better."

Tim stared him down. "I like you Rick. You seem like a pretty good little fucker, and it's not like we're not hanging out here almost every day anyways. You show me your board after you fix it up and I'll let you know whether or not I'll teach you how to ride. Deal?"

The smile practically burst through his cheeks. "Deal!"

Cool as a cucumber he hopped on his lame board and headed off toward home. As soon as he was out of sight, he flipped the board into his hands and high-tailed his little ass as fast as he could to his garage.

"I'll fix this board up." Grabbing a screwdriver and plopping himself down on the floor, he began to 'de-pussify' his skateboard. It didn't take long before the plastic side-rails, and nose and tail guards were tossed to the side.

"How the hell am I supposed to loosen up these trucks?" He rifled through the tool box trying to find something that would loosen the bolts.

"Fuck…this is on there tight." Thrusting the full torque of his body against the wrench, he heaved forward. "C'mon…c'mon."

With a jolt that almost sent him flying across the floor, the nut on the truck loosened. Success. Never a doubt.

After dealing with the hardware issues, he found a couple of cans of spray paint.

"Yeah…I can't ride with those guys with this kiddie-shit picture on here. They'd all laugh like hell." He took the silver can to the top of the board, and the gold can to the bottom, covering up any trace of its former 'pussiness'. The next day he was back at Devon's garage.

"Fixed up my board."

"Let me see." Tim took the board out of Rick's hand and gave it the once over. "Nice job. This'll work much better."

Rick was proud as shit, and he hung out with the boys every chance he had that summer, learning to board, learning to smoke, and generally learning a bunch of stuff that he'd have been better off not learning. He was well on his way to joining the 'skater' crowd and being a new neighbourhood nuisance.

"Fuck, I'm out of smokes," said Tim. "You got any Devon?"

"Nah, I'm all out too."

"Shit." He turned to Rick. "You got any kid?"

Even though he'd told the guys he smoked, Rick hadn't actually done the deed yet. Not that he was scared, he just hadn't had the opportunity, or the smokes. But he did know where he could find some.

"Nah," he answered pretending to check his pockets. "I'm all out too."

That night as he was sneaking around town, he purposely made his way to a particular trailer that was on his paper route.

"I knew they'd be there." He eyed the pack of smokes sitting on the glass table under the awning. Without making a sound he crept up alongside the trailer, and swiped the pack of cigarettes from the table, depositing them deep into the front pocket of his hoodie. He didn't have a chance to smoke any that night, so the minute he returned home, he tucked them away in one of his secret hidey-holes. A couple of nights later, with the smokes firmly in the front pocket of his pants, he made his way to the middle of the field next door to his house.

"There is no way I'll letting those guys know that I haven't smoked before." He pulled a cigarette out of the pack, held it to his lips, lit a match, and took a deep inhale.

"Holy fucking hell!" The smoke billowed from his gaping mouth as the nicotine vacuumed into his lungs, scorching a sinful path. It didn't take long for the nausea to creep up from the pit of his stomach and party with the new guest.

"Jesus…"

He dreaded the thought of taking another drag but he had to. He had to master this as soon as possible so he didn't look like an inexperienced little shit. Almost as bad as the first, the second drag sent him into a fit of coughs and gags. It was all he could do to keep the puke from erupting.

"Yeah…I don't think I'm going to be doing this too often." Of course, that would change, and over the next couple of years, it'd become second nature. But for now, he was a definite amateur, perfecting the cigarette dangling in the side of the mouth look, so at least he'd look cool.

To support his new habit, he needed a constant supply of smokes. He didn't figure he'd be able to rely on snitching them from the trailer guy forever, yet, the fourth time he showed up, there was a full unopened pack on the table and a brand new lighter. When he went to collect the fee for their newspaper subscription, there was a half a carton sitting on the table, and a few months later, a full unopened carton. Rick never charged them for their paper again. He never once spoke to his secret cigarette Santa, or offered thanks, but he figured they had an understanding, and cigarette Santa saved a bundle on his newspapers. The cigarettes were just a generic knock-off, but at that time, Rick didn't give a shit. A smoke was a smoke, especially when you were now the fucking coolest kid on the street because you kept your older teenaged buddies supplied. That gives a kid a lot of credibility, and makes him a favorite in the group.

He might have been a street rookie, but he'd proven that he'd come through when needed, and could be trusted and counted on. That was important. It made him feel important. But it also set a precedent. Ricky will do it won't you Ricky? He can get that for us, can't you Ricky? Ricky's the man. He's our boy. He's got fucking spunk that kid. He'll do anything if you ask him. He ain't afraid of shit. And that was the problem. When you're not afraid of shit, and your peers keep pumping up your ego, bad things happen. Things that shouldn't happen. All because you want to be accepted. All because you want to be a part of something that's different from your daily fucked up life. Jack and Jill. Adam and Eve. Jekyll and Hyde. All part of the same entity, all part of the same dichotomy ripping through his heart.

CHAPTER ELEVEN

When you're locked up and sequestered from society, you quickly discover who is really on your team and who is just there for notoriety of 'kind of', 'sort of' knowing a killer. Rick continued to receive mail, and since his move to Charlie Mod had even gotten a few phone numbers and was able to chat with some of his old friends. It hadn't taken long for his girlfriend Crystal to move on, not that he blamed her or expected anything different. He didn't have a right to ask her to stay committed to him; still, it stung. Some of his friends, mostly from ROTC wrote pledges of support to 'stand by his side forever' and while the gesture was welcome, the sentiment of course didn't last. Still, at the time, it was a glimmer of light and hope, the feeling that maybe, just maybe, he wouldn't be forgotten. His friends were just as confused about what happened as he was, and they had their troubles understanding the why behind it all. Rick was a good friend, someone who was always willing to listen, give advice, and lend a hand. But his friends never really knew the truth about Rick. How much of his life he'd kept hidden, how much of his life he was unwilling to share, not necessarily because he didn't want to, but because he was incapable of relaying those deep-seeded emotions. Rick knew how to help others, they just didn't know how to help him.

A small support group sprung up at the school, offering assistance to those who needed help in working through their feelings about what happened with Rick. None of his 'real friends' went, choosing to deal with their pain and confusion on their own, and were actually quite dismayed at the number of 'friends' who suddenly appeared out of nowhere, devastated and forlorn about their good buddy Rick Watkinson. Sometimes people can't help themselves. For someone who kept a very tight circle of friends, these 'pseudo' supporters lacked sincerity and seemed only out for their own personal gain, especially juxtaposed against those who were really hurting, like Amanda or Kristy. Amanda had been like a little sister, and it killed Rick to know how much pain she was in because of him. And Kristy.

Rick and Kristy hadn't even really met or became friends until late 1994 but the closeness and experiences they shared created an empathic intimacy between them. If anyone knew Rick, it was Kristy. Then there was the falling out; stupid reasons and misunderstandings that shouldn't have even mattered. She was hurt. He was hurt. And they'd never been able to heal those wounds. He came to her the morning after the murders because he couldn't turn himself in without saying goodbye. Receiving her letter in prison had opened the door to a reconciliation, and the two wrote back and forth. When Rick was finally given telephone privileges, he called her every day and they were able to sort through what happened to them, and he was able to help her understand what had happened with him. The closeness, intimacy, and the love returned, and this time, the two teens didn't back away from it. They arranged for her to visit in late January, and Rick was over the moon to see her, and to hold her in his arms.

"Kristy. Jesus it's good to see you!"

She took a few steps forward, not out of hesitation but trepidation. "Can I come closer? Is it allowed? I don't want to get you into any trouble?"

"You can come closer Kristy. We're allowed to touch." Rick smiled at Kristy's mother. "Thank you so much for bringing her Nora. I know you didn't have to."

Her warm return smile put Rick at ease. "I thought it was important for both of you. We support you Rick, and only want the best for you. I'm just going to wait out here in the hall. Give you two a chance to talk."

"So…" she said giving him a hug. "How have you been? I mean, I know we've talked on the phone and stuff but it feels weird seeing you here…and in that jumpsuit. It's just going to take me a little bit to get used to."

"I know. And I totally understand…I mean I get it. It still feels weird for me. The whole thing is fucked up."

Kristy tried to force a smile but failed miserably.

"It's okay," he said. "I know there isn't really much we can say about it. It happened and well, I'm probably going to be in here for the rest of my life."

"Don't say that Rick."

"Well it's true."

"But…just don't think that way okay? I can't stand to hear it."

"I'm sorry Kristy. I'm sorry for everything. I'm sorry that we let our fucking friends get in the middle of us…and I should have never listened to them."

"I know…me neither."

"But that's all in the past now right? I mean…you're here because you want to be here right?"

"Of course Rick." She leaned in close. He could smell her.

"I'm glad. Damn it's so good to see you. I've had so much time to think since I've been in here and I've thought a lot about you."

"I've thought about you too."

"You have?"

"Ya. And I've thought about how everything might have been different if we'd gotten together that summer. Maybe I could have helped you and you…you wouldn't be in here now."

"Oh Kristy."

"I'm serious Rick. Maybe I could have stopped you from spinning out of control."

His lips found hers and for a moment they were lost in each other.

"No Kristy. There was nothing you could have done."

Kristy's visits meant so much to Rick. Holding her in his arms, kissing her lips. He had wanted it to be her for so long; cared so deeply. Now they had each other. Except they didn't. Not really. In their teenage foolishness, they believed they could overcome the past. The events. The feelings. The guilt. And for a time they did, but the air of their visits was always tinged with a sense of melancholy and sadness. So many what ifs.

"I want to be able to trust you Rick. I want to let you in but I need you to always be honest with me and tell me the truth."

Rick wanted to believe he could let her in. He tried. But so much of his life was hidden behind the locked doors of his heart. Whether it was feelings, experiences, or events, some of these doors needed to be kept locked to protect those he loved. He just wanted to protect her. Sometimes, the less people knew, the better. Kristy understood, and rarely asked him to open those doors. She just wanted to know how many doors she was dealing with, even if she didn't know for sure what was behind them. She didn't like secrets. She didn't like surprises.

****

Bob made no secret of his love for Rosemary, and just a few months after his divorce was finalized from Brenda, he and Rosemary were married at a private farmstead just outside of McMinnville on July 1, 1990. Beautiful in its simplistic elegance, the natural vista cast a serene backdrop for the white lattice archway littered with fragrant flowers. Ricky scoured the guests for any familiar faces but came up empty.

"Where's Grandma and Grandpa?" asked Jimmy.

"Don't know," said Rick. "I thought they'd be here but I guess not."

"I don't see anybody I know," said Jimmy.

"Me neither. I think there's some people from his work but that's all. They probably hate him as much as we do."

Neither boy wanted to be there. Decked out in suits and ties, they were merely part of the 'happy family' charade; two families coming together under the beauty of the Oregon countryside. But it was all just bullshit. Watching his father stand up there in front of all those people, swearing his undying love and loyalty to Rosemary, the adulteress, made Rick want to vomit. Weren't those the same words his father had spoken to his mother? He'd broken that loyalty once already, and here he was, spewing the same garbage out of his mouth once again. And to make matters worse, they had to stand around and not only listen to it all, but pretend to be happy. It was too much.

From the very beginning the boys had never really even given Rosemary a chance. Their perception of the relationship and the events surrounding the divorce were so skewered, that Rosemary could have been Mary Poppins and it wouldn't have mattered. She was 'the bitch', and any chance of letting her into their lives in a positive light was scorched by their internal rage, a rage fueled by a scorned ex-wife, who didn't hesitate filling the ears of her young children with her own wrath and indignation. Rick hated that Rosemary looked beautiful in her dress, and he hated the way his father's eyes got this weird glossy twinkle when he looked at her. He'd never looked at their mother like that, at least not in a very, very long time.

"Do you Robert take this woman to be your…" Rick shut the words out. He didn't want to hear. He just wanted to get his part in the ceremony over with and go home.

"I do." Blah. Blah. Blah.

"I do."

"You may now kiss the bride!"

The boys flipped the latch on the wire cage, releasing a flock of doves into the sky.

"Aww…look at that. Aren't his boys sweet? Such a perfect moment."

And that was it. It was official. Bob was remarried; all hope of their family ever getting back together again, shattered. The white purity and innocence of the soaring doves only served as a stark juxtaposition to the charred blackness of Rick's heart. They were the lambs, him and Jimmy. The lambs of God, and the lambs led to slaughter, sacrificed by their father for a supposed higher and 'just' cause – his happiness. Bob had made his choice, and with it, sent the innocence of his oldest child spiralling into a grave pit of experience. It wasn't his fault of course. Bob had no idea the severity of the damage all of this had caused. He was unhappy in his marriage, so he took steps to correct that, and in turn, hoped that his sons would understand. But they didn't understand, and he didn't try hard enough to make them.

The reception was a celebratory and grand affair. Bob and Rosemary fed each other cake, posed for pictures, and partook in the general merriment as newlyweds do. As the evening wore on, and the booze continued to flow, Bob thought it would be a good idea to try out his wedding present from his new wife – a .22 Ruger Long-rifle with a small scope.

"Let's have some target practice!"

One of the men nailed a plastic milk jug to a tree not far from the back balcony of the house, about twenty-five yards.

"Jesus! Nice shot!" The men took turns plunking at the jug, seeing who could knock it down.

"Hey Rick," smiled Bob. "Want to take a shot?"

Like any young adventurous boy, Rick wasn't going to miss the opportunity to try his hand at the rifle.

"Just set the barrel on the balcony here Rick," said Bob. "Be real still. Check your aim through the scope. That's it. And when you're ready…"

Rick hit the trigger, and a split second later, the jug spun off the tree.

"Jesus son! What a shot!" Bob ruffled Rick's dark hair. "Did you see that boys? My son, a crack shot on the first try!"

The pride swelled in both father and son. It was a moment. Their moment. One that hadn't happened in a very long time, and here it had happened on his father's wedding day; a day that was supposed to be all about the bride and groom. But Rick had stolen a moment from her, and he was damn happy. He had no way of knowing the irony of that moment, that in exactly sixty-five months, he would hold that same .22 Ruger in his hands, take aim and steal their lives. Innocence lost. Experience gained.

"Oh how was it boys," said Brenda hugging the boys the minute they got home. "Was it awful? I bet it was just awful. I'm so sorry you had to go. I didn't want you to, but your father insisted."

There wasn't even an attempt to put a positive spin on the occasion, just negativity and sorrow, which only added to the grief the boys were feeling, and the rage that was simmering in Rick's soul.

"Let's pray. God will give us guidance. He'll tell us what we should do."

Brenda didn't need to look to God for answers, the answers were clear and concise. They needed to move on. Brenda needed to move on. As God's child, she needed to lay aside her hatred, forgive Bob for leaving her, and walk a new path into the future. She'd asked the boys to forgive their father, yet somehow, she could not practice her own preaching. The constant weight of her sorrow only pushed Rick deeper into his own despair. He felt what she felt twofold. He heard the distain in her voice, he heard the disparaging comments about his father and Rosemary, he felt her pain. He lived her pain, and it was too much. Too much pressure for a kid to handle. He needed an outlet, somewhere where he didn't have to be the son of a bastard father or the son of a God-fearing mother, somewhere where he could just be Rick, and find out who the hell he really was.

He found his solace in the night, where the darkness hid his pain, and festered his angst towards any who would exert their authority over him. His rebellious defiance found a home roaming the streets; his mantra of "I will not be destroyed and I will survive" played out in conjunction with other like-minded souls. Maybe it was his way of blowing off stream or a rebellious backlash to the constant negativity he felt. At night, on his own, there were no rules, no outside influences or expectations. The night gave him freedom. It didn't change the weight he carried around in his soul or his feeling of extreme emptiness, but it gave him the freedom to do and experience whatever he wanted, limited only by his own personal boundaries, which often times were non-existent.

The paradox of his life grew. In the daytime, he had to ask permission to do anything and was always subject to parental and social restrictions but at night, it was just him, and he held all the power. The psychological shift had begun, and the deeper this shift became, the more Rick came to resent any form of authority, and actually saw authority as an unnecessary burden. And why not? Sneaking out was a piece of cake. His mother, sleeping under the same roof, just a few rooms away, had no clue, and Jimmy was too scared shitless to breathe a word. What eleven-year-old, especially a naturally curious one, wasn't going to jump at the chance to get away with shit he isn't supposed to? That was part of the charm, part of the lure. No one was telling him no. No one was pulling him back. No one stepped up to check his behaviour. Not his father, and certainly not his mother. He was on his own, making his own life choices, following his own path.

The nights that summer were glorious, and Rick ran amuck without any boundaries or limitations. Fences? No big deal. No trespassing signs? Fuck them. Darkness? Danger? Roofs? Alleys? Police? Fuck them especially. Climbing up on top of a broken-down eighteen wheeler, and running the length of the trailer, just to see if he could? Hell fucking yeah. Rick began hiding a small backpack in the shop at home, stuffing it with rope, and various tools he could use to get to those 'hard to reach' places. When the clinking of the tools made too much noise as he was booting his ass out of those 'hard to reach' places, he began wrapping the tools in rags to help dampen the noise. Sometimes it worked, sometimes it didn't, sending him into a frozen silence when they happened to click at an inopportune time.

The warm, dry McMinnville summers made his venturing almost a compulsive act. In the winter, he had to worry about gloves and hiding wet clothes when he came in. That shit gave him pause for thought and sometimes kept him in, but in the summer, there was nothing chaining him down. His young eyes had long ago been trained to focus and function in little or no light, so even a thick cloudy night was no match for his unwavering exploration. So far, he had avoided the orchards. They were dark, even for him, and generally creepy as hell with all those trees and low hanging branches.

"Fuck. I have to go sometime." He looked up at the brilliant full moon. "I'll be fine. It's only a bunch of trees, and I've spent my whole life running through the forest."

But Dell Smith's orchard wasn't the forest back in Washington. Smith's orchard had a history. There was talk of slaves, and of course the stories. No one knew for sure whether the stories were true or just folklore meant to scare the shit out of adolescent children. Either way, the mystery of the orchards fascinated Rick, and there was more than a tinge of apprehension and fear as he readied himself for his adventure.

"I don't think I need the backpack but I'd better take this small knife…just in case."

He put the sheathed knife in his pocket beside his trusty old Swiss Army knife, and took off down the road behind his house. At the edge of the neighbourhood, the concrete road turns to dirt at the foot of the orchard. Rick entered with ease, crouching down beside the first tree to survey the situation, both in sight and sound. The last thing he wanted was for one of Smith's dogs to sense his whereabouts and come running.

"Jesus it's quiet. Almost too quiet. Fuck."

With the moonlight filtering through the trees, Rick was able to make out shapes in amongst the shadows. Slowly he began to leap frog from tree to tree, stopping at each new trunk to listen and watch, making sure that he was the only thing out there, his senses on high alert and in tune with his environment. There were no fears, stories, or other contriving thoughts running through his head, he was completely fixated on the physical sights, sounds and senses. He moved deeper into the orchard.

"What the fuck was that?"

His body froze in place, a statue of fear. The sobs continued. A young girl. Sobbing uncontrollably. Somehow Rick knew at once that the sound wasn't of this physical world. It enveloped him, and all other thought and emotion vanished in its eerie clarity. He had no doubt that somewhere close by a young girl was sobbing. He could feel the sound. The realness of it. At that moment, nothing else existed but her expression of pain, drawing Rick in, magnetized by the lure. He couldn't just turn and walk away. He should but he couldn't. On automatic, his feet shifted forward, step by step, closer to the sobs. Unlike his experience with the demon in the shed, Rick didn't feel a sense of dread or hostility. The continuing sobs drew him closer. His psyche on high alert.

In the intensity of his sensory concentration while creeping through the orchard, Rick had inadvertently opened his sixth sense just enough to pick up the frequency of the physic impression left in the orchard. Because he felt and believed immediately that the input he was receiving from the 'otherworld' was real, he further opened his third eye and gave himself to the second sight.

As he crept forward, the moonlight seemed to brighten, and everything took on a bluish hue, the shadows lessening, with things becoming more vibrant, yet at the same time blurred, with less definition. Branches and tree trunks seemed to bend at odd angles, losing their natural shape. He blinked his eyes, hoping to gain a clearer focus but it never came. His feet took him forward into this strange new realm. With every step, his perception completely changed, as if the shield over his mind's-eye had been lifted, a visor raised that gave that particular sense full capacity, while diminishing his own physical senses. Both fascinated and terrified, Rick moved slower, unsure of what might lie ahead, but too intrigued to stop. Then she appeared.

Almost in the exact center of four trees, in clear view of the moonlight, sat a young girl, naked, her legs folded beneath her, her arms hugging herself as if shivering in the cold. Her chest heaved in sync with her sobs, her blond hair matching the pale tone of her flesh. With her head slightly bowed, and eyes half closed, she looked as though she was gazing in a daze at the ground before her. Her tears. Suspended in the moonlight, each tear that fell from her eyes glowed, leaving soft translucent trails down her face until they fell from her lips and chin, gently splattering in her lap. Mesmerized, Rick's own young eyes followed the trail of tears.

"Jesus."

His heart leapt at the darkish red stain smeared on the tops of her thighs and legs.

"Blood."

His own body shuddered at the realization. He could feel the dryness of the stain. Old and painful. Traumatic. Rape. It was as if the very violence and malice of the event seeped from the stains on her skin and permeated the air. As he stared at the blood, Rick's senses caught the shadow of another presence directly behind the girl, about three or four feet away. With a narrow bald head, large fishlike bulging eyes, and pointy ears, the creature was the most hideous thing the boy had ever seen. His blood ran cold. The body of the thing was amphibious, as if moulded from a humanoid frog, not fat but squat, and it sat hunched over with long claw-like fingers, it's skin glowing in the light as if covered by a slick, glossy slime. Rick didn't move. The evilness of the creature made the boy's entire frame feel weighted. A soft guttural rasp, almost like a gargling, escaped from the creatures' half opened mouth.

Rick crouched lower to the ground, trying his best to sink into the surroundings and not be noticed by either. The creature didn't seem aggressive, and wasn't touching or acting violently towards the girl, but appeared to be inhaling a type of vapour that wafted from her tear-stained cheeks. That's why her tears stood out so much to Rick. Not only did they glow in the moonlight, but it was as if a faint steam rolled off of her face, a barely discernable smoke exuding from her sorrow. As the creature inhaled the smoke, it seemed to be feeding off her sorrow, using her pain to further his own existence. Turning his attention back to the girl, Rick noticed what he thought must be three claw marks down the front of her chest, barely visible beneath her crossed arms. As his 'sight' zeroed in, he realized they weren't claw marks at all but three separate lacerations that met a network of other slash and stab wounds covering her sides and upper abdomen.

"Jesus Christ Almighty God."

Nothing else existed while he took in the scene of this young victim sitting there in the orchard, too wracked by sorrow, pain and trauma to even think of trying to get away from the demon that was feeding off her misery. Watching the scene, Rick was frozen in shock and terror, not so much in what he saw but the realization that everything in front of him was in fact real. He knew it was. He felt it was. No imagination could ever make up what he was experiencing, or replicate the overwhelming emotions of fear, terror, pain, and sadness that soaked the area. He could feel what she felt. The thick, heavy air suffocated his breath, intensifying and magnifying the situation. It was as if the borders between sorrow, agony, terror and anguish were not defined, but overlapping, amplified and screaming all at once. Everything radiated from the girl, and Rick felt like he was slowly being swallowed by it all, like soon, he too would be lost to the abyss.

Fear rose. He had to save them. He had to save himself.

"Jesus Lord, Son of God! Please protect me and protect this girl…" The words flowed unabated. "Christ please deliver us from this evil. Pour your love down and save that poor girl. Free her from this evil…" He didn't even have to think, the words just leapt from his mouth like the waters from an eternal spring. "Feel her pain Lord, have sympathy for her. Feel her pain Lord oh Christ."

Raising his eyes to the heavens, he poured his entire heart and soul to God in a desperate desire to free this young girl from her pain. Real tears streamed down his own face. He prayed harder. He prayed louder.

"Hear me oh Lord! Jesus Christ our Saviour! Free her! Free her! Free her!"

The child collapsed to the ground. He searched for the girl, but the vision was gone. Everything had changed. The soft breeze gently swayed a single leaf on the branch above his head, and the leaf was sharp, its edges defined, crystal clear and physical. Gone were the blurry distorted edges of the 'other side'. He felt completely dry inside, empty, and light; the heaviness and thickness of the air gone, the freshness of a McMinnville summer night returned. He turned once again to the spot between the four trees. It existed. And the very physical realization that a rape had occurred in that very spot hit the boy full force. A rape that Rick was quite sure she didn't survive. He may not have been able to see any blood on the soil or other signs of struggle, but he had no doubt that right there on that very spot a serious crime against innocence itself had been committed. For the rest of his life Rick would never know whether or not the Lord had merely closed his mind's-eye to save him from witnessing the event, or if the Lord had actually answered his prayer's and took the young girl's soul away.

A wave of terror engulfed the child, and he took off running through the orchard, not caring in the least who or what might see him. Without breaking stride, he cut across the property of the church next door, and didn't slow one bit until he'd made it to the gravel lot right next to his house. A quick scale of the fence and he was safely in the side yard of his house, next to the barbeque area.

"Holy shit." His heart pounded through his shirt as he leaned against the support beam of the covered porch and tried to catch his breath. Heaving and coughing, he couldn't get the air back into his lungs fast enough. The time ticked. He had to get back up on the roof and into the safety of his room before his mother heard him and came looking. Still winded, he pulled his way back onto the covered porch, then silently open his bedroom window and creep in. The light from the desk lamp blistered the darkness of the room.

"Are you okay?" said Jimmy throwing his arms around his big brother.

"What are you still doing up?"

"I couldn't sleep. Are you okay? You don't look so good. I've been so worried!"

Rick had to think fast. He certainly couldn't tell Jimmy the truth.

"Yeah, I'm okay now but something just scared the living shit out of me. I got chased by a big dog and he almost got me, that's all."

"Geez Rick! That's awful!"

"Yeah but don't you worry. Everything is fine now." He gave Jimmy a hug and changed into his pajamas. Since they'd both had bad experiences with big dogs, he figured that Jimmy bought the story. He was only seven after all. They stayed up and talked for a little bit longer, and Jimmy seemed at ease.

"Night Jimmy."

"Night Rick. Glad you're home safe."

Exhausted from his adventure, Rick fell into a deep, deep sleep. He never forgot what he saw that night, nor would he ever tell anyone, not his mother or any spiritual advisor. The pain was too real, too raw. He also never forgot the effect it had on him, the deep sadness, and undeniable truth that horrible things happened to young innocent people. His situation paled in comparison to that of the young girl, but the whole thing only reinforced his sadness, and the one extreme direct consequence of that encounter was that he never forgot the overwhelmingly suffocating emotions that clung to that place in the orchard. They were so tangible and overpowering, and he would never forget that feeling of almost being swallowed by their existence.

Even at such a young age, Rick recognized what had been done to that young girl and he hated it. Hated the thought. Hated the pain it caused. And most of all, he hated the person who did it. As he grew older, this translated into an intense disgust and hate for any rapists, sexual abusers or predators. He also became fiercely protective over females who'd been raped, abused, or taken advantage of. They didn't even have to necessarily tell him of the abuse, he could just feel it. That night also showed Rick that he wasn't alone in his pain. That some people were victims just like him, and some people had pain and sorrow that far surpassed his own. The realization didn't diminish his own pain, in fact, the knowledge of how deep the ocean of suffering went was a burden that made his own, only that much harder to bear. He'd thought he'd hit rock bottom. Turns out, he was still at the top of the ledge.

CHAPTER TWELVE

"What the fuck Rick? I thought you were going to be honest with me?" Kristy could hardly talk through her tears, her voice muffled on the other end of the phone. "Why didn't you tell me?" The pain in her voice killed him. "Elmo told me everything. You should have told me. I thought I could fucking trust you!"

"Kristy, please calm down."

"No Rick. I won't calm down! Guns? Explosives?"

The situation was far worse than Rick had thought. Not only had Elmo told Kristy everything, but he also shot his mouth off to the Alaska State Troopers. This was not going to end well.

"I can't explain things to you right now Kristy…not over a prison phone and certainly not in front of your mother if you came to visit. I kept you in the dark to protect you. It was before I even came to Alaska."

"Bullshit! I thought I could trust you. Jesus Christ Rick. I'm so done."

"Kristy no! Wait!" The line went dead.

"Jesus fucking Christ!" Rick knew he was in some serious trouble. The goods hidden in the cistern from 'The Team'; if the police found out they'd all be in trouble. It would have been impossible to explain why. They just wouldn't have understood. "Fuck you Elmo! I need to call Strom. Fuck. I don't have his new number. Amy will." He picked up the phone and placed a collect call to Oregon.

"Hi Amy." She started crying as soon as she heard his voice. "Listen, I need Strom's new number. Do you have it?" She rattled it off without hesitation. "Are you okay?"

"What the fuck do you think?"

"I'm sorry I haven't called or written…I'm just not trying to rub shit in your face…I'm sorry."

"I fucking hate you Rick. I fucking hate that you threw away your life. You should have called me. I would have jumped on a plane and came and got you right away. You KNOW that!"

"I didn't know…I didn't know how things would end…"

"I can't fucking talk to you right now…" The line went dead.

The words cut through his heart, and an immediate wave of despair shrouded his soul. But there was nothing he could do about it right now, he had to call Strom back in Oregon.

"Hello?"

"Hey."

"What's up Bro? Are you all right?"

"Shadow."

Rick only had to say that one word and Strom knew exactly what he was talking about. Long ago they agreed on a code word, their 'kill-switch' to use in the event any of them got captured for any reason. There'd be absolutely no communication between anyone, and up until now, Rick hadn't received any mail or calls from any of them, and he certainly didn't expect to.

"Everything. Immediately," said Rick.

Elmo didn't know any specifics, but he knew enough that if law enforcement had wanted to do some digging, they could have. They'd all been careful and covered their asses, but Rick wasn't about to take any chances.

"Okay…well."

"Listen Bro," said Rick. "This is going to get expensive so I'm going to let you go."

Strom took the cue. "Alright Bro, I love you man."

"I love you too Bro. Take care."

"Yep."

And that was that. All ties severed. Strom would know what to do, and Rick trusted him. He'd take care of everything. Rick went back to his cell and waited for the shit to hit the fan. It didn't take long.

"All right Watkinson! On your feet!" said Sergeant Robinson.

"What time is it?" said Rick rolling over.

"Five thirty. Bright and early. Roll up your property and let's go. You're being relocated."

Rick didn't ask any questions and they didn't volunteer any more information. He figured it'd be best just to keep his mouth shut. He wrapped up his meagre belongings in his bed sheets and walked with them to the sally port.

"Bravo Mod. Your new home. Cell four."

The sliding door clanked behind him. Rick had lasted exactly forty-seven days out of a slider cell, and in general population.

"I guess I'd rather be in the Hole, than the psych ward."

Bravo Mod in Cook Inlet was where they housed the 'worst of the worst' of pre-trial detainees, and most people in Bravo were stuck there, almost indefinitely. There's only fourteen cells in Bravo, seven on top, and seven on the bottom, and the stairs and upper tier are covered to the ceiling in a steel grated mesh so that no one can be shoved over the top tier to the hard concrete below. Stationed at the desk next to the yard entrance, a CO kept constant eyes and ears over the area. An inmate couldn't say shit without everyone else in the mod over hearing; the quarters were that tight. Some of the most violent offenders in all of Alaska passed through Bravo. The guy who just happened to have the Alaskan record for brutal assaults on other inmates, and the bro who had just football punted a State Trooper in the face with his combat boots during a court hearing. These were the types of guys Rick now referred to as his neighbours. In prison for a mere eighty-two days, in with the worst of the worst, and he hadn't yet turned seventeen. Surely, there had to be a more appropriate process.

The first day in Bravo Rick was given access to the phone since the CO's hadn't yet been told why the kid was even there, or what his restrictions were.

"Hey Kristy. It's Rick. I know you don't want to talk to me but I need to know that you're okay."

"I'm fine." Her voice sliced through the air with a vindictive edge. "Elmo called the prison last night and told them you had weapons and explosives hidden somewhere, and that they needed to lock you away in maximum security right away."

"Are you fucking serious?"

"Well I'm assuming you do?"

Rick didn't answer. "What does it matter Kristy? You already assume that I'm guilty and that Elmo's telling the truth? Right?"

"He also contacted the State Troopers and is going to give them a statement of what he knows. I thought I could trust you. We're done."

Heartbroken, Rick returned to his cell. No wonder he'd been thrown in the Hole. The Department of Corrections doesn't wait to confirm this type of information; they just act and sort out the details later. Rick knew that eventually the suits would be down to interrogate him, so to save Kristy anymore trouble, he shredded and flushed every piece of mail she had sent him. He kept maybe six or seven letters from family and friends but ditched all the rest. He couldn't take any chances, and he was loathe that someone else might get caught up in the messes he had made. As an extra precaution, he slept with his little address book tucked into his sock, that way if his cell got raided in the middle of the night, they wouldn't know who he'd been communicating with.

"What's this?" said Rick taking the paper from the guard the next morning.

"It's your writ of purgatory kid," laughed the guard.

Rick sat at his desk and scanned the paper. He'd been placed on Ad-Seg 8. Reason? 'Escape Risk'. 'Investigation pending'.

"Escape risk? Jesus." He cracked a small smile. They really must think he's some sort of criminal mastermind. All at the tender age of sixteen. If anything, being in the Hole gave him some prison cred, and that had to count for something.

"Ah seriously? No phone or visits at all? What the hell."

The DOC pretty much had him by the balls for as long as they wanted. From here on out, he had to ask permission to do almost anything. For one hour a day, he was allowed to go out to Bravo's isolated enclosure for some 'rec' or take a shower. The other twenty-three would be spent in his cell, pondering his transgressions. While Rick was expecting a cell raid at any moment, it'd be days before they even came to question him. By then, Rick didn't care. He had lost the one person in Kristy who he sincerely believed was the love of his life. Lost her due to misplaced trust in another, someone who had sworn never to betray him. Some fucking friend Elmo turned out to be.

"Shackle him up. Seems like you have some State Troopers paying you a visit."

Fettered in leg irons and belly shackles, the guards escorted Rick out to the sallyport interview room. He'd been preparing himself for this encounter from the moment he'd been thrown in the Hole. No one was going down for his alleged misdeeds except him. The Troopers wasted little time laying out their case.

"Now if you don't cooperate, we can easily throw some Federal charges on top of what you're already facing. Where are the guns and who else is involved?"

Rick stayed silent.

"Listen punk! We know you're not smart enough to pull something like this off on your own and had to have some outside help. Give us some names."

"I have no idea what you're taking about," answered Rick. "I don't know anything about any guns and no one else was involved in anything."

"Is that so?" Rick could tell the officers were getting pissed off. "You know we can make sure that you never get out of the Hole again don't you?"

"I don't know what you want me to tell you. I have no idea what you're talking about."

"You're only hurting yourself Watkinson. Do you have any idea how much dirt we could dig up on you? If we wanted to?"

"Then why don't you?"

"Listen you little shit, I've had just about enough of you!"

Rick just kept his cool and didn't give an inch. He knew the cops didn't have shit on him. They always dig up any shred of evidence they can before interrogating a "possible" source of information or lies. Rick had been around enough to know how to play their game.

"So you know nothing then?"

"Nope," said Rick. "Not a thing."

"Then have a nice life in the Hole you little fuck. Get him out of my face."

The guards took Rick back to his cell no worse for the wear. He'd made it through another test in prison; he'd held his ground and didn't rat out a soul on the inside or out. He leaned up close to the air vent in his cell, otherwise known as the prison telephone line. He needed to send word back up to the boys in his old mod.

"All is good. The Troopers know nothing, and will never know anything. They got nothing out of me."

In prison, integrity is everything, and keeping your mouth shut in the face of adversity is the highest virtue. From the very beginning Rick understood this, he'd lived on the streets for far too long not to understand the consequences of being a snitch. And that reputation, and that respect, born that cold February 1995, stuck. Little Rick could hold his mud, he wasn't a rat, he was someone, even when shit was serious, that could be trusted. That meant a lot in prison. Respect and reputation. Sometimes, it's all a guy had.

****

The dichotomy of Rick's life continued that summer of 1990. Days spent swimming, flying down the slip and slide, and water balloon fights with his buddy Dan. There were forts to be built, trees to be climbed, and general mischief to be had. All in good fun, all quite normal. At least from the outside. For Rick, even though he enjoyed them, the activities were just a mere distraction and temporary relief from the brooding, oppressive atmosphere that had soaked his life. He felt a constant pressure, like his emotions pressed out from within, suffocating and overpowering. He had no explanation nor a remedy; just a feeling of sinking deeper and deeper beneath the waves that jaded and lessened the overall amount of joy he had as a child.

Sure there was laughter, fun and play, but it always seemed to be just a temporary, fleeting high, a brief moment before the current sucked him back under. The experience in the orchard didn't help. Rick had to accept that his gift was real and that he could see things that others couldn't and probably wouldn't choose to, even if they could. He had no idea how to cope, and was too damn frightened to even tell anyone about the experience, especially not his father or Rosemary. They'd all think he was fucking crazy. And if he told his mom, then she'd have him out fighting demons even more. He'd be their 'golden child' in the crusade. He didn't want any of it. He just wanted to be normal.

Why? Why could he see and how? What was the point of this 'gift'? How was he supposed to use it for God? So many questions, none of which had any straightforward answers. The elders told him to 'pray to God' and when he was ready or when it was time, God would give him the answers. But the great Jehovah was silent. There was no response to his prayers, no sudden flash of insight. Was the child just supposed to sit there and be patient and deal with these horrors and 'powers' all on his own? Rick needed a practical solution, not just

Bible verse reasoned mechanics. He needed something concrete. Something his eleven-year-old brain could comprehend, not more bullshit words. So he did what he thought was best. He shut down. If he just ignored that part of his life, giving it the least amount of acknowledgment or thought, then it would just go away. It had to. Didn't it?

The incident in the orchard put a halt to Rick's ninja activities for almost two weeks, and when he did eventually venture back out, he stuck to the sidewalks and lit pathways. One night in early August, he thought he'd check out the park just a few blocks from his home. The park wasn't a huge space, large enough for a play fortress and a couple of swings to keep the neighbourhood kids occupied. He noticed them the minute he rounded the street corner. Two figures gently swinging on the swings, smoking cigarettes.

"Fuck. What do I do?" At first, he was a little unnerved by their intrusion on his secret night life. Not wanting to seem skittish, he walked straight towards them. They saw him coming and cut off their conversation.

"What's up youngster?" said the girl.

"Not much," answered Rick.

"Wanna smoke?"

Rick took the smoke. He was nervous as hell but did his best to look calm and cool.

"I'm Charisma, and this here is Tom."

"I'm Rick."

"What are you doing out so late Rick?" said Tom. "Haven't ever seen you around before. How old are you?"

Rick took a drag, trying not to choke on the smoke. "I'm eleven…but I've been sneaking out of the house for a while now…just wandering around and shit."

"Why are you wandering?" said Charisma, her long light hair collapsing on her shoulders.

"I dunno. Just to see shit. I haven't really lived here all that long…and don't really know anybody, so was just trying to see where things were you know?"

Charisma, while she looked like she was around sixteen, was really only twelve, and Rick could tell right away that this wasn't her first night out on the streets. She had this 'don't give a fuck' attitude which of course drew Rick to her, much to the dismay of Tom. Tom was fifteen and starting high school in the fall. He'd been born and raised in McMinnville, and only lived a few blocks from the park. He was a bit of a dick, and treated Rick like a little shit nobody. Rick was an outsider who needed to prove his worth.

"Ever stole any shit?" said Tom. "Bet you haven't. I've stolen all sorts of shit."

"Well I ain't a pussy if that's what you're asking. I've stolen shit."

"Tom leave him alone," said Charisma.

"What? I'm just trying to get to know the kid. See if he's for real."

Right away, Rick knew he'd have to step up his game to even be considered a 'cool' kid on the streets. Stealing smokes from a trailer was one thing, actually breaking and entering somewhere was a totally different game.

"I'm not afraid to do anything," said Rick. "Just haven't had the opportunity yet."

They chatted for about an hour, smoking and swinging on the swings. Charisma was the first real runaway Rick had ever met. Her mother lived in Sheridan, and she knew who her father was, but had never met the guy.

"We just got in a really huge fight, so I fucking left and came here," said Charisma. "Been staying with friends for about a month now I guess." She didn't give up who or where, and Rick thought that was cool as hell. She had secrets just like him. Finally, someone he could identify with.

"So are you out every night?"

"Most," said Rick.

"Want to meet up tomorrow night and meet some of our other friends?"

"Ah fuck Charisma. Seriously?" said Tom.

"Shut up man. I like the kid." She leaned in and gave Tom a lingering kiss, partly just to shut him up, and partly just to get her way.

"Sure," said Rick. "That'd be cool."

"Okay…then tomorrow night. Meet us here at midnight."

As soon as his new friends were out of sight and he could let his guard down, Rick took off running for home, filled with excitement and anticipation. Any apprehension he might have had was washed away by his fascination with Charisma, if that was even her real name. She had an edge about her, a story to be told, and was certainly unlike any girl he'd even encountered. Tom may have been older and far more experienced but Rick sensed Charisma was the one in control.

The next night, with Jimmy fast asleep, Rick opened the window and made his escape into the warm night. Bounding along the sidewalk, his mood was light, his mind open to new opportunities.

"Where the fuck are they?"

His brown eyes scanned the perimeter of the park. Nothing. Sitting on the swings he waited. And waited. Waited. Nothing.

"God damn it. They were just fucking with me. You stupid idiot, they're not coming." He slid off the swings, hung his head, and slowly took off for home. Humiliated. Angry. Embarrassed.

"Why would they want to hang out with me? I'm nothing but a punk ass little kid."

The more he thought about it, the more he knew he'd have to prove himself worthy to hang with them. He wasn't a pussy or a coward. He'd show them that.

"I don't care who it is. I'll show them."

The next few nights he made sure to detour by the park, just in case, but their absence only added to his disappointment. He never waited around though hoping they'd show up because that'd be a pussy thing to do, and he was better than that. About a week later, on his way to the highway, Rick turned down the street towards the park."Hey…whatcha been up to?" said Charisma walking straight to him.

"Not much. You? You want a smoke?" He'd been carrying an open pack of crappy ass GPC cigarettes since he'd first met them in the park. Always needing to impress.

"Thanks," said Charisma. Tom leaned in and lit both cigarettes. "We're heading to meet some friends. Want to come?"

"Yeah…that sounds cool. Sure."

Just a few blocks from the park, McMinnville had a small movie theatre. With the front parking lot partially concealed by woods and the back paved area completely shielded from the highway by the building itself, it was a perfect place for kids to gather undisturbed. Rick had been by a few times on his travels but the place had always been empty. This time, they joined a group of four other kids whom Rick judged to be mostly sixteen or seventeen. He was definitely the raw rookie. Behind the dim moonlight, Rick could hide the fact that he didn't quite know how to fully inhale his smoke nor did he have any idea what 'blasted', 'blazed' and 'sloughed out' meant. He'd learn them all eventually, but on that first night, he was quite happy to hang in the shadows.

Meeting and hanging with these other kids pulled Rick into a life of perfect contradiction. Their complete disregard for authority, love of freedom and the night gave him some kindred spirits in a world he thought he lived alone. By day, Rick lived in a strongly Christian household, where morality and being Christ-like reigned supreme. At night, his world was full of skaters, rebels, runaways and stoners, who cared little for society's rules and nothing for God's rules. Listening to 'satanic' music and engaging in every activity condemned to them, Rick had found brethren. Fascinating and exciting, he had never encountered this type of lifestyle or people before, and it lured in his free-thinking spirit.

Being a small city, it didn't take Rick long to learn the who's who of the night crowd, and that every person knew a 'guy' who knew another 'guy'. The more shit you did, the cooler you were, and all Rick wanted was to be cool. To be accepted. To feel like he belonged and fit it. No one gets points for being chicken shit and sitting on the sidelines. As one of the youngest, Rick's ass was on the line. He had to put out or forever be sequestered from the 'in' crowd.

"I'll do it."

"For twenty bucks," said Tom.

"Fuck yeah," said Rick. "I'll do it for twenty bucks." He'd do it for free if it meant gaining respect, especially from Tom or Charisma.

"Okay. About a block from the park is this house with a back laundry room. The house has this white tree and a red door. You can't miss it. They never lock the back laundry room door, mainly because they're always home. I happen to know that they just got this brand new stereo system, not like an amp and speakers…but like a boom box. You know what I'm talking about?"

Rick nodded.

"It's in the front living room."

"How do I know you'll pay me?"

Tom pulled a twenty-dollar bill from his front pocket. "I give you my word. The same stereo goes for eighty in the stores, so you'll be saving me sixty bucks. You'll be fine. There's no dogs, and they have no idea who you are. If they see you, just book it and you won't get in any trouble."

Rick didn't think. He didn't even hesitate. Game on.

He lit up a cigarette once he left the park and inhaled a bit more than usual, trying to draw as much courage out of the nicotine as he could. The dampness in his hands began to build, and with every step, his heart beat a little further against his black tee shirt.

"You can do this Watkinson," he said. "Piece of cake. You NEED to do this man. Shut that fucker up for good."

He walked all the way past the house, noting the juniper bordered chain-link fence and the darkened windows. Keeping to the shadows, he made his way around to the side. More dark windows.

"Nothing but a wooden fence back here. Neighbours can't see shit." The dull, half burnt out light overtop the back door gave him pause for thought. "Well if they can't remember to lock their back door, then it's probably no big deal that they leave a light on."

In complete ninja mode, he carefully opened the back door and slinked inside.

"The fucking dryer is on which means I can't hear shit…but which also means they can't hear me. Fuck." Did he continue or hit the road? "Ah fuck it. I'm getting that stereo."

Slowly, he turned the doorknob and opened the inside door about half an inch. Nothing. Opening a crack just wide enough to slip his tiny frame through, he stepped through the door and pulled it closed behind him. No old man in underwear on the other side. He was safe for now. With the living room at the end of the hallway, he only had to worry about the closed door on his left. Light on his feet, he crept down the hallway and found the stereo sitting on an end table between a sofa and a chair. Giving a quick look at the configuration of wires, he followed the power cord to its place in the wall socket and pulled it out. With quick, agile movements, he snatched the stereo with both hands, balanced it against his chest, and made his way back through the hallway. A small tug pulled against his left foot.

"Shit!" One of the long cords from the detachable speakers had become wrapped around his left leg. He stopped, unhooked the cord from his foot, looped it around his arm to get it off the ground, and continued up the hall. Next problem. Opening the inner laundry room door, while not dropping the unit on the floor or accidently popping one of the speakers off its hooks. Balancing the unit on his knee, he opened the door wide enough for both him and his loot, then quickly snuck through, silently closing the door behind him. His escape from the laundry room to the safety of the night was painless.

Cutting left out of the laundry room, he walked at a quickened pace back through the neighbourhood to the park. A young kid walking down the street with a stereo in his arms was not an innocent action, so he tried to keep out of the light and into the shadows. He had no idea who might be creeping out their windows and catch a glimpse. His only strategy was to clear the area as soon as possible.

"I wonder if that fucker will even be in the park? Well if he isn't, I can always drop this bitch from the slide and break it into a thousand little pieces…or better yet, I could take it home, hide it in the shop, and then sell it myself. I could probably get way more than twenty bucks for the thing."

The point was moot when he rounded the street corner and saw Tom standing by the swings.

"See, I told you he'd do it!" said Charisma. She gained points for saying that, and Rick liked her even more.

"Nice bro," said Tom handing him the twenty.

"That's fucking cool dude," said Tom's friend.

That's all he needed to hear. 'Bro', 'fucking cool dude'. Rick was hooked. He'd just done his first robbery and he didn't even really know it. As an eleven-year-old, the difference between burglary, robbery, and armed robbery were lost on him. He wasn't chicken shit, and he did have the balls to go up into someone's house while they were there and steal right from under their noses. This really wasn't all that different from the time his mom made him break into the neighbour's house and look for signs of Satan, except this time it wasn't in the name of God. All those years of practicing stealth had really worked, and the philosophy of 'ghost' was rock solid, even though he hadn't yet formulated the name or ideal of 'Ghost' in his mind yet.

All Rick knew, at age eleven, was that by being a ghost, you robbed people of the opportunity to react if they weren't even aware of what was going on or who was there. His doctrine of invisibility was born. He liked it. He liked the rush, the power, that untouchable feeling of being able to get away with anything if he took enough care. He was already getting away with sneaking out at night, this was just a little something more. There wasn't a doubt that he knew it was a sin to steal, but the vengeful rebellious side of him didn't give a fuck. He'd had things stolen from him before. Didn't Rosemary steal his father? She got away with it, so why shouldn't he? He was just taking back a little of what was owed to him. Didn't God rob him of having peace because of his gift? He was just getting even.

But there's an inherently dangerous consequence to being able to blame all of your troubles on God or any higher power. It robs a person of accountability, and being forced to face the reality in purely realistic terms. The bottom line was that Rick liked the euphoria of that night. When Tom slapped that twenty dollars into his hand, it felt more like a million bucks. And in a kid so desperate and distraught, so wanting to fit in and find a place in the world, that feeling was a drug, a drug so powerful it instantly began to take hold. Through one small act of defiance, Rick had gone from a nobody to a somebody, and that was the best fucking thing in the world. It makes a kid feel important, like nothing in the world could bring him down.

If he was sneaky enough, he could do or get away with anything – so he thought. But overconfidence breeds sloppiness. He'd already spent the twenty bucks on cassettes full of cool music, which of course he had to keep hidden and listen to in secret, since Brenda only allowed Christian music in the house. Always secrets. Always one life clashing against the other. Daytime rules, nighttime desires. Rick could do 'adult-like' things like sneak out of the house, smoke and rob houses, but in the end, he was still just an eleven-year-old boy who liked playing with G.I Joes. So when a whole new collection came out at the local Payless, he was determined to get them. Over the course of the next few weeks, he proceeded to rip off almost an entire squad of G.I. Joe's. Nonchalantly, he'd stroll into the store wearing a large jacket, his typical loose jeans, and simply stuff one of the guys down his pants when no one was looking.

Efficient and ingenious. But with repetition, he became careless and sloppy. He'd thought the bank of windows on the second floor were just offices, and that the people in those offices would be working away, hunched over their desks, and not paying attention to a little shit like him out on the floor. After tossing a couple of guys into his coat, he leisurely walked around the store, pretending to look at stuff, as he headed towards the magazine and gum rack.

"What's in your jacket son?" said the man in the store apron.

"Um…nothing."

"I saw you put them in your jacket, give them to me."

Rick knew he'd been nailed, and for the first time worried about the consequences. As soon as he pulled out one of the G.I. Joe's, the other one fell out of his waist band. He picked them both up and handed them to the man.

"Come with me. You're in big trouble." He led Rick back into some first floor offices. "Sit here." The man pulled out a paper and placed it under the stainless-steel clip on his board.

"What's your name?"

Rick thought about lying but he figured the guy was going to call the cops anyway so it'd be best if he didn't. "Rick Watkinson."

"Where do you live?"

Rick answered all his questions honestly and politely.

"Where are your mother and father?"

"I think my Mother is at work and I'm not sure exactly where my Dad is right now. He's a pilot and he's really hard to get a hold of." Rick did not want his father coming down to the store to pick him up. Bob would kill him for stealing, at the least.

"Don't you know that it's wrong to steal?"

"Yes."

"Then why did you do it?"

"I don't know."

Brenda was unable to get away to come and get Rick, so she sent her friend Jill to gather her sinful son.

"I'm so sorry sir for Rick's behaviour," said Jill. "He really is a good child. He comes from a strong Christian home. He's just had some troubles lately. You see his parents just got divorced and he seems to be struggling…"

"I understand," said the man. "These things happen."

"Of course, we'll compensate the store for the value of the G.I. Joe's. How much? About ten dollars? There's no need to call the police now is there?"

The man shook his head from side to side. "I'll let him off with a warning for now but don't let it happen again. If we had caught you on the surveillance camera, we probably would press charges." His eyes bore down on Rick. "Do you hear me? Next time, you will not be so lucky. Also, I don't want to see your face in this store again."

"Yes sir. I'm very sorry sir."

Jill led Rick out of the store and into her red Subaru hatchback. Rick didn't want to discuss anything but he knew he wasn't going to get off that easy. Jill remained calmed.

"I'm quite disappointed in you Rick," she said as they drove to her house to await Brenda. "Stealing is a sin…and you know better than to sin against God don't you?" Rick nodded. "You must not get caught in the snare of sin."

Troubled by the incident and his developing rebellious spirit, Jill chose to see the good in Rick and that the bad was just a by-product of his anger and his pain. She was, of course, correct. Rick was genuinely a good soul, but at the moment his soul was lost and floundering. He needed support and guidance. Real support and guidance in a physical, emotional, and tangible way. A part of him was sincerely sorry, and he did feel bad about disappointing people with his actions. And they didn't even know about his nightlife. He was also sorry that he'd been caught. That was the real kicker for him. In getting caught, he'd let himself down, and that was something he could never do. His unabated faith in himself was all he had. When Brenda finally arrived at Jill's they discussed not the act itself, but his soul.

"We must pray for him."

The women prayed over Rick intensely, asking God to cleanse his soul, and not condemn him to eternal damnation.

"Ask the Lord for forgiveness Rick," said Brenda.

"Lord please forgive me for my sins."

"Lord please hear our prayers. Cleanse this child's soul and make him whole again. Spare him from the wrath of the devil, and bring him to the light."

When it was all said and done, Rick was deemed cleansed and 'brand new'. His soul had been saved and he was no longer under the threat of damnation and hell. The evil and sin were gone. For his part, Rick was left with a two-week grounding but more questions. If he'd been 'cleansed' and made to be brand new, then why did he still have the same sneaky, dark, manipulative, deceitful thoughts? Was part of him actually corrupt and truly inherently evil? Was it so deep within his soul that God couldn't even reach it? And why was there a part of him that was so totally incapable of being Christ-like? No matter how much they prayed, no matter how much they believed, or recited verses, or studied the Bible, it never got rid of Rick's desire to do whatever he wanted and to be above the laws of society and morality. Prayer may have washed away the sins, but it didn't wash away the sinner, and every time Rick looked in the mirror, all he saw was someone inherently corrupt and rotten. If God, the one true saviour, couldn't help him, then who the hell could?

CHAPTER THIRTEEN

Segregation only meant that Rick was moved away from the general population, and by no means signaled an end to his interaction with other inherently corrupt and rotten sinners. God couldn't help him in here. If he was going to survive, he'd have to use his wit and his smarts, and just like with Tom and the other street kids, he'd have to prove his mettle. He either had the balls to cut it, or he didn't. The choice was Rick's. He'd already gained some serious points for getting thrown in the hole in the first place and not being a rat. Still, some of the older, more seasoned convicts wanted to know what this youngster was made of. Like his life on the streets, he was constantly tested.

All kinds of violent and volatile men lived in Bravo, and Slug was no different. He wasn't nicknamed Slug because he was fat and lazy, but because he'd had a history with shotgun shells. In his early twenties, Slug was a highly violent, bonafide gang member, the kind of guy it was best not to annoy. When a prisoner is 'out' for his shower time, it's customary to do little things to help your fellow man, like pass notes, books and magazines, or bring the phone. There were four phones in Bravo, technically two for upstairs and two for down. With extra-long cords, the phones could be stretched right up into the cells from the wall. Made the day go by a lot quicker if you could lie in your bed and talk on the phone all day.

"Yo kid. Bring me up the phone," said Slug.

"Yeah no problem man," answered Rick. "I'll do it when I'm done cleaning my cell." He only had an hour and he had a bunch of shit he wanted to get done before his door got locked again.

"I said bring me the God damn phone! Do you fucking hear me punk?" Rick ignored Slug and kept on cleaning. "Jesus fucking Christ man. Bring me the God damn fucking phone right now!"

Rick didn't like the demanding or aggressive tone coming from the top floor.

"Hold the fuck on!" he replied.

Slug went quiet.

"Problem solved," thought Rick.

He took another fifteen minutes or so to finish cleaning his cell, then grabbed his shit to go shower, and on the way to the showers, like he promised, grabbed the phone for Slug. Rick didn't expect Slug to be happy that he'd made him wait, but he also didn't expect him to go off like a caged animal in the zoo.

"You think this shits funny you little punk," he said punching the plexiglass window and jumping around uncontrollably.

Rick didn't flinch but just scowled and looked at him like he was crazy.

"I'll beat you so bad you'll see the next life." Slug continued to beat the plexiglass and berate and threaten Rick.

"When I ask you to do something, you do it. You understand me? If I say jump, then you say how fucking high! This is one nigga you do not want to fuck with punk!"

Unamused, Rick continued to hold his ground, not showing a single sign of intimidation. When a person subconsciously believes that their life is forfeit, then they really don't give a fuck if they die. Rick's lack of reaction only enraged Slug even more.

"You think you all that don't cha you little bastard punk?" He turned his back, lifted the floor drain in his cell and pulled out a nine-inch shiv. That got Rick's attention. It was an impressive weapon. Not that Slug could even reach Rick with it at that very moment, but the fact that he could easily kill him with that weapon if given the opportunity, certainly did register with the teen. Still Rick held his ground and didn't move.

"I'm going to fucking gut you, you motha fucker!" Slug danced back and forth waving the shiv around in a fanatic frenzy. "I'm gonna poke so many holes in you they ain't even gonna be able to recognize your corpse."

After a few minutes, Slug lost some steam and settled down a little.

"Are you done?" said Rick. "Look dude, I ain't no one's bitch, and I was doing something. Do you want the fucking phone or not?" Gutsy, and not all that smart, but Rick figured, what the hell.

Slug lost it.

"How dare you, you little fucking punk talk to me that ways! Some punk ass sixteen-year-old kid talking to me that way?"

Rick left the phone dangling from the rail top and went to take his shower. He could still hear Slug ranting and cussing him out over five minutes later. Finally, one of the guards heard him and went up and handed him the phone just to shut him up. It wasn't the smartest or even the most disrespectful thing he'd ever said but no one was going to boss him around like that. If he gave in once, then Slug would gain the upper hand and think he could get away with shit. Chances were pretty good that at some point both him and Slug would end up in the same room or living unit but Rick knew that you couldn't allow fear to cause a person to bow down and be anybody's punk. At about five foot ten and around two hundred and twenty pounds of strength, Slug probably could do all the things he threatened. Still, the last thing Rick could afford to do was to show fear.

With Slug on the phone, that meant the front slot was open on his cell, when

Rick had to walk by to return to his own cell. He could easily reach him with the shiv now. Rick visualized how he could defend himself, running through the scenario of how he'd grab Slug's fist with one hand and then elbow drop with all his weight and try to break his arm. If he planned it right and executed, he might just be able to pull it off. Slug gave him nothing more than a glare as he walked by, and Rick returned to his cell without incident or instigation.

The next day as Rick was out of his cell, Slug yelled down.

"Yo kid. Holla at me before you lock down." His voice was calm and patient, a total one eighty from the day before.

On the way for his shower Rick stopped outside Slug's cell. "What's up man?"

"Man, you got a lot of heart youngster. You impressed me yesterday. You didn't even flinch when I was wailing at ya. Not an ounce of fear. You didn't even blink when I waved that shank in your face man!"

Rick sort of laughed. "Well at the time, you couldn't even reach me."

"Still man. That was heart…and heart is everything in here man. And true heart is rare in here man, even amongst us hardened cons. I like you youngster. If anyone fucks with you, just let me know."

"Thanks man for that." Rick went to the shower feeling pretty good about himself. He'd gained a very valuable ally, just by not flinching. Not that it'd been all that difficult. His own father had threatened him countless times, his face beat red with anger, his fists clenched ready to strike. In a few instances, he hadn't been able to hold back his anger and outright attacked his son. Rick had just given Slug that same deadpan, placid look he'd given his father a hundred times before. This time it counted for something, and instead of more anguish and anger like with his father, it gained him respect. Slug went to bat for Rick more than a few times in the coming months, and made sure everyone knew that although the youngster might be a scrawny wet-behind the ears cracker, he wasn't scared of shit.

****

"Think I'll like this new school Mom?" Rick said as he tied up his shoes.

"I'm sure everything will be fine," smiled his mother. "You're in Grade 6 now, your old school only went until Grade 5. You're growing up so quickly!"

"What about Jimmy? Who's going to look out for him with me not around?"

"I think Jimmy will be okay. And you'll see each other when you get home from school."

Rick had no idea what to expect at McMinnville Middle School. He liked the fact that it was literally just a quick hop over their back fence, and across the highway. He could make it in less than five minutes if he ran. The school was definitely a step up from his last school, in size and structure. Classes were now 'periods', there were different teachers for different subjects, and an actual schedule with electives. The school housed kids from grade 6 to grade 8, and from the first day, it was clear there was a pecking order and established hierarchy.

When the lunch bell rang, Rick grabbed his food from his locker and headed into the cafeteria, choosing a seat on the top tier of tables, giving him an excellent vantage point across the entire space.

"Hey kid. Beat it. This is our table."

Rick looked up at the group of eighth graders. "Go fuck yourself. I was here first."

"You better watch your fucking mouth," said another boy. His demeanour and stature clearly demonstrating he was the 'coolest' of the bunch. "Don't you know who I am?"

"I don't give a fuck who you are, and unless you want to fight about it, you should just fuck off." Rick was already in too deep to back down now.

"Then let's take this out front tough guy."

Rick was more than happy to follow the older kid outside, and the older kid's friends were more than ready to see this little shit get his face smashed in.

"Okay here are the rules," said the kid. "We're just going to grapple. No punches, and if you make me bleed, I'll put you in the fucking hospital."

Rick sized up his opponent. The kid was a good five inches taller, real athletic looking, and had an air of confident about him. Rick was pretty decent at grappling, and he figured his lower center of gravity might actually be an asset.

"Okay, you're on," Rick answered.

The match lasted all of three seconds. With a ring of about twenty kids around them, the kid stepped in for a hip-throw, and Rick went into him and reversed it, grabbing his hoodie and attempting to flip him right over his own back. In an instant, the kid dropped his weight and suplexed Rick, landing with his elbow in Rick's stomach, completely knocking the wind out of him.

"Want some more?" the kid said grinning.

Between coughs, Rick shook his head no. The kid helped him to his feet, then shook Rick's hand.

"I'm Brock. I'm on the varsity eighth grade wrestling team. I probably should have told you that. Nice reversal by the way. You almost got me."

"Thanks."

"You should try out for the school wrestling team. You're pretty good." Brock's declaration was loud enough for all the kids to hear, which pleased Rick greatly. "Listen, about the cafeteria seats…Only the grade eights and varsity kids are allowed to sit up in the high tier…sort of an unspoken rule you know? We weren't just fucking with you. That's the way it's always been here."

"Yeah I get it now."

"See ya around."

Brock and his buddies assumed their seats at the top, and Rick took up an invitation from another group of kids to sit a few steps down. He was still sitting higher than ninety percent of the rest of the cafeteria, so he didn't see it as a total submission to the rules. Once again, he'd stood up for himself and gained the respect of his peers. It was a common theme for Rick, and he took pride in these accomplishments more than anything else. Always looking for that vindication, that he isn't a nobody. Always ready to prove himself, and stake his claim.

The next day, Rick took his seat on the second tier and opened his lunch.

"Hey. Can I sit here?"

Rick took no notice of the taller, older kid, and kept minding his own business.

"Did you have fun with Brock yesterday?"

Rick sneered at the kid. "It would have been funner to dump him on his head."

The kid narrowed his eyes upon Rick's. "What if I could teach you how to do that?"

"And why would you want to do that?"

"Because I recognize heart when I see it, and I hate to see good heart to go to waste. My name is Simon."

"I'm Rick. I just started here. I'm in grade six."

The two spent the rest of the lunch hour talking about martial arts, what exposure Rick had, and Simon's more extensive background. At least five foot five, Simon was exceptionally tall for a kid in grade eight, and his pale skin contrasted sharply against his black hair and greenish eyes.

"My dad knows martial arts. Tae-kwon-do…so he's taught me some things. And he's also used it to beat the shit out of me a bunch of times. No big deal though. He just drinks too much and sometimes, you know, he just gets out of control."

"Dude, I'm sorry."

"I got used to it a long time ago. Doesn't bother me anymore. I guess that's maybe why I don't like seeing smaller people getting picked on you know? I'll train you if you want. I'm serious."

That was not an offer Rick could pass up. Martial arts and being able to beat the piss out of everybody was every young boy's dream, and to be given the opportunity to learn some new skills beyond what he tried to pick up from television and the Ninja Turtles, was something he wasn't saying no to.

"I'm in!"

"Okay, well how about you meet me on that small hill at the side of the school, after school."

"I'll be there for sure man. Thanks!"

As soon as the end of the day bell rang, Rick was out the door and busting his ass home to let the babysitter know where he'd be. About fifteen minutes later, he was back across the highway to the field by the baseball diamond.

"Sorry man, I just had to run home for a sec."

"No worries Rick. Personally, I try to stay away from home as much as possible."

Over the next few months, Simon and Rick spent a good deal of time hanging out after school. Sometimes it'd be three or four times a week, and sometimes it'd be every day. Once and a while, they'd even go all the way to Wortmann Park, where there was complete seclusion and they wouldn't be bothered. Simon's training wasn't by any means formal, and it focused more on situational fighting, like 'here's what you do when".

"Never back down Rick. Always be aggressive. The best defence is to just keep coming at the person in a relentless, merciless offense. Okay, come at me as hard as you can."

Fending off Rick was fun for Simon, and gave him an outlet for his own pent up aggression. Most of time Rick ended up on his ass with the wind knocked out of him, but that never stopped him from trying. Simon's height and reach always gave him the advantage over Rick, yet the younger kid was scrappy, and this disadvantage taught Rick to use his brain and develop more intense strategies during the scraps. Simon taught Rick a lot about fighting, and a lot about life. You didn't show off, and when you began an attack, you didn't let up until your opponent was incapacitated.

"Don't hold back. Always go for the kill. And never brag. No matter how good you get. Never brag. Don't talk about knowing how to fight. Surprise your opponent, and if it's time, then attack with ruthlessness."

Rick took it all in. He respected Simon, not only for the lessons but for the struggles the kid had to endure at home. They became close friends, and occasionally they'd hang out at each other's houses or in the evening. Rick respected Simon's ability to repel peer pressure and not smoke. That made him cool.

"Wanna sneak out some night and meet up?" said Rick.

"Aww man, I can't. My father is always home and if he found out or caught me…Jesus, that'd be the end of me. I do my best not to give him any excuses to beat the shit out of me."

Rick thought about his own dad. If he lived with him, he figured things would pretty much be the same as Simon. Bob didn't drink like Simon's dad, and Rick thought his dad was maybe a little better at controlling his temper, but there'd be no way in hell he'd put up with his son roaming the streets at night. There'd be hell to pay for that, and probably some steel bars on his bedroom window. He understood where Simon was coming from and respected his decision to just stay put.

"So I have something for you," said Simon one day as they were on the hill. "Open your hand."

"Jesus Simon! Are you serious? These are fucking awesome!" Rick took the nun-chucks and flipped them around in the air.

"They're padded so you can practice and not hurt yourself, but they're authentic dude."

"Wow Simon…I don't know what to say?"

Rick cherished those nun-chucks, and was touched by Simon's gift. Simon was authentic, a real good dude, and like Rick, he had heart.

Between hanging out with Simon, soccer practice, and school, Rick's nightly excursions slowed a little. He still had his paper route but it was a complete pain in the ass getting up at five in the morning, six days a week, especially when he didn't get home some nights until around two in the morning. Midway through the winter of 1991, he'd had enough and just quit, besides there were easier and much more lucrative ways to make cash. Rick continued to meet new street kids and expand his circle of influence, and a few of kids he met even went to his school. For the most part though, his new friends were mostly older and either in high school or had dropped out. He still ran into Tom and Charisma but really, he ran with whomever happened to be out that night.

The best part of having older friends was their access to cars. Suddenly, the world expanded and Rick was able to go places he'd never been. Catching a ride across town was as easy as asking, but that meant you were at the mercy of the driver, and if that driver changed plans, and decided not to go back your way, then you were shit out of luck. Rick learned that lesson quickly. Krysta had begged him to come to a party over by the hospital, and always wanting to impress, he obliged, not thinking or even caring how he was going to get home. When three A.M. rolled around, and his driver decided he was heading in a different direction, Rick knew he had no choice but to hit the pavement and start hoofing it. Of course, it didn't help that he was totally unfamiliar with the area, so had no clue about shortcuts. Two hours later, he climbed back through his bedroom window, just in time to change his clothes and head out on his paper route. He just couldn't say no to people.

Word spread quickly that he was game for anything and especially loved being sneaky. This lead to some genuine offers as well as some of the older kids taking advantage of him. Knowing he couldn't say no to a challenge, Rick was the go to guy for things the others wouldn't or couldn't do. The challenges became a sport, and like in any sport he tried, he had to excel and he had to be the best.

Sometimes he'd steal things from homes or stores in exchange for money or trade, whether it be watches, lighters, smokes, clothes, backpacks, tapes, Sony Walkman's and headphones. Basically anything a teenager could want but didn't have the money or the inclination to buy. It made Rick feel good to fulfill these requests.

"Hey dude, see if you can pick me up a new Walkman…"

"Hey, when you get a chance…"

Rick did his best to cater to them, and with every heist, his reputation and respect grew. His success rate made him very popular, and his income grew, both in cash and goods. He never really thought of the consequences of getting caught, not what the law would say or his parents. He really didn't give a shit. It was all just a game, a game he was damn good at. It was almost a newfound form of freedom for him, learning quickly that with enough patience and creativity, nothing was beyond his grasp. It gave him a sense of power, and a sense of control. The guys depended on him for shit, and that made him feel important. He proved he was good enough. His father may not want him around, but these guys did, and they did because they knew the crazy little fucker had heart, and in the end, heart was all that mattered.

****

Rick needed all the heart he could muster as he spent his time in the hole, awaiting his trial. It was almost like his first days on the streets all over again. Everyone had a story, and everyone just tried to navigate through as best they could. Rick spent his time in Bravo surrounded by many people, society would deem horrific. The dude who'd killed a cab driver during a robbery, and the two guys who were contract killers. Then there was the extremely violent 'enforcer' who collected drug debts and blood money. Another guy, ex-military, had killed a woman in broad daylight, then licked the blood off the knife while witnesses watched in horror. These became Rick's people. A 'normal' member of society probably couldn't imagine having an actual conversation with any of these individuals, yet as a con, you have hundreds of conversations with hundreds of different types of societies' worst. Prison has a way of desensitizing, where associating with types of people capable of extreme violence becomes no big deal and normal. This was Rick's new world, these were his new friends and comrades, and to meet one more murderer was just as common as walking past a guy on the street. The crimes become irrelevant. Nobody really cares what got you into prison, it's all about how you act once you're behind bars.

'Tremor' had plenty of experience with the prison system, both in Alaska and down in the Lower 48. He knew how to play the game, and had done some time in the real old school prisons in the continental United States. Vicious and uncontrollable, his six foot two inch and two hundred and thirty-pound frame loved to fight and beat people senseless. He was in Bravo for chasing a little weasel around the prison gym, just so he could beat him for fun. Tremor hated the cops and terrorized them any chance he had, always talking shit and threatening all manners of torture and retribution.

Yet despite all this, Tremor was also one of the most eloquent, mild-tempered, and reasonable people Rick had met so far. The two spent hours talking about life philosophy, emotional baggage, and how to see clearly in life with an untainted perspective.

"I have something for you youngster." He handed Rick a small book. "Read it. Read it a lot, and take to heart what it says."

"The Spirit of Tao."

"The Tao is all about balance, and finding a path or a way to achieving and maintaining it."

"Thanks Tremor."

That small gift, that small token of paying it forward, saved Rick's sanity, setting him on the path to help overcome and make peace with who he was and what he had done. The kid was about as unstable and imbalanced as they came, and though he really didn't understand the deeper implications of some of the content until his third read through, the message sparked something in him. He had always admired the East, both for its martial arts, and for the discipline and philosophies attached to them. Looking back, he wished his parents had enrolled him in formal martial arts classes. Training with Simon back on the school hill was one thing, but to truly benefit from the structure, discipline, and self-control, he needed more. Rick had desperately needed structure and discipline in his life, right from the get go. He yearned for it but it never came until it was too late, until he was too far gone.

The peace, tranquility, and power behind the Tao, and the way of the warrior found a home in Rick's thoughts, and in many ways he subconsciously associated the tranquility with the hollow nothingness of Ghost. The stories of the Eight Immortals, Lao Tzu, the concept of Yin and Yang, and attaining Wholeness within the self were all things he could appreciate and would come to love. That one little book began an intense period of soul-searching and self-discovery, and literally saved his mind and his sanity. Nowhere did it mention that all one needed to do to become whole was pray to God, and for the first time in his life, he understood how hard he was going to have to work to set his life on the right path. The 'Spirit of Tao' didn't promise to absolve him of his sins, instead it gave him the tools to begin to forgive those who needed forgiving – his Mother, his Father, and most of all, himself.

CHAPTER FOURTEEN

Back in Grade six, Rick didn't have the 'Spirit of Tao' to guide his ways, he was still fully immersed in the spiritual warfare for Christ. Sometime during the school year, the focus switched from defensive warfare to offensive warfare. Up until then, everything had been protective in nature, from the years of donning their spiritual armour every morning before school, to praying over their house, themselves, and their church. The goal was to purify and clean, rid any trace of Satanic influence. For Brenda, that wasn't good enough. She wanted the entire town of McMinnville free of the devil's hold. The battle wasn't localized, it was world-wide, and if she had to win the war against Satan one small city at a time, then that's what she would do. And thus, the offensive program of the spiritual warfare began.

Instead of letting the evil come to them, they began to seek it out. They had done this a few times in the past, but now the campaign began in earnest. Part of the tactical advantage that they now had at their disposal was the ability to specifically locate, see, and drive away actual demons – through Rick. Brenda had no problem putting her eleven-year-old son at the forefront of these experiences, if it meant they'd gain the upper hand on Satan. God would take care of little Rick and his soul. He'd provide him with the peace the boy needed after the ensuing traumatic experiences. They just had to pray and all would be well.

It's one thing to pray against demonic influences or sins, things that are just concepts or intangible ideas. A whole other dynamic exists when a shape, form, or substance is put to such things. For Brenda and the Potter's House crew, an adult movie or bookstore was a 'den of iniquity, or a 'house of sin'. The place saturated with the spirit of lust, and this spirit needs to be removed. They could pray all they wanted, but they needed Rick and his 'gift' to seek out the demons and ethereal spirits. While both Jill and Brenda were sensitive to the general feeling of a place, they relied on eleven-year-old Rick to identify the source. He was the hunter, the leader of the pack, always first to the scene and bearing witness to the sights.

"It's a gift Rick. We need you," said Brenda. "You've been given this gift and a very special role in the war. We cannot win this war without you."

So even though it scared the hell out of him, Rick relented and let himself be used as a bloodhound demon hunter. He wanted to help, and therefore in a way, he almost embraced the role. Maybe it would finally give his 'gift' some purpose and meaning, a burden worth bearing. He could only hope.

On weekends and in their spare time, the troop, Jack, Jill, Sarah, Paul, Brenda, Jimmy, and Rick, would hop into the car and seek out evil. Just a regular Sunday afternoon football game. When they found the evil, they'd call down the Holy Light of the Almighty to purge and cleanse. Then, it was on to the next stop. For Rick, who actually saw the skulking beasts and winged creatures, the process bordered on abuse. Already filled with so much pain and torment, he was forced to witness such raging evil, and this could only have left a detrimental mark. If he had tried to explain this all to an outsider, they wouldn't have believed him. The whole concept of 'sight' surpasses anything the normal senses can comprehend, and brings one into a realm that is unknown. But those non-believers could never dispute the sight because in truth, they had no idea themselves. We want to believe in angels, yet no one wants to fathom the idea of demons or satanic minions. It just doesn't fit the model.

Rick knew that if he tried to tell others what he saw, people like his father, or Simon, or his other friends, they'd laugh in his face and call him fucking crazy. How can one possibly describe a bat-winged hyena, with a face covered with black skin, who reeked of burning dung, with squirming crimson tendrils? It was laughable, yet this is what Rick saw. He didn't want to, but he did. And he didn't just see it, he felt it. He felt its hatred at Rick's very existence, and that hate burned like an ice cold dagger in his soul, like all they wanted to do was to rip that very soul from his body. These feelings had such a weight, such an intensity, that Rick felt as if he would suffocate. The pressure bearing down on his limbs, on his heart, on his head. It was too much.

"God has given you this gift. You must bear the burden."

"But the nightmares?"

"God will protect you and make it okay."

The group knew he could see, and they simply expected the good Lord to protect the child and make it okay. Never mind the tremendous scars, God would take care of those too. Just pray and Rick will become whole again. Except when he doesn't. Except when he's haunted by the images, and the sounds, and the smells. Except when those images, sounds, and smells come alive when he sleeps, adding to that constant, tormenting pressure. Rick never suffered any physical wounds or damage at the hands of the enemies, but what was there to protect his mind and soul from the simple fact of even knowing that this 'other world' even existed? Nothing.

But Rick was never one to back down from a challenge, so he sucked up all the courage he had, and put on a brave face.

"God must have given me this gift for a reason...and I must have a special place in His war. Why else?"

So Rick suffered the experiences and knowledge of what was, and saved the rest from having to. What if it'd been Jimmy who'd been given the gift? Rick didn't even want to think about that. No, if it had to be anyone in the family, it was best that it was him. He could handle it. He was brave. He was strong. He was a warrior.

With the change in war tactics, a new physical aspect was introduced to their training, based on the idea that matters of the Spirit rode on the physical breath of a person. In metaphysical circles, it is believed that an infant's first breath is when its soul actually enters and inhabits the body. At the moment of death, the belief is that the human body actually loses weight as the soul departs. The Christian doctrine practiced by the Potter's House congregation believed that one could inhale and exhale spirits, and that through this breath, they attached themselves to one's soul. The result was when one was possessed by a spirit of sin or a demon, and one was being laid hands on and prayed over in an effort to cleanse that spirit, they must keep their mouth slightly open, breathing in through their nose, and out through their mouth, so that the spirit could escape.

Terrified of what he might be breathing in on their demon hunts, Rick began to hold his breath. Except that holding his breath didn't stop him from smelling, feeling, and fully sensing the essence of the demon. Despite the 'valve' being closed, it was like he couldn't escape their presence, and their essence seeped in through his very pores. There was no stopping them. He had no protection. And that scared the living shit out of him.

Their crusades took them to various venues throughout the city. Oftentimes, it would just be Jill, Brenda and Rick. In this case, either Jill or Brenda would feel out the bad vibes or evil of a place ahead of time, and when the opportunity arose, they would go visit the spot and pray over it, seeking any specific signs or causes of demonic influence. Rick was always there to confirm and precisely locate, describe and identify any actual demonic presence that might be lurking. Change the demon to a deer, and the weapon to a rifle, and really their excursions were no different than a day hunting in the forest. Of course, the demon wasn't a deer, and a shotgun was powerless against their foe. But in either case, Rick was the hunting dog, sniffing, chasing, and cornering their prey. Not every place they visited had evil lurking in the shadows, and more often than not, there might have been a 'feeling' of evil, but no actual demonic presence. Rick enjoyed those days. Those were the nights he at least had a shot at sleeping.

Bolstered by the constant preaching that God would protect him, Rick believed he could witness the demons in relative safety. By no means did that negate the traumatic impact that seeing such evil 'in the flesh' had on his young impressionable psyche, but there was almost a morbid sense of fascination that drove him to continue the hunts. That, and he really had no choice. How was he going to say no to his mother, or to Jack and Jill? Doing so would mean he had stopped doing God's work, then he would cease to have protection and thus become completely vulnerable to the satanic influences.

"Today Rick we're going to McMinnville Middle School," said Brenda.

"My school?"

"Yes. Just you and I."

The group had long marked the various schools in town as important places to cleanse, since children were more susceptible to satanic influence.

"Children are the future," said Brenda, "so we must ensure that they are not dragged into the wiles of the devil at an early age. Look at you Rick, and the way you walk with the Lord, and have stayed away from the evil and temptations."

"Look at me?" thought Rick. "If only she knew the truth."

Brenda and Rick walked the short distance from their house to Rick's school. They wandered behind the school to the play area by the gym.

"Rick stop. I feel something." She closed her eyes. "Pray."

"Christ please wash away any taint of evil from this area. Cleanse it of evil and restore the good." Both were deep in concentration, the words spewing out as they spoke in tongues.

After about five minutes of praying, with Rick not sensing any real presence, they moved on to the hill where Simon and he always practiced their martial arts. Sensing nothing, they walked slowly towards the corner baseball diamond. Just as they passed a tree, Rick caught a glimpse of something shifting around in the dugout.

"Mom, I think there's something there."

The late afternoon sun left everything bathed in small orange hue but to Rick, there was an obvious pattern of darkness in the dugout, far beyond any normal shadows. As they moved to within ten yards, this darkness fully took shape, and Rick saw what appeared to by a blood-hued gargoyle in black smoke with disproportionally huge ram horns. Its skin glistened as if it was made of a solidified blood-wet substance. As soon as the creature noticed them, Rick felt a seething, blistering rage, so hot, he actually felt as if his own body was about to blister and explode. Immediately, he began to whisper to the Lord in tongues, and calling on the Lord's protection.

"Rick! Don't get too close!"

Rick had no idea that he'd even been walking towards the creature, spellbound into submission by its aura. The demon squatted down towards a corner of the dugout, smoke thickening around him as if he was trying to shield himself.

"By the power and blood of Christ! Demon leave!" shouted Brenda.

The demon caught Rick's eye, and snarled. The heat seared Rick's body, boiling his blood. They intensified their prayer.

"Oh Lord hear us now! Demon leave!"

With a flash of brilliance, the demon jumped through the closed roof and landing on top in a feline predatory stance, ready to pounce. Rick couldn't move. Or breathe. Then in a burst of wing and smoke, he shot up off into the sky and disappeared.

"Thank you God for your deliverance and your protection," whispered Brenda. She couldn't see the demon but she had felt his presence leave. "Rick, why are you looking at your arms? Are you okay? Did it hurt you?"

"No. I was…I was just seeing if my arms were blistered. The heat. It was just so hot. I felt like I was going to explode." Rick had felt a weight and a pressure with the demons before but he'd never experienced such a physical reaction to a spirits' presence, and it scared him.

"Let me see." She gently took her son's arms. "They look okay."

"Do you think I could actually get hurt by one?"

"I don't know for sure Rick. I certainly felt as if that demon was choking me that time as I sat in my chair reading the Bible."

It was the one and only time Brenda had ever seen a demon. She'd been reclining in her easy-chair in the living room when a small impish creature, no more than a foot tall had spontaneously jumped on her lap and began to physically choke her. She immediately called to the Lord for protection, banishing the creature to where he came.

"I did feel him though. It was so odd," she said. "I felt as if I couldn't breathe."

"But I never understood how you were attacked while you were praying?"

Brenda quickly changed the subject. "Come on, we'd better get home to Jimmy."

His mother never offered any explanation, and the thought concerned the young boy deeply. He'd been taught that when you were communicating with the Lord, you were automatically protected by his divine presence. The heat he'd felt throughout his body that day was real, and the possibility of suffering physical harm or torture at the hand of demons was not just something born from fear or fantasy. He checked his forearms once again. God had protected him this time, but what about the next? Still, he had to keep the faith and trust in the Lord. He was doing his work, and he would protect him. He had to.

The assault on the schools continued, only this time the entire troop attended, and the school was the local McMinnville High School. For high school aged kids, the devil was everywhere, from television, to movies, to books, and to modern rock and roll. They were an especially vulnerable group. The troop arrived after school hours but before the building had been locked up for the evening. Jack suggested they just roam the halls slowly and pray. The high school wasn't overly large, but Jack spilt the group in two so they could cover more ground. Neither Jill nor Brenda had ever been in the school before, so there was no foreknowledge of any hot spots. The goal was just to ask the Lord's favour and blessing upon the school, its teachers, and its children.

Not particularly enthusiastic about being there, Rick was really just going through the motions, walking along, his senses not primed and ready.

"What was that?" The hair on the back of his neck bolted up, and the dark energy radiated, seemingly from everywhere.

"Mom," he said turning his head slowly. Midway through the turn, his head froze as his eyes caught a glimpse of the creature. "Oh my God." Blocked by shock and fear, the words stumbled back down his throat. He'd never seen or felt such a large presence before, his slight arms and legs shaking from an extraordinary vibration emanating from down the hall.

"What is it Ricky?" said Brenda.

"It's huge. Like massive. Almost blocking the entire door of the classroom. And it has a hood. Like a big black hooded robe! Mom, I'm scared. I've never seen anything like it before."

Rick couldn't see the creatures' eyes or face, but a strange bearded snout, almost wolf-like, protruded past the darkness of the cowl, and two cloven feet, pointed, almost as a small deer, extended past the bottom of the material.

"It has a sword! A great wide double-bladed sword!"

"Jesus Lord…help us…" Brenda closed her eyes and prayed.

Heavy with chaos, the air around the creature thundered, matching the pounding of the child's terrified heart. The demons he'd witnessed in the past had never carried a weapon.

"Lord Christ Almighty, cleanse this air…cleanse this school…protect us all oh Lord God Almighty…"

The creature raised his arm, extending one pointy clawed finger directly at them.

"You shall pay."

"Ricky!!!!" screamed little Jimmy.

Brenda's eyes flashed open. "Where Ricky where? Where is it?"

Rick pointed to the door but the creature had already slid back through the solid steel and disappeared. As the creature moved, the scrape of the sword against the linoleum floor paralyzed Rick, as he felt the same scrape along his spine.

"Stay behind me," said Brenda.

The boys crept in behind their mother as she slowly walked towards the doorway.

"Lord Jesus…cleanse. Lord Jesus…remove this creature from our midst…"

Brimming with terror, Rick took a glance over his right shoulder.

"Mom!"

The beast shifted gears, and took position behind them. Brenda looked confused, as if she hadn't expected the beast to move with such rapidity.

"But no…I feel it here," she said.

The creature locked his gaze against Rick's, trapping the child in holy demonic terror. Brenda watched her oldest son's pupils dilate until they had completely wiped out the innocent purity of the whites.

"Okay, Ricky okay."

Slowly the group, Brenda, Jimmy, Rick, and Paul, turned back towards the creature.

"Lord God," said Paul. "Lord God. Lord God. Lord God. Lord God. Lord God." His amplified, incoherent ramblings see sawed back and forth between tongues and praying, annoying and distracting Rick. He wanted to just tell him to shut up. He needed to focus. It was just him and the creature. If Rick let up for just a second, he might lose the creature, putting them all in great peril.

The group inched closer to the long hall dissecting the main one. As they hit the mouth of the hall, the creature moved again. Rick flashed his head wildly as the creature reappeared directly in front of him, so close Rick could practically gaze up under the hood.

"Jesus Christ Almighty."

The child's frame dwarfed under the shadow of the seven-foot-high monster. He couldn't move. He couldn't breathe. The creature raised his arm once again, his pointed finger a mere foot away from Rick's forehead. In a demonic smile, it opened its jowl ever so slightly, revealing the side of its sharp canine teeth. The child could feel its eyes piercing down. Drawing him in, drawing him closer. The black cloak heaved in and out, and with the rise and fall of its chest, the creature let out a gargling, growling sigh.

"Right here!" screamed Rick. "He's right here!

A rush of divine energy blew past the boy as Paul and Brenda turned towards Rick. The creature disappeared. Panicked, Rick flashed his frantic gaze in all directions, trying to figure out where the creature might show up next. The seconds ticked away. He was losing time. Rick felt sure that the next time the creature appeared, he'd have his blade drawn, ready to strike.

"Sarah!"

Rick's mind jolted to the other half of their party. Sarah was out there somewhere roaming the halls with her mother and father. He had to warn them. He had to protect her. Without hesitation, he took off running. The aura of the presence hadn't decreased one bit, and Rick was terrified the demon would catch him alone, and skewer or behead him. His fear only drove him to run faster.

"Are you alright?" said Jack placing his hand on the panting child's shoulder.

"I saw him. He's huge and horrific. I had to make sure you guys knew."

"What did you see?" said Jill. Rick recounted his experience, all the while trying not to make eye contact with Sarah. He felt foolish now. She knew that he had risked his own fear and harm for her.

"You're a brave boy Rick," said Jill. "Let's go find the others."

Rick took the lead as the four of them made their way back through the halls. They met up with the rest, then veered off towards the cafeteria at the front of the school. The presence still hadn't changed, and the surge of adrenaline and shock had left poor Rick shaking.

"I want to go home," said Jimmy, tears streaking down his pale, terrified face.

"Let's just sit for a while," said Brenda. "And hold hands. Let's take comfort in us being together."

They sat around the cafeteria table for about fifteen minutes. The presence lightened but never fully dissipated, and the air still hummed and felt wrong. Rick did his best to regain control of his breathing, and take stock of what had just happened. They had lost. For the first time, they had failed. That demon had a hold over the school that it was not willing to relinquish. They hadn't been powerful enough to drive it away. The Lord hadn't been powerful enough to drive it away. The thought disturbed Rick greatly. God was supposed to be all-powerful, nothing could stand before him. And if that was true, then was it God's will that the high school remain possessed? Would he deliberately ignore the prayers of his faithful and put the children of that school and them at risk? Was there some other purpose? What the hell was his plan? Rick brooded all the way home and just couldn't let the incident go for weeks. He'd never felt a demon or presence so powerful, not even from God himself. He was rattled. He didn't understand. His confidence in their 'assured victory' was severely rattled, and his overall view of their holy war, and their spiritual crusade became a little darker and more jaded. His eleven-year-old brain just couldn't rationalize, and the nightmares wouldn't let him forget.

CHAPTER FIFTEEN

Regardless of how much Rick was drowned in the propaganda of Christianity and engaged in spiritual warfare, there was always a part of him that didn't fully commit. He just couldn't.

"You were born with the spirit of rebellion," his mother would say.

A proper and good Christian boy Rick's age would probably read their Bible every night before saying their prayers and going to bed. He'd wake up fresh eyed, complete his morning prayers, then dutifully await the Lord's message and visions in his dreams. Rick was not that child. He was never that child.

Some of the street kids were put off by the winter cold but not Rick. His games rarely took a break because of the weather. Charisma had somehow disappeared and he rarely saw Tom and his group of friends anymore. He still hung with Krysta. She hated being at home, so there were nights they'd meet up and just walk and talk. When it was just the two of them, she was often subdued and had more of a depressed spirit, which completely contrasted her upbeat, social butterfly persona when they were in groups. Just another kid trying to impress, and doing their best to fit in. Like Rick, she hated the world, and the two would spend hours just ranting and raving about how fucked up things were with everything. He never mentioned his religion, and he certainly never mentioned his 'gift' or the things he'd seen. While he was honest with Krysta, he could never fully reveal himself, never fully open up about who he was, and that meant he kept so much still bottled up inside. Incidents and visions like those at the schools only added to the pressure cooker building beneath his veins.

During the winter of 1990- 1991, Rick continued to take occasional contracts from the older kids, stealing mainly clothes, tools, and the things they themselves didn't want to risk stealing. But for the most part, Rick spent the majority of the winter wandering the streets alone, perfecting his ninja skills. Donning his ninja outfit, a black kimono over a hooded sweatshirt, black gloves, shoes, and black sweatpants, he'd spend the nights refusing to be anything but invisible. He'd even scored a black balaclava to cover the bottom half of his face, and took to performing diving summersaults over hedges and cursing himself when he made a sound hopping a fence. He was hard core. Most kids his age played pretend ninja, goofing around in their backyard or jumping over couches in their basement. But Rick? No Rick took his pretend play aspirations and transformed them into reality. His play was for keeps and anything in his way or anything that struck his fancy was up for grabs. Christmas provided an opportune time for a bored, little shit to cause havoc.

"I don't think anyone will mind if I just rearrange some Christmas lights and decorations?" he laughed. "All in good fun of course."

The little impish ninja became the little impish Grinch. The residence that hung strands of white lights around the small tree in their front yard awoke to those same lights tied between the trunk of the tree and the fence post on the other side of the yard, completely blocking off their driveway. The fool who used large multi-coloured outdoor bulbs would find strands of them criss-crossing the road in the morning, unplugged and easy prey for an unsuspecting vehicle. There was the house where the glowing Santa and his reindeer magically flew from the front yard and somehow on the roof of the mini van parked in the driveway, still glowing, still filled with Christmas cheer. Lights looked way better in the gutters, instead of hanging from them, and wreaths belonged in trees, after all, most were made of branches and pinecones. He was especially pleased with the giant glowing candy cane that he moved down the street, and then hung from a street light about thirty feet in the air. Sure it was immature and childish, but it was funny as hell.

One night, a few days before Christmas he came upon a residence whose owner had left his ladder perched up against the side of the house.

"Stupid fool," he laughed. "What were they thinking?" The kid couldn't resist, and in a flash he was up the ladder creeping across the roof. "Now what do I do with these lights?"

He thought about draping them down so they'd hang off the roof, or maybe wrapping them around the chimney. Ultimately, he decided on something a little more destructive. One by one, he began unscrewing each light bulb, then tossed it the fifteen yards or so out into the middle of the street. For someone so ninja, the sound of glass shattering on asphalt was not exactly a silent endeavour, and it didn't take more than five crashes before the front door flew open and the shoeless, shirtless fifty-plus male occupant came charging out.

"Get down from there you little bastard!"

He ran to the ladder, but Rick was one step ahead, and had dropped from the twelve-foot roof, landing in a shoulder roll on the dew covered grass. Perfection.

"Don't you run!"

Rick bolted around the corner of the house, with the man in hot pursuit only about ten paces behind.

"This is going to be an easy race!" thought Rick. Except he hadn't counted on the nunchuku he had draped around his neck to come flying off mid flight.

"Shit!" He couldn't just leave them. They were a gift from Simon, and no real ninja leaves their tools behind. He skidded to a halt, scooped them up, then dropped into a low stance, spinning the chucks around his body and arms in a 'kata', then flipping them back in the rest position over his right shoulder. It looked cool as hell when the martial arts guys did it on television, so he figured what the hell, he might as well try it too. He had no intention of using the chuck, but if it made the guy stop and pause, that would give Rick an extra step when he took off again. The guy couldn't see that chucks were actually foam and harmless.

"Whoa! Little motherfucker!" said the man raising his hands before backing away and running straight into the front door of his house.

"I'd better get the fuck out of here before he comes out with a shotgun or calls the cops!" thought Rick. Hopping the fence into the trailer court, he took off for one of his hidey-holes.

"Jesus that was close!" He couldn't help but laugh, remembering how wide the man's eye became when he started swinging the chucks. "He must have thought I was a real ninja. Now that is fucking cool."

He didn't see the old man again that night, nor any patrol cars but he gave the area a wide berth on his way home just to be safe. That was also his last time fucking with people's Christmas lights that year, figuring the rest of the neighbourhood would be sufficiently warned and be on the lookout for the little ninja dude.

This Christmas marked the second one since the divorce, and despite the still tumultuous relations, both parents made sure to spoil the boys with toys, and be at peace. Bob and Rosemary had recently purchased their first house together, a two-story affair on about five acres of land, not far out on a sharp corner of Baker Creek Road. The upstairs was much like a normal home, but the downstairs was single, wide-open room the full length of house, probably originally someone's shop. Without any stairs to the main floor, or a bathroom for that matter, a person had to walk all the way outside and come in the front door, or take the stairs to the back deck, which at the time were rotten and actually falling apart. When the boys came to stay, this is where Bob saw fit to let them sleep. Graciously, he did supply a couple of rickety old spring-loaded cots and a couple of sleeping bags.

"I'm just going to pee outside man," Rick laughed to his little brother.

"I don't like peeing outside."

"Would you rather have to climb up those shitty old back stairs in the dark?"

"I'll just pee outside."

"Yeah, that's what I thought."

Besides whatever toys or staples the boys happened to bring with them, the space was barren. No chairs or tables, a right comforting, cozy space for two adolescent boys. No wonder they never wanted to visit. And how often were Bob or Rosemary going to venture down in the middle of night to check on the boys to see if everything was okay, or even if they were still there? Oregon in the winter can get pretty cold. So the boys were shoved in the basement, while Bob and Rosemary enjoyed the true comforts of home upstairs. Out of sight, out of mind. Some true bonding and restitution going on. What were the boys supposed to think? How were they supposed to feel? Bob and Rosemary may have purchased a house, but they never made it into a home, at least not when the boys came to visit.

"Well? How do you like them boys?"

"Wow! This is awesome! Are you serious?" said Rick ripping the Christmas bow off his brand new eighteen-speed mountain bike.

"Of course!" smiled Bob. "Your brother's is exactly the same, just a little smaller. Sorry I couldn't wrap them but I had no idea how to wrap a bicycle!"

Rick loved his bike, and Bob couldn't have picked a better gift for his son. His old BMX bike was okay but this one blew the old one to shit.

"We'll just keep them in the woodshed and you boys can ride them here when you come visit."

"What?" said Rick.

"They're to stay here. And you can have the privilege of using them when you come to visit."

"That makes no sense. I ride my bike all over town delivering my papers and stuff. This bike would make it so much easier."

"If the old bike is seeming to work, then I see no reason why it can't continue to work."

"But Dad! That's unfair! You get us a Christmas present and then won't even let us take it home and use it! We can't be bought off if that's what you're trying to do."

"Watch your mouth Rick."

"Whatever, keep them here…I don't even care."

Except that he did care. He cared a lot. He could really use that bike at home, and his Dad was just being a prick 'again' by not letting them take them. It's like he did this shit just to piss Rick off, just to make sure Rick knew who was boss. Eventually Bob relented and ended up buying a bike rack for the roof of the Wagoneer, so he could bring the bikes when he picked up the boys. Still, the whole ordeal didn't help mend any of the old fences that desperately needed mending, another opportunity lost. In the ensuing months, the four of them did go on several bike riding outings, whether it was just a casual ride through a wooded park, or even in town.

While Jimmy was still too young to do any serious trail riding, Rick would have loved the opportunity to just get out there and do some serious rock hopping with his Dad. The outings were scenic and mostly peaceful, but there was still an air of extreme tension in the air. The boys were only there because the law said they had to be. Talk was sparse, and both boys were quite often subdued and withdrawn. Words became a match, where one swift strike and toss into the smouldering air ignited a fight or confrontation, so all sides found it easier and safer, just to stay quiet and say nothing.

Had Bob known about Rick's extensive nightlife, he would have had plenty to say to both Rick and Brenda, and probably the court. But he didn't know, so Rick was free to continue doing as he pleased. In early spring, he met Slate, and was introduced to the world of the 'whigger' – a white kid that acts like a black kid. About seventeen, Slate was a hard core whigger, with his saggy pants, ghetto slang, and love of gangsta-rap. Slate had a car and rumour had it that he'd actually been 'jumped-in' and was part of a bonafide gang up in Tigard. Too small and too country, McMinnville didn't have any real gangs, so Slate was a bit of an enigma and something new.

"Yo youngster. I've heard of you man. You've got quite the little reputation going on. Actually, that's why I came down here. I hear you is fearless man and can get shit that nobody else can."

Rick just smiled. "I do my best." It was all he could do to keep his pride from bursting out. He was in. One of the go to guys.

"If I think it's doable, then I'm game. But I'm not walking out of no Payless or Radioshack with a big ass stereo system on my shoulder."

"What about cars man?"

"Cars? I ain't stealing no cars? I can't even drive yet!"

"No, no," laughed Slate. "I mean like plates and hubcaps and shit." He pulled a huge gold chain from under his baggy T-shirt. "And hood ornaments. Look at this Lincoln symbol hanging from this chain. That shit is cool man."

Rick had never seen a hood ornament hanging from a chain before but he had to admit it looked pretty fucking cool.

"See you wear them as necklaces or hang them from a chain off the side of your pants. You can use it as a weapon in a street fight if you have to. It's like a status symbol man. And there's a huge market. You could make some serious cash."

Rick didn't really care what Slate wanted the shit for, he just knew that he offered him $50 per hood ornament, $75 for a licence plate, and $150 to $200 for a full set of rims. That was some serious dough, and it beat getting up at five A.M. every morning and riding his little ass all over town. Rick could easily pull in $500 to $700 a week just by being a sneaky little shit. For an eleven-year-old, that was some sweet ass cash. And even more than that, his nights now had purpose and a sense of fulfillment. He wasn't just passing time wandering around, he was working, getting shit done. He was the man, and damn, that made him feel important.

Slate would tell Rick what he wanted, and then Rick, sometimes even that same night, would go out and fill the order. With his wire cutters, a long flat-head screwdriver, and a small compact Philips screwdriver, he was pretty much ready for anything. Right across Highway 99, maybe ten minutes from his house was a used car lot, and just on the other side of the Town Center shopping complex was an actual dealership with spiffy new cars, and the best rims in town. Plates and hood ornaments were easy and small, and he could fit a tonne of those in his backpack. He even started bringing towels with him to wrap things in so they didn't chink and make noise. Rims were a different story. They were bulky, heavy, and wouldn't fit in a normal backpack, so there was never a quick getaway, and Rick did not like dropping merchandise to run.

While it was all still a game to Rick, it was about this time that it really occurred to him that the game had hit the next level and he was no longer just doing petty theft. The stakes were higher, and the consequences greater. Cars were expensive, and to replace the shit he was taking cost a great deal of money. The threat of jail was real. But only if he got caught. That was the kicker. He didn't intend on getting caught. He'd spent the better part of a year practicing his ninja skills and moving through the neighbourhood sight unseen. He'd just have to work a little harder, up his game.

As a very cerebral kid, Rick began taking note of angles of sight, lighting, potential cameras, the way sound carried; what could be heard and what couldn't. Meticulous in his planning, meticulous in his execution. Planning escape routes, the quickest, and the most effective. Plan A, then plan B, and then a plan C. Mental chess. What happens if this happens? Where do I go if this happens? Which way do I run? What if it gets blocked off? What's the best route that a car can't follow? What if he slipped and fell?

Often, he would cruise by the target, escape into a shadow, and study the area for a good fifteen to twenty minutes. Waiting, watching, thinking things through until he had all the variables resolved. The used car lot was only really good for stealing plates from cars parked on the backside where there was a high chain-link fence with barren fields behind it. Lots of shadow. Easy to get lost in. Licence plates took time to unscrew, and for some he even needed a crescent wrench. That meant spending more time in one spot. He had to account for that. Always planning to the last detail. Nothing out of place, nothing he hadn't accounted for. He was only really comfortable with getting rims from the dealership because it had a back maintenance area with no windows and no apparent camera angles, and woods right across the street. If the cops showed up, he could easily ditch the rims and run off into the dense woods. No one was going to find him in the woods, getting lost in the trees and the undergrowth was his all-time speciality.

Being the smallest and easiest to grab, ripping the hood ornaments was by far his favorite swipe. Ten in his backpack was an easy five hundred bucks, and not at all hard to pull off in a couple of nights, a single night if he wanted to be reckless. Slate would sometimes even drop him off on the other side of town smack dab in the middle of an area that was ripe for the picking.

"Yo man, I need fifteen plates in three days. Think you can pull it off?"

"Of course."

Rick only got $800 for that run because Slate did help him out a bit. Still, $800 for three days' work. Not a bad deal at all. School dropped even further down the priority list, and it was no wonder he was half-asleep and failing most of his classes. Sometimes he'd go out and just stockpile some ornaments, just so he had a little stash of the popular requests, a little exercise in supply and demand.

"Now this is a nice shiny white Lincoln."

Rick didn't really like stealing from cars in an apartment complex. Too many windows and too many variables. The lights may be off, but that didn't mean someone wasn't lurking by the window, watching his every move. Still, the complex had a good escape route and backed onto the loading docks of the Town Center shopping complex. Lots of nooks and crannies for a wiry ninja kid to squeeze under. The reward was worth the risk. The Lincoln sat in the middle of the parking lot. Lincoln hood ornaments were always in high demand, so whenever Rick had the opportunity, he took advantage. Normally all he had to do was pull back the ornament, snip once with his wire cutters, then take off running.

"Shit!" The first snip didn't quite make it through the wires, so he had to snip again. "Got it." With the ornament in his pocket and the cutters in his coat, Rick was already at the back end of the car, walking briskly.

Footsteps. Rick whirled around.

"Hey! He's stealing from my car! Stop!" Rick thought the middle-aged guy was about to blow a lung.

"Fuck!" Rick faked left, then took off running for the back of the complex, climbing up on the power box and then up over the fence. He landed with a hard thump on the concrete of the loading docks and froze. Nothing.

"Well that was easy." Walking briskly, Rick turned his route and headed home. He'd gotten no more than fifty feet when the same white Lincoln came barrelling around the corner, careening over speed bumps.

"Jesus Christ!"

Rick was caught dead to rights, and the car showed no signs of slowing down until he'd bowled straight through his target. He took off at a dead sprint in the opposite direction, taking a hard right to the front parking lot of the plaza.

"Should I go in the Safeway? Maybe I can lose him in there…Fuck…they can just block the front doors and I'm done. Can't corner myself in like that…"

Before Rick could even finish his thought, the car was right there, braking hard. Panting and gasping for air, Rick needed a few seconds to collect his wits. The guy thought he was surrendering, and stepped out of his car.

"Someone go in and call the cops!" he said to a few of the bystanders. "This little punk stole from my car!" As the guy rounded the front of his car, Rick took off right back in the same direction that he came, back towards the loading docks.

"You little fucker!" The guy hopped back in his car, not realizing that Rick could hop fences all night long if he had to.

Rick went straight back to the apartment complex, hopped the huge fence, then looked for a place to hide.

"I've got time, I've got time. It's gonna take him a minute to drive back around. Fuck. Where do I go?" He spotted the group of large garbage dumpsters. Sitting on a concrete block and surrounded by wooden fences, Rick didn't hesitate. It wasn't the most elegant hiding spot, but figuring the guy would expect him running or walking, it would cross them up. All he could do was sit and wait. And wait he did. He heard the Lincoln circle by three different times over the course of about thirty to forty minutes. Pretty soon the guy would figure that Rick wasn't on foot anymore. He had to move.

Climbing out of the dumpster, he ran to the south side chain-link fence and juniper trees. As long as he stayed behind the loading docks and in people's backyards where there were high fences, shrubs, and no sight line to passing cars, he'd be alright.

"And if they catch my scent again, I just won't go home. I'll go right past, through the trailer park, behind the bank and theatre. No way a car can get through there."

Practically his playground, he knew the west-side of Highway 99 way too well, and if he stayed on his feet, and just kept moving, nothing was going to catch him. He needn't have worried, he'd outsmarted them all once again, and made it home without incident.

"Dude man! You got to be careful," laughed Slate. "Don't get caught slippin' man."

With a stellar reputation and rolling in the dough, Rick became a little concerned that he might actually become a target for the other street kids who needed cash of their own or just got a little jealous of the attention the little shit ninja was getting.

"Do your parents know that you're purchasing this knife?" said the store clerk.

"Of course they do," said Rick.

"How old are you?"

"Fourteen," he lied.

"Alright then. Here you go."

For forty well-earned dollars, Rick had legitimately purchased his own four-inch lock blade and a nice leather belt-loop case.

"This baby is mine! And bought with my own money!" He loved the freedom and independence that came from having his own income; the power to do whatever he wanted.

"Now I need a belt."

He'd never worn a belt before and always thought they were preppy and unnecessary. Now they served a purpose. With a stack of cash in his pocket he strolled into Payless and found himself a nice black long leather-weave belt, that after he'd worked it in a little, had a tail that stretched down his left thigh a good six inches.

"That looks fucking cool. My new trademark."

With his long baggy T-shirts, no one ever realized that he was carrying a four-inch blade at his side. Not his mother, not his school, and especially not the other street kids. They'd think twice coming at him now.

The more Rick worked, the more the cash collected. A kid could only buy so many toys and crap, especially since he had to hide much of the stuff he purchased. If things just started mysteriously appearing in his room, Brenda would surely just think he stole it, and there was no way he could tell her that while the stuff he bought was legit, the money he used to buy it was not procured in a legal manner. Still, he had a lot of money, and since the divorce money had been tight for Brenda. As the man of the house Rick felt if there was some way he could contribute and help her out, then he should. How better to show his love and support? Prove his worth? Show that he had stepped up in his father's absence and been a man?

So one day, he laid a hundred-dollar bill and five twenties on the dining room table and waited. He knew his mother had walked by the table several times. He knew she'd seen it.

"Rick, what's this?" said Brenda, breaking the five-hour stand-off.

"It's just a little money to help out with things." His reply was simple and uncomfortable.

"Where did you get it?"

"That's not important."

"What do you mean it's not important? Of course it's important! Did you steal it? Is it drug money? I can't believe you did this? Do you not understand how wrong it is to steal? How you have offended God? I cannot believe that my son has become a criminal…"

Her mind went wild with accusations, and as Rick offered nothing to deny or substantiate any of them, she continued to rant and rave, bringing herself to tears.

"Just the presence of this money here is wrong. Oh Jesus, Lord, Almighty! Cleanse this child of sin!" In that instant, he knew his relationship with his mother had changed, had been irreparably damaged. "I'm not taking it. I'm not even touching it. It can stay right there until you take it back!"

Hurt and crushed by her reaction, he answered, his voice barely above a whisper.

"Then it can stay right there…"

He walked out of the house, leaving the two hundred dollars on the table. He'd only wanted to help. He knew things were bad, and that she was doing her best, and he had the money, so he could help. It was his duty. Later that night as he climbed the stairs to go to bed, he saw the money untouched on the table. When he woke up in the morning, it was gone. She never said a word, and Rick never mentioned it again.

It always remained their little secret over the years; the times random money would just appear on the kitchen counter or dining room table. Maybe she was embarrassed about taking money from her pre-teenage son, or maybe part of her was just scared wondering where the money came from. Either way, she always took it, and it made Rick feel proud that he was able to contribute. He wanted to help his family financially, he was more a father to his family in that way than his own father. And if Bob had found out, that would have been the end of her custody with the boys. It was all such a risky business.

Brenda's attitude toward her son changed that day. He was no longer her 'little Ricky', and even more, her little warrior for Christ. She had lost a part of her son to the world, a part she knew nothing about, a part she couldn't control. What had gone so wrong? He was her golden child. Had she failed in her teachings? Had God failed them both? No, God would never fail them.

She took the money, and didn't ask questions. She didn't say a thing when new toys or clothes now appeared in Rick's room. He didn't have to hide them anymore. She just turned the other cheek, avoided the answers she knew she didn't want to hear, and the answers she knew she couldn't face.

CHAPTER SIXTEEN

Losing Kristy was a hard blow for Rick, and made the loneliness of prison that much more pronounced. One by one, his 'old life', his old friends, disappeared. He never realized how hard it was to do time, and to try and stay in touch with the outside world. The stress of not being able to do anything to affect the outcome of anything happening in that world. Sure, he could listen and offer his advice, but he could never be a part of it and truly make a difference, and that killed him. The older cons told him it was just best that he forgot about that life altogether, tell the friends, tell the lovers, tell everyone to just move on and forget about him, until he could get out and become relevant again. It's a way of distancing the one's you love from your punishment. Why should anyone else suffer for your mistakes?

As a separate 'state', prison exists as a world within a world; separate rules, separate customs, a separate culture. When someone does time, they become immersed in the prison world, and to the extent of their isolation, it becomes all they know. It's like being pulled underwater, and forced to learn not only how to swim, but how to breathe the air in that water. Amphibious in nature, prisoners know there is a world beyond prison, and most cling to the memories of their time in that world. But while they are in prison, they are truly immersed in the ocean of their reality, little tadpoles trying to grow legs and arms as fast as they can, just so they can survive against the big frogs.

The only way they can maintain contact with those on the surface is through mail, phone calls, and for the lucky ones, visits. Each time that sort of external stimulation occurs, it's like rising to the surface for a little breath of fresh air. But that breath of fresh air is brief, and not sustainable against the oppression of the world below, so the prisoner sinks back under. Further and deeper with each passing year. Every time a prisoner walks out of a visit, hangs up the phone, or sets a letter down, the outside world disappears, and they're dragged back under the waves. The barrier goes up, and they're right back to being a convict, cold, occasionally cruel, and always on guard. Sometimes the change is so clean and abrupt that it causes great consternation.

But for those that choose it, these breaths of fresh air can represent a light, and the light bears love and hope on its wings. A hope that maybe there really is a life after this one. The warmth of knowing that you are still worthy of being loved and cared about, that you're important enough to deserve someone else's attention, whether you believe that or not. Some prisoners choose to shun all of this and just stay immersed in the prison world, and sometimes to an extent, things are easier to deal with this way. Rick didn't agree. Maybe it was his youth, maybe it was inexperience, or maybe it was just his belief in redemption, but he decided to continue to take these breaths of fresh air, and to not deny the outside world while he was condemned to this one.

So when he lost Kristy, and one by one his other friends started losing interest, thoughts of being totally forgotten shook him. He knew what he'd done had been a horrible act, and he didn't blame people for forgetting about him, but the realization and loneliness haunted him. But not everyone gave up on the teen. Back in early December, while he was still in the psych unit, he'd received a letter from Brenda and Amanda Young. A freshman during Rick's junior year, Amanda had been a cadet in the ROTC unit and he'd been the one responsible for teaching her how to march and handle a rifle in formation. In the three months they'd known each, the two had gotten close, Rick acting more like the pain in the ass older protective brother.

"Young! Drop and give me twenty!" He'd smile as Amanda dropped to the gym floor for twenty push-ups cursing his ass, but smiling all the same.

Full of compassion and support, the letter from Amanda and her mother was sincere.

"I don't care what they say, I won't turn my back on you…"

Rick cherished those words. As a parent, Brenda was very understanding and empathetic, reaching out to Rick in a way no other parent did. Most other parents were apprehensive about Rick, and a few, like Crystal's parents, had even forbidden contact. Brenda was different. Something about her words told Rick that she knew and understood his pain. At the time, he didn't fully understand why, and really, it didn't matter. All he knew was that he'd found a rock to help him through this madness. Brenda gave him full permission to call and write to her daughter and left him with a standing offer.

"If you need anything, don't hesitate to ask. It's going to be okay Rick. We'll make it through."

Rick had no idea how it was going to be okay but he believed them. The two of them did such a good job of comforting Rick as he was trying to come to terms with the weight of his crime. The guilt, the shame, and the regret over his actions was beyond tremendous, and Rick felt that he didn't deserve to live. Coupled with being locked in a cell, twenty-three hours a day, with around thirteen of Alaska's worst offenders, everything was drama and violence and negativity. This was his future. Grim and dark. Intense depression seeped even deeper into his soul, but a different depression than the previous six years. Then he had been depressed, hurt and angry over betrayal, over what had been done to him. Now the depression was over what he had done to others, and the combined fact that he couldn't even fathom a future in this worthless place; feeling like he didn't deserve any future at all.

Reading the 'Spirit of Tao' had begun to open up the darkness but his soul was still so lost and desperate.

"Why?"

"Why did I do the things I did?

"Why did I behave the way I did?"

"Why did my father leave when I was ten years old?"

"Why had I spent six years hating him?"

"Why did I give him a bullet instead of a hug?"

"Why?"

"Why?"

"Why?"

In seeking the answers, the Tao forced Rick to be objective, to sacrifice the self and see things as they were instead of how his sixteen-year-old mind had trapped himself into believing them to be. The arduous journey of awakening would take months, even years, to fully formulate, but he had taken the first step, and that's what really mattered. Trying to make sense of his life, his whole life, and why things had turned out the way they had. He didn't have to be lost. His sorrow didn't have to own him. It didn't have to define him like it had in the past. And as these realizations and the awareness began to form in his mind, he began to liberate himself from the Ghost that he had become, and truly begin his spiritual journey to becoming a man.

Brenda and Amanda were the personal link on his journey, the living breathing voices of encouragement that ran through his mind, and picked him up off the ground when things got too heavy or low. Twenty-three hours a day is a long time for anyone to spend alone cramped in a small cement space, thoughts can become crooked, and feelings can warp. It was Brenda and Amanda who provided the light in this darkness. Both pledges of support, especially from two unsuspecting sources, touched Rick deeply. They became his fresh air and hope, keeping him from being completely sucked into the muck of the prison sea. And that sea certainly was filled with muck.

"Hey Spokane," said Rick one day as they were chopping it up in the Bravo common area. "Did you see the new dude they just brought in?"

"The really tall white dude with the bald top and mullet? The one that looks like a fucking creep? Yeah...I saw him all right." Sixteen like Rick, Spokane had been thrown in the hole because the system didn't know where else to put him; a common problem with juveniles in the adult prison system.

"I'd stay clear of that dude man," said Rick. "I just don't get a good feeling."

A few days later a note found its way under Rick's cell door.

I saw you the other day. And I'd really like to do things with you, if you know what I mean. You're so young and so fresh. Unspoiled with your creamy white skin. I bet your ass is wonderful. Hard and tight. The perfect fuck. I dream about shoving my cock in there so deep that you scream in pain and pleasure. I've got money if that's you want. If you're interested, meet me in the shower. I promise I can make it worth your while. I bet you like having your dick sucked by a man don't you? If you're not like that, just act like I never asked.

"Jesus fucking Christ! What the fuck? Fucking creep! Jesus Christ." Rick held down the vomit creeping up his throat, shaking his head in a violent repulsion. "Fucking creepy, fucking flaming homo…Jesus Christ that's disgusting!"

After he'd calmed down, his young mind wrapped itself around the proposition; how easy it was for people to take advantage of others. Some weirdo meets some young kid, and almost immediately solicits sex. What if the guy hadn't even bothered to send the letter, and had just attacked him in the shower or something?

"Now I got to watch my fucking backside literally, all the time. Jesus fucking Christ."

Definitely an uncomfortable, disgusting feeling. He couldn't just say no and be done with it. He had to let the guy know that shit like this didn't fly in his world. While more than a tad embarrassed and feeling quite nervous, he had to share the note with Spokane.

"I got the exact same note dude!"

"Are you fucking kidding me?"

"I wish I fucking was. Seriously man, what a fucking creep."

"We can't let him get away with that shit Spokane."

"I agree man. He needs to be made an example of. If we don't stand up to freaks like him, then who will?"

"Okay…which one of us is going to be the bait?"

"I'll do it man," said Spokane. "I'll get him in the shower…"

"And then I'll come up behind with a weapon and initiate…"

"And we'll both give him the beating of his life, and send the bastard on a one-way trip to the hospital."

"Tomorrow. We do it tomorrow."

Spokane answered his note, and let the fucker know he was interested, putting the plot in motion. Maybe they were too obvious or suspicious in their planning, or someone had overheard, but the dude had a change of heart and asked to be put into protective custody.

"I'm afraid for my life!" he told the cops. "Please, please don't let me out with the rest of them."

Once word got out that he'd cowered and gone PC, the mod went nuts, screaming at him for being a homosexual coward piece of rat shit. The commotion went on for days. Some of the older cons threatened his life. It was one thing to be a homosexual in prison; it happened all the time. It was quite another though to be a homosexual and accost the youngsters. That was unacceptable. When it came out that he was in prison for being a child molesting pedophile, the shit really hit the fan, and his fellow inmates wanted him dead. After about three days, they transferred the fucker to a whereabouts unknown.

Rick found out later that the pedophile had given a full debriefing on him and Spokane, and told the Department of Corrections that not only were the boys going to beat him, but that they'd planned to sodomize him with a broom handle. He'd also read the paper, and knew about Rick's case, and told authorities Rick had admitted to him that Rick had raped Rosemary's body after he had shot her. From the evidence, authorities knew this was a complete lie, but it didn't stop the pedophile from offering to testify against Rick in his trial as a character witness. In one of the evidentiary hearings, the District Attorney asked the judge to add the pedophile to the witness list. Everybody in the courtroom knew his statements were blatantly false.

"This is complete bullshit," replied Judge Sanders. "I'm not even going to entertain this! I've had firsthand dealings with this man and I know that he is a sick, opportunistic person, and I would be offended if you even try to bring him into my courtroom!"

"But Your Honor…"

"If you bring that man into my courtroom, I will make sure Mr. Watkinson gets a mistrial. Are we clear?"

It was clear to Rick that if he ever ran into the Pedophile again, he would attack, and he would make him pay. It was also clear that in prison, lies triumphed over truth, and those willing to rat or give any sort of inside information were taken at their word over the accused. Actions first, questions later.

"Put these on Watkinson," said the guard handing him a pair of red clothes.

"What? Why? What have I done?"

"Just put them on now, then grab your shit. You're being moved."

Without any accusation, hearing or reason, Rick had been 'maxed out', which meant at least an automatic year in the Hole.

"To where?"

"Bravo-1 where you'll have a nice little camera in the corner of your cell so we can watch your every move. Sounds comfy doesn't it?"

Rick wanted to tell him to fuck off. Put on every restriction the DOC could think of, he couldn't use the phone, lost all visit privileges except from his attorney's, and was shackled in handcuffs or belly-chained with leg irons every time he left his cell. For the next month, he was completely cut off from the outside world.

"What's the reason man?"

"Per the Superintendent's orders," answered the cop as he slapped a big sign on the outside of Rick's cell door.

MAX. ESCAPE/MARTIAL ARTS RISK. All Restrictions to be enforced without exception. April 1, 1996.

Rick didn't learn the story of his Max-out until a few weeks later when one of the guards let him in the loop. The night of March 31, someone had 'bombed' the yard, launching packets of live .22 caliber bullets from the hill overlooking the prison yards. Someone had landed on the roof of the prison and in the Worker's Yard, right next to Bravo's. Who used a .22 caliber long-range rifle in their crime? Rick. Who was already in the Hole for escape risk and trafficking weapons and explosives? Rick. Where did they land? About forty feet to the right of where he'd be able to get a hold of them. The Alaska State Troopers had still been trying to get Elmo to testify against Rick for his allegations; he'd yet to skip the state though his life had been threatened twice. Therefore, the rational conclusion was it had been big bad Rick Watkinson, the sixteen-year-old criminal mastermind who had had firearm ammunition thrown on the roof of Cook Inlet. It wasn't him of course, although he did know exactly who it was, not that it even mattered. Rick fit the profile far too well, and as long as the Administration punished someone, they really didn't give a shit whether or not they got it right.

The wedge between him and the outside world deepened. Everything that had been brewing inside of him began to bubble. Five months before, he'd killed his parents, and as the numbness and shock began wearing off, he was left confused and searching for answers. His remaining friends and family were slowly abandoning him and disappearing from his life. The psych ward. The Pedophile. Bravo. The red jumpsuit. Getting blamed for shit he didn't do. Thrown in the shithole of Hell.

He tried to keep it all in but it was too much. He exploded. Lost his shit. His 'don't give a fuck' meter blew through the roof. He didn't care anymore. Didn't give a fuck. He acted out. He had absolutely nothing to lose, he couldn't get any lower than he already was. His aggression mounted, daring and enticing the cops to try and stop him. A few of them even tried to reason and talk some sense into him, but really most of them couldn't blame him. They'd been expecting it. Throw a sixteen-year-old kid in prison for the rest of his life, then throw him in the dungeon inside that very prison, and tell him he's lucky he's still being fed? They were surprised he'd lasted this long. Tough little bastard. A real survivor.

Part of Rick was so lost, hurt and confused, that he wanted to make the COs kill him. But they didn't. Instead, they sprayed him, beat him up, hog-tied, or threw him in a straight-jacket.

"Just kill me for fuck's sake!"

Fate wouldn't let that happen. He began to believe that he was cursed to live. Ghost. An immortal being trapped in an eternity of living hell. Rick didn't give a shit what the correctional officers in Bravo thought of him. He had enough, and didn't shy away about expressing his displeasure with them, and his own life.

"What do you want you cock sucking, punk ass faggot-licking pig?"

None of the officers were immune to the constant berating, and sometimes the entire fourteen members of Bravo would get going at once.

"Cock suckers. Fucking pigs!" Rick tossed an empty shampoo bottle through the open slot in the cell door.

Anything he could do to cause shit he did, from popping his sprinkler and flooding his cell, to throwing his trash under the bottom of the door. With nothing but time on your hands, and no reason to care about anything, it becomes quite natural to occupy yourself with the most disruptive, destructive activities. Some of the guards were cool and didn't take the shit personally but most did everything they could to get back at the disturbers. The morning of April 19, 1996, as Rick was out in the yard, the officers raided his cell for a very non-routine search. Hidden inside an Old Spice deodorant container and wrapped in toilet paper, Rick had kept a few little do-dads, such as a small metal clip, and a spring, nothing that could really amount to anything but that didn't stop them from trying.

"Mr. Watkinson, we're writing you up for a B8…possession, use, or instruction of weapons or escape implements."

Everybody knew the charges were a tad overstated but in this little battle the officers won, and Rick was given ten days of punitive time. Punitive time was harsh. No commissary, reading material, except religious, and no phone calls or visits except from attorneys. Rick was already on so many IDRs that he couldn't do half the shit anyway and barely noticed his ten days of punishment. Three days later he flushed a sheet down his toilet and flooded his cell. Intentionally, just to be a prick.

"Lock him in the showers while we clean up this mess."

When Rick returned to his cell it was empty.

"What the fuck?"

"Don't mess with us Watkinson. We've been patient but we've had enough. You're on dry cell until further notice."

Except for his toilet, the entire cell was empty. No bed, no blankets, no desk, no nothing. They even shut off his fucking water.

"We'll issue you water three times a day at meals," said the officer. "So if you're going to take a shit, I suggest you take it then because any other time, it's just going to sit right in there with you!" He smiled.

"Cocksuckers…"

They dry celled Rick for a week and they hoped maybe he'd settle down, but no such luck. The officers didn't know what to do. Rick continued to be just as much of as asshole as he'd been before. Always kicking and throwing both objects and obscenities at them. Writing him up for every little thing he did was more work than it was worth, so they never ever bothered. They had to try a new tactic. On May 1st, they gradually began giving him back some of his privileges.

"Look, we're releasing some of the IDRs in an effort to calm you down. You can't go on like this. If you keep getting write-ups, you're going to rack up the punitive time, which means no visits or phone calls ever. Now, I'm pretty sure that's not what you want is it?"

Rick missed his phone calls with Amanda and Brenda, and he desperately wanted a visit, to see someone from the outside, and breathe a breath of fresh air. As much as he didn't want to admit it, Rick was vulnerable, he needed the sense of strength the women provided. He needed their light, and he needed their hope.

****

Invulnerability through invisibility – the very essence of what would become Ghost. The more he could disappear and fade into his surroundings, the more successful his night time ventures would be. He became obsessed with finding or using anything that might give him an advantage in the game. It was never about becoming a 'better thief', and even though he stole things, he never even considered himself a real criminal. The fascination was in the lure of being able to go anywhere and do anything he wanted, to be incapable of being found no matter what the circumstances were. That's what gave him the power. That's what he craved. Anytime he had a chance to add tricks and tools, he did. A decent rugged flashlight, a pair of skin-tight tactile gloves, binoculars, rope, surgical taping, knives, tools, and lighters, anything cool that he could imagine some ingenious purpose for.

Most of the stealing Rick had done so far had been from large stores and businesses. As young rebel-headed kids, this was acceptable because they were all part of the Establishment, the Machine. Besides, they all had insurances, were chain stores with millions of dollars and dirty CEOs at the top, so the kids didn't feel bad about ripping them off. They were practically Robin Hood. At least, that's what they told themselves, and how they justified their transgressions. It was different stealing from Joe Blow citizen, and expressly forbidden to steal from amongst your own; that broke the code, the honor system. But theft for revenge didn't fit the code, so when one of Slate's homeboy's asked Rick to pull off a job against another guy he knew, Rick accepted.

"In the garage of the house is a Firebird. I'll give you seventy-five bucks for the hood ornament and then we'll work out a price for whatever tools you can grab. The guy's a dick and I know he'll be real pissed about losing the ornament."

"Deal," said Rick.

Armed with a green army canvas duffel bag, the two drove by a little after one in the morning.

"Looks clear. And you're in luck, the idiot forgot to close the garage door all the way."

The guy parked aways down the street, and silently and slowly, Rick snuck back to the house. For a scrawny almost twelve-year-old, sliding under the gap of the garage was a piece of cake.

"Fuck! Why didn't I bring my flashlight you stupid ass! It's pitch dark in here!" The ambient light spilling under the garage door was barely enough to see the outline of the back of the car, let alone work by. He debated just turning out and giving up but since Rick was Rick, he wasn't easily deterred by a challenge. He had to improvise.

"If I'm fast, I should be able to get away turning on the light. Now I just have to find where the hell it is." Striking a match, he immediately saw the switch on the back wall.

"Bingo!" His initial glance at the ornament, which laid flat on the car hood wasn't promising. "How the hell am I going to get that off without scratching everything?" Fighting to wedge the screwdriver under the emblem, he had to see how the thing was attached so he could get it loose.

"Fuck. Two pegs. This bitch is probably bolted to the inside of the hood. Shit." Rick tried the driver's side door. He needed to pop the hood.

"Shit. It's locked." His eyes scanned the multitude of tools and gadgets hanging from pegboards on the garage walls.

"A hacksaw should do it."

While it wasn't going to be as quiet as he would have liked, he thought he'd better at least give the hacksaw a shot. Slowly and carefully sliding the wire thin blade between the ornament and the hood, he began to move the saw back and forth. The noise was noticeable but not that bad. Suddenly, the wedged screwdriver holding the emblem up gave way and flew into the air, sending the emblem crashing flush against the hood. He managed to catch the screwdriver from smacking against the concrete floor, but he couldn't do a thing to squelch the loud, sharp squeak of the hacksaw. Snatching the duffle bag, he scooted to the edge of the garage door, crouching low, and waited, listening for any signs of movement within the house. Nothing. No sound, no movement. All appeared calm.

With his heart racing against his chest, he moved back to the Firebird to finish the job. Five, ten, fifteen minutes passed. Then twenty, twenty-five, thirty. Finished. Burying the emblem deep in his pants pockets, he dropped the hacksaw into the duffle bag. He knew time was tight, and that he needed to get the hell out of there, but he just couldn't help himself.

"Hmm…what other goodies do we have kicking around here?" He tossed a bunch of wrenches, a hammer, a hex driver kit, and a bunch of other stuff into the bag. "Now what do we have here?" He turned the army green hilted serrated survival knife around in his hand. "Oh this is definitely going home with me!" Instead of throwing it in the duffle bag, he tucked the knife into his waistband. What they didn't know, didn't hurt them. Without turning off the light, Rick slid under the door, pulled the bag though, then walked back towards the car.

"Where the fuck are they?" The car was gone. "Jesus Christ. They couldn't even bother to wait."

No matter, it just meant that he had a shitload of stuff for himself now. After he was a safe distance, he tossed the duffle bag over his shoulders, feeling like fucking Santa Claus. A couple of blocks later, the car pulled up along.

"Why didn't you wait assholes?" said Rick hopping in the back seat.

"We thought you got chicken and bailed man. It was taking so long, we figured you probably got caught."

Rick pulled the ornament out and tossed it between them on the front seat.

Slate slugged his friend. "See man, I told you he'd get it!"

Slate's words made Rick feel unstoppable. He told them the story, then described all the tools and cool shit he'd grabbed, including the knife.

"You guys can have all the tools. I don't want anything for them but I'm keeping the knife."

"Yeah man, no problem. Here's your seventy-five bucks."

Rick didn't even care about the money, his attention fixated on the knife. It looked authentic military. He should have felt bad, stealing from someone who didn't deserve it, especially when that knife could have been a veteran's, passed down to his son or grandson. Rick didn't care, about anything really. Free shit was free shit, and an even bigger rush when such cool shit could be found in a random home. The only lesson he took out of that night was to plan ahead, visualize and walk himself through what he might need. As soon as he was able, he found a small zip-up sheath of hacksaw blades, and added them to his bag of tricks. Anything he could find to make the job easier, to lesson his chance at exposure, and increase his invincibility. No one was going to be able to catch Ghost. He held the power. He held the control.

CHAPTER SEVENTEEN

"I've signed us up for a week of summer camp."

"A week?" said Rick.

"Yes, a week. It's a Christian camp being organized through Bethel Baptist Church. We're all going. I think it'll be good for us to get away as a family and to deepen our connection with God."

A week away in the prime summer months would cost Rick some serious cash and opportunity. Still, there was nothing he could do about it. High up in the hills, the camp lay in a heavily wooded, very natural area, which did appeal to the outdoorsman in Rick. The camp itself was small, with only four cabins, a large bed and breakfast type dining hall, and then up a slight hill, a covered equestrian ring about half a football field in length with stables, an office, and a game room.

When they arrived, all the boys were scuttled into one cabin, the girls in another, and the adults in the others. Each day had a program of scheduled services and prayer groups, as well as activities, just some good wholesome Christian fun. Being a Baptist camp and not an affiliation of Potter's House, the atmosphere was more laid back, happy, and certainly less militant. No speaking in tongues or casting out demons. No pressure, and no being suffocated in the wiles of eternal spiritual warfare. Just a tranquil enjoyment in fellowship and faith. Rick could relax. He felt safe here. No one was looking for him to be anything more than a kid at a camp.

One night all the kids talked the adults into letting them have a combined sleep-over in the game room. Nothing salacious, just a chance to have all the kids together, tell scary stories, and generally goof around.

"With this rain, and thundering and lightning, it's a perfect night for ghost stories," said one of the kids turning off the lights.

"Dude, I have a plan," said Craig whispering at Rick. "Wait a little bit, then make up an excuse to leave…"

"Then I mess around outside and scare the hell out of everyone!"

"Yes. Are you in?"

"Of course," said Rick.

He waited until midway through the first story before he made his announcement. "Yo, I'm just going to get more snacks from the boy's cabin. Be back in a bit."

Nodding and mumbling, the others gave their acknowledgment, and Rick left.

The cold rain against his warm skin quickly left him shivering, but he had a blast scratching on the outside wall, rustling the bushes outside the window, and knocking things over in the barn.

"Oh this is going to be awesome!" Rooting around in the barn, he found a shovel which he proceeded to stick in the ground handle-first. "When the lightning flashes and this bitch lights up, they're going to shit their pants!" Killing himself laughing, his brain flew into overdrive trying to come up with an even scarier stunt. He looked around, scoping out his options.

"I bet I can use that tractor to get on the roof…" In a few leaps, he was up the tractor, and crawling around on the sheet metal roof. "Fuck, how am I going to do this?" Crawling on his stomach, he wormed his way, head-first to the edge of the roof right above the games room window. The roof slant wasn't all that severe, so that even though he didn't have anywhere to anchor his feet, he was still able dangle his upper torso over the edge.

"It's only a ten-foot drop. I've seen worse."

Letting his arms go limp and fall parallel to his head, closing his eyes, he drained all expression from his face in an attempt to appear dead and pale as a cold corpse. He nailed it.

"Holy shit!" someone screamed from inside as a flash of lightning illuminated his image through the window. Screams.

"Holy…fuck…"

"Oh my God…oh my God…oh my God."

Three flashlight beams danced across his face.

One of the guys opened the window. "Rick, dude are you okay?" Rick didn't move a muscle. "It's not safe to hang out there like that and you're freaking out the girls."

"Shit…he's not moving. What the hell is going on?"

Rick's strength was waning and he could feel the metal ledge of the roof scraping against his hips.

"I'm going out there."

"Me too."

The minute the flashlight moved away, Rick made his move and let the rest of his body slide off the roof. Landing on his shoulders, he rolled inwards towards the building, lying flat against the outside wall.

"Oh my God, he just fucking fell! He fucking goddamn fell!" yelled one of the girls.

Amid the terrified girlish screams, the overhead lights flicked back on. But Rick was already gone, snake crawling down the wall away from the game-room and all the way around the backside of the stables.

"Where the hell did he go?" said Craig, the senior member of the search party.

Even he was shocked and confused.

By the time the search party got to the stables, Rick had already hightailed it around the corner and was running around the entire outside perimeter of the equestrian ring. Looping back to the side entrance, he snuck back into the actual riding area, tucking himself in the deep shadows next to the door. Waiting. Waiting for the final triumph, the coup de grace.

"Seriously man," said Craig. "I don't know where the dude went."

Talking loudly and freaking out because they hadn't found a trace of the little ninja, the group returned to the side door, perplexed and muddled. Arielle was the first one through. Rick leapt from the shadows, grabbed her arm, and conjured a blood-curling scream. Arielle screamed like someone was trying to kill her, wind-milling her arms in a furious defence.

"Get off of me!! Get off of me!!"

Craig grabbed the girl and pulled her away, as Rick retreated back into the riding area, his gut about to bust in hysteria.

"You little fucker! You scared me half to death!"

"Dude…that was awesome man."

"Yeah, seriously," said Craig. "Awesome. Little more than what I had planned but cool just the same."

"Well I think he's a little fucker for doing that…"

There was just no pleasing the women in the crowd. Rick didn't care. It was worth it. He'd won and he was proud.

"You looked like a fucking ghost hanging there man."

Ghost. There it was. The name didn't stick quite yet, but that night, the seeds were planted. For as haunted as he was in his own soul, he drank up the power that came from haunting others, and being invisible to a world he felt had forsaken him. Mirroring these great highs, were great lows, always lurking, beneath every smile, behind every laugh, waiting to manifest in their own demonic way.

"Hey, so today we get to try the swing!"

"The swing?" said Rick. "What's the swing?"

"Seriously man? You don't know? C'mon then if you want to try it."

Of course Rick wanted to try it. Did they even know him? Deep into the bush, the boys climbed the path up to the top of the steep hill to the edge of the ravine. Moored to the trunk of a tree was a thick rope with a massive knot on the bottom.

"This is the swing."

Rick peeked his gaze over the edge of the ravine. It was deep, very deep. So deep, that if you fell off that swing, chances are you weren't going to be walking away in one piece. Brain splattering deep.

"They let you swing from this over there?" said Rick, his arm pointing over the ravine.

"Ya of course!"

Those Baptist's were crazy fuckers. One by one, each kid took a turn. Two other kids holding the rope while the rider got on, and then two there to catch him on the way back. Rick eased his way to the edge of the cliff, and looked down into the abyss.

"Jesus," he thought. "That would be messy if someone let go. Like really messy. I wonder how that would feel, lying there, your whole body broken and bleeding, not being able to move. Would you even survive?"

He could see the body lying there. Battered, bruised, crushed. He could see his body lying there. Quiet, still, not moving. All the pain in his life would be gone. Somebody handed him the rope.

"It's your turn dude."

He took it. All he had to do was let go. He'd fall and it would all be over with. All the pain, all the sorrow, and all the anguish in his life would be gone. He only had to let go of the rope. He saw himself lying there at the bottom. Quiet, still, dead. Finally, at peace. He'd never known how truly miserable he was until that moment. He'd never fully realized the hate that filled every inch of his heart, and the deadness that filled his soul.

"He destroyed us. He changed everything. He doesn't love me? Would he even give a fucking shit if I died?"

He readied for the jump; his sweaty palms greasy on the rope. He just had to swing out a little, then let go. Fuck it would be easy. That would show him. Make him feel so fucking guilty for the rest of his life. He destroyed them, so now his eldest son would return the favour and destroy him. So easy. Just let go. Just let go.

Rick took a few steps back. He'd take a run at it. Get out as far as he possibly could. It'd be easier to let go then. His eyes scanned the other kids, all laughing, and full of excitement, full of hope. The swing was just a ride for them. Nothing more. Fuck them. Fuck them all. He'd never felt so detached.

In four strides he was off the edge of the ravine. Soaring. Free. He just had to let go. It'd only hurt for a little bit on impact, and then he'd go blank. He was sure of it. The rope swung further. He had to make a decision. Now. Time stopped. His father, his mother, little Jimmy. His father. If Rick let go, then his father would win. He wouldn't ever have to look Rick in the eye again, knowing what a fucking bastard he'd been. His mother, Jimmy. Who would take care of them? Who would be the man of the house? They relied on him. They needed him.

The rope swung to the apex. He just had to let go. Every inch of him wanted to let go, begged him to let go. Pleaded with him to let go. Momentum brought the edge of the cliff closer. All the kids still laughing and smiling, exhilarated. He would never be one of those kids. He knew that. Something inside of him was different, he felt it then, at eleven years old. He couldn't explain his feelings, he didn't know the why himself. He just knew that deep down inside he was different. He had a darkness that shrouded his entire being, yet his soul burned hot and bright with rage. Why couldn't he handle the divorce? Why did he feel so betrayed? Why did he hate so much? Why all the darkness? Everywhere, all the time. The rope swung back closer to the edge. Now. Let go now.

No. He couldn't. He wouldn't give in. If he let go, then he'd always be that kid that everyone felt sorry for, after the fact. They'd think he was weak, and he wasn't weak. He could deal with shit, he'd been dealing with shit for a long time now. Angels, demons, his father, his mother; whatever came his way. He wasn't a quitter. He didn't take the easy way out. Ever. His dad took the easy way out by leaving, and he was not his father. Not now, not ever. Fuck him. Fuck them all. He'd live, because he was better than that. He'd just continue to tuck all his feelings behind the placid, calm shell he'd carefully constructed. He'd just continue to be Ghost, defiant and unfazed in the face of the storm.

"Fuck man! That was awesome!" said Rick landing his feet on solid ground.

"It's awesome right?"

"Yeah man! That was just the coolest. Never felt better!"

Grinning and brimming with bravado, he strode over to a giant oak tree and plopped down against it. No one would have ever guessed he was about ready to puke his guts out. He hardy slept at all that night. It was everything he could to keep himself from sneaking out of the cabin and disappearing into the night. Into his element. He just wanted the peace and the stillness to combat the swirling in his head. He'd almost let go of the rope. He was close, really close to just letting in go and ending it all. The experience scared him to death, and made him realize how different he was from the other kids. Why did he have to be this way? Parents divorced all the time and kids handled it, they dealt with it. They learned to move on. Rick couldn't move on, and he couldn't let go, and he had no idea why. Still feeling detached and sombre, Rick took the first chance he had the next morning to get away for a bit.

"Can I come with you?" said Bethany.

Although he wanted to be alone, he couldn't say no to Bethany. She was too cute, and the first time he'd laid eyes on her, he felt the tingles of young love.

"Sure, c'mon."

The late morning sun painted the landscape in a bright orange hue, almost as if the world was in a giant halo. Rick led Bethany down the path past the stables and into the sheltered valley, the tall trees acting as an umbrella, as the soft green moss, silenced their footsteps.

"Do you like critters?" said Rick.

"Depends what kind of critters you're talking about?"

Rick took out his small pocket knife and dug into the failing bark of a fallen, massive rotting tree trunk. "These kind of critters," he said holding up a snail on the blade.

"Gross."

"It's not gross. Look at him. I'm not going to hurt him. Look at his shell. That's where they live you know."

Rick was only too happy to impart Bethany with his ecological wisdom, after all, he was a man of the woods. He showed her a newt, and a centipede, and a host of bugs, and they both laughed when a tree frog sprouted across their path.

"Look at him go!" she said.

"Yeah they're fast and can jump like crazy." Spending time with Bethany made him thankful that he decided not to let go of the rope yesterday. It was the small things about her. Her smile, her laugh, the way the freckle on her cheek danced when she talked. The innocence of youthful attraction. Perhaps there was still some goodness left in the world? Maybe you could take all these small moments, add them up, and they'd outweigh all the bad? Was that even possible? Rick didn't know, and he was tired of thinking. In this moment, he just wanted to exist, to be with Bethany, enjoy the woods, and forget about everything else in his life. He relaxed. He let go. He let his guard down.

It happened slowly, as it usually did. The gleam of sunlight had caught his eye in just the right way to enhance the glow of the surroundings. He hadn't expected it, and hadn't even felt any of the eerie forewarnings. His mind blurred, then snapped with clarity, and the other world opened. Illuminated with a light yellowish aura, everything buzzed with life and energy. Patterns of energy blossomed out from every nook and cranny, as the sharp lines of perception failed and existence became a blur of life. Distinct shapes dissipated into varying densities of energy, lost in radiating pools of force. He'd never seen anything like it. The life force stopped his breath, the beauty of the forest captivating every bit of his own energy. Light. Life. Every other experience he'd ever had, had always been in the darkness, or in the shadows. This was showing him light, showing him life. There were no demons lurking, the forest pure as the innocence of Bethany's heart. He looked at her. The sunlight caught her hair as she moved slightly. Then he saw her.

The beauty of the forest paled in comparison to the beauty of the energy radiating from the girl. Flesh and blood seemed to melt into varying degrees of coloured resonance. The very form of her body glowed, the hues of her spirit exploding in various shades of pink, yellow, and gold. Mini-suns had replaced her eyes, orbs emitting the brightest pulse. The yellows and greens of the surrounding flora mixed with her own life-force, melding in harmony. She was beauty. She was peace. She represented everything good and innocent in the world. Bethany was hope.

Ten heartbeats later, it was gone.

"Are you okay?" she asked.

"Yes. I'm fine." As his vision returned, and the forest began to regain its shape, his soul was touched by the sheer beauty and tranquility of the moment.

"It's so peaceful here isn't it? So beautiful."

"Yes, it is," he answered.

Was this a sign from God? Up until this point, Rick believed that his second sight could only be used to detect the forces of evil that dwelt in the dark. But there had been no darkness in the forest. He'd stood in broad daylight, in an environment outside of any spiritual influence, good or evil, with his 'eye' in full bloom. How? Did all things, including nature, stand in the etheric 'other world'? Did nature stand outside of the normal war fought between the light and the dark? It had been beautiful, splendorous, unclaimed – and simply was. That he could see nature's glory by itself and that his gift wasn't only to see spirits was the most refreshing thing in the world to him. Rick didn't know whether God had allowed it as a breath of fresh air, especially after the heaviness of yesterday, or if his gift was really a gift that he possessed irrespective of God's will. The ripples and echoes emanating from the surrounding organic life brought him to a peace and beauty he'd never thought was possible.

Moved by the passion of the moment, Rick overcame his shyness, reached over and met Bethany's lips. Short and sweet. Innocence at its utmost. They giggled.

"We'd better get back," said Rick reaching out his hand. "It's almost time for lunch."

She smiled, taking his hand in hers. It was all just a crapshoot. Good days, bad days, light, dark, evil, innocence. All he could do was muddle through the muck, and hope for the best. Feeling the warmth of Bethany's hand, he knew that today was a good day, and he was going to hang onto every moment for as long as he could.

****

"Hey Watkinson," said the guard. "You got some visitor's."

"Seriously?"

"Yep. C'mon over. You know the drill."

Too excited about the thought of seeing 'normal people', Rick didn't even wiggle as the officer slapped on the full leg-irons and waist chains over his red 'MAX' jumpsuit.

"Let's go, up to booking."

When he saw the two beautiful women, his heart jumped. "Amanda! Brenda! Oh my God! I'm so happy to see you!" The officer led them all to a small booking booth, right under the watchful eyes of Master Control. "Thank you for coming. Seriously, it's so good to see some friendly faces."

"I didn't think they'd have you all chained up like that?" said Amanda. "Can't they let you go? You're not going to hurt us!"

"I wish," said Rick. "It's okay. It's just standard procedure. It's fine."

"No it's not fine," said Amanda.

Brenda squeezed the hand of her daughter. "How are you doing Rick? We were worried when we didn't hear from you for such a long time. Is all that over with now?"

"I hope so but you never know what's going to happen in here."

"One day at a time then Rick. One day at a time. We believe in you and we have great faith in you. You just have to hang in there. We're not going anywhere."

Brenda always seemed to know exactly what to say. They didn't see Rick as a murderer, or some sort of evil terror, they saw him as a person who needed just as much love and support as anyone else. They cared about him. For Brenda, Rick was a wounded bird. From her own life experience, she knew that sometimes things happened in life that pulled you off one path, and set you on another. What Rick did was horrible, but in her mind, there had to be a reason, there had to be some background. His life didn't just start at chapter twelve, 'Murder's Parents', it had to begin at chapter one, and she was willing to open her heart and open her understanding to this clearly troubled teen. It was the least she could do. She knew in her heart that it was the right thing to do.

"Wrap it up people," said the guard sticking his head through the door.

"Just a few minutes more man, please?" said Rick.

"Sorry. Rules are rules."

"It's okay Rick," said Amanda. "We'll come back right Mom?"

"Of course we'll be back!"

"It's your birthday soon right?" said Amanda.

"Yeah in a few weeks," said Rick.

"Well we'll be back for that," said Brenda.

"I'd like that."

"Let's go Watkinson," said the guard.

"Okay, well I gotta go. Thank you both so much for coming. Honestly, you have no idea what this meant to me. I'll call you as soon as I can…and again.

Thank you."

Amanda and Brenda truly had no idea what their visit meant to Rick. After so much time in the Hole with no communication, and the stale stench of loneliness fogging every thought and action, just seeing the ladies gave him a lifeline, a small glimpse into an increasingly foreign and forgotten world.

Rick almost forgot it was even his birthday. Prison twists all sense of time and occasion. Routine becomes the norm, and the things that once mattered get shoved to the back burner. Or maybe it wasn't that he forgot his birthday and more like he didn't want to remember. He didn't imagine the DOC would be pushing a cake through his tray hole anytime soon. There wasn't a whole lot a person could send someone in prison gift-wise, maybe a card, a magazine or book, or a deposit to their commissary account.

"I hope you like it," said Amanda with a smile.

Rick tore back the paper. "The Tibetan Book of Living and Dying?"

"It's written by Soygal Rinpoche," said Brenda, "and it's about helping people through death and how to truly value life. It's all about his own experiences, and offers some great wisdom and insight. Maybe give you a bit of a different perspective on things."

"Thank you both. I truly love it."

The book changed Rick. Most of his Eastern studies and interest up to that point had been from a martial arts angle, so being introduced to Taoism and now Buddhism, was something new and extremely interesting. He'd never realized how different 'Eastern' and 'Western' thought were in their approach and in their messages, with Eastern thinking being much more holistic, and less selfish or "I" based. The messages resonated, and reading and re-reading 'The Tibetan Book of Living and Dying' and 'The Spirit of Tao' that Tremor had given him before, slowly began to crack the steely casing of his ghost persona, enlightening the darkness, banishing it back to the underworld.

His mother of course sent him a black leather Bible, his full name gilded in gold on the lower right hand corner. Just what he wanted. The Bible came complete with essays, references, and a short concordance. She'd even highlighted some Bible verses.

> *"The LORD looked down from his sanctuary on high, from heaven he viewed the earth, to hear the groans of the prisoners and release those condemned to death."*[3]

"The Lord will always be there for you Rick. You just need to call upon him and he'll be there. God hears you, and he WILL free you someday if you continue to put your faith in him."

[3] Psalm 102:19-21.

For the last three years, Rick had deliberately pushed God away, so he wasn't just going to throw up his hands and beg for forgiveness. God hadn't helped in the past, why bother now?

"Just give him a chance Rick"

"Thomas said to Him, 'Lord, we do not know where you are going, so how can we know the way?' Jesus said to him, 'I am the way, and the truth, and the life; no one comes to the Father but through Me.'"[4]

It's not like he didn't have the time to read. For his mother's sake, he'd give the Lord one last chance. He'd commit to reading the Bible cover to cover, with an open mind; it was the only way he could decide for himself whether or not it was all bullshit. No pressure from outside sources, no one looking over his shoulder wondering what he thought of this and what he thought of that. Just him and his conscience. Then, and only then, would he decide if he wanted to continue serving the Lord. Sometimes he read for a couple of hours a day, and sometimes he'd binge and get lost in the stories and history for the whole day. Much of it had already been drilled into his head, but there were large chunks he never knew.

'Sons of God' coming down and mating with the 'daughters of men'? Giants? 'Ashura' being a consort with temples next to Jehovah? The river Kidron running red with the blood of her priestesses? Genocide against the Caananites? Abraham being from the Chaldeans and worshipping in groves? These were things he'd never been taught in Sunday School. As he read, his list of discontent grew, and he soon realized there was a whole lot he didn't know about the Bible and history according to God, things he would have to investigate for himself before he could ever call himself a Christian again.

What struck him most was the ignorance of modern Christians, people like his mother. Sure they knew all the popular stories that the preachers told again and again, and they could quote a Bible verse to fit every situation.

"That scripture is 'God-breathed' and shouldn't be questioned."

If that was the case, then how do they explain a God who says, 'Thou shalt not murder' and then orders the mass executions and genocide of entire tribes? Again and again and again.

"Now go and smite Amalek, and utterly destroy all that they have, and spare them not; but slay both man and woman, infant and suckling, ox and sheep, camel and ass"[5] *"And they utterly destroyed all that was in the city, both man and woman, young and old, and ox, and sheep, and ass, with the edge of the sword"*[6]

[4] John 14:5-6.
[5] 1 Samuel 15:3
[6] Joshua 6:21

"And we utterly destroyed them, as we did unto Sihon king of Heshbon, utterly destroying the men, women, and children, of every city"[7]

How could that be? Unless God meant, 'Thou shall not murder unless I sanction it and say it's okay.' God forbid all other idols and says temples are not even necessary to love and walk with him yet, he has a sacred idol built to himself and one of the grandest temple designs ever known. Things just didn't add up. It took Rick almost three months to get through the entire Bible, and all he had to show for it was a shitload of questions, and notes that needed further explanation. He couldn't blindly commit, not until he had answers. His mother would just have to keep praying for his soul on her own.

"Hey youngster. We heard it's your birthday today, so we got you a little something. Meet us in the yard at rec…and bring a battery and some staples."

Rick smiled at the other prisoner. A battery and staples could only mean one thing. They'd gotten him a smoke. The boys had gotten together and rolled Rick a giant kick ass smoke. They'd even thought to write Happy Birthday down the side.

"For you youngster. Sorry we don't have a light. You're going to have to see if you can spark one from the battery and staples."

It took him a sec to get it going but before long, it was glowing bright. He offered it around.

"That's all you youngster, enjoy that shit."

And enjoy it he did. That first inhale sucked every ounce of oxygen out of his lungs. Glorious. A cloudy day, Rick stood up against the window next to the stairway that ran inside the mod. Another deep inhale, his thoughts lost in the clouds.

"Oh shit," someone mumbled. Another pointed to the window. Rick turned his head, exhaling a big smoke ring against the glass, right in the face of the guard standing on the other side. The guard looked awfully pleased, his hands on his hips, the scowl turning the corner from his top to bottom lip. Knowing he was fucked one way or the other, Rick tipped the cigarette towards him in a mock salute.

"What's up?"

"Watkinson! Put that damn thing out!"

Rick took another long drag. "Yeah, I'll get right on that." He knew he had time. He was in a prison yard with seven or eight of the most dangerous felons in Alaska, and the guards couldn't come in the yard without restraining and escorting them one at a time. Rick calmly finished his birthday cigarette, then dropped the evidence down the small drain. By the time he was finished, the

[7] Deuteronomy 3:6.

squad had been assembled.

"Okay, which one of you assholes was smoking?" screamed Sgt. Robinson, waving his can of mace as he stormed out into the yard.

"No idea man."

"Don't know what you're talking about."

"No one smoking out here."

The boys had Rick's back.

"It was Watkinson," said the original guard.

"Me?" said Rick. "You're blind man. I think you're mistaken."

"Fine," said Sgt. Robinson. "If you're not going to talk, then line up. I want to smell your breath on the way in."

"You sure about that man?" someone laughed. "That's just nasty!"

No way Rick was getting out of this one.

"Write Watkinson up for an E4, smoking where prohibited, and a C7, possession, use, or introduction of contraband."

"Put it on the tab," laughed Rick. What did he care? He was already facing 198 total years. Fuck them. It was his seventeenth birthday, and he'd enjoyed his present.

Later that day he'd tried to call his mom but no one answered, which was strange because they knew it was his birthday, and her and Jimmy knew he'd be calling. They had to be there, they just didn't bother to pick up.

"Shit happens, I guess."

He tried again the next day.

"I'm so sorry I didn't pick up yesterday Rick. I just…just couldn't talk to you. I didn't want to answer the phone because your Grandpa Barnes died yesterday…and I wasn't ready to tell you."

Complete numbness.

"He died of heart failure Rick. I…I just…I'm so sorry. And on your birthday too. Almost the exact time you were born. Just four minutes earlier. Quite eerie actually."

Rick dropped the phone on the receiver. It was his fault. He'd killed his grandpa. This was the Lord's punishment for having taken two lives. He could deal with the prison sentence, but he couldn't deal with the guilt that his actions had broken his grandpa's heart – literally. Captain William Roy Barnes, USN retired was the only other male figure in is life that Rick looked up to as a hero and a mentor. Rick became the son William never had, someone to walk in his footsteps or at least bear a legacy that he could be proud of. Grandpa Barnes knew Rick had eventually planned to join the Navy, and Rick wanted nothing more than for his grandpa to be proud of him. And then Rick threw it all away. Rick was his hope, and Rick had failed him. Barnes was a war hero, awarded the

Silver Star, and the highest medal of honour a non-citizen of France can receive during the Second World War. His grandson? A killer.

"He lost his heart because of me."

The whole thing might seem rather irrational, fanciful, and even a little self-important to those on the outside, but for Rick, the blame was real, it was concrete. Why else would he have died on his birthday? A coincidence? Hardly. The Lord was laughing at him. Sneering even.

"See what happens? See what you've done? You killed your father, you killed Rosemary, and now you've killed your beloved grandfather."

"Beloved, never avenge yourselves, but leave it to the wrath of God, for it is written, "Vengeance is mine, I will repay, says the Lord"'.[8]

The Lord re-paid Rick all right. The anchor of guilt is enough to keep any soul weighed in the void of darkness. No matter what Rick did to better himself in the present or the future, to try and right the ship, that anchor would never be lifted, he could never atone for his father, Rosemary, and now his Grandpa Barnes. A few weeks later, a Coast Guard cutter took the ashes out to sea off the coast of Oregon. Rick wasn't there to see him off, but his mother took a photograph of the ashes being poured into the Pacific Ocean. The ashes floated on the water, then disappeared into the sea. He carries the photograph still.

"Alas, he's gone, he slumbers 'neath the seas.
I hope he's gone to heaven. God be pleased.
Mourn not for him, he's better off, he sails with more divine.
Faithful in duty, contented with his mind,
Died lamented by those he left behind.'[9]

Haunted by betrayal and sorrow, hatred and demons, was he supposed to look to a God who only loved you if you were his faithful slave? As hard as he tried, Rick could never wipe the blood stains from his hands or from his heart. The remorse was real. The guilt too much. He wanted to die – to just give in to the anchor and sink to the bottom of the sea.

[8] Romans 12:19.
[9] Taken from an old Naval poem

CHAPTER EIGHTEEN

The week at summer camp introduced Rick to a God filled with love, laughter, and hope; quite a contrast from the inherent hell of the Antichrist and the Four Horsemen of the Apocalypse. A breath of fresh air, the camp gave him hope in a Christianity that was rewarding and happy, a reason to hang on. But it didn't last. The minute he returned, it was right back to the grindstone and donning the armour against the devil. His carefree childish gait gave way to the languor of oppression, his heart and head heavy with the weight of lost souls. They were his responsibility, and he knew it. He could see. He could save them, even if he couldn't save himself. This juxtaposition agonized the boy. Made him sick to his stomach. The pressure unrelenting. Maybe it was his soul for all the others?

In the midst of his perennial confusion, his 'gift' hit full bloom, spiralling out of control. At the grocery store, driving in the car, school, the public pool, anywhere and everywhere, it didn't matter, the other side refused to lie dormant. He didn't understand the why or the how. All he wondered was why me? And how come? Being constantly exhausted didn't help. The minute he let his consciousness slip, the spiritual world sprung alive with energy, spirits, demons, vibrations, auras, and whatever else lay beneath the surface of our understanding. The world would fade, sharpness would turn into jagged fuzziness, then a re-focus to the other world. The demon with its claws dug into the guy buying milk at the corner store, or the old man waking with a spirt by his side, almost as if he was walking his dog. Did they even know they had company or were they oblivious? Rick wasn't oblivious. The extreme energy from the sounds, lights, people, and mechanisms cascaded and bombarded everything, yet no one seemed to know. And if they didn't know, then how the hell were they supposed to care?

Rick cared. He cared too much. Took everything to heart. It was as if the entity that attached itself to the unknowing soul was a direct reflection of their own inner pool of madness. He could see those drowning in their sorrow, their parasite dull and slothful; an embodiment of their own debilitating depression. People filled with malice and hatred had a being seemingly very alert and aggressive, always on the watch, always on the prowl. Many of the beings he saw walked alone, and just 'followed', feeding and gaining strength from whatever misfortune they could find. With no way to shut the other world out, Rick felt trapped in the middle, still a member of the land of the living but able to see and witness a sub-level of a normally blind existence.

He began to hate public places, or anywhere with crowds or a lot of pedestrian traffic, preferring the solitude of his own aloneness, withdrawing even further into his protective shell. Not only did the night become a freedom for him, but it became a time of peace, a time when he could be alone and wander through the world without having to witness all the horrors in it. He tired of trying to reason it out. Why had God given him this 'gift'? Rick truly believed that God wanted him to see and witness all these things. For what purpose? So he knew just how fucked up everything really was? Just how lost the world really is? There was no way he could save everyone, and there was no way one little warrior for Christ was going to stand up to all the evil in the world. Is that what God expected? Or was he just the reality check? The person who could confirm to all the believers that the war was real, and that the good guys were getting their asses kicked.

"Why is the world filled with such evil Mom? Why can I only see demons and bad things? Isn't there supposed to be angels? How come I never see those? Is there even any good in the world?"

"Mankind has turned its back on God, and because people just keep rejecting His Will and Word, Satan was able to gain an increasing foothold on earth. Think back to the Garden of Eden and the First Sin. Man chose to defy God, and was shunned from the perfection of the Garden. Then there was Sodom and Gomorrah. The list goes on and on. Look at all the examples from the Old Testament where God would punish those who turned from His light. They never listened, and they never learned, so they had to pay. Then, he gave his son Jesus to show us the path to redemption and to give us a way to be saved. We must embrace him, that's our only option. Stay with the light, or be condemned to hell. It's simple really."

"So if you don't find Jesus, then there is no hope?"

"Yes. The darkness can only be lifted if we rid the world of the wiles of the Devil and turn back to God. Put it this way. When it's dark in a room at night, what's the first thing you do?"

"Turn on the light?"

"Right! You turn on the light and the darkness goes away. So if you let Jesus, the Light, into your life, then the darkness will go away."

But Rick loved the darkness. He craved it. He did everything in his power to roam in the darkness as much as he could. The light only brought a world he didn't understand, and a world he didn't want to live in. He was fucked.

"See Rick. I think in a way, God has allowed Satan an increasing presence on this earth. He wants his faithful to be strong and tested, so that when the end comes and Revelations begins, we, the faithful, will be ready and battle trained. With our help, Christ will triumph as he leads the Armies of God over the Prince of Darkness. In the meantime, we are the resistance, the persecuted, who strive to uphold God's Will in a world where everyone else had shunned it. And your incredible gift is proof itself of God's wondrous powers!"

It all made sense. Rick never doubted the existence or power of God. And all the evil and sin in the world was proof of how mankind had turned their backs on God. No one really cared about God anymore. People went to church on Sunday's because that was the thing to do. Asking them to be 'good Christians' the rest of the week was a little more than they were willing to give. They didn't really believe there was a war going on, and people who believed in 'speaking in tongues', spiritual healing, and 24/7 for Christ, were fucked up zealots. They didn't see the danger like Brenda and her cohorts did. They didn't feel the impending doom. They just went about their merry lives oblivious to it all.

Rick could only dream of such an existence. The misery and depravity seeped into every facet of his existence. Not only did he live in a broken home, and have a father who betrayed and destroyed their family, he lived in a world where he was completely surrounded by the same evil and wickedness that caused his father's betrayal in the first place. Rick couldn't escape the evil or the misery, and the more he tried to reason everything, the more he fell into deep depression. There was no help, nowhere to turn. His father would just tell him to 'man-up' and don't be a baby, and his mother would just tell him to pray harder. They didn't understand, didn't see how far he'd fallen, or maybe they just didn't care, both wrapped up in their own issues.

Exhaustion took hold. He didn't give a rats-ass about school, instead, living for the moment he could sneak into the darkness and his freedom. There'd be times he didn't make it back to the house until four in the morning, then spend the rest of the day in jumbled, groggy haze. And the longer he stayed in a haze, the more his gift ran wild, and the more his gift ran wild, the further he sunk into the pit.

"Why is he doing this to me? What does he want me to see?"

With no true guidance, the boy would make some far-off conclusions that only reinforced his negativity and false perspective of the whole thing. He sank deeper. The severe depression, introverted mind, exhaustion from lack of sleep, and the spiritual world-view only helped to facilitate the gift, and in combination with the emotions he was experiencing, and the way he was encouraged to use it, it's no wonder how quickly the gift spiralled out of control. What he didn't realize, and wouldn't realize until long after it was already too late, was just how close to the edge his gift had pushed him. He was dangling, and no one was there to throw him a rope.

"I think you're really going to enjoy this book Rick. It's a bit frightening and goes into quite a bit of detail but I think you're old enough and spiritually strong enough to handle it."

"A Divine Revelation of Hell."

"It's about a woman who says God called to her and had actually given her a guided tour of Heaven and Hell."

"Are you serious?"

"Yes," said Brenda. "It was quite an experience as you can imagine."

Rick couldn't put the book down. He could totally commiserate with the author, Mary K Baxter. God had chosen her to see things as well!

I will try to describe the looks of these evil beings. The one speaking was very large, about the size of a full-grown grizzly bear, brown in color, with a head like a bat and eyes that were set very far back into a hairy face. Hairy arms fell to his sides, and fangs came out of the hair on his face. Another one was small like a monkey with very long arms and with hair all over his body. His face was tiny, and he had a pointed nose. I could see no eyes on him anywhere. Still another had a large head, large ears and a long tail, while yet one more was as large as a horse and had smooth skin. The sight of these demons and evil spirits, and the terrible odor that came from them, made me sick to my stomach. Everywhere I looked were demons and devils. The biggest of these demons, I learned from the Lord, were getting their orders straight from Satan[10]

Her vivid descriptions resonated with his impressionable mind. He had seen these things too in one form or another. The sights, smells, heat and fear she felt, Rick had felt. Her experiences were real, and for him it was a relief that he was not alone. Every step she took, he took. Every sight she saw, he saw. Hanging off every word, he feared at any moment his own Third Eye would open, and he too would be taken to Hell in his dreams. The torture, torment, punishment, and misery. There was no hope.

We came to the next pit. Inside this pit, which was the same size as the other one, was another skeleton form. A man's voice cried from the pit, saying, "Lord, have mercy on me!" Only when they spoke could I tell whether the soul was a man or woman. Great wailing sobs came from this man. "I'm so sorry, Jesus. Forgive me. Take me out of here. I have been in this place of torment for years. I beg You, let me out!" Great sobs shook his skeletal frame as he begged, "Please, Jesus, let me out!" I looked at Jesus and saw that He too was crying. "Lord Jesus," the man cried out from the burning pit, "haven't I suffered enough for my sins? It has been forty years since my death."

Jesus said, "It is written, 'The just shall live by faith!' All mockers and unbelievers shall have their part way, but you would not listen to them. You laughed at them and refused the gospel. Even though I died on a cross for you, you mocked Me and would not repent of your sins. My Father gave you many opportunities to be saved. If only you had listened!" Jesus wept. "I know, Lord, I know!" the man cried. "But I repent now."

[10] Excerpt taken from Chapter 3 of "A Divine Revelation of Hell" by Mary K. Baxter

"It is too late," said Jesus. "Judgment is set."[11]

The deepest and harshest torments were dealt to those who had loved the Lord, but then turned away. God had given them his forgiveness, yet they refused to repent. God would show no mercy.

When she was a young woman, I called her, but she continued to do evil. She did many wrongs, yet I would have forgiven her if she had come to Me. Satan entered into her, and she grew bitter and would not forgive others. She went to church just to get men. She found them and seduced them. If she had only come to Me, her sins would all have been washed away by My blood. Part of her wanted to serve Me, but you cannot serve God and Satan at the same time. Every person must make a choice as to whom they will serve."[12]

Rick had a personal relationship with God, yet he knew there was darkness inside of him, and worst of all, he liked doing what he wasn't supposed to do.

They loved darkness rather than light[13].

Did Rick love darkness rather than the light? The sneaking out, stealing, and getting away with all the things he wasn't supposed to do. That was his pleasure. God loved the world. Rick had grown to hate it. Was he already making a subconscious choice to serve Satan over God? No. He loved God. He did. Fuck he was confused.

Wasn't God supposed to reward his faithful? Why had he rewarded him with a traitor for a father and a shattered home? Why had God subjected him to this suffering and sorrow if he was supposed to be his chosen warrior?"

Jesus said, "My child, in My name, evil has to flee. Put on the whole armor of God that you may be able to stand in the evil day, and having done all, to stand.[14]

He had done everything God had asked of him. Yet, if he was being truly honest with himself, he had to question why he liked to sin so much. He liked the darkness, he liked sin, and he didn't want to have to answer to anybody, even God. Would he spend his entire life knowing and seeing what others could not? Fighting in this spiritual warfare, only to have his soul judged too corrupt in the end? Would it be his mangy flesh dripping from his skeleton as he burned in the Lake of Fire? Did he even fucking care anymore?

You are lost in this place of torment. There is no way out of here.[15]

There it was in black and white. There is no way out. So lost in his own sorrow and depression, the last thing he cared about was what God wanted or what was going to happen when he died. He already felt dead, so really what was the difference? His hell was now.

[11] Excerpt taken from Chapter 4 of "A Divine Revelation of Hell" by Mary K. Baxter
[12] Excerpt taken from Chapter 3 of "A Divine Revelation of Hell" by Mary K. Baxter
[13] Excerpt taken from Chapter 8 of "A Divine Revelation of Hell" by Mary K. Baxter
[14] Excerpt taken from Chapter 17 of "A Divine Revelation of Hell" by Mary K. Baxter
[15] Excerpt taken from Chapter 10 of "A Divine Revelation of Hell" by Mary K. Baxter

You are lost in this place of torment. There is no way out of here.

Why would God give him this gift, expect him to fight in his name, yet punish him and rip his family apart? Why would God give him a soul that loved so much to dwell in the night, yet demand he walk only in His light? It made no sense. Was he, at twelve years old, expected to serve some 'higher purpose' while bearing a burden of eternal sorrow that most mortals couldn't shoulder? Was he a martyr? That's how he felt, and there certainly wasn't anyone telling him different or guiding him down a different path. He didn't find out until years later that "A Divine Revelation of Hell" was just a bunch of made-up Christian propaganda horse-shit – a fact that infuriated him and drove him even deeper into his depression. His mother had presented the book like it was gospel, and the words had a profound impact on his life at the time. Then it turned out to be a lie. Just like his father's love for his mother. Just like his father's love for him. It was all just a fucking lie. A big fat fucking lie.

He accepted his fate. It was the only thing he could do. Even after reading the book, he knew he just wasn't going to be miraculously scared straight. He was already lost, already damned. His only hope was that maybe the Lord would take pity on him for the burdens he carried, and that Heaven would find a place. God would either show favour to him or throw him away. Regardless of what he chose, God couldn't magically erase the burdens Rick bore, the sorrow or emptiness he felt, or the fact that he had to be a ghost. Hatred itself was a sin, yet no matter how many times Rick prayed, God couldn't or wouldn't erase the hatred the boy felt in his heart for his own father.

"Pray for forgiveness," said his mother. "The strength to forgive him."

"Why?" thought Rick. "Why should I forgive him? Why should he get to be happy and prosperous in life while we're cold and miserable? Why should I forgive him for his adultery and betrayal when, unless he gave his life to God, the Lord wasn't going to forgive him either?"

All reading "A Divine Revelation of Hell" did was convince Rick that he was truly damned, and that he'd always been damned. The Lord knew all of it before it ever happened. He'd planned the whole thing from the very beginning.

"Yes, we have free will," said Brenda, "but God knows the outcome, and has known from the beginning. God is the alpha and the omega. He sets everything in motion according to His Will."

"So he knew that my father was going to rip the family apart," thought Rick. "He knew I would end up with this gift, and he knew I would see all of these things and be tormented in my mind and heart? He knew I would suffer this way?"

"Everything is all in accordance to God's Will and higher plan. Why do you ask Rick?"

He couldn't answer, and the fact that his own mother had no insight into his emotional state was troubling. A child isn't self-aware enough to realize the warning signs of withdrawal and introversion. But a parent is, or at least should be if they're paying attention. Rick was able to communicate and socialize well enough, but by this point, he was so trapped inside himself, that he was buried alive and gasping for air. His exhaustion, his preference for being alone, his failing grades, his dismissal of life in general. The condemnation. The signs were there. He needed help. He needed guidance. All he got was that he needed to pray. He was tired of praying. God didn't give a shit anyways. His faith was falling, and it was falling fast.

****

"I deserve the Hell that awaits," said Rick smacking his towel against the side of his desk. "First, I kill my father and Rosemary, now Grandpa Barnes dies. Who the fuck is next?"

It was all on his shoulders. Sure Grandpa Barnes was 83 and had lived a good life, but did he have to die on Rick's birthday? It felt like some cruel deliberate joke. Prison would be the least of his punishment. Guilt. Regret. More guilt. Poison. That's what he felt like. Poison. Would the dominoes continue to fall? How many lives had he destroyed? How many sons and daughters, sisters and brothers, grandchildren now had to grow old without their loved ones in their life because of him and what he did? The bricks of guilt built a tower of regret. He couldn't escape the thoughts. He couldn't escape how he felt.

"Look at what you've done."

Tangible in his own psyche, the guilt and the fear shrouded everyone he ever knew or loved. Who would be next? This wasn't just some fanciful fascination, Rick truly believed Death had hitched its smarmy tentacles into his backside, following every move he made, waiting to hack down anyone he loved. Add to the total. Increase the carnage. Add more bricks to the tower of regret. Living became a chore. He couldn't risk anyone else being hurt. The only way to end it all would be to end his life. Right now. If he were dead, then no one else would ever have to suffer for his debt in life. He could go to whatever Hell awaited him, and the punishment would be his and his alone. No more suffering for anyone. He couldn't stop the pain he'd already caused but at least he wouldn't be responsible for any new pain. He'd promised Amy he'd never take his own life. Damn it.

"Why the FUCK did I not make the cops shoot me when I had the chance! All I had to do was run. They were practically begging me to run. Jesus. It would have stopped."

He could still make them. It was possible. He just had to think of a way. Scenarios ripped through his brain like fire. He would run. No, they'd just catch him before he could make it up the fence. He could try and hurt someone. No, he didn't want to cause any more pain to anyone, even the guards. None of the things he thought of would get him killed, they'd only get him sent right back to Mike Mod, although this time he'd be strapped to a board and pumped full of drugs.

"No fucking way."

That wasn't enough punishment. Living in a chemically induced stupor, would alleviate any of the pain and suffering he felt, and that couldn't happen.

"I need to suffer. I need…no…I deserve to die. Amy would just have to understand. She'd get over it. I'll just kill myself." He slammed his fist against the wall. "Fuck that! I won't be a fucking coward! A killer and a coward? No fucking way. Jesus Christ!"

Weeks passed. The internal war raged. How does one make peace with, and at the same time stomach life when it's not something you deserve?

"As I walk the rain is my temple, the ocean my altar, the lakes and bays my sacred grounds. Sacrifice is my Way, pain restores my Soul, taking it from others, my happiness and fulfillment."

Rick set the pencil down beside the freshly written words on the paper. He'd always instinctively equated water with emotion, and rain with sorrow. Buddha taught him of 'samsara' the ocean of suffering. The sense of drowning in his own head had permeated his entire life, so why should it stop now? Death, drugs, meds, they were all an escape from suffering. In order to make peace with his life, he had to suffer, there was no other choice. You don't just take someone's life and be okay with that. You don't just cause the level of pain and loss that he did without having to answer for it in some way – within yourself. Society would see that he suffered behind bars, but he was the only one who could ensure that he would suffer within his own soul. That is the only way he could reconcile living. He felt the burden of his guilt, and he took it seriously. If that's what crushed him in the end, then that's what would have to happen.

God became a symbol of his past transgressions, and in his place, he worshipped a new Goddess. The Goddess of Suffering. He would deliberately seek out suffering in all its most potent forms and worship fervently at Her altar. She would be the one he served and sought after, the One his very soul belonged to. In everything he did, he decided he would take the harder road, and would purposely seek out pain and hardship, never shying away from physical or emotional hurt. And in this suffering, in belonging to Her, he would find his redemption. And in his redemption, he would honour the ones whose lives he had cost. There would be no coward's way out. Never. He would honour his father, he would honour what he had taken from Rosemary and her family, and he would honour the life of his Grandpa. All this would be accomplished by forcing himself to live, to suffer, to sacrifice, and most important of all, to die a good man.

Rick knew there really was no true redemption for what he had done, nothing that could bring the three of them back. All he wanted, at the end of the day when he was dead and buried, was to be able to look his father and grandpa in the eye.

"We're proud of you Rick. Proud of the man you've become."

It would all be worth it then. Every hardship, every ounce of suffering would have meaning. Finding meaning in his own life was only part of the redemption process. He had taken three lives, so in return, he somehow had to save three lives. He owed the world three. An eye for an eye. It didn't matter how he saved them, physically, emotionally, or spiritually, he just had to save them. A sacred debt he must repay.

After weeks of intense self-reflection, on June 6, 1996, sixty-one years after his Grandpa joined the Navy, and fifty-two years after he'd participated in the D-Day invasion off the coast of France, Rick made the decision. He would live, he would suffer and sacrifice, and repay his sacred debt to the world. And he made a promise, the single most important promise of his life.

"Dad, Grandpa Barnes. When I die, you both will be able to look me in the eye and tell me you're proud of me. I make that promise now, and it's a promise that I always intend to keep. I have wronged you both. I know that. And I am sorry…more than either of you will ever know. I take full blame for what happened, and I promise I will spend the rest of my life making it up to you, and honouring you both."

In that moment, after uttering those words, Rick felt a sense of rebirth. He would never totally be able to put the past behind him, but the day signalled the beginning of a life-long journey, a journey through which he would seek to find the real road to the only thing that truly mattered – redemption.

CHAPTER NINETEEN

Rick first laid eyes on Strom during their sixth-grade choir class. Rick loved music, especially the new Fender Strat electric guitar that he'd gotten for his twelfth birthday, but choir class was for girls and sissies. Strom felt the same way. A slight kid with dusty brown hair, his brown eyes shone with a mischievous glow. In those eyes, Rick saw a kindred spirit, someone who didn't give a fuck about authority, and too stupid to be scared of anything. Like Rick, Strom was a survivor, coming from a broken home, his parents recently splitting. They both loved the woods, and more importantly, they both loved the night.

Strom lived across town, so both boys spent a great deal of time trekking on their bikes, finding excuses to get together. Strom had a buddy they called 'Cajun' because of his apparent family history, although no one really knew if Cajun really was Cajun or if he just liked to shoot the shit. Cajun lived much closer, not far from Bethel Baptist Church, so his house frequently became the meet up spot. He didn't have as much freedom as Strom and Rick, and Rick felt that Cajun was always a little envious. His parents were in a happy, stable relationship, and he couldn't quite relate to how Strom and Rick were feeling. His dad was also a State Trooper, not exactly ideal for a son hanging around with a couple of adolescent hooligans. Strom lived with his mother, who was frequently gone, and really didn't give a shit what he did. Another bonus.

"Hey Mom, can I stay at Strom's tonight?"

"Will his mother be home?"

"Oh sure. You really think she'd leave us alone all night?" The laughter was about ready to pop.

"Alright then. Go ahead."

It'd only taken the boys two or three nights of sneaking out to realize there had to be a better way. By the time they'd walk across town, half the night would be blown, and they wouldn't have any time to do anything. They were still too young and 'not cool' enough to bum rides from the older kids, so they'd do the old-fashioned thing and just have sleepovers, except that sleep was never really in the cards. Strom's mom was almost never home, either over at her boyfriend's place or up in Portland. A drinker, she didn't care what they did as long as nothing got destroyed or they didn't burn the house down. The boys had free range, and they loved it. That summer was the first time Rick had been able to stay out all night, then come home and sleep all day. It was awesome. They didn't have to answer to anybody, could smoke indoors, and Brenda was none the wiser. As far as she knew, Rick was in bed by nine, and eating pancakes and strawberries for breakfast at seven.

The boys (including Cajun as much as he could make it) took to terrorizing McMinnville. Their goal was simple; find every little hidey-hole in town, and pretty much go anywhere and everywhere, especially if they weren't supposed to be there. The storm drains and sewers across from the hospital, the three-tier parking garage next to the Civic Center, the Library, the public pool, the stadium, the park, the college, anywhere, and everywhere was fair game. "No Trespassing" were not words in their vocabulary. A fence was just something to climb and a locked door was just something that needed a little creativity.

"Dude," said Strom. "A construction site."

"That's a new one. Fuck man, let's go."

"Yeah those fuckers are always leaving their shit behind."

If it wasn't bolted down and was even remotely cool, then it was gone. Utility knives, hammers, drills, bit-sets, whatever tools they could find went into their stash bag; whatever made it easier to get into other places. Dismantling a vent or prying through a window just to get into a building, not even to take anything. Sometimes they'd just move something out of place, just to say, 'we were here', and then try and leave absolutely no trace as to how they got in. It was game, a giant ninja game.

"They're going to piss their pants when they find the circle of display cases in the front hall."

"Jesus Rick that was a brilliant idea!"

"All those trophies look like they're having a fucking meeting!"

"We're good man."

And they were good. Any idiot could take a brick or hammer and shatter a window, but how many, and at twelve years old would take a hack-saw blade and cut the bottom cap off the door hinges to literally dismount a glass panel door. Their creativity and craftiness made them the 'go to guys' for any job that might seem suspect or complicated.

"Is this doable?"

The boys would give each other a glance. "Of course it's doable. How much ya payin' us?"

A definite sense of pride filled the boys when they were asked by the older kids to do a job. Gave them a sense of accomplishment. It was nice to be wanted.

All of the pranks they pulled, from filling car interiors with the entire contents of a fire extinguisher, to re-arranging shit for no reason, gave them an outlet for their pre-teenage angst. They never once thought of the damage faced by the car owners, nor did they see how despicable their actions were. They didn't have the insight, they didn't have the filters, and they didn't have the maturity. Young, stupid, and full of apathy and hatred for the world, they made others pay for their own individual suffering. Was it right? Of course not, but at the time, none of it mattered. It was all about power, and taking back every last bit that they'd lost. They didn't need drugs or alcohol to give them a high, they just needed to feel in control. They never 'stole' the bikes to ride them around or take possession. They merely just 'relocated' them to the bottom of the ravine by the old railroad bridge. A quick toss, and the bike bumped and rattled its way down to its new resting place. People had paid hard-earned money for those bikes, but the boys couldn't give a shit. Locks and chains just added to the challenge and to the fun. No second thoughts, never a concern on how anyone else would feel. No one cared about them, so why in the fuck should they care about anyone else. Everyone and everything was fair game.

"Let's egg some drunks," said Strom. They'd tired of doing the regular shit and needed a new adventure.

"What, like just get some eggs and start tossing?" said Cajun.

"Fuck no man! We'll scout it out. Find a good vantage point and nail them. It'll be a fucking blast!"

"The Blue Moon Tavern," said Rick. "Over on Third Street. There's drunks coming out of there all the time. Maybe we can get up on a roof or something?"

"Third Street?" said Cajun. "I don't know. It's awfully busy down there and there's so many lights. Besides, the cop-shop is just over on Second Street. If my Dad ever caught us…"

"Don't be a chicken shit Cajun!" said Strom. "Who says we're getting caught anyways?"

"Cajun did have a point" thought Rick, "The downtown area was pretty bright, not many places to hide in the shadows, and there were a fuck load of apartments. You could never know who might be watching or who might have heard something."

"It'll be a challenge, that's for sure," said Rick. "Not saying we shouldn't, just that it'd probably be best to scout it out for a few nights first."

"I agree," said Strom. "We'll go tonight."

"I can't tonight," said Cajun. "I have to be home."

"No worries man," said Rick. "Strom and I'll take care of it."

Strom and Rick waited until it got dark, then set up on their reconnaissance mission. Despite all their adventures, they'd never taken on the roofs before.

"I don't know about you man, but I'm scared shitless!" said Strom. "I don't know quite why?"

"Maybe because the cop fuckers are just down the street, and the last thing we want is to get trapped up there like a fucking cat. Just be careful and be quiet."

"How we going to get up there?"

"I don't know yet. Just look around…see if there's anything we can climb on."

"Dude!" said Strom. "A fire escape ladder."

"Perfect. If we stand on that dumpster, think we can reach?"

"Dunno, let's see." Like a nimble sprite, Strom clambered up the side of the dumpster. "Fuck. I can't reach the bottom rung."

Rick dug into his bag of tools. "Here, toss this rope around the bottom rung. That'll help."

"You're a genius man," said Strom laughing.

Rick smiled. He knew. In no time, Strom was scaling the ladder and throwing his legs over the top of the building and out of sight.

"Piece of cake!" he said peering down through the shadows to his friend.

"Just give me a sec." Rick threw the bag over his shoulder and climbed up onto the dumpster. The whole thing was too easy, like God wanted them to go up there.

"What a view," whispered Strom. "You can see fucking everything from up here!"

"We need to secure an escape route," said Rick. "The fastest and the safest way down."

"The same way we came looks pretty good to me."

"Yeah," said Rick. "But what if that way is blocked?"

"True. Let's look around."

In full stealth mode, the two boys snaked across the roof. Most of the buildings on Third Street were uniform and flat-roofed, tightly packed with maybe a six-foot alleyway in between, and a forty-foot drop to the ground.

"We're going to have to jump if we want to position ourselves right across from the target," said Rick.

"Are you scared?" said Strom with a wry giggle.

"Fuck no!" Rick tightened the straps on his backpack, walked back to the middle of the roof, then took off running. As his feet left the ground and he soared through the air, he wanted to scream with pure adrenaline. He was high. He was in the air. He was fucking Spiderman, leaping from tall buildings. He hit the other side with a thump and a roll, his smile exploding onto his face. Strom landed a few seconds behind him.

"Jesus, that was awesome!"

"Look at that," said Rick pointing to the front doors of the Blue Moon Tavern. "It's perfect. Straight on target. That little ledge at the top of the roof will give us at least a little bit of cover."

"Rick…look over there. The hydro wire. We can use it as a zip-line during our escape."

"Are you fucking crazy?"

"You know I am man!" The power cable ran from the top of the two-storey flat roof to the top of a one story pointed roof. "It's only about thirty feet or so. It'd be easy."

"It'd probably work," said Rick walking to the edge of the roof. "But we need something to hang on to. We can't just grab the wire…we need something that'll slide."

"It has to take the friction and the heat without burning through or breaking. So that leaves rope out of the question. Maybe a belt?"

"Not sure it'll be strong enough?"

"True. I guess we're just going to have to scrounge around and find something."

The boys leaped back across the buildings and descended the same way they came up. The zip-line would have to wait until the night in question. They may have been crazy little bastards but they weren't stupid. They weren't going to attempt sliding down the cable until they knew it was at least sort of safe. About a week later, while digging through a construction site, the boys found their prize.

"Rick, look at these! They'll work perfectly!"

"What are these things?" he said turning the heavy metal object over in his hand. "They look like horseshoes but also some sort of clamp. They're sturdy as hell…"

"And, look we can hold on the edges like this and the cable can go in the middle."

"Metal on metal. I dunno man. That could be risky."

"We'll test it all out first. It'll be fine. We'll just send Cajun down first! You and I'll be fine!"

"Yeah," said Rick laughing. "I'm sure he'll love that idea!"

The metal on metal did worry them both. The horseshoe clamps would easily hold their weight, and because of the width and metallic surface, it would easily slide down the cable. If the wire was live or had enough conductivity though, they could be looking at a few thousand volts of energy surging through their skinny asses.

"We could duct tape the handles?" said Strom back at his mom's place a couple of days later. "That would help a little wouldn't it?"

"I guess. Couldn't hurt."

They wrapped the handles of the horseshoes with a good solid dose of the magic tape and prayed it would be enough. They'd find out the hard way if it wasn't.

"Are you sure you're up for this Cajun?" said Strom. "Your dad's a cop bro.

You sure you want to do this?"

"Yeah, what the fuck. These are the same assholes that cause shit. My dad just ends up arresting them anyway."

"Good point," said Rick. "We'd be helping him out then." The astute logic of twelve year olds was never-ending.

Operation Egg Toss was set to commence in three days. Both Rick and Cajun had gotten permission to sleep over at Strom's place, and his mother would be in Portland. The coast was free and clear. The anticipation grew as the night approached. It's like they'd been planning some sort of Special Forces military raid or something.

"I hate waiting!" said Cajun tossing the pillow onto the couch in Strom's basement.

"Relax bro," said Strom throwing the pillow back at his friend.

"You brought the eggs right Rick?" said Cajun.

"Yeah I picked them up on my way here. Quit your worrying! Pass me a smoke Strom. I'm out at the moment."

Strom tossed him one from the pack on the side table. "Need a light?"

"Nah I'm good," said Rick. "You know me, I've always got some fire."

They passed the time smoking and watching some television. Strom and Cajun got into a roaring argument about whether or not DC Comics were better than Marvel comics, and who was the fiercest guy from the X-Men. Rick was more of a G.I. Joe guy, and didn't really know anything or give a shit about comic books, so he just hung back laughing, and let his friends go at it.

Rick gave his watch a quick glance. "Ready boys? It's 22:30 hours. Time to roll."

The three of them hopped on their bikes and tore out of the garage. They figured a quick getaway was easier with bikes, and they could get places faster than on foot. Strom and Rick knew every nook and cranny of McMinnville, and where a cop car could and couldn't go.

"Park your bikes here," said Rick. "Between these bushes and that other dumpster. Make sure they're not in the light."

Strom led them back to the same fire escape and dumpster. Rick handed him the rope.

"C'mon Cajun, you're next bro."

Now Cajun wasn't the nimblest of kids, and while he wasn't fat, he was quite a bit taller and about 30 pounds heavier than the wiry Strom and Rick. More of a linebacker to the other boy's wide receiver.

"Shut the fuck up will you Cajun? Jesus man."It took almost two minutes to get up him on the dumpster, and another five (while he was standing on Rick's shoulder's) to get him up the fire escape.

"What?" he grunted. "I'm trying man. But I'm not used to this shit man. You guys are just little fuckers."

"Shut the hell up and be quiet! You're killing us bro! Strom…grab his arm. We've got to move."

Armed with his trusty backpack, Rick scampered up the ladder right behind his friend. Rick set the carton of two dozen eggs next to the ledge, while Cajun went to check out 'the jump'.

"You guys are fucking ass crazy! I can't make that jump. Jesus…I don't even like heights! Not doing it man. Not doing it."

"Okay," said Strom. "Totally cool. I get it. We can change plans. If it's better for you to wait down by the bikes and make sure our getaway is clear, then that's fine. No biggie. Seriously, it's okay."

"Yeah bro," said Rick. "No big deal."

"But then you guys would be having all the fun?"

"Well," shrugged Strom. "What do you want to do then?"

Cajun paused. Fuck he didn't want to jump. He'd clean shit his pants if he had to do it. Either that or they'd be calling an ambulance to scrap his ass off the cement below.

"I have an idea," said Rick. "We'll take our thirty feet of rope here and tie part of it around this PVC exhaust port. Strom and I will jump, and then take up the rope. Cajun, you loop it around your arm a few times. When you jump, Strom and I will run back with all the slack, so if you don't make it, we can pull you up. Sound good?"

"I guess," said Cajun.

"You'll be fine bro," said Strom patting Cajun's shoulder. Cajun couldn't see the indecisive smirk on his friends' face. Truth was, the exhaust port would probably snap under Cajun's weight, and if he did fall and they had to pull, the force would probably break the kid's arm. It was a win-win scheme all the way around.

"C'mon. Let's go test these clamps."

Strom jumped across the roof and headed for the cable. It'd been his idea, so he got to do the testing, and see if indeed, they were going to electrocute themselves. Holding a clamp about eight inches above the cable, he took a deep breath, then dropped it. Nothing. No sparks. Strom then pulled out a roll of copper wire, and uncoiled a good five feet.

"If I get blown off this roof, you motherfuckers better call a fucking ambulance."

He took another deep breath, then let the copper wire fall against the clamp and the roof at the same time. Rick and Cajun could only watch, their hearts racing and stopping, racing, then stopping. Slowly, with both feet firmly planted on the rooftop, he reached out and grabbed one of the duct taped handles. Nothing. Not a spark.

"All clear bro's," he said with a grin. "Fuck that was intense wasn't it?" He jumped back to the other side. "Let's have some fun!"

The goal of the whole operation was to actually egg a couple of drunks coming out of the bar and get away with it. Some pretty elaborate planning for about two seconds of glory. In their minds, the scorecard consisted of how many drunks they could bulls-eye without giving away their position. Rick was up first. Crouching below the eighteen-inch ledge, he waited for a target to exit the bar. As the watchful wingman, Strom hid in the shadows at the corner of the roof where he had a perfect vantage point of the street.

"Get ready…" said Strom. "Target at two o'clock!"

Rick bolted up from behind the ledge and let it fly. "Shit!" The egg splatted against an adjacent pole, sending a torrent of sticky yolk and white up against the target's sandaled feet.

"What the fuck?" The man turned and stared up the street. Rick flat out hit the deck, while Strom had both hands trying to force back the laughter that bursting from his mouth.

"Jesus little fucking pricks? Where the fuck are they?"

"Dunno man," said his friend. "Across the street?"

For the next four minutes, the two men searched behind every car and alcove along the street, never once looking up.

"Fuck it man, the little shits are probably long gone by now."

"Ya, let's get the fuck out of here."

As the two men slowly sulked away, the 'Egg Brigade' quickly re-grouped and shifted positions.

"Your turn Cajun," said Rick handing him the carton.

Cajun crouched low, an egg perched in his right hand. Waiting. Waiting. A few people entered the bar but none came out. Five minutes, then ten, then fifteen. Twenty. The door opened a sliver. Cajun re-cocked his arm. With some difficulty, a salt and pepper haired drunk stumbled out the door and onto the street. Zeroing his radar, Cajun squinted his eyes, then rolled his arm back and let that fucker fly.

"Whoomp!" Right smack dab on the intended's neck.

"Jesus! Fucking Bloabandjiekl (or whatever that was)," said the drunk pointing to the Heavens.

The boys gutted themselves laughing. The dude just kept pointing to the sky and muttering unintelligible words. Rick shoved the corner of his jacket into his mouth, his eyes crying with laughter.

"Jimmy! Man what's wrong," said another man exiting the bar, followed by a couple of his buddies.

"Jesus fucking…bird?" He pointed skyward.

"What?"

Jimmy wiped the egg shit from his neck. "I got shit on."

The men guided Jimmy back into the bar. The boys just couldn't stop laughing. When the stone sober bartender came flying out the door, the boys all hit the deck, and held their breath. Shielding his whale pale face with his black-mesh ball cap, Cajun peered over the ledge.

"He's going back in," he whispered. "Probably to call the cops."

"What do you want to do?" said Rick. "We still have so many eggs?"

"If we wait, then every fucking cop will be here looking for us," said Strom.

"They're gonna see our bikes," said Cajun.

Strom smiled. "I say we fucking unload, and then split."

"I'm with ya bro," said Rick, matching the mischievous grin. Employing full scale assault tactics, the boys busted every last egg on the front of the bar and sidewalk, all the while killing themselves with laughter.

"Let's get the fuck out of here!" said Rick.

"Jesus, I can't jump shit, I'm laughing so hard," said Cajun. Rick and Strom took off and cleared the gap in the buildings without difficulty. "Seriously man, I can't do it!"

"Cajun! You wrap that rope around your arm and jump now!" said Rick. Cajun looped the rope around his arm a good five times, holding on with a death grip. "On three, two, one, GO!"

Cajun hauled ass as fast as he could across the roof, landing with the thump of a rhinoceros on the other side, almost taking out his two friends in the process.

"Jesus man! I thought the idea was to be quiet?" laughed Rick.

"C'mon you guys," said Strom clipping his horse clamp to the power cable. Rick and Cajun paused. The moment of truth. Strom was either going to make it safely, or bite it into the side of the wall if the cable sagged too much. With a quick step off the ledge, Strom was whipping down the cable like a bat out of hell.

"Jesus! He's flying," said Cajun.

"You're up bro," said Rick. "Careful on your landing."

With the extra weight, Cajun rocketed even faster down the cable, almost taking Strom out at the bottom. Rick clipped his hook, smiled, then took the leap. He was made for this kind of shit. The boys leapfrogged from roof to roof, then finally to the ground where they mounted their bikes, and took off into the night. Trying to stay off the streets, they wheeled their way through alleyways and parking lots, all the while killing themselves laughing.

"Jesus man!" said Rick ditching his bike, and flopping onto the grass. "That was fucking awesome!"

"You should have seen your face Cajun sliding down that wire," said Strom. "I thought you were going to shit your pants right then and there!"

"Too fucking funny," Cajun answered. "I wonder if my Dad will say anything about it?"

"No way they know it was us," said Rick. "We're just too good for that."

The boys waited at the park for a good fifteen minutes, then mounted their bikes and headed back to Strom's house. It'd been a night to remember, one of those experiences that sealed the bonds of friendship and trust. They were a brotherhood now, tried and true, and for the first time really, Rick felt like he belonged and had people he could count on. Guys that had his back. People that wouldn't disappoint him or let him down. Tonight had been a fucking blast. Hilarious. What none of them realized at the time was how this bond of brotherhood would carry them into far more serious situations, situations they wouldn't laugh at, and situations that would even break their hearts.

CHAPTER TWENTY

Redemption. Rick knew his final destination, but he had no clue how to get there. Making the decision to live, and to make the rest of his life worthwhile didn't undo seven years of severe depression and negative psychological programming. It didn't give him all the answers, it just gave him a goal, a direction, and something to strive and fight for, and that was more than he'd had in a very long time. The burden of his guilt didn't ease, nor should it. He killed them; that would never change. The guilt seeped into his subconscious. He began to dream. Horrible, vivid and violent nightmares. He was hunted. He was back in Washington at the house on Federal Way, soldiers storming the streets, shooting, killing. He flew up the stairs and hid in the bathroom. Footsteps. Closer, closer, closer. A gun cocked. The door opened. The bullet ripped through his stomach, shredding it to pieces. Hot blood spilled over his cold, lifeless body.

"Jesus Christ!" His hand clenched his gut but there was no blood and wound, just a searing, intense pain. "What the fuck just happened?"

He tried to go back to sleep but the clamminess of his skin, and the unsettlement of his psyche kept him sitting on the side of his hard cot. The dreams continued with a disturbing frequency. One night he'd be shot to death, the next he'd be stabbed with a serrated hunting knife or blown up. Nothing he did during the day could stave off the terror of the night. Was this part of God's punishment? Was this part of his suffering? Real world life for unconscious death. The pain felt so real, the images so crisp and clear; the burden of his guilt manifesting itself in a perverse and masochistic subconscious need to punish himself for all he's done in his life. There was no point in telling anyone about them, and certainly no point in complaining. He knew he deserved them, and if they dogged him every night for the rest of his life, then it was a small price to pay. At least he had a life to live.

As May rolled into June, and his intense soul searching continued, Rick calmed, and the clouds began to clear ever so slightly. Even the corrections officers noticed a difference. Rick was tired. Too tired to cause any shit, and too tired to deal with the repercussions of any shit.

"I'm glad to see things seem to have calmed down a little Rick," said Randall Patterson, Rick's Public Defender and the lead on his case. "The last thing we want is for you to be hauled into the courtroom for your trial wearing leg irons and belly chains. It doesn't leave a very good impression on the judge. You have to keep yourself together kid."

"Any change on the amount of bail?" said Rick.

"No. It's a million dollars, payable in cash."

"So where do things stand right now with the case?"

"I've brought on another public defender, Wally Tetlow. He's a good man and a good attorney. We've also hired a private investigator by the name of Frank Waite to interview people and investigate the facts. I'm also arranging for a counsellor to come and chat with you. Her name is Gwen, you'll like her. We just want to get your side of the 'why' and also I think it's a good idea that you have some emotional support and just someone to talk to about anything you might want to talk about. You can trust her. The trial is going to be difficult, I'm not going to sugar-coat that for you, and from now until we go to trial, I can't stress enough how you must be on your best behaviour. Don't give them any reasons. Also, thank you for the thirty-six-page report on the fights with your Dad and your domestic history. I'm sure that must have been difficult to write."

He had no idea. It had taken Rick almost a month to write those pages, and it had been hell. More old wounds ripped open, spilling into the new wounds, creating havoc with past, present, and his future.

"Can we talk about the fights?" said Gwen. "About the abuse."

"It wasn't abuse," said Rick. "We'd just get on each other's nerves and he'd end up snapping. Most of the time I deserved it."

"Rick, whether you believe you deserved it or not, does not make it right! No parent has the right to hit their child like that, no matter what. What about the name calling and how he made you feel?"

"What about it? I felt like shit but I should have been able to handle it. No big deal."

Gwen just shook her head. "This kid is a mess," she thought. She did her best to make him open up but he was still so guarded, and she knew he was being very selective in the information he was revealing. She never thought he was lying, just withholding. There had to be more to it, there had to be more going on to cause such a violent outburst. Something deep and dark was missing.

Of course Rick never told her or Wally or Randall about his 'gift' or his religious upbringing. And he sure as hell wasn't going to tell that psychiatrist they sent down to the jail, Dr. William Vicary. It wasn't a good time to interview Rick. Sure, he'd made the decision to move forward, but making the decision and then actually talking about what happened were two completely different animals. He didn't know Dr. Vicary, and he sure as hell didn't trust him. How was this doctor supposed to understand the way Rick thought? Rick didn't even quite understand it himself. He couldn't explain everything to this man over the duration of a couple cups of coffee and a few cigarette breaks. It just wasn't possible – nor quite that simple.

****

Young Rick's life continued to be a study of juxtaposition. Parents inside the house praying, while their young teens huddled in the back bushes drinking whiskey and beer. Sin really was just a three-letter word, and besides, who gave a shit, when all they had to do was pray for God's forgiveness. A beautiful little scheme. God would forgive anything and everything, as long as you asked him nicely enough. Pray. Pray. Pray. Pray. All they did was fucking pray. Pray for forgiveness. Pray for all the sinners. Pray for mercy on thy evil soul.

"Where are we going Mom?"

"There's a house that needs our help. Jill and I both can feel the strong presence of Satan."

With the sun long since set, Brenda pulled the car alongside the curb opposite the run-down two storey red brick house and shut off the engine. Flanking the front door windows were two 'curtains'. At only twelve years old, Rick had no real understanding of what the Nazi swastika flag meant, but he did recognize the pure evil represented by the other black flag with the goat-headed pentagram on it. These Satanists were the real fucking deal. They didn't just entertain evil by rejecting God, they invited its presence and actively sought to embrace and further it.

"We're not getting out of the car are we?" said Rick.

Generally, he didn't scare all that easy but for some reason he couldn't stop the ice cold chill seeping through his veins. The wavering shadows cast by the numerous trees and shrubs only added to the ominous and dreadful creepiness of the moment. Even the gleam of the streetlights vaporized into the thick fog of darkness.

"No," said Brenda. "We're staying put. Are the doors locked?" Rick gave a quick glance and nodded. "We must pray. Just remember…the Lord will protect us."

"I sure hope so," said Rick under his breath.

They began by simply praying in tongues and focusing on drawing down the cleansing blood of Christ. Fear hammered his every breath, weighing his lungs, and drying even the slightest stitch of moisture. Dread was everywhere. His mind completely focused on the evil, Rick had the urge to see. He wanted to be brave and stare the pure wickedness in the eye. God would protect him. As his experiences mounted, he had developed a weird sort of fascination with seeing demons, and even though he dreaded the occurrences, he felt he that he *had* to see. Partly as a defence mechanism, to make sure the little bastards weren't sneaking up behind them, but mostly it was a morbid fascination and obsession with knowing what was actually out there in the unknown.

As they prayed, Rick began to look deeper, opening his mind and his soul. Fear propelled him forward. Searching, reaching, waiting. He'd never been so terrified. Shaking. Praying. Lord protect him. Blue light reaching out from behind the Veil. His vision brightened. He'd entered the unknown. Immediately confused by the lack of spiritual activity around the outside of the house itself, Rick's senses caught hold of a strange blood red hue streaked with gold emanating from the seams and cracks around the windows and the front door. As their prayer deepened, the same reddish-gold light appeared to almost mist through the four non-curtained second storey windows.

Tucked behind the mist, strange colourless symbols and glyphs began to appear and scroll by as if someone had simply cut a shape into the misty light. Void of substance, yet still sharp and defined, the images scrolled as if on an electronic bulletin board, some shapes larger than others, and others seemingly taking the form of letters. A message? Rick had no idea what it all meant, yet was captivated by the sheer power radiating from the images. Drawn to the power, his chant in tongues lost its focus and became an incessant drone, meaningless in thought and words. Just as God could cleanse and set his territorial boundaries, the Devil was hell-bent on protecting what was his.

For the weapons of our warfare are not carnal, but mighty through God to the pulling down of strong holds; Casting down imaginations, and every high thing that exalteth itself against the knowledge of God, and bringing into captivity every thought to the obedience of Christ[16]

The Devil readied his troops. Rick could only watch in horror as the red-gold light intensified, and the creature appeared through the mist.

"Jesus Christ Almighty."

Not six feet from the front of the door, a pale-grey, completely hairless being, knelt down with one arm straightened and resting on his fist. Black eyes stared at the car with an aloof indifference.

I know you're there but there's no way you're going to fuck with me. Laughing. Taunting God. Taunting those fuckers who think a little prayer to God is going to save them. The black eyes bore deeper.

"Um Mom…"

"Jesus, our Lord…cleanse this house from any evil that may dwell within its walls…Oh Lord Jesus…"

The creature shifted his weight but not his gaze, his pale skin opaque against the red-gold background.

[16] 2 Corinthians 10:4-5 King James Version (KJV)

"Holy fuck."

With a wry smile, the creature rose from his crouch, unfurling his massive, muscular seven-foot frame. The intensity of his sheer power and presence terrified the twelve-year old. His blood ran cold.

"Thank you Lord for protecting us and for your Will to stand up to evil. We will prevail against the dark forces…Thank you Jesus, thank you Jesus, thank you Jesus…"

"What the hell was she talking about?" thought Rick. "Stand up to evil? She has no clue what it lurking out there!" It was true. While Brenda could maybe feel a presence, she had no insight into what was really happening on the other side. The fact that she truly believed their prayers had even the slightest impact against this creature, or others for that matter, deeply disturbed Rick.

"Mom, we need to go."

What you do matters not to me. You shall not prevail against me.

"Now Mom. We need to go NOW!"

The icy fingers reached out towards Rick's heart, and he felt himself lean forward against the car door in the back seat. He was powerless against the supreme confidence of this terrible evil. Penetrating deep. The evil. The hopelessness. The mocking laughter. Why was God not protecting him? That was his promise. A wave of nausea blurred his vision. The sharply nailed fingers came closer. Laughter. Calling him. Jesus. Mocking blankness.

"Thank you Jesus. The work of the Lord continues as we cleanse Satan's evil from this earth."

Brenda opened her eyes and finally turned on the car engine, slowly driving away from the curb. The black eyes held their gaze until the car rounded the corner, and like a magnet losing its charge, Rick fell into the seat. Scared, horrified, and downright traumatized, he sat in silence, trying to comprehend what just happened, and how God could have let that creature get so close to his soul. Being lost in the black pools of his eyes, and that piercing cold indifferent glare made him feel more alone and insignificant than he had ever felt before in his life. God didn't care about his soldiers. He sent them out there to fight, but why? Nothing they could do would ever truly matter, the evil was just too strong.

None of that seemed to matter, as Brenda and the Potter's House warriors raged on throughout the summer. Every experience, every prayer, and every inkling of evil weighed heavy on the boy's conscience. Not every venture was as frightening or dynamic as the 'Satanic House' incident, and sometimes he wouldn't 'see' anything at all. Much of the time it was the things he saw during his normal waking hours or when he wasn't necessarily out demon-hunting that were the worst and most disturbing. Evil was everywhere, and as the incidents mounted, the pressure of it all pushed him deeper and deeper into despair and damnation. God? The light of the world? How could there be any light when all he ever saw was darkness? And worse, the oppressive militant Christianity he was being fed at home gave him no break from the constant strain and stress. It was all he knew, and really, there was no one else stepping in to tell him otherwise. Not his father, not Rosemary, and not his mother. He tried to hold it all together but everyone just expected so God damn fucking much from him. He was the golden child of the movement, the one with the gift. The one that would lead the cavalry. Except, he didn't want the job, but when God calls you to a higher power, you have no choice.

"For many are called, but few are chosen."[17]

They all believed that Rick had been chosen. He'd been given the gift of sight hadn't he? God had a plan for him.

"Before I formed you in the womb I knew you, and before you were born I consecrated you; I appointed you a prophet to the nations."[18]

So much pressure, so much expectation for someone who still played with G.I. Joe's and was only a few years removed from believing in Santa Claus. But when you were chosen, there was shit you could do about it.

"Where to today?"

"Your school," said Brenda. "I know we were just there not too long ago but we can never be too diligent, especially when it comes to our children."

Convinced that evil constantly lurked in schools, Brenda had actually considered removing both children and homeschooling instead. That way they would be protected. She could keep them safe. If she just didn't have to go to school herself or work, then she would have. Another reason to blame Bob. To complain. He'd left her high and dry, and took pleasure in doing so. Things should have been so much different. As she slowly drove the car by the side of the school, they began to pray in earnest.

"Lord with all your will and the blood of Jesus, wash this place clean and protect the kids that attend. Protect them from any demonic influence. Keep them safe oh Lord, oh Lord, oh Lord…" The prayers manifested into speaking in tongues and then back to prayers.

"Jesus Christ Almighty, protect these children, these wonderful Lambs of God. Protect them from the sins of evil and the darkness of the devil. Cleanse this building, cleanse this school yard where they run and play…your innocent children Lord. The Lambs…"

The midday sun pelted against the front windshield, reminding Rick that he was shuttered up in this hot, steamy car, when he should have been out riding

[17] Matthew 22:14 English Standard Version (ESV)
[18] Jeremiah 1:5 English Standard Version (ESV)

bikes with Strom or just goofing around, enjoying his summer vacation.

"Rick? Are you concentrating?" Brenda steered the car around the corner of the school.

"Jesus Christ!"

The massive fourteen-foot monster standing near the flagpole caught him completely off guard. Rick had to double-take to make sure what he was seeing was real. He'd had no warning at all, no slow bleeding into his sixth sense. One second it was bright sunshine, green grass and chirping birds, and the next, this terrifying sight.

"Mom! There's a demon! Right there!" His arm shot out in the direction of the beast. Brenda stopped the car in the middle of the street and began to pray. Instantly catching the demons' attention, it turned to them and sneered.

"What's it look like?" said Brenda in a panic.

"It's the biggest thing I've ever seen before! It's around fourteen feet tall, with brown muscular skin…like a lizard or a snake. And its fingers…they're long with claws. Maybe a foot or so."

"Jesus Lord protect us…"

"And…and…it's sort of hunched over with this ape-like body but it's covered in spikes and black talons…"

"Lord God protect us. Cleanse this creature from our midst…"

"It's got this bald head! But everything is so gross! Its face, even its teeth and fangs are black…and there's this purple tongue. And its wings! Oh my God! They're massive! They almost drag on the ground. Oh Mom! I've never seen anything like this before!"

"Stay strong Rick! God will protect us! Pray son pray!"

As their prayer reached a fevered frenzy, the demon bellowed a deafening, aggressive howl. A boundary had been crossed. The battle cry.

"Did you hear that?" said Rick. "Oh Mom, I feel like I have worms squirming in my stomach."

"Jesus Christ oh Lord…"

"Make it stop! I can feel the noise inside of me! It's hurting."

The demon caught Rick's gaze and stepped out from behind the flagpole. It wasn't fucking around. It was coming straight for them, its fiery breath turning Rick's stifled cry into steam.

"Mom?"

Time stopped. A brilliant flash of golden light, holy light, struck from the heavens like a spotlight, circling the creature, and halting it in its tracks. In awe, Rick watched as three lithe winged angels descended down upon the light, their very skin golden and glowing with their silvery white armour. Words failed to surface from the boy. All armed with swords, they kept one hand free, as they seemingly floated down in an almost peaceful, serene manner, their sapphire blue eyes focused on the target, their hair alive in reddish flames. Their assault on the bellowing demon was anything but peaceful. While the creature swung his long clawed arms, the angels deftly dodged away unscathed, without even a flutter of their white fluffy wings, their own swords systematically carving the demon like a Thanksgiving Day turkey. With every cut, gobs of crimson blood spewed in a vaporous steam, falling to the earth and pooling around the creature. Too fast and furtive, the angels made quick work of the demon, shearing his wings, and cutting deep across his scalp with their razor sharp swords. As the blood drenched its skin, the demon flew into a hissing spin, bellowing and screaming like a banshee, until there was nothing left but a stench-filled mist. The pools of steaming blood strewn across the pavement slowly vaporized and disappeared into nothingness. Stunned to silence, Rick watched in awe as the angels danced in a circle above, then crossed swords where their foe had once stood. With a quick bow to one another, the angels shot back up their beams of light and disappeared into the heavens. The glorious bright light was gone, and the scene appeared as if nothing had even happened.

"Rick? Are you alright?"

He couldn't speak, nor take his gaze off the scene of the battle. After uttering the word 'mom' he'd gone catatonic. Brenda had tried to get him to speak, to look at her, and tell her what was happening but all she got was emptiness. He'd quit praying entirely and was completely gone, staring out the window, unmoving, and unresponsive. The whole thing had frightened her more than she dared let on to her son. She knew he'd seen something, and that something was probably horrific and terrifying. She'd felt the presence herself, and she felt her son's fear. There was nothing she could do. What could she? He'd be fine. God would protect him. That's where all her trust lay.

"Did it leave?"

"Yeah."

The image of the awesome glory and spender of those angels, seeing them there, 'in the flesh' was something that would stay with the boy forever. He'd never forget the blood either. It was the first time he realized that spirits and demons could bleed – like humans. Were demons just transformed sinners that God could not save? His mother had told him that his father had left them because he had a demon inside him. What if that demon never left? If his father didn't accept Christ and be saved, then maybe he too would eventually morph into a hellish creature. The thought made him sick. He hated his father, but he also loved him too. Why Bob chose not to free himself from that burden of evil Rick could never understand. Would his father suffer the same fate? Being cut down by the defenders of Christ?

Seeing the demon bleed made the war so much more real to him. They were no longer dealing with simple entities or a presence that he had the ability to 'see'. These spirits, the angels and the demons, could fight, bleed and die just like life in the physical world. The war of the heavens between Michael and his angels and the 'Dragon' and his angels, as mentioned in Revelations[19], was suddenly a real event and not just some metaphor. The reality of the spiritual violence that day changed Rick, bringing home the importance of all the spiritual teachings and the priority of the warfare they raged. His fear of the 'other' amplified tenfold. If spirits could cut and harm each other could they also do the same thing to people? The thought terrified him. People watched movies like "The Exorcist" and "Poltergeist" and left the theatre scared but believing in Hollywood magic. Rick left knowing the truth. Possession was possible.

His young mind spiraled with scenarios. What if these spirits could lacerate your soul or manipulate the physical environment around and indirectly cause harm? With no doubt of their existence, his concentration turned to the possibilities of their evil. How could he stop them? The demon at the school had appeared without warning. If it happened then, there was no reason it couldn't happen as he walked to the store or played in the park. The only solution was to ask the Lord for protection. He began to see his spiritual armour not as a metaphor but just as real as the armour he had seen on those angels. He had to believe in the blood of the lamb, and that it would seal and keep him safe. The world was just too dangerous a place now without it. They had called to Christ, and he had come and vanquished their foes. The power of that moment was too hard to deny or push away. He'd seen it. He'd felt the terror, and he'd felt the light. There was no denying the Lord now. The incident at the 'Satanic House' had shaken him – it had seemed so impregnable, like the power and the demon they'd encountered were simply mocking their prayers. In the past, demons had always fled before the power of Christ and their prayer, but that demon just stared at him with an amused, cold indifference, defiantly daring them to challenge him. This insolence had fractured Rick's faith in God's power a little. Was he really all that supreme? Could he really protect them?

Seeing the angels completely decimate so gargantuan and powerful of a demon, showed Rick that if "He" wanted to, God could destroy his foes at any time, and without the slightest bit of injury to the good guys. That power drew him closer, kindling a fire deep inside, an affirmation of his faith and a certainty that he wanted to be on the winning side. On the Lord's side. He became excited about his faith and his destiny with the Lord. He'd been given the sight. He'd been chosen. It was time to finally step up and accept his path.

[19] Revelation 12:7

Trust in the Lord with all your heart, and do not lean on your own understanding. In all your ways acknowledge him, and he will make straight your paths.[20]

His faith would be strong. Unwavering.

For to this you have been called, because Christ also suffered for you, leaving you an example, so that you might follow in his steps.[21]

He would channel all his pain and all his suffering. He would run to the outstretched arms of his Lord.

Because, if you confess with your mouth that Jesus is Lord and believe in your heart that God raised him from the dead, you will be saved.[22]

He would save those who needed saving. Show them the light – somehow – God would show him the way. God would give him the tools. He would give everything his little twelve-year-old heart and soul could muster. All for God. All for the war. All for eternity.

[20] Proverbs 3:5-6 ESV
[21] 1 Peter 2:21 ESV
[22] Romans 10:9 ESV

CHAPTER TWENTY-ONE

"Do I have to go?"

"Not if you don't want to Rick," said Brenda. "Now that you're twelve you have the legal right not to go visit your father if you don't want."

"But then Jimmy has to go still right?"

"Yes, Jimmy still has to go."

"Don't make me go with them by myself," said Jimmy, panic bursting from his wide eyes.

"I won't make you go alone buddy."

"You promise?"

"I promise."

In the two years since Bob left, the boys had only visited their father and Rosemary the absolute bare minimum, and only at all because the law said they had to. Brenda loathed to see her children walk out the door and into the waiting car of 'that man'. In her heart, she wanted Rick to stay home, to reject Bob like he had rejected them, but Rick was right, he couldn't let Jimmy face that horror all on his own. The two years since Bob left had done nothing to lessen Rick's hatred of his father, and in fact had only stirred the simmering pot. As a Christian he was supposed to forgive. As a twelve-year old boy who'd lost his father, he just couldn't. The same arguments, the same confrontations.

"I don't want to be here."

"No matter what you think, I am still your father!"

Every time Rick heard those words his blood boiled. Yes, Bob was his flesh and blood, but that was it. Bob could never truly understand that for Rick, hearing those words only affirmed his hatred.

"You're right," thought Rick. "You were/are my father, and if you had ever really given a fuck about being my father, you wouldn't have left us high and dry!"

Fear kept the words inside his head.

"Life goes on Rick. The fact is I'll always be your father and you just need to deal with it."

Bob was right of course, but it was this black and white attitude, this sense of never even giving a shit about what his son thought, or how his son felt, that drove Rick crazy and only deepened the rift between them and fueled the resentment. The boy couldn't help the way he felt, he didn't know, and certainly hadn't been taught any other way of dealing with his emotions. With both father and son wired like an elastic band, all it would take was a side-ways comment, a resistant gesture or a simple act of defiance, and the band would snap. In an instant they would be yelling and screaming at each other, their tempers running rampant and out of control. Bob fed into the frenzy by not being able to just walk away, and always having to have the last word. The boy was twelve years old, and letting these petty arguments explode into a volatile mess was all on the parent. He was the adult, he was supposed to be the grown-up.

"Why don't you just go live your life and leave us alone!" sneered Rick.

They were in the living room of Bob and Rosemary's Baker Creek home. Like always, they'd been arguing about the divorce, and Rick was remembering how him and Jimmy had first refused to go with Bob, and Bob threatened to move to Madrid.

"You little son of a bitch!"

Bob rushed forward a good three paces and with both hands shoved the boy as hard as he could. Rick stumbled back a good five feet but managed to keep his balance. Instinctively, he took a defensive karate pose, just like Simon had taught him when they practised on the hill by the school.

"What? You trying to be a tough guy?" Incensed at this defiance of his authority, and Rick's willingness to defend himself and not back down, Bob took a step forward and raised his right fist.

"Yeah? What are you going to do huh?" he yelled, his crimson cheeks barely holding in his anger, spit frothing at the corner of his mouth. "You think you're a tough guy huh? Come on, give me your best shot!"

Rosemary burst in from the kitchen. "Oh my God! Stop! Stop!"

It was too late. Rick had been challenged. He knew his father thought he was just some puny pussy who didn't have it in him. Rick would show him otherwise. With a quick, low crescent-sweep, the bridge of his foot connected with Bob's left knee, instantly dropping him to the floor, writhing in pain.

"Oww!" yelled Bob, his hands cupped around his left knee.

"What's happening? What's happening?" said Jimmy flying in through the front door. He'd heard the commotion all the way out on the front yard.

"Nothing," said Rick, his voice barely audible.

He walked past his brother, out the front door and around the side of the house to his basement bedroom. Hurting his father was not in his original plan but he also wasn't going to just let him believe that he would cower and stand down to his threats. By this time, Rick had already spent a great deal of time running the streets, and he knew a great deal about how to protect himself. Never show fear. He flopped onto one of the military style cots that had been thrown down there for him and Jimmy to sleep on.

He didn't care. Numb emotions. Numb thoughts. His only real concern was whether or not his father was going to come down later and try and beat the shit out of him. Maybe pull out the belt? It wouldn't be the first time. Sullen and lost, Rick laid on the cot for a solid five hours waiting for round two to begin. There was always a round two. Jimmy came down to check on him a few times but Rick wasn't really in the mood to chat or go outside and play. The anger and the rage kept him pinned to the cot. Sometime after dinner (that he didn't have) the basement door opened and Bob limped in and sat down on Jimmy's bed.

"Hey Rick. Can I talk to you?"

Rick didn't respond.

"So listen, I'm sorry that things got out of hand, and I'm sorry I let them get that far. But I am your father, *never* hit me again." Another threat.

"As long as I don't feel threatened, I won't."

Bob tried to stay calm. "I don't care if I have a knife in my hand! You NEVER retaliate!"

The boy looked his father dead in the eye. "If you ever come at me with a knife, I'll make sure you never do it again."

Bob leaped to his feet, lunging forward, his carnivorous stare ripping through Rick's flesh, ready to beat him to a pulp.

"You stupid son of a bitch…you're not worth it."

Without emotion Rick watched him wheel around and storm out of the basement.

"Fuck you. I hate you."

They're just words Rick tried to convince himself. But those words hurt, and they stuck with him. Had he ever really been worth it? Is that truly how his father felt about him? It all made sense now. That's why it was so easy for his father to leave. They just weren't worth his trouble. Not worth it. He'd never loved them. He'd never loved Rick. It was all just a big fucking game. For show. He. Never. Loved. Him.

"Good morning Rick!" said Bob. "Did you sleep well?"

Rick just stared at his father in disbelief. "What the fuck was he talking about?" he thought. "Last night he was ready to rip him apart, and today he's acting like nothing even happened?"

The incident was never mentioned again. Rick came to loathe this aspect of life with his father. Shit would happen, then it would all be swept under the rug. No big deal. Except it was a big deal. How was Rick ever supposed to learn how to deal with his emotions, or learn from his mistakes, when they were never properly dealt with or even acknowledged? Always on his own. Always being left to figure shit out for himself. No instruction. No positive examples. He already believed that Bob and Rosemary were fake, and that their material wealth was just a fake happiness, so why should their domestic life be any different? All just an act. All for show. He'd never loved him. Why shouldn't they act like a family who could get along and act like nothing was wrong? That was the easy way out. Then again, wasn't that just like his father? Just take the easy way out, and not dig in and really try to work at something worth working at? It was obvious to Rick that in his father's eyes, he wasn't really worth working on. Hadn't he told him that just the night before?

Ignoring the elephant in the room was a constant theme with Bob and Rose. It made Rick's skin crawl. He hated that there wasn't any resolution, and he hated that they had to be fake around them and act like the fucking Brady Bunch, when in reality, they were always just one disdainful look away from an explosion. But that's how Bob and Rose 'moved past' their problems – just act as if they weren't there. For Rick it wasn't enough. He couldn't just ignore them. The anger and the resentment was always there, with each unresolved incident only adding fuel to the fire. He'd go Ghost so he could play along with the façade because it was far easier to be dead inside, than to give a fuck. Years of burying the anger. Years of burying the resentment. Never any resolution. Never any understanding of why things happened the way they did. One day the dam would break. Too much pressure, too much unresolved misery. He'd never loved him. End of story.

With his withdrawn, inhibited persona, Rick knew he lived on the fringes of social acceptability, especially at school. People found him dark, mysterious, and unreadable – just not the sort of kid who wore his heart on his sleeve. He didn't dress like most of the other Grade 7 kids, didn't care about wearing name brands or even acting and socializing like the other kids did. He wasn't mean or unkind, just inhibited. He knew no one could even begin to understand him, the darkness he harboured, the void, and the demons that haunted him, both while he was awake and in his dreams. He just couldn't identify with the other kids. He had groups of people he hung out with like the skaters, outcasts, runaways and street-kids, but his only real friends were Strom and Cajun. They just let him be who he was and didn't ask questions. And he had God.

Potter's House had continued to grow and slowly expand since its foundation in McMinnville. A sister church, twenty minutes north of town in Newberg, had also been growing, so the decision was made to combine both congregations and look for a larger building. They settled on some space at the McMinnville National Guard Armoury, which at full capacity could fit about three hundred people. With the combined congregations, the new church had about 220 people, a far cry from the 15 that attended Connelly's Potter's House. The 'Potter's House' brand of churches was expanding nationwide, so the new church fit right into their vein of progressive evangelical thinking. Armed with a new pastor, Kenneth Foley, one of the heavy-weights of the movement, the church attracted many new members both from McMinnville and the surrounding area.

"It's God's blessing that he and his family have decided to come to McMinnville. God is smiling on us."

With the church housed in the National Guard building, the setting took on a very 'militarized-for-Christ' sort of vibe, with Foley taking the lead and the congregation wholeheartedly diving in. Services were structured, an opening prayer followed by a praise and worship lead by the church band, then a fiery sermon, then more heavy prayer, then more praise and worship, then a farewell prayer. Rick loved the praise and worship segments the most, as the church band cranked it into high gear. More advanced than most church bands, they had keyboards, a drum set, tambourines, at least two vocalists, a bass, a guitar, and a middle-aged guy jamming on the tenor sax. It wasn't long before Rick's own saxophone talents were discovered and he was asked to join them on stage during the services. It took him awhile to get comfortable playing in front of such a large crowd but music and performing came naturally to him, so he made the adjustment with ease. It gave him confidence, boosted his self-esteem to be playing with the adults. People knew who he was, and for all the right reasons.

Rick felt at home in the 'Armoury Church'. No longer just a rag-tag bunch out fighting an invisible and impossible war, there was comfort in numbers, and psychologically, the boy felt they stood more of a chance against Satan. Playing sax in the 'Praise and Worship' group, meeting new faces and friends, encouraged him, and shone hope at the end of the tunnel. The burden of his gift became a little bit easier to bear. He became more involved in church functions and events, not shying away from the mission. On multiple occasions he found himself participating in outreaches, where they'd spilt into small groups and go door-to-door handing out pamphlets and preaching the good word of Jesus Christ. Doors would be slammed in their face and abusive comments thrown but Rick knew not to take it personally. What could they expect from the lost? More often, they'd be greeted warmly, they'd share their message, and even sometimes even pray with new converts or those in need. Selling the same propaganda he'd heard since birth, the same message he'd bought hook, line, and sinker. It troubled him why some people told them to go away. Did they not want to be saved?

With his heart on fire for Christ, Rick took his work for the Lord seriously, and really tried to make an effort to put God first. The Armoury Church had opened new windows, showing him that there could in fact be a positive and non-despairing Christianity, and one could maybe find joy and love in Jesus. He didn't totally abandon his subversive nature but he did give God an honest try. How could he not? Especially not with the prophecies. The church believed in messages from God, sometimes given in two parts, once in tongues, and then a translation, or sometimes just a calling to allow the Lord to speak through them.

"Young Rick Watkinson stand up," said Pastor Foley one Sunday morning during one of his sermons. When a preacher such as Foley told you to stand up, you stood up. Highly respected in the evangelical community and the church, Foley had all the makings of a church superstar and someone clearly blessed by the Lord - the good-looking wife, the gorgeous daughter, a nice car, designer suits. And he was one hell of a preacher! Full of fervour, enthusiasm, and a persuasive, charismatic way of getting his message across.

"It's okay. Stand up son." Foley walked down the aisle toward him, microphone in hand. "I have words from God to share with you."

"Words from God?" thought Rick. "For me? And me alone?"

Foley placed his hand on the boy's shoulder. "God has given me a great prophecy for you son. God has a great calling for you. A special calling. Let me ask you something. Do you walk with the Lord?"

"Yes."

"Do you sometimes stray from the Lord?"

Rick bowed his head. "Yes…sometimes."

Foley leaned in close to Rick, the microphone tight in his hand. "God has told me that if you walk close with Him, you will be a great warrior for Christ! A leader of His work and His Will! And," he paused, "one day, quite possibly his armies!"

Rick smiled, his chest pounding. Brenda grabbed for his hand, tears fell down her face.

"You've told me that you've strayed from the Lord on occasion. I encourage you to never stray again. Never break faith in the Lord! If you stay close, He will ensure a life full of great works and rewards, and an honoured place in heaven when the end of times have passed! This I tell you. The word of God himself, as relayed through me, His faithful servant."

Rick tingled.

"Let me place my hand on your forehead. Congregation, let us pray. Lord God you have spoken to your child Richard Watkinson. You have placed him in the light and shown him the mercy of your word. Help him to follow you, and walk with you, as he journeys through his life. With this prophecy he has been chosen Lord. He has heard your words. His accomplishments will be great and mighty oh Lord. Bless him oh Lord! Lord God above bless this child! Amen."

"Amen."

Rick opened his eyes. The congregation seemed to be aglow with the power of Christ. He was aglow with the power of Christ. Out of all the boys in the church, he'd been chosen. God had words specifically for him. God had given him the sight, and now he'd told him he'd be a leader. A general in the Lord's army. God did have a purpose for him. He did have a plan. Only twelve years old and destined for greatness. At least God thought he was worth the effort.

Time and time again, Rick received these prophecies, these words from God. The second time was during a lecture by Doctor James Dobson, a highly respected member of the national Christian community, less evangelical and more conservative, but certainly someone whose words carried great weight. After his 'Focus on the Family' presentation, Dr. Dobson sat down with a small group for a question and answer period. After addressing Brenda, he turned to Rick.

"I can tell that you have a very special relationship with God. I can feel it. Christ has a heavy calling on your life." While much more soft-spoken and less dynamic than Foley, Dobson's message to the boy was the same. "If you allow Him to…and you keep Him close, God will use you in many magnificent ways. These are His words through me."

In the spring of 1992, the Armoury Church had a guest preacher, a man who made his living travelling around the country and spreading the word of God to 'on-fire' churches. Another highly reputable and respected soldier of God, he exuded a power and charisma like no other preacher Rick had ever seen.

"As we end this prayer, I would ask those oh Lord who have heavy hearts, those who need to repent or need your special guidance Lord or those who just wish to receive your blessing oh Lord…I would ask those people to come up to the front and kneel before the congregation. Those with a special calling…and perhaps need direction from our Saviour. Join us."

Rick's heart had been feeling heavy. He'd had another argument with his father, and he felt so lost alone. Without really thinking, he stood up, solemnly walked to the front, and kneeled before the pulpit. The preacher went from person to person, laying hands and praying. He stopped when he got to Rick.

"Young man, stand on your feet before your Saviour Lord Jesus Christ."

Rick stood. Again, the only one out of a group of forty at the pulpit, and the three hundred others in the congregation.

"God has a message for you, a prophecy, spoken through me to you. His words." The preacher closed his eyes, then slowly re-opened them, as if awakening from a peaceful dream. "The Lord is proud of you. He knows your heart is pure. You are not forgotten. He wants you to know that you are not forgotten. We speak often of 'Israel' and the Lord wants you to know that the origin of that word, of the name Israel, and how it means 'soldier of God'. You will be such a soldier. Many battles you will fight. Many of those battles with be traumatic and leave their mark on your soul. But God rewards those marks, he sees them, and he honours their pain. And for someone who receives such marks on God's behalf, you will have a great reward in Heaven. You will find honour in being a great warrior for Him…to help eradicate the evil on this earth…the demons that lurk in the soul. You must never turn away from Him or be deluded by the wiles of the Devil. You have a mission, and it is a great mission for God."

He placed his hand on Rick's head. "Do you accept this mission and the pain you will endure as a soldier for Christ?"

"Yes," said Rick in a quiet resolute voice. "I accept this mission for Christ."

"Kneel down son." Rick kneeled before the pulpit as if he was being knighted in King Arthur's court. "My friends," said the preacher stretching out his arms, "let us pray for this young boy who has answered the call to be a soldier for Christ. Thank him for his heart and for the sacrifices he will make on behalf of our Lord. Bless this child. Bless this child. Bless this child."

Overwhelmed and confused, Rick's mind raced.

"Was I really chosen by God to be a mighty warrior in His name and lead His armies into battle?"

"What was my destiny?"

"Was this why I had such a disturbing gift and had to endure seeing what no one else could?"

"Why me? Why was I always the one being chosen?"

"I don't know if I can handle all of this. I'm just a kid."

Rick wanted to believe the prophecies he was given. They felt so surreal that they had to mean something? In one sense, they did give him hope. Hope that somehow all of 'this' would be worth it someday. On the other hand, there was always the nagging thought, the one that ate away at him day and night. He never spoke of it to anyone, but always felt that the pastors were somehow naïve to the real struggles of the war. Could they really see? Did they really know? No. Rick concluded that they didn't know. They didn't know how the nightmares plagued his waking hours or how disgusting and infested humanity has become with malignant evil. But most of all, they didn't know the only feeling he had in his heart, when he truly allowed himself to feel, was a burning furnace of hatred towards his father and the God who allowed him to leave. How could Rick love the Lord when he hated him so desperately? How could he love someone who plagued him with images and an ability he never asked for? They all wanted him to reach for the Light, to believe in the Light, without being aware of the tangible darkness he had inside himself. He tried. He really did. He didn't want to be or feel this way.

"You must forgive your father Rick," said Brenda. "The hatred will destroy you. You have to allow God to cleanse that hate from your heart and soul, and lift the burden from you."

And he tried. Fuck did he try. Again and again and again he prayed and prayed and prayed, and repented, then prayed some more, then repented. Just to be free of the hate and darkness that filled his heart. And no matter how many times he felt the warm glow of Christ's love or the power of the Holy Spirit flow through him, it was only ever temporary, a fleeting reprieve. Nothing really mattered because nothing ever changed. He still saw the things he saw, he still hated his father, and he still hated the fucking world and the fake ass people who lived in it. He tried to believe in the prophecies, he desperately wanted them to become true. He wanted to be special, to be what God wanted him to be, but it would never last.

Brenda and Jill still dragged him along on their demon hunts, him being the 'spotter', the soldier for Christ who could identify evil where it stood. As his walk with the Lord grew, his eye quite often remained opened and alert. Everywhere, at school, at the grocery store, even at church, his eye would catch the evil spirits preying on the weak, tempting and prodding them. Sometimes he'd see the Lord's servants in all their glory and splendor, but they were so rare and infrequent, that it became far too easy to believe that the world and humanity really did belong to Satan. The preachers could preach all they wanted, and lay hands on everybody that knelt at the pulpit, but it was never going to be enough. The world was too dark. He was too young. He was just one kid. How in the hell was he supposed to bring all these sufferers to the Light? Especially when he was still filled with so much darkness? Stay with the Lord. Walk with Lord. Keep him close. These are your prophecies. Spoken by God himself.

Regardless of whatever promises and prophecies the Lord threw his way, the part of Rick that suffered and remained dead inside, would always remain just out of reach for the Lord's light. He wanted to let it in. He wanted to truly believe but he was so confused. Always so much confusion. And always a juxtaposition. One side versus the other. One Father told him he was worth it, the other said he wasn't. Who was he supposed to believe?

CHAPTER TWENTY-TWO

Despite his commitment to God, Rick wasn't about to give up his nightlife or the fun shit that came with it. Smoking pot, drinking beer, and getting in the odd scrap or two was a welcome stress relief for the kid. He loved the challenge of doing things he wasn't supposed to do, and the more someone told him no, the more incentive there was to do it. He and Strom didn't get the nickname 'Crazy Little Fuckers' for no reason. They were always doing shit, pushing the limits, trying to prove to the older kids that they weren't pussy's. When Brenda first signed Rick and Jimmy up for gymnastics lessons, Rick was mortified, at least until he saw all the equipment and the other kids running around doing wicked ninja jumps and flips. He longed to take martial arts but McMinnville didn't have any dojos that Rick knew of.

One night as Rick was helping the gymnastics instructor sweep up the white grip powder from the floor, Rick noticed a heavy-set Hawaiian man coming into the gym with a group of people.

"What do those guys do?" asked Rick.

"Oh there's a martial arts class that uses the gym after us."

Right away, Rick knew somehow he had to get in that class or at least talk to the instructor. From the master event schedule, he found out when the classes occurred, and he and Strom just happened to stroll around about a week later when the class was finishing up.

"What can I do for you boys?" said the Hawaiian. "The building is about to close."

"Well," said Rick. "My name is Rick and this here is my friend Strom and we're both real interested in learning martial arts. We don't have any money to take any classes but we could set up and take down stuff and clean up after your classes if you gave us a bit of private instruction on the side."

"Hmmm. I don't know. Do you even know what form of arts I even teach?"

"Well no."

"My name is Peter Akimo and I'm one of the most experienced Aikido instructors in Hawaii. I just moved here to Oregon not too long ago and just decided to offer some instruction as a way to make some extra money."

"My Mom is dating a guy who used to live in Hawaii," said Rick.

"Oh yeah? What's his name?"

"Iopeka Patrick Jo'e"

"No bloody way?" said Pete. "I know that dude! Known him for years and years. Yeah, we go way back him and me. That is one dude houlli. Did he tell you that he was a third Dan, ranked a black belt in Jujitsu?"

"No way?" said Rick truly surprised. The guy they called 'Hawaiian Joe' seemed the epitome of passive and not all that motivated. Brenda had been seeing him for a few months now and Rick didn't really have any sort of opinion about the guy one way or another. The more Joe kept his mother occupied and off his back the better.

"Well if you know Joe, then I'd be happy to help you boys out and teach you a little something."

"Seriously? That would be so cool! Thanks so much man!"

Every day Rick and Strom were free, they'd go after class and hang out until the other classes were finished, and then set up for Pete. Sometimes they'd stay and watch the class or clean other parts of the building, and if that got boring, they'd go find mischief, then show up afterwards and clean and put everything away. Pete didn't hesitate to bust their asses and earn their lessons, but Rick was grateful for the instruction and did whatever Pete wanted him to. Pete was a straight shooter, something Rick liked and respected. Sometimes after clean-up he'd show them a few moves or teach them a few philosophical points, and sometimes he'd even have the boys over to his house on the weekend for some lessons on his front lawn. Pete mostly taught them what he liked to call the 'jujitsu of practicality'. He wasn't big on fancy moves, showing off or being held to rigid rules of art or form, he taught the boys what worked, more of a street smart Aikido. The boys learnt how to face down every day opponents in the streets, what to do when they were attacked with weapons and how to respond with the precise effectiveness that would scare the hell out of their attackers. The boys loved every second of it.

"Every part of your body is a weapon," said Pete. "Your hands, your feet, your knees, your elbows, your head. But the most important weapon of all is your mind. You must be able to outthink and outsmart your opponent. Now, let me ask you a question. What are the two things a man can't fight without?"

"His head and his feet," said Strom.

"Wrong," said Pete turning to Rick.

"Umm his head and his hands?"

"Wrong again! A man cannot fight without sight and air. If he can't see or he can't breathe, then he can't fight back and you win. Every opportunity you can, the first thing you do is attack the eyes and the throat like this." He demonstrated on Rick. "But…and listen to me very carefully boys. You are only ever to employ this technique if you are in serious danger. Never use it maliciously. And I mean that. If I ever find out you've been stupid and doing shit like this just for fun, I will hunt you down and beat the shit out of you. Is that clear?"

"Yes sir," they answered. Pete had said it in a joking way but the boys knew he was serious. Pete beat the crap out of them every lesson just so they knew how much things could hurt, and so they'd learn to respect the skills they had. It had been a long time since Rick had looked up to an adult the way he looked up to and admired Pete. He was a no-nonsense guy. Six months later, when the gym building got rented out to a permanent tenant, forcing Pete to move on, Rick was devastated. Pete was making a difference in their lives, and he cared about their welfare, and suddenly he was gone. Their lessons and just spending time with Pete had filled a void in both Rick and Strom's life, and when he left, Rick lost the adult male guidance he so dearly missed and needed.

Of course, he always had the guidance of the church. After the Christmas celebrations died down and the year rolled over into January 1992, the Armoury Church decided to hold a baptism. Being born into a Christian family, Rick had been baptized at birth but as individual child of Christ, he had never yet 'chosen' to be baptized on his own merits. To be baptized as an adult (or adolescent in Rick's case) symbolized a literal cleansing and washing clean with the Holy Spirit. As the excitement within the church built, the church authorities had to find an actual location to hold the baptism. McMinnville didn't want the church using the public pool for their spiritual event, so they ended up securing an outdoor pool at a motel about forty minutes north in Tigard.

"I think it would be wonderful for you Rick. For all of us as a family."

"I'm not doing it," said Jimmy.

"That's fine Jimmy," said Brenda. "Maybe when you get a little older. Rick?"

"I don't know yet."

"Okay, well I'm leaving it entirely up to you. If you want to, you can, if you don't, then that's okay too."

"Do I have to decide right now?"

"Of course not. The Lord will be ready when you decide."

For the last little while, Brenda had been feeling uneasy about her oldest son. She worried about him and his anti-social, withdrawn, and angry behaviour.

"You can't let the hatred take hold of your heart Rick. You have to learn to forgive and let go."

Brenda had no idea how fucked up her son really was at this point in his young life. She knew it was bad, and it even scared her sometimes, but she could never really know just how scarred Rick's mind, heart, and spirit had become. No one could. He lived in a world that many thought theoretically impossible, one that even most Christians couldn't even fathom truly existed. Angels and demons. They were just stories weren't they? Symbols and metaphors from the Holy

Book? Not for Rick. Brenda had no idea how much their excursions into evil affected Rick. She meant no harm, she truly didn't. She believed with all her heart and soul that Rick had been given these gifts for a purpose, and it was his destiny to fulfill that purpose. For Rick, these images only added to his deepening depression. How was the child supposed to walk the halls of his middle school knowing what he knew, and seeing what he saw before? All those creatures lurking around, feeding off the innocence of his young, helpless peers, and him helpless to save them, helpless to save himself. Why make friendships and why reach out when everyone and everything was so fucking doomed. Sure the angels came, but not nearly as often as they needed to. It was all just too much.

"I think if you receive the Holy Spirit again Rick…that…maybe it will finally ease your burden. Ask God to cleanse your soul and remove the hatred that burns in your heart. I know it's been rough for you. But let God in. He can make it all better. You just have to let him son. Trust in him. Trust in the Lord with all your heart and lean not on your own understanding; in all your ways submit to him, and he will make your paths straight. Proverbs 3:5-6"

He'd heard that verse a thousand times, and he'd repeated it in his head a thousand more, yet nothing ever changed. He still felt the way he felt, and he tried not to question, and just accept, but his was not the personality to just blatantly accept things he didn't understand. Maybe if he was older? More mature? Maybe then he'd be able to understand why God gave him his gift, or why his father left, and more importantly, why he couldn't get past it and move on. The idea of cleansing appealed to Rick, just not in the manner his mother was thinking.

"I'll get baptized," thought Rick, "and instead of asking God to cleanse my heart and soul, I'll ask him to cleanse me of this stupid fucking damned gift! I don't want to 'see' anything anymore. I want the 'eye' closed for good. I just want to be a normal kid! Why can't I just be a normal kid? 'The Lord giveth, and the Lord hath taken away; blessed be the name of the Lord'[23]. Isn't that what the Bible says? So if he gave me the gift, then if I ask nicely, he should be able to take it away?"

The logic seemed pretty clear and convincing in his young head. He'd still fight for the Lord, just not on the front lines. He needed a break, it was time for someone else to step up and take the reins. He dreamed of living the life of a normal kid and not being trapped in this endless war of the heavens. The gift only made his frustration with God grow. He didn't dare tell his mother of his plans; he was even afraid to utter the thought out loud in case God heard and was then forewarned of his escape.

[23] Job 1:21.

As the day approached for the baptism Rick became even more withdrawn and quiet. What if God wouldn't release him? What if this was all part of His plan and the gift was a necessary burden of his calling?

"No. If God truly loves me then he'll understand how much this is killing me and he'll set me free. He wouldn't ever want me to suffer like this. Jesus said, 'Let the little children come to me, and do not hinder them, for the kingdom of God belongs to such as these.'[24] I want to come to you God but you're asking too much. I can't handle it. I need your help."

As Brenda drove the three of them to Tigard, Rick tried to stay positive. God loved him, he'll set him free. Wasn't that what they always preached? 'The Lord is the Spirit, and where the Spirit of the Lord is, there is freedom'[25]. Freedom. That's all he ever wanted. The freedom to do as he pleased, believe what he wanted to believe, and to be the person he wanted to be. Trapped in this living hell was wearing him down, and he couldn't take it much longer. At some point, the dam would break. He just had no idea how or when.

Over twenty parishioners gathered around the pool, with everyone having brought another set of clothes and a towel. In order to fully receive the Holy Spirit in an adult baptism, one had to wade down in the water and be completely dunked fully clothed. Many of the other spiritual warriors of the church, like the Connelly's were there for moral support. One by one each of the participants would take off their socks and shoes, wade down into the pool just over waist deep, be prayed over intensely, and then dunked backwards to receive the cleansing power of the Holy Spirit. With the sun not able to peak through the covering clouds, most people came out of the pool not warm and fuzzy with the Spirit, but cold and shivering from being in a cold motel pool in the middle of January.

Wearing jeans and a t-shirt, Rick stayed back, quietly waited his turn and prayed with all his might.

"I know I'm supposed to be a warrior for you, a mighty leader in the armies of God, but I don't want to see anymore. I've seen enough! Please God…Please God! Take away the gift of sight. I don't want this gift any longer. Give it to someone who is older and knows how to handle it. I can't handle it Lord. I've tried but I've failed miserably. Please, please, please ease this burden for me. It's all I ask. Please Lord please…I'm begging you."

As he prayed, he spoke in tongues, and spiritually prepared himself. He'd never wanted anything as bad as he wanted this. He wanted it more than he wanted his father back and to erase the divorce from ever happening. Perhaps if

[24] Luke 18:16
[25] 2 Corinthians 3:17

he didn't have the pressure of the sight he'd be better able to deal with his longstanding emotions towards his father. Perhaps if he didn't actually 'see' demons, he wouldn't have been able to visualize what haunted his father and made him leave in the first place.

"If God really loves me, then he'll understand how badly I need to be rid of this. He'll understand."

"It's your turn Rick," said Brenda. "May God be with you."

He took off his boots and socks, and slowly slid into the water. The chill of the water didn't even register.

"Please God. Please."

"Come stand before me," said Kenneth Foley. Brenda and Jill followed Rick into the water. "Lord, let the divine power of the Holy Spirit rush forth and cleanse this man…."

"Yes Lord," thought Rick. "Cleanse me off this gift."

"By the power and the blood of the Lord Jesus Christ, wash his mind and spirit clean…"

"Yes Jesus…wash it away and cleanse my mind and soul…"

With their hands on Rick's shoulders, Jill and Brenda joined in on the prayers, pleading for his young soul to be cleansed. To be renewed with the Spirit.

"Please Lord!" Rick prayed silently. "Please take it away!" His heart pounded.

"NO!" The voice of the Lord thundered in his head.

The next few seconds were distorted. His breath short and pulsing. God had spoken to him. No? Rick's heart ripped like thunder splitting the sky. All sense of essence and substance inside of him evaporated, leaving him empty.

"In the Name of JESUS!" yelled Foley, pushing Rick back by the forehead and dunking him under the water. The second the water closed over his face, his eyes flashed opened. His third eye, wider and brighter than it had ever been. White thunder light flashed through the wispy grey clouds revealing a cyclone of spirits dashing and darting about as glorious angels and hideous demons bloodied the sky with red. Only underwater for a couple of seconds, for Rick it felt like an eternity that he couldn't escape; the vision so lucid and absorbing, like the water magnified and made his consciousness part of it.

"YOU WILL ALWAYS SEE!"

The deep resounding boom of the Lord's command echoed through every inch of Rick's body and soul.

"No!" Rick screamed.

And it was then, in that one damning moment that eternity broke into pieces and he began to cry, still staring up into the heavens. Time resumed its sordid tick as they brought him back up out of the water, his broken and defeated soul sobbing uncontrollably.

"Thank you Jesus! Thank you Lord, blessings from the Most High! Thank you for your grace and glory!" Foley, Brenda, and Jill just kept repeating the words. "Thank you Jesus! Thank you Lord, blessings from the Most High! Thank you for your grace and glory!"

Damned and defeated, trapped by a God whose Holy War was more important than a young boy's sanity and peace, Rick cried uncontrollably. The door of hope slammed right in his face. That was it. That was the moment. God had forsaken him. He didn't care about His little children. He only cared about himself. He never loved him at all.

"Oh Rick!" said Brenda. "My son! I have my son back!"

Rick didn't blame his mother for her reaction. It was only natural she thought he was crying because the Holy Spirit had broken through the dam and cleansed Rick of the hatred and bitterness of the divorce. She had no idea what Rick asked the Lord. So they all stood around him, giving heartfelt thanks and praise to the Lord God who'd just condemned this little boy to living out the rest of his life in a ghoulish nightmare. Shivering with cold fear and horror, Rick slowly made his way up the pool stairs. Sarah met him at the top with a towel.

"Here. Wrap this around you. You look freezing." Her smile oozed empathy, none of which even registered on the boy.

He didn't matter. His desires, sanity and peace were unimportant. He was just a tool to be used and abused by a 'merciful' God. He had been condemned to walking between two worlds and forced to keep his gift, so he could better be utilized in the war between God and Satan. The feelings of hatred had been planted, but he was still too numb and empty to even begin to feel that hate. All he knew, standing there dripping wet, was that he was damned and forsaken, that his want and will as a person didn't matter. His Father didn't love him. Never had. The tears continued. Betrayed by a Father. Again.

The importance of that moment never dawned on Rick until much later. It was a huge turning point and monumental milestone in his life, just as important, if not more as the divorce itself. He'd never tell his mother what really happened that day, it was too hard to explain, too hard to even imagine. He wanted to protect her. Protect her from the truth that her God was a selfish, uncaring bastard. The truth would crush her. He couldn't do that. So he'd bury it. Deep with all the other emotions and feelings he couldn't think about or deal with. As far as Brenda was concerned, the Lord God saved her child, cleansed his heart, and granted him the ability to forgive. Oh how wrong she was.

Forsaken. Rejected. Not worth it. In God's eyes, in his Father's eyes, he wasn't worth it. The love of Jesus Christ was supposed to be infallible, a perfect love, the ideal. Rick could deal with the imperfection of his love for his father, but when God showed him that His Will was more important than Rick's sanity, it shattered all of that. God was no longer good; he was just an ambitious tyrant. A Satan wearing white. All of these feelings only added to the numbness and depressed sense of self, and in a way gave him a twisted sort of melancholy acceptance of it all, and made him never want to come back to life and feel again. What was the point? Terminally ill in his heart. There's nothing you can do about it, so you accept it with a sort of laughable helplessness and hopelessness.

At the time, Rick never thought he could 'die' any more than he already had. God took care of that, squeezing out every last bit of hope for a normal existence with a single word. No. There was no up, only down, only continued submersion in a pool of stagnant water, where the air was soiled with hate and contempt. He couldn't breathe, rational thinking didn't matter. Authority was bullshit. Why should he care? Why did it matter? The greatest authority in his life didn't give a fuck about him, so why should he give a fuck about anything? Why should he be more forgiving than His most 'merciful God'? He'd asked for help. He tried to reach out. He wanted to be free. He wanted things to change. But it was out of his control. He had no choice. YOU WILL ALWAYS SEE! The path to righteousness slammed shut by the keeper himself.

When Rick walked with the Lord, his walk was not filled with light. The Lord promised him light. Jesus said so himself.

Again Jesus spoke to them, saying, "I am the light of the world. Whoever follows me will not walk in darkness, but will have the light of life."[26]

Rick followed the Lord but he walked in darkness. He walked in the shadows, existing only as a shell of a human, unable to feel, unable to let anyone's light through to his aching heart. He'd reached out. He'd prayed. He'd done everything he could think of to be free of the burden. The Lord said no.

"Fuck you, I'll just walk alone."

[26] John 8:12

CHAPTER TWENTY-THREE

"I'm getting married," said Brenda.

"To Hawaiian Joe?" said Jimmy.

"Of course that's who she means," said Rick. "Who else do you think she's talking about?"

"The wedding is in June. Aren't you just both so excited?"

"Yeah," thought Rick. "Real fucking excited."

Joe wasn't a central figure in the boys' lives, and both Jimmy and he couldn't stand the guy, a fact they made apparent with their little jokes and nicknames. He was complete opposite of Bob, and they thought he was stupid and docile. Of course, they never really gave him a chance, and anyone their mother brought home would pale in comparison to their father. To Joe's credit, he never tried to play the Step-Dad role, he knew it was better and much safer to keep his distance. Joe had two much older children of his own back in Hawaii, so he wasn't all that into raising a couple more, especially with Rick getting in more and more trouble. The attitude, the fight at school which got Rick suspended for three days, watching Brenda pull out the switch to whack the kid again. Even Joe had to admit that she got Rick good that time. The wooden spoons didn't work anymore. The last time she tried to spank Rick with a wooden spoon, it broke, and the kid laughed at her. The strong thin branches of the apple tree made great switches, and for the moment, it was the only way she could really discipline him.

Ever since the baptism, and then the fight at school, Rick had been moody, his pride wounded by the apparent defeat. If his fucking nose hadn't bled so much, he wouldn't have looked like such a pussy, and man, he hated looking like a pussy. He couldn't wait. He was just itching for someone to start something so he could prove his worth and set the record straight. Martin, from gym class just happened to walk into his sights when the mood was ripe and his anger seething. They had a little scuffle during class and the teacher had to intervene and tell them to cool it. After class, as they were all walking back across the grass, Martin and Rick started talking trash.

"Weak ass bitch," said Martin.

Rick knew he couldn't let that one go. "Oh yeah? Come fucking bitch me then pussy!"

Martin flashed across the field, dropping his book bag, and squaring his hands. "Let's go you little fucker. Right now."

Rick smiled, calmly setting his own bag at his feet. Martin lunged at Rick and attempted to throw at haymaker, a big mistake against someone twice as fast as you. Rick blocked with his left forearm, then gave him a quick jab to the throat with his right. The second Martin raised his hands to grab for his throat, Rick grabbed the back of the kid's head with both hands and bounced it off his knee, his forehead taking the brunt. The kid was out cold before he kissed the grass. Calm and cool, Rick picked up his school bag and walked away like nothing had even happened. The self-confirmation that he could be a flawless bad-ass fighter had him glowing inside. It was powerful to take on the enemy and win for a change. He was Bruce fucking Lee.

"Holy shit! Did you see that? Watkinson is a fast and vicious little fucker!"

"Remind me not to piss that dude off."

Rick swelled with pride as he heard the school chatter. It made his day and redeemed his honour. Watkinson was a dangerous fuck.

"But he just left him there and walked off? Who does that?"

Someone who doesn't care. Someone who is empty and unfeeling. Martin started it, and Rick finished it. End of story. Word of the take down even reached Rick's street friends, pumping up his reputation and his pride. No one would call him a pussy again.

Brenda and Joe married that June in a nice happy ceremony. Rick was glad for his mom, if Joe made her happy and took some of the household pressure from him, then that was one less thing he had to worry about. Merely three years since their family fell apart, both parents had remarried, and Jimmy and Rick found themselves in the undesired position of tolerating step-parents that they didn't necessarily care for. Bob and Brenda had moved on. Rick stayed stuck in the past, unable to accept these new family dynamics. Both he and Jimmy just wanted things back the way they used to be, but as Rick knew all too well, you don't always get what you ask for, even if you pray real hard.

Bored of his desk job at Evergreen International, Bob applied to fly 747s for Japan Airlines, and spent the majority of the summer in an intensive flight school and training. Rick didn't want to admit it, but he was proud of his Dad for making it through the selection process and to the flight school. Being a pilot and flying 747s was still fucking cool in any kid's eye, whether he was a shit ass father or not. Bob worked hard to get where he was, and the whole ordeal was incredibly stressful and time intensive. Besides a few short bike trips and some visits to the house on Baker Creek, Rick didn't spend a great amount of time with his Dad that summer, which suited Rick just fine. With his Dad away, his Mom more or less occupied with her new husband, Rick and Jimmy were pretty much free to do whatever the hell they wanted. This was the summer that Rick fell in love – with fire.

Fire fascinated him. The way it started, the way the flames danced, the way certain items ignited or fueled. At any given time, he and Strom had an assortment of lighters, matches, and occasionally some butane and lighter fluid. This obsession with fire lead to experiments with all things fun and flammable, from sprinkling non-dairy creamer over their lighters to make a fire-cloud, to dangerously using cans of WD-40 and other aerosols as flamethrowers. Reckless and out of control.

Along with a bunch of their new 'pyro friends', the boys did anything and everything they could to feed into their anti-social, 'world in flames' complete-anarchy ideology. They considered themselves anti-establishment anarchists who hated the government and all things authoritarian. And to a teenager with absolutely no conception of real politics, the term anarchy just sounded cool. Rebellious teenage angst to the extreme. Just having turned thirteen, Rick finally felt a part of this teenage rebellion. The group reveled in the idea of a world lost in chaos, every man, woman and child out for themselves. Of all people, Rick knew this to be true. He'd seen the chaos first hand, and he knew that the only person or being you could ever truly rely on was yourself. God wasn't going to help you out of the chaos. He's to blame for creating it in the first place. This whole idea of raging against the world, raging against society, and raging against those with higher power and authority resonated deeply with Rick. Tired of giving in, tired of not having any control, he was in a fighting mood.

In the spirit of true rebellion, the group left anarchy symbols and their own group identifying 'stick fox' symbol everywhere they could; sometimes in spray paint, sometimes in lighter fluid and fire. It was their way of spreading the chaos and signifying to any and everyone who may see it, that their agents were here and hard at work. Unwilling Christ warrior by day, willing pyromaniac anarchist by night – not a well-suited combination. Their pyromania and anarchist tendencies infected everything they did, and if you wanted to hang out in the group, then you'd be expected to partake. No pussies allowed. This sort of rigid, take no prisoners ideology was the perfect outlet for at least some of Rick's anger and pain. He took to drawing Stick-Fox cartoons, where Stick-Fox became the 'spirit of fire' who lit up and consumed everything. Eventually, he added 'Pyro-Demons' who possessed people or mysteriously started havoc to wreck large scale devastation. Fire, rage, destruction, demons. The seeds planted so early in his youth, finally begin to sprout and blossom.

With the Light forsaking him, all he had left was the Darkness. In his mind, there was no escape. Fire would be the only light he needed. He wanted the world to burn and everyone with it. What did it matter, everyone was going to Hell anyway. If God's 'chosen ones' had to pay this kind of cost to get into His exclusive club, then he could have it. Rick didn't want any part of it. The mould had been cast, the hate festered too long. All the good things he had in his life were dwarfed by the darkness that had swallowed him like Jonah and the Whale. Except, he had no intention of escaping the whale. The darkness understood him far more than the light ever would. The Lord may have owned him, like a master owns a slave, and he prayed because he had to, went to church because he had to, and fought in God's war because he had to, but it didn't mean he had to put his heart and soul in it anymore. This feeling of forced destiny only fueled the fire of his resentment.

If only he'd recognized all these feelings when they occurred, maybe then he could have afforded a gradual release of the volcanic tension. Instead, they festered on a subconscious level, Rick unaware what they meant, or how they applied to his daily decision making and rational thinking. He'd spent years training himself to believe he was dead inside, that he couldn't feel. He didn't question the why or try to explain or reason; he didn't have the maturity or mental capacity at that age. His emotions were demons themselves, lurking in the dark corners of his soul. To force them out and admit that they even existed would open a whole other war that he wasn't ready to face. The divorce, the betrayals, being lost and forsaken, fated to see and to suffer; it was far easier to remain dead and just believe that he couldn't feel. He believed that he had successfully detached himself from his own emotions, he believed that Ghost was real, and that's all that really mattered. He had no idea the psychological damage he was doing to himself, and no one bothered to step in and get him the help he needed.

All of this manifested itself in a reckless, destructive teen, who rejoiced in danger and chaos. It didn't scare him, none of it did. The Pyro group was already out of control, randomly lighting shit on fire, being careful that no one actually got hurt, but enough that society would recognize and fear the unseen spirit of Pyro. Always walking in the shadows, avoiding the light. Stealing, breaking into buildings, going places they had no business going, all just for the fun and the challenge of it. It was never about actually hurting anyone, and more about breaking every barrier of authority. No one would tell them what to do. No one. Especially not the cops. Never allow yourself to fall into enemy hands, cops or other persons. Ever. Unbreakable rules. Do what you want, just don't get caught.

The more Rick did, the more his reputation grew, the more he liked the feeling. Being important. Being needed. Being wanted.

"I know a kid who can pull that job off," she said, her dark long hair flipping to the side.

"Yeah right." The older college kid had been running his mouth and bragging about this ridiculous job that only he could have pulled off.

"No seriously," said Selena.

"Oh yeah? Who?"

She pointed her cigarette towards the scrawny kid leaning up against the car. "Rick and his buddy's man. They're like fucking ghosts. They can pull off anything."

Ghost. Just hearing the words sent a rush through Rick's body. It was the second time he'd had someone direct that word towards him. Ghost. She'd fucking nailed what he felt in side. He'd already begun to think of himself as a spirit or ghost-like, but it had yet to become his identity. Until today. As if who he was on the inside had manifested enough on the outside that, even without knowing what was going on inside of Rick, someone could know and acknowledge the very nature and essence of who he was. For Rick, this was one prophecy that came true.

"I like that," he said interrupting the conversation.

"What?" she said confused.

"The shit you just said about ghosts."

"Oh, well I just think it's fucking cool how sneaky you guys are. They should just call you Ghost."

And there it was, the nail in the coffin.

"Yeah, that would be cool," said Rick. "You can if you want to."

"All right," she smiled. "Well I'm out of here! See you later Ghost."

It didn't take long for the moniker to spread, and the more Rick heard himself referred to as 'Ghost', the more it affirmed his own belief that he was dead inside. His inner nature, who he was, and what he did, became his identity. Rick the person slid away, and Ghost, the enigma took his place. All his friends thought the name just fitted his stealth, ninja-like activities, they had no idea it was the ultimate representation of how he truly felt inside – hollow, empty, desolate – like a Ghost.

"Hey Rick," said Brenda. "I've borrowed another book for you to read. Sorry it's a little beat up but it's the message that matters. It will help you understand what's really out there."

"As if I don't already know," he mumbled. "Thanks."

"Oh you're welcome honey. I know sometimes you struggle, and as your mother, it's my duty to do whatever I can to help you through it."

Missing its front cover and the title page, the book was about a woman who'd been a member of some sort of satanic cult and had been 'scared straight' and turned to God for help and forgiveness. The book explains how during some heavy drug experimentation, she'd become exposed to the 'satanic religion' and it had captured her attention, luring her in quickly and completely. During her years with the cult she witnessed and experienced a myriad of horrors, from rituals cursing people with the blood of slain goats, to sacrificing human infants, ritual sex with virgins on the altar, female sex slaves, child prostitution, drugs, murder, and demonically possessed 'priests'. Threatened with death, she managed to escape the cult, and turned her life over to God. With its vivid descriptions and first person account's, Rick had little doubt that all of these horrors occurred, and it only reinforced the idea that 'they're out there' – people and groups who not only sin but who deliberately support and seek to spread Satan's evil across the earth. The enemy. The Soldiers of God must always be on the alert.

The woman in the book was just one soul saved. But there were just so many, and the task just so intoxicatingly overwhelming. Armageddon was near. The Second Coming was coming; it was just a matter of time. They had to be ready. They had to be prepared. They read pamphlets, and books, watched movies and listened to lectures over and over. The 'End of Days' were close, life on earth as they knew it was coming to a close. One day, all the peoples of the earth would wake up to seas churning red with blood, comets raining from the sky, and every inch of land, and every inch of water and sky, and indeed every soul, would be fodder for gain or loss in the Great War. Only those who'd given their life to God would be spared the wrath. Bob had never given his life to Christ, nor Rosemary. They would be subject to this horror. The pictures grew in young Rick's mind. The despair deepened.

No one could tell him that any of this wasn't true, that it wasn't real. It was all he knew. And those who rejected the ideas, like his father, they were just being naïve, brainwashed by the devil, lost souls. Rick accepted all of this without question. Why would he question it? He saw firsthand what it was like. He knew all about the angels and the demons. The descriptions of the satanic practices given by the woman in the book all fit what he'd be taught, and it was both fascinating and frightening to read how successful these people were in building the Devil's empire. If Christ could build an empire, then it made total sense the Devil could as well.

Whether or not the woman's account of her experiences was truthful had no bearing on the young boy. He hung on every word, and to him at the time, every word was real, and that's all that mattered. Not only did he have to worry about fighting Satan on a spiritual level, and saving souls from sin, now he learned that Satan had warriors that could do the exact opposite of what they were doing. For every place cleansed with the spirit of the Lamb, they could soil with a curse. For every soul saved, they were tainting one with their sex, greed, and gluttony. Every prayer to God was countered with a prayer to Satan. It didn't stop, it would never end. There was no hope. Paranoia crept into Rick's young mind, and made his view of the world and spirituality suspect. His rift with God deepened. He still went to church, prayed, prophesized, and did his part as God's little warrior but he didn't trust him – not one fucking bit.

God really didn't care about him, he'd made that point abundantly clear at the baptism. He was just a pawn for God, used without any regards for his own personal well-being. Tired of it all, Rick felt his resolve slipping, his willingness to battle lessening. God's betrayal weighed heavy. Rick never believed he was personally possessed by demons or anything, he was simply possessed by the images and visions of them, and it tore him to pieces. This only increased his propensity to sin. He smoked, he drank, sucked back the odd joint or two. He didn't care. He snuck out, he lied to his mother, he stole things. It was like a big fuck you to God. He told himself that God had to take the good with the bad. If he was going to force him to be a part of his war, then Rick was justified in forcing God to accept his behaviour. God couldn't expect Rick to bear all these burdens, all the heartache, betrayal and madness like a docile and accepting soul. If God created Rick and had chosen his destiny with his own hand, then he had to have known the boy would lash out.

A part of Rick believed that he was meant to be forsaken and endure all these things. All this suffering would turn him into a better and more understanding soldier. By surviving his own personal hell, he would be tested, and a stronger warrior for the Heavens. That had to be the reason God was doing this to him. Why else? With those thoughts, he shrunk even deeper into himself, numbed it all out, and died a little more, just so he could survive the madness and misery that he'd accepted as his life. He just wanted the misery to stop. Unfortunately, all he could do was soldier on, soldier on and go Ghost. There were no other choices, no other options. His life was not his to live.

CHAPTER TWENTY-FOUR

Soldier on they did. Despite its enormous growth, some members of the Armoury church, including the original Potter's House gang, felt they still weren't doing enough. Going to church, praying and being 'good Christians' was just the minimum expectation. God wanted warriors in the field. That meant a summer of going door to door spreading the word, giving out pamphlets, and ministering to any who would listen. Despite all that had happened, there were still times that Rick felt on fire for the Lord, and his youthful exuberance made him a fervent and persuasive witness to God's glory and power.

"You have a gift Rick," said Brenda. "You are just so good at sharing the word. And I'm not the only one who says that. Jack, Jill, Pastor Ken. We all think you were born just for this role. There is just an inspirational power flowing through you."

When Rick preached and prayed with people, he did so with one hundred per cent of his heart. He wouldn't back down, and he wouldn't take no for an answer. Failure was not an option. With Bob away at flight school, there was little disruption to God's work that summer.

"Jill and I have been talking," said Brenda. "I think we should concentrate on Wortman Park. We've both had bad feelings about that place, and with all the trees and hidden spots, only the Devil knows what's truly going on there."

"But don't people just go to Wortman Park to have barbeques and play soccer and stuff like that?"

"That's what they want you to think son. But there are a lot of souls there that need saving, trust me. And with all the people that hang out there, it's a good opportunity to just preach the word and bring more souls into the fold."

With thick patches of forested areas and a small stream running through it, Wortman Park was a summertime favorite for McMinnville residents who enjoyed walking or biking along the cement paths or gathering under the many canopied picnic areas.

"It's not the real public areas we're worried about Rick. It's the sex and the drugs that happens in the more isolated sections of the park. They think we can't see them, but let me tell you, God knows they're there."

Often they would all walk through the park in the afternoons or early evening's, seeking out 'shady' characters, or those who looked like they needed saving. Most times they would just end up praying with or over the 'lost', those who'd either didn't know God's love or who had fallen from it. They'd even coerce a few to attend church the next Sunday, and a few they saved by the blood of the lamb right there on the park grass.

"The clock is ticking," said Brenda to a group of unsuspecting souls.

"Ticking for what?"

"Ticking to the end of days. Have you been saved? Have you found the salvation of Christ?"

"Fuck off woman and leave us alone!"

"Bitch…"

"God is watching! Be saved now or feel the wrath of God! Walk away from Satan!"

"We like Satan."

"But we haven't much time left before the Lord returns! There will be war! There will be terrible, horrible things! Come with us now! Let us fill you with the love of Christ."

"For the love of Christ lady, leave us the fuck alone!"

"They'll be sorry," said Brenda turning back to Rick. "They have no idea what's in store. God help them."

"God help them," answered Rick.

Salvation through implied terror and damnation was always the best. It had worked on Rick, so why shouldn't it work on everybody else?

"That music they were playing is going to send them to Hell."

"Yes Mom for sure," said Rick totally hiding the fact that not only did he know the songs they were playing, he listened to them on a regular basis with his friends. A part of him longed to feel the freedom, to sit back and blast whatever type of music he wanted.

Some people listened patiently before they responded with a curt 'no thank you', while others were two seconds away from throwing their beer bottles or a nearby rock directly at a group members head. Always on high alert these days, Rick's eye continuously picked up demon activity. Sometimes the demons themselves appeared sad, worn, and lethargic, mimicking the inner nature of the hosts they inhabited. Others were as angry and brutish as their person, enjoying the confrontation and aggression. Rick would point out those possessed, and the group would then pray over that person, most often in tongues, whether they'd consented or not. Trying to rid a person of demon possession was tricky business. Demons weren't nearly as territorial over a location, like the school, as they were over individual souls. Physical places could be tainted, cleansed, and re-defiled a thousand times over but a person's soul was sacred ground not to be played with. If that soul was filled with Satan, there was no way in hell he was going to give it up without a violent and brutal fight. The demons never went easy, and more than once, they would threaten or attempt to intimidate the group by cursing against them in their own infernal tongue. Of course, the only person who could see and hear this all was Rick.

"What are they saying now son? Are we making any progress? I can feel it! I can feel it!"

The words of the devil are not sweet and comforting. They burn with the acid of hate and disgust.

"We are protected by the Blood of the Lamb Rick! The demons are powerless against us!"

"But what about my sanity and my soul?" thought Rick. "Who is going to protect that? Who is going to make me un-see and un-hear the things I have? Not you mother. Or Jill. And certainly not God."

The only time the demons didn't flee was when the host had voluntarily resisted exorcism and refused to let go of their own afflictions; a few even reveling in the group's powerlessness against their own personal choice.

"You will not defeat me. This is one soul you will not be taking. I have won." The words boomed through the boy's head. "Leave now."

"Pray Rick pray!" said Brenda.

"It's no use Mom. This one is gone. We need to move on. Now."

Rick learned a great lesson on these ventures – human will is a powerful thing. When unwavering and unassailable, even the power of God himself cannot force one's spirit to relent and bend. If one could stay strong in their beliefs, and not give in, they had a chance against any power, good or evil. Fortunately for the Christ crusaders, most people were weak, and their defences down, their will drained to the last drop. They knew they'd fallen from grace and lived a life of sorrow and misery under Satan's thumb. Some had been possessed so deeply, and lost for so long that they didn't believe they even could be redeemed. Cleansing those souls was a painful and precarious process.

One damp and rainy afternoon while scouring the park, the group came across a young woman in her mid-twenties.

"You look so sad my dear," said Jill. "We're here to help you? Can we pray for you? Christ is here to save you." The woman looked with no emotion. "I can see from the look on your face that you're in pain, and that this pain is weighing you down. It is weighing you down isn't it?" The woman nodded. "Drugs? Addiction?" The woman nodded again. "Let us pray over you. You don't want to keep living this life do you my dear?"

"No," she answered weakly. "I don't."

Brenda reached out here hand. "Come with us. Let us find somewhere peaceful where we can all pray."

"Bugger off lady," said one of the guys sitting next to her. "She's fine and you're all fucking crazy to be preaching to people in the park. We don't want you and we don't need you here."

Rick had seen the demons lurking the moment they'd walked up to the group. As the ladies spoke to the woman, her demon raised its ears defiantly.

"Honey," said Brenda. "I can see that you want to talk. Let's go somewhere where we can talk and pray."

"I'd like that," she answered.

"You're fucking crazy to go with them baby," said the guy. "Are you serious?"

"Leave me alone Steve. You like when I'm all drugged up and fucked up don't you? Well I don't. And I'm tired of it. So tired of it all."

"Have you ever known Christ?" said Jill.

The woman nodded. "A long, long time ago. I'm sure he's completely forgotten about me."

"Never," said Brenda. "The Lord never forgets about anyone."

"Really?" thought Rick. "I know that's a lie."

"Let us help you find the Lord once again," said Jill. "Come with us."

The minute the woman reached out to take Jill's outstretched hand, her demon became visibly and aggressively annoyed. As they reached the clearing, and Brenda and Jill crouched down with the woman and began to talk, the demon rose to full height and began walking towards its host. Almost the same height as the woman, its matted grey skin flexed taut over its exaggerated bony structure and jagged brow. Its lobe-less, spiral-like ears sunk into the sides of its head, while its putrid yellow eyes bore a fiery gaze that ran Rick's blood cold. Leathery wings with bat-like hooks spread out from behind its gargoyle body, while its clawed hands and feet were adorned with long spindly fingers. Even with its forged teeth dripping black poison, it wasn't the scariest creature Rick had even seen, but it was one of the most aggravated and angry. Had they not been protected by the Blood of the Lamb, Rick had no doubt this creature would have gleefully tore them all to shreds. Despite the damp day, the air in the clearing seared with a stifling heat and hatred.

As the woman poured out her soul to Brenda and Jill, the demon lurched up from behind, embraced her in its arms, and sunk the full length of its claws into her ribs and breast.

"Jesus Christ!" said Rick.

The woman sobbed uncontrollably, her body shaking with torment and despair. The demon sunk its claws in deeper, delighting in her anguish.

"I've been raped more than once and I've had two children…but I lost them both prematurely." Her words sputtered out between the sobs. "I'm so lost and alone…and I don't know what to do or where to turn. I don't want to live like this any longer…"

The demon turned its yellow stare to Rick, as it whispered in the woman's ear, and dug its claws in even deeper.

"Just try and take her," it seemed to be saying. "I will rip her to shreds if you so much as take another step closer."

Rick dug his shoes into the soft grass, crossed his arms and clenched his fists, refusing to show fear, and furious at the pain the creature was causing her. His heart bled for her. No one should have to suffer like that, to feel so lost and broken, a kindred spirit to the core.

"Do you want to be saved and cleansed by the blood of the Lamb?" said Brenda.

"Yes," said the woman. "I want to be saved."

The demon shrieked, digging his claws in even further. With its wings fully extended, the demon hunched over the woman, black liquid dripping from its pores, landing with a searing smoke on the woman's tender skin.

"Rick," said Brenda. "Come pray with us."

As they all began to pray, the woman cried out in unison with the demon; hers in pain, his in rage. The creature refused to let go and began stabbing his nails in and out of her as if it was trying to claw its way up the ledge of a cliff. As the claws manoeuvered in and out of her body, a bluish-black luminescence poured from the holes, staining the creatures nails. Rick knew it could only be the essence of her Spirit. He feared deeply for her. The creature would rather kill her than leave her. The battle lines were drawn. Right now the love of Jesus was keeping her whole, though her emotional and spiritual agony was excruciating. As they increased their intensity of prayer, Rick could see the demon being pulled back at his neck and throat area, as if some force was trying to pry him away and pull him off the woman.

Praying deeply in tongues, Rick's sight was no longer in the physical, the gateway to his mind's-eye wide open and active. The child just wanted her torment to end. With every thrust of its flapping wings, the woman's shoulders were thrown back, her back arched, her wails bordering on hysteria.

"Oh my God!" she screamed, not in religious ecstasy but in sheer tormented pain.

"Dear Jesus, please let her live!" said Rick. He'd never seen anyone in such physical and emotional anguish, and he truly worried she wasn't going to survive.

"Free her Jesus! Free her!" shouted Brenda. "Free her now!"

"Free her Jesus! Please!" screamed Rick.

With a sudden jerk, the demon flew straight back and slightly upward through the trees at a furious pace, as if the invisible hand of God had reached down the heavens and grabbed the beast by the collar. The woman jolted forward.

"Oh God, oh God, oh my Lord Jesus," she wailed.

Rick could see the wounds through her clothes, leaking her essence, and as his outstretched hand came to rest on the back of her head, he finally knelt down too. Spellbound, he watched the wounds instantly begin to heal as her body and soul calmed down.

"Shhh," said Jill wrapping her arms around the woman's shaking body. "It's okay. You're safe now."

Rick had never experienced anything like that before. For the first time ever, he truly thought the woman might die during the extraction. It was a lot for him to witness. This time God prevailed but it took every ounce of their power and prayer. They just as easily could have lost. It was close, very close. This woman wanted to be saved, but so often people like their demons and feel empty without the symbiotic relationship that slowly ruins them. They may be oblivious to their own spiritual reality, but subconsciously, they revel in sin because sin is comfortable and it makes people feel good. Being a believer in Christ is hard work, and it's why, in the end, the Devil will win every time. The War over people's souls isn't won by showing them the Way, the Truth, and the Light, but by what they're comfortable with, and what takes the least amount of effort to maintain. The Lord gives you a bed of nails on which to lay your weary head, while the Devil tempts you with a mattress plush with velvet and roses. For most, the choice is simple. Eternity is just an afterthought when temptation is always knocking on the door.

For Rick the questions always festered. Why would God create such a world where his children, whom he supposedly loved, suffered so much? Was this really necessary? The answers given by his church were not satisfactory to his young and troubled mind. God created two perfect people in Adam and Eve, free of hunger, thirst, pain or misery, ignorant of good and evil; and then gives them a way to make them 'fall'. Then God creates the snake, an adversary, to purposely undermine and tempt them to take the opportunity to disobey God, and do the one thing that could condemn humanity to a world of pain and suffering.

"You engineered this situation knowing that we will fall? Why?" thought Rick. "So we each must spend our lifetimes earning our way back into your good graces? It just doesn't make sense."

"Why mom? Why does God do this to us?"

The answer was always the same. "God is too powerful and advanced for us to comprehend. We can't know or understand why he made all of this happen. We just have to accept that it was necessary and trust in His Will."

Rick wasn't satisfied. "So you're telling me that the woman who I just saw with demon's claws literally impaling her body and attempting to rip out her very soul is necessary? That is God's Will? That all of the people who reject or lose sight of God…or those who may never have even really ever learned of his love…must burn in Hell for eternity? That is necessary?"

"That is why we must never stop preaching. Why we must never stop trying to save."

"But what about those we can't get to? Is that their fault then? Why should they have to suffer so much then?"

"We just have to work harder son. This is our responsibility. We are the soldiers. We are the one's God is trusting to work on his behalf. You must never give up Rick. You must never lose the faith."

Rick still didn't understand. "So all the people who are raped and murdered, or starving or whatever. All this is necessary for God's higher purpose?"

"It is son. I can't tell you exactly why…but it is all just part of the plan."

Rick walked into his bedroom and closed the door.

"Well I think the plan is bullshit then. God wanted that woman to suffer? God wants me to suffer? It just doesn't make any fucking sense? God didn't have to create Satan or the Tree of Knowledge of good and evil. He didn't have to give us a way to fuck everything up. He didn't even have to allow pain and suffering or demons to exist. All for some supposed 'Higher Purpose'. What the fuck was that all about? All to fight a war and emerge victorious against Satan…when he created Satan in the first place? What the hell?"

Rick could accept that he was just one little person and maybe it was too difficult to comprehend the divine plan but any way in which he tried to reason it all out, it just didn't make sense. He tried to make sense of it all, he really did, but he just couldn't. The older he became the more he just couldn't put blind faith into something that had no real answers and such an ambiguous ending. Rick came to two conclusions. One, God couldn't expect people to accept all of this because everyone was trapped in their own level of human understanding, and two, it was unfair that while everyone was trapped in this inability to understand, they were also forced to be trapped in the suffering and misery forced upon them. He'd always been taught that being a 'good Christian' was all about choice; choosing to walk with the Lord instead of living a life of excess and sin. But in Rick's eyes, he didn't choose to exist, he didn't volunteer to participate in this war, so why was he and others forced to endure all of this bullshit just to appease God?

"You have to trust me or I will punish you like no other."

At thirteen years old, Rick was beginning to see through the bullshit, and form spiritual opinions of his own. There had to be more to the story, than what he was being told. He knew that. But at the moment he was trapped in what he'd been taught, in his own realm of experience and understanding, and all he really knew was that things didn't add up and they certainly didn't make sense. His apathy toward God began.

"Why were demons allowed to freely roam the earth but angels had to be called to help us?"

"Sure Christ died for our sins and suffered three days of torture on the cross…but that was one man and I'm sorry but there have been people who have been beaten, raped, and suffered all their lives…far worse than Christ ever did. His torment alone is worth more and somehow eases the collective suffering of billions of people throughout humanity's history?"

It all made Rick furious. He could see the demons using people as their playground and God just standing around letting it all happen. He was told to simply have faith.

"You motherfuckers don't understand! You don't see what I see! You have no idea how bad it is. You think you know, you run your mouth off hypothesizing, but you don't know shit until you can witness it first-hand."

The bitterness began to grow. His blood father was gone, and his spiritual Father had condemned him. Nobody knew the truth about how and what Rick was feeling. There was no one to talk to. His mother and the church had been no help in answering his questions, and he didn't dare breach the subject with his father. Bob would have yanked both boys from Brenda in a second had he known how deep into the pit of Christ the family had fallen. It's one thing to believe, and it's okay to believe in a higher power. It's not okay to become so wrapped up in that world, that your sense of reality becomes distorted, and your childhood happiness is replaced with condemnation and a tormented and lost soul.

"Mom, why did daddy leave?"

"Daddy had a demon inside of him."

CHAPTER TWENTY-FIVE

Rick longed for guidance. Not just any guidance however, he longed for some sort of adult guidance that he could relate to. He found that guidance in youth group leader Kevin Nichols. A mid-40s hippy like character, Kevin was real. He didn't pretend to be someone he wasn't, and never sweated the small stuff in life. A lover of rock music, guitar playing, and everything alternative, he immediately found a willing student in Rick. Kevin never told the kids what to believe and he certainly didn't use any psychological terror tactics to get his ministering across. He asked the kids questions, questions that made them think and face themselves. They all loved and looked up to Kevin, and for Rick especially, Kevin was the only adult that didn't treat him like an out-of-control insignificant child whose thoughts and beliefs were just misguided. Kevin listened. And he understood. He'd been a kid once as well, and in fact, in many ways was still just a big kid himself, which is part of the reason he endeared himself so much to the boys.

They all did some seriously fun shit when they got together, and while some of the parents didn't agree with Kevin's tactics, the kids listened to Kevin, especially Rick, and took him far more seriously than he did any words from his own parents. Kevin never stopped being a 'good Christian' or loving God. He'd pray with the boys, and he'd often speak of God without preaching or using evangelistic tactics. The guy was sincere and Rick never once doubted him or the depth of his faith. He inspired the boy. Kevin showed them that you didn't have to give up who you were, you could still be cool and fun, and love and walk with God. That was a huge revelation for Rick. His experiences had always been so painful and so black and white. You had to do this otherwise you were doomed. Kevin offered a softer, kinder approach to God and to life in general, one that Rick could understand and relate to.

"Can I talk to you boys for a second?" said Kevin motioning to Rick and Strom. The boys followed him out to the back deck of his country home.

"Did you boys steal from the store on the way up here?"

Rick hung his head. He could never lie to Kevin. "Yes. We took some Swisher Sweets and a rock magazine."

"What makes it okay for you to take something you didn't earn?"

"I don't know," said Rick.

"Listen boys, I'm not going to yell at you, and I'm not going to call your parents. I just want to talk about it and try and make you understand how I see it. You may not believe me, but it's so much more satisfying to earn things in life. Do you think it's really fair to take something somebody else worked for without compensating them for it?"

"No."

"How would you feel if that was your stuff that you'd worked so hard to get and someone just came along and took it? You'd be angry right?"

"Yeah…I guess I would."

"I can't stop you from stealing or doing anything really…but next time you're about to hock something…just take a minute and think about this conversation. Think about what we've talked about...and put yourselves in that person's shoes."

Both Rick and Strom felt like shit as Kevin made his point. The boys didn't stop stealing but they did become more ethical about who they stole from and why. Baby steps. Rick lost count of all the moral, spiritual, and practical lessons Kevin doled out during their time together. Kevin pointed out the possible consequences of their decisions, and really made them think of what could happen. His approach, methods, and explanations went a long way with the boys, and left an indelible mark on Rick's life. If only the boy could have spent more time with Kevin and less time crusading for Christ.

"I want to pray at Witches Rock," said Brenda. "Cleanse it if we can."

"Today?" said Rick.

"Yes. It's time."

His mother had talked about visiting the rock for a while now, and from the beginning Rick didn't have a good feeling about it. The rock was supposedly sacred, and used by witches and Satanists for their ceremonies. Out towards Sheridan on Highway 99 East, the rock lay in the lush green countryside a little south of McMinnville. Low grey clouds coated the sky, remnants of an earlier summer shower, and everything had that cold, wet but fresh feeling. Not wanting to be left out, the sun was doing its best to poke through the clouds, throwing everything into a sort of twilight. Pulling off the highway, Brenda parked in an open space near the paved walkway up the hill to the site.

The rock itself was an anomaly in the surrounding geography, an enormous piece of solid granite laying on its side weighing tonnes. About five feet tall and about twelve to fourteen feet in diameter, it looked like a medieval table fit for a family of giants. In the smooth valley plains, and small creeks of the countryside, it certainly looked out of place. To a Christian, the rock was probably one of the most significant sources of evil in the valley. Of course Brenda would eventually seek it out to cleanse. It was only natural.

Halfway up the path they started praying in tongues. With each step, Rick felt the rock calling with an eerie, icy chill, almost as if the rock itself was an ancient sleeping giant.

"Be careful son. Do not underestimate the power of the forces here."

Rick waited and braced himself, expecting his eye to open at any moment, revealing a myriad of horrors. But it was silent. No demons, no spirits on the rock or anywhere in the vicinity. A violent shiver shook his small frame, as the rock radiated a pure cold evil, almost like a force field drawing kindred's in, and keeping enemies away. They continued circling the stone, praying in tongues, uncertain if anything specific would occur, and wondering what they should do next. Rick stared at the side of the rock, pulled by its magnitude and its undeniable force. He had to touch it. He couldn't help himself. Without even thinking, Rick reached out his hand and placed it on the side of the granite.

"Jesus Christ!"

A frigid black ice screamed through his veins, quickly freezing him in place. He couldn't think. He couldn't breathe, pull away or even scream. His soul felt as if it had reached absolute zero and an infinite heaviness plunged his heart downward into the earth, right out of his body. Desolation and anguish washed over him, and life, meaning, and hope seemed to just disappear.

"It feels like me. The rock feels like how I feel inside. It feels like death."

He had no idea how or why, or whether it was really happening or whether it was all in is head, but he stood there transfixed by the sorrow and soullessness pulsing from the rock through his hand to his heart, and back again, as it sucked whatever life he had left. Noticing Rick's pallor, Brenda slowly made her way behind the boy, intensifying her prayers. Two minutes? Ten minutes? Fifteen minutes? Rick had no idea how long he stood there before he was able to remove his hand, losing all sense of time, and reality.

"Rick."

Gazing upon the stone with a look of both curiosity and intense fear, Rick pulled back his hand, regaining a sense of self-awareness. It's like he'd outwardly felt what he was becoming inside, and it scared him to death. Powerful and real. The cold, stark reality of his future. They finished praying, but the desolate nothingness stayed with Rick, not just for that day but for all the days to come. He didn't dare tell his mother, she wouldn't understand. He didn't even understand. Was the rock trying to tell him something? Was it able to somehow tap into his inner self? Like the ghosts of ancient past seeking the ghost within his soul. Rick had no clue. All he knew was that he'd never felt so cold and empty in his life.

As the summer wore on, Rick's reputation on the streets grew. He was the kid that would and could do anything. Need something ripped off? He was your guy. Smart, feisty, and full of vigour, Rick challenged authority every chance he got. Cops were pigs who deserved to be messed with. Respect? Why respect someone who doesn't respect you. His legend grew, and as his legend grew, so too did the expectations of having to live up to it. Rick was always up to the challenge. His quiet, subdued nature made seem him mysterious, and being dark and mysterious also made him dangerous. Being seen as dangerous was fucking cool. And while the very nature of street life was to be cautious and suspicious around people, everyone trusted and confided in Rick. There was no doubt that by this time in Rick's life, he got more trust, love and respect from the streets than he did anywhere else, including home. More and more, these people, the 'rebel' lifestyle, the underground, anti-authoritarian culture became his home, especially as the dynamics of his own home life began to change.

"Jimmy," said Brenda shaking her youngest son on the shoulder. "Where is Rick? It's after midnight!"

Jimmy hung his head. "I don't know."

"Jimmy. Where is Rick? I know you know where he is!"

Jimmy pointed to the window. "He's out there."

Brenda pulled back the curtain and saw the open window. "Out here? As in he's outside roaming around?"

"Yes." Terrified and tired of keeping his older brother's secrets, Jimmy spilled his guts to his mother.

"For how long? Are you kidding me? Lord Jesus help me!"

Brenda grabbed the screen from its perch on the roof, slammed it back in place and barred the window. How could she not have known? How could she have missed this? Three years? What on earth was that boy doing out on the streets all night. The thought made her shake with anger and with fear. Not her son. Not her Rick.

"Lord, I pray for that boy. Please guide him home safely."

When Rick climbed back onto the roof a couple of hours later at two in the morning, he knew right away the gig was up.

"Son of a bitch." He didn't even bother knocking or trying to wake up Jimmy. He couldn't be angry, he'd had a good three-year run. Both sliding glass doors on the patio and deck were locked.

"Damn, she's waiting for me behind that front door. Oh well…not much I can do about it."

With a deep breath, he placed his hand on the front door handle and turned the knob. No movement.

"God damn. She's really pissed."

With every other door to the house locked, Rick tried the door to the GEO Storm car.

"Thank God." He opened the door and climbed into the front seat. He had half a mind to teach his mom a lesson and take the car for a spin, but his need for sleep overpowered that decision. That he was going to catch hell in the morning was a given, but he couldn't really be angry. The fact that he'd managed to sneak out undetected around three hundred plus times since he was ten and a half years old was a pretty good record. Sneaking out was now a thing of the past; his ninja had been busted.

"How could you Rick? Why? I just don't understand! How could you do this to me?"

Rick said nothing.

"Sneaking out? Why? Can you please explain?"

"It had nothing to do with you."

"Nothing to do with me? What about your little brother? Do you have any idea how terrified and worried he is about you every time you sneak out? How can you be so selfish? What do you think the Lord thinks about this?"

Rick truly did feel bad about Jimmy but he didn't really care what the Lord thought.

"You're grounded until further notice!"

Rick took the punishment because he knew he deserved it, but it wasn't going to take giving up his street life. It meant too much to him, it was all that really mattered in his life. The real fight became whether or not Rick would keep going out at night. In his eyes, Rick was a thirteen-year-old 'young man', who'd already stolen, ran from the cops, and had an esteemed image and friends on the street. He didn't give a fuck about society or its normal requirements that he be a good boy, go to school, and do as he was told. The rebellious, anti-authoritarian, 'I don't give a fuck' attitude was already too deeply ingrained, and to be quite honest, he really didn't care. Didn't care what anyone thought, including his mother. She was lucky Rick even still lived at home. It wasn't like he hadn't thought about leaving for good.

He was Ghost, and he was going to do whatever he wanted, the way he wanted – catch him if you can. He knew he had his mother up against a wall. If she told Bob what their oldest son was up to, he'd flip and demand custody, and there was no way she was going to let that happen. For all he'd pissed her off, Brenda wasn't about to lose Rick. She loved him, and she needed him, and more importantly, in her heart she still believed that she could save him. She had to save him. Brenda never stopped believing that she could. And that was the bond, the connection. Whatever happened in his life, Rick loved and would always try and protect his mother, no matter what. She didn't leave them, she had no control over his 'gift' or how God chose to use him – none of that was her fault. For Rick, no matter his mother's faults, she never stopped trying to bring him to the light, to show him the way she had found love and peace in her life – through Christ.

Brenda did what she thought was best for her children. There was no malice or ill attempt. She loved her son deeply and wanted to see him be the best he could be, and live up to his divine potential. Were her methods questionable? To some parents perhaps, but she did what she thought best based on her own knowledge and experiences. Her intent was pure. Even at a young age Rick understood the difference. While Bob's intent bordered more on power and control, Brenda was all about love and joy, peace and light. She wasn't about to give up on her boy, not now, not ever. She wasn't perfect. Neither was Rick. And he pushed the limits as hard, and as often as he could.

Brenda's mistake was not taking charge right after the divorce. She gave him too much leeway, too much rope, and like any young boy would do, he took full advantage of it. She let the Lord guide her decisions instead of rational, logical thinking. It is fine to let faith lead your spiritual life, but it shouldn't take a parent almost three years to realize their child is sneaking out at night and leading a completely different existence. That is just cold hard, lack of parenting, and a failure to protect a child from society and himself. What if something serious had happened to the boy while he was out? Once or twice is understandable. Kids are kids. Even a dozen times might be explainable. But over three hundred? That figure is inexcusable. Incredibly lucky that Rick managed to return each night relatively safe and sound, Brenda could have been faced with the full wrath of Child Services had they known. And now Rick had her by the ass. He had all the power in their relationship, he had all the control. He'd spent almost a quarter of his young life doing what he pleased and he wasn't about to give that up. Not for her, not for anyone.

Rick loved his mother, and he'd protect her to the death, but in his mind, he was already too old and too far gone to let her tell him what to do. She'd had her chance. She let it slip away. She'd had her chances to regain control. Where did Rick come up with the money he'd left on the kitchen table? He didn't have that many papers to deliver. She knew he didn't have another real job. She had to have known that it was acquired under dubious circumstances? Yet, she took it. And she kept taking it every time Rick laid it on the table.

"The LORD will provide".[27]

Turning a blind eye was much easier than facing the truth. The truth was just too much for her and her faith to handle.

Rick quit sneaking out. No more screen windows and quietly dropping down from the roof. No. If he was going to go out at night, from now on, he was going to use the front door. If his mother even tried locking him out again, he'd just quit coming home all together. An unspoken understanding. Rick could just come and go as he pleased and no questions would be asked.

[27] Genesis 22:14

"Just please don't quit school. Be responsible and keep your grades up."

He could do that. What a kick-ass arrangement! He got to do whatever the hell he wanted, when he wanted, the complete freedom he'd always craved, and all he had to do was half-ass it at school. The bare minimum. Homework? Fuck it. Didn't matter. He'd do whatever he had to do before class started. All he had to do was pass school and take care of the house. Rick could do that with his eyes closed. Did he force her hand, or did Brenda just give in because she recognized that her son was a young man she couldn't control and didn't want to face the consequences? She could have gotten help. She could have discussed it with Bob. Yes, he would have been furious, and yes she may have lost the boys, but at least Rick may have gotten some help before he'd fallen any further. But none of that happened, and none of that mattered to Rick one bit. Why would it? He was free to live the life he wanted. No restrictions. No boundaries. No control. He was Ghost.

CHAPTER TWENTY-SIX

With the shackles of his bondage removed, Rick sped towards a complete freefall. Young, popular, and more than a little rash, he was driven by his 'devil may care attitude', and crazy enough to take on anything. If he wanted it, he got it. The word 'no' just wasn't in his vocabulary. His mother never told him no, so why should he listen to anyone else? In fact, even attempting to tell him no only spurred his curiosity and wantonness. Never without a smoke dangling from the corner of his lips and a can of Mountain Dew in his hand, his habits led to a constant need for money, and the only way to get money was to do 'jobs' for whomever was paying the price. Small store shelf swipe jobs manifested into medium jobs, which manifested into serious shit, the kind that got one's ass sent off for a stay in juvenile detention. Rick thought nothing of it.

"You want me drop in ninja style from a skylight onto the floor of a car dealership so we can haul the safe out? Sure no problem. I can do that. Thanks for the $1700 fuckers!"

Unstoppable. With the money and the prestige that came from pulling off such a heist, he no longer considered himself a child. He was an adult, a man, capable of earning a living, providing for his own needs, and making his own decisions. Except he wasn't an adult. He was a thirteen-year-old boy full of delusional grandeur about where thirteen-year-old boys stood in the hierarchy of the social order. This delusion gave him power. This delusion spiraled him to greater risks, and greater accomplishments in his eyes. There was nothing he couldn't do or at least nothing he wouldn't try. With no one to stop him or at the minimum step in and say no, why wouldn't he think these things? Self-preservation. His father had betrayed him, and his mother, bless her intentions, left his guidance to a God that Rick clearly believed had forsaken him. The only one he could trust, the only one he could truly count on was himself. Sure he had Strom, Cajun, and some of the boys, but they didn't know. They didn't know the true torment of his soul. For them, 'Ghost' was just a moniker for their friend; they had no idea how deep the discourse ran within Rick's identity. They would never know. Ghosts don't talk.

Rick spent the majority of his haul on new tools and equipment for his trade, a pair of black fourteen eyelet boots, better bags, and a good supply of smokes. No longer feeling like a snot-nosed kid working out of a garage, he was an entitled professional and a real menace to society. A confidence boost. He was the man.

The guy who could get shit done. He was riding at the top of the roller coaster. Invincible. It didn't matter who, and it didn't matter what. Rick was ready to fuck shit up.

"She needs us man," said Havoc. "He fucking raped her and beat the shit out of her. Her boyfriend. That fucking God damn Spic! Then he gave her to two of his fucking friends! You in bro?"

One look at Sunrise's swollen face, and the hollow look of pain in her eyes, told Rick all he needed to know. "Oh yeah. I'm in."

Three days later, Rick, Havoc, and Strom caught up with the boyfriend and two of his buddies. It wasn't pretty. They beat them to within an inch of their lives, and then beat them some more. They didn't care, they didn't hesitate. They were there for Sunrise.

"Hey you kids! They've had enough! Stop that shit and get down the road before I call the cops." The guy stormed out his house waving his paper. "Stop!"

After a few more well placed kicks the boys turned and meandered down the road leaving them bleeding and broken on the pavement. Justice. The cops never came and asked them about it, even though everyone in town knew what they'd done. Power. Admiration of their peers. The legend grew.

"They're threatening to retaliate," said Strom. "We need to start packing."

With his stash, Rick purchased matching .38 Walther's handguns for $250 along with some ammunition. He knew it was a very dangerous step forward, but it was also the next logical step in the evolution of what they were becoming. There was no turning back now. The ante was raised. Death begets death. This wasn't a pretend game of cops and robbers, and the youngsters weren't running around with plastic Hasbro toy guns, this shit was real. With the purchase of the weapons, they'd put themselves at that level, and at that risk. None of them old enough to need a razor but apparently old enough to need a gun. With the purchase of the guns, things began getting serious. If it was so easy for them to get guns, then it'd be just as easy for their enemies to get guns too. They had to step up their game, play by a higher set of standards. The focus shifted from a purely offensive infiltration to defensive consequential thinking. Now, nothing was ever done without thinking of the consequences. No longer could Rick and the boys afford to do things haphazard or fly by the seat of their pants. If the consequences of their actions were potentially prison or death, then they needed to treat them with the utmost severity and respect.

"We need to start an organization," said Rick reaching over to light Strom's smoke. "Fucking us against the man."

"Yeah bro for sure."

"Like the military. You know the Special Forces. They do some cool ass shit. And they know a lot."

"Tonnes of cops are ex-military," said Strom.

"Exactly. If they play the game at the highest levels, then we need to do the same."

"Military guys are cool. They fight for the same sort of shit that we do. Sucks that they all sell out and become cops."

"Pigs. Who think they know everything," said Rick. "We need to be one step ahead of them. Always. No excuses."

"I agree man, I agree."

"We're just protecting ourselves."

"Yep," said Strom. "All about survival."

With the makings of the 'organization' firmly in place, the boys nabbed every book, magazine, and piece of information they could on the elite forces of the military, law enforcement, and intelligence agencies. Already obsessed with the topic, Rick dove head first into the task, relishing in the idea and challenge of besting the best at their own game. If they could level the playing field, the more untouchable they'd be, especially to the common criminal or criminal organization that may wish to compete or seek vengeance upon them.

An easy recruit to the organization, Cajun taught them everything he knew from his dad being a cop. All of this wasn't just a spur of the moment decision, the boys spent hours and hours talking about it, and trying to recruit others to their cause.

"You're all fucking crazy," said Havoc. "I want nothing to do with it."

"Clover?"

"The US military sucks. It's the IRA you need to follow."

"The IRA?" said Strom.

"The Provisional Irish Republican Army," said Clover. Almost four years older than the boys, Clover held the position of 'knowing the most' and being respected strictly because of his age and the army green trench coat and tall black combat boots he wore. He knew shit, and the boys listened. "The IRA know how to work behind enemy lines. My family has direct blood links with the originals, and my people have spent their lives bleeding and dying in their fight against British tyranny."

"No way bro," said Rick. "That's fucking cool shit."

"I see what you guys are trying to accomplish here. I get the agenda…but you're going about it all wrong. Read about the IRA man. They'll teach you some real useful shit."

The boys took that under advisement and welcomed Clover to the group. With its free refills for coffee and both a smoking and a non-smoking section 'Shea's', a little restaurant right on Highway 99 became organizational headquarters. The owners and waitresses knew the boys were underage but they were cool and never called the cops, even when the boys were there during school hours. Out of respect and thanks, the boys always left a big tip and never once caused a ruckus. They weren't there for trouble, they were there to go over plans and strategies. They'd sit for hours and hours talking about history, revolutionaries, patriots, law enforcement, tactics, the military, and really everything imaginable under the sun that had anything to do with their new area of interest.

"We need to operate and think like a paramilitary unit," said Clover taking a deep drag. "That's the only way to guarantee our safety and security."

"And we need to study and learn all the best elements of the best," said Rick.

At the time, the boys had no idea what their conversations would turn into, if anything, but the fertile soil of what would become known as "The Team" was dug, raked, and ready for seeds. For now, it was just an exercise, a way to feel as if they were coming of age, and a way to feel like more than just common criminals; a sort of justification for their actions. 'The Team' solidified their way of life and gave them an agenda and a way of thinking, being and doing. These early conversations and meeting of the minds were extremely formative for Rick, and would colour the rest of his life, including the events that led up to the fateful day. Efficiency, organization, elitism, planning, an obsession with the militia, acting 'above' any form of authority and unaccepting of any rules, laws or limitations – all of these pre-existing traits in his personality blossomed and took complete hold. Coupled with the already dark, brooding, and emotionless Ghost, the stage was set for a very unique and powerful chemistry just ready to explode. The hands of time powerless against this ticking bomb.

The dichotomy of Rick's life continued, and in the early winter of 1992, he was enjoying a twisted sense of popularity – his deeds and reputation made him a celebrity both at church and on the streets. Even though his personal relationship with God was strained, with the church crowd, he was the dark young man, shinning in Christ who played the saxophone every Sunday with the 'Praise and Worship' team. He'd become a fixture within the church, and combined with Brenda's reputation of being one of its most deeply spiritual warriors and the repeated prophecies over his head, everyone assumed that young Rick was a white knight, and ignored the tarnish on his armour. On the streets, his tarnished armour only solidified his sterling reputation. Everyone knew that he had 'done things' even if Rick was loath to talk about those things himself. And the less Rick talked, the more the myth and legend of some of those things grew. Some even knew he'd started carrying, though that was something he never advertised. Even the older kids treated him with respect and a certain amount of reverence; his guts and grits meaning way more than the number of years he'd been alive. Not many knew both sides of Rick's life, he was careful who he did and did not let in to each.

Jackie was different. She'd moved with her mother to Lafeyette around August and had started attending the McMinnville church with one of her friends at the beginning of the school year. She also hung around with Destiny, who happened to be a young street protégé of Becca, a close and trusted friend of Rick's. Becca adopted Jackie and "Dez" like little sisters, immediately taking them under her wing. The streets could be a mean and dangerous place without support. The archetypical 'church girl', fourteen-year-old Dez was desperate to break free from her strong Christian family and experience the real nuances of life.

The same age as Rick, Jackie grew up in a single family home where her mother's boyfriends didn't think twice about having the child service their needs whenever they felt like it. Angry and sullen, Rick immediately felt a kindred spirit hiding behind her mesmerizing green eyes and dirty blonde hair. She was a bad ass – smoked cigarettes and weed, drank, cussed like a sailor, and experimented in all sorts of substance abuse. There really wasn't anything she wouldn't try or say no to when it came to booze and drugs. More of a wild flower than a potted plant, Rick felt the need to take care of her, and keep her safe, as much as he possibly could. The guard dog role made him feel important, like someone needed him. The perfect match, the two hit it off the moment they met, and over the next few months became inseparable. Jackie and Ghost. Ghost and Jackie.

"You're going where?" said Jackie.

"Alaska," said Rick. "My Dad just moved there, so now Jimmy and I have to spend our Christmas break flying up there and visiting."

"I don't want you to go."

"You really think I want to go? I mean seeing Alaska will be sort of cool but I sure as hell don't want to spend a second with my father."

"Can't you stay?"

"Nope. We have to go. Stupid fucking law."

Successfully finishing his flight school training with Japan Airlines, Bob chose Anchorage, Alaska as his flight base, where the airline had offices and made a routine stop on its Pacific route. Bob purchased tickets for the boys, and after the hour's drive to Portland, they were on a flight to Seattle. Despite Bob being a pilot, the boys really hadn't flown that much, and this was the first time they'd flown by themselves.

"Maybe we should just miss our flight?" Rick joked as he bought his little brother some fries during their layover at SeaTac airport in Seattle.

"You think we could?" laughed Jimmy.

"It'd be sort of fun to hang out here for a little while and wouldn't Dad be pissed?"

"Oh he'd be more than a little pissed," said Jimmy. "He'd kick our ass!"

The boys laughed and joked but they knew the consequences would be real and severe if they weren't on that flight to Anchorage.

"Did you boys have a nice flight?" said Rosemary turning around to the backseat of the car.

"It was alright," said Rick.

"Were the skies clear enough to see the mountains?" said Bob.

"Yeah," said Rick. "It was pretty cool flying in seeing all the ice-covered mountains, and then all of a sudden there was just this city covered in white. There's snow everywhere here! And man is it cold!"

"Welcome to Alaska son," laughed Bob.

The drive up to Doggie Avenue and the new house felt long, mainly because it was hard to distinguish anything specific or interesting amongst the cloud of white.

"See up there," said Bob slowly down and pointing. "That's Hill Top Ski Area. You boys aren't going to mind spending some time on the slopes are you?" Bob and Rosemary were doing their best to make the trip enjoyable. Maybe with a new house, in a new city, things would be different.

All Rick noticed as they drove was how upscale and rich the surrounding neighbourhood was. And as much as it went against all he and "The Team" ranted and seethed about, he had to admit that he was impressed. The house on Doggie Avenue was a serious step up from the broken down affair back on Baker Creek Road. Sitting up high on a hill, the huge glass windows overlooked the entire city of Anchorage. With its three bedrooms, two baths, and large back deck, it stank of money, money that his father had refused to give his mother to help with their care.

"Fucking unbelievable," he seethed under his breath.

It was like his dad and Rosemary were just rubbing the child support battles in his face all over again. He had the money; that much was clear to Rick. His father made a conscious choice just not to give any to his own children. The thought made Rick sick, and intensified his hatred, not only of his father but how money controls everything in life. His father used money to prove a point to his mother and to make them all suffer. For Rick and the members of 'The Team', wealth was a symbol of everything that was wrong in society. Did the cops ever pick on rich people? Hell no, it was always people who had nothing. People like Rick and his friends.

This first trip to Alaska wasn't horrible, and the boys spent much of the time with Bob and Rosemary on the slopes learning to ski. To his father's dismay, Rick fell in love with the 'rebel sport' snowboarding, and really wanted nothing to do with the snobbish and preppy sport of skiing. The week and a half passed rather quickly with both sides doing their best to pretend they were enjoying each other's company. Still it was a start. The arguments had been few, and if Rick was legally bound to come and visit his dad in Alaska, then at least he could look forward to shredding it on the slopes.

Once back from Alaska, Rick returned to school and returned to his duties as scout master for the demon hunters. Brenda and Jill had heard that one of the dormitories at Linfield College was entertaining devil worship and witchcraft, all led by a Satanist. Of course, they had to go check it out. Deemed too dangerous for the children, only the adults and their hunting dog Rick made the midnight trek. Finding the right building, the crew piled out of the car and made a plan of attack.

"If anyone asks," said Jill. "We're all here to see a family member. That way if we go inside or walk around the building, it won't seem out of place. We don't want to raise any suspicions."

"Whatever," thought Rick. "As if anyone's parents or family stopped by to visit at midnight."

The demon hunts had lost their lustre for the teen. He'd already pretty much seen and heard everything he possibly could, so he was more worried about running into someone he knew and getting thoroughly embarrassed. The college scene in McMinnville overlapped pretty heavily with the street and party scene, and more than a few times, Rick had purchased smokes and alcohol from someone who attended the college.

"This place is creepy," he thought as the heavy oppressing air surrounded him. "Like seriously weird."

As they walked around the perimeter, Rick noticed the building beginning to pulse like it was alive and breathing.

"This building is possessed," he said to his mom. "It's dangerous. I think we should leave now."

"We'll pray son."

His warning only made the group pray harder. Rick joined them. He could never really tell during these forays when he actually stopped praying, it just always happened. One minute, he'd be praying his little heart out, and the next, his tongue would freeze. Today was no exception. He watched in horror as they came out of the windows, over the roof, and through the doorways. A dozen or so grotesque forms bound and determined to protect their territory and beat off these Godly intruders.

"Umm…Mom," said Rick. "They're here and they're forming a circle around us! They're coming fast!"

Jill hit the grass, her legs unable to support her spirit in the face of such evil. Brenda and Jack flew to her side, placed their hands on her shoulders, and prayed to the Almighty.

"Lord protect us from these spirits! All hail mighty God!"

The darkness flashed with an intense brilliance of white, as three Godly presences descended from the heavens to do battle. In an instant the air flooded with a breathless intensity, more terrifying than Rick had ever witnessed before. The demons attacked the angels with a deathly vigour, striking with all the might of Satan.

"Easy win for the angels," thought Rick. "They were backed by God's Kingdom and all his might." Yet, he watched in horror as both demon and angel blood spattered the sky, walls and ground; guts and gore dripping from the mangled forms.

"Jesus Christ!"

The first angel fell lifeless to the ground, defeated.

"We are all going to die!" Rick couldn't move. He couldn't even scream, his voice locked in a steel vault of fear. He'd never seen an angel die before. Never even though it was possible. He was next. He could feel the horrors searching for him, searching for his gaze, like they knew, he knew he was about to die. A second angel down. Torn to shreds by the claws of Satan's glory.

"Jesus Christ Almighty save us!"

With the spirit of its fallen comrades, the third angel spread its majestic wings and went on the attack, thrashing and lashing at any demon that dared to even come close. One by one they dropped in death until only four remained. The combatants eyed each other, then the surrounding carnage, with both sides finally backing away, an uneasy truce observed. The angel hovered near Brenda and the Connelly's, while the demons retreated to the safety of the walls. Through his fogged haze, Rick could hear Jill sobbing, her body slumped on the ground like a ragdoll. Brenda with tears in her own eyes.

"I think we should leave now," said Jack, still thanking the Lord for his Will and his work.

"Rick," said Brenda. "Are you okay? You're white as a ghost."

Shaken and stunned by what he'd just witnessed, Rick needed to get away. To be alone and process what just happened. And he needed a smoke. He needed a God damned fucking smoke.

"I'm going to walk home," he said turning on his heel and taking off into the night.

"Rick!" yelled Brenda.

"Come back Rick," said Jill. "Rick! We need to talk about this!"

Ignoring the voices, he dug in his pocket for a Marlboro, and flicked a light. With the first drag he went completely ice cold, numb inside. Everything he'd thought he'd known had just been shattered. All his life he'd been taught to believe that God's Will and might were irrefutable forces in the universe. Every Sunday they sang songs about how 'none could stand before Him' and how all His enemies would be crushed. The only reason Satan and his followers existed was because God allowed it. A cruel and morbid test for His children. Never did His followers doubt their God's invincibility. In fact, they were told to never doubt His invincibility. Faith would take care of everything. You believed, and God would take care of you. He would never let His children fall if they turned to Him in faith. Never. That was the promise.

Give your burdens to the LORD, and he will take care of you. He will not permit the godly to slip and fall.[28]

It was all a lie. A great big fucking lie. Rick had just seen it happen with his own two eyes. Two of God's angels, fragments of His Holy Will, torn to shreds in agony and slain by the same demons who were not even supposed to be able to stand against them. God wasn't invincible. He wasn't infallible. He didn't always win. What the fuck?

Rick's head swirled, trying to decipher some meaning.

"I know what it means," he thought. "It means that God can't even protect us if the numbers and circumstances aren't right. It means that all of the stories of the Wars in Heaven, when Michael and his angels fought the dragon and his angels were bullshit. Victory had never been guaranteed. It also meant that our victory at Armageddon wasn't either. Why the hell were we even bothering to fight then?"

He had been betrayed. Once again, Rick had been betrayed. His world and his beliefs had been turned completely on their head. All this time he'd been led to believe that he was fighting for the winning team, that in fact, there was no way that they could lose. He'd believed that he'd been suffering all this time because he had been 'fated' to and he was an instrument of God's Will, no matter how severely that calling afflicted his soul. But if God's Will was fallible, if even His instruments, the holy angels could be defeated and destroyed, there was no longer any unbreakable fate or Will that necessitated all that he had endured. It had all been for nothing. The spell had been broken. God didn't have his shit together. He wasn't 'everything and all things'. He wasn't omnipotent, he wasn't omnipresent, and he certainly wasn't all powerful. His Will wasn't a guarantee against anything. It had all been lies. Big giant fucking lies, and no amount of Bible reading or fiery sermons was going to undo what he'd just witnessed. They'd all lied to him. The Bible, preachers, Jack and Jill, his mother. All liars. All perpetrators of the betrayal.

His entire life, from the time he was born and baptized, had been devoted to

[28] Psalm 55:22

God. He knew more Bible verses than he could count, and had been donning his spiritual armour since he was six years old. Everything for God. Everything for Christ. For at least five years, he'd been God's little warrior, and for the last three years he'd been told his 'gift' was instrumental to God's work. His young, programmable mind had believed everything. Every message, every verse, every prophecy. But none of it had been true. The entire time, they'd all lied to him about the extent of God's power; that nothing could stand against Him or His angels. The betrayal Rick felt was real. He hadn't asked for this war, he hadn't volunteered. He'd been told service was compulsory and that the wounds he bared during this service would only be rewarded once his life was over, and he was taken to heaven.

"God's power is fake. What the fucking hell."

The realization shook him to the core. There was no winning side. There was only pain, misery, sorrow and sin – and plenty of carnage to back it all up. And death. Lots and lots of death. Nothing but violence, war and suffering. All in the name of who's 'right'. Fuck who's right. Before tonight he'd never questioned who was right; his own suffering had been a necessity to fight the Holy War, the good fight that would guarantee everyone, including his father, a place in heaven. But now he knew. There was no guarantee. Not God's Will, his might, or even his protection. Because he could be defeated and resisted, they could too. All those demon hunts, when they'd been so close to such horrific danger, Rick thought they'd been protected, that God would be there and never let anything happen to them. All lies. A life of lies. A life of betrayal.

The light was still on when Rick walked through the front door.

"Are you okay?" said Brenda sitting in her chair, Bible in hand.

He couldn't even look at her.

"No." The words hardly made it past his throat as he walked up the stairs to his room.

Something snapped and irreparably changed his soul that night. He would never look at God, Christianity, his mother, or his own life the same again. For the rest of his life, Rick would refer to that night as 'The Turning'. Turning away from God, turning away from his mother, and turning away from everything that he'd ever known. His level of doubt, cynicism, and disdain for it all, cemented in his heart. He'd never felt so trapped. He'd never been given a choice in anything. No one had ever really cared how he felt or all the pain he'd suffered on their behalf. For their cause. They'd always just wanted more. More than he could give. They just kept pushing and pushing. What do you see Rick? You're going to do great wonders for God, son. You are a chosen one my child, touched by God himself. Well they could all go to hell. He didn't fucking care about any of it anymore. From now on he'd make his own path, his own choices, and live his own life. No one would tell him what to do or how to behave. Why should he listen to anyone? They were all liars. Every single fucking one of them.

CHAPTER TWENTY-SEVEN

By February 1993, Jackie and Rick's friendship had grown into an intense puppy love. Her the broken soul, and him the protector, they became inseparable. She was his 'foxy girl' and he was her 'Ghost', and together it felt like could really survive their adolescence and possibly even make something of it all in adulthood. Both drowning in sorrow, misery, and depression, and sharing a seriously angry and rebellious side, they couldn't have been a better fit for each other, even at just thirteen years old.

"If our parents ever try to move," said Rick. "I think we should run away to Seattle."

"I'm totally down for that. I don't ever want to be apart from you Ghost. Ever."

"Me neither babe, me neither."

Rick cared for Jackie more than he'd ever cared for anyone in his life. Unlike his parents or any of the others who'd betrayed him, he knew he could count on her. She'd always be on his side, no matter what. And he'd always be there for her. The more he thought about it, the more he did want to escape and just leave McMinnville. Part of it was to rid himself of that part of his life, the church, the divorce, and where all the lies and betrayals began, and part of it was to satisfy his wandering spirit. He hated to be tied down, feeling trapped in any circumstances or surroundings. He'd fully rejected God, and even told Kevin one night during the spring break retreat that there was no hope he'd ever return to that path. It was the first time he'd said the words out loud. There was no reason to stay. He knew he could get the money together and he and Jackie could end up pretty much anywhere they wanted, just the two of them. No one to answer to, no more lies, no more hurt for either of them. It would be hard, but he'd make it work. Hadn't he been the man around the house taking care and providing for his mom and brother for years now?

The day started out like any April day, the sun was shining and the Oregon weather was just starting to hit its just right phase. Jackie and Dez had spent the night with Becca, who dropped them back at Dez's house after Dez's parents had left for work.

"Hey Ghost…I'm at Dez's now," said Jackie over the phone. "Come over. I want to see you."

"You guys have been up all night partying haven't you? I can tell."

"Yeah," she laughed. "We've been tripping a little."

"Okay, I'll try and get there as soon as I can."

Rick caught a ride with Ben, one of the older kids who just happened to be heading up through Newberg. He didn't give a shit about missing school or his responsibilities, especially since he already had it in his mind that him and Jackie were leaving soon anyways. None of it mattered. He just wanted to spend time with the love of his life. Sure, thirteen years old is young to be supposedly falling in love but any that knew Rick, knew that when he gave his heart to something or someone, he gave every piece of him. Jackie had become the center of his life, his hope, his future and his dreams.

When he got to Dez's place, the girls were already acting as wild as hell. On top of the drinking they'd done the night before, Rick could tell they'd dropped acid. Jackie was never one to turn anything down.

"What have you guys been doing?" he said talking over their hyper-active hysterical laughter. Immediately he shifted into babysitter mode, assessing the situation and doing what he could to keep his 'foxy girl' safe through her trip.

"Fuck man," said Dez. "Anything here we can huff?"

"Yeah!" said Jackie. "Let's find something to huff."

"No way am I letting you girls sniff anything. You're way too high already. What you need is some breakfast."

He went into the kitchen, pulled out the frying pan, and started to make some eggs and toast.

"Baby," said Jackie draping her arms around his neck and giggling. "We need some squirrel piss for our Mad Dog and I want some munchies."

"You want Mountain Dew?" He and Strom had named their favourite soda squirrel piss a long time ago and the moniker just stuck.

Jackie flashed her doe eyes. "Yes please."

Those damn eyes got him every time. "Alright. I'll be back soon," he said giving her a peck on the cheek. He turned down the stove, checked his wallet, turning back for one more look before he walked out the front door.

"I love you Ghost."

In that moment, Rick couldn't have been happier. He loved her too. Jackie was truly the first source of real happiness he'd had after the divorce, and a huge part of him believed she'd be the only source of happiness he'd ever need. Strolling into the convenience store without a care in the world, Rick couldn't keep the smile off his face. Everything was a perfect as it was ever going to get. Picking up a two liter of Mountain Dew, some Cool Ranch Doritos, and a few other candies and snacks, he was set.

"Thank you very much," he said to the clerk. "I don't need a bag."

With the two litre in one hand, chips in the other, and the candy in his pockets, he walked back feeling light and free.

"I got the…" He heard Dez sobbing. "Dez?"

Two steps in the front door he saw her lying in the middle of the living room floor.

"Jesus Christ Jackie!"

The chips and soda fell to the ground as he ran to her side.

"Oh my God!"

Coughing and sputtering like she was choking on her own oxygen, every inhalation sent her body into spasms. A white spittle, almost a froth seeped on her lips, which were already starting to darken and lose their vibrancy.

"Jackie!" He took her in his arms and tried to make eye contact but her eyes were already lost to the back of head. He turned over his shoulder and yelled at Dez. "Is she choking?"

"I don't know," she sobbed. Her tear-streaked face panicked as she held the phone to her ear talking to 911.

He could feel Jackie spasm in his arms. He did his best to still her before laying her flat to perform CPR. Performing it on fake dolls in training was nothing to trying to preform it in a real life situation. Determined, he tipped back her head, holding the back of her neck to keep her steady but her shaking body was making it nearly impossible to keep her steady.

"Jesus Christ Jackie! Please hold still! Damn it! Let me help you!" Her body in a complete fit of seizure, he did his best, alternating between pumping her chest and giving her breath through his own lips. Every time he breathed in her mouth, it seemed to go nowhere, like the passage was blocked, and her lungs just refused to take any oxygen. After a frantic minute or so, Rick could feel the cessation of her breathing. The rise and fall of her chest still, the spasms done. Her small body trembled, her eyes a rollercoaster in their sockets, rolling around uncontrollably as if probing for something that was lost. He took her in his arms, hoping his voice would spark some life into her fading soul.

"Please come back to me baby…don't leave me. C'mon Jackie." His face not a foot from hers, he held her so tight, willing her to live, searching for any signs of life and hope. "Jackie…please. Don't go…we've made plans. We can leave…you and me together…we'll go wherever you want to go…"

Then at once she was silent. No breaths, no trembles. She was gone. Rick just knew.

"Please baby…" He touched his head to hers. "Jesus Jackie."

His own chest closed against his breath as he laid her gently on the floor, stood up and walked out the front door. He couldn't stay there a moment longer. He couldn't bear to see her lying so lifeless. It was all just too much.

"Ghost?" said Dez.

He didn't even turn around and acknowledge her. He couldn't. He just kept walking, heading towards McMinnville, twenty kilometres away. He didn't even hear the sirens for at least another minute or so, but it didn't matter, they wouldn't help her, they couldn't help her. She was already gone. Nothing mattered, nothing would ever matter again. She was gone. The love of his life, his Jackie. He'd felt her fade and leave right there in his arms. He'd watched it happen, helpless to make it stop. Thirteen years old and Jackie was dead.

So lost and numb, Rick was lucky his feet knew how to put one in front of the other. He couldn't think, he couldn't breathe, he couldn't feel. A single tear trickled down his face.

"What the fuck is wrong with me? I can't even cry like a normal person. Jesus Christ."

He wanted to break down, he wanted to sob, to cry like a baby, but the numbness of his heart trapped any tears in a vat of ice. His legs just kept walking and walking. His head just kept spinning and spinning. She was gone. Miles past before he reached in his pocket and took out a cigarette. Instant guilt flooded him. He could smoke and she couldn't. There was no turning back, no reversing what had happened. The realization began to sink in that she would stay dead, and he was damned to go on living, except the huge part of him that died along with her. Rick knew she didn't do it on purpose, and had she been given a choice, he knew she would have chosen to live, she would have left with him instead of leaving him behind. So much sorrow, so much suffering, at such a young age. He felt so small, so insignificant, more than he'd ever felt before in his life. All he wanted to do was evaporate and die too. Then they'd be ghosts together. Forever.

April 6, 1993 changed Rick forever. Whatever childlike innocence he may have still harboured deep down in his soul disappeared. Since the divorce, he programmed himself to shut down emotionally, and lash outwards when he experienced moments of intense pain and loss. By thirteen years old, he hated his father, despised him and everything he stood for, but he'd never taken his sorrows out in self-inflicting manner. Instead, he converted that pain into a seething hatred directed at the man responsible for it. He didn't get to choose who his parents were, he just woke up one day and they were there. But he did get to choose Jackie. He chose her because he wanted her to be in his life, not because she had to be. Now she was gone. That was the difference. That's what made the horror of her death so intense and traumatic.

There was no crying, there was no feeling sorry for himself. There was only a bludgeoning manifestation of hate. Someone had to be responsible. Someone or something had to shoulder the blame. An object at which he could focus all of his hurt, sorrow, and resultant aggression. And there was resultant aggression.

The divorce had made Rick lash out, but that was nothing compared to the angst and anger he felt now.

An eye for eye, tooth for tooth, hand for hand, foot for foot, burn for burn, wound for wound, stripe for stripe.[29]

Vengeance consumed him. Yes, Jackie was the one who took the drugs that morning, but Rick refused to accept this explanation. It just wasn't a big enough scope for him. There had to be more. Besides, it was hard to exact vengeance on someone who was already dead. The drugs. They were to blame. And all those involved, from the people who bought her the drugs, to the people they bought the drugs from, to the people who decided that creating synthetic drugs and distributing them in the first place was a good idea. The question of who killed Jackie became the only thing that mattered in his life. It was her mother, it was all the men who had touched and abused Jackie, it was Dez, Becca, and all her friends. It was society in general, and the social conditions that put her in a time and place where it was okay and acceptable, and even cool for a thirteen-year-old girl to get drunk and high. It was everyone for not making the world a better, more tolerable place. It was him for not discouraging her or keeping her safe.

"I hate myself." He repeated the words over and over again in his head. "I am a failure."

Long had he uttered the words, 'I hate my father', 'I hate the world' or 'I hate God' but 'I hate myself' was a new statement, and one that tore directly to the depths of his tortured soul. He couldn't even succeed at the one thing that he was good at – protecting people and keeping them safe. He could never ever forgive himself. He could never bring himself to forgive others. He never spoke to Destiny again, and the few times they were in the same general vicinity, she couldn't bring herself to look at him. She knew he held her partially responsible. It took until the end of the summer for Becca to work up the courage to approach him.

"Ghost, I'm really sorry about Jackie."

He raised his head, looked directly into her eyes and said nothing. It was never going to be okay. He never even got the chance to say anything or make peace with Jackie's mom. She had Jackie cremated immediately and then moved back up to Portland, no funeral, no memorial service, no chance for anyone to give her daughter a formal goodbye. All Rick wanted was a little memento, something physical to remember her by, but he was left empty-handed.

Rick knew in a roundabout way who they had gotten the drugs from, what circles and individuals, but his blame and hatred expanded to encompass any and

[29] Exodus 21:24-25

all who sold dope to the public. Heroin, coke, PCP, acid, crank, speed, whatever, all of it became known as the 'Angel of Death'. Anything that caused addiction and lead to disease, death, and misery. But the biggest blame he saved for the Angel of Mercy himself – God. In Rick's young and deluded mind, he was sure that God 'took' Jackie from him. Why wouldn't he think that? It fit everything that had happened and everything he believed. Not even three weeks ago, he'd publically denounced God for the first time. God knew all didn't he? And if he knew Rick's heart, then he knew Rick was straying, and finding happiness and an identity in something else, a lifestyle and a girl outside of Him and His Will. God had lost him. He'd lost His little golden warrior. God wasn't going to stand for that. No way in hell. So the best way to punish Rick was to take away the one thing, the one person that made him happy. Jackie. It all made perfect sense to Rick, and resonated so strongly in his soul.

People might call bullshit or even call Rick delusional, but for someone who had been trained, who had been brainwashed into thinking *everything* that happened in existence was a 'spiritual matter' in accordance with God's Will, this was a logical conclusion. For Rick to interpret Jackie's death as a direct attack by God on his life was not a stretch. The hatred and feelings of betrayal boiled hotter than the fires of hell. Rick felt God's wrath, and in his mind, God's taking of Jackie was a direct act of war, which was fine, because if God wanted war, then he was going to get it.

> *For the weapons of our warfare are not carnal, but mighty before the Gods for the casting down of strongholds, imaginations, and every high thing that exalts itself before my own Divine Will.* [30]

And while he outwardly raged, he also drew himself further inwards, sharing nothing with anyone. Any hope of him resurrecting himself from the depths of despondency as Ghost was lost forever. The shadow grew, and at times he became so quiet and withdrawn that he seemed to fade from existence. He refused to speak of Jackie's death with anyone, not even Strom, but everyone knew it was there, and it wasn't hard to see how quickly the walls secured even further around his heart. No one had the guts to bring it up, and no one including his mother suggested he seek help. No one would ever admit that perhaps he was in trouble.

Everyone knew why he was upset, and the loss he had to feel, and now in a way, it made it okay and even expected to him to seem troubled or lost. Everyone treated it as a perfectly acceptable part of him. Except it wasn't normal, and he shouldn't have had to deal with all of these things on his own. It was too much. Way too much for an adult to handle, let alone a thirteen-year-old boy.

[30] 2 Corinthians 10:4-6

Jackie's death spurred Rick into action. First thing to go was his own experimentation with hard drugs and anything that wasn't natural. Never again would he ever ingest anything, or take anything that didn't grow out of the ground. His drinking and pot smoking became rare occasions. He made his hatred and disgust of drugs extremely apparent to everyone, even at full blown parties, and most everyone just shrugged it off as him being extreme.

"Mom, I need to talk to you. I'm telling you now because I'm trying to be honest and upfront, and I don't want to hurt you…but I'm done going to church."

"What? What are you talking about? You can't just walk away. I know you've been through a lot lately but…"

"Mom. I'm done."

"But why?" A dark sadness filled every crevice of her face. The golden light no longer shone as bright.

"I have my reasons and I don't want to talk about them…I'm just tired of it all. It's just getting way too heavy for me. Too much and I need some time away…"

"But you'll be back?"

"I don't know." He lied. "Maybe I just need a break." Up to this point church had been a mandatory requirement. Not anymore. Brenda had to have seen how broken her son had become, how changed and withdrawn he'd become. She had to have noticed.

"Maybe we should pray about it?"

"I don't want to pray about it."

Brenda sighed. "Well you're almost fourteen, and if you don't want to go to church, I can't make you. I just hope one day you find your way back to the light Rick. Darkness is no place for a soul to live. You should know that."

And there it was. Even his own mother knew he'd been lost. She acknowledged his independence and her own lack of control as a parent. She couldn't make him go. In reality, she couldn't make him do anything anymore. He was free to do whatever he pleased, live his life with reckless abandon, and she wouldn't say or do a thing. He also knew that she'd never stop praying for his soul. Praying that he'd come back, ignorant to the amount of damage that had already been done. There was no turning back now. No light in heaven could ever penetrate the coal mine of his soul.

Done with drugs and done with church, he was half tempted to be done with school. Only his buddies still attending kept him from completely dropping out of society. But as time wore on, he became more isolated from even his friends. When he skipped school, it was most often alone, just needing the time to get away. Too many of the older kids provided a constant reminder of Jackie, so he stopped taking rides and hanging out. The only one he could truly count on was Strom. The two boys stayed close, well as close as Rick would let anyone get.

A mere couple of weeks after Jackie's death, Brenda began her tradition of accepting homeless waifs into their home. Call it 'Christian charity' or 'The Lord's Work' but for some reason, she thought it part of her service to God to take in strays and those in need. Never mind that her own son was someone desperately in need. Perhaps she thought that she'd already done all she could for the child. Drop out street kids, Richard and Chris weren't bad people, they just couldn't get their shit together in life. Nineteen and pregnant with a baby girl, Chris and the baby's twenty-one-year-old father Richard, were both addicts who had wandered all over the west coast and somehow ended up in McMinnville in the capable hands of the Potter's House. They gave the church a good sob story, and being 'good Christians', asked God for mercy and the church for help. Of course, their story was actually well rehearsed, and they were only 'Christian' in the sense that they went to churches and prayed, and were 'reborn' by the love of Christ whenever they needed something.

"You can stay in my spare bedroom," said Brenda.

Rick didn't have a problem with Chris or Richard themselves, just the idea of his mother accepting strange people into the house in the name of the Lord. He knew what that Lord had done, and he knew just by looking and Chris and Richard that the Lord didn't really play a huge role in their lives. They were Rick's type of people. Richard had been living on the streets since he was thirteen and had been involved in his share of violence and close calls. Just the sort of person Rick could latch onto and learn the tricks of the trade of street life. Where to sleep, who to steal from, how to tell when someone is home or has an alarm system. The guy was a treasure trove of information. The two of them would spend hours out in the shop smoking an absurd amount of cigarettes, listening to Motley Crue and Queensryche, the big brother figure teaching the sponge-like little brother everything he knew.

An addict since she was in her teens, Rick also gravitated towards Christine, the embodiment of the life Jackie had just left behind.

"Why did you do it?" said Rick. "Take all the drugs."

"I don't know," she said. "I guess I just wanted to forget about a lot of things…and the drugs made it easy."

Rick spent hours and hours picking her brain, asking about her life, and why she'd done the things she'd done. He needed to know everything.

"Fuck man, by eighteen I'd tried just about everything you could possibly try…mushrooms and I've smoked a bunch of shit too…like resins, coke, tar, crack, speed…taken pills, and even spent almost a year smoking China-white."

"Jesus Christine!"

"I know. And that stuff makes you do some crazy shit. I'm not proud to say this out loud but yeah…I was this guy's whore. I was miserable. And I can't tell you how many times I almost died. And you know what? I didn't even fucking care. But I care now. All I care about is this little girl growing inside of me. It's all that matters now."

Rick wondered if Jackie had lived how things might have turned out for them. Would they have become Chris and Richard? Rick needed to understand everything. He needed to know why Chris made the decisions she did. Every little thing he could discover about the drug scene, how it worked, what drugs were worth what, and how someone got them. He had to understand it all. Gain insight. Infiltrate and gather intelligence on an entire culture. Sure he'd already been introduced to some but it wasn't enough, not nearly enough to do the damage that he planned on doing. Fight, conquer, and get revenge. He hadn't declared war just yet but the motivation and desire to seek retribution burned hot in his heart.

He could thank his mother. All those years he'd been sneaking out at night and roaming the streets trying to find himself and his calling, and low and behold, his mother brought the streets right into their own home. God bless her. He may not have been on track to graduate middle school but he sure as hell got a high school diploma in 'streetology' and the dope scene. The timing couldn't have been better. The fire, the passion, and the motivation. After a month with Chris and Richard, his thirst to know transformed into a decisive path. His next war and battle plan fully formulated. What better way to avenge and honour Jackie's death than to wage war against the sinister force that had taken her life? He couldn't do all that much to avenge his hate for his father or society in general except rebel and be a nasty little bastard, but he could do something about Jackie's death.

No one would ever know. He was Ghost wasn't he? A master of the night, and a keeper of secrets. He could bear the burden of knowing what nobody else knew, and never allude to the fact that anything was there. He'd been doing it for years. He'd turned sneaking out and breaking into places and getting away with it into an art form. He was 'of' the streets, he knew the people and he knew the game. Fucking drug pushers. He had no problem making up the rules as he went along. No one would know a thing, not even his friends. Pure brilliance. He had to do it. For her. And for his hatred of what it did to her. He would stop at nothing. His methods just as evil, dark, and menacing as the drugs themselves. He would show them all.

Whoever fights monsters should see to it that in the process he does not become a monster.[31]

[31] Friedrich Nietzsche

CHAPTER TWENTY-EIGHT

While Rick raged against the monsters of the outside world, the monsters within his soul raged against him. Jackie's death only intensified the turmoil. The 'first betrayal', the divorce, had set him on the path to loss and darkness, but so much had happened since, so much more had been thrown on the heap. So much more that he couldn't take, that he couldn't deal with, that he just didn't understand. The betrayal by God in the pool. The betrayal by his mother, the church, and all those religious guides who misled him from the beginning. And now? Now he'd lost the one thing that promised to make it all better, the one person who'd brought him happiness, and the one person who'd brought him hope. Hope that literally died in his arms. It was too much.

She'd been taken away from him on purpose, Rick knew that much for sure. He hated his father for destroying his family. He hated his mother for lying and using him for His agenda. He hated God for cursing him with his 'gift' and forcing him to take part in a war he'd never asked to be part of in the first place. He hated the world and society for being so fucked up to allow kids to take drugs, and he hated most of his 'friends' for letting Jackie die, and then going right back to 'business as usual', as if she never even existed. The depression mounted. Everyone knew the kid was hurting. Everyone knew the kid was in serious trouble and in serious pain, but no one stepped up. No one stepped in. The pain consumed him. The coldness of his heart steamed against the furious inferno of his soul. He could feel himself slipping, coming apart, and starting down a path that could only end up in more pain, destruction, and loss. He wanted it all to stop. He begged it all to stop.

May 18th, 1993. He told himself that he was only going out to the shop to train, to practice martial arts, and to just let off some steam. That's what he told himself anyway. Feeling frantic, hectic and overwhelmed, his small frame buzzed as if charged with a metallic ringing. Stripping away his shirt and shoes, he drove his right hand into the speed bag hanging from the ceiling beam.

"Fuck!"

Spun out and torn up, every inch of his body felt the need to destroy someone or something. Bloody, violent thoughts flashed through his mind like an electrical storm.

"Whack!" His elbow crunched the bag. Sweat dropped to the concrete floor.

A flurry of punches, a fluster of kicks. Someone's face being destroyed, ripped apart. Rage. His body flipped off the floor in a series of aerial kicks, crescent moons, and reverses. His pulse raced. His heart bled. All of it needed to stop. To end. Glistening with sweat, he moved away from the speed bag, his body engaging in a series of frantic sweeps and combinations, deliberately trying to exhaust himself, calming the rage. But with each movement, the rage grew, picking up momentum, culminating in a wild abandon.

"Jesus Christ! Make it stop!"

He wanted to cry. Jesus fucking Christ he wanted to just lay down and cry. Let it all out. But the tears wouldn't come.

"Am I even fucking human? Why can't I cry? Why can't I feel? Why can't I be normal?"

He just wanted to be with her. To be in her arms. To see her smiling green eyes. To hear her laugh. To make dreams together. His hand reached out to the top of the work bench. His fingers clasped the handle of his large buck knife. Dazed and despondent, all rational thought gone. Chest heaving, he fell to his knees in the middle of the floor, both hands wrapped in a death grip around the hilt, the blade downward, aimed at the center of his chest.

"I need it to end. I can't do this anymore. I can't fight. I'm too tired. It's just too much. I need to die."

The tip of the blade inched closer to his skin. He needed to die before his rage completely took hold and made him the predator. Killing himself would quell the fires. The storm would stop. The misery would be over. He'd never be used again. He'd never be betrayed again. And, he'd be with her. He stared hard at the blade. It shimmered in the glare of sunlight through the shop window.

"Will anyone even care? How long will it even take before they find me? Lying here. It's not like they miss me when I'm gone anyways. I'm sure they're not even going to miss me now." He stared in fascination at the blade. "I wonder what it will feel like…when the blade is in my chest…It'll hurt for sure…but then I'll go numb I guess…maybe bleed out. I wonder if I'll cry then?"

He just had to thrust it forward. One. Two. Three. It'd all be over. There'd be no more pain. Deep breath. One. Two. Three. Just thrust it down! He could do it, he just needed to concentrate. Heaving uncontrollably, his chest reached out and nicked the blade, almost willing it to find a home deep within its confines. Three. Two. One.

"I can't! I can't do it! Jesus Christ! I'm sorry baby. I'm so sorry. I can't let them win…I just can't. If I die, then they win! They all win! My father…my mother…God. Everybody wins but me! Maybe that's what they want…but I'm not going to give them the satisfaction. No fucking way. I'm not going to be just another tombstone marker somewhere…where they just come to visit now and then…standing over it…pretending like they even fucking gave a shit…like I never even existed. That'd probably make them all happy…to believe I never even existed. Well fuck that! Fuck all of them! No way am I letting them off the hook that easy. They all need to pay for what they've done. If I don't make them pay…no one will. They'll just go on with their fucking lives…acting like none of it even happened. I will not let that happen. I can't let that happen."

Rising to his feet, he slowly lowered the blade to his right side. As he turned, he flicked the blade up, caught it in his hand, and fired it towards the garage door as hard as he could, the sharp edge slicing his palm as he threw it. The shop thundered as the knife hit its mark. That was the answer. It had to be him. He had to be the one to strike the blow and become the instrument of vengeance. Even if he had to do it on his own – he would be the one to make them pay for all their lies, their betrayals, and the pain. Rick wrapped a rag around his bloody hand and went right back to training.

Vengeance is mine; I will repay, saith the Lord.[32]

"Fuck what the Lord thinks! Who takes vengeance out on Him? Who holds Him accountable for His misdeeds?"

No. Rick would take care of vengeance with his own hands. He would make sure everyone paid exactly what they owed, especially God. Already feeling damned and forsaken, Rick didn't give a shit about forgiveness or playing by anyone else's rules either. They'd never considered his well-being when they made their choices or used him for their own gain, so why in the hell should he consider anyone else's? At the time, Rick couldn't see how selfish his decisions really were. No one else cared about vengeance and making the world pay. Those were his thoughts, his reaction to what he'd been taught, and what he knew. How do you fight evil? You arm yourself. You become a warrior. You spill blood, and flail about, ripping and tearing anything and everything to shreds; anything that stands in your way. You take your problems to God. You watch him use violence to fight His war, and if it's good enough for God, then it's sure as hell good enough for you. Talk about your feelings? Talk about what was bothering you? Hell no. One doesn't talk about their feelings. They pray about them. They go to God, let him lead the way. And he shows you how to solve your problems, how to rid the demons. You don't take a soft tone and tell them to please go away. No, you rip those mother fuckers apart. Tear them to shreds. You spill blood. You seek vengeance. That was God's way. And in his pain, and in his despondency, it became Rick's way. All he knew, he learned from His Father.

Man might know one thing were his sight less dim;
That it whirls not to suit his petty whim,

[32] Romans 12:19

That it is quite indifferent to him.
"Nay, does it treat him harshly as he saith
It grinds him some slow years of bitter breath,
Then grinds him back into eternal death.[33]
What men are they who haunt these fatal glooms,
And fill their living mouths with dust of death,
And make their habitations in the tombs,
And breathe eternal sighs with mortal breath,
And pierce life's pleasant veil of various error
To reach that void of darkness and old terror
Wherein expire the lamps of hope and faith[34]

If only he'd had more insight into his own depressive state of mind. Locked in the idea that his destiny was bound by a fallen fate, Rick became the fallen angel, violence and retribution his calling cards. Two days later on the night of his fourteenth birthday, Rick and the boys literally painted the town, then lit it up with fire. It hadn't been planned, just a spontaneous night of complete chaos and carnage. They spray painted at least twenty of their signature 'stick foxes', their very own pyro sign, then set out to cause some shit. After a bit of a street brawl, they found themselves walking through the Taco Bell drive through, fueling up on food and more caffeinated beverages. By four in the morning, they'd been from one side of town to the other, made a commemorative fire of fused plastic to Kurt Cobain using six of his albums, lit a twenty-four-foot anarchy sign across three lanes of Highway 99, and were sorely disappointed when it burnt out long before any traffic came by. By sunrise, they were at McDonald's buying breakfast and hanging out in the playground.

"Don't you guys have to go to school or something?" said one of the cashiers as she walked by to change the garbage cans.

"School?" said Rick with a fuck you smirk. "We've already graduated."

Unamused the woman just shook her head and walked off with the sound of rebel laughter in her ear. It was far too early in the morning to give a shit about some smart ass teenagers. And that's exactly what they were. Smart ass, rebellious, 'don't give a fuck about anything' vagrants. They'd go to school if and when they felt the need to grace the school with their presence. No one was going to tell them what to do or where to be. Conformity was not a familiar or well-used word in their vocabulary.

When he finally wandered home two days later, he found his mother had taken in another stray.

[33] "The City of Dreadful Night" by James Thomson (VIII 42-47)
[34] "The City of Dreadful Night" by James Thomson (XI 1-7)

"Sarah? What are you doing here? Where did Chris and Richard go?"

"They moved on I guess. Your mom said I could stay here for a while. Things with my mom haven't been great and dad is away…so…"

"My mother offered you our spare room."

"Yeah. Are you mad?"

"No not at all. Just surprised I guess."

"Yeah well…things aren't always what they seem Rick."

"Tell me about it."

"Where have you been anyway? Like seriously, don't you have to come home at night?"

"I don't have to do anything I don't want Sarah."

"I can see that."

Rick and Sarah had grown distant in the past year. She always had her eye on some older guy and Rick was always out with his wild-ass friends. Things had certainly changed in the three years since they met at Potter's House, and his Mom befriended her parents Jack and Jill. No longer the sweet and innocent church girl, she was now fifteen, finishing her first year of high school, and openly talked about getting pregnant and running away. Apparently, God was doing wonders in her life as well.

Over the next few weeks, they spent time hanging on the roof beneath Rick's bedroom window, chatting and reconnecting.

"You should go back to school Rick. It's important. Don't be a dropout."

"I haven't dropped out Sarah. I just only go when I feel like it, and lately, I really haven't felt like it okay?"

"Just don't throw your life away. I couldn't stand that. You have to finish school. You can't do anything without it. It's only four more years Rick. That's not a lot."

"Listen Sarah, I appreciate what you're trying to say but I just don't care. My life is what it is…and what I do with it is my business. I'm not trying to be an asshole but you don't know everything, and I don't expect you to understand. I live my life the way I want. I do what I want, when I want. I don't give a shit what anyone says…I really don't."

He proved that point by taking a two week break from school, only showing up for the final two days of the year.

"Nice to see you Mr. Watkinson," said his teacher.

Rick just smiled. They could all fuck themselves. He'd just spent a glorious two weeks wandering aimlessly through town like some sort of haunting wraith, just looking for shit to get into. It didn't take him long. Not far from his house, back beyond the park where he'd first met Charisma and Tom sat a private garage and junkyard. Too curious not to leave it alone, Rick snuck into the large wooden structure to have a look.

"Just a bunch of pulleys, winches and shit. Some nice tools though." Not really interested in anything the shed had to offer, he spied a fifteen-foot camper trailer amongst the rusted out, piled up vehicles.

"Now that looks promising!" Sitting up on a couple of cinder blocks, the trailer door was locked tight with a welded heavy duty clasp and a huge Masterlock.

"Fuck. Hmm…let's see." Never one to walk away from a challenge, Rick eyed the space between the ground and the bottom of the trailer. He smiled. "Silly dude for putting this trailer high enough off the ground where some little shit like me could wiggle right underneath. Stupid fucker!"

Grabbing a crowbar from the shed, Rick wiggled his way under the trailer and began to dig and pry away at the rotten floor boards. After a concerted effort, he managed to make a hole large enough for his wiry frame to crawl through. It was time well spent.

"Look at this fucking jackpot!" Without missing a beat, he carefully packed fives knives, a machete, a slew of lighters, and a bunch of packs, hats and miscellaneous gear in his knapsack. His best find was a bad ass, old school twelve gauge Remington shot gun.

"Can't ever turn down a gift like this," he said slipping it down the side of the pack. "And what do we have here?"

His brown eyes zeroed in on a huge moonshine jar full of change, mostly quarters. Filling every pocket he had in both his pants and his knapsack, he carted away as many of those quarters as he could. The jar was way too big to move all at once, so he returned to the scene of the crime a few more times to fill his pockets. He had to keep returning; spending hours and hours in the arcade playing video games used up the stash rather quickly. The good stuff from the haul he hid in only the best places, especially the shotgun. With quite a few places on their property his mom was never hip to look, Rick knew his gear would be safe from prying eyes. Never for one moment did he feel bad about taking it. He didn't care. Why should he? He'd put that gear to good use, give it a purpose. Stockpiling weapons and gear was just part of the plan, a necessity to fight the war.

The group's 'first strike' went down during the final two weeks of school. They had defined their war and its objectives a few weeks before, and now was the time to select a target and act. Eight months of meetings, intellectualizing, plotting and theorizing, all leading up to this moment. They'd talked enough. It was time for action. Everybody knew 'Darin', the major weed dealer for McMinnville, and the boys knew exactly what parties he'd be invited to and when his house would be empty. It wasn't hard to gain the intelligence, all they had to do was hang out with the right people, listen, and keep their mouth shut. They knew exactly where Darin lived, and the fact he had a golden retriever named Buck. These boys weren't fucking around. Their game was real, and they aimed to win.

"Creek," said Rick. "You wait down here in these heavy bushes and stay the fuck out of sight. You're our point bro. Use the two-way radio and let us know what's coming."

"No problem. I'm on it."

Under the cover of darkness, Strom, Cajun, and Rick, all dressed in head to toe black, snuck down the street and back around the house. Both Strom and Rick had their .38's and Cajun had the bad ass Remington shot gun Rick had just swiped.

"Remember," said Rick. "No one fires a shot unless someone confronts us with a gun or something deadly. And if the pigs show up, the only shots fired are suppressive…just to provide cover so we can get away. Got it?"

Entry to the house couldn't have been easier. A quick crowbar to the already unhinged backdoor, and they were in.

"Hey Buck," said Strom handing him a doggy bacon bone. "Shhh…no barking okay. Good boy." Buck obliged and wagged his tail instead.

Like a miniature SWAT unit, the boys first 'cleared' each room of any hidden surprises, then gave the signal to Creek.

"All clear from here," he whispered through the radio.

"Keep the flashlights low," said Rick. "We don't want the neighbours to see the lights, have a shit, and call the cops. Now let's get to work."

Finding the weed was a piece of cake. Darin had at least two pounds of pot stuffed in multiple shoeboxes in his closet. All the dope went into a duffle bag. In a small compartment behind his headboard, they found a .45 and under the couch a beautiful .308 Marlin. It even had posts and rings for a sling.

"Find the cash boys," said Rick. "We need to find the cash. I know it must be here."

"I can't find it anywhere," said Strom.

"Keep looking bro, keep looking."

They'd given themselves a half an hour time frame but that quickly turned into two hours plus as they tore the house apart looking for more drugs, guns, money, and any other shit they deemed worthy of scooping.

"Son of a bitch," laughed Rick as he stuck his hand under the bottom drawer in the refrigerator and pulled out a thick wad of bills. "Sneaky fucker."

"How much?" said Cajun.

"Not sure. We'll count it later. I'm sure there's more here but we'd better get the fuck out of here. Been here way too long already."

Cajun nodded.

"Strom. Dude...let's go!"

Using cover and the railroad tracks, the boys made it back to base and spent time in the shop relaxing and drinking Mountain Dew.

"Fuck man," said Strom. "That was too easy!"

"I think we've found our calling. Fuck that was awesome. That was the big time and we pulled it off like no shit."

"How much cash?" said Strom.

"Seven hundred," said Rick. "Small bills. I say we each grab a bill and then put the rest in the war chest for future supplies and expenses?"

"Fine with me," said Cajun.

"Yeah I'm good," said Strom.

"What about the weed?" said Creek. "What are we going to do with that?"

Figuring out what to do with the weed was the hardest part of the whole night. All of them, except Cajun, enjoying smoking and had on many occasions, and between wanting to smoke it, and knowing how much money they could get for it on the streets, it was a difficult decision.

"If we smoke this or sell it," said Rick, "then we're no better than Darin or the people that sold the shit to Jackie and Des. How can we call ourselves true vigilantes? We'd be fucking hypocrite's man...just as hypocritical as the fucking government. I say we dump it. It's the right thing to do."

"Where?" said Strom.

"How about that creek up on Dell Smith's property?" said Cajun.

With all in agreement, they took the duffle bag and made their way out to the creek. After a small, solemn ceremony, they dumped all the weed into the water, proving their integrity and their honour in their war against the enemy. Their first blow had been swift and hard, a smashing success, no hiccups, and no one had any idea who had actually robbed Darin.

"I think he owed some dude some money up in Newberg. Guess they came to collect."

"Yeah, well I heard he ticked off some guys up in Portland."

"Either way, they got his ass good!"

No one had even the slightest inkling that the real culprits were standing right beside them; the four youngsters in the crowd. The success and ease of it intoxicated them all. More power than they'd ever felt in their lives. What was Darin or any drug pusher going to do? Call the cops? No fucking way!

"Umm...yes excuse me officer but I just got all my guns, two pounds of weeds and a shit load of cash ripped off. Can you help me catch who did it?"

As long as the boys kept wearing their skin tight gloves, did a clean run not leaving any shit behind, and kept their mouths shut, they never had to worry about getting caught. None of them were the bragging type anyway, and this mission, this war, was far more important to the greater societal good than two minutes of fame on the streets. Pulling off the gig made them feel like the good guys. They were doing society a favour. The police were grossly incompetent and no one else was doing a thing. Someone had to step up. Why not them? With that first run complete, the charter of their organization "UPIU" was locked in. They would subversively steal the resources of drug dealers right out from under their noses, and undermine their operations in a wholly clandestine way. Seemed simple enough.

"Thank God school is out," said Strom taking a swig from the bottle of Jim Bean. "Now we can do whatever the hell we want."

"Like we didn't already bro," said Rick laughing. "Hand me that bottle. When is your mom getting home?"

"Who the fuck knows man. But just to be safe, let's get the fuck out of here."

They took the 'borrowed' bottle of Jim Beam and headed out to the nearby field.

"This is all just so fucked up," said Strom laying back, looking at the stars. "I mean my life, your life. We ain't got nobody but each other, and I sure as hell don't trust saying any of this to anyone but you."

"I know bro, I feel the same way. It all just fucking sucks. My life sucks. I hate this God damn fucking world. It's a piece of shit."

"Pass me a smoke."

Rick handed him a smoke, then lit one up for himself. Of all his friends, Strom was the one he confided in the most. They'd been through a lot together and both felt like no one in their lives, especially their parents gave a shit. They didn't usually talk about their woes but occasionally they'd have a philosophical night where they'd let it out and wear their hearts on their sleeves. Laying out there in that field, looking up at the stars, and talking about how much their lives sucked and how they hated the world, these two couldn't have been more lost.

"Fuck man," said Strom. "I'm going to puke."

Rick only smiled, knowing he was two seconds away from expelling the contents of his gut as well. Too many smokes and too much booze was way more than their young systems could handle. It was excess for the sake of excess. No one was there to rein them in. Not in life, not in anything.

"Fuck man," said Rick wiping his own mouth on the back of his sleeve. "That was fucking nasty."

"Honestly…I'm not sure I've ever been this sick from drinking before. I feel like hell."

"You look like hell too bro," said Rick with a grin.

"Fuck off," laughed Strom. "Go look in a mirror asshole."

"I think I'm done."

"Done what?"

"Drinking. Smoking. All this bullshit. I hate feeling like this."

"Yeah I feel ya bro. This shit is bad for us."

"Let's make an oath. Right here, right now. No more smoking or drinking for a year."

"A year?"

"Yeah, why not? Seems like a good number. I can do it if you can do it."

"Well I can do it…so yeah…okay…one year."

And there it was, a pact between brothers. After years of puffing nonstop, Rick quit smoking cold turkey. No one could ever question his commitment to a cause he believed in, and if the Team was going to operate at a high level, and be worthy of being black op vigilantes, they and especially he needed to be at his best. No questions, no excuses. His life continuing the pattern of juxtaposition. A year ago, he was smoking, drinking, and toking the noble weed. Now he wouldn't touch the stuff. His 'higher calling' meant too much. And for the first time in his life, his higher calling had nothing to do with God, Jesus, or the Holy Spirit. For Rick, a welcome relief.

Their missions kept them busy throughout the summer, and when they weren't actually executing their plan, they were gathering information and trying to understand how the drug supply lines worked. Robbing someone's house for guns, money, and drugs was all good but it was a dead end if they just hit it and left. There had to be more punishment. Eventually, the dealer would just get more drugs from their supplier and the whole operation would just start all over again. For Rick and the boys, part of the fun was seeing just how much their activities were fucking up the dope community. Many times a supplier would give drugs to the dealer's, and then get paid when the drugs were sold, meaning the dealer technically owes the supplier for the product. When your dope suddenly vanishes, as a dealer, you're left in a bit of a pickle because more often than not, you don't have enough cash lying around to pay the supplier off. Of course, this ticks off the supplier, who isn't happy about not getting his money, and much strife and violence ensues. All to the delight of a bunch of fourteen year olds who are causing all this shit in the first place.

This wasn't enough. They desperately wanted to move up the chain of command and find out who the actual suppliers were, information that people in the trade didn't offer up like a piece of gum. An uphill battle, but certainly not enough of a deterrent to stop operations. Being resourceful, the boys began hitching rides out of McMinnville to the much bigger cities of Portland and Salem. Having outgrown their own small town and surrounding places ages ago, they were eager for some new turf and some new explorations. There's a shitload of adventure to be had in the big city, and expanding their circle of friends and circle of influence was always a plus.

Strom and Rick began hanging out even more with the older kids who made the hour or so trip to Portland on a regular basis. Not only did they get to explore a new playground, while they were hanging with them, they picked up key bits of information on where everyone was getting their drugs. More than a few times they were in the very vehicle that was transporting a significant quantity back to McMinnville. This made it super easy to track the drugs, but also quite dangerous because the guys they were riding with knew that they knew.

"We gotta wait bro," said Strom.

"Yeah, I agree. Our ass is done if we strike right away. They'll totally suspect us. I say we wait…like for at least a month…"

"By then they'll have forgotten that we were even in the car and probably will have even made another run by then."

"But we'll still know where it's going and that's the main thing."

"Fucking right man."

"I have to say though, this hitching or paying for rides fucking sucks."

"I hear ya bro," said Strom. "What are you thinking…cause I know you're thinking of something."

"Well…what if we borrow one now and then. Just when we need it. I'm not saying all the time…just when we can't find anyone to take us or we don't have the money to pay for a ride."

"Bro…you know no one has their license right?"

"So? When has a small obstacle like that ever stopped us before?"

"True," laughed Strom. "Very true."

Stealing cars was the next logical step, especially for Rick. He'd been stealing from cars for the last two or three years, so why not just take the whole thing. Problem was, none of their core group knew how to steal or hot wire a car. They'd have to look for outside help.

"Sure…I know how to hotwire a car," said Clover with a wry smile. "I've pulled the gig once or twice."

He gave the boys some decent pointers on how to get into the vehicle and then how to hot wire it.

"Once you get a car, come on by and I'll teach you how to drive."

The first car the boy's stole was from a used car lot, junk yard in Newberg. Beat up and sputtering, the old Lincoln had working air conditioning and a radio, and that was good enough to make them all feel like tough little shits. Carefully, they drove the car down to Sheridan where Clover was now living. He gave them each a crash course in driving like a real licenced driver, some customs of the road, then took him on an errand back to McMinnville.

"We'd better ditch it soon bro," said Strom.

"Yeah, it's been four and half hours," said Cajun.

"Agreed," said Rick. "Not a bad first outing."

They drove Creek home, then abandoned the car just outside of McMinnville.

"You got the Pinesol?" said Rick.

"Yeah," said Havoc. "I got it."

"Okay," said Rick. "Wipe everything down. Put some on your fingers too…to wipe away the oil. And grab all of Clover's cigarette butts. We can't leave anything behind."

"This was the best fucking night!" said Strom. "Total freedom man!"

"I know bro," said Rick. "Fucking best feeling in the world. We can go anywhere and do anything we want now."

"Let's drive one of this babies across America!" said Cajun.

"You got money for gas?" said Havoc laughing.

While the boys did steal their fair share of vehicles, it was always as a last resort, and wasn't the preferred method to get where they needed to go. Still, now it was an option. They called them 'T-Motes" for 'temporary mode of transportation' and that generally was all they were used for. Psychologically, they had broken a huge barrier. They owned their lives now. The power and feeling was intoxicating, especially for Rick. Before the summer was over, he was dreaming of just getting the fuck out of McMinnville, and leaving everything behind; his mother, his father, God. But he couldn't. He couldn't leave 'The Team'. They were his brothers; they were his family. Strom, Cajun, Havoc, and Creek, they were the ones that kept him from just taking off. Rick didn't give a fuck about anyone or anything else. The side of him that wanted to forget his old life and start fresh, desperately longed for a complete cutting off of everything before that moment; to just act like none of it had ever happened. But he couldn't forsake the boys. He couldn't leave his brothers. He stayed because of them but his heart was already deeply entrenched elsewhere, where he was free of limitations, expectations, invisible wars, and what was socially acceptable. Somewhere where he was free to roam, free to think and feel, and not have to hide who and what he really was. Somewhere, where he was just free to be himself.

CHAPTER TWENTY-NINE

Rick had known of Thanatos for over a year, as he was a popular staple amongst the street kids, but he'd never had the chance to meet him. Typically clad in a black trench coat, with long greasy hair down past his shoulders and a brooding sinister look on his face, Thanatos was one dark, dangerous dude, a bonafide Satanist, whose very name meant 'the incarnation of death'. Rick, 'the little warrior for Christ', would have donned his armour and prayed his ass off for the kid, but 'the I don't give a fuck Rick' was more than willing to meet his acquaintance.

"So Charisma tells me you're a drummer?"

"Well I play drums…"

"I need a drummer for my death metal band. You interested?"

Rick didn't know what to say. Technically yes, he played drums and owned a kit but he would never call himself a drummer. Worse, Thanatos represented everything Rick had been trained to see as the enemy. The guy looked like the incarnation of the devil himself, every inch of an evil Son of Satan, reveling in pissing Christians off, and spitting in the face of their weak God. Rick knew even associating with Thanatos was a huge left turn from his upbringing, and even though he'd forsaken God, and couldn't give a fuck about what He wanted, this was crossing a huge line. It was like deliberately choosing to become one of the 'Fallen', as if he was one of the angels at the beginning of creation who chose to serve his own will instead of God's, and thus cast of out heaven.

"Fuck yeah! I'd love to play in your band man!"

The first time Thanatos took Rick out to his father's 'compound' was an extremely eye-opening experience. Out in the middle of nowhere, Thanatos' father had purchased a huge piece of property, built a homestead, and then secured the perimeter with a large barbed wire fence, just on the edge of a thick forest. A perfect example of resistance and territorialism at its best, and the exact type of anti-government place that Rick and the boys dreamed of owning.

"You don't even live in the main house?" said Rick.

"Nope," said Thanatos. "My place is attached but it's pretty self-sufficient. I have my own kitchen, living room. All that sort of shit."

"Nice man nice. I'd love that set-up at my place."

"C'mon in."

"Holy fuck man, this place is dope. Look at all the computer shit! And an entire room full of amps and guitar equipment. This is wicked."

Besides the abundance of computer components and music equipment, the thing that caught Rick's eye the most were the satanic banners hanging from the walls. He recognized the huge poster of the idol Baphomet and Necromantic Keys but not much else.

"How can this dude have all this satanic shit, and just be so nonchalant and normal about it?" thought Rick. "So openly allied with the devil and isn't afraid to show it. Jesus…my mother and Jill would be screaming fucking bloody terror right now. Me…little Christian warrior…right smack dab in the den of the enemy."

It hadn't been that long ago that he'd been actively praying and waging war against this exact type of satanic stronghold, and now here he was walking through one as a neutral party and potential friend. The tables had certainly turned. Still he felt it. The totally erect hair on his arms and legs confirmed that. He felt the undeniable power of the place. But it wasn't what he'd been taught. There was no decrepit or disgusting siphon feeding off of Thanatos, just an exuding power as if he himself were in command of all situations at all times. For as dark, dreary, and junked his place was, there weren't demons lurking in every corner. Instead, Rick detected more of an ambiance of freedom and independence, as if nothing could take hold here unless Thanatos had wanted it to. The banners and the flags exuded an air of dark authority, as if daring anyone to question their power and their depth. Everything had a sinister feel to it in nature but it wasn't uncomfortable or threatening, more on a spiritual level, like a warning. Rick, the golden child of God, heeded that warning, kept his mouth shut, and acted as if everything was all perfectly natural.

"In here man," said Thanatos opening another bedroom door.

"Whoa. That's a nice drum kit."

"Give it a try."

He put on some deafeningly loud metal and told Rick to play along. Rick did the best he could but there's a huge difference between playing grunge and punk alternative to playing death and thrash metal. He wasn't too far off but certainly wasn't up to par.

"You've got some potential," said Thanatos "but you've got a lot of work to do." He walked over to the speaker, picked up a handful of CDs and handed them to Rick. "Take these home and practise to them."

Rick had never even heard of half the bands on the CDs. This was serious shit, and CDs like this were very hard to come by unless you were part of a certain scene. Obviously, Thanatos was part of that exclusive group. The existence of these CDs did prove to Rick that the Christians hadn't lied about everything, there definitely was a satanic metal scene. Satanic, lawless, and brutally aggressive, the anti-Christian 'black metal' certainly wasn't something Rick dared blasting about the house. Just listening to it, hearing the words, feeling the meaning of the violent beat, Rick was drawn in and he couldn't stop. Too forbidding, exotic, and foreign, he needed to find out just how deep the darkness truly went. He had tasted it before, even been touched by it, but always from the outside, and always as a warrior. Now he had the chance to explore it from the inside, to stand at its center and finally find out who exactly were the monsters he'd spent his whole life fighting.

"Hey bro, you like to read right?" said Thanatos one day as they were sitting around his living room.

"Yeah. I don't mind reading at all."

"Have you ever read this book?" Rick's hands went numb as Thanatos laid a copy of 'The Necronomicon' into them. "You can borrow it if you like."

'The Necronomicon' was only the most feared, most evil, and most dastardly piece of work ever written according to his Christian dogma. Reading this book, even holding this book, signalled the point of no return, a horrific whisper on the lips of every devout Christian. Mentioned in his short horror stories by H.P. Lovecraft in the early 1920s, the book is mainly known as a fictional textbook of magic, and among other things, contains an account of the 'Old Ones', a group of Gods, their history and how to summon them. Much mystery surrounds the actual authenticity of the book and its origins, and to someone like Rick, it represented something completely foreign and new. In his rigid, militant Christian upbringing, Rick had been taught that any other God or spiritual practice other than Jehovah's was a machination of the Devil. Even Greek, old Roman, Egyptian or other indigenous 'pagan' Gods were false idols meant to lead people and cultures away from the One True God. This was Christian law. No exceptions, no other explanations.

For Rick to have this small book in his hands, this book that spoke of the Ancient Ones and Sumerian deities, how to tap into their power and wisdom, and contacting lost demons and such was pure blasphemy. He would go to Hell. A forgone conclusion. His first lecture on Sumerian mythology came from Thanatos, who despite being a high school dropout was fairly well-read. He had read works like Budge's 'Egyptian Book of the Dead' as well as studies on Chaldean and Babylonian religious ideas. Rick had no clue what he was talking about and the ignorance he felt on the subject only made him thirst for the knowledge that he didn't have. Here he thought he knew it all. He'd been brought up heavily indoctrinated and extremely well-studied in Christian belief and mythology (with a crash course on demonology and spiritual warfare), but the most he could tell you about Egyptians and Babylonians was that they were evil cultures who at one time had both taken the Hebrews, God's chosen people, as slaves. Their history, Gods, and culture were totally left out of the equation.

"Christianity wouldn't even exist if it hadn't been for Rome man," said Thanatos.

"What the hell was he talking about?" thought Rick.

For the first time, Rick was introduced to the idea that things existed before the Bible or Christ had even been thought of. He'd always been taught that God, the Bible and Christ had always come first, and that anything that existed outside of this idea had been an abomination that had come after. His mind so warped and bent by pigeon-holed doctrine, he couldn't even conceive that *anything* had existed before Christianity and the God of the Hebrews. He just didn't know. He just hadn't been taught. No one bothered to tell him any different. He'd been clouded by a close-minded, uneducated Judeo-Christian extremist mindset; his mind had never been opened to any other sorts of possibilities. Insanity.

As he sat there listening to Thanatos, fingering the cover of the evil book, his life changed. More than ever he knew there was one thing he couldn't be or remain in life – ignorant. He had to know. He had to understand where all this came from, how it all developed, and where it all began. A huge change, a massive psychological shift. There were things outside of the Bible that were worth knowing. Christianity and the Bible were not all there was. Fueled by his own previous experiences, especially 'The Turning', this moment, this realization had a profound effect on his psyche. He had been so warped, twisted, and disenchanted with his militant-Christian upbringing that this catalyst flipped a switch in his head, and suddenly he was possessed by the spirit of exploration, an unquenchable thirst and desire to know all that had previously been forbidden to him. He vowed to never again be ignorant, lost, uniformed or under-educated, especially concerning the spiritual, religious, or philosophical. Never again. The 'point of origin' and 'from whence it came' became obsessions for him, and more important, never again would he take anyone else's word for anything. Not a preacher, not a teacher, and certainly not God. Parents, teachers, holy men, and the devout. They'd all lied and betrayed his trust from birth, and all so he could fulfill their vison and agenda. Never again.

Even at the time, he never realized how deep the Christian indoctrination had been. No one would openly admit or say the words 'brainwashing', but that's what it was. Pure and simple. From birth, a young mind programed to believe only what it was told by those he trusted, those he believed in. Now, at fourteen years of age, he could feel his worldview shift. He could feel the light seep into the darkness of his brain, and he liked how that felt. He began his own holy inquisition. He would still exorcise demons, but they would be the demons of ignorance and propaganda. He would see and know things for what they really were. It would be a difficult journey, and the deprogramming wasn't going to happen overnight, how could it, when it had been so solidly shoved up his ass for his entire life. But under the intense and accumulative pressure of events; 'The Witches Rock', the 'Second Betrayal', the blood of angels, the 'Turning', and now the opening of his eyes to the 'Before', the hold of such indoctrination had snapped. Finally. The time for putting up with anyone's shit was over. God could fuck off. His father could fuck off. All of them could fuck off. He didn't care.

That summer, 'The Team' stepped up their assaults, and with each successful mission, the legend and the brotherhood grew. The dope robberies and the violence became the lore of a local turf war between the local drug dealers and some foreign asses trying to dig in on their territory. No one had a clue that a small group of six barely teenaged boys were in fact perpetrating this war, and that it had nothing to do with turf, money or business. It was all about vengeance and power – a way to be above and outside the rest. The theme rang true to Rick's own life and his own heart. Gaining control. Taking back a life he never thought was his to live. Changing fate and changing destiny.

Jessica had only been a runaway for a few months before Rick met her. Quiet and withdrawn, her biological father had been sexually molesting her for the past few years.

"I just couldn't take it anymore, so I ran away."

"Is this the first time you've ran?" said Rick.

"No. I've run before but every time I go back it's worse. He beats the shit out of me and then…well…you know…"

Rick seethed. Only thirteen years old, Jessica wasn't a bad girl, and far too innocent for street material, but here she was hanging out with the wrong people, too scared to go home or to the police. If things didn't change, she'd end up strung out on dope and whoring herself out. Easy prey for the nasties.

"Look at me Jessica," said Rick gently pulling her chin up. "Do you want your father to never touch you again?"

"What? How?"

"I'll just talk to him, you know, man to man, and get him to see how much he's hurting his little girl. I'll tell him the truth…what's going to happen to you if you're forced out on the streets instead of safe at home."

Rick knew every word was bullshit the minute it left his mouth, but he said what he needed to say to convince Jessica he meant her father no harm. Three days later they hitched a ride to Newberg and walked through the squeaky chain-link gate.

"What if he yells and threatens you?"

"Don't worry Jess. He won't yell. I've got this."

Relaxed and with his hands in his pockets, Rick walked to the door and knocked. The second her father opened the door and saw his daughter, Rick knew he had to change tactics. It was that sick look on the man's face. Rick couldn't take it. He'd come to seek vengeance. The man hadn't even let go of the door when Rick's right elbow slammed across his forehead, knocking him six feet back into the living room. Without hesitation, Rick pounced before the man could catch his balance, striking his knee and kicking his arm out from under him. Blow after blow. Rick was relentless.

"What are you doing?" screamed Jess. "Oh my God!"

Rick couldn't hear her, on complete automation, he struck his target, time after time after time.

"What's going on in here?" said Jessica's mother racing in from the kitchen.

"You fucking piece of fucking shit! You want to touch your own daughter? You mother fucking child molesting fucking punk!"

With blood and blows flying, both mother and daughter stood there. No one ran to call the police. No one ran to call the neighbours. They simply stood there, the mother with her arms folded across her chest. That bastard had it coming and she wasn't about to intervene. This only fuelled Rick. The fact that this man's own wife believed he deserved the beating, filled Rick with a holier rage. His purpose was even more righteous. He wouldn't just be saving Jessica; he'd be saving her mother too. Broken in the initial scuffle, Rick snatched the carved wooden pole from the floor lamp lying on the floor.

"Don't fucking touch her again!" The pole struck its mark as Rick descended into a hypnotic chant-like state. "Don't fucking touch her again!" Blow. "Don't fucking touch her again!" Blow. "Don't fucking touch her again!"

"Stop…please…. stop…"

Rick grabbed him by the shirt, pulled him up, and bore deep into his eyes. "You EVER touch your daughter again, and I'll be back to fucking kill you!"

The sheer terror in the mans' eyes let Rick know that his message had gotten through. With a release of his hand, the man fell back to the floor heaving and almost in tears. Mission accomplished. Rick turned and walked out of the house, not even stopping to make eye contact with Jessica.

"I fucking hate you!" she screamed.

Rick put his hands in his pockets and just started walking home. He had no doubt that she would hate him for what he did, but neither did he doubt that that bastard would ever touch his daughter again. Sometimes you have to take a situation to the furthest extreme in order to express the severity of it and break the ice in people's mind's. He'd done that. Rick also doubted that any of them ever stopped to talk about 'why' it happened, but each of them knew with absolute clarity, and no one under that roof could deny it was happening or happened ever again. Jessica quit talking to Rick but she also quit running away and stayed in Newberg to finish school. No longer tortured and withdrawn, she began to be just another girl, and the sight of that made Rick happy. He had no clue how to save himself, but he was damn good at saving others.

That was his job, his mission. Saving others. And Jessica was just one example of how he solved problems and dealt with conflict. It wasn't always through violence but it was almost unquestionably through extremes. He never talked or bragged about the shit he did. It was never about that. It was all his burden to carry, and he wasn't in it for the recognition or glory. He was Ghost. Already lost, damned and forsaken, there was no reason for him to hold back and not do the things that no one else would dare to do. He had nothing to lose. In his mind, suffering was his way, pain restored his soul, and protecting others was his fulfillment. There was no reason to worry about his deeds or how quickly they were going to send him to Hell, because, in his heart, mind, and soul, he was already there.

CHAPTER THIRTY

"Come sit down boys, I want to talk to you," said Brenda.

"Is everything okay Mom?" said Rick.

"I hope it will be. Your Grandpa Barnes has been having some troubles with his heart lately…you know with the surgeries and the stroke…so we've decided that it's best if he and Grandma come up here and live with us in Oregon. There's a heart specialist in Portland he can go to, and with Grandma having trouble with her memory, I just think it would be better for him to be closer so I can look after them better. Is that okay?"

"Are we all going to live together in this house?" said Jimmy.

"No, we'll look for a bigger house that we'll all be more comfortable in. Grandma and Grandpa will help out with the cost. I think the move will be good for all of us."

"Still here in McMinnville though right?" said Rick.

"Yes, yes. Although we were thinking of maybe looking for somewhere outside of the city limits. Maybe something with a little bit of property."

The wanderer in Rick loved the idea of having a bit of property to roam, even if it meant he'd be further away from the action of the streets. The first time they walked through the 'High Heaven' house, Rick knew it was his home. Located about seven miles outside of McMinnville up in the lush wooded hills it truly was a 'High Heaven'. The woods surrounding the area were never-ending, a perfect playground for a kid most comfortable with the land and the outdoors. The house itself was two stories with four bedrooms, three bathrooms, an awesome cobblestone fireplace, two hot tubs, and a swimming pool. Built on a hill, part of the downstairs was a basement, and the other half was a full granny flat with stairs connecting the upper and lower levels.

"This place is amazing," said Rick. "I can't believe we're going to be living here."

"Well you can thank your Grandpa Barnes," said Brenda. "He's always been very smart and very careful with his money."

"Thank you Grandpa Barnes," Rick smiled as he stood on the top deck overlooking the forest. "This is paradise."

About the second week of August, Brenda flew down to San Diego to help her parents finish up their affairs and get ready for the move up north. With everything ready, she would drive them up to Oregon to their new home. The whole process was going to take around seven to nine days, which left Jimmy and Rick in the care of Joe for far too long. With Joe working down in Salem for ten hours a day, the boys had free reign of the McMinnville house. Rick spent the first day at home entertaining Jimmy before realizing how much more he could be doing.

"I need my own vacation," he said. "Time to just do my own thing."

He packed a large internal frame backpack, and all of his camping, hunting, and survival gear that he could including his rifle.

"Let's see…I need enough water and jerky for at least five days and fuck yeah, I'd better bring some Dew and other good stuff to eat."

"Where are you going?" said Jimmy.

"Out to the new place. Wanna come?"

"Just the two of us out in the wild? I don't think so. Mom is going to freak when she finds out."

"So tell her then where I am. I don't care that she knows."

"Are you sure that's where you're going?"

"Yeah, I promise you Jimmy. I'm just going out to High Heaven to camp in the woods. I'll be there when everyone pulls up."

"You're going to go all by yourself?"

"Sure, why not? It'll be fun."

"I don't think I'll ever understand you Rick."

Rick laughed. "I think you're right."

Rick had arranged for Elisha to drive him out to the property late in the evening so he could literally set out on his adventure at night.

"You're fucking crazy man," said Elisha. "There are cougars and mountain lions up there you know…and God knows what else!"

"Exactly. What better way to challenge myself than to start at night when I know it'll be the most dangerous and intimidating."

"Be careful Ghost," she said giving him a hug and a peck on the cheek.

"Now what fun would that be?" he grinned.

As her taillights faded off into the night, darkness and silence settled in. No crickets chirping, no dogs barking, no sirens howling, just the brief rustling of the faint wind through the moonlit pine boughs. Elated with freedom, Rick's first exercise was to stalk the house, getting to know every nook and cranny of the exterior and surrounding area, like an animal marks its territory. No one was going to know those woods better than he did. Freedom gave him power, and power gave him invincibility.

Leaving his pack against a tree, Rick scoped out the house, pretending it was occupied, attempting to gain every access and vantage point. Always a planner and tactician, he began to analyze the best cover and stealth approach to the house. After checking out approaches, he spent the next few hours finding every imaginable way to break in. With Brenda having the only set of keys, the house was locked up tighter than a drum. That is, to someone who didn't have Rick's skill or ingenuity.

"Let's see…that door on the upper back deck looks easy enough, and the window on the other side is missing a dowel-rod. And Jesus, this garage door has way too much play. Piece of cake."

By three in the morning he'd had his fun breaking in, and left an Oberto's teriyaki beef jerky wrapping on the front living room table.

"I'm sure Mom will see this right away," he laughed. "She'll be so pleased!"

Slinging his backpack over his shoulder and while he still had the cover of darkness, Rick set out for the abandoned fire lookout tower, not only to figure out how abandoned it actually was, but to see if it would make a good outpost and training center. Sticking to the thick cover of the forest and refusing to use a flashlight, Rick made it to the post in a little over an hour. Of course, he could have just walked the two minutes up the gravel road from the house but that wouldn't have been very sneaky, and he would have been in plain sight of at least three different houses – not the way a stealth operator works.

"This is fucking awesome!" said Rick peering up at the hundred-foot wooden structure.

With two large radio towers and a barbed-wire fence surrounding the central house and antenna, the area was a virtual playground for tactical manoeuvers for the budding anarchists. With no signs of life, Rick wasn't all that worried about getting caught, but for added protection he slept on top of the highest flat bunker, just in case someone showed up for work in the morning. At about five in the morning, he spread out his sleeping bag and caught some well deserved sleep.

"Shit, it's raining." He checked his watch. "Five hours. Not a bad sleep at all."

Quickly rolling up his sleeping bag and re-attaching it to his pack, he made for the cover of the woods to continue exploring the beauty. The area was as close to untouched Oregon wilderness as one could get, and Rick had it relatively all to himself. Peace and serenity. Paradise. It wasn't long before he found the small creek running down the west side of their property.

"This'll be my central landmark. If I ever get lost, I can just reverse directions back to the creek and follow it back uphill to the house."

Easily covering over five miles down and back that first day, Rick discovered that the little creek which was no more than a foot across at its source, became much closer to a small river around twelve feet across at the bottom of the valley. Steep and slippery, Rick climbed his way back up the slope.

"This place looks perfect for a base camp. I'm what…probably a good two and half miles downhill from the neighbourhood, and with the creek running fast, there's no way anyone is going to smell a fire."

With enough tree cover to keep out the light drizzle, Rick set up camp and built a small fire, not even bothering to build a shelter.

"So peaceful and quiet," he said digging a stick deep into the moss. "I could stay out here forever. Fuck society man. Fuck it all. I have everything I need right here. It just feels right. Tomorrow I'm going to pick up that trail of deer scat and tag me some venison."

It wasn't until late afternoon that he finally caught on the trail of what he believed to be a herd of deer. Blending completely into the forest he slowly and carefully followed the trail, his breath as silent as his footsteps. A little after nine in the evening, he came upon a large steep grassy vale pouring down the hillside. Although it was still damp and extremely moist out, the clouds had broken and there was just enough moonlight to illuminate the herd peacefully grazing below. He set his sights on the three-point buck.

"Damnit…turn around will ya," he whispered. "I'm not about to shoot you in the ass."

Surveying the situation, he decided to take one of the younger bucks first with an easier shot, and then hope the big buck leapt up and hesitated enough to give him enough of an angle to take him out.

"You got this man…you got this." Steadying his breath, Rick hooked his finger around the trigger. "Shit. I can't see the crosshairs. They're getting lost in the shadows. Fuck it. Just take the shot."

A quick pull of the trigger sent the young buck on his side and the rest of the herd, including the prized three-point scattering. Rick fired a couple more shots in desperation, hoping for some good luck but came up empty.

"Motherfucker!" Only the wind was around to hear him howl.

With the young buck dead, Rick spent at least forty-five minutes searching the woods below the clearing making sure he didn't tag anything or anyone else. Collecting his shells, he began the long arduous task of dragging his kill back to the base camp, a journey that took the entire night. By the time he made it back, every muscle in his body ached, every last bit of energy exhausted.

"Fuck. How in the hell am I going to hoist this beast up in the tree?"

Using boating rope and his dwindling adrenaline, Rick pulled the deer up in a tree so it dangled at least eight feet off the ground. No small feat. Securing the rope to the bottom of the tree, he collapsed into his sleeping bag, and fell into a deep and satisfied sleep. He'd bagged a buck. Tomorrow he'd be eating fresh venison.

Waking with a euphoric smile, Rick set out to skin his prize. The only problem - he'd never skinned a deer before. Sure he'd watched a show and read some articles, but there was a huge difference between watching and doing.

"Wonder how much it's going to smell and how much blood?" His biggest fear was the scent would attract some unwanted friends like a cougar or a mountain lion. "I'd better clean my gun and re-load just in case."

Setting the gun nearby, he carefully lowered the buck to about a foot from the ground, and then built up the fire with a whole lot of wet moss and kindling in hopes that the smoke would cover up the smell of what he was about to do, and to keep the flies away.

"Well here goes nothing."

It was messy. And bloody. Admittedly, he butchered that poor thing in the worst way possible. Skinning a deer was much, much easier to watch than to do.

"Jesus fucking Christ this is disgusting. And hard. I don't have the right tools."

It took him about three hours to get the majority of the good meat out of the carcass, and as for his glorious plans for the remaining skin, they'd been completely fucked over. After piling the meat on an olive coloured drop wool blanket, he wrapped everything in a small tent tarp.

"I think I got all I need. Now to deal with this carcass."

Lowering the buck to the ground, he untied it, then looped the rope through the rivet holes on another tarp, and tied the tarp tight around the dead animal.

"Good luck at even a fly getting in there!"

Dragging the corpse about fifty yards from the camp, he spent another couple of hours digging a hole and burying the remains as best as he could.

"Look at me," he laughed. "I'm a fucking mess. The boys would love this for sure!"

Stripping down to his pants, Rick washed in the bitter cold creek water, dunking and scrubbing his t-shirt to a semi-clean state. Armed with a pot of water, he re-built the fire and began the task of drying his shirt. He hadn't thought to bring another change of clothes, one of the only things he didn't think of.

"Now, how am I going to cook you?" he said eyeing the pile of meat.

Between the machete and the hatchet, he was able to construct a decent little tripod cooking platform, both to hang the pot over the fire and to make a spit. It took forever, but by mid-evening he'd boiled water for a well deserved cup of instant coffee and charred the hell out of a piece of venison.

"If I cook the fuck out of it, that should take care of any diseases or maggots or shit. At least I hope it does."

Popping a can of Mountain Dew and taking a huge bite, Rick celebrated his day and a half of hard work. The meat had never tasted better and he was proud of himself. He could survive out here if he had to. Yeah he'd do things a little different next time but he could do it if he so desired. Another option. Another real and doable option. It was fairly smooth sailing from then on. He had food, drink, and a safe and relatively dry camp. Content and at peace. Emotions he hadn't experienced for a very long time. Everyday he ventured back up to the house to check on things and see if anyone had shown up. The constant treks around the area made him increasingly familiar and harmonious with the area, and while he continued to 'hunt' he didn't take anymore kills. There was no need. He had enough meat, and when it came to nature, he would only take what he needed. Nothing more. He had no vengeance against the land or those who dwelled in it.

By the seventh day he noticed activity up at the house, so after much deliberation, he packed up his gear and headed up. It would have been so easy to just pick his shit up and keep heading west towards the coast and deeper into the Cascade Mountains. The woods had been so peaceful, and so incredibly fulfilling for him, that he wouldn't have been happier to just leave society and the world behind, and take off into the green abyss forever. But he couldn't. He couldn't leave the ones he loved. But it wasn't his mother or brother or any love of family that made him reappear. Hell no, it was his love and loyalty to 'The Team' and the brothers he had found in Strom, Havoc, Cajun, and Creek. He couldn't disappear on them and abandon the brotherhood. Loyalty and honour.

"How nice of you to come home and grace us with your presence," said Brenda. "My good gracious, look at you! You stink."

"Safe trip?" said Rick with a smirk. "I'm just going to go have a shower, and then I'll be out to help move boxes."

Brenda was not amused by her oldest son's behaviour. Seeing him happily march through the back door with his large backpack, carrying a bonafide hunting rifle, and smelling like a dead animal only reinforced how much of her son's life she knew nothing about. Where did he get the rifle? How on earth was he able to survive in the woods like that by himself for a week? No lecture or grounding would change anything. At least he came home. Whether it was the woods or the streets, her son was rebellious enough to not come home, to never come home, and she knew it. She was losing control. And that's where she made a serious miscalculation in her thinking. She thought she still had a chance, she thought she still had some say. She was never more wrong. She'd lost control ages ago. Maybe even as far back when she first took the money Rick brought home. She just couldn't bring herself to admit it.

Rick's journey in the woods had been a reinforcement of his independence. He'd probably spent more time out on his own than he should have, although he certainly didn't do it maliciously or for spite, the time spent was just an extension of his psychological needs. It was the final act. Once and for all he'd cut the cord of dependence and solidified his belief that he was a sovereign individual. He'd already turned his back on God and severed his dependence on Him, and now it was time to take that next step. Rick knew he could survive on his own, whether it was on the streets or in the mountains, and the choice to come home would be his and his alone. He could take any car he wanted and drive across the country. He had enough money to hop on a plane. Now he had just proven that he could survive out in the wilderness. He could just walk out into the woods in any direction and thrive. He could live and survive one hundred per cent on his own – at fourteen years of age. He didn't need anybody. Complete power and independence.

There was an unrivaled freedom that came from not needing anybody. Each of these experiences gave Rick the realization that he was smart enough, and skilled enough to make it on his own. He didn't have to be dependent on anyone. He was his own man. Power and freedom. Hand in hand. The only time someone had power over him was when Rick let them. When he allowed them that privilege. When he humoured them. Such thoughts and feelings were so liberating, they bordered on euphoric. All his life he'd been under the power and control of someone else. He had to do things because that's the way things were. He had to love and obey God. He had to live by His Will and His Words. He had to love and respect his father simply because he was connected to him by biology. Society deemed that he had to go to school and get good grades to be successful. The number of 'had to's' and requirements on his life seemed infinite. No longer. Not anymore. He wasn't dependent on anyone or anything.

God could kiss his ass. He had no time for a tyrant in the sky. His father could go to hell. He left and forfeited his right to tell Rick what to do. And even his mother, although he loved her, he was coming to understand her 'sickness' of being a delusional Christian. Society could really kiss his ass. He didn't need its recognition or acceptance; he was a Ghost amongst them. Rick had countless reinforcement for all his views, which made him all that more confident that he didn't have to answer to anyone. But why was he so different? So extreme? Other kids didn't think this way. Other kids could reason, they were given choices, left to make some of their own decisions in their own upbringing or at least given explanations for decisions made on their behalf.

"But why?"

"Because He's God."

"Because this is what the Lord wants. There is no questioning His Will or His way."

"Because I'm your mother. Do as you're told."

"Because I'm your father. You have no say."

"Because, because, because."

Growing up in such an arbitrary manner, with arbitrary rules enforced for arbitrary reasons, Rick was assumed to be an ignorant pawn whose station was only to follow directions.

"You are God's Little warrior."

"But why me?"

"Because, that is His Will and His Way. Don't ask questions. Just accept and do. Asking questions only tells the Lord that your faith is not strong and perhaps you don't love Him like you should. Rejoice always, pray without ceasing, give thanks in all circumstances; for this is the will of God in Christ Jesus for you. Do not quench the Spirit."

But it was all bullshit. He knew that now. He'd already seen too much. Too much hypocrisy, too much corruption, and too much delusion to merely accept 'because' as the answer to anything anymore, especially when it concerned God. From this point on, rebellion wasn't just an adjective for Rick, it was a mantra, a way of life. It became his worldview and his philosophy, as ingrained in his being as the need to breathe. No one was worthy of power and control over his life, and any semblance of obedience on Rick's part was only an act meant to keep the peace. Ghost was beholden to no one but himself.

Except he was. Or was he? Although Rick had stepped away from God, there was still no question in his mind that God existed and controlled everything. Rick knew with absolute clarity that he was not 'right' with God, and that he was purposely outside His Will and away from Him, and therefore was 'wrong' in his life. Regardless of how justified Rick felt in no longer working as a warrior, he was still wrong for turning away from the light, and thus, by proxy, was damned and forsaken. There was no getting around it. One does not completely rid their psyche of fourteen years of indoctrination in a flash, so the feelings Rick had of it being 'too late' for him were very real. He believed his soul was already too torn, his mind already too damaged, and his heart already frozen over. Lines had been crossed. Redemption unattainable. The sense of spiritual dread and forbearing overwhelmed him. God was going to punish him, that much was certain. It was just a question of where and when. And each day Rick waited for the hammer to drop.

Pounded into his head from birth was the Christian ideal of 'either / or' – and in a person's walk through life, they either belong to God or they belong to the devil. Rick wanted to belong to neither but with God out of the picture, that left only one alternative. In his mind, his soul and his life belonged to the monster he'd spent his entire life fighting against. God would make him pay for that. He'd have His vengeance. And with God out of the picture, the Devil was free to torture and have His way, seek His own vengeance for what Rick had done to Him in the past. When would the demons come? What evil would they bestow on the young boy's soul?

For fourteen-year-old Rick, these thoughts were real. They haunted him.

They cursed him. They stalked him. He was always waiting and wondering. When would it happen? Would it be more horrible than the things he'd already seen? A mind this full of angst and torment begins not to care what happens to him. It takes risks because those seem like nothing compared to what might lie ahead. When a life is worthless who the fuck cares what happens? He didn't want his life. He didn't want his soul or his memories. So why not kill himself? Why not just end it all? Because the torment in life was much easier than the torment he'd face in death. Death would only signal the beginning of an eternity of torment in Hell. He had offended the Devil, more times than he could count. The Devil was waiting with open arms for his arrival.

He'd have to wait. Rick wasn't about to 'tap out'. He wouldn't run from his reality and prove to God and the Devil that he was too weak to make it in the world. He couldn't let God or the Devil or any amount of pain and suffering drive him away. To do so was being a coward, and Rick wasn't a coward. No matter how doomed or forsaken he may have felt, he was still a warrior, and warriors don't quit. Ever. They don't take the easy way out; they keep on fighting. Giving in or giving up wasn't an option no matter how tough things got. Warriors took control and they fought back against the tyranny and injustice. And if they did go down, it was with guns a blazing.

CHAPTER THIRTY-ONE

The start of high school in September did nothing to quell Rick's behaviour, and more often than not he found himself in both morning and afternoon detention. Staying out all night roaming the streets tended to interrupt one's sleeping time, so Rick made sure he always caught a few winks in class. That is when he actually got on the bus and made it to class. It was just too easy to hide in the brush at the end of the driveway, and then disappear into the woods once it had picked up Jimmy and headed into town. As long as Rick was back at the end of the drive when the bus arrived after school, none was the wiser, except the school and Jimmy.

"You're going to get in trouble."

"Really?" said Rick. "And who's going to tell on me? You"

"Yeah. Me."

"Don't make me laugh," said Rick. "You know that if you say one word to Mom I'll beat the living shit out of you."

Jimmy and Rick were very different. While Rick had grown up his mother's little warrior, Jimmy had grown up as her innocent little lamb, a 'do-gooder' who didn't like doing anything wrong. Rarely did they do anything together anymore, and their relationship wasn't close. Rick could be a definite asshole, and Jimmy was scared of his unpredictability. But on another level, Rick was just into things with a bunch of people that Jimmy couldn't hang with. There was no way he'd ever even dream of getting his little brother involved in any of the shit he did. He loved him dearly, even though his actions towards his little brother sometimes suggested otherwise.

"I mean it. You say one word and I'll beat you to a pulp."

"I hate you Rick."

"I know you don't really Jimmy but if it makes you feel better to say it then go ahead."

"It does make me feel better. I hate you." Jimmy made the wise decision not to ever snitch on his brother missing the bus. What did he care what his brother was doing? It was his life.

In his first month as a freshman at McMinnville High School, Rick had spent almost everyday in detention, often just to get out of taking the bus and going home that night. He was also skipping at least two full days of school a week, staying up in the woods of High Heaven. Sometimes he'd go on long excursions, and sometimes he'd stay right next to the house. On September 29th, 1993 Rick decided he wasn't getting on the bus and instead slinked off into the woods to an encampment he'd made a few days earlier. He'd made a small clearing and pitched a tent into the bushes, providing it the maximum natural camouflage. He'd also built a small fire pit, ringing it with wet mud and a few large rocks. After waiting a couple of hours until his mother left for work, Rick sparked up the fire to get warm and have something to eat. Three previous fires had given the pit a nice base of ashes and he was able to build a nice little fire. At no time did he ever leave anything important at any of his encampments. He just never knew who might be out in the woods and stumble upon his space. Tired of reading, he let the fire die down, then took two pots of water, dumped them on top and then covered everything with dirt. Satisfied with his work, he spent the rest of the day tracking coyotes, before stopping by the camp one last time to zip up the tent and make sure the fire was out. By three-thirty he was back at the end of the drive waiting for the bus. The next day at school his mid-day class was interrupted by his furious mother.

"What on earth do you think you're doing?" she said pulling him out of class. "You almost burnt down the entire neighbourhood!"

"What are you talking about?" said Rick. He truly didn't have a clue.

"Were you up in the woods yesterday? Answer me and make it the truth!"

"Yes I was…but..."

"Did you light a fire?"

"Yes I did but I put it out. I swear I did. I poured two pots of water on it and smothered it with dirt!"

"Well it didn't work. And don't think you can lie your way out of this one. They found a bunch of your stuff…I can only presume it was your stuff at the site. I can't believe you'd do something like that Rick! What have you become?"

Rick knew he was screwed. His fingerprints were all over the cans of food.

"I didn't do it on purpose Mom. Honest. I'm not lying. I would never intentionally burn down the forest…I love that place. How much burnt down?"

"Well, you're going to have to convince the Forest Services people. And our neighbours the Klein's want to see you hang. They're thinking about pressing charges. Mr. Klein saw the fire and called it in right away. They caught it early. I think it was a patch about thirty by forty feet but I'm not exactly sure. What in the hell were you thinking anyway?" Brenda began to cry.

"I'd been skipping school and camping down the hill from the house. I put the fire out Mom. I don't know how the hell it started back up."

Brenda knew when her son was lying, and this wasn't one of those times. The drive up to the house from the school seemed exceptionally long.

"I believe you Rick. I believe you didn't mean to start the fire, but the first thing we need to do is go and see Mr. Klein."

Mr. Klein met them halfway down the gravel road.

"My son came to apologize."

"I don't want his fucking apology!" he said before turning toward Rick. "I want you to stay off my fucking land. Do you understand me?"

Rick looked the man square in the eyes. "Don't worry, I won't be back."

"I mean it," said Mr. Klein changing his tone. "I just don't want you to be in the woods and get shot for trespassing by my son or something."

"Mr. Klein, I can assure you that there would be no reason to shoot Rick."

"Well…I'm just giving him the warning…It's been a very dry and dangerous summer up here and you need to be extremely careful with your woodcraft."

"I understand sir. It won't happen again."

"It better not."

"You know I have to ground you," said Brenda as they were walking home. "I don't know why…it's not like that even works anymore."

They both knew Rick was going to do whatever he wanted, regardless of what Brenda or anyone else had to say. If he stayed home and obeyed the rules it was because it was convenient. If he went to school it was because he wanted to either see his friends or stay in town, not because he cared about his grades. If he walked off into the night or stayed in the woods for a week, there was nothing she could do about it. Still, Rick felt bad about the fire and the money it cost them. But more than that, he felt dumb and foolish for appearing so incompetent, especially in his own element.

"Yeah I understand," he said. "I truly am sorry Mom. Are you going to tell Dad?"

"I don't think there's any reason he needs to know. I do want you to speak to the Forest Ranger Service though. They want to speak to you."

"Yeah okay."

Well meaning and genuine, Officer Lee sat Rick down at school the next day. He didn't try any sort of bad ass cop routine, and didn't even have a tape recorder.

"I just have to read you this little slip of paper before I ask you any questions if that's okay? You know…just to be safe and to make sure we're following procedures. I've already spoken to your mother and she gave me parental consent."

"Okay," Rick nodded.

"You have the right to remain silent. Anything you say can and will be used against you in a court of law. You have the right to an attorney. If you cannot afford an attorney, one will be provided for you. Do you understand the rights I have just read to you?"

Rick nodded yes. He could feel his chest tighten as a pang of fear and confusion shot up his throat. It was just a campfire.

"I just want to start out by asking you a few simple questions about the fire in the woods. First off, when did you start it?"

Rick answered all his questions honestly, and in this case, he didn't have anything to hide. He told him about skipping school and making the campfire to get warm and cook some food. Officer Lee wanted to know what sort of fuel Rick used to get it started and the procedure he used to put it out.

"I swear sir that it was an accident. I put out the fire and made sure I smothered it with dirt. I have no idea how it started up again. I swear I don't."

"Okay that's fine. Now, I have to ask you about some other fires we've found in the past."

"Okay."

"These are much more of a concern to me. We've found a number of campfires up at the lookout and even one in the actual tower itself. Would you happen to know anything about these?"

"I have no idea sir," said Rick. He and the boys never made campfires at the lookout, it was too close to other houses immediately down the hill and the sight or smoke would draw attention.

"Are you sure son?"

"I am positive sir. I have never set any campfires up at the lookout and that is the truth. I've certainly been up there with my buddies but we've never set any fires. I do know that people go up there all the time. College kids making smores and stuff."

"So you're saying you have no clue. You do understand that having a fire on private property is one thing but arson on a state or Federal structure or building is a federal offence."

"I have no idea about any of those fires sir," said Rick. This would explain why Officer Lee read Rick his Miranda Rights. Because of the campfire, Rick was now their primary suspect in a string of other fires around the area. Great. That's all he needed. The one time he doesn't break the law intentionally and now he's getting pinched for it.

"I hope you don't son because you can get yourself in a lot of trouble playing with fires, especially up there at the lookout tower. Like many boys your age, I think you like playing with fire but I want you to think very long and hard about the consequences. You seem like a good kid. Just be careful okay?"

"Yes sir, I will."

The interview lasted all of twenty minutes, and there was never any threat of charges. It had been a close call, and he'd have to be more careful. Of course, it didn't take long for the rumour spread to around school that Rick had tried to burn down his neighbour's property, and Mr. Klein's son, Chris, was at the forefront. Older than Rick and feeling quite tough, he confronted Rick in the school bathroom, trying to stir up trouble.

"I'm going to thrash you, you little fuck," said Chris spitting in Rick's direction.

"Look, I told you it was an accident."

"Fucking little liar."

After a brief scuffle and exchange of blows, Rick had had enough of this asshole spreading rumours and causing trouble. He was done.

"Come at me again Chris and I'll fucking bleed you dude," said Rick flipping out the butterfly knife he'd borrowed from Strom. Rick wasn't playing and Chris knew it.

"Man, stay off my fucking property and no more fires."

"I will," said Rick calmly. "But if you don't let this go I'll kill your bitch ass and I'm not joking."

Chris hesitated. "Fuck you man, I'm done." He turned and walked out the door.

Not ten seconds later, Strom and Havoc burst through the same door, just as Rick was putting the knife away.

"Jesus, you didn't stab him did you?" said Havoc.

"Did you see any blood asshole?" Rick answered. "Nah, he's fine – it wasn't all that. I had no intentions of using the knife. I just wanted to make sure he knew it was over."

And Chris did know it was over. He never spoke to Rick again. Once again, the whole school knew about the incident, which only added to Rick's image and mystique of being one dangerous little motherfucker. If only they knew the truth behind the image, that these outward bursts of emotions were like little releases of steam from a volcanic inferno brewing below. But they didn't. Know one did. Except God and the Devil.

It had been almost a year since the 'Turning'. He had quit going to church, opened his mind to new horizons, and his participation in the demon hunts had ended. He'd even moved out of town, up to the hills where it was peaceful; a place veritably untouched by the War. It would make sense that the torment within his heart would lessen. But nothing in Rick's life ever made sense, and he was still as afflicted and full of despair as he'd ever been. The sight had not left him, neither had the visions, the betrayal or the feeling of being stalked by something he'd fought so long against. It was hard for him to even describe the feelings to himself, let alone anyone else.

Imagine for the first fourteen years of your life you're taught only one thing – that the worship of one object was all that mattered in life. Let's say this object was a rock, and that worship and faith in that rock was all one needed to get by in the world and nothing else mattered. That the rock was invincible and should it choose to wield its power, nothing could stand before it. And anyone who doesn't believe in, or speaks out against the rock is evil and will be punished eternally for doing so. So, being raised knowing nothing but the rock, unquestionably taught that this is 'the way'. The rock is all you have and you must have trust in it because the very axis of your entire world revolves around it. The rock is your world. It is your everything.

And then, the rock shatters. It's ground to dust, and in an instant you learn it was all false. The rock had been none of the things you had been taught. It was, and it had been all a lie. Imagine how that discovery would shatter your world, cause you to become unglued and trust no one or nothing. All you'd ever known was the rock, and now all you knew was how easy it was to be deceived, lied to and betrayed. How adrift would you be? Would you be floundering? Sinking? Unable to grab a hold of anything real or positive? Now imagine that this object isn't just a rock, it's a God, it's a being, it's a Spirit – something so powerful it's rooted in the beginning of time.

And now just for kicks, pretend that because you worshipped and loved this rock so much, because you gave it your soul, it returned the favour by giving you a gift. A gift that allowed you to see through the murky reality to the underbelly of existence, whether you wanted to or not. It'd be like deep-sea diving to the very deepest darkest depths of the ocean, where light doesn't exist because the darkness is impenetrable. Creatures lurk in the unknown, and because no one has seen them in person, no one can really dispute whether they're real or not. And this stone is supposed to protect you from these creatures, from these beings, but it's buried so deep in the murk that it's powers are useless, and it turns out, they always had been.

Rick's eyes had been opened to a world behind a world, and he simply couldn't forget what he had been shown or could see. And knowing that God or the stone was false, who or what was going to protect him from the horrific things he saw? Who was going to keep them at bay? Nothing. Nobody. They were free to haunt his every waking moment. He still saw them, still heard their snarls and the clicking of their talons. Every time he went into town, to school, was around his friends, anywhere there was living souls, he saw them and felt their presence. And they could sense his. They could feel the emanations of fear and being forsaken, and they would taunt and leer at him with predatory glee. Breaking ties with God didn't close off the other world to Rick, it simply set it adrift. It was all still there. Waiting. He had to do something to relieve some of the pressure and lighten the weight of his affliction. He couldn't stand it any longer.

When the family moved to the High Heaven house, Rick decided to appropriate one of the 'tack' rooms in the barn for his own special space. Only about seven by ten feet, the room was originally meant for horse saddles and gear but Rick had other plans. He found some random boards and plywood and with a hammer and nails, sealed shut the doorway so that the only entrance was through the ceiling which opened to the barn rafters. He nailed more boards and unused closet doors to the top, leaving a small three by three foot opening in the center for him to drop down into. To cover up the window, he nailed a solid green canvas across the frame, blocking out all light when draped down. For added security, he didn't bother making a ladder or any means of climbing onto the ceiling, so the only way up was to kick yourself up off the neighbouring wall, grab the ledge and pull yourself up. Easy for a kid that was part ninja, not so easy for anyone else, especially Brenda or Joe.

In this little fortress, Rick stashed a fold out chair, candles, and various necessities. He covered the walls with posters, pictures, and articles that he knew there was no way in hell he'd be allowed to hang on his bedroom wall. Without knowing it or even realizing it, he had psychologically constructed a sort of temple to all those things he worshipped or were forbidden to him; a sort of sacred space that contained all his fascinations.

On November 2nd, 1993, Rick made his cease fire and pact with the forces of evil. It was something he'd been thinking about for months, how to relieve some of the pressure and some of the pain. In the end, he decided that if he had to co-exist with the forces of evil, then he'd let them know that he was no longer a threat or someone they had to worry about. Rick was out of the war for good, and he wanted and needed all parties to know. He'd had no ritual instruction or training, just the instinctual knowledge that such a pact would require blood and some sort of talisman to represent the bond. A few weeks before, he'd found a simple gold-plated ring with a large black onyx stone in Joe's horde of meaningless garbage. He wouldn't miss it. The ring fit perfectly on the middle finger of Rick's left hand, looked masculine, and even had a bit of an evil look about it. The ring would remind all those on the other side that he was 'off limits' and they could expect no harm from him.

Rick sat cross-legged on the floor, inhaling down to the tip of his toes, sucking every last bit of air in, then out through his nose. This was a big moment. Huge. Bigger than any one decision he's ever made in his life. There was no turning back. No crossing back over the line. This was it. For a full twenty minutes he sat there, breathing in and out, thinking, contemplating, until he was in a near catatonic state. This wasn't just for the now but would have ramifications for all his eternity.

"What choice do I have? God abandoned me and after what I've seen and done…how can I put my trust in Him. I have no choice. I have to do this. I just can't take it anymore. I'm not going to make it. I'm not going to survive the pain."

Rick set the ring carefully in the center of a large stainless steel bowl. Filling the bottom inch of the bowl with lighter fluid, he began to pray – not to God but to Asmodeus, the King of Demons. He didn't want to make this pact with the 'opposite of God' but wanted to contact and make a deal with an actual 'person' because this was personal. It wasn't just some selling of the soul to the generic devil, this was real and this was for keeps. As he prayed, he cut the meat of his left hand below the thumb and mixed his own blood with the lighter fluid until it was a deep red colour. He prayed to Asmodeus the same way he'd spent his entire life praying to God, kneeling down on the concrete floor, beseeching Him to listen to his request.

"God has failed to acknowledge me. You Asmodeus, please hear my request. I swear to never again use knowledge or my abilities against you or your interests, and in return I demand that you return the favour and leave me alone. LEAVE ME ALONE! I know that you will always be around me but please act as if I don't exist. Make me as much of a ghost to you as you are to the rest of the world."

"I've been misled and drawn into this War by lies and manipulation. It was not my choice. I have severed all ties with my former master. I will never be a problem again, nor will I fight on either side. I just want out. I just want to remain neutral."

"Please Asmodeus…please seal this pact and cease-fire with your own power and leave a mark or some sort of signal in the ring so that those who see it will know that I am no longer in this War, and those that break this cease-fire…this pact will have to answer to you."

When he believed that enough blood had fallen into the bowl, Rick pulled out his lighter and touched the contents. The lighter fluid instantly burst into flames, and Rick held the bowl a loft in his hands, continuing his trance-like prayer. As the bowl began to heat, the pain and burning sensation radiated down his hands and arms. No longer able to withstand it, the bowl slipped from his grasp and landed with a crash on the concrete before him, red fluid splashing off the side and towards him. Still aflame, the bowl rocked back and forth before finally settling back on its base.

Sitting in silence, Rick watched the flames eagerly eat the rest of the fuel, then die a slow lingering death, licking the sides of the bowl as if not wanting to waste one-minute drop. The ring. Rick peered into the bowl, not really knowing what to expect. Refusing to wait any longer, he grabbed the ring and held it in the palm of his hand. Dead cold. Not a drop of heat. Nothing. The black chill was disturbingly familiar, as if his hand was back on the Witches' Rock. Without hesitation he slipped the cold, black ring on his finger, knowing the instant it slid into place his fate was sealed in eternal black ice. That was it.

Did it work? Did the demons leave Rick alone? Yes, immediately. He still saw them but he was no longer threatened by them, and over time, they simply became no longer important to see. His Third Eye became less hyperactive, less paranoid and sensitive, and eventually was as nonchalant or normal as seeing a cat or dog being walked down the street. They were still quite disgusting to be sure but with an absence of fear, his fascination was at the forefront, which simply fueled his obsession to know and understand what he was dealing with or witnessing. Curiosity replaced trepidation and in the end he was able to relax and much of the spiritual pressure lifted from his weighted soul. Did this happen overnight? Of course not. Was it all in his head? Who's to say, but the idea that he believed in what happened is all that really matters. And he couldn't deny that whenever he used his sight the black stone on the ring glowed with a strange glacial essence, and in any confrontation he had with a demon, they seemed to back off, as if the ring itself had the power. That alone was proof enough for Rick.

Whatever the proof, whatever the evidence, it was a step Rick felt compelled to take. That's how torn and gutted his soul was. He didn't make a pact with the devil to join him in his evil practices. No, he asked the devil to stay the hell away! To leave him be. He wanted no part of God or Satan. Just as he sought to free himself from the shackles of dependence on others by spending a week in the forest, he sought to free himself from the shackles of any power, good or evil. He wanted the freedom to make his own choices and be his own man. He was tired of it, tired of it all. The weight, the burden, just everything. Fuck his parents, fuck society, fuck the drug dealers, fuck God, fuck the Devil. Fuck them all.

CHAPTER THIRTY-TWO

"Jesus Christ boys! Run!"

The job hadn't gone well. Hadn't gone well at all and in the cold late November night, three teens sprinting their asses off were quite easy to detect.

"Where's our fucking ride?"

"I don't know man but we'd better split up and get the fuck out of here!"

"Son of a bitch, son of a bitch, son of a bitch," Rick muttered as he turned the corner and headed south down the street. "How the fuck am I going to get out of this one!"

If he didn't get off the street soon, he was screwed, and Ghost wouldn't be a ghost anymore but a documented and registered felon. He needed to think. Where could he hide? Then it hit him. It was risky and it was either going to doom him or save his ass. Either way, the chance was worth it. He quit running, walked into the street on a red light, opened the door of a green Subaru, and hopped in the passenger side.

"Drive," he said slumping low in the seat and pulling the Walther out of his coat.

The young blonde woman in the front seat looked unfazed and a little more than pissed. It wasn't the reaction Rick was expecting, and he instantly worried that this hadn't been the best decision he'd ever made. He had no clue whether she was going to simply open the car door, get out and flag the cops, or slap the shit out of him and risk getting shot. She did neither. Rick kept a close watch as she checked the rear-view mirror, picking up the flashes of red wailing police lights. When the light turned green, she calmly put her foot on the gas and pulled out into traffic like she was driving home after picking up some bananas at the grocery store. Rick sunk lower into the upholstery and took off his hat, trying to be as unnoticeable in the passenger seat as possible.

"Where?" she said in a rather venomous tone.

"I don't fucking care," said Rick softly. "Just away from here."

She glanced at Rick again with a slight air of disappointment but didn't reply. They drove in silence for the next fifteen minutes.

"You know you can put the gun away," she said. "You shouldn't be putting yourself in a position to have to shoot someone anyway."

Rick put the gun back in his pants. "Sorry. Shit just got a little hairy back there and I didn't see another way out." He was embarrassed and felt surprisingly shy in her presence.

The girl sighed and relaxed her shoulders. "Well don't tell me what it is because I don't want to know."

Rick knew then that she was special. Instead of being scared and fearful for her safety, she was angry at him and knew better than to ask about the specifics of his crime. She was a keeper. Still skittish and scared as hell himself, Rick was at least comforted in the face that he hadn't traumatized her.

"I'm just going to drive around until you figure out where you want to go. My name's Amy by the way. You don't need to tell me yours 'cause I'd hate to make you have to shoot me." A wry grin crept on her face. "And I have way too much planned for my life."

Rick didn't know how to respond. Already feeling confused and guilty about the whole thing, she was making it worse by being so nice and comforting.

"What would make you put yourself in this kind of position anyway? You don't seem like the type of kid to carjack people? Trust me, I do know the type. I have a little brother. He's back in juvenile hall in Wyoming…that's where I'm from. He was such a sweet kid growing up and then he started hanging around with the wrong people, making stupid decisions and doing stupid things. Got into drugs and the gang life. He stuck a gun in my face once before too. Told me he hated me. It hurt you know? Broke my heart. I only ever wanted what was best for him. Anyways, that's one of the reasons I decided to move so far away to go to college. Was tired of dealing with it. All of it. My mom and dad and their drinking, and all the other shit and trouble they got into. I didn't and I don't want that sort of life for me you know?"

"Yeah," said Rick softly. "I get it."

"I mean…I know how easily it can happen. One minute you're good and then the next minute something happens and everything is shot to shit. I think of my little brother all the time and wonder if there was something more I could have done to help him…"

"You probably did all that you could do," said Rick. "Or at least all that he would allow you to do. Sometimes it's hard helping people who don't want to be helped."

"Is that you? Someone who doesn't want to be helped?"

"I don't know," said Rick. "I think I'm better at helping other people. It's just easier."

For the next forty-five minutes the two talked as Amy drove, with Rick slowly feeling more comfortable in the conversation but still not wanting to give up any specifics. In the end, they were both laughing and chuckling. Amy's anger completely gone.

"Hey listen," she said. If you want to lay low for a bit and catch some sleep, you can crash at my apartment and leave whenever. I'm not going to do anything weird like call the cops on you or anything."

It was a set-up. It had to be. Lulling Rick into dropping his guard. For all he knew she could have been the daughter of a cop and she'd made up the whole 'little brother' story. Paranoia played a video of scenarios in his head, screaming reasons to not accept her offer.

"Yeah," he answered. "That'd be cool. Thank you."

The two times he'd connected with her big soft green eyes, there was nothing but understanding and compassion. He took a risk and decided to trust her. Once he said yes, the whole dynamic changed and it was like she was back taking care of her little brother again – which is exactly what Rick became. As she drove southwest into Beaverton, they talked longer and shared stories and ideals, even delving into what kind of music and bands they liked. Nineteen, Amy had been studying journalism and politics at a nearby college for just over a year.

"I know it's not much," she said opening the door to her apartment, "but it's all I can afford. I would have loved to live on the other side of town but not much I can do about it since I'm pretty much on my own."

"That's okay," said Rick. "I like the place."

"You hungry? I think I have some leftovers…sorry I need to get groceries."

"Leftovers are fine."

The two shared some snacks and a couple of glasses of orange juice, talking for hours and hours about almost everything.

"What's your name?"

"Ghost."

"No. I mean your real name. If you're going to spend the night on my couch, I want to know your real name."

"It's Rick. Rick Watkinson."

"And where are you from Rick?"

"I live in McMinnville."

"McMinnville? What on earth are you doing running from the cops all the way out here?"

"It's a long story."

"Well we have all night," she answered.

Rick opened up. He confided more in her that night than he ever had to anyone. She just had that look, that personality that told him she had his back, that she understood, and more importantly, she was willing to listen to what he had to say. She cared. She could relate. The only adult that ever did. She gave a damn about what he was telling her, and not once did she judge him or scold him or tell him that if he prayed more, things would be better. She rewarded his honesty with love and compassion. By the end of the night, Rick's broken soul opened and he cried while she held him. It was the first time he'd cried since the divorce, even since Jackie. And as he cried into her chest, they forged a bond. They became family – big sister and little brother. And that bond meant everything to him, and she meant everything to Rick. If she needed him, he'd be there. If she wanted a mountain moved, he'd do it. Anything.

"Nice. Well Rick, I'm exhausted so I'm going to head to bed. Here's a blanket and a pillow. The couch is pretty comfortable, not too many bumps or lumps."

"I'm sure it'll be just fine," said Rick. "I just appreciate this so much."

"No problem kid. Have a good sleep and try and stay out of trouble at least until the morning."

Rick laughed. "I'll do my best."

He watched her walk into her bedroom and shut the door. For the first time in a very long time he felt safe. He felt like he was somewhere he belonged. While Amy went to school the next morning, Rick used a nearby payphone to check in on his buddies.

"We thought you'd be pinched bro or were dead in some alley."

"Nah bro," said Rick. "I'm fine. Still up north but will be back soon."

He waited for Amy to get back from her classes, and then the two of them had a very serious talk about what happened the day before, who he was and what he did. The talk continued all the way back to McMinnville.

"Listen Rick," she said handing him a piece of paper. "Here's my address and my phone number. There's an open invitation. If you're in the area and need a place to crash, you're more than welcome to come over."

"Thanks Amy," he said getting out of the car. "Here's some money for gas, and here's my phone number. If you ever need anything, I don't care what it is, call me and I'll be there."

Amy gave him a hug and a peck on the cheek. "I don't doubt that you would Rick. I don't doubt that you would."

Rick called her at least every other day to check in and make sure she was okay, and to let her know that he was alive and well, and tried to make the trip to Beaverton as much as possible. About the third week of December, right before Christmas vacation, Rick found himself on Amy's doorstep. Amy was just making breakfast.

"Rick, hey!" said Amy. "Come on in."

"Thanks Amy. Oh hey Tom."

Tom only scowled. As Amy's boyfriend, he wasn't all that fond of the 'little brother' showing up unnoticed. Sort of dampened the mood and the chances of getting laid. Tom was a druggie, a drop out, and inches away from going to prison at any time. Pretty much an asshole in Rick's view.

"Tom, I'm not cutting classes. And especially not for three days!"

"Oh come on! It's almost the break anyway. Come down to Eureka with me and party. It'll be fun."

"Tom, honestly, I'm not going to California just so I can party."

"Jesus Christ Amy."

Tom wasn't taking no for an answer.

"Tom, I'm not going. You party too much anyways. I'm not into it like you."

"Oh, so now I party too much? What the fuck Amy?"

As the arguing escaladed, it ran the gamut of grievances. Amy didn't like how much Tom partied, or his low-life behaviour and general irresponsibility. Then it turned to money and who had been pulling more weight in the relationship. The arguing turned to yelling, and the yelling turned to hurtful words, things being slammed, and plenty of heightened emotions. Rick sat motionless on the couch. The tape rewound in his head. His parents. All those huge blowouts in California when he was little, his father sitting in the car threatening to leave. All the fights and yelling in Washington which culminated in the divorce. His own blowouts with his dad. So much fighting. So much arguing. He hated it.

"Stupid bitch."

"Watch how you talk to her dude," said Rick calmly.

"Stay the fuck out of this you little shit."

Not saying another word, Rick sunk deeper into the couch, his complete silence hiding the rage brewing inside.

"Fucking bitch," said Tom shoving Amy across the living room.

Like a burst of molten lava bursting from a volcano, Rick flew from the couch, cleared the coffee table and landed square on a startled Tom, tackling him to the floor in a flurry of elbows and knees. Much larger and stronger, Tom flipped Rick onto his back and drilled him twice with his clenched fist. Rick had to do something, and he had to do it fast before he ended up eating shit. Bucking hard, he launched Tom forward, then grabbed a mostly empty wine bottle off the coffee table, and cracked his opponent across the head, dazing him. Plopping himself across Tom's stomach with his arm across his chest, Rick continued his assault, hitting him a good three or four more times, splitting his head open.

"Ghost! Jesus sweetie STOP!" Amy screamed, running over and wrapping her arms around Rick from behind, pulling him off before the wine bottle made another descent. Rick dropped the bottle and stood over Tom with a pointed finger.

"You don't ever fucking touch her again!" He stormed out the front door and sat on the landing steps to cool down.

"Little fucking asshole!" Rick heard Tom say.

"I'm done Tom," said Amy. "I'm done. Get your shit and get out of here."

A furious Tom emerged a few minutes later, washcloth to his bleeding head.

He ignored Rick, got into his car and took off. Amy followed him out the door, sitting down beside a still panting and heaving Rick. She lit up a smoke, took a drag, then offered it to Rick. Although he'd sworn off them for a year, the situation warranted a drag.

"I thought you didn't smoke?" said Rick.

"I don't. They're Tom's. They fell out of his pocket when you flying squirrel jumped him." She let out a chuckle.

"Sorry about that," said Rick returning the laugh. "I don't know what happened. I mean I do…but…I just hate fighting. Like arguing. I just can't stand it and it gets me so angry."

"You know," she said her voice turning quiet. "You had me really scared in there. I was screaming for you to stop the whole time, and you didn't hear me until I called you Ghost. I had said Rick like five times…but you never responded."

Rick went silent. The fact he didn't respond to Rick anymore, even from someone he had a loving and trusting relationship with, hit him like a tonne of bricks. It was the realization that he didn't identify himself as Rick anymore – Rick was dead – Ghost was all that was remained. Ghost was who he was now, and when it really mattered, Rick wasn't around anymore.

"I'm sorry Amy. I never want to scare you."

He hadn't just scared Amy; he had scared himself. He'd drifted so far from the reality of who he was, that it was now impossible to bring that person back. Amy tried. God she tried. At every little step, she did what she could to keep Rick alive. The only time she ever called him Ghost was when she knew he was about to do something bad or dangerous. It was always Rick. And in that, it was her unspoken promise that she wasn't giving up on him, even if he'd given up on himself.

"Don't be my Ghost," she'd say when they parted.

"I won't," he'd always answer.

But he could never truly make that promise. It was far too late in the game. So much had already happened, so much that he just couldn't sweep under the rug. There was no water under the bridge for Rick, it was a full scale raging river, out of control and on a path to blow the bridge completely to hell.

By the time January 1994 rolled around Rick was operating at Mach speed. Staying out all night with the team and then popping caffeine pills just to try and make it through the school day. Obsessed with their 'war' he was willing to do anything and everything he could to take it up to the next level, and if that meant staying up all night, then so be it. The night also meant complete freedom and immunity, and for Rick, there was nothing more powerful and exciting than that. Nothing was going to stop him. Not parents, not society's rules, and certainly not the need to sleep. Being the best night predator and operator he could be fueled his desire, pushed him to test the limits of his body and his physical capabilities.

Time at home was just for resting and relaxation. Brenda wasn't pleased. A rift began. Despite being married to Joe, Brenda still saw Rick as the man of the house and the one who should be taking care of the fixing and upkeep of the property, including the newly purchased horses. Rick felt differently. He did do his fair share of work. Wasn't it him and Strom who cleared out and got the cisterns working? Wasn't he the one who fixed up and painted the barn? Wasn't he the one who had to clear the brush and shit so the horses would have somewhere to graze? He did his share, the lion's share actually.

Their arguments increased in frequency and intensity, Brenda trying to regain control, and Rick having none of it. He loved his mother and was fiercely protective of her, and loyal to her, but he had other shit going on in his life, shit that was important to him. She's the one that wanted the damn horses in the first place, so why was it Rick's job to be the one to have to clean the stables all the time? He didn't even ride them. The answer? Because. Well Brenda could take her because and shove it up her ass. No one in heaven or on earth was going to have autonomy over Rick any longer. He was his own man. End of story.

He did his best not to cause his mother grief but sometimes shit just happened. Sometimes he didn't know his limits and he pushed things too far. One night in late January, he and Strom were at a house party in Portland, over on the east-side. As they were just standing there chilling, a cute little punk rocker girl walked in, tears streaming down her face. Always the gallants, the boys went over.

"What's wrong?" said Rick to one of her friends. "Is she okay?"

"Her stupid ass boyfriend punched her in the chest and threatened to rape her."

"Jeff is such a fucking punk. He hits her all the time," added another friend. "He's threatened to kill her a bunch too."

"One day," said the first friend. "I'm afraid he just might do it."

"What an asshole," said Strom.

"Take my piece bro," said Rick.

"What are you going to do?" said Strom.

"Wait for him to show up of course. You in?"

"Of course."

Rick just couldn't stand to see someone in pain and hurting, especially at the hands of an asshole boyfriend. The capes came on, and both he and Strom swept in to save the day. When Jeff showed up at the party looking for Nicole, Rick knew he'd made a serious miscalculation.

"Fuck bro," whispered Strom. "He's fucking huge."

Easily six feet tall with long muscled arms, Jeff looked like a dude who'd done plenty of hard labour and heavy lifting in his life.

"Fuck," said Rick.

"You gonna back down?"

"Hell no." Rick couldn't back down, not now. He'd already shot of his mouth, and vowed to confront the prick. No way he was walking away and looking like a pussy. Sucking in hard, he made his way to the center of the front cement walkway, assuming the position. The audience took up positions a safe distance away.

"Tell Nicole to get her ass out here!" said Jeff throwing open the chain-link gate. "I'm not playing this shit!"

"Why?" said Rick full of calm bravado. "So you can beat on her some more?"

"I'm going to beat on you if you don't get out of my way you little runt!"

Rick should have walked away. He shouldn't even have gotten involved but his stubborn arrogance was too much for any sort of rhyme or reason.

"The difference is I hit back you punk-ass faggot! Come get some!"

And Jeff did. Blow after blow after blow. Rick got in a few good shots, even swept Jeff's legs out from under him but that was it. The dude was just too big and too strong, a bruiser flipping Rick around like he was a rag doll. Blood exploded from Rick's bottom lip, his chest empty of air from being slammed to the ground.

"He's had enough dude," said Strom. "Kick rocks."

Jeff paid Strom zero attention and continued to rain fully extended blows to Rick's head and torso.

"Jeff! Dude, he's got a gun!" someone yelled.

Jeff looked up. Strom held the gun at his side, turning it a little so Jeff could see the full profile.

"I said beat it motherfucker." Strom was cool, so fucking calm and cool.

Jeff slowly got off Rick, his eyes furious with rage. "I see you punk-ass kids around my girl and I'll fucking kill you both!"

Strom didn't blink. "Whatever dumbass. Get the fuck out of here."

No doubt Jeff could have taken both Rick and Strom on in a fight but he wasn't stupid, and he wasn't about to get himself shot, so he backed out of the yard and took off.

"You crazy fuck," said Strom helping Rick up.

"Thanks bro. You saved my ass."

"No problem. You alright? I mean do we need to go to the hospital? You look like shit."

"Nah, I think I'm okay. Don't think anything's broken."

"I'm sorry you had to stand up to that jerk," said Nicole. "Are you okay. Jesus look at you. Anyone have a cloth for the blood. I'm so sorry he did this too you!"

"It's all good," said Rick. "Just don't go back to that prick if all he's going to do is put his hands on you."

Nicole did end up breaking it off with Jeff which gave Rick some consolation for the thrashing he took on her behalf. Not everyone was pleased or sympathetic to his chivalry.

"What if Strom hadn't been there dumbass!" said Amy.

"I know you're angry with me…"

"Angry? No I'm not angry Rick, I'm furious! That guy could have killed you! You're hurt!"

"But I was standing up for Nicole!"

"I don't give a shit. Once again, you put yourself in a dangerous situation when you didn't have to. It has to stop. You can't save everyone Rick."

"No," thought Rick. "But I can sure as hell try."

Amy helped clean up the wounds, then made them all a good dinner but she wouldn't let it go and continued to lecture Rick all night. At the same time, she knew it wasn't going to change, it was just his way. Protect the innocent and prey upon those who prospered or took advantage of their vulnerabilities. No one deserved to be victimized, and at the time, Rick was idealistic enough that it didn't matter how big or how many, he took on whoever was profiting from human misery. It was an outlet for his own pain and suffering.

"What happened to you?" said Brenda as Rick walked through the door the next day.

"Got in a fight at school."

"Oh Rick, not again! What this time?"

"Over a girl."

He wasn't lying. Of course, he wasn't being completely truthful either. Just another thing to add to the list of things she didn't need to know, a list that was a hell of a lot longer than it probably should have been, and a list his father knew absolutely nothing about. Secrets. So many secrets.

CHAPTER THIRTY-THREE

Rick and the boys weren't scared of shit. Whether it was retaliating against a group of skinheads who'd been talking trash to them after a failed recruitment effort, or defending themselves from gangs like the Latin Kings and the Crips, they never backed down. To back down showed weakness, and to show weakness on the streets was like putting a bullet in your own head. It just couldn't happen. They were too determined, too committed to the cause.

"Yo bro," said Havoc tapping Rick on the shoulder. "Some Crip nigger is about to go at it with Creek."

A group of them, including some of the girls had decided to go down to 'The Bowl', an extremely popular club venue in east Portland. On any given night there would be up to one thousand people hanging out in the joint, drinking, chilling, and getting downright rowdy. The Crips felt like they had some sort of territorial claim on the place, and to any of the girls that happened to be there.

"Leave her alone," said Creek. "She's with us."

"Is dat so white boy? I don't think you know who you talkin' to."

As Havoc and Rick fought their way through the crowd, more Crips came over and formed a semi-circle around Creek and Jesse, the girl he was trying to protect.

"You scared white boy?" said the Crip pulling out a shiny knife. On cue, several Crips in the crowd whipped out their guns, and starting waving them around, while jabbing threats at Creek. But Creek wasn't backing down. Without even thinking Rick pulled his weapon and leveled in straight at the back of one of their heads.

"You dumb motherfucker. You even think about hurting my friend and I'll splatter your brains all over this concrete floor."

The Crips went to make a move but were countered by Strom's gun in the back of another head. A Mexican stand off but the boys had the upper hand.

"Oh my God," said Jesse through tears. "Oh my God! Oh my God! Oh my God!"

Seconds seemed like minutes as each waited for the other to back down.

"We gonna cap yo' asses you fucking white pussies. This is our turf and we's gonna do what we want and no little punk ass is gonna stop us."

"Man," said Strom. "We're just here to have a good time and didn't start this bullshit. You assholes were the ones starting the disrespect. Why don't you just leave and everyone can go back to having a good time?"

Knowing they really didn't have a choice, the Crips backed down.

"This ain't over's white boys! We'll be seeing you's again real soon." The first Crip turned to Jesse. "And I fo sure will be seeing you agin."

Rick never did handle threats very well, and the anger boiled. Furious at the situation, he wanted retribution. Jesse hadn't done a single thing wrong. She was innocent, and there was no way in hell Rick was going to let them get away with victimizing her.

"Bro," said Strom. "Let's go. Security is coming."

Rick shoved the gun back in his waist band and like two ghosts, he and Strom evaporated into the crowd. They found the rest of their group, and told them it was time to go.

"We'll meet you out front," said Rick. He and Strom continued out the back of the club, then circled around to meet everyone in the front. "Keep your eyes peeled bro. I'm sure at some point we're going to have some trouble."

Other than the vibration of bass radiating out of the building, the outside was quiet and peaceful.

"Let's go," said Strom to the group. "We'll tell you what happened in the car."

As they piled into their two different cars and drove away, a dark green Escalade pulled out behind them.

"Jesus Christ," said Creek. "We've got company."

Not used to being followed by a bunch of Crips hell bent on revenge, the driver of their car panicked, sped up and veered off on a side road. The cat and mouse game was on. When they turned, the Escalade turned. When they sped up, the Escalade sped up.

"I can't shake them!"

"Let me out as a decoy and then haul ass," said Rick.

"Are you fucking crazy," said the driver.

"Yeah no way Ghost!" echoed through the back seat.

"Do it," said Strom from the front seat. "Slow down when you hit this next corner."

The other vehicle in their group had already peeled off back to the hotel, and Rick knew if he could slow the Escalade down, the vehicle he was in would get away too. He already had the door ajar when the car took the final turn. Pushing the door open, and rolling onto the hard pavement, he had about three seconds to find some cover next to a garbage can. He took out his gun. The Escalade pulled around the corner, speeding up as it went past. Rick let it get about fifteen yards before he opened fire, shattering the back window, and sending everyone inside ducking for cover. The tires screeched to a halt. Rick was over the fence and out of sight before they even opened the door.

"Jesus fucking Christ," said Rick as he walked towards the hotel. "Jesus fucking Christ!" His head was spinning. Out of control. Furious. "Jesus fucking Christ!"

He couldn't take it anymore. All of it. They'd just gone out to have fun tonight. No one was looking for trouble, they weren't looking to break any laws or cause any harm, yet they'd come closer to death than all the missions combined.

"All over some nigger hitting on a girl trying to mind her own business. Jesus fucking Christ!"

Needless. Rick absolutely hated people preying on other people for no reason. It burned his ass. Those who thought they could bully any and everybody. And why? Just because. Preying on the innocent. Adrenaline only fueled his rage. Rage only fueled the madness. His thoughts became disjointed, an ever increasing darkness shrouded any rational thought. The slippery slope became even more precarious.

"Are you okay man?" said Creek.

"Yeah, I'm fine," answered Rick slouching into a chair and slapping his pistol down heavily on the table. "I shot up their ride. No, I didn't hit anyone."

Everyone, including Strom and Creek, could tell Rick wasn't in a chatty mood, and left him alone. He just wanted to be alone. Jesse sat down and stared at him. Rick could tell she wanted to talk but he just didn't have it in him. The rage was too much, the anger and despair too close to boiling out.

"Thank you," she said, her eyes full of tears.

Rick nodded.

"Hey bro," said Strom. "We're just going to get some munchies. Wanna come?"

"No."

Rick walked to the bathroom, took a piss, then washed his face with cold water. The cold water hissed with steam as it splashed against his red-hot skin. His eyes met the mirror. They had no idea who that person in the reflection was. Madness. He waited until they'd all left, then sat back down, seething and spinning so hard he couldn't even think straight. Was he even there? What was the point of anything? All of it bubbled and simmered. All the years, all the heartbreak. God was a lie, love was a lie, life was a lie. He didn't give a fuck and none of it mattered. It needed to end. He needed to end it.

A rabid caged animal, tearing the chains of his own soul, he believed he was a danger to society and to everyone else he loved. It was so easy for him to pull the trigger at the car. So easy and so dangerous. There was no sadness, no despair, only a maddening fury and conviction.

"It's all just so meaningless and senseless. I just need to get put down. I'm a menace, an ice-cold raging demon. I need to die. I need to end it all."

Without hesitation, he scooped up his pistol from the table, put it to his right temple and pulled the trigger. Click. Nothing. He pulled it again. Nothing. He tried again. Nothing. It didn't fire a single fucking round.

"Son of a bitch!"

He couldn't even kill himself properly. With a giant heave, he threw the gun straight through the glass of the closed window and out into the parking lot. Insanity. The crash of the shattering glass brought him back to reality. Cops, hotel staff, onlookers. It was time to go. He snapped back into tactical ghost mode, did a sweep of the room putting all their personal items in a backpack and took off. Grabbing his gun from the parking lot, he briskly walked down to the street corner to head off the car as it came back.

"We can't go back to the hotel," said Rick climbing in.

"Why?"

"Because I broke the window, I'm sorry."

"Fuck Ghost," said one of the girls. "What the fuck is wrong with you?"

He couldn't even begin to answer her question.

"Just drop me at the closest bus station," said Rick.

"You sure?" said Strom.

"Yeah. I'll meet you guys back in town tomorrow. I just need to disappear for a while."

They dropped him off at one of the stations the ran south-west to Beavertown. Rick bought his ticket, then slid into his seat, shaking.

"What the fuck just happened?" he thought. "What even happened this entire night? I can't even kill myself! Why am I still alive? How am I still alive? No way that gun should have been empty. I know I refilled the clip when I was walking back to the hotel. Is this part of my punishment too God? You won't even let me die? Have I no control over anything in my life?"

He couldn't calm himself down. He couldn't shake the experience of the night and a failed suicide attempt.

"I am a complete and utter fuck up."

Rick got off the bus and walked the rest of the way to Amy's. He was sitting on the couch when she came home. So cold and quiet.

"Rick? Jesus are you okay?"

Amy sat down beside him, putting her arm around his shoulder. He felt her reach down his back and pull the gun from his waist band. She set the gun on the table.

"It's going to be okay Rick."

He just stared at the gun. Mesmerized and bewildered that Amy even knew he had it, and numb because not a few hours before, he'd had the barrel against his head and pulled the trigger. Three times. He should have died. There was no logical reason he was still alive. None. In his mind, when he pulled the trigger, he had every confidence and no doubt that he was going to die. And in that moment, something happened to him, the moment he pulled the trigger and heard the click. He realized that his life had no value, no meaning. He had deliberately tried to kill himself. He had pulled the trigger, not once, but three times. He didn't back down, he didn't panic and chicken out. He pulled the trigger, and it failed. He failed.

He had gone through with it, and in his mind, that meant that his life meant nothing. And believing that your life means nothing is both a frightening and liberating thing. Who cares what you do? You've shown the ability to throw your life away on a whim, to face the fear of death and not blink. Everything after that point is meaningless. He'd pulled the trigger. He should be dead, except he wasn't. He took no pleasure in cheating death and certainly didn't see it as an opportunity for renewal or a changing of his ways.

"What happened Rick?" said Amy. "Please tell me. Please open up to me."

So he did. Rick sat on the couch with Amy beside him, and told her everything. The betrayal, Jackie, his hatred of his father, the War. He told her everything he could in the span of eight hours. There were no tears, he was flat, just matter of fact, straight up, this is my life. Amy spent much of the time crying, sensing his despair, her heart aching for his sorrow.

"Promise me Rick. Promise me you will never ever take your own life! Promise me."

"I promise," said Rick.

"No matter how bad things get! You can never turn the gun on yourself again and commit suicide! I don't care how bad things are. We'll find another way to get through it. Promise me again."

"I promise Amy," he said looking through her tears. "I promise. I swear to you."

"You have no control over it Rick. I mean death. It's its own thing and it will come when it's your time. Our lives aren't ours to take, we're just here on earth…like living on borrowed time, and the best we can do is make the most of it while we're here. And think about it Rick. Karma. Think about karma. If you'd really done all that bad, and you were meant to die tonight, then you would have. But you didn't die. Why? Because it's not your time Rick. You have so much to give, and you have such a big heart, and you do so much to help and care for others…but you need to take care of yourself too. You have to let go of some of this anger and rage. Can you do that? For me?"

"I'll try," he answered.

Amy tried to help. She tried to get through to him but the walls were so dark and deep that it proved near impossible. He heard her words, and he meant to keep the promise, but not because he didn't want to die, that would never change, but because he believed that his fate and his karma were to suffer. Killing himself would make him a coward, and he wasn't a coward. He was strong, he was brave, and he'd handle all the cold, searing pain because that's what he was meant to do. Even though he'd left God far behind, he couldn't leave the idea or the doctrine of God's Will and God's Way, the dogma ingrained too deep. He may not have made the connection at the time but it was there; the idea that he had absolutely no control over his life or the path it took. Was it God? Was it the Devil? Karma? Fate? The who's, what's and where's didn't matter, it was the how's and the why's. How was the rest of his life going to unfold, and why did it all have to hurt so much?

"Hey bro," said Strom a few weeks after. "I forgot to tell you that while you were in the bathroom at the hotel, I took the full clip from your gun and replaced it with my empty one. I'd forgotten to bring my other full clip from McMinnville, and I figured since you were staying back, you wouldn't need yours. I didn't want to be out in the open without enough ammo you know?"

"You changed my clip? Are you serious?"

"Yeah, sorry bro. Why what's wrong? You look kind of sick." Rick told him about that night and attempting to take his own life. "Well I guess that I'm glad that I forgot my extra clip back home. Seriously bro. I'm glad I did what I did. Don't do that shit again okay?"

Rick smiled. "No worries bro. I guess it just wasn't my time."

After the incident at the Bowl, the Team laid low for a while and steered clear of Portland. It was almost spring break anyways, and spring break meant a trip up to Alaska whether he wanted to go or not. Tickets had already been purchased and if Jimmy and Rick refused to go, they'd feel the wrath of their father, so the second week of March, they packed up their gear and headed to the airport. Rick felt like an actor in a play, just going through the motions, hoping to hell he could get to the last act without a major blunder. He didn't want to go, the movie in his head still stuck on his suicide attempt and the fact he was still alive. Seeing his father only angered him and increased his pain. Never the entire cause of his despair, his father was certainly one of the roots, and with every visit and every encounter or blow out, the roots squeezed tighter and tighter around Rick's chest.

The break away from Portland was what Rick needed, even if it meant having to spend time with his father. Rosemary and Bob did their best to welcome the boys and make it a fun and positive time, but to Rick's hateful fourteen-year-old mind, it was all for show. He could never see past the past, or even try to acknowledge that Bob and Rosemary were trying to make the best of a bad situation. To Rick it all just seemed so fake and it made him hate them all the more. They all 'acted' like they were happy to see each other, when in reality, the only person who really wanted the visits to happen was Bob. He wasn't giving up on his boys. He just couldn't let them go and allow them to fade out of his life. Of course, this wasn't how Rick saw it. All his hurt and jaded soul saw was someone who was refusing to give up power and control over his sons' lives. Rick never had the emotional maturity to see any of that. Justified or not, all he saw was hate.

Bob and Rosemary took the boys to see the sights, visit some landmarks and museums, and catch a few movies, the usual stuff a parent does who's trying to grow and culture their child. The best part of the trip was a two-day excursion to Alyeska, the largest ski resort in Alaska. They were joined by the Roth family, who had a son a year younger than Rick. The two boys had a ball exploring all the runs and got into their fair share of fun, wintertime mischief. For the first time in a very long time, Rick allowed himself to be a kid. There were no guns, or Crips, just fights with snowballs, tumbles down the awesome mountainside, and warm cocoa by the fireplace in the lodge; the kind of experiences that childhood should be full of. It's too bad that Rick was such a hateful little shit and couldn't appreciate the moment for the pure pleasure that it was. But he couldn't see. He was too blinded by the past, his heart hardened against any sort of outreach by his father to create lasting memories.

Upon his return to Portland, Rick and the Team jumped right back into their War. It wasn't enough to just go after the small dealers anymore, they wanted to push the limits and take down some of the big players. They took risks; sometimes the risks paid off, and sometimes they had to abandon the job because the risks were just too great. It was never about the amount of money they collected, or the drugs they confiscated, or about the cool weapons they added to their stash. It was about being the best, being elite, being the force that gets in and gets out without leaving a trace. Feeling invincible, on an incredible high, and full of power. Nothing could stop them, nothing could take them down, they were just too good, just too smart, just too invisible.

Around early May, Jana ended up in the hospital. Her and Rick had dated for a while but she'd always wanted more from Rick than he could give. She wanted to know what was going on behind his shielded soul, and Rick just wasn't ready or willing to let her in. Jana was a party girl, a full-fledged 'try anything' sort of girl, someone for Rick to don his Superman cape and try and save. Except, Jana didn't want to be saved. In the end, it just didn't work, and Rick walked away, leaving Jana mad as hell and hating his guts. But now she was in the hospital, six months pregnant with some other guy's baby, and the doctors weren't sure they could keep either her or the baby alive. The toll of drinking, smoking, and partying both before and during her pregnancy was too much for her fifteen-year-old body, let alone a developing fetus. She was in rough shape. She didn't care if she or the baby lived. She wanted to die. Rick couldn't walk away this time. He had to care for her.

He'd visit her several times a week, often every day, and at first it was awkward. There was so much guilt. Rick had tried to get her to slow down. She just wouldn't listen, and now she had to face Rick sitting at her bedside, knowing he was right. But at least he came. Her friends? Her classmates? Charlie, the father of the baby? All nowhere to be found. It was Rick who sat by her bedside, even if it was just in silence. He was the one that was there for her, cheering her on, and hoping the little being inside of her would pull through. He brought her chocolates and candy and always made sure she had fresh flowers. He'd tell her stories, and sometimes even sing, anything he could to calm her down and get her to relax. None of the nurses believed that the baby wasn't his. No kid cares that much if he didn't have a stake in what happened. Rick let them believe what they wanted, and it became his sacred and sworn duty to be her guardian and protector. Regardless of whether she was his girlfriend or not, he had already lost Jackie, and he wasn't about to let Jana or her unborn child slip through the cracks.

CHAPTER THIRTY-FOUR

"We've got a bit of a trip planned," said Bob with a smile. "I think you boys are going to love it."

Rick wasn't so sure. He loathed having to spend any of his summer holidays with his father and Rosemary, especially now with all the shit going down with Jana.

"Where we going?" said Jimmy.

"Well," said Bob, "we're going to tow the Nomad trailer up the Alcan Highway all the way to Alaska so we can park it beside the house in Anchorage. But before we do that, we thought we'd take you boys down to Lake Powell, right on the border of Nevada and Utah. Rose's friends', Tom and Sheri have a lease on a house boat, so we're going to stay on that, do some sight-seeing and touring around.

Rick had to admit, the trip sounded pretty cool. He loved the water, and Tom and Sheri had a motorboat moored to the houseboat, so they could use that for excursions out onto the lake and to explore the expansive Lake Powell network of waterways, canyons, and smaller dead-end desert fjords. The boys had fun waterskiing, booting around on some rented Ski-Doos and for Rick, climbing Gunsight Butte. The area ended up being their 'parking space' for three days, and Rick wasn't leaving until he'd climbed it. He told everyone he was leaving in the morning at daybreak, packing a small Thermos of ice-cold water, some basic medical supplies, and the camcorder into his backpack.

"This is amazing!" he said fitting his hands and feet into the centuries old nooks and crannies lining the clay hills beneath the Butte.

With the red clay and sandstone blistering in the summer heat, Rick was able to get almost a third of the way up without much effort. The rest after that was pure freestyle without the benefit or safety net of climbing gear. Even leaving around six A.M. it still took about five hours to get as high as he could go, stopping on a fairly precarious rock shelf only about forty feet from the top and about two hundred feet above the water. Crawling slowly on his belly, he got a camcorder shot straight down at the boats moving through the water below.

"Jesus! What a view! The houseboat looks like it's about an inch big! Wow, wouldn't the boys like to see this."

With the rock scorched from the midday sun, the road down was far lengthier and far more treacherous than the trip up. With his water supply dangerously low, heat exhaustion became a real possibility. But he made it, just the sort of extreme shit he lived for, just one of those things he had to do for himself.

After their fun on the houseboat, the group docked, unloaded, and each of the respective families went their separate ways. The Watkinson's had a four-thousand-mile drive awaiting them through half the United States, up through Canada, and then along the Alcan Highway. Four thousand miles was a long time to be trapped in a car, and without any 'outsiders' along, the walls came down, and the façade of a happy family faded. It was never that they didn't or couldn't have fun as a 'family', it was just that it was always so fleeting and overshadowed by the fact the boys didn't want to be there, and if it were up to them, wouldn't even have gone in the first place.

So when Bob and Rosemary took the boys to the Science Center in Edmonton, Alberta, or let them spend the day in the giant indoor water park at the Edmonton Mall, they did have fun, they had a good time, and they smiled and laughed like kids do. But there was always that underlying tension, that one wrong word, one wrong gesture, that could set the fuse. Rick couldn't just turn off the hate and rebellion towards his father and Rosemary because he'd gone tubing down a water slide. It was all too deep, all too intense, and sooner or later, someone would snap.

"Bob, look at them," said Rosemary. "They look like homeless little waifs. I'm not going into the restaurant with them looking like that. Can they not be decent and put on a pair of pants instead of those shorts?"

As usual, the boys ignored her. Even Bob shrugged off the comments saying it didn't matter. It wasn't like they were going to eat in a five-star restaurant, they were out in the middle of nowhere at some jack-hick spot.

"Fine, then I'm not going to eat with you guys!" she said slamming the trailer door shut as she took off outside. Bob sprung to attention.

"Go put some pants on boys."

"Why?" said Rick.

"Because we should look nice for people wherever we go."

Rick scoffed. "Why? These people will never see us again, so who cares?"

Bob knew Rick was right. "Just put your God-damned pants on."

"I'm not dressing up like a stupid rich boy just because Rosemary can't stand second-best!"

Rick opened the trailer door and walked off to the nearby river, passing an arms-crossed and glaring Rosemary sitting in the car on the way by. Then as if her disgust wouldn't let her look at Rick any longer, she charged out of the car and back to the trailer.

"Glad to see your getting somewhere with him Bob."

Egged on by her rudeness, Bob walked over to his son, rekindling the conversation by the edge of the shallow but wide and very cold river.

"She always looks down on Jimmy and I," said Rick. "And you always take her side! You never stand up for us, it's always what she wants. Bottom line, I'm not dressing up just to go to some stupid restaurant and she can bitch all she wants!"

"You don't disrespect her like that! Do you hear me? And if I tell you to do something, you do it!"

"Fuck you and your stupid fucking wife! I'm not doing shit for you!"

"You stupid fucking punk kid!" Bob lunged at Rick, shoving him into the river. Before Rick even had a chance to react, Bob grabbed hold of his arm and was flinging him around, dragging his bare legs across the rocks. "You stupid dumb fuck kid!"

In the manifestation of his anger, Rick pictured himself reaching up and breaking his father's arm. Horrified at where his mind had gone, Rick immediately let his body go limp and his mind blank, so he didn't retaliate.

"Son of a bitch fucker! You listen to me do you hear! Stupid dumb fuck! Fuck! Fuck! Fuck!"

"Daddy stop!" yelled Jimmy running out of the trailer. "Let him go! Stop hurting him! Don't hurt my brother!"

Rather amused, Rosemary watched from the doorway of the trailer. "Bob, let him go."

Bob looked up at Rosemary, then threw Rick's arm down, leaving the boy sitting in the frigid water.

"Jimmy go to the trailer now!"

"But.."

"Jimmy now!"

Jimmy looked helplessly towards Rick. Rick nodded for his little brother to do as he was told. Bob followed Jimmy inside and slammed the door. Soaking wet, Rick got up from the river bed and walked to dry ground, fighting back the tears. That was the first time he'd ever thought of really hurting his father and it scared the shit out of him. The trailer door opened, Rosemary threw out a towel, then slammed the door shut. Rick dried himself off and wiped the blood off his scratched up legs, half-laughing at himself for crying, and half crying even more.

"Fuckers."

Making his way over to the bank of the river, he walked about twenty feet down stream, found a secluded spot, and sat down with the wet towel over his freezing legs. Shocked by the cold, they'd stopped bleeding almost instantly, leaving a network of scratches down his legs. Cold and shaking, Rick sat there for almost an hour before his father walked over with a ceramic plate of food.

"Let's try and have fun the rest of the trip."

Rick didn't say a word. Bob stood for a moment, then turned and walked back to the trailer. No 'I'm sorry', no 'are you okay?', no nothing. That night, when Rick finally came back into the trailer, Bob and Rosemary acted as if nothing had ever happened and everything was just Brady Bunch perfect. Jimmy knew different, and Rick would never forget the terrified look in his little brother's eyes. The can of worms had been opened, with neither side realizing the coiled cobra lurking on the bottom. The river incident was the first time Bob had ever actually struck Rick, and put his hands on him in anger. Yes, he had spanked him with belts before and 'disciplined' him physically, but it had never been the result of him losing his temper and attacking. This was new, and it opened a door and made violence a viable option between them.

When Bob held Rick by the arm in the water, Rick wanted to hurt him. He wanted to break his arm, but regardless of how deeply he hated him, he was still his father, and in his mind there was a definite psychological line that forbids a child from striking a parent. Sitting alone on the riverbank, shivering, Rick realized that for Bob, violence was an option. He didn't hesitate throwing his kid into the water and tossing him around like a doll. If Rick pushed, his father was fully willing to put his hands on his son, and that made the boy boil.

"After everything he's done to hurt us. To both Jimmy and I, he thinks he can do that too? Like it's his right? When he broke his oath, and he left and abandoned our family, he forfeited the right to be my father. He's just another regular fucker as far as I'm concerned. I will never let him touch me again."

But what sickened Rick the most about the whole incident was that Bob and Rosemary just acted like nothing had ever happened. That night, the next day, the rest of trip, not a mention, not a breath, not an admission of guilt or remorse, no acknowledgement at all, it was back to the Academy Award performance of "The Happy Family". Act like you care, act like you want to be here, act like you love each other. The only one who wanted the act not to be fake was Bob. He desperately wanted his children in his life, and for them to be able to get along with the woman he loved, except he was the only one fighting the battle. None of them, including Rosemary, wanted the same.

"I want him all to myself," said Rosemary. "You boys interfere with that, and that was never part of the plan."

She only tolerated their presence because she loved Bob and wanted him to be happy, but the boys weren't naïve, they could feel the icy vibe she so expertly threw. How were they supposed to feel? In their eyes, this was the woman who showed up in the passenger seat of their father's car a week after he left? She was the reason that he left. Anything she said or did, whether genuine or not, was going to be perceived in a negative manner.

Regardless of how they all really felt, the act continued the rest of the way up the Alcan Highway. It wasn't that Bob didn't love his boys, that was never in question, but he was trying too hard to fit a square peg in a round hole, especially when it came to Rick.

"Thank God," said Jimmy as the plane took off from the Anchorage airport. "That was some trip."

"Yeah little bro. I'll be glad to get back home to my life. Three weeks is way too long to keep this shit up. I'm exhausted."

"Are you okay Rick? I mean…"

"Yeah Jimmy, I'm fine. Don't you worry about me okay?"

"But you don't understand Rick, I do worry about you. And about you and Dad. I worry about what might happen."

Rick had no response. Truth was, he had no idea how things were going to play out. So much was wrong, and no one knew how it make it right. Rick couldn't fathom forgiving his father. Rosemary had no clue how to get the boys to accept her. Jimmy was caught in between everyone, a victim of his own emotions and loyalties. And Bob couldn't figure out how to get his boys to forgive him, and really feel like a family instead of just playing make-believe. Broken and dysfunctional. No one knew how to heal, no one even knew where to begin. The only answer, the only alternative on the table was to live in a fantasy family, where, when they were forced to co-exist, they at least gave the appearance that they could stand each other. The truth? No one gave a shit about that. It was all about appearances. It was all about wearing pants to the restaurant because you should care what other people think – because that's the shit that's important.

For all the stress and anxiety Rick faced on his three-week vacation, it was nothing compared to the mess he arrived home to on June 24. Jana had been taken for an emergency C-section the day before. Extremely premature and underdeveloped, baby Andrew was immediately put on life support and placed in the neo-natal unit. Things did not look good for the little tyke. It killed Rick to see Andrew's tiny body full of tubes and wires.

"What has this poor kid done to deserve any of this?" he thought. "Jesus Christ. Look at the little guy. Even if he manages to pull through, he's going to have a tough go. He's just so sick."

Jana wasn't much better.

"How are you feeling?" said Rick.

"Like shit. They keep pumping me full of these antibiotics and won't let me go home. Did you see Andrew?"

"Yeah, I did. Cute little guy. Looks like you I think Jana."

"I haven't even seen him yet. Didn't even get to hear his first cry. They told me…the doctors…that he's probably not going to live you know…Andrew. I feel like such a fucking failure. I did this to him."

"C'mon Jana, you can't think that way."

"I'm such a fucked up person. I've fucked up so bad. Nothing even matters anymore."

Rick tried to console her but her depression and feelings of guilt were too deep to let him in. He felt horrible.

"Has Charlie been up to see the baby?" said Rick.

"Yeah, who the fuck are you kidding? I only had three people come up the entire time you were gone, and one of them was some wacko who left me that book on the table there."

Rick glanced at the title. The Book of Mormon. Jesus, that's all she needed to hear, about how God would make everything okay, and if it wasn't okay, then it was still okay because it was all a part of God's plan.

"I'm sorry Jana. I'm sorry I had to go away. I didn't want to, trust me, but it's my Dad. He would have had a fit if I didn't show up, and would have probably caused a bunch of shit for my Mom."

"It's okay Ghost, honest. It doesn't matter. You're here now. All the rest of them can go fuck themselves."

Bitterness and sorrow oozed from every one of her pores. Rick could see it. He knew how that felt. Just like him, Jana didn't care whether she lived or died, but unlike him, she had another life to think about. Rick worried about little Andrew. With Jana too far gone and lost in her own head, who would care for the boy? Rick went down to see the baby.

"Excuse me," said the nurse. "Can I talk to you for a second?"

"Sure," said Rick.

The nurse held out a piece of paper, Andrew's birth certificate. "The boy needs a father, and whether you're the one who got her pregnant or not, you've shown more concern to Jana and that baby than anyone else."

Rick looked at the blank space where the name of the baby's father went. "You're serious? You want me to sign my name as the baby's father?"

"Yes, I do. You're the best option they have."

Rick took a deep breath. She was asking him to legally register as Andrew's father and accept a huge title and burden of responsibility. He didn't know if he was up for that, and he certainly didn't want to lie on something so sacred. But he couldn't leave Andrew out in the cold either. The kid didn't do anything wrong, the exact definition of innocent. He took another deep breath.

"I wouldn't want you to put me on there without Jana's permission," said Rick. "But I give you my word that I'll raise that baby as my own. I won't let him down. Ever."

With tears in her eyes, the nurse smiled and nodded, then walked away with the paper in her hand. What could he do? Walk away? That was never going to be in the cards. He'd been too close to the situation from the beginning to back out now. More than that, he knew in his heart that Andrew was his responsibility, regardless of what was ever on any piece of paper. At fifteen, he was fully prepared to take care of him as if he was his own. Maybe this was part of the grand plan. Sort of a do over. Maybe it was a good thing that the chamber in his pistol had been empty. If he'd had killed himself, then what would have happened to Andrew?

"I can do this. I can be his Dad. I can take care of them. Maybe I'll even marry Jana and formally adopt Andrew in the future…I mean not today…but someday, when the time is right."

Rick continued to visit them at the hospital and was the one Jana leaned on when she was finally well enough to get out of bed and go see her son for the first time.

"He's so tiny," she cried. "Oh my God. What have I done to him?"

"He'll pull through Jana. I know all the tubes are scary, and I thought the same thing when I first saw him but you get used to them…you just have to look past them you know…and see him…see Andrew."

After Jana was released from the hospital, Rick would walk with her to see Andrew, and there were many times he just went to visit the boy on his own, just to spend time with him, and let him know that he wasn't alone. That someone in the world gave a shit about him. He didn't ever want him to feel lonely. The call from Jana's mom came the morning of July 7.

"We took Jana to the emergency room last night."

"Why?" said Rick. "What happened?"

"She overloaded on pills, and was trying to drink herself to death."

"What? How could she? With little Andrew…"

"Andrew's dead Rick. He died yesterday afternoon…about twenty minutes before Jana arrived to visit him."

"Jesus Christ no."

"Jana came right home and started drinking and popping pills. She couldn't handle it. We called the police because…well…I just didn't know what to do. She wouldn't go on her own. Took three people to get her into the hospital. That was at around ten last night. I don't know what to do. She's a mess Rick."

Numbness spread throughout Rick's body. He couldn't think, he couldn't move, he couldn't talk. He was prepared to be that little boy's father, and now he was gone. Not even two weeks old, and gone. What had Andrew done to deserve the life he'd been given? And what had he done to deserve it being taken away so soon. He'd done nothing. He was innocent. There was no sin in that little soul, no hate, no vengeance. But there was sin, hate, and vengeance in Rick's soul. He wanted payback. Andrew didn't cause his own death; therefore, someone was responsible. He could think of two. Jana and Charlie.

Charlie, he wanted to find that prick as quickly as possible and beat the living fuck out of him. How could he get Jana pregnant and then just leave her alone? Not even give a shit about what she was doing to her body and the little person growing inside. Not even try to stop her or get help? Rick did the best he could to fight the feelings of hatred towards Jana. He understood her depression, he understood the pain she was in. He'd put a .38 to his own head four months prior, so he got it, he got the desperation in her heart. But his actions hadn't fucked up someone else's little life. It was one thing to forsake his own life, or someone else who deserved it, but not an innocent. He couldn't get past that. But that didn't mean his own heart didn't ache for Jana's pain. He could only imagine the guilt and responsibility she was feeling for losing Andrew, for costing him his life and his future. Rick fought between wanting to reach out to her and never wanting to see her again.

"Mom, can you drive me into town? I've got to go see Jana. Andrew died."

Brenda dropped Rick off near the hospital, and the first thing he did was swipe a pack of Marlboro 100's from the corner store.

"I guess my clean streak is over," he said stabbing one in his mouth and lighting up. He didn't care anymore, didn't care about what they might do to him, didn't care about a God damn fucking thing. He choked back a second one before going into the hospital.

"Please be careful with her Rick," said the same nurse who'd asked him to register as Andrew's father. "She's fragile."

Jana was awake when Rick walked in. She immediately turned her head away. "Why are you here?"

Rick pulled up the stool, not saying a word.

"What…are you just here to tell me told you so? Fucking go away." Her voice ached with tears.

"I'm not going anywhere," he answered quietly. "And neither are you."

Jana whipped her head around to face him, furious.

"What's the fucking difference between you getting yourself killed and me killing myself Ghost? What the fuck does it even matter?" As her eyelids closed, they pushed a stream of tears down her cheeks. "I killed my own baby. I'm such a fucking horrible person."

Rick moved to her bedside, letting her cry in his trench coat as he held her. All the anger in the world couldn't stop him from aching right along with her. He hated seeing her like that. It was killing him. After a solid five minutes of weeping, Jana pushed Rick back.

"I'm such a horrible person, I deserve to die." She looked away, not able to face him.

Rick returned to the stool, silent. There was nothing he could say, nothing could make any if it better. He didn't even know the words. Slowly, as if expecting something, Jana turned back towards him, her eyes pleading.

"You're right Jana. What happened was horrible. But dying doesn't do anything to make up for this."

Without another word, Rick turned and walked out. He didn't have anything more to say. He didn't say it as an admonishment or with spite, it was a simple fact and a challenge. She could end her life now, and it would accomplish nothing, except two beings would have died instead of one. Or, she could live and try and make Andrew's death mean something. Rick left knowing that he would never be back, he wouldn't seek her out or try and shadow her life to make sure she was okay. The pain was just too much. He was done.

Staying Ghost was the only way he could cope. He had to block out the emotions screaming within, he had no other choice. He'd go mad if he didn't. And the easiest way to do that was to hold onto his hate. Hate everything. Drugs and alcohol, the people that pushed them, and the society that pushed people to use them in the first place. They all had to pay – taught a lesson. Andrew's death only reinforced Rick's War and the vengeance with which he fought. There was no way he could make any of it okay. So much had happened, so much shit had sailed down the river that it was too late to turn back. The betrayal, the demons, the loss, Jackie, Andrew, his own transgressions – the real sins that no one knew. All he could do was continue to hate, continue to fight, and continue to deny that his emotions even existed.

CHAPTER THIRTY-FIVE

With Andrew's death, Rick spiralled further into hell. He threw himself, and his ravaging hatred into the War. The boys knew what had happened with Andrew, but had no real idea how to help their friend or get through to him. Who does at fifteen? So they told him they were sorry and that everything was going to be okay, except it wasn't. They did what they could, what they had the intellectual and emotional capacity to do. It wasn't enough. Nothing they did could have ever been enough to break through the icy shield Rick created. With every passing day, he became angrier, more violent, bitter, and distant. The death of Jackie and Andrew were already too much for his young troubled heart to take. Hadn't God punished him enough? Apparently not.

The boys were up in Portland, just hanging out and chilling. They weren't there for a mission; they weren't there to cause any trouble. They took a wrong turn, and walked down the wrong street, at the wrong time.

"Yo motherfuckers! Wat you think you doin' walking in our hood?" The Mexican ran his hand over the bill of his sideways baseball hat and laughed. "Boys…you see these punks walking like nothing? Wat da fuck is that all about?"

"Ah fuck," thought Rick. "Not another bunch of pussy-ass Mexican thugs trying to be tough." He just wanted to tell them to shut the fuck up with their 'gang-talk' and incoherent 'nigger-jive' made all the more laughable because they weren't even black and probably had never even stepped inside a real ghetto.

"Are you listening to me? You punk-ass motherfuckers?" The Mexican drew his gun.

"Chill out man," said Strom. "We're just passing through."

"We're not trying to start shit man," said Havoc. "Back off."

The boys were just being relaxed and nonchalant, just trying to get them to leave them alone. None of them had drawn their weapons. All the Mexicans had theirs cocked and ready. Out of the corner of his eye, Rick scoped the dude with the 12-gauge shotgun. The back-up, behind cover, in their blind spot. The same tactic the boys had used a hundred times. Then the truck moved. Not in the plan. The guy panicked and fired his shotgun. Point blank. Time stopped. The slug cut through the air, piercing all boundaries of reality and sensibility.

"CREEK!" yelled Strom.

Creek dropped to the cold hard ground, half his head blown to oblivion, splattered against the side of the truck. Strom screaming. The blood pooling.

Creek dead on the pavement. Strom screaming for their brother. The blood pooling. Voices. Yelling. Screaming. Jesus Christ. Jesus Christ. Jesus Christ.

"JESUS FUCKING CHRIST!" Rick whipped out his pistol and starting firing. His mind a blur. Disbelief. More yelling. More shots. Falling back. Getting the hell out of there. Creek laying dead in No Man's Land. No one could help him now.

"Strom! Get the fuck out of there! Havoc! Jesus Christ move!"

Rick would have stayed and killed every last motherfucking one of those Mexicans had he not been so concerned about the rest of his brothers. So many shots. So much screaming. Complete chaos. So unexpected. So unprovoked. So needless. Creek, their brother, 'The Punisher' dead on the ground, the bullet ripping through his head like it was nothing, like it didn't care about the consequences of its actions, like Creek's life hadn't even mattered. They couldn't do anything to save him. No ambulance, no medical unit, no amount of prayers to God could bring him back. His young life snuffed out in a brutal attack, for no fucking reason other than 'turf', territory and image.

Helplessness set in for all the boys, especially Rick. He had no opportunity to stop what happened. He didn't even see it coming, there were no signs, nothing. The guy got spooked and fired. None of them really believed that the Mexicans had planned for it to go down that way, they seemed just as shocked as the boys. None of that mattered. Creek's death destroyed them, and destroyed an already destroyed Rick. Losing a friend so suddenly, so violently, and so senselessly killed him inside more than anything else. It didn't have to happen. Just like Jackie didn't have to happen, like Andrew didn't have to happen. Creek didn't have to die. Ghost no longer became a defense mechanism, it was a survival mechanism, something Rick had to keep in place just to keep going, just to continue, to keep himself from falling to pieces.

Nobody said a word as they piled in the car and headed back to McMinnville. They had to just leave Creek's body, alone and cold on the pavement. Too many police, too many questions. They hated to do it.

"He'd understand," said Havoc. It didn't make it any better. He turned on the radio but the song only reinforced the silence in the car and in their hearts.

Bury me softly in this womb
I give this part of me for you
Sand rains down and here I sit
Holding rare flowers
In a tomb... in bloom
Down in a hole and I don't know if I can be saved
See my heart I decorate it like a grave
Oh, you don't understand who they thought I was supposed to be

Look at me now I'm a man who won't let himself be
Down in a hole, feeling so small
Down in a hole, losing my soul
I'd like to fly,
But my wings have been so denied
Down in a hole and they've put all the stones in their place
I've eaten the sun so my tongue has been burned of the taste
I have been guilty of kicking myself in the teeth
I will speak no more of my feelings beneath
Down in a hole, feeling so small
Down in a hole, losing my soul
I'd like to fly but my
Wings have been so denied
Bury me softly in this womb
Oh I want to be inside of you
I give this part of me for you
Oh I want to be inside of you
Sand rains down and here I sit
Holding rare flowers (Oh I want to be inside of you)
In a tomb... in bloom
Oh I want to be inside...
Down in a hole, feeling so small
Down in a hole, losing my soul
Down in a hole, feeling so small
Down in a hole, out of control
I'd like to fly but my
Wings have been so denied[35]

It was only natural to want to hit the rewind button and go back and change what happened. But how far do you rewind? Back to that morning and then take a different street? It is an accumulation of life choices? What if they never got into the violence? Would it have stopped Creek's death then? What if the Team never formed? What if Creek had never started hanging out with them? What if his own life choices had been different? What if they had decided to collect Legos instead of guns? What if? What if? What if? So many what if's and no real answers, just an intense and incredulous feeling of utter helplessness. There is no rewind button. If there was, Rick would have already rewound the last five years of his life, maybe more. But he couldn't. There was nothing he could ever do to change any of it, and that sent him spiraling even deeper.

[35] 'Down In A Hole' by Alice in Chains

They talked about taking revenge, adding gangs to their list of take-downs, fire-bombing the apartments where they lived, but that was just as senseless as Creek's death. People would get hurt. Innocent people. People that were just in the wrong place at the wrong time, just like Creek. And as angry and as broken as they were, the boys weren't really killers. Their targets had always been things – money, drugs, guns. They never directly targeted people, and taking out people just because, would put them in a whole other stratosphere that none of them had the stomach for, even now.

"Fuck it hurts," said Strom. "I miss him bro."

"I know man. There's just no words," said Rick.

They'd all met up to go visit Creek's headstone, walking three miles in the rain, silent, somber, and smoking. Havoc brought one of the original collector's editions of "The Punisher" comics, and with a little lighter-fluid, they burnt it as an offering.

"Just something for you to read on the other side bro."

They all spoke their peace to Creek in their own way, with Strom hanging back the longest, just staring at the tombstone, always so philosophical about death. In their hearts and minds, they all knew that nothing would ever be the same again. The effect on their lives and mentality was one of finality.

"I guess there really is a point in time when there's no longer any takebacks," said Strom on the walk back. "Like we've gotten away with doing so much…avoided the shit that could have happened."

"Always came out on top," said Havoc. "I didn't think anything could touch us."

"Except this time," said Rick. "Not this time."

Karma really was a bitch. Their air of invincibility was gone, demolished. Testing the odds wasn't fun anymore, it was now just a matter of time before they all got popped or some more bad shit happened. All just a big long waiting game. None of them were cowards, none of them would back down in the face of death, but the thrill was gone. Now it was just work.

Creek's death wrecked Rick. If he was indifferent and apathetic before, now he'd reached crisis proportions. Nothing mattered. Absolutely nothing. Jackie's life hadn't mattered. Andrew's life hadn't mattered, and now Creek's. None of it had fucking mattered. God hadn't cared about any of them, and sure Jackie and Creek were no angels, but Andrew? What the fuck did he do wrong?

What then shall we say? Is God unjust? Not at all! For he says to Moses, "I will have mercy on whom I have mercy, and I will have compassion on whom I have compassion." It does not, therefore, depend on human desire or effort, but on God's mercy. For Scripture says to Pharaoh: "I raised you up for this very purpose, that I might display my power in you and that my name might be proclaimed in all the earth." Therefore, God has mercy on whom he wants to have mercy, and he hardens whom he wants to harden[36].

How was Rick supposed to have compassion, when the Lord didn't even show compassion? Was Rick supposed to elevate himself above even God and not develop a hardened heart? Too many years of indoctrination kept these thoughts close to his mind. Nothing he could do, 'no human desire or effort' could change the course of anything, only God's mercy. But letting a two-week old baby die is merciful? Being merciful would have been not letting Jana get pregnant in the first place, as messed up as she was. Merciful would have been letting Rick be the one to take the bullet, not Creek. There was no mercy, there was no fucking mercy or compassion at all. Not with God, not with life. None of it mattered. Despondency trumped any sort of rational thought.

Go to school? What the fuck for? Clean your room? What the fuck for? Do your homework? What the fuck for? Why? Why bother? Nothing society or his parents deemed important meant anything to him. How could it? The shit he'd been through was too heavy, too real, and the pettiness of the world just made him want to puke. Nobody understood where he was at. A black hole, sucking the life out of itself, drifting into oblivion. He wanted to die. He didn't even care about existing anymore.

By the end of July, he was back to smoking two packs a day. He'd sit on the back deck puffing away, his mother just shaking her head, then walking away. What did he care what she thought? She'd never stood up to him before, so why start now? Truth was, he was way beyond talking to – there wasn't shit anyone could say to him. Not his mother and definitely not his father. They were all too late, way too late. He started drinking again, carrying a flask full of Smirnoff or Jameson wherever he went. He never drank to get drunk, and he didn't need it to get numb, he was already numb enough on his own. He drank because he was so cold and empty inside, and the alcohol warmed and filled him up. What else was left? There was no love, no God, no hope, no faith in anything. Not even in himself. He no longer lived, he merely existed. Spirits and fumes, like a ghost, haunting and hating, his heart a black abyss.

"What do we do now bro?" said Havoc. "I mean…it's just going to be so different without Creek.

"Yeah," said Strom.

Rick took a deep drag on his cigarette. He knew what he had to do. Without Creek, and Cajun down with a broken leg, they were flying on broken wings and broken spirits. He'd gotten them all into this, and he'd have to be the one to shut it down, at least their involvement. The boys just didn't have the same drive as

[36] Romans 9:14-18

him, the same manic dependency to avenge all those who had fallen or been hurt by the drugs. It was his war and he knew it. He could never walk away but he couldn't continue asking his brothers to risk their asses and their lives for something he just couldn't let go of. It was all way too personal for him.

"We have to shut it down," he answered. "It's just gotten way too risky and it's too hot."

"What about all the shit we have?" said Havoc.

"Well we can't sell half of it because it's stolen," said Strom.

"So we keep it in the vault, who knows, we might need it one day, and it's pretty fucking safe where it is. We'll divvy up the cash, and if you need to borrow any of the gear, just let Strom or I know, and we'll keep tabs on it and add it to the list of inventory."

"So that's it then? Like we're done right here, right now?" said Havoc.

"Nah," said Rick. "Let's have one last little bonfire up at basecamp…you know…and we'll toast to everything we've accomplished…and to…Creek…we'll drink to Creek…and we'll drink to us. To the Team GKF."

No one at the bonfire even pretended that the war was over for Rick. They all knew he wouldn't stop, that he couldn't stop, and that they were powerless to even try and stop him. For Rick, he felt it rise within him like the spirit of a man possessed, and maybe he was, it certainly wouldn't surprise him if he was. He just knew what he had to do, he'd cut the Team loose and go rogue, continue the fight on his own, be a one-man army. The fifteen-year-old welcomed the fight, and all the pain, sorrow and suffering that came with it.

"Hey brother," said Strom pulling Rick away from the bonfire. "You need me…you know I've got your back."

Rick knew without a doubt he did, and as they stood there with their arms around each other's shoulders watching the fire, he knew that Strom was the only true brother he'd ever really have, thicker than blood and family. But he'd never take Strom up on his offer, from here on out, he was flying one hundred per cent solo. His choices, his consequences. After years of going 'Ghost' emotionally, it was time to go completely Ghost both physically and socially, sovereign and answerable to no one. No one knew where he was, who he was with, or what he was doing at any given time. He would show up places completely unannounced, hang out for a while, maybe grab a shower or catch a nap, and then would disappear just as suddenly. Deliberately not telling anyone where he was going, including his mother, Rick lived his life in a complete state of darkness and mystery, completely embracing his Ghost persona and everything it stood for.

Rational thoughts began to give way to a more feral, crazed madness, so intense that those close to him even began to pull away, scared of who he'd become, locked in a state of mania and paranoia. All it did was drive him further away and hammer the wedge between himself and society. He was gone. So far gone. No law, edict, ethic, or moral norm, nothing society generated or declared, meant anything to him. The 'rules' of life and mankind no longer existed. Prone to the furthest extremes of violence, not vindictively, but simply because he didn't care if he lived or died, he did whatever he wanted, but never without purpose. Completely alone.

Being alone was nothing new to him. Had he not spent years exploring the woods behind the Federal Way house, or stalking the neighbourhoods at night in McMinnville? He wasn't troubled in the least, in fact, he welcomed the solitude. He was tired of having to always watch out for others, of being the one that people leaned on to take care of them. The girls, his mother, the church, the whole fucking spiritual race. He'd be the man of his own domain now, thank you very much. Rick relished the innate freedom that came from not having to worry about anyone else's well-being or safety. Life was less complicated. If he got hurt or ended up dead in a ditch somewhere, who cared? Who really gave a fuck? It sure as hell wouldn't bother him if it happened.

Armed with angst and indifference, Rick burnt and haunted his way across Portland, Tigard, Salem, Amity, and McMinnville, leaving unexplainable wreckage in his wake. Things would spontaneously come up missing with absolutely no explanation. A pile of dope soaked in gasoline in a bathtub. A missing firearm and a stash of money. A stash-spot destroyed. Drywall cut through. Windows smashed or dismounted. A stolen car at the bottom of a ravine, the truck charred with burnt dope. He was the Grinch Who Stole Christmas, sneaking through the Whoville of the drug world, snatching up anything and everything that remotely furthered his cause. He welcomed fate or the lucky motherfucker who would finally find and kill him. Bring it on.

Madness. Mania. Nothing he did would ever be enough to negate the necessity of his mania. Nothing could bring Jackie back, nothing could change what happened to Andrew or Creek, and nothing could make it as if his Dad never left or that he'd never seen or stared down demons. Nothing. Now, he was the demon, a wandering spirit spreading his own suffering across the land. He couldn't stop himself. He couldn't just sit by and do nothing, his actions driven by the most extreme level of compulsion. This would be his legacy, and his fate. He would make the world pay. He told himself that maybe if they all had something to fear, they would stop, so he gave them something to fear. The meaning went so much deeper than just ticking off some drug dealers. It was about everything – his mother and her war, his father and the betrayal, God. The connections ran so deep and so fluid, that he couldn't even sort through them anymore. A jumbled fucking mess.

"Hey, you got a sec?" A grey Crown Victoria with a whip antenna pulled up along side him with the window rolled down.

Instinct told Rick to bolt.

"You're not in any trouble. I just want to talk for a moment. No Miranda, no arrest."

Rick glanced through the window and met the eyes of the plainclothes cop, although he knew right away he wasn't some sort of city cop, but more of an investigator or a detective. Keeping his cool and his wits, he leaned in the window.

"Why what's up?"

The officer squinted his eyes and studied the boy for a moment. "I know some things that may help you make some smart decisions." That caught Rick's attention. "There's a coffee shop up on the corner. I'll meet you there."

Rick watched him drive away. The guy seemed genuine enough; no manipulation or treachery in his voice, and he hadn't even demanded that Rick get in the car. Rick fought every warning bell screaming in his head. It was not a good idea to sit down and have a polite one-on-one conversation with a cop. What the hell was he thinking? The cop was already parked and waiting inside by the time Rick got there. The whole thing had a 'you're fucked' written all over it, but Rick was far too curious to pass up the opportunity.

"Thanks for not running," he said pushing a hot coffee across the table. "I'm not here to arrest you." As he spoke, he casually set his badge on the table. "So you're the one they call Ghost right?"

Rick shut down, everything icing over. The walls were up. "I'm not in the habit of answering questions, but I think I know who you're talking about." Confirmation without actually confirming anything, just in case there was a tape recorder lying about.

"Fair enough. I don't expect you to trust us. The fact is, we're pretty sure we know who you and your friends are and what you're up to and we can't say we really mind."

Rick clenched everything in his body. The statement hit him hard. It was almost as if the Portland Police Department was giving the Team their blessing.

"I'm not sure I know what you're talking about," answered Rick.

"Believe me, we wish we could be a lot more hands on at times, but the law is the law." There was no doubt in Rick's mind that this guy knew exactly who the Team was and what they were doing. "Still, what you kids are doing is dangerous and highly illegal…and not everyone is as understanding as we are. In fact, a few are gunning for you."

Rick could barely even process what he was hearing. He had no idea the cops knew anything. "Who's doing the gunning? The good guys or the bad guys?"

The officer stared at Rick for a moment while taking a sip of coffee. "Well the bad guys for sure, but the good guys too. The bottom line is that we can't have a bunch of juniors running around doing our jobs for us."

Rick sat in silence, too overwhelmed by the conversation to even speak.

"So, regardless of how fun it may be," he said tapping his badge with his forefinger, "I'm advising you to stop." He paused to let that sink in. Rick had no real response except to deny.

"Look, I really don't know what you're talking about but if I see Ghost and his friends, I'll be sure to let them know."

The cop wrinkled his brow, perturbed by the answer. "Okay, guess that's the way it is." He leaned across the table, his voice distinct and serious. "You guys are being investigated hard by a number of different people, and if you give them an angle, they'll lock you up quicker than shit, okay?" He leaned back and took another sip of coffee. "You kids need to take a vacation, enjoy your lives, chase some girls or play sports. The shit you've been up to isn't a game."

Sensing the man's genuine concern, Rick softened his tone a little. "They're done anyway."

The officer stared a moment before picking up his badge and cigarettes. "Just make sure you are too. I'd hate to have to be the one who tagged you someday." He didn't wait for a response, walking out of the coffee shop and back to his car.

"God damnit," said Rick. "What the fuck was that all about?" He took out a Marlboro and flicked his lighter. He needed a long deep drag to calm himself down. Their entire shroud of secrecy shattered, he surmised about how the cops were able to point the finger.

"It must have been Creek. We're they investigating Creek's murder and then stumbled upon who we were and what we were up to? Did someone squeal?"

The thought made him sick to his stomach. It seemed as though the cop had some pretty specific intel that could only have come from an inside source. Cajun? Clover? Havoc? He knew there was no way Strom would have said a God damned thing.

"Maybe one of the boys got in a jam and need to trade some info to save their own ass?"

Of course, it was all just speculation and conjecture. What he did know for sure was that Team had been compromised, and thus, for his own survival, he needed to go completely underground. His sense of paranoia exploded. Cutting ties with everyone, except on the most superficial level, no one could ever say with absolute clarity where he was at any given moment. He attended the first day of school that September, mainly just to see who his teachers were and what kids were in his classes, but by the third day, he was officially a high school drop out. He didn't care. He didn't give a fuck. The minute he turned 18, he'd walk into the nearest recruiting office and join the Navy. He just had to make it on the streets that long.

Except for Amy and Strom, he trusted no one. Everyone else was suspect and subject to turn on him when shit went down. All of this just drove him further away and deeper into his loneliness and solitude. A complete strangers' car or house was far better than a friends'. The further he delved into uncharted territory, the safer he felt. Mania. Paranoia. He thought if he just kept moving, just kept running, he'd be okay. He'd survive, he'd make it to the finish line, and finally find a home in the military. So he ran as fast as he could, as fast as his legs and his furious mind would let him. But it was never fast enough, and it was never far enough. He just couldn't out run the demons lurking within his own heart.

CHAPTER THIRTY-SIX

"Where have you been?" screamed Brenda as Rick rifled through his dresser drawer.

"What does it matter?"

"And so what…you're a high school drop-out now? You think that's acceptable?"

"I don't care what's acceptable. School doesn't matter. Home doesn't matter. None of it matters."

"What has happened to you Rick? I don't even know who you are anymore. You've strayed so far. It just breaks my heart."

Rick was way past giving a shit what his mother thought, and he knew exactly what the 'strayed so far' meant. God. She used to speak of the spirit of rebellion and how they must fight against it, and yet here her own son, her own flesh and blood, her own Christ's Little Warrior, now completely embodying that spirit and more. For Brenda, God was still the answer to all things, and if Rick was living in sin and rebellion, the only way to fix it was to get right with God. Fuck that. He'd heard that song and dance his entire life and he was done, no longer having the patience or tolerance for any of it. God was the cause of everything wrong in his life. Why couldn't his mother see that? Rick had no intentions of getting right with God. None.

"I'm still your Mother Rick, and you will do as I say."

"Yeah? So I guess I have you to blame for bringing me into this fucked up world then don't I?"

Brenda's face shattered, struggling to regain its composure. She'd tried to be sympathetic, now it was time to get stern.

"If you can't live by my rules, then you can't live under this roof!"

Rick peered up from the drawer with an amused snarling glare. "Oh yeah? Well I guess I'm not living here anymore then, am I?"

Brenda knew she had lost. Her boy was gone. She watched him continue to pack his things, her head screaming for answers, and searching for the right words.

"God can make this all better Rick! You just need to turn to Him and give yourself back to Him! It's not too late! In God's name Rick! Stand down and see reason!"

"Fuck God!" he screamed.

Brenda's open palm shot out and connected hard with her son's face. Stunned and shocked, Rick took a step forward.

"Don't you ever fucking hit me again!"

With a look of pure indignation and authority, Brenda promptly hauled off and slapped him in the face again, as hard as she could. Without even thinking, Rick shoved her shoulder hard with his right hand, sending her flying up against the wall. Brenda grabbed her shoulder as if she'd been pierced with the blade of Satan's own sword, her face awash her tears. Slowly, she slid down the wall to her knees, too weak and shocked to stand any longer. In her mind, all doubt was erased. Her son had actually become one of the demons they had fought so hard to eradicate. He'd gone to the other side. Rick grabbed the rest of his gear, and leaned over his mother on the way out the door.

"I said, don't fucking hit me."

With that, he was gone. Gone from her house, and gone from the house of God. He did feel horrible about shoving his mother, and for what it was worth, he loved her dearly and had always protected her. But the God shit was just too much. He just couldn't take it any longer. A part of him felt relieved, to finally get his feelings about God on the table, and a final breaking of ties that would set his soul free. Rick knew he was going down at some point, fate would catch up to him, it was inevitable, and with his mother and Jimmy out of the picture, it would just make things easier for them.

He left that night fully believing that he'd never be back. He'd already been mulling over plans. Maybe head north to Portland? Or Seattle? Or maybe head south along the Cascades or even disappear into Canada. Wherever he went, he wouldn't bother anyone. He just wanted to wait out the time until he was old enough to join the Navy. All he knew for certain was that he was free. His past was dead, and he'd never have to deal with it again. Not his mother, not his father, and not God. He was finally his own man, and the future was all his.

He spent the frigid night sleeping in a ditch down in McMinnville. He did it on purpose. With the ditch acting as a shallow grave, he laid there, wrapped in his trench coat, chain smoking until he was sick, letting his past seep out his pores and into the cold earth. Once and for all he would be free. In the morning, he would awake to a new life, a re-birth of sorts where Rick Watkinson would be a mere memory. Maybe he'd get lucky and freeze to death in the ditch, either way, he welcomed this rite of passage into a new world of his making.

As the misty morning dropped its dew on his forehead, Rick rose like a spirit, like a Ghost. Immediately, he knew things were different. He was a homeless teenager, on the run, and completely fending for himself. In the past, he'd always had a 'base camp' to return to, to fall back on. It was no longer Rick not wanting to go home and cooking up lies and excuses as to where he'd been, now, he'd been deliberately thrown out and Brenda had made sure that Rick knew he was no longer welcome.

"Fuck her. Fuck them all. I got nothing and nobody over my head now! No school, no parents, no rules, no fucking authority. All I got to do is dodge the cops…and fuck...I've been doing that for years."

True inexhaustible freedom. Exhilaration. He soon found out that it wasn't all one big party, and it sure as fuck wasn't fun. Now he had to worry about his basic needs. What was he going to eat that night? Where would he sleep? Clean his clothes? Have a shower? How could he make his wad of cash last as long as possible? Sure he could drink as much as he wanted, but he didn't. He needed to stay sharp and focus on his own survival. Rabid paranoia set in. Were the cops on his trail? Was someone going to give him up? Bouncing from place to place, he made sure to make his stays short and sweet, especially if there was someone there he knew.

First it was Portland for a week, then a few days in Tigard, then back to McMinnville, and despite the hardships and anxiety, he was loving every minute of it. Being completely immersed in the unknown and new was a welcome relief to his troubled soul. On the streets, he was home. It was who Ghost was, and no one could stop him. In his mind, he had a handle on everything, but nothing was further from the truth. He needed help, he desperately needed someone to step up and show him a different way to live, that there could be a compromise between Rick and Ghost, that it didn't have to be strictly one or the other. He wasn't going to respond well to threats or ultimatums. He didn't want to change who he was or what he was doing, so telling him he 'had' to do this or he 'had' to do that would only result in failure.

Ten days after Brenda threw him out, he was walking down Highway 99 with some friends, wearing some brand new clothes, and some brand new boots. His pack full of food and supplies, he was feeling good about his life and his situation.

"Jesus Christ," he said as a blue GEO Storm pulled up in the parking lot in front of them. "Wait here guys. I'll go see what my mother wants."

As he walked over, Brenda got out of the car. There were no hugs, no hellos.

"You doing all right out here?" She leaned against the car and crossed her arms.

"Yeah Mom, I'm fine. I'm making it okay."

"Have you been able to eat and stay clean?"

"Yeah, I do just fine at taking care of myself in case you hadn't noticed. Been doing it for a while now."

Brenda tried to ignore his stinging sarcasm. "You know you can come home as soon as you can follow the rules?" Her tone was soft.

"Mom, I'm probably never coming home…that's just the way it is. I belong out here."

"Well," she answered after a long, somber pause. "You know that I love you Rick and God loves you too." She just couldn't keep God out of it. Why couldn't this conversation just be about her and him. Rick seethed at the mention of God and completely shut down.

"I love you too Mom," he said as he turned and walked away.

With a broken heart, Brenda got back in the car and drove off. She never did realize that he was more at home on the streets than anywhere. He'd been doing it since he was ten years old. And really, Brenda only had herself to blame. She's the one who took the money. She's the one who came to rely on funds Rick earned while out at night. She had to know he wasn't selling Girl Scout cookies. Five years later, her attempts at tough love were way too late. She had her chances to reel him in, to get him help, and to shift his path, but her 'God-coloured' goggles blinded her to the severity of the situation. And when she couldn't pray it away, she just threw up her hands and gave up.

"Hey Rick," said the school security guard. About a week after seeing his mom, Rick had stopped by the cafeteria to hang with Strom and bring him up to date. "I'm not going to stop you if you run but your Mom reported you as a runaway, and I'm obligated to report you every time I see you."

Anger spread across his lean face. "Alright, I'm gone. Thanks for the warning."

"Why don't you just go home son? It can't be that bad?"

Rick turned and glared at the guard. "I'll be home when I'm buried in the ground and make it back to Hell!"

Within seconds, he was out the door and gone.

"Damn her! What the fuck?"

While on one hand it wasn't a big deal, it's not like it was a felony warrant or anything, but now the McMinnville Police Department was obligated to stop him and take him in whenever they saw him. It just complicated things, and drove him deeper underground and away from any sort of safe place or anyone that might be able to offer him help. Even if Rick wanted to stay somewhere and was allowed by parents, he couldn't take the risk because they could be charged for harbouring a runaway. His paranoia cultivated. His options shrank. He took to sleeping during the day and travelling by night, catching rides with God knows who, going God knows where.

"I need to get out of here. Go to the city and just get fucking lost."

September turned to October, and Rick knew he had to make a serious move, decide once and for all where he was going, and what he was going to do. It would be a huge change and cost him a bunch of friends but it was time. He was tired of running, he needed to go where no one knew who he was, and where he could make a fresh start.

"Seattle here I come."

Not content to leave without saying goodbye to his friends, Rick walked into McMinnville High School on October 9th, 1994. He should have just sent a postcard. All the boys were there, and it was tough saying goodbye.

"When will you be back bro?" said Strom.

"I don't know bro…not for a long while I think. I just gotta go up north for awhile."

At the time, no one had inkling just how far up north he'd be going, and that it would be for the rest of his life. He was being proactive, doing what he could to get out of the mess that was his life and start anew.

"Shit Rick," said Strom. "The principal is here with security.

"Don't run Rick," said the security guard. "We're not going to call the cops on you. We just really need to talk."

"Your mother wants to talk to you Rick," said the principal. "No games. She just asked us to see if you'd be willing to talk to her. Nobody else involved."

Super hesitant to even entertain their bullshit, and a little pissed off that they ruined his good bye with his buddies, he shot a glare in their direction.

"No cops?"

"No cops," answered the principal. "All we want you to do is come with us to the office and wait for your mother to show up."

"Alright, but if I see even a single black and white, I'm gone, and I wouldn't advise getting in my fucking way."

He gave Strom one last hug and followed them to the office.

"She wanted us to see if you'd be willing to go out to breakfast with her, no strings attached. She just wants to talk," said the principal.

Rick dropped his guard just enough. "Fine, call her."

What could it hurt? He was fully capable of getting up and walking away, or getting out of a moving car. He done it before and he do it again if he had to. Brenda was at the school in ten minutes flat.

"If you don't like what you hear Rick," she said. "We can just part ways afterwards."

"C'mon Rick," said the principal. "What can it hurt?"

"It's just a conversation Rick," said Brenda.

"Fine. Let's go."

A free breakfast at a restaurant and if he didn't like the outcome, he was gone? He could do that. His extreme love and fierce loyalty to his mother got the best of him. For old times sake, he'd have one last breakfast with the woman who had everything to do with making Rick the way he was now. Then he'd be gone. Off to Seattle and a brand new life.

"Let's just put our differences to rest Rick. We can make this work. I know we can."

Rick said nothing.

"We can change the rules. You want to smoke? Okay fine, I get that, but please just not in the house. We can sit down and figure out what classes you want to take at school. If you don't want to take it, you don't have to, I just want you back in school. You'd like that wouldn't you? You could see your friends on a regular basis…"

"I see my friends on a regular basis now."

"But it'll be different this time Rick, I promise. I won't push you to do anything you don't want to do and I'll even…I'll even sign the waiver so you can get into the military when you turn seventeen. I know that's what you have your heart set on. That's a whole year you won't have to wait! How does that sound?"

Rick just nodded, but he liked the idea.

"I just want you home Rick. Both Jimmy and I want you home. We miss you. Please son. Please Rick. Please come home. We'll make this work. I promise with all my heart that things will change and we will make this work."

Rick looked into her pleading eyes. Maybe things could work? As much as he liked being on the streets, home was home, and he didn't want to leave if he didn't have to. He'd been prepared to get on bus or hitchhike his way up to Seattle, but why leave if he didn't have to? Everyone and everything he'd ever had was in Oregon. Strom, Cajun, Havoc, Dustin and the band, Amy, Selene, his woods, the base camp, the look-out, the ATV, and the house that would one day be his. His whole life from the age of ten onward had been in Oregon, and if Brenda was willing to rescind the runaway status, and accept him for what he was, why wouldn't he take it? He could at least give it a chance, and if it didn't work out, them he could always leave. She made it sound so sweet, so enticing, especially to a kid who hadn't slept in a warm bed in almost eight weeks. She was willing to give him his sovereignty, and they'd work together to solve their issues.

"Okay," he said. "I'll come home."

"I love you Rick. I love you. You know that right? I'll always love you, no matter what."

They hugged, then left the restaurant to go home. A sense of relief swept over him as he walked into his bedroom, and dropped his gear-bag on the floor. For so long he'd had to watch every step, and constantly look over his shoulder. Now he was back home with a warm bed, free food, a bathroom. It was the fucking Hilton compared to where he'd been. He made some food, had a hot shower, then made his way back to his bedroom. All he wanted to do was stretch out and chill on his bed. As he was walking past the office, he heard his mother on the phone in her back bedroom.

"His father is on his way down from Alaska right now. I'm really worried about what's going to happen."

Rick stopped dead in his tracks. "Son of a bitch! She sold me out to Dad!" Without saying a word, he immediately went to his room and began to repack, this time for good.

"Fucking son of a bitch. I can't even believe this! How could you let yourself be so fucking stupid Rick! You should have known it was a trap!" He was furious with himself for letting his guard down, and even more furious at his mother.

"She played me. She fucking played me. It was all bullshit! All of it. She just said all that shit so I'd come home, and she wouldn't look so bad in front of Dad."

It was all true. Brenda had played him. Bob was already on a flight to Oregon, and her conversation with Rick was just to save face, and her own ass. If she could at least get Rick to come home, then she wouldn't look a complete incompetent parent, and she might be able to hang on to Jimmy. So she said whatever was necessary to get Rick to come home, never meaning a single word. Another betrayal. He had believed his mother, even trusted her, and now she fucked him over, yet again. The sooner he left this cesspool, the better. Brenda heard him packing and was soon in his doorway begging him not to go.

"Rick, you have to understand my position! What choice did I have? Please just stay and face your father. We can do it together!"

"Yeah, fucking right Mom. He wouldn't be flying down here if he wasn't coming to get me. You should have told me he was coming. Now I'm gone for good!"

"Rick please! We can stand up to him!"

"Really? You mean like all those times you stood up to him in the past? You have no fucking clue. You lied to me! What makes you any different than him? He betrayed us, now you betray me? It's all a big fucking joke…but lucky you, you won't have to deal with me anymore. The both of you can go to hell!"

"Rick! Please just listen to me!"

"Just get out. I mean it, get out now."

Not willing to test his anger, Brenda walked out of the room, and Rick slammed the door behind her. The only weapon she had now was to hide everything and anything she could that might aid in his escape. The car keys, his boots, the ATV keys, all went into her closet where he couldn't find them. Rick lay on his bed, waiting for his chance to run. He had no idea what time his father's plane landed, and it was only an hour's drive from Portland to McMinnville. If he could just make it to nightfall, then he'd be off into the woods where no one would ever find him. Brenda kept her ear to the door and checked on him numerous times. She knew he was going to run, and she couldn't let that happen. Bob would kill her, and Jimmy would be gone for sure.

Rick tired of waiting. So after Brenda stuck her head in his door one last time, he made his move. He uncovered his second pair of boots, threw on his trench coat, and went to work on the window in his bedroom. Slowly sliding his window open, he lowered his duffle bag with a rope, then followed behind, silently dropping the fourteen feet to the ground. As he hit the deck, he heard a car pull into the driveway.

"Fuck! Game time!"

But his first decision was a bad one. Instead of just heading for the forest on foot, he took off for the barn to hotwire the ATV. All he could think of was leaving this fucking place as soon as he could, and getting to Seattle. He'd drive the ATV out past the logging roads to the coast and then turn north. When he ran out of gas, he'd just walk or hitchhike, and once he got to Astoria, he'd cross over into Washington, and be gone for good. He knew his father would chase him in a vehicle when they realized he was headed up the hill, which is why Rick grabbed his 10-pump Airsoft BB gun. If worse came to worse, he could spider the windshield and make pursuit near impossible. The only thing he hadn't thought of was a flashlight, and without one, hotwiring the ATV was a no go. Precious time ticked away.

"Fuck! Just start you motherfucker!"

The barn was the first place Bob and Joe looked. With the barn to his left, a brambled-covered steep cliff to his right, and a triple-strand barbed-wire fence behind him, he had no where to go. He held the Airsoft rifle out to the side, hoping in the darkness, they'd mistake it for being real and hesitate just enough to give him time to bolt and dive through the fence behind him.

"Give me the gun Rick," said Bob holding out his hand. Rick threw it over the fence in a complete act of defiance. "You're coming with me to Alaska." Bob took a few steps forward, fearless.

"I'm not going anywhere with you, you fucking traitor! Don't fucking touch me!" In one swift motion, Bob and Joe lunged at Rick, grabbing him by the shoulders. "Let me go you fucking prick! I'm not going anywhere!"

"Don't talk to me like that! I'm your father!"

"And you're a fucking bastard who has no right to call himself my father! Now let me go!"

Kicking and screaming the entire eighty yards back to the house, Rick made his position and his feelings quite clear. But Bob made his position clear as well, cuffing Rick in the back of the head as hard and as often as he could. Delirious rage. Once they got back to the house, Bob pinned Rick against the wall, his forearm across the boy's throat.

"Don't talk to me that way, I'm your father!"

"Fuck off!"

Jimmy only added to the chaos, running around, hysterical.

"Jimmy!" said Bob. "Stop screaming and go to your room now!"

Rick had no intention of going down without a fight, and after they dragged him across the room to a chair, the argument began. Full of fury and rage himself, Bob stood over his son, his finger waving in his face, explaining how things were and what was going to happen. There was no attempt to diffuse the situation, to calm Rick down, to find any semblance of order. Bob just began the lecture, and the ultimatums, and the threats, his face red and bulging with anger and adrenaline.

"Fuck you!" yelled Rick lunging at him like a wild animal.

Grabbing both Rick's shoulders, Bob slammed his son back in the chair with a force so violent, Rick's back hit the window crank, flinging his head against the wooden window sill. For a moment, Rick couldn't breathe, and his head spun in a grey tizzy. Struggling to regain his composure, Rick brought his forearm to his split lip, wiping away the blood that began to trickle down his chin. With his father standing over him ready to crack the shit out of him if he even moved, and Joe, a 3rd Dan black belt guarding the front door, the situation was hopeless.

"Please Bob! Don't hurt him anymore!" pleaded Brenda. "This isn't necessary!"

"Shut the fuck up Brenda! You've already done quite enough here don't you think?"

At one point, Rick thought Joe might intervene on his wife's behalf, but apparently he really didn't give a shit how his wife was getting berated by her ex-husband. Joe wasn't going to say a thing. He just wanted the kid gone too.

"I'm not going," said Rick. "I'm not going to Alaska, especially with you! Do you hear me!"

"Yes you are Rick. I will not have my son living like a tramp anymore. Not going to school? What the fuck are you thinking Rick?" He turned to Brenda. "How in the hell could you let this happen?"

Brenda had no answers. So much for the 'we'll stand up to your father together' talk. She cowered like she'd done each and every time before. Rick didn't blame her. His father could be a scary son of a bitch when he was angry, and he was fucking angry.

"I will never consent to going with you."

"You think I need your consent?" Bob laughed. "You have no choice in the matter. Do you hear me? No choice! The law is on my side and I'll take it there if I have to, don't think I won't." He stared at Brenda.

"Maybe it's best Rick," she said softly. "Things aren't working out here. Alaska can be a brand new start."

Fucking bitch. Rick had lost. His whole world shattered. Not only was he forced to give up every little bit of freedom he'd enjoyed, he was now forced to go live with the man he hated most in life, the one he blamed for ruining his family and his life, and his whore Jezebel wife. How could this possibly end well?

If anything, Rick needed the intervention of counsellors, he needed a program, some sort of regimented structure, where outside distractions were minimal. He needed to have time in a safe and caring environment, to sort through his feelings, to come to some sort of understanding and internal compromise. But none of this was offered to him. Nobody even thought of the idea. Bob believed everything would be solved with a little parental discipline and proper parenting. He had no idea how far gone his son was, he had no clue of what Rick's life was truly about, he had no inkling of the war, of the demons, of Jackie, Andrew or Creek. He knew none of it, and quite frankly, he didn't even bother to ask. Discipline, structure, and rules – that was going to solve everything. He had no idea how fucking wrong he was.

"Go pack your stuff. We're leaving this house tonight."

Rick had no choice but to listen. He grabbed his clothes, packed some of his other belongings, and then was marched out to the car.

"What about my stereo and guitars?"

"I'll have your mother ship it up as soon as possible."

Rick heard the locks click as he settled into the front seat. Bob wasn't taking any chances. Rick was his POW, a captured prisoner, and he was going to do everything in his power to make sure he got his cargo on the plane first thing in the morning. Neither said a word as he drove the short trip down to McMinnville and the Best Western on Highway 99. Marching Rick inside, Bob pushed a table in front of the door, stacking all their luggage on top. He wasn't messing around, and rightly so. The second he saw an opportunity; Rick was planning to bolt. There was no way in hell, he was getting on that plane, and he had zero intentions of living with him in Alaska. The sooner he broke free and got back to living on his own, the better it would be for everyone.

CHAPTER THIRTY-SEVEN

"Jesus fucking Christ," Rick muttered. "You can't keep me here."

"I sure as hell can keep you here," said Bob. "You're coming to Alaska with me and you're going to start over. You're going to finish high school and choose a career. I'm not having my son wander around the countryside like some homeless waif."

"And I get no choice in this whatsoever?"

"Well seeing as you've already made some very questionable choices, I think it's best to take any sort of decision making out of your hands at the moment."

"I know exactly what I'm doing! You don't think I have a plan? Or know what I want to do?'

"Well then, let me hear it."

"I want to join the Navy."

"That's great but you still have a ways to go before you turn 18. Is your plan to just run around the streets digging through garbage cans?"

"I don't dig through fucking garbage cans."

"Watch your language with me Rick."

"Why? Why should I? What does it matter? You don't understand me, you've never understood me, and you've never even really tried! It's always 'you're going to do this' and 'you're going to do that'! You never ask me shit! I don't want to go to school. School means nothing to me! I can learn more about whatever I need to without being in a classroom. It's all bullshit!"

"It's not bullshit Rick."

"But it is! Why are grades so important? Because society tells us they should be! And I don't give a shit what society says or expects!"

"You say that now but you'll change your mind. It's just a phase."

"It's not a phase! Jesus it's not!" Rick turned away from his father. "You just don't get it. You never have. You don't give a shit about my opinion or what I think, so not sure why I even bother. It'll never change. You think I'm just being some snot-nosed rebellious kid…getting into trouble just because? Fuck that. And I'm not going to Alaska."

"I'm done talking about this Rick. You're either moving to Alaska with me or I'm dropping you off down at the police station. I know they're looking for you."

"Yeah, mom turned me in as a runaway. Big deal."

Bob glared hard at his son. "You and I both know it goes way beyond that.

I know more than you think I know."

"What the fuck is he talking about?" thought Rick. "How in the hell does he know anything?"

It wasn't beyond Bob to bluff, but the sternness on his father's face and the sharp tone of his voice told Rick all he needed to know. But how? How could he know anything? Especially in Alaska? His mother didn't know shit and she lived in the same house. Had he been in touch with the cops in Portland? Cajun's dad? How much did the McMinnville police really know? Fuck. His paranoia exploded like a raging tornado.

"Just who the fuck can I trust in this life?" he thought.

The only clear-cut answer was himself. He sure as hell couldn't trust his mother, and anything he told his father would only be used against him. His friends? Someone had snitched before, so they were out, except for maybe Strom.

"I have no one. I am completely alone."

He made up his mind, although he really didn't have much of a choice. He couldn't just let his father turn him in to the cops, he'd have to take his chances in Alaska. It wouldn't be for long. As soon as he could gather up and stockpile enough gear, he'd be gone. He'd walk back to the Lower 48 if he had to. Being locked up in Alaska forever was never in the plan.

The next morning, October 10, 1994, Bob escorted Rick on a plane bound for Alaska. Rosemary met them at the gate.

"Hi Rick. Welcome to Alaska! Did you have a nice flight?"

Rick's eye's bore through the charade. "It was fine."

"I've told Rick," said Bob, "that things are going to be different from now on. It's a clean slate and a new life for him. For the three of us."

"Great," thought Rick. "They're both laying it on pretty thick. Act positive like nothing was ever wrong". Same old deal. Same old tactic. Fake it. Fresh off the streets, he was still too raw for such games and bullshit. He wasn't having any of it.

"I think we all know that I don't want to be here and all this 'new life' bullshit is just that, bullshit. You can try and act like we're all one big happy family but we all know it's a lie. It always has been and always will be. I know she doesn't want me here. She's never wanted me in your life and that's fine with me just so you know. I really don't give a shit."

"Well that's your choice then Rick," said Bob. "Bottom line is that you're now in Alaska and there's really nothing you can do about it. You may not believe me, but we want this to work out. I know that I haven't been able to spend as much time with you over the years as I would have liked but you're here with us now, and like it or not, it will be a fresh start. Yes, it's going to take some compromise, and that means you too, starting with what you're wearing."

"There's nothing wrong with what I'm wearing," said Rick.

"It's not exactly what the other kids are wearing up here," said Rosemary. "And they look ratty."

"So what?" said Rick. "It's what I'm used to wearing and they're comfortable."

"Let's not argue about it now," said Bob. "Just wait and see what she picked out."

Rick could only imagine the type of clothes image-loving Rosemary picked out, and when he walked into his 'new' room and saw them laid out on the bed, he wanted to puke.

"Are you fucking kidding me? Polo shirts with the alligator? Slacks? Oh, and what a lovely pair of shiny white Nikes." He folded everything up and tossed it in the corner. It'd be a cold day in hell before he was caught wearing any of that shit and looking like a fucking prep. No fucking way.

"You're not sitting at this table looking like that," said Rosemary when she called him for dinner. "This is not a barn."

In her defence, Rick did look like shit. Roaming the streets for two months, wearing clothes barely hanging together and boots that should have been thrown out ages ago, Rick looked a dirty, grimy, mess. With a partial shorn head at the sides, and then hair down to his shoulders at the back, he looked completely out of place sitting at the pearl white dining room table with its gold-rimmed China. He didn't give a shit. They were the ones the ones that brought him there, so they could just screw it. None of this was his choice. None of it.

"Unbelievable," said Rosemary shaking her head. "I take the time to buy you some new clothes and you refuse to wear them. I ask you to clean up and look at least presentable for dinner and you show up looking like this? A thug? You are nothing but an ungrateful young punk and a loser! Why your father even bothers with you I have no clue! Look at you! Look at that hair! It's unacceptable!"

For the next five minutes, Rosemary ripped a strip off of Rick, all while Bob sat and said nothing. Rick kept his mouth shut as long as he could. If he didn't get out of there now, something bad was going to happen. He knew he was going to blow.

"Get back here and sit down!" said Bob as Rick got up from the table and headed for the stairs. "I said get back here!"

"No! I'm not going to listen to that fucking whore bitch and watch you just sit there!"

Before Rick could even take another breath, Bob tore across the floor and caught him on the stairs, grabbing one arm and clotheslining him across his chest with the other, sending him flying to the floor. As Rick lay on the ground, Bob wound up and backhanded him across the face.

"Don't you ever call her that again! Ever!" Bob screamed, spit flying, shaking his son by the arm like a ragdoll.

"Don't you ever hit me," answered Rick in a very low, stern voice.

Bob threatened another backhand. "I'll hit you as much as I want."

"And you'll die," thought Rick, sniffing the blood from his nose back down his throat.

Bob stared at his son, waiting for a reaction, then let go of his arm. Without a word, Rick got up and walked down to his room, still sniffing blood, hell bent on not letting his father know that he'd hurt him. He wasn't about to give him that satisfaction. His 'new life' in Alaska was off to a fucking wonderful start. If this was what he had to look forward to, then he'd be better off leaving now. Fucking bitch. From the moment he arrived, she just expected him to conform, to flick a switch and be someone else. Well he couldn't do it. The truth was he hated both of them. Despised them for what they'd done, and what they represented. Rosemary hated him right back, found him shameful and vile. A new set of clothes wasn't going to change that. And Bob? Poor Bob was caught in the middle. He loved his son, and he loved his wife, and he refused to give up on either of them.

The next morning Bob and Rosemary acted as if nothing had ever happened. Everything was just sunshine and roses. It drove Rick nuts.

"So I see you're not going to wear the new clothes?" said Rosemary.

"No, I'm not."

"Okay then, will you at least wear new jeans and flannels if we buy them for you?"

"Yeah, I would."

"And we need to do something about those boots."

"Well I did have new ones, but they're back in Oregon. Mom hid them on me so I wouldn't leave, so I had to grab these ones. I guess I could stand for a new pair."

"I have some errands to run today, but tomorrow we'll go shopping."

"Okay."

The next day, Rick and Rosemary went shopping; three new flannel shirts, three new pairs of Levi's Silver Tab jeans, new socks, new boxers, new T-shirts, a new winter coat (although he'd never give up his black trench coat – he'd almost died in that thing), and a brand new pair of fourteen eyelet Wolverine boots. And if he hadn't been such a hateful little prick at the time, he may have even been grateful. It was good shit, top of line clothes. But in his skewed mind, the clothes were only to keep up appearances. He never for once believed that they actually cared enough to want to buy him nice things. His mind and reasoning just wouldn't allow it.

Because of how the divorce was handled and the intense negative reinforcement he'd received for years, Rick steadfastly and religiously believed three truths. One, his father was a 'traitor' who had forfeited his right to even be his father, or have a say over his life. Two, Rosemary was a 'home-wrecking whore' and the epitome of evil snobbery. And three, he hated both of them, and was only ever capable of hating them. There was no give or take to any of these beliefs. Black and white, no grey. Never any gray. If he even tried to let them in a little, it would break everything he'd ever been taught or what he believed to be true, and with so much upheaval and misrepresentation of the truth in his life already, he wasn't about to give up these core truths. There was just too much emotion riding on these truths. Nothing was black and white. Ever.

The whole thing was doomed from the start. If trying to get a regular, rebellious, hateful, pissed at the world teenager to bend on any of their ideals was hopeless, then imagine trying to get Rick, former 'Little Warrior for Christ' turned 'pact maker with the Devil', 'let's start a militia group to get back at drug dealers and pimps', Watkinson to change. Bob and Rosemary had no clue what they were up against. No clue. Rick needed help. He needed to be deprogramed from his beliefs. He needed intense levels of therapy and psychiatry. Truthfully, how were Bob and Rosemary supposed to know? They didn't know the half of what Rick had been through, they knew nothing of what he'd seen both in this world and beyond the Veil. And he wasn't about to tell them. Ghost would never talk to anyone about what he really thought or how he really felt. How could he? He was so withdrawn and locked inside of himself, that even breathing a word about any of it caused him intense pain.

How do you get through to someone like this? How do you get them to understand that they don't have to think and feel this way? Years of brainwashing, the building up and shaping of these beliefs, seeing them reinforced by everything he perceived, had only cemented their truth. The best course of action would have been to send Rick away, to some sort of boarding school or military school, to get him out of the domestic situation and away from the people who had in his mind, wrecked him. Somewhere other than at the home with the parents he was so hateful towards. Brenda had failed miserably with her 'God is the answer' doctrine, and now Bob was on the same course to failure trying to stubbornly hammer a square peg into a warped hole. He was never going to succeed, and had Brenda not been so selfishly concerned with her own image as a doting mother, she would have been honest with her ex-husband as to just how gone their son was. She put herself before her son, just as she always had, and he paid the price. Bob and Rosemary paid the price.

"What's this new school called?" said Rick.

"Robert Service High," said Bob.

"I suppose it's a preppy school right? Where all the rich kids in Anchorage go?"

"That I don't know," said Bob. "But it doesn't matter. That's where the kids from Hillside go, and that's where you're going to go. Everyday. Is that clear? I won't have you skipping classes like you did in McMinnville or getting away with the garbage you got away with. I'm not your mother. Is that clear?"

Rick nodded. He didn't feel like arguing. He wasn't looking forward to any school, let alone a rich preppy one. He was just going to have to wait it out until he could get enough gear to head back south.

"I don't think you're going to hate it Rick," said Bob. "In fact, there's a program there that I think you're going to love."

"I doubt it," said Rick.

"We'll see," said Bob.

After the initial tour of the school and meeting the principal and his teachers, Bob and Rick walked into a tiered classroom adorned with flags and military paraphernalia.

"Hello," said a man in a uniform. "My name is James McBroom but everyone calls me Top."

"Hello Mr. McBroom," said Bob shaking his hand. "I'm Robert Watkinson and this is my son Rick."

Rick shook his hand. He felt an uncommon twinge of nerves. Top invited them to sit at some of the desks.

"So, I hear you think you want to go into the military? Is that right son?"

"Yeah," said Rick meekly.

"Yeah what?" replied Top. Rick was confused. "You meant 'Yes sir', didn't you?"

"Yes sir," answered Rick immediately. An ex-Marine and a Drill Instructor who had seen combat, Top wasn't fucking around. He was a man who demanded respect. Rick sat up straight in the chair, pulling his shoulders back; he knew he'd already lost points for appearance.

"JROTC stands for Junior Reserve Officer Training Corps," said Top. "Have you heard of the program before?"

"No sir," said Rick.

"Well here at JROTC we take a lot of pride in what we do and how we act as young men and women. Title 10, Section 2031 of the United States Code states that 'the purpose of JROTC is to instill in students in secondary educational institutions the values of citizenship, service to the United States, and personal responsibility and a sense of accomplishment. Students will acquire an understanding of what it takes to become a leader, work in a team, and the importance of physical fitness. We want you as cadets to be ready to serve our country and support our national objectives."

This man was speaking Rick's language.

"Taking JROTC for a number of years and progressing through the ranks can also grant you the ability to rank higher, if you decide to pursue a military career. But you have to earn it. Nothing is given for free and we demand your very best. Each branch of the United States Armed Forces maintains a Junior Reserve Officers' Training Corps, and here at Robert Service High School, we're all Navy."

"Are you serious sir?"

"I do not lie son."

"I just meant that my Grandpa spent thirty-five years in the Navy and it's where I want to go." A glimmer of hope and belonging tweaked its way into Rick's heart. Maybe, just maybe he'd found somewhere where he belonged, where he fit in.

"Here at Service High we have a competition Rifle Team, armed and unarmed Drill teams, and all our cadets have uniforms, rank, and a chance to be awarded ribbons and medals. Like I said, it's not a free ride, you're going to have to work for every last bit."

"I'm not afraid of hard work sir. I welcome it."

"Good to hear son. Oh, and one other thing. You're going to have to do something with that hair."

"Yes sir!" said Rick with a grin.

The next day, Rick got himself down to the barber shop for a 'high and tight' Marine style haircut. He didn't even blink at having to cut off his hair. It was more like an honour. Sitting in that chair, listening to the buzz of the razor against his head, he began to let himself entertain the idea that maybe Alaska wasn't such a bad thing.

Walking into Service High the next day, Rick had no idea what to expect. While looking way better than he did, he was still dressed like a grunge skater dude from the lower 48, and had a definite urban appeal. He had that look of someone who'd been places and done things, especially to kids who for the most part had never ventured out of Anchorage. But Anchorage was nothing like Portland or Seattle. It wasn't littered with slums, ghettos, or projects that a regular lower American city had, and with the temperature below 32 degrees Fahrenheit, half the year, street life was generally non-existent or highly discouraged if you don't want to freeze to death.

"Hi," said Rick. "I think I'm supposed to share your locker."

"Hi," answered the petite girl with pony-tailed strawberry-blond hair. "I'm Natalie."

Natalie and Rick hit it off right away. Both a little rough around the edges, they found common ground, and forged a friendship. Through Natalie, Rick was introduced to a new circle of friends, and he met even more when he made the Jazz Band after the first tryout. But his shining glory came in JROTC. For a young man who'd always dreamed of joining the Navy, this was the real shit. His first day he was taken to the Supply Room and issued a full uniform complete with rank – Seaman's Apprentice – shoes to shine, a peacoat, and a navy-style cap. He couldn't have been happier.

Pouring every ounce of his heart, he became a star cadet, taking to the structure and discipline like it was second nature, flawlessly standing at attention, saluting, and memorizing the ten 'Orders To the Sentry' within the first week. With his focus and dedication, other JROTC students were drawn to him, and he made many new friends. There were a few hiccups of course.

"Can I see you in my office cadet?" said Gunner the lead instructor.

"Yes sir!"

"I noticed during your pull-ups that you have something on your belt there."

"Yes sir. I have a four-inch lock blade knife and a Leatherman tool." Rick was scared. Knives in school were illegal, and Gunner had the power to cause him some serious trouble and get him kicked out of JROCT.

"Don't ever let me see them on your person again. Is that understood?"

"Yes sir! Thank you sir!"

Rick had dodged a major bullet. The Leatherman tool that he never took off for anyone, he took off for JROTC, no questions asked. That's how much he respected Gunner and the honour of the command. He wasn't going to do anything to jeopardize his involvement, or his rise through the ranks. He would do anything for JROTC, include walking three miles in the bitter Alaskan cold to get to a Halloween dance. Bob and Rosemary would have driven him but they had a tennis match scheduled and couldn't get away until later. By the time he got to the restaurant, his eyes were frozen red and his whole body chilled.

"Dude! You walked here? From the Alaska Club? Are you fucking crazy?"

"I've been known to called a little crazy before," Rick stammered.

"You can't do that here bro, it's cold out. You know this is Alaska right?"

"Yeah," laughed Rick. "It wasn't that bad." Of course, none of them had any inkling that he'd slept in freezing-cold ditches and windowless abandoned buildings before, or that he'd walked fifteen miles from Newberg to McMinnville on more than one occasion. Three miles in sub-zero temperatures was a piece of cake. It had been worth it, the other kids gave him cred and his popularity and acceptance soared. No longer was he an outsider from the lower 48, he was Rick, the cool new guy who was down for whatever and didn't mind contributing in any way that he could. It all meant the world to him, and he soaked up every last bit of the attention.

But something in his life was off. Since his youth, he'd always idolized a military mind-set and needed an enemy to fight against. He needed a war to be apart of. After the divorce, there was nothing holding his mother back from engaging him in God's War in a daily, if not hourly manner. It had consumed him, and when he'd finally had enough and it had taken its toll, along came Jackie and his war against the disease and addiction that killed her and plagued society. To Rick, these wars were real, and he fought them both with all the passion and energy he had.

Moving to Alaska was a fresh start; no friends, no contacts, no past scores to settle. But with no enemy, there was no war, and he only had those who betrayed him to hate. There was a void, a massive void. A void quickly filled by Bob and Rosemary. All his life's conflict, resistance and struggle now centered on them, amplified by the misguided belief that all of this had started with his father anyway – his betrayal, his abandonment, his selfishness. They had set Rick on this path. All his angst, his propensity to not give a single inch and offer no surrender, his combative, resistive nature, all zeroed in their authority and rule over his life.

Oregon equalled independence. Alaska equalled stringent and stifling control. It only made him resent and resist them even more. The only thing he truly had was JROTC. He embraced and gave himself to everything it stood for, far more fervently than any other of the other cadets. It really wasn't a surprise though, everything he did, if it was on his terms, he did with passion, and the cadet program was no exception. That's how he met Kristy.

A little hellion, Kristy Braman was given the task of bringing Rick up to speed on the intricacies of the Drill Team. As her cadet, she was responsible for making sure Rick didn't look like an idiot, and for correcting him when he fucked up, and she loved every minute of it. She hassled him and he threw it right back in a fun and playful way. From the very beginning, they just got each other, there was something about her, that Rick identified with. He couldn't yet open up, but with Kristy, he felt at least a glimmer of hope that maybe someday he could.

But the turmoil inside kept brewing. To think that everything was going to change or be forgotten just because he was in a different state was pure craziness. Regardless of how well he integrated into the Drill Unit or made new friends, there was just too much of his old life missing. Strom and the boys. The nights on the street. There was just too much of who he was, and what he was, that remained hidden in his new life. No one had a clue who Ghost was. How do you tell your new friends that you used to rob houses for guns and drugs? How do you tell them about Jackie, Andrew or Creek? Or that you see angels and demons? You don't. All that shit stays stifled. But just because you don't talk about it doesn't mean it's not there or that it's not still burning a searing scar on your heart and in your psyche. And how do you cope? The only way you know how. You go with what's familiar. You slip back into old habits, unable to forge a truly new path because your feet are stuck and sinking in the quicksand of your past.

CHAPTER THIRTY-EIGHT

"Hey Watkinson," said the guard unlocking the steel prison cell door. "Your lawyer is here to see you."

Rick had been meeting with his lawyers Wally Tetlow and Randall Patterson quite a bit lately. The trial was coming up, and they were doing their best to try and get the facts straight, and formulate their understanding as to what happened, not only on the night of the murders, but to Rick himself. Rick hit the jackpot when Wally Tetlow was the public defender assigned to handle his case. A young graduate of the California Western School of Law, Wally believed in standing up for his clients' rights and treating them with dignity and respect. Rick had done a horrific thing, no doubt about that, but Wally was determined to show the court the underlying circumstances behind Rick's actions. Wally and his co-counsel Randall Patterson knew the task wasn't going to be easy but they had to give it a shot. He was just a kid. There had to be some explanation, some sort of mitigating factors.

"Hi Rick," said Wally motioning for him to sit down at the table. "How are you holding up?"

"I'm all right I guess."

"Okay good," said Wally. "I want to go over more of your time in Alaska and the months leading up to the murders. Is that okay? The more Randall and I know the better we're able to help you."

"Yeah, I get it."

"I think the last time we spoke you were talking about your time in the JROTC and how much that meant to you, but that you still felt out of place and missing your old life."

"Yeah," said Rick. "I loved JROTC. It was my life and it meant the world to me but I did miss my friends and my old life. I started sneaking out at night again, which was much harder than at home because even though my parent's headboard was the opposite of my window, the sound carried like a bitch through that wooden house. You could hear everything."

"And did you sneak out when your father was home?" said Wally.

"No way! I wasn't that stupid."

"So things were bad at home then?" said Wally.

"Well, as I got more involved in Drill and ROTC, I spent less and less time at home, which was fine with me. The less I had to be there, the better. And I started hanging around Kristy a lot."

"Kristy Braman?" said Randall.

"Yeah, Kristy Braman. She'd been instructed to help me in Drill when I first got there and we just sort of became really good friends. She was someone I could confide in."

"Did you tell her about you and your father fighting?" said Wally.

"Not on purpose, no. I didn't want anyone to know anything."

"So how did she find out then?" said Wally.

"I think was around February…things had been pretty rough at home with my Dad on my case about my grades and Rosemary on my case about everything else. I knew Rose didn't want me there…she made no secret about that. I mean, nothing big happened between October and February between Dad and I…just shoves and slaps, and some punches to the chest."

"Just shoves and slaps and punches?" said Wally with a raised brow. "And you didn't think that was wrong?"

"Well it just became a part of life you know. I'm sure I deserved a lot of it. I could be a mouthy little shit, and I knew Dad couldn't control his temper, so I just took it and never fought back."

"Why didn't you fight back?" said Wally.

"I don't know. I think deep down inside I did have some sort of love for him. I don't know...I was so used to just keeping my emotions in. And we were both used to it. Most of our arguments ended with some sort of physical contact. I think we both got used to it, and he got used to me not hitting him back. When I think back on it, it was weird you know? He felt justified slapping me around but if I hurt him back, he'd have flipped his lid. Still, with him, I always had trouble standing up for myself. I'm honestly not sure why because if anyone else had done those things to me, I would have beat the living shit out of them."

"So about the incident with Kristy?" said Wally.

"My Dad and I had a huge blow up. About my grades of course. The discussion inevitably turned into another hot argument and I got sick of it real fast. They just wouldn't listen to me. They never wanted to hear what I had to say, it was always just listen and do what they said. I never really felt apart of any of the conversations. Anyway, I stood up from the table and said 'Screw this, you win, goodnight'. I just didn't want to deal with it anymore. Of course, my dad thought I was just doing it to defy him so he screamed, 'Sit back down until you're told to leave!' 'Fuck you' I said. Then I kicked the wooden chair so hard it broke and left a nice sized scrape mark on the wall behind it. It was more like a hole in the drywall…and I can see why my dad was pissed. And man was he pissed. He flew into a rage and started screaming, 'You want to break this house, I'll break you!'"

"He said that?" said Wally. "I'll break you?"

"Yeah…then after he said it, his fists came flying through the air and started wailing on my back. I'd purposely turned away from him…he hit me so hard that he drove me across the downstairs and almost into the washing machine. I think he only hit me about seven or eight times…but it was so hard. He was out of control, like he couldn't even stop himself."

"Only seven or eight times?" said Wally. "Rick, you understand that even once was too many times right?"

"Well I did break the chair so…"

"That doesn't matter," said Randall.

"Anyways, the bruises he left weren't that bad…but I did have to sleep on my side that night…and the whole thing just got to me. I'd hardly slept and by the time I saw Kristy at the end of school the next day, I was feeling pretty worn out. She noticed right away that I was down and came over and gave me a hug. As soon as she touched the bruises on my back I winced and pushed her away. I didn't mean too but it hurt like hell. She asked me what was wrong and I told her nothing but she knew better. She pulled me off to the side away from the other kids and told me to lift up my shirt. At first, I said no, but she kept insisting so I turned around and lifted both shirts. Some other kids had come around, saw the bruises and asked me what happened, and I just told them that I fell out of a tree. Kristy knew right away that I was lying. I told her I'd talk to her after Drill practice."

"And did you?" said Wally.

"Yeah. I told her everything. Like about the divorce, the pain, and the fighting."

Of course, the 'everything' he told Kristy was not the truth. He didn't confide in her about the angels and the demons, or any specifics about the Team. She knew he had a best friend down south named Strom and that he'd had a pretty violent and dangerous street life, and did shit that could have either gotten them shot or thrown in prison, but never any specifics. Kristy came to know the real Rick more than anyone else would, both in Alaska and down south, and was the first to start calling him Ghost again. With both of them in relationships with other people at the time, (Rick was dating a girl named Jennifer at the time), there was no expectation of anything more, and they could just concentrate on being friends. Rick trusted her; he felt comfortable and safe.

"So Kristy knew about you and your father?" said Wally.

"Yeah, she used to beg me not to escalate or feed into any of the fights we had. She gave me one of her rings to wear, and she'd told me 'never get blood on it', meaning my dad's blood. She made me swear I wouldn't."

"So you and Kristy were close then?" Said Wally.

"Oh yeah," Rick answered. "Extremely close. I wasn't a crier but I cried on Kristy's shoulder…more than once actually."

"Can you tell us about that?" said Wally.

"I think it was back at the beginning of May. The arguing with my parents about grades and school performance really never did stop. The only thing I performed at with excellence was ROTC because that's where my heart was…but Dad and Rose didn't seem to care about that or how high I'd risen within the Corps in such a short time. Ask anybody, I was good. I was completely dedicated, and would do anything I had to for ROTC. I worked hard, I really did. Anyway, it was another tiring day after Drill practice and another discussion about my grades. They just never let up. We were having dinner and it was relatively calm until after dinner, and the kitchen had to be cleaned. Things just exploded between Dad and Rose. Dad didn't agree with one of her suggestions on what should be done, and they started yelling and screaming…slamming things around the house. I didn't want to listen, so I walked out the front door for some fresh air and a much needed cigarette. When I returned about a half an hour later, they were still going at it."

"They'd been fighting the whole time you were gone?" said Wally.

"Yes, it sure sounded like it. When I walked back into the room, they turned all of their anger on me. Started yelling at me about being a 'teenage punk'…"

"Who called you that?" said Wally.

"Rosemary. Those were her words. She was mad I left in the middle of a family discussion. Dad was caught in the middle. He sort of understood why I left…but not wanting to start a war with Rosemary, he took her side. Again. Like always. They were screaming at me, and I was so ready to just dodge out again. I was just so tired of it. I turned to walk down the stairs, and by this time, I just didn't even care enough to say anything. Neither of them even noticed until I was halfway down the stairs. Dad lost it and screamed at me."

"Do you remember what he said?" asked Randall.

"Oh yeah, he said, 'Don't you walk away from me when we're talking to you!' I just laughed and said, 'Look, I'm sick of this shit. If you're going to ground me, then do it. If not, get off my back and drop it.' He didn't like that response and charged at me on the stairs, calling me a 'little son of a bitch'. I knew he was gonna be pissed the minute I said it but I seriously was done listening to them fighting."

"Did he catch you on the stairs?" said Wally.

"I turned around just as he raised his backhand to me but this time." Rick paused and took a deep breath. "This time, I wasn't going to let him do shit. I reached up and blocked his shot. I was calm and deliberate. I had no intentions of going on the offensive, I was strictly in defensive mode. He looked surprised and sort of paused for a second, then came around with his other hand and hit me square in the chest."

"Jesus," said Randall.

"It was my turn to be surprised. He knocked the wind right out of me. I was two steps lower than him…still standing and trying not to suck air or cry. He pointed his finger and yelled, 'You don't ever retaliate against me, ever!' I just glared and said 'Fuck you'. It wasn't loud or anything, more just under my breath, but he heard it, and I thought for sure he was going to beat the living shit out of me…but instead he turned and stormed out the front door. Slammed it so hard that a painting on the wall almost fell. Rosemary took off after him, calling his name and running down the driveway. I just went to my room."

"Was that the end of it?" said Wally.

"He came into my room awhile later, still mad as hell, and he told me, 'You go to school tomorrow and start working on your grades! Is that understood?' I didn't answer him right away…I just sort of glared at him before I said yes. As he was walking out my door, he said, 'you'd better'. Then he slammed it like hell. I wasn't going to tell anyone about what happened but it was on my mind the whole day at school, and I kept counting down the hours before I'd have to go home and face him again. Kristy asked me if anything was wrong, and I just couldn't help it, I started crying. I'm not a person who cries, let me make that clear. I can handle a lot of shit…but that day, I just couldn't hold back, and I cried on her shoulder. It only happened a couple of times after that, that I cried on her shoulder I mean, usually I just cried laying on my bed or while I was playing my guitar."

"So the abuse really got to you then?" said Randall.

"Abuse?" said Rick. "I never saw it as abuse really. We fought and he smacked me around. I should have been able to take it and deal with it…but all of it together. Like when Dad wasn't home, Rosemary and I never talked about it, actually we hardly spoke at all. But when Dad was home, it was a constant battle zone. Either the three of us fighting about school and my grades or them fighting about money. It was constant."

"Besides the physical altercations," said Wally. "Was there ever any other sort of consequences?"

"Oh yeah," said Rick. "I'd get grounded, like they'd say, 'you can't go anywhere for a week period' but while they were out, I'd spend all day and night talking with my friends on the phone. Eventually they got hip to what I was doing and started taking the phone cord, but I just went out to Dad's cupboard of electronic gear in the garage and grabbed a new one. Rosemary found out, and just started taking the whole phone, receiver and everything. I didn't make things easy on them, I know. I borrowed the car keys while Rosemary was away, went down to the store and bought my own phone, which I then kept hidden in my room. Eventually they found that too. I took the car too. I made copies of the keys for myself and then used them for short trips into town. I still didn't have a phone, so I took a pair of my Dad's aviator headphones with the boom-mike, and then spliced the wires to another adapter to get voice and sound. I figured out how to trick our home computer into making phone calls, and then I could talk to my friends."

"Pretty smart kid," said Randall.

Rick smiled. "That was part of the problem. I always seemed to be one step ahead of them and it drove them crazy. But they didn't realize how independent I was, like how much I'd had to fend for myself, and be the man of the house after the divorce. I just did what I thought needed to be done. My grades were shit, I don't deny that, and both my parents and my teachers knew I could do better, and it just pissed them off that I didn't try and that I didn't care. I had my own goals, and I knew what they were, and that's all that mattered to me."

Rick tried to be as honest as he could with Wally and Randall, but there were so many things he couldn't tell them. They wouldn't understand all the spiritual stuff nor was he about to spill the beans on all the activities of the Team and jeopardize his brothers in any way. Just wasn't going to happen. While everything he told his lawyers was the absolute truth, it wasn't the complete truth. He wasn't even close to understanding the complete truth of his life himself, so how in the hell did he expect his lawyers to understand?

On the surface, it seemed like his time in Alaska had been great, and in many ways it had. He loved JROTC, and he met a bunch of great friends. There were even times when him and his Dad got along, and went running up Flattop together. If only it truly had been a fresh start. If only there hadn't been so many memories and hurt from the past. He just couldn't escape it, no matter how hard he tried. And God forbid he let anyone in, truly let them in.

Lori, a girl from JROTC had gotten close. They were both outsiders and formed an instant connection, and an unlikely duo. The two weeks they spent together as an 'item' were brief but intense. Lori wanted to know everything there was about Rick and she sensed right away that he was hiding so much. She wanted the key to unlock his hidden mystery. She read his dark, dreary poetry and listened to his songs, wondering what the words meant and what their significance was. A deep and passionate person, Lori was both obsessed and fascinated with them, and Rick in turn. Rick let her in as much as he could. Then he panicked. Got scared as hell. He couldn't let the relationship continue. So he walked into school and dumped her, like a real asshole. It was the only way he could do it. She never understood the real reason. Another secret. Lori had come so close to kicking in the door and forcing Rick to let her in, and he couldn't let that happen. He wasn't even ready to face all the emotional and spiritual pain and trauma, and he'd been through it, let alone face it with somebody else. He just couldn't do it. So, he pushed her away. He banished her from his life without any explanation, and in the coldest way possible, and she hated him for it. He had to do it. He had to protect his inner sanctum and preserve Ghost. He didn't know any other way to survive.

"And how did the school term end?" said Wally. "Did you pass?"

"Yeah, I ended up passing. Dad and Rosemary weren't thrilled with the final marks but I did it, I passed everything. If I didn't, then I wouldn't have been able to move on and stay with my ROTC friends. That was the main reason, the only reason I even gave a shit actually. It wasn't because of my Dad's harping on it. I didn't care what he said."

"And then it was summer and you didn't have to worry about school anymore," said Wally.

"Exactly. Summer took a lot of the burden off, being out of school. There was less pressure for sure."

The summer began innocently enough with Rick, Kristy, and their friend Matt deciding to climb Flattop. Rick had done it a dozen or so times by himself, and a few with his father, but never with friends. Being that Rick was technically responsible for others this climb, Rosemary lent him the family cell phone in case of emergency. He tucked it in his knapsack along side some snacks, drinks, and some other gear. While Flattop is steep in some areas, the trail is so well worn, one rarely has to actually climb or touch the rock with their hands. They took their time going up, and spent an hour or so at the top enjoying a warm but cloudy day.

"I love this view," said Rick. "I could spend all day up here. So peaceful." He picked up a small pebble and chucked it as far as he could. "Hey want to make the trip down a little more interesting?"

"How so," said Kristy.

"Well," said Rick. "We could go down the backside?"

"I'm in for that," said Matt.

"Me too," said Kristy.

"Perfect! Let's go!"

The backside of Flattop that faces Ptarmigan Peak is a hell of lot steeper and definitely something that had to be climbed. Starting with a small ravine cut into a sharp cliff, it slopes down into a boulder-strewn grade of about sixty degrees before levelling and hitting the treeline. They took their time finding the best route down, bracing themselves on rocks and ledges, taking chances but not being too crazy.

"Fuck!" said Rick looking in his backpack. "The phone is gone! Son of a bitch!"

"What? Where?" said Kristy.

"Who the hell knows," said Rick. "I'm dead. I'm so fucking dead. That phone was like my father's prized possession."

"We'll find it," said Kristy, knowing full well what the consequences might be if they didn't.

"You guys stay here," said Rick. "I'll back track and see if I can find it."

For forty-five minutes, Rick searched and searched, back-tracking to the point where he would have to start climbing again. Nothing. He couldn't image where it might have fallen out. Frustrated and a little panicked, he started back to join Kristy and Matt. In his typical reckless nature, he raced down the mountainside like he was part snow-leopard and part mountain goat, leaping and jumping. About halfway down, he caught something with his foot, tripped and lost his balance and rolled. Since this wasn't the first time he'd ever fallen or jumped off of something, he knew to tuck and shoulder roll. Relaxing his body, he went where gravity took him, shooting like an out of control car, especially the last twenty yards.

"Jesus," he said finally coming to a stop. A little dizzy, he was more concerned about the cell phone and the hell he was going to have to pay for losing it.

"Oh my God Rick, you're bleeding!" said Kristy.

Not knowing what the hell she was talking about, he followed her gaze down to his left arm to find a perfect thin-lined slice, starting at his thumb, skipping over his watch, and continuing up his arm.

"Aw fuck," he said. "Jesus Christ. This is the last thing I needed to have happen!"

He didn't let it show but he was concerned. The gash on his thumb was at least an inch and half wide, and deep enough to bleed like a bitch. It didn't look or feel pretty. Stitches for sure.

"Help me take my shirt off will you?" He wrapped the shirt around his arm to help stave off the bleeding.

"Here," said Kristy. "Put my flannel on. I'm not wearing it. But don't get any blood on it!"

They made it back to the parking lot without further incident but Rick was starting to get worried. Matt's parents weren't coming to pick them up for at least an hour, and the gash was right across where someone would slit their wrists. He needed to get it cleaned and see how badly it was bleeding, then he'd know if he needed to freak out or not.

"I can't wait for your parents Matt. I can make it back down to my place in about forty minutes. I have to go. This thing is bleeding like a son of a bitch."

"Well I'm not letting you walk back on your own!" said Kristy. "What if you pass out?"

"I'll be fine."

"No way," said Matt. "Kristy goes with you. I'll wait here for my parents. You guys go."

"Are you sure?" said Rick.

"Yeah, positive. Hurry up bro. Go take care of that."

Back at the house, Rick dug out all the gauze and medical supplies he could find. Rosemary was out until late evening and Bob was on a flight, so it was Kristy and him.

"I can't find the peroxide," said Rick.

"Well we need to clean it with something more than water. Where do your parents keep the alcohol?"

"No way. They'll kill me."

"I'll back you up Rick. This is important. We need to clean the wound."

"Fine. Top shelf in the far right kitchen cupboard."

Kristy grabbed a bottle of Smirnoff.

"You're out of your fucking mind if you think you're going to pour that over me."

"Oh shut up or I'm going to kick your ass!"

"Well give me a swig first then." He unwrapped his arm. "Okay, ready." The minute the alcohol hit he wanted to vomit. "Jesus fucking Christ!"

"Oh quit your bitching and acting like a girl," Kristy laughed as she dabbed and irrigated the wound as carefully as she could. "What do you think? Stitches?"

Once the wooziness left, Rick took a closer look. "I think I'll be okay if I just wrap it really tight. I don't really want to go to the hospital. I'd have to call Rosemary and she'll be pissed…I mean I still have to tell her about the phone. I don't want to push it."

When Rosemary came home later that evening, she didn't give a shit about his injury. Did she ask to see it or even suggest they go to the doctor to have it checked out? All she cared about was the phone. She just kept going on and on about trust and responsibility.

"Have fun explaining this to your father."

She sounded happy, like she was glad Rick lost the phone. Made her day, and proved that he was nothing but a worthless, unreliable prick. Rick vowed not to give her the satisfaction.

"You know what?" he said. "I'm either going to find the phone or buy a new one!"

"Yeah right," she laughed. "Good luck with that."

"Fucking bitch," thought Rick as he laid on his bed, his arm throbbing. "I'm going to find that god damned phone. I'll prove her wrong."

As soon as dawn broke, Rick was gone. Fueled with a healthy, hardy breakfast, and a glass of orange juice, he jogged up the trail to the parking lot, the whole time replaying yesterday's climb in hopes something would step out and jog his memory. When he reached Flattop, he mirrored everything they'd done the day before.

"I'm almost positive it didn't fall out on the way up," he thought. "We weren't in the back pack for anything."

Making his way to the top, he scoured every bit of the rock. Nothing. It had to have fallen out on the way down. He slowed to a snail's pace and kept his eyes peeled, combing every inch of their path on the way down the backside.

"Too bad the fucker wasn't bright yellow instead of grey and black just like the rocks. That'd make things a little easier."

About a third of the way down he found it, just lying on a boulder as if it was part of the landscape.

"Fuck you Rosemary!" he laughed. He gave it the once over, checking for damage. "Holy shit, I am one lucky dude! Not even a scratch!" The final test was to make a call.

"Hello?" said a sleepy voice.

"What's up sleepy-head?" said Rick. "You all warm and still tucked in?"

"Where the hell do you think I am dumbass?" said Kristy.

"The better question is, where do you think I am?"

"I have no clue."

"I'm on Flattop. I found the phone!"

"You're shitting me!"

"Nope…it was just sitting there."

"Unbelievable. I can't believe you climbed Flattop and with your arm and hand. What the hell Rick? It must be so sore. Are you crazy?"

"I think you know the answer to that question," he laughed. "And it doesn't hurt any more now that I found the phone."

"Well hang the damn thing up and get down the mountain will you? And be careful! No more injuries!"

"I will Kristy. Love you!"

"Love you too, dumbass."

Rick set the phone on the kitchen table. Rosemary glanced over but didn't say a word. Score one for the worthless, unreliable prick.

CHAPTER THIRTY-NINE

After their bonding experience on Flattop, Rick knew he had to make his true feelings known to Kristy. He loved her. He loved her more than he'd ever loved any girl. He couldn't imagine loving or wanting anyone the way he wanted Kristy, and all that mattered was that they quit denying the connection they had. He was ready to give himself to her, to completely open up, and let nothing stand in their way. He saw Kristy as his future wife, and the mother of his kids. She gave him a hope, a light, that he hadn't had since he was a young boy. He even bought a ring as a sign of his commitment. He could see himself living a long and happy life with her, with Ghost just a distant memory.

"Hey can I talk to you a minute?" he said pulling her into Angela's kitchen.

"My mom will be here soon, what's up?"

"I love you Kristy."

"I know you do Rick. I love you too."

"No Kristy. I mean I really love you. I want more."

He took a deep breath and laid it all on the table, leaving no room for any doubt as to how he felt. Everything that remained unspoken between them, he spoke, he brought to light. As her mom sat in the driveway waiting, he slid the ring on her finger.

"Will you be mine?" He looked deep into her eyes. "I can't tell you how much I want this to happen…how much I want you to be mine…and for us to be together as a couple. We belong together Kristy. You know we do."

He leaned in a gave her a long, soft, slow kiss. There was no taking it back now, it could never be just friendship again. He took her into his arms and they hugged, her crying on his shoulder.

"Asshole," she laughed hitting him on the shoulder, just as she'd done a hundred times before.

"Wait. I want you to have this too." He handed her a folded up piece of paper.

"What is it?"

"Just something I wrote out and wanted you to have, that's all." He'd given her the lyrics to White Heart's 'Gabriela',

All those empty streets I have wandered down
Restless nights and lonely dawns
Seems like forever I've looked for you

Now the dream that I've been waiting for has come true
The dream is you
Gabriela, angel of mercy
She comes to my night on wings full of light
Gabriela, my love and my friend
Come take my hand, may the dance never end
Gabriela...
Now I hear your voice sing inside of me
The missing song I could never be
I see you thru the mist of my grateful tears
Even in those lonely times when you're not here
Your face appears
You are so near
Gabriela, angel of mercy
She comes to my night on wings full of light
Gabriela, my love and my friend
Come take my hand, may the dance never end...
Oh Gabriela
If we were born to another time and place
Somehow my Lord would lead me to the love and grace
Of my Gabriela
Gabriela, angel of mercy
She comes to my night on wings full of light
Gabriela, my love and my friend
Come take my hand, may the dance never end
Gabriela...

He watched her get in the car. The moment over. He knew it was possibly the most important moment and move of his young life. He'd taken a chance, put himself and his emotions out there. He knew he'd never meet a girl like Kristy again, and he had no doubts that she could make all the pain, suffering, and loss worth it in his life. She only had to let herself fall and believe in them as much as he did; to tear down any of the walls that were left, and allow them to be all they were meant to be. That's all he wanted, and all he believed. Now he just had to wait and see if she believed it too.

He would know soon enough, the minute they saw each other again, he'd know instantly. He spent the night wrecked with anxiety and anticipation. He'd never wanted something so much in his life. This was his chance to finally dig himself out of the depths of his despair and move forward. It wasn't going to be easy, but with Kristy at his side, he knew he at least had a fighting chance. He saw her sitting, sullen and alone, on the hill as he rode his bike down to the school for softball practice. His heart sunk. He wanted to throw-up. He pulled up slowly, laying down his bike. She stood up and faced him, a lost sadness swimming in her eyes. She just stared at him, unable to find the courage or the words, before pulling him into a hug.

"I'm sorry," she said pulling away. She tucked something into his hand, a note folded around a small circular object, then turned and walked down the hill to join the rest of the softball team, trying to act like nothing was wrong. Except everything was wrong.

"What the fuck just happened?"

His already fragile world shattered like a glass ornament, a million broken pieces scattered on the grass. Rick had no doubts as to their closeness or the fierceness of their love. He'd never been as close to anyone in his life as he'd been to her, physically, mentally or emotionally. As intimate as lovers without being sexual, they were best friends who trusted each other and felt safe enough to let each other in. It was a no brainer. Yet, there he was standing there, holding the ring.

He couldn't even think of going to practice and just pretending nothing was wrong. Slinging his backpack over his shoulder, he pulled out a cigarette, trying to steady himself for the wave of emotions he knew was coming. Opening the note, he pulled the ring out first and just stood there staring at it. So much hope had been put on that ring, a new circle of life, a new beginning. Kristy did her best to explain.

"Try and try as hard as I might, I couldn't make myself fall. I pushed and pulled, pleaded and begged, yet my heart wouldn't let me."

Rick recognized the line as one from a song she always used to quote. He kept reading. She was scared. Scared they'd go too deep, that it would be too much, that it would take over and leave nothing left. Scared to trust and to give in. Scared. It all came down to fear. It wasn't that the love and passion weren't there. It wasn't that she didn't want it. She was scared of the consequences. She hadn't spurned their love because it wasn't powerful enough, she spurned it because it was too powerful. Cracks of anger split his soul as that familiar icy sensation filled his veins and made him numb.

"Motherfucker!" He wanted to scream at her. "I'm scared too but I love you too much to run from this, from us."

He sat in complete silence, lighting a second smoke, allowing her words and the moment to sink in. She had all night to think of and formulate an answer, and this was the best she could come up with. Cowardice.

"I'm not saying never…I'm just saying not now…"

Kristy just didn't understand. Rick's life was about now or never. There was no 'maybe later'. It was always about now or never. Missed opportunities usually resulted in catastrophes that made 'later' impossible.

"Everything I love gets robbed from me. Every fucking time! Why can't anything ever work out?"

And now Rick had been robbed of the one thing he almost never allowed himself to have – the light of hope. All because the girl that he loved so deeply was too afraid to give herself to him. She was too afraid of him. Rick played for keeps and she wasn't ready, or in his mind, she wasn't willing to even take the chance. He wasn't worth it. He wasn't worth the fight. He didn't mean enough to her to even try.

"You're a coward Kristy."

Cowardice would never be an acceptable answer to Rick, and the minute she handed him back that ring, no matter what happened in the future, it was too late. She'd lost his heart. He folded the ring back up in the note and tossed it in his backpack. He sat there for the longest time, watching her practice down on the softball diamond, and puffing on his cigarette.

"What now?"

Devastated and alone, not only had he lost the love of his life, but he'd also lost one of his best friends, his confidante. Forsaken again. There was no hope for happiness left in his heart. All the light, all the glimmer, all the hope for a new beginning had been snuffed out. Died. All that was left was Ghost. It wasn't even worth trying to be anything else.

"Fuck this, I'm outta here."

Rick hopped on his bike and headed home. When he got there, he went straight to his room, and hardly came out until the next morning. He didn't eat. He didn't sleep. He really just wanted to destroy the world, like his had been destroyed. He plugged in his electric guitar, making the strings wail like the pain in his heart. His head wouldn't stop spinning. He couldn't comprehend what was happening to him. Why she didn't love him enough to even try. Manic. Depression. Uncontrollable thoughts. He read and re-read the letter. A thousand times. Wondering. Why? He held the ring, twirling it in his fingers, hoping that somehow it would speak to him, give him the answers that he so desperately craved.

"Damn it! What is wrong with me? Am I really that much of a monster that people are that fucking afraid of me?"

All he wanted was to be loved. Loved in the way he loved others – with everything he had. He tried. He really did. He wanted to be free of the internal thunder. He thought he'd found a way, a slight crack that he could perhaps slip through. He was wrong. Why? He needed answers.

The next morning, after a solid breakfast, he was out the door. No pack, no water, no phone, not even pepper spray, just his boots, his shorts, and a flannel wrapped around his waist in case he got cold. For the third time in a week, he was headed back up into the mountains, but this time, he wasn't aiming for Flattop, that was too easy, not dangerous or powerful enough to give him the answers he needed. He was headed for Suicide Peak. He needed a challenge, he needed to know that he was worthy and capable beyond mankind's expectations. He needed to know that no matter what anyone thought of him, they couldn't compete with who or what he was.

He took the trail jogging, running up Flattop like an obstacle course. His blood pumping. Stepping off the backside of Flattop, he was still jogging, continuing along the ridgeline into unfamiliar territory. Keeping the pace, he ran all the way up the ridgeline parallel to Ptarmigan across the valley, leaping and skirting over cliffs and rocks. The threat of slipping and falling was real. The threat of a serious, life-threatening accident was real. No one would ever find him. He had no way to get help. No one even knew where he was. He didn't give a shit. He kept on pushing.

He attacked Suicide Peak with a vengeance, as if by simply getting to the very top, he would conquer the sleeping dragon in his heart. Without any proper gear, the climb was absolute madness. There were times he was on sheer rock faces, times he had to backtrack and find another way. Times he had to jump a precipice, and by pure will alone, not slip and fall. It was truly the greatest climb of his life. Standing at the top of Suicide peak, he watched a Lear jet fly below him on its approach to Anchorage. It rattled him. Made him realize just how high he was. He felt dizzy, a little off kilter.

"Jesus Rick," he thought. "What the fuck are you doing up here?"

Taking a deep breath, he refocused, calming his pulse and his head. The sun glinted off the plane, a moment of ultimate beauty that he'd never forget. It took him twelve hours of moving fast to ascend Suicide Peak, with no food or water. There were numerous times he considered sealing his fate, just purposely making a wrong step, and meeting a gruesome end. If he couldn't have what he wanted in life, then why continue to live it? In Kristy, he had found the one person he believed he could make it with. He believed and knew in his heart that if they were together long enough, he could eventually tell her everything; the demons, the death, the suffering, the loss. Ghost could finally find release.

Kristy had been the one person, the only person, he had wanted inside, and didn't fear – yet she feared him. As he stood at the top of the peak, he had a very real discussion with himself about the deepest mysteries of life, death, and love. Was she worth killing himself over? Was she even worth his love? Was it even worth loving someone this way and allowing them space in your head and heart? With his heart and his muscles aching, he always came back to the same conclusion.

"No one is going to break me. No man, no woman, not this fucking mountain. If I can do all the shit I've done, and survive all that I've survived, then it's not in me to be filled with weakness. It's everyone else and their inability to rise. Fuck them! Why should I be diminished by lesser beings? Why should I suffer or be broken due to their ineptness? Their lacking or their cowardice. Fuck them. If I can conquer all, then those who choose not to, are simply unworthy of my time and my love."

It all came down to one simple premise.

"If you're too scared to stand up and risk it all. Don't waste my time and don't get in my way."

From that moment on, his life was ruled by the will and the courage to strive. He had proven himself, and until someone could prove themselves to him, they were unworthy of his attention. Of course, all this was just another way to shut people out and keep his emotions tucked away. It would be a cold day in hell before he ever gave anyone the chance to get inside again, if inside even existed anymore.

On the way back down the mountain, he stumbled upon a small patch of yellow blanket flowers, growing an altitude where most other vegetation said the hell with it. He picked the largest flower, and carefully slid it into his wallet. Courage and hope. It would be his symbol. Nothing could ever break him. But also a hope that maybe one day, someone would be just as willing to fight for him as he was for them. Those flowers fought like hell to grow and exist amongst the rocks and boulders. If they could do it, so could he.

The climb down was even more treacherous than the ascent, and took him close to six hours. He'd left around five in the morning, and thought it'd be a feat if he returned before midnight. Luckily the sun doesn't really set in Alaska during the summer, so there was always a bit of light to guide his way down. The entire experience thrilled and exhilarated him, and no one or nothing could ever take the experience away from him. He knew he was going to catch hell when he got home, but he didn't care.

"I went up into the mountains. I just needed some time alone."

He never told Kristy or anyone else that he went all the way up Suicide Peak, it was none of their business, and besides, they would have thought he was crazy. He also never told anyone how close he was to breaking that day either. How he'd walked such a fine between life and death. It would have been so easy. But he didn't, he didn't break, and that's all that mattered. Kristy begged and pleaded with Rick to tell her where he'd been. He refused. She'd lost her right to know.

He wasn't sure where he'd picked up the old German pocket dictionary but he decided it'd be a good place to store his flower. He tucked it in the page right under the word 'gespenst', the German word for ghost, a moving and symbolic gesture of the day, and his life moving forward. His attitude changed. It was all about him. He became selfish. Until someone could prove to him that they were worthy of his time and attention, it would be 'Rick' first from then on. Fuck his parents, his friends, Kristy, God, and all the 'higher powers' of his life. Fuck the military if they weren't willing to take him. Until someone proved to him, that they could love and live as hard as he did, fuck them all.

A part of him still hoped that someone would be Kristy, that one day she'd choose not to be a coward. But until that day came along, or someone outshone her, the whole world could kiss his ass. Ghost retreated even further into himself, becoming even more remote, reckless, and sardonic. An insensitive, unaffected, asshole. People had proven to him that they were hollow, and until someone proved their substance, he just assumed it was lacking. His world became dark and disdainful. Isolated. Inaccessible. He doubted everyone and everything. Everything anyone did, no matter how innocent, had an ulterior motive. He trusted no one. He listened to no one. The walls were up, and they were as thick and deep as the hell that burned behind them. All he had left was himself. Fuck anyone who didn't like it. Nothing mattered anymore. Nothing.

****

Meeting with lawyers always drained the hell of out Rick. It killed him to have to recount what he did or even think about what he was going through leading up to that fateful night. He still couldn't even believe that it happened, that he actually shot his father and Rosemary. He wanted to die. If it hadn't been for Amanda and Brenda's support, or his own mother's desire to see him as a free man, he would have told his lawyers not to even take his case to trial. The legal shit overwhelmed and confused him. His desire to fight was nil. In his heart, he knew he deserved far worse than what the prosecutors were threatening. In his mind, he deserved to die, twice, if that was even possible; to suffer a horrible death, twice over for what he did. The most he would suffer by law would be one 198 years, and even then, to him, that wasn't enough.

He gave his lawyers the go ahead to prepare a defence, to prepare for trial. For them, he did it for all those that kept telling him to live, although he had no idea why they even cared, or how they could still love him. He couldn't stand to let them down again, so he'd at least try. He was resigned to dying in prison, that's all there was to it. Rick knew he'd broken his mother's heart, and knew that she was wrecked with guilt over what happened, and the part she played in his fall.

The state had already offered him a deal. Plead out to first degree murder in the death of Bob, get ninety-nine years solid, but then no time for the death of

Rosemary. Nothing. Zero. Like she was an after thought and of little importance.

"How can they even offer me that?" said Rick.

"Well, they're not sure whether the bullet you shot through the door was the one that killed her," said Randall. "If it was, then that would be second degree murder. The autopsy report isn't clear on the point."

"But I killed her. I did it!"

There was nothing Rick wanted more than to go back to that night and change everything. Stop himself from doing what he did. Try to understand what was in his head and in his heart. He was certain he wasn't himself and he wasn't in control. None of it made sense. Something took over, a primal rage, his subconscious. Whatever it was, he wished he could go back and take it all back. And not just because he had gotten caught, but because it never should have happened. His father didn't deserve to die. Rosemary didn't deserve to die, especially Rosemary. Sure, they'd had their trials but she went against her original impulse, let Rick in, and gave him a chance. It wasn't a perfect relationship or situation to say the least, but they could have made it work. He wondered what her family would think about the state's offer. 'Yeah, sorry, her life wasn't worth any punishment'. It was bullshit. It was all bullshit.

"So? What do you think? Do you want to take the deal?"

"Absolutely not," said Rick. "I won't do it."

"That's a smart, bold move Rick," said Randall. I think we can get you better. You'd serve 33 of those 99 years for sure, but I think once they hear our case at trial, and hear the mitigating factors, we can get you better."

Rick didn't care. He didn't turn down the deal in hopes he'd get less time, he turned it down because he couldn't stomach not doing any time for killing Rosemary. In his mind, he deserved to do more time for killing her, than he did his own father. Bob was the one who had betrayed his family, he deserved a bit of the hate Rick harboured, but Rosemary didn't deserve any of it. She had simply come into his life and done the best she could to deal with the fallout. She was an innocent bystander to the war, and the ultimate victim in Rick and Bob's inability to make peace. If he could, Rick would get down on his hands and knees and beg for her forgiveness. The guilt was almost more than he could take.

As the pre-trial months passed, he found solace in books, especially those on redemption and Eastern philosophy. No matter what happened, he had a lot of time ahead of him to reflect upon what he'd done, and the person he'd become. He never wanted to be Ghost again. He didn't want to be lost or dead inside anymore. He didn't want demons, including his own, to be able to laugh and sneer at his downfall, and their unfettered ability to wreak havoc on his life. Balance. He strove for some semblance of balance, that would at least allow him to move forward, to gain perspective, and to ultimately change his life. His mind was in shambles, tortured, guilt-ridden, full of shame and regret, the depression unwavering. He wanted peace. He craved peace. He wanted to be able to live with himself and not feel like he'd been defeated in his life. He finally made the decision that he did want to live, he wanted to make his loved ones proud, and the only way to do that was to take the power back and achieve some kind of equilibrium.

Finding this balance led him to question, 'Why?' Why did his father divorce his mother? Why had he been given his Gift? Why did he hate God so much? Why had he given his father a bullet, when he should have given him a hug? Why was he even alive, when clearly he deserved to die? Stripping everything away, everything down to the core, these were some of the fundamental questions he had to begin to try and least understand. As much as he liked to think he was a rebel, and that no one controlled him, the answers to these questions and the influence they had upon his life were really what made him the person that he was. This lesson was hard for him to stomach. He'd spent his entire adolescence shunning all forms of control over his life, adamant that he would control his own destiny. He never understood until now that he was just a by-product of these events and outside forces.

"Live your life instead of your life living you."

Rick had some very serious lessons to learn, and was in for a very serious reality check. Just when he'd thought he'd had it all figured out, he had to cut through his own bullshit and admit that he didn't know it all. He had to challenge all of his most foundational beliefs and conclusions from the very beginning, and seek out the actual truth of his life. The task was daunting. But if he was ever going to move forward, he had to start somewhere, and for him, that began with the question why, and to ask that question with a clear head and no preconceived notions.

Each day he strived for understanding and answers. He began to meditate with vigour, starting at five minutes, and working his way up to a full hour. For a former child of the night, mornings became his favorite time of the day, when the prison was its closet to absolute quiet. In his meditation, he had found his mind to be an absolute tangled mess of anger, guilt, betrayal, and horror. The hatred burned in him like a furnace. In his life, he had come to conclusions, erected beliefs, all of which fueled the fire. The ghosts within him haunted the Ghost he became, the demons taunting him, the images of all he had lost, flashing their constant presence. All he could do was to let go of the emotions and focus on the questions, letting the answers come.

The divorce? Looking back on it, it was a simple conclusion. Bob was no longer happy. He was no longer in love with Brenda. If he was, then he would have never left. Seven years after the fact, Rick could finally see how different his parents were. Bob, so athletic, was always on the move, seeking better, faster, evolving, finding adventure and exploring life and the very limits of human capabilities. Brenda, the religious zealot, content to sit at home, pray, walk with the Lord. Her quest in life was wholly spiritual, while Bob's was physical and technological. They had drifted apart, especially when it came to religion, they began to fight. Rick figured the only reason he stayed around as long as he did was because of him and Jimmy. Was he an adulterer? Probably. But did he deserve to die for it? No. Rick knew better than anyone that everyone sins and fucks up once and awhile. Did him divorcing Brenda mean that he didn't love his kids?

"No."

The realization blew Rick's mind wide open. Sure Bob had handled the divorce like shit. His fighting against paying child support just to make Brenda miserable, and trying to manipulate the kids into going with him was wrong. But Bob was human, prone to mistakes and short-sightedness, not the perfect archetype that Rick had needed him to be.

"How many times could he have just turned his back and decided we weren't worth the trouble? He had money, he could have lived anywhere in the world. There were so many fights, and so many hardships. Why didn't he just leave and cut us kids out of his life? He couldn't. He loved us. He loved me. That's why he came down to Oregon. To save me from myself. That's why he risked his marriage to Rosemary, and brought so much bullshit and strife under his own roof…to make sure I didn't fuck up my future. Jesus Christ. Dad."

Rick then realized, in his cold solitary cell, how much he truly loved his father. Through all the misery and betrayal, he loved him. If he didn't then he wouldn't have cared that he left. He wouldn't have cared when his father kicked him out that night. Rick loved his father, and desperately needed for his father to love him back.

"What a fucked up selfish reason to take his life. He wouldn't love me the way I needed him to, and I shot him for it. Jesus. What have I done?"

For seven years, Rick 'had' to believe that his father was a traitor and a piece of shit. He 'had' to hate him and deaden himself inside to deal with the pain of his loss. He 'had' to believe that his father only wanted control and to exert his authority over Rick because he was his father, and that was his right, to mould him the way he thought he should be.

"That wasn't it," thought Rick. "Jesus Christ, that wasn't it at all. Dad made mistakes but he never turned his back on me, not once. He just wanted to find happiness in his life. He deserved that. And I killed him for it. Jesus Christ, I killed him for being human…and for not loving me the way I selfishly needed him to love me. Now he's gone…and I'm the reason. You stupid, selfish, fucking asshole."

Rick would have to learn to live with that realization. But at least his mind had finally reached that point of understanding. The mind is really just a cage that we fill with all these different beliefs and so called truths. If we're not willing to open the cage every once and awhile, then we become locked in the safety of that narrow-minded thinking. We have to make the world make sense. We have to understand things, especially when they hurt us or cause us loss. But often our understanding, our conclusions, and the assumptions we create to try and make sense of things, are so far from reality, that we lose total sight of reality itself. For many different and wickedly complicated reasons, Rick lost sight of reality, he failed to unlock the cage until it was too late. Now he was faced with living in a cage of another sort for the rest of his life.

CHAPTER FORTY

With summer holidays in full swing, Jimmy had flown up from Oregon for a few weeks.

"When are Dad and Rosemary coming home?" said Jimmy.

"Not until late. They're gone all day."

"What do you want to do then?"

"Well I'm sure as hell not going to sit around here all day and do nothing. I'm going out. Natalie just called and a bunch of people want to get together but they don't have a ride."

"Well you don't have a ride either Rick?"

Rick laughed. "Don't be silly Jimmy. I am the ride."

"Rick no! Dad will kill you if he finds out."

"I guess I'll take my chances."

"Rick seriously. Please don't do it!"

"See ya Jimmy."

Rick reached under the bed and grabbed the secret set of keys he'd had made for Rosemary's Corsica.

"What if you get caught dumbass?" said Natalie piling into the car with three other friends.

"I don't plan on getting caught."

Rick spent the afternoon and early evening ripping around Anchorage with his friends. Everything was fine until it started to rain. No big deal. Rick would just drop his friends off a little earlier, then head back home in time to dry the car. Having a blast, Rick decided to show off a little, and crashed a twenty-foot puddle just in front of the roller-skating rink.

"You know that was full of mud right?" said Natalie laughing.

"That's why I did it!" said Rick.

"You know the car is going to be dripping with mud right?"

"I'll get it cleaned up, don't you worry."

"Oh I'm not worried…about me"

Rick knew he had beaten his parents home. All the upstairs lights were off, just the way he told Jimmy to leave them. Pulling the car into the garage, he stopped slowly so he wouldn't smear any mud on the pavement.

"Jesus, this is worse than I thought." He grabbed a towel and dried off the still dripping car as best as he could. "Fuck, look at the floor!" He took the broom and started sweeping all of the mud and water around, in hopes that it would dry faster. Forty-five minutes later and the undercarriage was still a mess. He was fucked. Midnight on the dot, he saw the lights of the Suburban.

"Oh shit." Grabbing his trench coat, he headed out the back, upstairs door. Jimmy didn't say a word, and he certainly didn't try and stop him. By the time he got to the side of the house, the Suburban was in the garage. Rick knew he had to disappear, and fast. Running down the driveway was out, so he quietly slipped into the thick brush covering the north side of the property. He'd be safe there. Halfway down to the road he heard the screaming inside the house, and then the slam of the front door.

"RICK! GET YOUR ASS BACK HERE RIGHT NOW!"

Bob was pissed. Knowing full well that Rick wasn't just going to saunter home, Bob ran out into the rain and down the driveway. Jimmy had told him that Rick couldn't have gotten very far, but with the rain and the darkness, Bob couldn't see a fucking thing.

"JESUS CHRIST RICK!"

Rick just kept on moving. Headlights met him as he hit the bottom of Upper O'Malley. Like a trained soldier, he dropped to the ground, still as the darkness. A taxi cab pulled up to the stop sign, paused, then turned and sped off. Just as he was about to lift his head, a second set of lights, dawned his silhouette. Bob and Jimmy stopped in the Suburban, a hair's breath away from Rick's hiding spot. Not a breath, not a whisper. Bob took his foot off the break and sped away. After watching them go, Rick trekked through the short cut, and headed to Natalie's place.

"Good, her light's still on." Rick climbed up to the second storey deck, and waved to get her attention. She almost dropped the phone, when she saw Rick standing there.

"You got caught didn't you?" she said.

"Well, let's just say, my Dad knows I had the car. He hasn't actually caught me yet." The two talked for awhile, then Rick heard the doorbell ring. He already knew who it was.

"Natalie! The door is for you!" said her father.

"Who is it?" she answered sticking her head outside the bedroom door.

"Bob Watkinson. He wants to know if you've seen his son Rick?"

Natalie went back to the bedroom window. "Get the hell out of here Rick, your Dad's at the front door."

With a single leap, Rick was on the ground running. For the next few hours, he ducked in and out of places, making his way down to the 7-11 where he bought some Mountain Dew and cigarettes. Knowing his father wouldn't come this far into town to search for him, Rick took to the streets and made his way to the

Diamond Center Shopping Mall. Closed for the day, but that didn't stop Rick from squeezing through a ventilation grate near the storage docks. Soaked to the bone, he needed to dry out. Wary of security guards that might be roaming, Rick cautiously made his way around the mall, finding himself a pair of shades, some coffee, and some pastries. Turns out, there were no security guards and he had free roam of the place until around seven in the morning. He didn't dare try to break into any stores, especially the ones that were shuttered, knowing full well that they were protected by alarms. Still, there were enough places to go and hide if need be.

For three days, Rick basically lived at the Diamond Center. Once and a while, he'd get picked up to go to a friend's house or to a party. It felt good to be back on the streets and have full control of his life, but Anchorage was no Oregon, and the street scene wasn't the same, and certainly didn't have the same opportunities for long-term living. Still, he had no reason to go back home, and if he was going to make it Alaska, then summertime was the best time to get to know the scene and get established. He drained his bank account of the few hundred bucks he had stashed, and treated his friends to some shit.

"You know," said Katie. "You really should call Kristy and let her know what's going on. I'm sure she's worried about you."

"I'm sure she doesn't give a shit Katie."

"Really Rick? Of course she does. Just call her. I know you miss her and want to talk to her. Quit playing games and just call her."

Rick tried to change the subject but Katie kept at him.

"Jesus, fine! I'll call her!"

Leaving Katie where she was, Rick found a pay phone and dialed the familiar number.

"Hey Kristy, it's me."

"Are you alright? I heard things haven't been going so well."

"Well I'm not sure what you've heard but I'm not living at home anymore. I've been staying at the Diamond Center."

"As in the shopping mall?"

"Yeah."

"You're an idiot. I'm coming over."

Kristy had her Mom drop her off at the Diamond Center, and the three of them, Kristy, Katie, and Rick, sat upstairs drinking coffee and chatting. The girls were fascinated at how Rick had first been able to break into the shopping mall, and second, that he was actually surviving.

"Are you even eating? Sleeping?" said Kristy. Rick could tell she was scared for him.

"Sure, I eat enough, and I really don't need that much sleep. I never have.

Just give me some coffee and cigarettes and I'm good."

The look on Kristy's face told him she wasn't buying any of it. She knew some of his history, and she knew it was only a matter of time before he started carrying again, and getting into trouble. He was going to run out of money at some point, and then what was he going to do? Rick saw her concern, and it made him angry. What gave her the right to even care? Why show him any love or concern for him after basically spitting in his face? Just sitting close to her was killing Rick. She was all he wanted, and all he couldn't have.

"Let's go to a movie or something," Kristy said breaking the silence. "I'll call my Mom, she'll pick us up and take us."

In the car, Kristy filled her mom in on what happened, half asking if Rick could stay with them for a while, just so he had somewhere safe to go. Rick could sense the hesitation in Kristy's mom, Nora, but not because she didn't want to help Rick, but because she knew the trouble that might come from harbouring a runaway.

"Let me think about it okay?" said Nora. "I'll let you know when I pick you up from the movie."

Rick paid for the three of them to see "Braveheart" and Rick knew by the end of the movie what he needed to do. The true love of William Wallace is killed, and after everything that happens, he loses her anyway.

"Why the fuck does it even matter?" thought Rick. "Those of us who are damned always lose what we really want, so is it even worth trying? When you literally feel like the universe is taking everything away from you, everything you love, is it even safe to love anymore?" He answered his own question with a resounding no. "Why even bother trying to go home. There's no love there. I'd rather live on the streets and have to beg and steal, then to live with them under the false pretence of love. Fuck that. I'm going back to running rogue. You always lose love eventually anyway, so what's the point."

After the movie, Rick had little hope for any sort of reconciliation with his parents, and he didn't even know if he'd even see Kristy again. His thoughts spiraled. Maybe he'd find his way to Oregon, maybe he'd get lost in Alaska. He didn't know how, but he knew that somehow he was going to make it, he'd find someway to survive until he could join the Navy and live his dream.

"I think I have the answer," said Nora as they all piled into the car. "There's a place called Covenant House. It's a small non-profit place here in Anchorage that deals specifically with runaways and homeless kids."

"Thanks, but no thanks Nora," said Rick completely tossing the idea into the no fucking way pile. In all his time out on the streets, Rick had never stayed in a shelter, and he wasn't about to start. He could survive on his own just fine, and a shelter meant paperwork and answering questions, neither of which he was very fond of.

"Rick please!" begged Kristy. "At least give it a try. You might like it, and at least you would get to sleep in a bed, and not a stairwell!"

"I'm fine Kristy. Trust me, I've slept in worse."

"But there will be other kids there as well…"

"She had a point," thought Rick. "What a perfect way to get to know the street scene."

Covenant House would be full of runaways, and kids that knew a lot more about the scene than Rick did at the moment. It would be perfect. He would please Nora and Kristy, but more importantly, he'd be able to do some legwork and buy some time to figure out exactly what he was going to do. Covenant House wasn't jail, and he could leave whenever he wanted, so he figured why not? More than anything, it was a strategic move that would leave him downtown, and in the mix, just where he liked to be.

"Okay, I'll go," said Rick.

"Thank you!" said Kristy sounding very relieved.

Nora drove to Covenant House and Kristy walked Rick inside. As they started the intake paperwork, she gave him a hug.

"If you need anything, ever, just call."

Rick nodded.

"Okay Rick," said the intake counselor. "Did something happen at home? Is there a reason you can't go home?"

"My dad and I got in a lot of fights, and I'm not living there anymore."

"What kind of fights? Did he hit you?"

"Just fights. Sometimes it got a little physical yeah…"

"Have you ever talked to the police about these fights?"

"Absolutely not."

"Would you be willing to talk to the police Rick?"

"Absolutely not."

"Look Rick, if you file a report with the police, then things are on record, and we can protect you. Then you can stay with us."

"I'm not talking to the police," said Rick. "If I have to leave, then I guess I have to leave."

The last thing Rick was ever going to do was to be a snitch, especially against his own family. He didn't need their protection, and the first rule of the streets was never talk to the cops, no matter what.

"We're not saying you can't stay Rick, at least for a little while. We'll give you what is called a limited Visa, which means that you can stay as long as we're not pressed to fill the bed. Now, because you won't file a police report, it also means that your parents can show up anytime and demand custody of you, and unfortunately, there's nothing we can do to stop it."

"I understand," said Rick.

He'd have to work quickly, meet some other kids and then get set-up on his own. He had no doubts that his Dad would eventually come looking for him. The first thing Rick realized was that these Alaskan kids were nothing like the kids from the lower 48. They might have been shit disturbers but packing heat and doing real shit was more of a fairy tale, then their reality. The second thing was, that for six months of the year, there was no street life at all. Nobody was stupid enough to try and brave the Alaskan winter. All Rick had to do was get enough money, and find a place to live. Piece of cake for a kid with his street chops. All he needed was some time. Time he wasn't going to get.

"I'm sorry Rick," said the intake counselor. "Your parents came in. They're picking you up Friday."

Rick pleaded his case. She wouldn't budge. There was no way he'd be able to find a job and get an apartment before Friday. He was fucked, he'd have to go back to Doggie Ave.

"Things will change Rick," said Bob at the Wednesday meeting. Rick had no choice but to believe him, and if that was the case, he was willing to give it another try. He should have known better.

"Hi Rick, how are you?" said Rosemary smiling as he climbed into the back seat. The exaggeration of her happiness was not hidden.

"Rick, son, so glad you're coming home," chimed Bob. "Everything is going to be okay and we're going to be just one big happy family."

"Yes!" said Rosemary. "Just one big happy family!"

Jimmy just looked at Rick. Rick said nothing. The entire ride home, the conversation was nothing but sunshine and rainbows. Rick wanted to puke, it was all so fake and full of shit, just like always. The charade lasted until the car pulled into the garage.

"What's your problem?" said Rosemary turning around to stare at Rick. "Everyone's in a good mood but you. Why are you just sitting there looking mad?"

"Rose now come on," said Bob tying to keep the happy vibe alive. "Let's just keep things calm and light here."

"No," she answered. "I want to know why he's acting like a spoiled brat. We're doing everything we can to make this work, and he's not even trying! Why are you in such a bad mood?"

"Can't this wait until we at least get inside?" said Rick.

"No, I don't want you taking one step into this house until you have an attitude adjustment!"

Rick hated the term "attitude adjustment" and was just about to lay into

Rosemary when Bob intervened.

"Just go inside Rick. Jimmy you too."

"My pleasure," Rick replied. "Anything to get out of this car."

Rick threw his bag on the floor and flopped on his bed. It did feel good to be back in his room again. The door opened.

"We're going for a walk," said Bob.

Father and son trudged up the block of houses to the Chugach Trail heading up towards Flattop; the conversation light and cordial. About half way up, Bob changed his tone.

"So why did you come back?"

"Because you said things would change, and if they do, then living here wouldn't be so bad."

"Well you could have done better in the car. Rosemary didn't appreciate that."

Rick's blood began to boil, and he had to hold his tongue from saying something that probably would have gotten him a punch.

"I don't care," he answered. "I'm sick of playing games, and I'm sick of living here, and one of those things is going to stop."

"What games?" Bob snapped.

"Just all the shit you guys pull. The being fake, the everything."

Five minutes later, the quiet conversation had exploded into a full-fledged screaming match. The more Rick talked about the problems, the more enraged Bob became.

"Well why do you have to be such a hard-little teenage punk about this!"

Rick lost it. "Because my stupid fucking snob ass parents only listen when I'm being a hard-little teenage punk because they're either deaf or fucking stupid!"

Bob jolted towards Rick. His lips quivering. "You don't talk about us like that, you ungrateful sonofabitch!" Without hesitation, Rick readied himself into a defensive stance. Bob looked with shock.

"You NEVER go against me!" he said coming at Rick, and grabbing him by both shoulders.

Anyone else, Rick would have had on the ground in two seconds, but Bob was still his father, and he just couldn't bring himself to hurt him. Bob drove him back across the trail with such force that Rick fell backward onto the ground. Bob was on him in an instant, his fist raised and aimed at his oldest son's face.

"I should break you in half right here and leave you."

Rick just looked straight into his father's burning, raging eyes, and said nothing. Bob wanted him to react, to say or do something, anything to justify, landing the punch. Rick wasn't giving an inch, and continued to be calm and cool, the complete opposite of his father, which annoyed the fuck out of Bob. Furious, he shoved himself off Rick, just as two hikers approached,

"Is everything okay here?" said the man.

"Yes, everything's fine," said Bob wiping his brow, and trying desperately to calm his breath.

"Are you alright?" said the female hiker, ignoring Bob and looking directly at Rick.

Rick wanted to tell her no, and suggest that they all kick the shit out of his father, but simply answered, "Yeah, everything's fine."

As soon as they left, Rick started back down the trail towards the house. Bob just stood there and watched him go. Rick went straight to his room, grabbed his fifty-pound hiking bag, and started tossing his shit inside. Turning the stereo up, he sat and waited, unsure of where to go, or what to do. After about an hour, Bob knocked on the door and walked in.

"Tell me if you're going to leave."

Rick nodded yes, then watched his father walk out of the room. That night, shortly after midnight, Rick put on his black trench coat, slipped through the window, then slung the hiking pack on his shoulders, picked up his guitar, and left, walking the same route he did exactly one week earlier. When he got all the way down to the 7-11, he called a cab. Only eight hours after he'd walked out the doors to go home, Rick walked right back into Covenant House.

"Rick? What are you doing back here so soon?" said the intake counsellor.

"I told you that going home wasn't a good idea, and well it wasn't."

They talked throughout the intake process, and the counsellor wanted to know why Rick was back. Rick relayed the events of the past few hours, but left out much of the detail, at least enough so that the police wouldn't be called. If the police were called, Rick knew he'd have to face his father again, and that was something he just wasn't going to do. Covenant House was adamant that he reported the incident to the police, and when he refused, they said he could stay the night, but had to leave in the morning.

Rick tried to sleep, but his tossing and turning mind, kept his subconscious from relaxing. If he couldn't stay at Covenant House, then where else could he go? Friends would eventually kick him out, Nora had already basically said no, and could he really impose himself on Top or Gunner, and just show up at their place? He just had to last until his 18th birthday. Surely he could do that. Besides, as much as he hated to admit it, he was tired of living on the streets. Alaska certainly wasn't McMinnville, and winter was always on the horizon.

He made up his mind. He would go back home, face it, and win, or spend eternity in hell. Those were the options he gave himself. He would go back and make things right. He would fix his family, just like he fixed things for everyone else. Even if he had to argue until he couldn't argue anymore, he would try and heal the enormous wounds. He could do it. He had to do it. He really didn't have any other options.

Rick hopped on the bus back to his favorite 7-11 store, bought a Mountain Dew, then began the long trek up Hillside towards home. About three hours into his walk, just as he was hitting Upper O'Malley, a car pulled up beside him and stopped. He was surprised as hell when Rosemary opened the passenger door from the inside.

"Did you want a ride?" This time her cheerful tone was real and as genuine as Rick had ever heard it.

"Sure, that'd be great."

Rick threw his pack in the backseat and got into the seat beside Rosemary. Immediately, she leaned across the seat and gave him a huge hug.

"I'm so glad that you're okay."

Rick had no idea what to do or say. He and Rosemary had never shown any sort of physical affection towards each other in the five years they'd known one another. This was definitely not her style. Was she truly glad that he was okay? Or was she glad because he came home, then it wouldn't reflect poorly on them anymore? Rick mulled this over. But she did seem genuine in her actions, like she truly didn't hate him, that she really did give a fuck. He wasn't used to that – not from the person he generally associated with the definition of being fake. And he hated fake.

When Rosemary backed away from the hug, Rick thought she looked as though she was about to cry. Not fake tears, but real ones. Genuine ones. Maybe she finally realized that Rick wasn't bluffing. Maybe it finally hit her that Rick wasn't being just some teenage punk that was purposely trying to piss them off, but that he truly was a serious, real and headstrong person, very similar to the man she fell in love with and married. Rick wasn't a child, and in many ways, he was way more experienced and mature than some adults. Rosemary's attitude towards Rick changed that day. They still fought and argued but it was more as equals, and always less severe.

With Bob away for work, Rick and Rosemary talked for hours that night, and even enjoyed their first real social dinner together. The 'you'll do as I say' tone softened to more of a 'what do we need to do to get along'. Cooperation replaced demands. Rosemary had never been allowed to discipline or be a real parent to Rick. He was 'Bob's son' and Bob reserved all rights to parent and discipline his son the way he saw fit. Except Bob was gone two-thirds of the time, leaving Rosemary to deal with the fallout and consequences. Rick and Rose had to decide how they were going to live in Bob's absences. And left to their own devices, they were actually quite successful, and even managed to have some adult conversations, and disagreements that didn't blow the stack off the roof.

"I was actually just coming back from dropping Matt and Kristy off when I saw you," said Rosemary.

"Matt and Kristy were here?"

"Yes. I wanted to talk to them. I needed to talk to them to try and find out what was going on with you or if they had any idea where you were before you came home the first time."

"And what did they say?"

"They told me you'd been living on the streets, and in fact, they think you're still there now. They don't know you've come home. You should probably let them know. I can drive you down."

Rick walked up and knocked on Kristy's door. The minute she saw him, she ran into his arms, embracing his wiry frame.

"How did you get here?" said Kristy.

"My step-mom dropped me off. She'll be back in a bit to pick me up."

Rick told Kristy what had happened, the walk on the trail, his dad and the fist, and the hikers.

"They wouldn't let me stay at Covie unless I filed a police report, and that sure as hell wasn't going to happen. I'm not ratting on my father no way."

"I get it," said Kristy. "But still…Anyways, I'm glad you're safe." She gave him a hug. "And I'm glad you're back home."

They talked until Rosemary pulled up in the lane. Kristy gave Rick another hug and a peck on the cheek. Rick held back the 'I love you' that was burning in his heart. As he watched her walk back into the house, he kept kicking himself for always holding back his feelings.

With Bob still away, the next week was the best week that Rick ever had in Alaska. He and Rosemary spent the week going out for coffee, renting movies, talking, and just getting to know each other. She even let him move out of the house and live in the trailer for the summer.

"You can have your own space, provided that you be respectful with the noise. We do have neighbours, and the trailer isn't by any means soundproof."

"Deal," said Rick. "Thank you."

For now, there was a truce. And for now, that's all Rick cared about. Peace and quiet. He had some space, was basically free to do as he pleased, within reason, and the fights and arguing were kept to a minimum. When Bob came home from his trip, he followed Rosemary's lead. Peace would be nice for him too. But there was always one thing that bothered Rick, especially through this calm. They never really dealt with their issues. They never really brought everything out into the open and laid it all on the table to be dealt with. Just because no one talked about it anymore, didn't mean that they didn't exist. It just meant that they were left to fester and stew, not a good combination in an already tumultuous soul.

CHAPTER FORTY-ONE

The truce didn't last near enough. A fight about answering a phone call from Kristy during dinner, and all the shit was once more flying. He had to answer it. Kristy needed him. She and her mother were in a bad place, and Kristy needed his support. There was never a question of being there for the girl that he loved. The day after the phone call and the fight, Rick was back on a flight to Oregon to spend some time at his Mom's. This was his chance to escape Alaska forever, but he knew in his heart that he'd be back. He'd be back because that's where his family lived. Not Bob and Rosemary. Kristy, Matt, Natalie, and all the gang from ROTC, they were his family now. They were all he really cared about.

What happened was a complete dick move, and Rick knew it. Kristy and he had been talking on the phone almost every night, just to keep up, and to check in on each other and make sure things were okay. About a week into the vacation, he told her he was going out with the boys for some fun.

"The same guys you used to hang around with?" said Kristy.

"Yeah."

"And what are you going to do? The same shit that you used to do?"

"Maybe."

"I'm not cool with that Rick. I don't want you to go out with them."

"And why would that be?"

"Because I don't want something happening to you and I don't want to have to worry all night about you!" Her concern was genuine, but Rick was enjoying being an asshole.

"That sounds like a personal problem, don't it?" he said.

"Then I guess we're not talking anymore, are we?" she answered.

"If that's the way you've got to play it. I don't see how that's really necessary."

"Rick please. I'm not going to spend the rest of my summer worrying about you. If you're going to go out with them, and put yourself at risk, then I don't want to know about it, and I don't want to talk."

Rick called her bluff. "Then don't. But I'm going to do what I'm going to do."

"Then maybe I'll see you at school."

"Yeah, maybe," said Rick.

"Bye."

She hung up before Rick could even reply. He wasn't really sure what possessed him to be such a jerk. Yes, the "Team" was getting back together for a reunion, but it was only to hang out and have some fun, nothing serious. He could have just told her that. Would have been simple. But he didn't want to. He wanted her to worry. He wanted her to suffer a bit. She had turned him down, and now she was trying to dictate what he could and couldn't do. That just wasn't going to happen. Maybe if she'd been his girlfriend, but she wasn't, so she had no right.

Once she hung up the phone, Rick knew it was a done deal. Kristy wasn't the type to go back on something she said. So because he felt vindictive, and decided to be a jerk, he lost the one person he could really talk to, the one person who really tried to understand. All the things he would have normally vented to her about, he now kept bottled up, simmering and brooding with everything else. His own self-sabotage. She was the only one who even knew he had feelings, let alone what they were. He felt the loss deeply. He was in love with her, completely and utterly in love with her, and now he'd basically just told her to screw off and mind her own business. Rick needed her. She was the only one who could hold his heart, and she was the only one who even had a chance in Hell of breaking down any of the walls he'd thrown up. Now, that option was done. The door slammed. In one phone call, he'd lost his best friend and the love of his young life. The road just became a little darker.

This time when he stepped on the plane to go to Alaska, he did so willingly. He was ready to go back home to his "family" – his friends and comrades in the Unit. His "family" in Oregon was broken, and didn't need him in the same way they needed him up north. One of the first things he noticed in Oregon was how everyone had seemed to get along just fine without him. Sure they missed him, but they didn't need him, and Rick needed to be needed. He thrived on it. It was the only way he knew how to operate.

So, he stepped on the plane. He had things to do in Alaska. He had a relationship to fix. He would make it right with Kristy. He had to make her get over her fear of loving him. She was everything Rick wanted, and who he believed he needed. Theirs' was a love of destiny, and he couldn't ever imagine loving someone else. And for someone who didn't show their emotions often, this declaration was a massive step toward unlocking the hidden chambers of his heart. If Kristy would only believe in them like he did, there wasn't anything they couldn't do or overcome. He just had to make her believe. He could do it. He could do all of it. Only twenty-one months stood between him and his eighteenth birthday, before he was on his own, and could join the Navy. Twenty-one months. Rick refused to fail. He wanted to be the best at everything. The best at Drill, the best cadet the Unit had ever seen. He and Kristy would repair the damage, and begin their future. All he had to do was survive. That was easier said than done.

The minute he set foot in the door, the arguments began. And they continued. Again and again, and again. Do this. Do that. Don't do this. Don't do that. Bob and Rosemary wanted him to take a break from ROTC, forget Drill Team, and go into sports. Rick liked sports, but Drill and ROTC were his life. He wasn't having any of that shit. Then it was about Jazz Band, and how much involvement he could have in that. Then it was homework, how many hours was he going to spend, and how long would he be grounded if he didn't maintain a 3.0 grade point average. They had new rules for everything. Even his allowance was regulated by how clean the downstairs was on Wednesday's. Not just any day of the week, but specifically Wednesday's. Rick didn't mind authority, in fact he thrived under it at ROTC, but in his mind, these were just stupid, petty bullshit rules meant to get under his skin, and remove any space or freedom he had in his life whatsoever.

"What are your grades like?"

"I have no idea yet Dad, we've only been in school for two weeks, and there's hardly anything that's even been marked yet."

"You're lying," said Bob. "You think you can hide the truth from us?"

"I swear! I'm not lying!"

With home such a war zone, school became his solace. He threw himself into ROTC and as a Petty Officer 3rd class, he was given his own squad of five to train. Top and Gunner even made him Drill Commander for drilling sessions, and he became responsible for teaching his platoon how to march. Everything was going great – except for Kristy. She refused to speak to Rick, actually even refused to acknowledge him if she didn't have to. After feeling the initial icy chill, he met her coldness with indifference, even though he was burning up for her inside.

"Act like you just don't care bro," he thought. "It's just a game she's playing. She'll have to talk to me eventually."

That eventually came on the night of September 15th, 1995. The whole gang had been at a party, and Rick and Kristy had been avoiding each other as much as they could.

"Rick," said Katie. "I think something is wrong with Kristy. You have to help. She's out laying on the street, saying that she wished a car would hit her. I just don't know what to do!"

"I've got her Katie." Rick found Kristy just as Katie had said, lying on her back in the middle of the road, her hands covering her face. He knelt down beside her.

"Kris, what the hell are you doing?" he said softly.

"I want to die! Leave me alone!"

Rick had no clue why she was so upset and depressed. She hadn't let him in in ages. All he could do was to reach out and try and make things better between them. After a long pause, collecting his thoughts and trying to pick just the right words, he decided to just go for it.

"Kristy, you know I love you."

Kristy moved her hands from her face, looked Rick straight in the eyes and laughed, a cold, sarcastic laugh.

"Yeah right!"

Rick's heart hit the pavement. She didn't believe him. She didn't see how much he loved her. He'd meant it. Every single word. And her response was to just laugh in his face and basically call him a liar. She turned her back to him. Rick went numb. He had no idea what to do, she'd never been that cold or distant with him before. After everything they had shared, after all that they'd been through. She'd been his soul, his 'person', the one who knew him the best, and now this nothingness and cold indifference.

Unsure of what to do or how to react, Rick lit a cigarette and took a few puffs, blowing the smoke at the back of her head. The longer he knelt by her side, the angrier he became.

"You know I do."

He tossed the cigarette onto the road, stepped over Kristy, and went back into the house. That was it, his friendship with Kristy was over, and any hope of a future together was gone. Had he really hurt her that badly during their last phone call? Seriously? He'd been a dick for sure, but it wasn't worth trashing their entire friendship over. Was it all just a game to her? Did she even feel anything for him at all? Had she ever? Rejection and uncertainty filled Rick. Again. Again with the rejection. His father, God, and now Kristy. He couldn't handle much more.

The rest of the night he was inconsolable. No one asked what happened, but they all knew. He'd gone out to win her heart, and he came back a dark and brooding mess. Ghost in full effect. That coldness, that 'I don't give a fuck'. His friend Crystal tried to console him, but it was pointless. He couldn't return her warmth or her comfort. Inside, he died a little more.

"Rick," said Andrea. "Your Dad is here."

"Fuck," said Rick grabbing his trench coat. He walked in silence to the car. Bob was fuming.

"I thought you were sleeping at Matt's tonight. So funny I should get a call from Matt's mother saying she caught Matt trying to sneak out of the house, so he could meet you back at the party? Is this all a game to you Rick?"

Rick didn't answer.

"Well are you happy?"

Rick didn't give a fuck anymore, and if he was going down, he was going to go down pissing his father off.

"Yes."

Bob slammed the car into drive and took off towards home. Silence. Rick knew it wouldn't last. Bob parked the car in the garage. The silence was done. Bob blew his lid. Rick just sat and stared straight ahead. This just infuriated Bob even more.

"Go to your room!"

Rick was fine with that. He loved his room. A little peace. That didn't last long either. Rosemary opened the door and gave him that 'bastard, look what you've done now look' that Rick despised. Then Bob stormed in for Round 2. Rick stayed quiet and just took it. Bob kept screaming.

"And why did all those kids look so spaced out?"

That was it. Rick couldn't hold back any longer.

"What the fuck is your problem? Three quarters of those kids are from ROTC and I bet you half of them have never even smoked a joint and you're sitting there making accusations against the best group of friends I have! Yeah, we march around drunk like stupid fucks!" On fire, Rick jumped off the bed, got right in Bob's face, and pulled up the sleeves of his trench coat. "Here, want to see my needle marks? Or maybe you want to take me down to APD to get a breathalyzer. FUCK! You don't ever accuse me of doing drugs, or my friends!"

Bob reeled back his fist but Rick was too quick, and blocked the first two blasts, enraging his father even more. Bob landed a shot to Rick's chest, driving Rick back onto the bed.

"You NEVER get up in my face like that you punk sonofabitch!" screamed Bob shaking Rick's arm, his fist raised.

"Fuck you!"

The ensuing slap sent Rick back off the bed. Like lightning, he was up on his feet and ready to defend. His eyes piercing daggers. That was going to be the last time he let his father hit him that night. Bob returned the stare, then stormed out of the room, slamming the door so hard, one of Rick's guitars toppled to the floor. An hour later, Bob stormed back into Rick's room, took all the usual gear – stereo, phone, and this time both guitars.

"You're grounded for a month."

What the fuck, Rick didn't even care anymore. Big fucking deal. That weekend began a very dark era for him. He quit caring almost completely and just gave up on everything. With the rejection by Kristy, the last piece of his heart died. He felt so cold. So alone. He just didn't ever want to feel anything again. All of the restrictions his parents put on him was child's play. School work was a joke. All of it didn't mean shit. All of the bullshit with his parents, schools, relationships, and petty drama, it was all nonsense. He'd already been running and gunning, been smoking since he was eleven, stolen cars, broke into houses, been shot at, 'suited up' and went in hot numerous times and in numerous locations. He'd watched friends die, right before his eyes, and even in his arms. Nothing mattered to him anymore. He was indifferent, untouchable, nothing seemed to phase him. His dad wants to belt him? Go the fuck ahead. None of it mattered anymore. He was done with everyone and everything, except his comrades at ROTC. They were all he lived for. They were all that mattered. Fuck the rest of the world.

He let everything go to hell. His grades, his attitude, and his judgement. When he 'borrowed' Rosemary's car to pick Crystal up from where she was babysitting, and then drive her home, he didn't care that he might get caught. And he did get caught. He didn't beat Bob and Rosemary home from their tennis match. Bob was already pulling back out of the driveway to come look for him when Rick pulled up along side.

"Get up that driveway now!" Rick thought for sure his Dad was going to put his fist through the window. The minute they were both back in the garage, Bob lurched out of the Suburban, ripped open the driver's side door of the Corsica, grabbed the keys out of Rick's hands, grabbed his other arm, and literally tore his son from the car, not caring that Rick's foot got caught between the seat. Twisting Rick's arms behind his back, with his keys digging into Rick's arm, Bob dragged his son to the back of the car, slamming him hard against the trunk.

"This is how the cops treat punks like you! This is how they treat you!" With the keys still in his right hand, Bob slapped the back of Rick's head. "Is this what you want?" The keys smacked hard against Rick's skull. "Is this what you want, you sonofabitch?" Bob suddenly realized he hit Rick with the keys, and let go of his arms.

"Oh shit, I'm sorry."

Rick just stood there, holding the back of his head, staring at his father, his eyes wide with disbelief. Bob calmed his voice, almost overcome by his momentary delve into madness.

"Goddamit, go to your room."

Keeping his guard, Rick slowly walked past his father and into the house.

"Damnit!" said Bob slamming his fist down hard onto the car.

Rick laid on his bed, still holding the back of his head. Thankfully he wasn't bleeding. Still didn't stop the throbbing pain though, both in his head and in his heart. What the fuck had just happened? Bob came in about twenty minutes later, calmer but still heated.

"I'm sorry for hitting you with the keys. But that doesn't excuse any of this. Your restrictions are on for another month. Try not to get in anymore trouble." Rick said nothing. Bob just stood there studying his son for the longest time.

"Rick, how am I supposed to control you?"

Rick wanted to answer, 'love me' but he couldn't get the words out, so he replied in smart-ass fashion, his most trusted defence mechanism.

"Well you could start by stopping hitting me."

Of course, Bob didn't take kindly to the remark, and another argument ensued, not a raging fist-fest, but an argument none the less.

"Fine," said Bob. "Just go to bed. I'm not getting anywhere with you."

Bob had no idea what he was truly up against. He loved his son, and was trying to get through to him, but he just had no idea how, and the current approach was an abysmal failure. He was up against a son who hated his guts, and purely out of spite, refused to let him win. A son who had already been through so much shit in his life, most of it completely unknown and hidden from his father, that he didn't believe he had to answer to anyone. There was no way of controlling him. Bob couldn't hope to understand who Rick was, or what he had been through, anymore than Rick could understand the choices his father made. The chasm between them only grew with each argument, with each fist. With neither willing to give an inch or change their tactics, the war raged on. And in this war, the sides were firmly established.

Rick had always protected his mother. No matter what. He may have disliked some of the things she had done, and had been resentful about her pushing religious dogma down his throat, but he would always step up and protect her, especially when it came to Bob. Because Rick was living in Alaska, Bob went back to the courts to petition his child support fees, reasoning that since Brenda had one less mouth to feed, she required less money. The courts didn't share his theory, in fact, when they found out how much money Bob made, they actually raised the amount he had to pay, making him pay more for Jimmy alone than he'd been paying for both boys. He was livid.

For once, Bob and Brenda had kept the dispute from the boys, and until Bob lost, Rick had no idea what had been going on. The issue of child support had always been a sore spot for Rick from the beginning, when Bob initially balked at wanting to pay anything to support his kids. It only deepened the hatred and disgust he had for his father. They all knew it was just an unspoken attempt to make their lives so miserable, that it would be easier to 'win' the boys over with money and 'things'. Foolish, and a complete failure.

Bob should have known better than to bitch and complain about having to pay more money, especially right in front of his oldest son.

"Why wouldn't you want to pay for Jimmy anyway?" said Rick. "You make a crapload of money. Why does it hurt you to give to your son?"

Bob exploded. "That's not the point," he said trying to defend himself. "This has nothing to do with Jimmy. I just can't stand the thought of giving it to her!"

Rick coiled, ready to snap. His dad was walking a thin line. The argument escalated, carrying on as they went down to the family room, voices high, tensions tight.

"She's a fucking bitch!"

"Don't you fucking talk about my Mom like that!" Rick screamed, taking an aggressive step forward, his red face exploding with rage.

"Your mother is a fucking bitch!"

Bob didn't even have time to react. In one swift movement, Rick took a low step forward and hit him in the ribs with both hands, a lightning fast double strike. Falling onto his back, Bob clutched his now cracked ribs, screaming in pain. Rick walked into his room, grabbed his trench coat, and headed out the front door, the wet snow melting as it hit the burning heat of his body. He didn't care that he'd hurt his father. He felt vindicated, and he'd protected and defended his mother. Always her saviour. Always her knight in shining armour. Always her little warrior. Fuck his father.

Bob and Rosemary finally decided it was time for some third-party intervention, and sent him to see Dr. Wieger, a psychologist. They hoped Dr. Wieger would help Rick open up and talk about what was going on inside. Fat chance. Rick wasn't having any of it, and when he could hardly open up to the people he trusted, what made anyone think he would just randomly spill his guts to some shrink? There was no way Dr. Wieger was getting anything other than a generic, boring response.

"Why are you having problems at school?"

"Because it's boring and I hate school."

"Why do you think it's boring? Don't you like being involved?"

"The only thing I like involving myself in is ROTC."

"Why do you have so much animosity towards your father?"

"Because he divorced my mother and destroyed our family."

"Why was this so hard for you?"

"Because I looked up to him, and he betrayed me, and he became a traitor."

Nothing about Ghost. Nothing about the deaths he'd witnessed. Nothing about the demons. Nothing of substance. Just telling the doctor what he wanted to hear. He never brought up any of the abuse because he never saw it as abuse. To Rick they were just fights, just altercations that sometimes got a little testy and sometimes got physical. Rick lived a life of conflict, and the issues with his Dad were just an extension of that. In his eyes, that's what he believed. He never saw himself as a victim, nor did he ever want anyone else to see him as a victim. Victims were weak. Rick wasn't weak. And even if he did perceive it as abuse, he was never going to rat out his own father. No matter how much he hated him, a person just didn't do shit like that.

It never dawned on Rick that as the adult, Bob should have known better, he should have reacted differently. It didn't matter. Rick didn't want to talk, and he resented being sent to see Dr. Wieger. Did Bob have to go too? Nope. Just Rick, because Rick was the one with the issues, and the only one who needed help. There was no doubt Rick needed help. There was no doubt he needed a severe intervention, but there was also no doubt he needed that intervention years ago. This last ditch effort was too little, and way too late. The vault was sealed. No one was getting in.

Early November, Bob was away on another work trip, leaving Rick and Rosemary alone. Rosemary had gone to tennis, and left instructions for Rick to clean and vacuum the house. Already tired from Drill practise, Rick wasn't thrilled, but he did it anyway.

"Rick!"

"Yes," he answered walking out his bedroom door.

"I thought I asked you to vacuum?"

"I did vacuum."

"Really? Then what are those paw prints on the carpet? Why can't you ever do what you are told! How hard is it?"

"Rosemary, I did vacuum. Cody must have just done this."

"You're a liar and you know it! And a stupid punk for thinking you could fool me!"

"I did clean it. The dog must have walked on it after I finished and went into my room. I'm not lying."

"Well I think you are. Just like you always do. I'll never believe anything you say because all you do is lie!"

Already fed up and tired of listening to her rant, Rick walked upstairs to get the vacuum cleaner.

"Don't you walk away from me when I'm talking to you!" Rosemary followed him up the stairs.

"Look, I'm going to get the vacuum cleaner because obviously I've lied about cleaning the downstairs, so I'd appreciate it if you'd just shut up!"

"What right do you have to talk to me like that?"

Rick turned to face his step-mother. "The same right that you have to bitch at everything and call me a liar."

The sting of Rosemary's right hand across his face left Rick rattled and in shock. "Never use that language around me."

If Rick hadn't been so shocked from the slap, he would have laughed in her face. He'd heard far worse come out of her mouth directed at him. Rick glared into her eyes.

"I dare you to do that again." He wanted to smack her back but kept his cool. "If you think the floors are that bad, then you can vacuum them."

He turned and walked back into his room. Shortly after, the vacuum cleaner roared to life making Rick laugh.

"I should have expected that."

As usual, the next day Rosemary acted as if nothing had happened. Until Bob called that night. Then the bitching began. Rick was just a punk who lied and never listened to her.

"Bob, I can't take much more. I should just go live with my parents!" Rosemary handed Rick the phone. "Your father wants to talk to you. He wants your side of the story."

Rick told his dad what had happened, and of course his father didn't believe a word, and completely sided with Rosemary. Tired of being chewed out for the millionth time, Rick was done listening.

"Fuck you, here's your wife."

He handed Rosemary the phone and went to his room, his father still screaming on the other end. He was tired. He was done. Nothing he ever did was right. Nothing he ever did was good enough. Even when he was right, he was wrong. That night just drove him deeper over the edge. Why bother? Why care? What does it all fucking matter?

He found much needed solace in the Drill Team. But that was the only solace he found, settling into a very cold, indifferent routine. Survival. Hunkering down in the blackness of an emotional fortress, waiting out the days, the hours, and the minutes until he could finally be free. Nineteen more months. Nineteen more months until he turned 18. The magic number. He just had to hold on.

But his mind was failing him. His sanity wavering. The isolation too much. He began to blank out, drift off, be of another place and time. He took to spending time laying in the mounting Alaskan snow, stretching out, his body sinking into the cold, welcoming him. One especially low night, all he could see was the snow around him, and the bare skeletal branches of the trees. The Northern Lights cast an eerie type of purple against the blackness. He wished he would just freeze to death. He'd be happy that it'd all be over.

"Just let me die."

There was nothing left for him. Nothing of substance anyways. Tonight, the misery won and he just wanted it all to end, to be carried away by the howling, vicious wind. His mind blanked, went its own way. His Third Eye opened. He had no control. He was now on a cross, chained and nailed. Suffering on the cross. Just like Jesus. Christ's Little Warrior. His own crucifixion happening in his own mind. Made of old oil-soaked railway ties, the cross stood in the middle of a frozen landscape of ice and snow. Solid white. Blinding white for miles and miles. Except on the horizon. There was a black spot, a cave, a way to the underground, its wolves screaming in the blackness. There was no peace. Not on the cross, and not in the cave. There would never be any peace. He had no idea how long he hung there, no sense of time existed. Was it days, weeks, years? Sometimes he'd climb down from the cross, unravelling the chains and pulling the nails through his frostbitten hands and feet. He felt no pain. He was numb. Then, he'd wander, stumbling through the ice and snow, just wandering, wandering forever.

The visions became frequent. He'd be in the middle of a conversation or at school, and then he'd be gone, once again, wandering aimlessly. And each time he came back feeling just as cold, just as alone as he was he when he left. He could still hear the wolves howl, almost as a reminder, the distant echoes of the cave calling him. The visions disturbed him, the losing of reality, the loss of control. At times, he would dream it or fall asleep in that vision, eventually waking up and not even remembering. He would dream of being shot, dreams so vivid that he'd wake with chest pains or stomach pains. Was God paying him back? The only way God was ever going to be happy was if Rick gave his life to Him, and voluntarily submitted himself to God's Will. But Rick had refused. And now he suffered. Constantly. The wolves howled louder. The wolves howled longer. They were calling him. He just wanted them to stop. To just fucking shut up. For all of them to just fucking shut the hell up.

That day. November 30th, 1995. The cafeteria. His father stomping in red faced and pissed. Pulling him out of ROTC, the only place he finally felt he belonged and had a home. Another betrayal. Then home. All the yelling. The fucking yelling between his father and Rosemary. About him. Always about him. His father throwing him out in the Alaskan winter without even money for a ticket back to Oregon. Him choosing HER over him. Again. Just like when he was a ten-year-old boy. He had spent six full years hating his father for destroying his family, abandoning them, and then trying to have some say over his life. He had forfeited that right when he left. And now six years later, his father was making the same choice again. Rick never wanted to move to Alaska with him. His father had forced that on him 'for his own good' – the same line he'd used the day he left. Bastard. Fucking bastard. He had taken him away from everything, ruined his life, and forced him to forge a new one. But none of that mattered to his father. He chose her. The spineless bastard chose her. Again. Rick was confused. He couldn't understand. And he hated his father for what he had done. Lying there on his bed. Just thinking. Just listening. Wanting it all to stop. For once and for all, wanting the pain to go away. Needing silence.

Then the dam broke. He couldn't control it, couldn't even really think or move. The years of hatred, pain, loss, depression, agony, apathy – all bottled up, swept under a rug. All the feelings of betrayal washed over him like glacier water, chilling him to the bone. This was the very reason he had 'died' six years ago; a family destroyed, loved ones abandoned, a son betrayed. It was why he had gone

Ghost in the first place. He couldn't take the pain then. It was easier to 'die' and act like he didn't feel at all. Except the pain was still there. Buried deep in a box he didn't even know existed. He had lied to himself about being 'dead' to his feelings. The emotions were all still there. Building. Waiting. Every friend he had lost, every defeat, every sorrow, every unfilled desire; he had trained himself as Ghost to feel nothing. None of it mattered. He had talked himself into believing that his emotions didn't exist. That he couldn't feel. But there, in that moment, lying on his bed listening to the incessant yelling, absorbing the second betrayal, his mind crazy with emotion, he couldn't deny the crashing waves of pain and heartache that exploded through his body. He was lost. Broken. Drowning. The tempest inside had completely taken control, and Ghost was replaced by a seething frenzy of feelings and memories.

He dimly remembered hearing the side door to the garage open and close, and the roar of a cold engine coming to life. Bob was going after her, leaving his crushed and shattered son alone, at a time when he needed the comfort and reassurance of a father; at a time when a son was screaming for an explanation, screaming for even just the slightest hint of love. Rick lay on the bed for another ten minutes or so, overwhelmed by memories and emotions, every minute past, a countdown to that moment when the soul is consumed, and all rational thought or consciousness is abandoned.

Around 8:30 the ripping of tires up the driveway and into the garage told Rick that his father and step-mother had returned. The minute the car doors slammed shut, the arguing continued.

"What the fuck are they still arguing about," thought Rick. "He chose her, I have to leave, so what is the fucking problem?"

Still raging on full steam, the intensity of the screaming match hadn't changed from the moment Rosemary had stormed out the house and into her car a little earlier.

"Just shut the fuck up. Seriously. Shut the fuck up."

The actual words they were saying didn't even register with Rick anymore. It was like they were being spoken underwater or the soundtrack had gotten stuck on slow motion. The pressure in his head pounded against his skull, threatening to explode at any moment. The feeling reminded him of looking past the 'Veil'. There was a fluidity that permeated everything; a blurring of reality where one couldn't really tell where the world of spirits and demons stopped and the 'real' world began. The shadows, the shapes, the vile energy clinging to everything – like swimming through a dark ethereal matter that possessed a restrictive quality but no substance. And now this dark seething matter broiled deep within his core, threatening to suffocate him from the inside out.

"STOP IT!"

It could have been the door slam, it could have been Rosemary's blaring sobs, it could have been the mention of his name, again – he didn't know – but somewhere in the midst of all the noise and commotion the spark flew and his psyche exploded. The rage over the betrayal, the infinite sorrow over being cast away, forced back, only to be cast away again, was too much. He was there, but he wasn't there. His mind wasn't right. He felt more like an observer to the experience, neither conscious of his physical actions or the wanderings in his brain – like there was no more room in his head for thoughts, and all he could do was watch.

Then it stopped. The yelling. The only thing that was able to distract his mind, stopped. Had they gone to bed? Was his father banished to the couch for the night? The sudden silence was deadly. Almost unbearable. Without anything else to listen to, the reverberation in his skull amplified, a constant and unending 'whoomp', 'whoomp', 'whoomp' equivalent to slow moving helicopter blades slicing through the air, sending long, painful vibrations racing through his body. Time had ceased to have any meaning; all he could feel was the numbing howl of pent-up emotions screaming in his ears. He tried to breathe, to somehow slow the building rage. He tried to intercept his thoughts with others. He tried to wedge his conscious mind back somewhere into the present. He couldn't. The crushing weight of his angst was too much for the experience of his sixteen-year-old mind. His head felt heavy. The pressure built. His vision blurred. The pressure built. His muscles tensed. The pressure built. The betrayal. The betrayals. Not again. Never again. Then, like a single steel cable, brittle and taught – he snapped and grabbed the rifle.

CHAPTER FORTY-TWO

Rick closed his eyes and tried to block out the droning voice of State Prosecutor Robert Collins. The State was laying out its case to the jury. Stating the 'facts', over and over. The facts were clear. Rick killed Bob and Rosemary Watkinson. He didn't deny it, never had, never would.

"The indictment reads as follows," said Collins. "That on or about the 30th day of November, 1995, at or near Anchorage, in the third judicial district, state of Alaska. Richard Roy Watkinson, with the intent to cause the death of another person, caused the death of Robert G. Watkinson. Count II, on or about the 30th day of November, 1995, at or near Anchorage, in the third judicial district, state of Alaska, Richard Roy Watkinson, with the intent to cause the death of another person, caused the death of Rosemary J. Watkinson."

Every word brought Rick back to that moment. Had he just walked away to cool down, none of this would have happened. Had Bob kept his guns locked up and safe, Rick would never have been sitting at that table beside Wally and Randall. So many what ifs. So much pain.

"At the conclusion of the state's case," said Collins. "You will have absolutely no doubt -- I submit you will have to the point of a metaphysical certitude that Mr. Watkinson intended to kill his parents. Did he have legal justification? In our case we will demonstrate beyond any doubt he did not. If the defendant, as the judge has previously instructed you, decides to put on a case, we will be entitled, and will put on, rebuttal evidence. Whatever defense, if any, they may want to claim, will be met by rebuttal evidence to show that his actions that night and during this time period were not the actions of a reasonable man, a man, adult, in the defendant's situation. Thank you, ladies and gentleman. Thank you, Your Honor."[37]

"Of course they were not the actions of a reasonable man," thought Rick. "And certainly not the actions of an adult. That's the whole problem. I was a kid. A lost and desperate kid."

Rick watched as Wally Tetlow gathered his papers and cleared his throat. He trusted him. Wally had shown his chops during the evidentiary hearings, proving they weren't about to roll over and just let the State have its way. Too bad the Judge stood in their way. Wally knew it was going to be a tough trial, an emotional

[37] Opening statements for the State taken from the Court transcripts

trial. Two people were dead, those were the facts. They were victims. But so was young Rick. He just had to prove it to the jury and hope they had compassion. They had to have compassion. They had to understand. They would understand once he told them why.

"Thank you, Your Honor. Ladies and gentlemen, this is not a whodunit case. You will not hear the defense once during this case tell you that this child seated at defense counsel table did not take the lives of his father and stepmother on November 30, 1995. And you will not hear the defense once say that, that is not a tragic event. But you will hear the defense answer the question that the state will not answer. The state can tell you what happened on November 30, 1995, but they cannot tell you why."

"You will hear, during the course of the evidence in this case, and during the course of the trial, exactly why Mr. Watkinson did what he did on November 30, 1995. Why would a 16-year-old boy, a likeable, articulate, intelligent, 16-year-old boy, with no prior involvement with the criminal justice system, do such a thing? Children are supposed to honor and respect and obey their parents. And parents are supposed to care for their children. They're supposed to shower their children with affection, with hugs, with attention, and with kisses. Not with fists, not by inflicting bruises, and not by emotional, verbal abuse."

"You will hear that not all parents do the job that they're supposed to do. And you will hear exactly what happens to a child who suffers an extremely bitter and traumatic divorce at age ten. You will hear what happens to a child who suffers years of physical abuse. And you will hear what happens to a child who suffers years of emotional and verbal torment. And you will have an insight into the state of mind of Rick on November 30, 1995."

"You will find that there are three victims in this case. They are not only the deceased, but Rick. And Rick was the victim of a violence that took from him at a very young age his self-worth, his self-esteem, and his connection with his family. But things were not always bad in Rick's life. Up to age ten, Rick's family was a very happy family. It consisted of his father, Robert Watkinson, his mother, Brenda Watkinson, and his younger brother. And they were all a family unit, and they were all together. And Rick in fact was his father's favorite son."

"He was not only the oldest, he was also athletic, he was intelligent, he was outgoing. He was a daddy's boy. And like most ten-year-olds, he respected his father more than anything in the universe. In addition to the respect that young children have for their fathers, especially young boys, his father was a pilot. He flew planes for a living. He was a world traveler. And to a ten-year-old boy that is extremely fascinating."

"Rick loved his father, but that changed in 1989. Because in 1989 Rick's father came back from an extended flight, came into the family home and he called a little conference in Rick's room. And he was seated in a chair much as I am standing in front of you now, and Rick and his younger brother were seated on the bed, and his mother was in the room. And he announced at that time that he was leaving the family. That he was divorcing the mother. And ten-year-old Rick began to cry, and the younger brother began to cry, and the mother began to cry. And you will hear how ten-year-old Rick actually grabbed on to his father's leg, crying, daddy…don't go, don't leave us. And how Robert Watkinson pushed his son away from him and said, son, this is in your best interests, and turned and walked out of the room."

"Rick and his younger brother and his mother stayed in the room for a while, obviously very upset, crying. And when they came out of the room, Rick's father was gone. He came back some two weeks later. And he came back with Rosemary. Rick's mother took this very hard, as did Rick, obviously. They had been married -- Brenda and Robert had been married for 23 years, when in 1989 Robert announced that he was leaving the family. Robert made a very, very good income and could support the family very well. Brenda did not. There were financial hardships on the family when Robert left."

"And then Brenda discovered that Rosemary was in fact a stewardess on the very flights that Robert was a pilot on prior to 1989. And that's really about all she heard about that. But in her mind she was convinced that Robert Watkinson walked out on her and her family for Rosemary. And she shared that pain, and she shared that loss with the two people that she just happened to live with, which happened to be a ten-year-old boy and his younger brother."

"Robert came back with Rosemary and wanted to take the boys on a bike trip two weeks after he announced that he was leaving the family, and the boys did not want to go. They did not want to go with their father who walked out on them, and they did not want to go with this woman that their mother had said took their father away from them. And there was a heated argument about that. Dad insisted that the kids go. The kids said, no, we don't want to go. And dad responded physically by pushing young Rick away again and saying that if you're not going to have it my way, then I'm not going to be in your life at all. And he left again."

"During the next year from 1989 to 1990 was an extremely difficult year for Rick and his mother and his younger brother. Rick's mother had to go back to school in order to earn a living to support her two sons. There were financial battles in the courtroom. Which anyone who has been through a bitter divorce knows about. And the kids were present for those. There were financial disputes about how much child support should be, and the children were present for all of that. During the next four years, from 1990 to 1994, Rick Watkinson began to display the signs of the mental effects that he was feeling as a result of the divorce.

He began to skip school. He began to have problems with other children. He began to run away from home. And during that four-year period he twice attempted suicide. And during that four-year period he adopted a new name for himself. He called himself Ghost because that's the way he felt. He felt that no one could see him anymore after his father had left and rejected him for Rosemary."

"In 1993 Robert and Rosemary got married and they moved to Anchorage. And during that point in time Rick's life was out of control. He was living on the streets of Oregon. He was running away from home all the time, and his mother became desperate. And she called Robert Watkinson in Anchorage and said, please help me here. And Robert began to berate her on the telephone. You're a lousy parent, you've never been able to control your son, and I'm going to come down there and I'm going to get him, and I will discipline him the way that he should have been disciplined a long time ago."

"And he came to Oregon. And when Rick found out that he was coming, he tried to run away again. He went out to the barn which was next to the house, and he started up a four-wheeler and was going to drive away, when his father, Robert, caught him. And he grabbed him by the arm, and he dragged him back into the house, and he immediately began the verbal abuse. He began to berate him. Rick responded. He told his father that he did not want his father in his life. His father had walked out of his life and gave up what he had with their family."

"His father became angry. Frustrated and angry. And he lashed out physically in front of the other people who were in the room, and struck Rick in the face, knocking him backwards into a windowsill where Rick hit his head and fell down into a chair. And that subdued Rick, which is exactly what it was intended to do. And then he continued to berate Rick, and continued to berate Rick, and actually stood guard over him for the evening and dragged him back to Anchorage physically the next day."

"You can imagine what life was like in that home. Robert and Rosemary Watkinson had a home on the Hillside, and that is where Robert brought Rick. Probably the last person in the world at that point in time that this young boy wanted to spend time with. The person who had walked out on him, and who abused his family. But Rosemary was there. And Rosemary could have made it much easier for Rick to live in that house. But you will hear that she did not. You will in fact hear from witnesses who know full well that Rosemary Watkinson and Robert Watkinson struck a deal when they were married. And their deal was that neither one of them would have children from former marriages in their new relationship."

"And Rosemary made a point of telling that to her friend. She actually made a point of telling that to the therapist. And she made a point to tell that to Rick's friends. You will hear evidence that Rosemary actually told Rick's young friends that she did not want him in her life because they had had an agreement that they would not accept any children from prior marriages. More importantly, Rosemary made it a point on numerous occasions to make sure that Rick knew that she did not want him in their relationship. Rick resented that as any child would. And that is the atmosphere that he had to live in from the time that he came to Anchorage in 1994 until 1995."

"And during that time the physical and the verbal abuse escalated because Rosemary did not want Rick in the home, Robert did. Rick resented Rosemary's resentment of him as a child, and he responded to that. And Rosemary responded to him. Robert did not want Rosemary disciplining Rick, and that was a source of contention between the two of them. So there was a vicious triangle going on here, and the more frustrated Rosemary became, the more she took it out on Rick. The more she did that, the more frustrated Rick became and responded back to Rosemary. The more that Rosemary took her frustrations out on Rick, the more that Robert took his frustrations out on Rosemary and on Rick."

"The beatings became much, much worse in the one-year period between 1994 and 1995 as Robert started taking his frustrations out on Rick. The beatings got so bad that on more than one occasion Rick's friends at school noticed bruises all over his back that you will learn were inflicted by Robert Watkinson. At one point during that year Robert took Rick out on a trail behind their house to have a father and son talk out in the woods away from other people. They got out into the woods, and Robert took this 16-year-old boy and physically threw him on the ground, and got on top of him and held him down with one hand, with a raised fist with the other, and was ready to strike him when hikers came by and prevented that from happening. And you will learn soon enough that that was not an uncommon experience in that house."

"You will also learn that the physical abuse came not only from Robert, but it also came from Rosemary, because as the frustrations got higher and higher, and the anger level got higher and higher, Rose escalated from verbal abuse, from tearing Rick down to actual physical abuse on more than one occasion during that one-year period. You will hear witnesses testify as to how Rose treated Rick when they were in the home. She referred to him on numerous occasions as bastard, as punk, and made a point of repeatedly telling him. I never wanted you here anyway, and I would get rid of you if I could but your father will not let me."

"One thing that Rick had going for him during that year -- the one thing that he had going for him was the ROTC program at Service High School. Because prior to that Rick's life was unbearable. And you will hear that he ran away on more than one occasion, and on one occasion actually went to Covenant House, which is a home for abused and neglected kids, troubled kids. And he stayed there for six days before he finally went back to that house on Hillside. Where else was he going to go? This is a 16-year-old kid in Anchorage with no relatives other than the people who are in that house. He had no choice but to go back. Back to the same verbal abuse, back to the same physical abuse. He was stuck."

"And the one thing that made his life an iota bearable was the naval ROTC program, Naval Reserve Officer Training Corps Program, at Service High School. And you will hear from his instructor that he was an excellent student in that program. He was an excellent leader of other students, and he enjoyed his time in the program. And he spent as much time as possible in the program so that he did not have to spend time in the abusive home. He began to focus so much on the ROTC program as a substitute for the family that he did not have that he began to neglect other things. He started skipping other classes so that he could attend ROTC activities."

"Ironically enough, it was Rick's focus on the ROTC program as a substitute for his family that actually triggered the events that happened on November 30, 1995. Because Robert Watkinson found out that his son was skipping classes on that afternoon, November 30, 1995. And as soon as be found that out, he jumped in his car in the middle of the day, drove down to Service, went storming into the foyer area where he knew Rick would be, and where Rick was practicing drill with the other ROTC students, and in front of all the other students physically took him out of drill practice and pulled him out into a foyer area, where he immediately began yelling and screaming at him where the other students could hear what was going on."

"Rick came back into the drill practice and asked his senior instructor if he could be allowed to leave. His dad held the door open for him to make sure that he walked out of the school. He physically escorted him to the car and began berating him again, and berating him, and berating him all the way home. And one of the things that he told Rick was you are no longer going to be allowed to attend the drill program or the ROTC program. He was going to take from Rick the one thing that made his life bearable."

"Then they got home where it should have ended. There should have been a restriction imposed, and that would have been the end of the story. But he continued to berate Rick, continually calling him names, telling him what problems he was causing with his marriage. On and on and on until Rosemary came home. And then Rosemary joined in. The same old story. You're ruining our marriage, I never wanted you here in the first place, and on and on and on. And then, of course, Robert and Rosemary get into it. They're arguing with each other about who has the right to discipline Rick. And that goes on and on, just as it had for the last year."

"And Rosemary gets upset and says, that's it, I've had it, I'm leaving, and storms out of the house, gets in her car and drives off. Robert's very upset. The last thing he wants to do is lose his wife. So he's going to go after her. And on the way out of the house he stops by Rick's room where Rick's laying on his bed· listening to the arguing, and be tells Rick, I've had it with you, you're out of here, you're ruining my marriage, and goes after Rose. And rejects him the same way that he had rejected him when Rick was 10 years old in 1989 when his dad pushed him off of his leg and said, I'm leaving the family, I'm leaving you. And he walked out. He walked out the front door and after Rose, just like he had walked out in 1989. And in Rick's mind once again Robert was rejecting him for Rosemary."

"Robert caught up with Rosemary. Rosemary and Robert came back to the house. Rick's lying on his bed. They start in arguing again. Rick is ruining our marriage. I never wanted him here in the first place. And on and on and on. All about how Rick was ruining their relationship.

"You will hear from an expert psychiatrist who has worked for the federal government, who has worked for the military, who is a professor and a lecturer, who will tell you exactly the effect that that traumatic divorce in 1989, that the issues of abandonment that Rick felt in 1989 and never got rid of, how the years of physical and verbal abuse affected Rick Watkinson. And you will hear that on November 30, 1995, Rick Watkinson was unable to control himself. He was unable to control what happened on that evening."

"You've already heard that in order to get a conviction on murder in the first degree the state has to prove beyond a reasonable doubt that Rick intentionally killed his father and his stepmother without legal justification. And we are confident that after you hear the why in this case, and after you see and hear all the evidence, you will be convinced that there was legal justification for what happened on November 30, 1995. And we're also confident that you will return a verdict of not guilty on both counts of murder in the first degree."[38]

"What happens now," said Rick turning to Randall.

"The State is going to call a bunch of witnesses and lay out all the forensic evidence, like the crime scene photos, the gun, all of that sort of stuff."

"I don't know if I can look at the pictures," said Rick. "It's hard."

"I know," said Randall. "Just close your eyes if you have to. You're doing great."

The State proceeded to call their witnesses one after one. The 9-1-1 operator, the first officer on the scene Trooper Lee Oly, Rosemary's friend Jeannie Roth, and the two medical examiners who performed the autopsies on the bodies. The 9-1-1 call by Bob was confirmed, Miss. Roth confirmed she was Rick's emergency contact number, and told the jury what wonderful parents Bob and Rosemary

[38] Opening statement by the Defence taken from Court Transcripts

were to Rick, and how involved they were as parents.

"Including Rick in family activities," said Miss Roth, "enrolling him in tennis lessons teaching him to fly, having a mystery type of dinner party put together and involving him as a part of that. Lots of involvement and including."

"Would you describe what sort of context you observed discipline, please?" said Collins.

"I would say just, you know, very normal, calm, kinds of request that might have been made. Like, you know, just -- more requests than discipline, you know. Maybe directives to help with setting the table, that kind of thing."

Judge Sanders was very sure to allow the State lots of leeway into her descriptions of Bob and Rosemary as parents, and their state of mind, all the while shutting down every objection the Defense made. But Randall was quick to poke holes in her story on cross examination.

"Miss Roth, my last question was if you remembered telling Trooper Baty that Rosemary would say things like, I could just kill him, I'm so frustrated I don't know what to do."

"I did say that."

"Do you remember describing Rosemary's parenting style as tough love?" said Randall.

"Yes"

"And do you remember talking about whether or not Rosemary was controlling of Rick?"

"No, I don't."

"Okay."

"I may have made some comments about it but right now I don't recall those."

"And do you remember making statements that Rick may have thought that he was being picked on?"

"What I remember saying was that my interpretation -- I certainly couldn't know how Rick was interpreting things, that I -- I couldn't know what was going on in his mind."

"Do you remember saying that it was difficult for you to answer questions like this because you were on the outside?" said Randall.

"Yes."

"Would you say that's generally true? That it's difficult to answer questions like this when you're on the outside looking in?"

"You can only answer, you know, with what you know and what you observe."

"Okay. Would that be why you don't have any knowledge of name calling, as an example?"

"Yes."

"Okay. Such as you don't know whether or - not Rosemary ever called Rick a bastard."

"I do not know that. I've never heard her say that."

"You don't know whether she ever called Rick a punk."

"I never heard her say that."

"You don't know whether she ever slapped him."

"I never observed that."

"Okay. You never heard Bob say anything like that to Rick."

"I did not."

"You never witnessed Bob punch Rick."

"No."

"Or hit Rick in any way."

"No. Absolutely not."

"Okay. But again, you're on the outside looking in. Is that correct?"

"I'm not a part of that family."

"Okay. Were you aware of an agreement between Bob and Rose not to have children in this fam -- in this relationship?"

"No."

"Okay. Do you remember telling Trooper Baty that Rosemary wasn't planning on being a parent?"

"Oh. Yes."

"Okay. Why did you say that?"

"When they got married, Bob did not have joint custody, and I think that the understanding was that the children would be visiting, but not living with them full time."

"That was the understanding between Bob and Rose."

"As I understood it yes."

"Thank you," said Randall. "Nothing further."

Randall made his point. Miss Roth had never seen any abuse, but she admits she was an outsider looking in. She wasn't a member of their lives, and certainly had no idea what went on in the intimacy of their private lives.

Trooper Oly walked the jury through the crime scene, describing where the bodies were, where all the gun shells were, and backing up his findings with photographic and video evidence, while Dr. Propst and Dr. Thompson walked them through the autopsies. All very detailed. All very factual. No surprises. John Goodwin, Rick's teacher at ROTC took the stand on behalf of the Prosecution and recounted what happened the morning of December 1, 1995.

"I -- I walked up to Rick and kind of put my arm around him and pulled him away from the other kids, and asked him if he was okay, what was going on. And he looked upset. Looked like he had been out that night, wasn't his usual clean-cut self."

Wally jumped on that statement during his cross examination.

"Okay," said Wally. "So you were very familiar with Rick's usual state."

"Yes, sir," said John Goodwin.

"His usual -- the way he usually looked."

"Yes, sir."

"Right? And the way be usually acted."

"Yes, sir."

"Okay. But he looked very different than he normally looked on the morning -- on December l when you first contacted him outside the ROTC classroom."

"Yes, sir, he did."

"Okay. Did it appear to you that he had been crying?"

"Yes, sir, it did."

"Did it appear to you that he was in shock?"

"Yes, sir, it did."

"He looked pretty shaken, right?"

"Yes, sir."

"And you'd said that he looked like he'd been out all night."

"Yes sir."

In response to Collins suggesting that Rick would have gone to Mr. Goodwin, a trusted confident, about the abuse, if there in fact was any abuse, Wally asked the teacher.

"Mr. Goodwin, would you find it at all unusual in your 18 years of experience for a child who had in fact been severely abused not to tell you that that was happening?"

"No, sir, I wouldn't."

"Why is that?"

"Because I -- I think most - my experience with children ·· most of them are -- are ashamed to -- to tell you that they're being abused, if they're being abused."

"A child would be ashamed to come to you and say, my father pounds me with his fist on a regular basis."

"I've never had one do that, no."

"Do you think that it would be fair to say that a child would be ashamed to admit that?"

"I think it would be fair to say, yes sir."

Rick didn't look himself that morning. Goodwin saw it right away. He was in shock. And as a veteran of the Vietnam War, Mr. Goodwin certainly knew the definition of shock. John T. Goodwin was a stand-up gentleman, someone who called it like he saw it, someone who cared about his ROTC students. It isn't hard to understand why a child doesn't tell others they are being abused, it's a known psychological reaction. Yet the State contended that since Rick never told John

Goodwin about it or Jean Roth about it, then it obviously never happened.

Judge Sanders was killing them. Constantly meddling, constantly giving the State hints and advantages. Randall couldn't hold back any longer.

"Judge, first of all, it's -- with all due respect, it's not your call to, as you've been so kind to point out over the course of this trial, to tell us how to try the case. If by -- the court has sort of envisioned what might happen on the stand when we -- when and if we put -- or if and when we put Dr. Smith on the stand. You've sort of gone with this little idea of what you think is going to happen. I'm not convinced that's what is going to happen, but certainly by standing here and the court now saying what you would do, or how you would ask those questions, the court is instructing the state on how you think the state could best effectively challenge one of our experts. With all due respect, Judge, I don't think it's appropriate for the court to be engaging in this kind of speculation as to how a witness may testify. Well, again, Judge -- and I mean no disrespect, but I wish the court would view us as being sort of the Bobby Fishers' of criminal cases and allow us to sort of anticipate the moves ourselves and make our determinations about what's going to happen in the future rather than constantly sort of second-guessing us in advance. That I think is helpful to the state, more so than it is to us, and I object to the court really participating in that kind of analysis."

"You tell him Randall," thought Rick. "This guy has no clue what a fair trial is all about. It's bullshit. He's bullshit."

The first week of the trial had been taxing on Rick. From just having to relive every moment, to seeing people he hadn't seen in sixteen months, like John Goodwin. He adored Mr. Goodwin, and it broke his heart that he'd disappointed his mentor, and put him in this position of having to testify against him in court. What the hell. He wanted so much to just sit with Mr. Goodwin and talk about ROTC, school, and life in general. Shoot the shit like a normal human being living a normal existence. That is, if he could even remember what normal was.

CHAPTER FORTY-THREE

The morning of March 24, 1997 started with the State calling Trooper Baty to the stand, who talked about searching out Rick's friends the night of the murder, and what happened when Rick arrived at school the next morning. He reiterated his impression of Rick's state of mind.

"There were no high type emotions or low type emotions, nothing where he was overly excited or -- or sad or anything like that. You know, none of the -- none of the -- the extremes that you would notice. Just a regular contact as if you and I were talking right now."

Sergeant Michael Marrs ran through the tape and video recordings of his interview with Rick with Collins again asking about Rick's state of mind throughout the process.

"During the first interview, which was the audio tape at the school, he seemed calm and rational to me, cold. I didn't notice anything -- any over-nervousness. I didn't notice anything that concerned me other than just having a conversation with him."

"Did he ever try and fall asleep or anything like that?" said Collins.

"Oh, absolutely not. No."

In cross examination, Wally immediately jumped on the trooper, questioning his interviewing training, especially when it involved juveniles and abuse. Rick had told him about the abuse on the trail, but Marrs didn't dig any further. No follow up questions. Nothing. He missed the signs.

"And so you didn't ask any follow-up questions on physical abuse," said Wally.

"What I asked is in the interview, sir," answered Marrs.

"Okay. You didn't ask what Rick's definition of physical abuse was."

"No, I did not ask that question specifically."

"You didn't ask him if he had been punched by his father."

"No, I didn't use those words, no."

"Or kicked by his father."

"No, sir."

"Or ever had bruises all over his body as a result of beatings by his father."

"No, sir, not in those words."

"No further questions," said Wally.[39]

[39] Questioning and testimony of Sergeant Marrs taken from Court Documents

Sergeant Michael Marrs didn't ask the questions he needed to. He only wanted the 'facts' of the case. The what, how and when. He didn't give a shit about the why. Maybe he felt that wasn't his job, not his place. Except it was. When you have a young man sitting in front of you, who's just shot his parents to death, one has to assume that there are mitigating factors to the crime. There had to be another story. Some sort of reason. Too bad Sergeant Marrs didn't even try to find out. Collins called a few more expert witnesses to testify on ballistics, fingerprints, and handwriting. Then, believing he'd proven all he needed prove, rested his case.

"And the state has rested," said Judge Sanders, "which basically means they have concluded their case in chief. The defense is going to now present some witnesses. And as I told you before, you'll recall, things are the same except they're reverse. So that now Mr. Patterson or Mr. Tetlow get to ask questions on direct. Mr. Collins gets to cross examine witnesses. And so I guess we're ready to roll here. We've got the first witness in the box, so do you want to swear her in."

"Ma'am," said the clerk. "For the record I need you to state your full name, spelling your last name."

"Brenda Jo'e. J-o-'-e"

"Miss Jo'e," said Randall. "How are you related to Robert Watkinson?

"Bob and I were married for 23 years."

Brenda gave the jury her account of how her and Bob met, and their early life together. She admitted to having a drinking problem early in their marriage but had been sober for a long time.

"Well, he wanted to practice and build his hours," said Brenda, "so he'd get off work and go fly, and then come home and go to bed and get up and go to work and go flying, come home and go to bed."

"Did this have an effect on your relationship?"

"Yes, it did. I started hanging out with some friends from work, and I started drinking a lot because they drank a lot."

"You drank a lot."

"A lot."

"Would you consider yourself an alcoholic?"

"Yes."

"Tell me about how that affected your relationship with Robert."

"Oh, very -- very much. He got very angry and he was always checking me out to see if I'd been drinking, and we got in a lot of fights about it. And he would always, you know, go through the house and try and find my bottles and pour them out, and things like that."

"Okay. Did you seek counseling at this period of time?"

"Not for a while, but then after a while I went to AA."

"Did that work for you initially?"

"Not at first. I had a couple of what they call slips, and you know, went out and continued drinking for a while."

"How long did this last? This problem."

"About a year or so."

"And how did Bob react to that?"

"As I said, very badly. He didn't like my drinking at all."

"Did he yell at you?"

"Yes, he did."

"Okay. Was there any physical altercations?"

"Well, sometimes he would pin me up against the wall and kind of hold me there and yell at me until I told him where my bottles were so he could pour them out. And then when I got upset and I wanted to leave, he'd throw me in the bedroom on the bed and lock the door."

"So he physically restrained you from leaving."

"Yes," said Brenda.

"Anything beyond that?"

"There was one night -- I don't even remember what we were fighting about, and he pinned me down on the bed and started choking me."

"Did you seek marriage counseling?" said Randall.

"No. Bob was never open to any sort of marriage counseling."

"Did you talk about it?"

"Yes."

"What was his reaction?"

"He wouldn't even like go talk to my sponsor in AA. I thought maybe to help him understand what was going on that - he could go talk to her. He never would."

"There were still no children at this time?"

"No."

"So, did you and Bob -- were you able to work through the problem of the alcoholism?"

"Yes."

"Did it on your own though."

"Yes."

"Did things get better after that? After you quit drinking?"

"Yes, very much."

Randall questioned her on disciplining the boys.

"Okay. Did he handle any of the discipline at all?"

"Only if it was something really big."

"Okay. Any specific instances you can remember?"

"Well, there was one time Rick and a friend did something they shouldn't have been doing out in the woods, and Rick wouldn't admit it. And he kept not admitting it for a considerable period of time. And Bob grabbed him -- he was like seven or eight I think, and picked him up in the air and shook him as hard as he could until Rick admitted he'd done it".

"Okay. What did Rick -- what was Rick's reaction to that?"

"He was scared to death."

"Did he cry?"

"Yes."

"I mean had his dad ever done anything like that to him before?"

"No."

"That was the first time."

"Yeah."

"And could you see a change in Rick after that?"

"Well, he told us the truth about what had happened. He was just kind of unglued for a while."

"And he was how old?"

"Seven or eight."

"When you say he was unglued, I mean that -- that could be any number of things. What do you mean by that?"

"Really upset, you know, and scared and everything."

"What about verbal -- how did Bob talk to the boys?"

"Well most of the time -- when he'd get mad, be tended to lecture and get really loud, and go on, and on, and on about something."

"Well, what kinds of things would he say? I mean when you say lecture, would he just say, you shouldn't do that, or…"

"Well, it was kind of – it's hard to describe it. It's almost like he'd make you feel like you were totally worthless. Totally worthless person, and you should never have done that, and you were horrible for doing it. This kind of thing."

"Is this the way he spoke to you?"

"Yes."

"And was that the way he spoke to the boys too?"

"When they'd get out of line, you know."

"And so what was it like when he went to work for Evergreen?" said Randall. "Did things change?"

"Very much so. Because, like I said, he was gone all the time. And that was very hard on him, and it was hard because the kids were older, and like Rick was in school. And he'd come home for a few days, and he'd want to go off someplace to do something, and I wasn't going to pull the kids out of school every time Bob came home and wanted to go someplace, you know, like camping or sailing or something. I just didn't feel like we could do that. So, I tried to really build Bob up and everything so that there wouldn't be that feeling. You know, to -- to kind of play dad up as their hero, and stuff like this."

"Do you think the boys did that?"

"Yeah, I think they really did."

"What about Rick? How do you think he viewed his father at that time?"

"Oh, especially Rick because his dad was an airline pilot, and he'd take him down and let him play in the simulator, and even took him board the planes, you know, and occasionally he would fly in little planes and -- and even let Rick fly."

"So you think Rick's relationship with his father was still good during that period of time?"

"Yes."

Through her testimony, Brenda revealed Bob's change in jobs, their move to McMinnville, and the state of their marriage. Things weren't great but she thought they'd be able to work through it.

"Do you know whether Bob ever had any conversations with the boys about divorce during that period of time?"

"Not -- not until just before he left."

"How did that come about? Were you present?

"Yes. A couple of weeks before he left, Ricky I guess did know what was going on and, you know, he realized his dad wasn't home, that he was staying somewhere else and all this. And so he point blank asked his dad if he was going to get a divorce. And Bob said, no."

"Do you remember how that conversation got started?"

"Yeah. Rick was like asking."

"You mean just like out of the blue."

"Well, Bob was going away again on another trip, and he was saying good-bye to the kids. And Rick asked him, and -and Bob said, no, that -- that things weren't going real well right now, and that he might have to -- he might go away for a little bit and get his head together, but he loved all of us and he wasn't going to get a divorce."

"Do you remember when that was that that conversation took place?"

"It would have been mid-August."

"When was the next time you saw Bob?"

"About two weeks," said Brenda.

"And where was he during that period of time?"

"Boise, Idaho."

"Tell us what happened when he came back."

"He came back and he came into the house, and he was really cold. I mean he didn't hug me, he didn't kiss me. He just kind of went, where are the boys. And I told him they were up in their rooms. And he went upstairs, and I followed him. And he sat them down and told them he was leaving, and he was filing for divorce."

"Where were you?"

"I was standing in the doorway."

"Had he said anything to you before he went up to the room to talk to the boys?"

"Not really."

"What do you mean not really?"

"Well, you know, where are the boys."

"He didn't tell you he was going to leave before he told the boys."

"No."

"So this is the first you heard about it."

"Yes."

"Where were the boys?"

"In their room."

"Where was Bob?"

"Bob went in and -- and sat like on a chair. Pulled a chair out in kind of the middle of the room."

"Did he hug the boys?"

"He kind of held them off really."

"What do you mean held them off?"

"Well, kind of, you know – kind of pu –well, pushed them back you know…"

"I mean the boys hadn't seen their father in two weeks," said Randall. "Were they trying to…"

"Oh yeah."

"…hug him?"

"Yeah."

"And he didn't return that."

"Not really. He just told them to sit down, and that's when he told them."

"How did he say it?"

"Just basically, you know, that -- that he was leaving and he was getting a divorce."

"What was your reaction to that?"

"I was devastated because right before he'd left he said he wasn't leaving and getting a divorce. So I thought, hey, everything's going to be okay."

"Emotionally what was your reaction?"

"I was crying."

"Hard? The boys were there."

"Yeah."

"What was their reaction?"

"They didn't -- I don't think they quite understood at first and -- and so Bob told them -- you know, told them he was leaving, he's moving out, he's getting a divorce."

"What did Jimmy do?"

"Jimmy was crying really hard. Really confused."

"Uh-huh. And Rick?"

"Rick too."

"Rick too what?"

"Crying and -- and really hurt."

"Did he say anything? Rick?"

"I don't remember. I – I know he probably did."

"After he made this announcement, what did Bob do?"

"Went and started getting some of his stuff together, put it in the car to go."

"Stuff like what?"

"Clothes and things like that."

"Loaded them up in the car," said Randall.

"Yeah."

"Where was Rick?"

"Well, we all followed him downstairs. And so we all followed him downstairs. And Rick -- Rick grabbed a hold of his leg."

"Whose leg?"

"Bob's."

"How did he do that?"

"Wrapped his arms around his leg."

"Was Rick standing up?"

"Yes."

"So he's got his arms around Bob thigh?"

"Yes."

"What was he saying?"

"Don't go. Daddy, don't go."

"And what did Bob say?"

"He peeled Rick off his leg, looked him in the eye and said, this is what's best for you, son."

"Peeled him off his leg. What do you mean by that?"

"Peeled him off his leg. Unwrapped his arms and shoved him away."

"How did Rick react?"

"About like he is now. Sobbing his eyes out. We were all sobbing."

"What did Bob do?"

"Got in the car and left."

“Drove away.”

“Yes.”

“Did Rick watch him leave?”

“Yes.”

Sitting there at the table, listening to his mother recount the moment was too much for Rick. The tears started and he was powerless to control them. All the hurt, all the betrayal of that moment came flooding back. It was just too much to take. He could see the anger in his mother’s eyes as she spoke about Rosemary.

“Bob pulled up in the driveway with Rosemary in the car, and wanted to take the boys out bike riding so they could get to know her better.”

“Had the boys met Rosemary at that point?”

“No.”

“What was your reaction to that?”

“I lost it. I couldn't believe he'd done that. I couldn't believe -- I mean he hadn't even filed for divorce or anything like that, and he pulls right into the driveway right at the bottom of the stairs with her in the car to take the boys bike riding so they could get to know her better. I -- I -- I'm sorry, I just lost it.”

“What did you say?”

“When he came up to the door, I asked him what she was doing here. And he told me. And I think I said something along the lines of how can you do something like this. How can you bring her over here like this?”

“Where were the boys at that time?”

“Standing right near me.”

“So, the boys overheard this conversation?”

“Yes.”

“Rick was there?”

“They were both standing right there.”

“Did they go with him?”

“No. They refused to go.”

“Why?”

“I don't know. Maybe they saw how upset I was. They were confused. They were upset. You know, all of a sudden he shows up on our doorstep and there's this big blowout. And so they refused to go with him. He tried to kind of make them go, and they kept saying, no, they weren't going to go.”

“What was Bob’s reaction when the boys said, no?”

“He said, then, all right, they weren't going to have a father, and slammed the door and took off.”

“How did that make you feel?”

“Horrible.”

“Were you upset with yourself for the way you handled it?”

"Yeah. I mean I was upset, period. Yeah, I was upset. The boys were upset. They were crying their eyes out."

"How long did they cry?"

"I think we went through it for about an hour after that."

"Did you ever make any negative comments during that period of time about Bob to the boys?"

"Probably. I don't remember specific -- specifically. I tried not to run him down and say things because as crazy as it sounds, I was still hoping he wasn't going to do it. That he wasn't going to file."

"So you had hopes of a reunification?"

"Yes."

"Did you express that to the boys?"

"Yes."

"You told them you wanted their father to come back."

"Yes."

"When did you finally decide he wasn't coming back?"

"July 1st, 1990. He married Rosemary."

"Any particular feelings like anger?"

"Yeah. I was angry, very angry. Angry at what he'd done to me and what he'd done to the boys, and I was scared because I hadn't worked since the children were born. And so I had like no job skills, no recent job history…I went back to school right away to - to finish up an accounting degree so I could get a decent job that I could support myself."

"Did Rick take on any extra responsibilities during this period of time?"

"He tried to," said Brenda.

"What do you mean he tried to?"

"He kept -- kept telling me he was the man of the house."

"How did that make you feel?"

"I kept telling him he was the mouse of the house, and he was 10 years old. I didn't want him to feel like he had to be the man of the house."

"What do you think he meant by that?"

"I don't know. It's like he was trying to take care of me."

"But do you think you did lean on Rick during that period of time?"

"Yeah."

"Was he emotional support for you?"

"Yes."

"Did that go on for a while?"

"Yes."

"Had you noticed any changes in Rick's emotional stability or anything like that?"

"Yes. He would -- would what they call, act out, you know. Kind of -- he had an awful lot of anger, and that would show sometimes when he was just, I don't know, starting to become a teenager."

"Did you think about counseling?"

"There really wasn't much money for a counselor. I took them to the pastor at church and stuff, but there really wasn't money to, you know, go out and pay 50 to 100 dollars an hour for a counselor."

"Did you ask Bob for the money?"

"Yeah."

"What did he say?"

"The same thing be said before, that be gave me enough money. And be didn't think Rick needed any counseling. He thought Rick would get over it."

"He said he thought Rick could get over it. What did you think?"

"I hoped Rick would get over it.... I talked to him, and I talked to the pastor at church, and the youth group leader, and things like that. Tried to get help at school, but they said there wasn't anybody available for him to talk to."

"Okay. And did -- was Rick doing other things at that time that had you concerned?"

"Yes. He -- he was cutting classes at school, and he was flunking some of his subjects."

"And what happened when you talked to Rick about cutting classes?

"Well, when -- when he knew I was going to find out how much he'd been cutting, a couple of times he ran away just briefly."

"Did he ever take off for any longer periods of time?"

"Right before he went to Anchorage, he was gone for almost a week. He went down into town."

"Did you talk to Bob about that?"

"Well, when Rick had been gone about a week and – Bob called. And I realized Rick wasn't coming home any time soon, and I didn't know really what to do. I really didn't. I felt like a total, complete, utter failure as a parent. I mean he'd blown school, he's living on the streets. And Bob called, so I told him what had happened."

"You told Bob that Rick was -- had run away."

"Yes."

"And what was Bob's reaction?"

"That he was coming down to get him and take him to Anchorage."

"When did Bob get there?"

"Towards evening. Middle of the afternoon.

"Was Rick still there when Bob showed up?" "He tried to run away. He went out to the shop and tried to get the ATV started."

"And when Bob and Joe found Rick out trying to get the ATV started, what did they do?"

"They hauled him back into the house."

"They hauled him back in?"

"Yes".

"Okay. Was there any conversation going on at this time? Were they saying anything?"

"Rick told him to fuck off. And Bob slammed him against the wall."

"Rick told Bob to fuck off, and Bob slammed Rick against the wall. How did he do that?"

"Shoved him back against the wall, and he had like his arm up against Rick's throat."

"Pinned him?"

"Yeah."

"Did he say anything to him?"

"Just that Rick wasn't going to talk to him like that."

"So he's got his arm up against his throat, holding him against the wall, and he's telling him he's not going to talk to him like that."

"Yeah."

"All right. What happened then?"

"We took Rick in the living room. And there was -- like the living room comes to a point, and there was a chair or settee, whatever you want to call it, and they sat Rick down."

"Who sat Rick down?"

"Bob and Joe."

"They were still manhandling him at this point?"

"Yes."

"Okay. They set him down, and what did they say?"

"I -- Bob was talking about taking Rick back to Anchorage."

"And what was Rick's response?"

"Rick told him to fuck off again."

"And what happened?"

"Bob slammed him against the window. There was a – like the hand crank kind, and slammed him against the casement and the window."

"How did he do that?"

"By…"

"Did he grab a hold of his shirt?"

"No," said Brenda. "By his shoulders, and slammed him…"

"So, what happened at that point then?"

"The crank hit Rick in the back of the head."

"And what did Rick do at that point?"

"He was holding his head."

"You'd just seen Bob and Rick fighting, specifically Bob pushing Rick around. Why didn't you try and stop him at that time?"

"I guess because I was still kind of intimidated by Bob. Bob was very -- kind of authoritarian type person. And, you know, we'd been married for so long and I'd always done what he said."

"How did your relationship with Rick change after Rick moved to Anchorage? Or did it change?"

"Yeah. I think he was really angry with me for letting him go."

"Let's go to December 1st, 1995. How did you hear about what had happened?"

"The school principal called. There was a message on my answering machine when I got home to call her back."

"Did you call her? What did she say?"

"She said that Bob and Rosemary were dead."

"What was your reaction to that?"

"I was stunned. I mean I -- I thought it was like a plane crash or car accident, or something like that. So I asked her, you know, how's Rick, where's Rick. And then she told me that they'd been murdered, and that Rick was a suspect."[40]

Rick couldn't imagine how his mother must have felt hearing those words. Bob and Rosemary are dead and your son is a suspect. From Christ's little warrior to cold blooded killer. God could not have been pleased.

[40] Questions and testimony of Brenda Jo'e taken from Court transcripts

CHAPTER FORTY-FOUR

The next morning Rick watched and listened as Kristy Braman and her mother Nora Braman, took the stand on his behalf. It pained him to watch Prosecutor Collins try to hurt their credibility and rip their testimony a part. Kristy had seen the bruises on his back. She wasn't a liar. None of them were.

"Jesus this is hard to take," thought Rick wiping his eyes with the back of his sleeve. "Too many people hurt."

"Ma'am," said the clerk, "for the record I need you to state your full name, spelling your last name."

"My name is Vivian Nitteberg. And the last name is spelled N-i-t-t-e-b-e-r-g.

"And your occupation."

"Well, I'm trained in Norway as a psychologist, but I'm not working as a psychologist here since I'm not licensed, so I'm doing some counseling work.

"Good afternoon," said Wally. "Miss Nitteberg. How long were you a psychologist in Norway?"

"For almost 23 years. I was a clinical psychologist, and I was working with children and adults, and their families for most of my career."

"Okay. And when did you come to the United States?"

"In January in 1995."

"Okay. And did you know Rosemary Watkinson?"

"Yes, I did."

"Did you become very close with Rose after January of '95?"

"Well, it -- I wouldn't say we were close immediately. But Rosie would take me places, and advised me how to -- to live here, and show me things, and introduce me to friends and – and, yeah, help me to -- to get along here."

"You and your husband John would have dinner at the Watkinson's house?"

"Yes, we would."

"Okay. And they would have dinner over at your house?"

"Yes, they would."

"Did you ever have an opportunity to see Rick with Rosemary?"

"Yes, I had."

"Okay. And how did Rick treat Rosemary when you saw them together?"

"She was - he was always very polite, very helpful and…"

"Okay. Did he -- would you characterize him as submissive?"

"In a way. I would say, yes, almost…"

"How about Rosemary with Rick? How would Rosemary treat Rick when you were there?"

"Most of the time she would treat him well, and sometimes she would -- I -- I recall sometimes when I felt she was kind of irritated with him and…"

"What do you mean irritated with him?"

"How can I explain that. Sometimes -- or a few times she –I felt I would like to say like, well, let that be or something because she -- I felt she was pushing him. Pushing him too hard. Yeah, like -- or she had -- well, this is difficult to explain."

"That's okay. You can take your time."

"I remember for instance -- and this would happen more than one time, and I reacted a bit to that because I felt she stretched him a bit like. When we were having dinner, Rick was always helping to do things around the dinner table. And then she would ask him to go and put on the CD so that we could have some music, and Rick would go down and do it. And then when he came back, she wanted another record on, and then and he sat down to eat, and she would say, it's a bit loud, and he would go down again, and put it not so loud. And so it was situations like that. And Rick never protested, and so I would think that my teenagers would at one point have said something to me about that, and I felt that she was pushing him in a way. And also I felt sometimes that - that good wasn't good enough. Like he would put in the dishes in the dishwasher, and do the things in the kitchen after we had been eating, and then she would go and do it over again because it wasn't done the right way. And it was the small things that I felt maybe wasn't so - so good all the time.

"And what was it that you thought was unusual about that –about the CD?" said Wally.

"It was more like he would be sent away from the table all the time and that it wasn't good enough in a way. And I think that I might have done it myself finally when I had asked him a couple of times or so. But he had to run up and down, and do these things."

"As Rosemary's friend, did you have any concerns about how Rosemary was treating Rick?"

"Yes, on some occasions I did."

"Can you give us an example?"

"I was concerned because I felt he was grounded a lot, and that I not always saw the reason for that after what was explained."

"Rosemary had expressed on numerous occasions – or Rosemary had appeared frustrated on numerous occasions with Rick, right?"

"Yes."

"So they were having problems in their relationship."

"Yes."

"Rosemary was having problems in her relationship with Rick."

"Yes."[41]

Wally questioned Mrs. Nitteberg on several other points but the CD incident stuck in Rick's head. He'd forgotten about it. Up and down the stairs. Up and down. Up and down. All while his dinner got cold. But he didn't complain. He was polite and did as Rose asked. It was never good enough. Nothing he ever did for her was good enough.

"Sir, for the record I need you to state your full name, spelling your last name."

"James Robert Watkinson, W-a-t-k-i-n·s-o-n."

"Do you go by Jimmy?" said Randall.

"Yeah."

"And how do you know Rick Watkinson?"

"He's my brother."

Rick couldn't listen. He couldn't bear to see his little brother on the stand having to go through all of this – for him. He hated it. He hated that Jimmy had to be up there. Randall was gentle and led Jimmy through his testimony.

"How would you describe your dad's attitude about Rick's schooling?"

"He was very angry about it."

"Okay. Did he express that anger to Rick?"

"Yes, he did."

"And how did he do that?"

"By shouting."

"What kinds of things would he shout at Rick?"

"He would say, you ungrateful little bastard, you'd better get your grades up."

"Okay. And how old was Rick at this time?"

"Rick was about 11 years old."

"Now, do you remember -- you also mentioned that they argued about the divorce. How often?"

"Very often."

"Well, I mean can you give us an idea? Did it come up every time you had visits with your father?"

"Yeah, that's about right."

"Every time."

"About every time."

"Okay. And what kinds of -- why were they arguing about the divorce? What -- who started it?

"I can't remember who started it most of the time. It just suddenly came up."

[41] Questions and testimony of Vivian Nitteberg taken from Court Transcripts

"How would the conversation go?

"Rick would be upset that my dad broke the promise that he made on the marriage vow to be with my mom forever."

"Is that how he would say it?"

"Yes."

"Okay. And what was your dad's response to that?"

"He would say he couldn't have stayed with my mom because he was unhappy."

"Okay. Would they shout at each other?"

"Yes."

"And what kinds of things would they say when they'd yell?"

"My dad would say that my brother didn't understand what was going -- what was going on."

"And would he call him any names during those arguments?"

"Yes."

"And what kinds of things would he say at that time?" said Randall.

"He would call him an asshole and a shithead."

"During these discussions about the divorce."

"Yes."

"And how old was Rick, again?"

"Rick was 11."

"Okay. How old were you?"

"I was seven."

"Do you remember your reaction to these arguments?"

"I would just sit and listen, and not say anything."

"Why not?"

"I was too uncomfortable to say anything."

Jimmy recounted all the incidents of violence and all the times Bob and Rosemary had called his brother names. Too many to even count.

"Do you ever remember discussions about your mother during this period of time that Rick and your dad and Rosemary would get involved in?"

"Yes."

"Okay. What kinds of things would they say about your mother, Brenda?"

"Rick would say that my dad shouldn't have divorced her. My dad would say that he had to because she wasn't athletic enough, and now he could have fun with Rosemary."

"This is the way your dad would describe the reason for the divorce to Rick?"

"Uh-huh."

"That your mother wasn't athletic enough?" said Randall.

"Yeah."

"Did you ever talk to your dad about Rick living up here?"

"Yeah. And how did that come about?"

"Usually I'd ask how Rick was doing on the phone."

"Uh-huh. And what would Bob say about how Rick was doing?"

"He would say that he was doing fine, and that his grades were getting up, and that everything was perfect. When I came up and visited, I saw that Rick's grades weren't up, the arguments about grades were still going on, and Rick was very unhappy living there."

"Do you have any idea why your dad would have told you things were going okay?"

"It was like a competition to him to show my mom that he could raise Rick better than she did."

"Do you ever remember specific things that Rick or your dad would say about the divorce when they would argue? Did any of those arguments ever turn violent?"

"There was one that almost did."

"Okay. And when did that happen? Do you remember?"

"I think summer of '95 maybe."

"Okay. And what -- how did that happen? What came about?"

"They were arguing. I don't know about what. And my brother clenched his fists and my dad raised his fists."

"They raised fists at each other?"

"Yeah."

"Did they actually hit each other?"

"No."

"Why not?"

"I ran in the middle and screamed at them to stop it."

"And what happened when you did that?"

"My dad grabbed me by the arm and threw me against the wall."

"What about the relationship between you and Rosemary? How was that?"

"Rosemary would often get upset at little things. She thought that I should be tougher and more athletic."

"Did she tell you that?"

"Yes."

"Did she ever criticize you?"

"Yeah."

"What kinds of things would she criticize you for?"

"She would say I was stupid if I ever did anything wrong."

"Like -- she would say you were stupid if you did something wrong, or when you did something wrong, she would say you were stupid."

"When I did something wrong, she would say I was stupid."

"Were there other instances where Rosemary called you stupid in - say in Rick's presence?"

"Yes. I was pulling weeds and I cut my finger on one of the weeds, and I went back to the house to get a Band-Aid, and Rosemary started laughing at me and calling me stupid because I grabbed the weed wrong."

"Did you get a Band-Aid?"

"She wouldn't let me."

"Why not?"

"Because I was so stupid I didn't deserve one."

"That's what she told you."

"Uh·huh."

"Did you ever get a Band-Aid?"

"Yes."

"And how did you eventually get a Band-Aid?"

"Rick convinced her to let me inside and get one."

"Did - were there other times when Rosemary criticized you in front of Rick?"

"Yes."

"Okay. When did that come about?"

"There was one time when I was sleeping in my room during the middle of the day, and she thought I was too lazy, and started calling me fat."

"Okay. Was she joking?"

"No, I don't think so."

"Rick heard this?"

"Yes he did."

"And what was his reaction?"

"He didn't say anything until after she left."

"And then did you and he have a conversation about it?"

"Yes."

"And what did he say?"

"He said she was stupid to call me fat, and that I wasn't fat."

"Okay. Did he make you feel better?"

"Yes."

"Did you think you were fat?"

"A little bit."

"Rick told you you weren't.""

"Yes."

"Okay. When people would come to visit, would things get better?"

"Most of the time. In most cases, yes."

"And when you say they would get better, or when you answered yes to that, what did you ·· what do you mean they would get better?"

"Well, we would be treated with politeness and respect instead of being treated almost like slaves."

"So, it would change the attitude that Rick or that Rosemary and Bob would have towards you and Rick?"

"Yes."

"How do you think you appeared to the visitors when they came to visit?"

"Like the Brady Bunch, the perfect family."

"Was that a show?"

"Yeah."

"Would the arguments start when they left?"

"Yeah. Like if we did something wrong while they were visiting, then we would get yelled at afterward."

"Was this the way it was when Vivi and John were there?"

"Yes."

"Was this the way it was when the Roth's were visiting?"

"Yes."

"You didn't have arguments in front of them."

"I don't think so."

"Nobody got called names in front of them."

"Not that I remember."

"Did Rosemary complain about Rick to you?"

"Yes."

"What kinds of things would she complain about?"

"How she was trying so hard to be nice to him, and how he would refuse her."

"Do you think she was trying hard to be nice to him?"

"No."

"So when she would say things like that to you, that how she was trying to be nice, did you tell her you didn't think she was trying to be nice?"

"No."

"Did you ever tell your dad that you didn't think Rosemary was being nice to Rick?"

"No."

"Why not?"

"Because if I said so, they would have probably started yelling at me."

"Did you talk to them at all about what was going on?"

"No."

"You didn't talk to them about the name calling?"

"No."

"You didn't talk to them about the arguments."

"No."

"Why not?"

"Because if I did say how I felt, which I felt they were wrong, then he would start yelling at me."

"Did he ever yell at you about that?"

"No."

"You just thought he would if you did."

"I was positive he would."

"And why were you positive that he would yell at you if you brought it up?"

"Because he -- he can't accept being wrong. If anybody says he's wrong, then he starts yelling at them."

"And when you say he, who are you talking about?"

"My dad."

"Did you visit in the summer of 1995?"

"Yes, I did."

"Did you talk to your dad about Rick leaving and going to Covenant House?"

"Yes."

"What kind of conversation -- how did that conversation go?"

"It went pretty smoothly. I -- I was trying to convince them that maybe they should take things a little easier on Rick and not really yell at him when they eventually did get him back."

"Why did you step in at this point when you hadn't before?"

"Because I was afraid for him more than usual."

"You were afraid for him when he came back?"

"Yeah."

"Afraid of what would happen?"

"Uh-huh."

"What did you think might happen?"

"I thought they might have an argument, and based on how the last one had almost gotten physical, I thought this one might actually get physical."

"Okay. Were you there when Rick came back?"

"Yes, I was."

"Was there an argument?"

"Yes, there was."

"How did that argument go?"

"I don't know because after a while they went for a walk outside."

"And you didn't see how it ended?"

"I didn't see it."

"Did you ever have any conversation with or hear Rosemary say, in front of Rick anything about the effect that Rick's presence was having on her relationship with your father?"

"Yes."

"How did that come about?"

"I don't remember how it started, but they -- Rosemary would argue that Rick was tearing their relationship apart because the only thing they argued about was Rick."

"That was the only thing they argued about?"

"All that I can remember."

"Did Rosemary ever talk to you about Rick being in the house and living there?"

"Yes."

"And what did she say about that?"

"She said she wanted him to leave."

"Why did she say -- did she say why she wanted him to leave?"

"He was a burden on her, and he was tearing my dad's marriage with her apart."

"She told this to you."

"Yes."

"How often?"

"I think only once."

"Do you remember when that was?"

"I was helping her cook in the kitchen."

"All right. You said earlier that Rosemary said that she was trying to be nice to Rick, but you didn't believe that. Why didn't you believe that?"

"Well, because she -- she was just rude to him. Like she -- she would cook dinner for me, but not for him. And she wasn't polite. She didn't treat him with respect."

"Did -- this incident you've talked about her making dinner for you, but not for Rick, was Rick there at the house?"

"Yes, he was."

"And did Rick eat?"

"Yes."

"What did he eat?"

"He microwaved something for himself."

"Did Rosemary say why she wasn't cooking something for Rick?"

"No."

"She made dinner for you two."

"Yes.

"But not for Rick," said Randall.

"But not for Rick," said Jimmy.

"Did Rick react to that?"

"Not that I remember."

"What was the general feeling in the house? Can you describe that?"

"Very tense, very hostile."

"Was that all the time?"

"Yes."

"Even when people were present and every -- when like family - visitors were coming over and everybody was being pleasant, it still had that feeling."

"No."

"It didn't have it at that time," said Randall.

"No."

"Why not?"

"Because we always put on that show, and we always felt better while we were putting on that show for the visitors."

"How about emotions in the household? Any?"

"A lot of anger, and sadness."

"Was there any good emotions in that household?"

"No."

"Did you and your brother ever talk about his feelings about the house?"

"Uh-huh."

"About his relationship with your dad?"

"Yes."

"And about his relationship with Rosemary?"

"Uh-huh."

"And what did he say about that?"

"He said he hated them."

"Do you remember when you first heard that from your brother?"

"I think it was summer of '95."

"Had you ever heard him talk about that before?"

"He said he didn't like them, but he never said he hated them."

"So, he's said before that he didn't like them."

"Uh-huh."

"Did that go back -- how far back did that go?"

"All the way to the beginning. All the way right after the divorce."

"What was your reaction when your brother said he hated your dad and Rosemary?"

"I didn't believe him."

"Why not?"

"Because I thought it was impossible to hate a family member."

"You thought it was impossible?"

"Uh-huh."

"To hate a family member?"

"Uh-huh."

"Do you still think that?"

"No."

"Why not?" said Randall.

"He showed me that it -- it's not impossible."[42]

The words stung and a deep ache radiated from Rick's heart. He never meant to teach Jimmy that. It's awful that Jimmy felt that way now because of him. But everything Jimmy said was true. He'd felt the wrath of Bob and Rosemary just like Rick, although thankfully not as severe. Jimmy had done a great job with his testimony, and Rick was proud of him for getting up there and being honest. That's all Rick wanted from everyone who sat on the stand on his behalf. Honesty. Tell the jury what they saw going on. No one needed to lie on his behalf. He was tired of all the lies. The lies are what got him into this mess in the first place.

"Sir," said the clerk. "For the record, I need you to state your full name, spelling your last name."

"John Richard Smith. S-m-i-t-h."

"And your occupation?"

"I'm a physician specialized in psychiatry."

Dr. John Smith, a definite expert in psychiatry and the same psychiatrist who interviewed Timothy McVeigh after the bombing of the Alfred P. Murrah Federal Building in Oklahoma City on April 19, 1995. Rick had no idea how they managed to pull it off but Wally and Randall had managed to bring in a major heavyweight in the field of forensic psychiatry. Rick had met with Dr. Smith over the course of a few days in mid-February. Very skeptical about speaking with anyone involved in the mental health industry, Dr. Smith made Rick feel at home, and made Rick comfortable enough that he wanted to talk to the doctor. When he spoke to counselor Ann Drake or Dr. Keith Wieger before the murders, he was very withdrawn and careful with his words, almost to the point of being paranoid. Less so with Dr. Vicary because Rick knew that the doctor was there to help him with the case. He had none of this apprehension with Dr. Smith. Talking to him was like talking to an old friend, or even his grandfather. Dr. Smith actually took the time to explain things and help Rick understand the things about his emotional reactions that still confused him.

Rick learned a great deal from Dr. Smith and the doctor did an amazing job in a short period of time understanding him. Their interviews over a two-day

[42] Questions and testimony of Jimmy Watkinson taken from Court transcripts.

period were extremely long, with plenty of monotony. Routine questions to provide a foundation and fill in the blanks, but the conversations they had were simply amazing. Talking for four to five hours straight can be mind-numbing but the way Dr. Smith got to the bottom of things was so interesting it made it all worthwhile. Starting at the very beginning, Rick talked about his early childhood, the divorce, and what he was like in his teenage years. They then covered the move to Alaska and what it was like living under Bob and Rosemary's roof. They covered almost all of the fights between Rick and Bob, and spent quite a bit of time on the day of the murders and the night in question.

Extremely detailed in his responses, Rick tried to leave no stone unturned. There were some things he deliberately left out or asked him not to include in his report. Rick mentioned losing some people over the years running the streets of Oregon but didn't go into great detail. Dr. Smith recognized that Rick was obviously trying to protect those 'lost', so he didn't push the issue. Thinking back, Rick should have been completely forthright and told Dr. Smith everything, as it would have truly helped him understand just how far he was gone, and the extent of his depression and grief. Rick mentioned spiritual warfare and how deeply his mother drug them through militant Christianity but he wasn't about to risk telling Dr. Smith about the demons, his gift, or the things he could see. He didn't know how Dr. Smith would react or what the consequences might be since the doctor did have the power to medicate; something Rick desperately did not want. The fact was, he was scared shitless to even talk about it. He should have, it would have made the picture that much clearer for the jury.

CHAPTER FORTY-FIVE

"During your 32 years' experience as a psychiatrist how many of those years would you say you've specialized in treating adolescents?" said Wally.

"I would say about 25 of those years," said Dr. Smith. "Although I see many adolescents right up to the present time.

"Dr. Smith, would you define for the jury what is meant by the term, physical abuse?"

"Physical abuse is meant -- by that is meant the infliction on someone, who cannot defend themselves adequately, a degree of physical punishment like hitting, striking, pushing, kicking, throwing, that goes beyond any expected or ordinary physical activity like the spanking of a child with one's hand."

"And if you would, please, define what is meant by the term, psychological abuse."

"Psychological abuse is a pervasive kind of attitude toward someone who, again, is dependent on you cannot escape you, in which you devalue the person, where you demean, where you cause them pain in excess of what might be necessary to teach, if we're speaking about children."

"In your expert opinion," said Wally. "what -- how does physical abuse on a child affect that child's development in later years, say as a teenager?"

"Well, it saps one self-confidence, for one thing. It usually generates a feeling that one must be bad as a human being. It also may create a considerable sense of fragility about one's body where then one becomes more shy or defensive about any threat to one's body. It certainly deeply affects self-esteem and one's feeling of independence."

"Is there any relationship at all, any interplay, between physical abuse and psychological abuse on a child as it affects the child's emotional growth?"

"Well, to begin with, it's unusual to find one without…it's unusual to find physical abuse without psychological abuse. It is more common to find psychological abuse without physical abuse. As far as them both affecting -- they do both affect maturation, maturing, self-confidence. There is an enmeshment often of someone who has been even psychologically abused with the abuser. I mean there are technical words for that, but it's basically a kind of overdependence and an inability to break free, a kind of an enmeshment psychologically with the abuser."

“I'm not a psychiatrist so you'll have to bear with me. In lay terms, would it be fair to say that a child who is being physically and psychologically abused by a parent will actually bond close with that parent?”

“Yes, they may very well.”

“Well, how can that happen?”

“Well, it happens because of an inability to escape the engaging, intense, attitude of the parent toward the child. That's one aspect of it. Children with a parent like that never lose a kind of desperate effort to please that parent, even though it may have become obvious to anyone outside the family, like you heard earlier, that that person could not please the -- the parent. But they will not give up trying because of their dependency on it, and the driving need from within a child to -- to receive ultimately some kind of approval or love from a parent.”

“Is it unusual that a child who is enmeshed with a parent like this, who is abusing them, is it unusual that they would keep on, and keep on, and keep on trying to please even when it's obvious that they cannot do that?

“Well. I would say up to a point that that's usually what happens actually.”

“What do you mean up to a point?”

“Well, ultimately you may mature to the point where you can leave home, or escape, or get into therapy, or if you're fortunate in life, meet someone who can help you comprehend what's happening. You often can't see that yourself.”

“Do adolescent males, who are psychologically and physically abused by their father, do these adolescent males exhibit any sort of common behaviors?”

“Well, some of the common behaviors may be an irritability, an over-aggressiveness because they may identify with the aggressor as a matter of fact. The abuser may be identified with so that they may then become abusers or more aggressive, more angry people. That's at least one aspect of what can happen with an abused child.”

“So, the abused child in essence becomes like the abuser.”

“Absolutely, in many cases unfortunately. Not always. I do want to say that.”

“Are there any other common characteristics of adolescent males who have been abused by a parent?

“Low self-esteem is -- is a rather common characteristic, and often a kind of feeling of helplessness, and that is, powerless.”

“Why would a -- an adolescent male who is being abused by a parent -- assuming they did get away. Say they ran away. Why would they go back to the same abusive situation that they ran away from?”

“Well, a lot of times they don't have a choice.”

“Is it unusual for an abusive parent to have periods when the abuser is actually being kind to the child that they're abusing?”

“Oh, no. As a matter of fact, that's especially common. It's even – well, it's especially common of course, in sexual abuse. But it is also not uncommon that an abuser or someone who may have an explosive temper, who they themselves may recognize they have trouble with, because often there is some pathology in the parent -- that is, psychological pathology in the parent who is being the abuser. It's not always because they're just an evil sadistic parent. It is often because they have problems themselves and can't control their temper. So that they may feel very remorseful and apologetic at times for the loss of their temper."

"During your career as a psychiatrist have you ever evaluated or counseled parents who in your opinion were in fact being abusive physically and/or emotionally, and simply did not realize that they were in fact being abusive?"

"Oh, many times, yes."

"So, sometimes you wind up with parents who are actually being abusive who just don't realize -it themselves."

"Absolutely. Or the kids don't realize it. Kids are also really embarrassed about abuse."

"Would it be unusual to see a father who was not aware that he was being abusive in counseling with the same person that he was in fact abusing?"

"No, that's not unusual at all. I see that a lot of times."

"In your experience, Doctor, is it the norm for adolescents who are being abused physically and emotionally to report that abuse to authority figures?"

"It is not the norm. The norm is the opposite. One of the major reasons that child abuse goes on, and especially during adolescence, is because it's not reported by anyone, including the person being abused."

"Given the veil of secrecy that you just spoke of, is it possible for a neighbor, or even a close family friend, to look at the relationship between an abusive parent and their child and say, this looks perfectly normal to me?"

"Yes, it is -- it is possible."

"Why is that?"

"You're talking about a friend who looks at a family. Well, number one, you can't see abuse unless there are scars or bruises or something showing up. Secondly, as I've already indicated, people will frequently put their best foot forward when other people are in the home. I think that's not an uncommon thing, especially if there's something to hide. So that you may not see it from that point of view. And not everyone will allow themselves to talk about this to even their best friends. Kids are more apt to do that than adults are."

"Doctor, let's -- I want to ask a few questions about your involvement with Rick Watkinson. Have you had a chance to meet with Rick?"

"Yes. I spent somewhere around nine, or a little more, hours interviewing Rick, doing a psychiatric evaluation and interviewing of Rick here at the Cook Inlet detention center -- pre-trial center. Then last night had not seen him since I came back to Alaska for this testimony. I wanted to talk with him briefly again about certain other issues that I wanted to make sure I had the facts clear on, so I talked to him about 30 minutes last night."

"What did these sessions with Rick consist of?"

"They consisted of an intensive psychiatric interview over a period of time which had to do with developing his history, trying to seek a better understanding of the internal workings of his mind and his brain, the way the mind and brain operate within him, as that shows its expression in his emotional life, in his thinking, in his behavior. So, I -- I did this through my knowledge of how to interview and evaluate a person."

"And did you in fact conduct interviews with other people?" said Wally.

"Yes. Well, I spoke with Rick's mother and his brother Jimmy, that you heard this morning. And I spoke with the gentleman that testified here just before I did, John. And spoke with his wife. I'm trying to remember…

"Vivi Nitteberg?"

"Yes. And I'm trying to remember if I'm leaving anyone out."

"What was the purpose of interviewing those people?"

"I wanted to collect as much information as I could about Rick, his behavior, the developmental history that I could get from his mother alone, and try to establish more in my own mind something about the family milieu in which Rick grew up because I knew from experience that murders within the family like this are usually a sign of family pathology, not just individual pathology."

"Well, why should the court or the jury even concern themselves with family history? Why not just focus on the night of the shooting, as the state has done?"

"Well, I didn't know the state had just done that. But as far as -- if you're going to understand, not from a legal point of view, but from a psychiatric point of view, any behavior, certainly a behavior as tragic and dramatic as this kind of behavior, then you're going to have to understand the developmental history of the person and the family milieu in which it occurs. It doesn't just occur in a vacuum. These things never do."

"Okay. And are you familiar with the term parricide?"

"It refers to the murder of one's parent."

"Is there anything different about parricide cases than say from other juvenile homicide cases like say where a juvenile walks into a liquor store and shoots somebody in a robbery?"

"Yes. Studies have ac -- there's a study -- I mean studies have been done on this, statistical studies. The major difference is that adolescents who murder a parent are found to be much more neurotic, had much more internal difficulty like depression, severe anxieties, being crippled by often family interaction."

"Did you have a chance to take a look at the videotaped interview that was done with Rick Watkinson down at trooper headquarters?"

"Yes, I did. I watched that."

"Okay. Do you have an expert opinion about how effective those interviews were in determining what happened, or why it happened, on the evening of December 1?"

"Well number one, I thought the video of the -- where the detective was sitting there and interviewing Rick on the video, I thought for the most part that gave a pretty good picture of what happened. I mean if you just mean the facts…of -- you know, you got your gun and shot and so forth. I thought that gave a pretty good picture of the facts. I thought it gave almost no picture of what emotional state Rick was in. He was calm. He was on the surface -- there was one psychological question asked, which I -- I was glad at least that was asked. They asked him if he heard voices. And he said, no. Because sometimes these things do occur in psychotic kids and are a result of command hallucinations. But Rick said, no, he was not hearing voices. So it's not a very good evaluation of Rick in terms of the way I would want to evaluate psychiatrically. But I thought it did give a pretty good picture of what happened. I mean as far as just the facts of shooting people."

"How effective do you think the interviews were in getting Rick to talk about physical abuse that he was experiencing by his father?"

"I don't think that was the intent of the interviews. Not the ones I read. And I think that was a very casual kind of approach to that."

"Well, didn't -- in the interview didn't the trooper ask Rick, have you ever been physically abused by your father?"

"Yes. Yes, he asked him. But that's all he asked him."

"Why shouldn't that be sufficient? Why can't I just say to an abused child, have you been abused by your parent, and that should cover it?"

"Well, if you're that naive in approaching an abused child, you will almost never get the correct answer, just exactly for what I've said. That is, in the vast majority of cases if you ask an abused child if they're being abused they'll say no, for the reasons I said earlier. Now, if Rick had been a psychopath and he wanted to really make himself look good, he could have talked about how bad his dad was beating on him, and threatened him, and so on and so forth. But he didn't do that. He's much more typical of abused children that he just hides it."

"How so? How is he typical of abused children?" said Wally.

"By not saying anything when he has a chance, even when it's in his own self-interest."

"Based on your interviews and your review of the police reports prepared in this case, do you have an opinion as to the parenting behaviors of Robert Watkinson?"

"I think that he had very limited parenting skills. I think that, for whatever reason, since I don't know his background and so forth, his personality was such that it did not lend itself to very rational parenting. And that primarily showed itself in terms of not just his absences - often that couldn't be avoided because he worked away -- but the quality of the time spent with Rick, especially after he became a teenager and after the divorce occurred. It was punctuated with periods of verbal outbursts, temper outbursts, and sometimes physical outbursts which involved hitting Rick. I think that was a product probably of his own personality. You heard some about that here from this stand from John yesterday when he talked about his perfectionism, his competitiveness, his inability tolerate imperfection in others, especially I'm sure his oldest son, since he basically was describing a highly narcissistic man."

"And were you aware that Rick had asked his dad – shortly before his dad sat them down and told them about the divorce he asked his dad, dad, are you leaving us? And that his dad said, no, son, I'm not leaving you."

"Yes."

"How do you think that that prepared Rick, or did not prepare Rick, for his dad then coming in and saying, I'm leaving you?"

"Well, it generated mistrust. It's the sort of thing -- although this man was not an alcoholic that you see in alcoholic families quite a lot -- in which you get unpredictable response at different times. And you often leave a child then feeling very insecure, not trusting their own perceptions, and in this case not trusting his father."

"In your expert opinion was Robert Watkinson inflicting physical abuse upon his son Rick in that incident where he went down to Oregon to bring Rick back to Anchorage?"

"Yes. There's no question that both the incidents -- I mean are inappropriate physical abusive episodes."

"Were there any other episodes…" said Wally.

"Rick's no saint, but you expect a father to control himself a good deal more than you do a 14-year-old or 15-year-old boy."

"Okay. Now, in your experience, when adolescents are talking about physical abuse that have been inflicted on them by their parents, is it the norm for them to recall every instance of physical abuse that they've suffered?"

"No. In fact they usually have what they call screened memories," said Dr. Smith.

"What does that mean?"

"That just means that they'll remember the –some of the most dramatic moments of the abuse. It becomes so normal in these families -- I mean it is the norm. It's not even -- I don't think Rick would have ever defined this as abuse.

He would define it as a conflict with his father. It is not ordinary for kids who are raised in this – these kinds of homes to say I've been abused. In fact, it's exactly the opposite. This is what happens between dad and I. It never occurs to them that there are families in which the children are not disciplined like that or where that kind of thing is not going on."

"So, would it -- given what you've just said about physical abuse becoming the norm for an abused child, would it be unusual if you were to ask an abuse child, have you been physically abused, for the child to say, no?"

"No. I mean that would not be unusual. You're correct. Especially if you use those words," said Dr. Smith.

"Why not?"

"Well, because a child doesn't experience themselves as being abused in the first part. If you said, tell me a little more about you and your dad and how you get along, let's take a look at -- at what's happened over the last couple of years with you, then you may begin to get some -- he may begin describing to you what happens, but he would not identify that as abuse."

"In your 32 years of experience in family counseling and adolescent psychiatry," said Wally. "How does Rick's experience with his father compare to other cases that you've worked on?"

"Well, that's a very broad question. You mean other cases in which children were physically abused?"

"Right."

"I would say it falls in about the middle third. I mean if you wanted me to rate it, I'd probably say it was -- if you -- from zero abuse to the most severe abuse I've ever seen, I would probably rate it about a five or a six."

"So you have seen cases where there's been much more serious physical abuse than we see in this case."

"Yes. There are cases I -- I wouldn't even call abuse. They're torture of children."

"Okay. Does the fact that there are more serious forms of physical abuse, does that mean that what occurred – what Robert Watkinson did to his son in this case was not physical abuse?"

"No, it does not mean that. And it doesn't really explain either what this specific boy, and his specific personality -- how he experienced and reacted to what was occurring. This abuse occurred within an explosive atmosphere. That is, I don't think that his father or stepmother hated him, or thought he was an evil little monster. I mean even though they called him names and so forth. And I think that often out of their own misunderstanding of how to parent him, and their own personality styles, they became explosive at times, and that abuse occurred in those - at those times. But I think they would really liked to have had a good relationship with Rick, and I think they did at times. In fact, I know they did because Rick told me they did."

"So, based on your review of the documents in this case, and all the interviews you conducted, you think that abuse would not have occurred by Robert or Rosemary as long as they didn't lose their temper. Is that basically what you're saying?"

"If they had a different personality style, or had been able to control their tempers and the impulse -- all three of these people have impulse control problems when they're angry. I mean it's very clear from the history and the family milieu that existed that they do. Yeah, I think if they had been able to control their temper, had different personality styles, if Rick had been less provoking, I mean if the system had been different, there may well not have been abuse."

"And when they'd lose their temper, they would then inflict the physical abuse," said Wally.

"That's right."

"Would it be unusual for abusive parents to take their kids on vacations?"

"No."

"Would it be unusual for abusive parents to take their kids jet skiing?"

"No, not in the context of what I've just described this particular kind of abuse as being. I mean I could tell you stories of abusive parents that would never do that, but certainly in this family that was -- that would be expected I think."

"Based on your review of the records in this case and the interviews that you've conducted, do you have an expert opinion as to the parenting behaviors of Rosemary Watkinson?"

"The information I have, which comes from her friend Vivian and from Rick, would be that Rosemary at times could be a very caring person. In fact, she was described at times as -- like one time on the telephone talking to Rick, as being almost flirtatious, like she was talking to a boyfriend. In other words, she - I think she was trying to describe that she was very kind. And then at other times Vivian would hear her, as you heard some also from John yesterday, being just super critical, demanding, demeaning, devaluing, toward Rick. So that she seemed erratic in her response to Rick. But remember, Rosemary was -- is the person that Rick believed, and his mother promoted that belief, who had destroyed their family and taken his father away from not only him, but his mother, who had a terrible time following that. And Rick was the oldest boy and felt very responsible for that. So, the issue here was not only Rosemary and her kindness or lack of it, or her hostility and so forth but it was also Rick had a history before he ever came there. And he had that simmering pot of anger inside him that be also had to deal with. And it was easy to focus it on someone if they're going to slap you, if they're going to ridicule you, if they're going to call you a punk. I mean it became a lightning rod not only in relationship to - her behavior, but the history of Rick by the time he got there. You know, our brain -- our mind and our -- its brain is always a product of everything that has happened to us up to that moment and how we react in the current situation."

"Did you also form an opinion as to the nature of the relationship between Rick and his biological mother, Brenda Jo'e?"

"Yes."

"And what is that?"

"Well, you know, Rick -- I'm sure as everybody has figured out by now, that Rick has very ambivalent feelings about most of the authority figures in his life. Ambivalence being mixed feelings. He's of two minds. And he was of two minds about his father, he's of two minds about Rosemary, mostly on the hostile side, he was of two minds about his mother, but mostly on the positive side. After all, his mother had stayed with him when his dad ran off and left him. He had overall been well treated by his mother in his eyes. But there was a side to Rick, as he got older, that he told me about, that I think he hadn't really told anyone else about, and that is that he felt very angry with his mother also. And I asked him what about. And he said he felt angry with his mother because she was so angry with his father and focused on it so much, about the divorce, and abandoning them, and in her mind at least finding adequate financial support of the family, that she was so angry and so critical of his father and Rosemary, that it made it very difficult for him to love his father and relate better to his father and Rosemary without feeling guilty about it. Because he felt he was being disloyal to his mother. So, he loved his mother, he enjoys his mother's support, but by the time he came up here be also had been fed this anger so long that he felt angry that his mother was so angry. He understood why she was angry, but that had persisted right on through up to the time he came up here and afterward."

"So then Rick's relationship with his mother would have affected his relationship with both his father and Rosemary."

"No question about it. It did. I mean they were lightning rods, and their abuse really gave a focus, but that wasn't the only source of his anger."

"If you had to describe the effects of the family dysfunction that we've been talking about, the physical abuse that Rick suffered, and the emotional abuse that he suffered, if you had to describe the effects of those things in a nutshell on Rick on November 30, how would you sum that up?"

"I would sum it up as his being full of hate and pain, because that's what happened."

"As a result of the divorce?"

"It went -- the core of it goes back to the divorce. But, of course, then there are multitudinous, continuing incidences. He has to leave Oregon. He doesn't want to. There's the physical violence between he and his father. And from the time he's a little boy -- it wasn't physical violence, but he related to me that whenever he'd wrestle with his dad, which he liked to do, his dad would get so carried away that even when he was like five or six years old, it wasn't like a little kid wrestling his dad, it's like his dad would pin him down and he'd feel tormented and helpless, and he would hold him there until he started crying and screaming. Now, I say that because it's important in understanding Rick. He always experienced his father from the very beginning as being overwhelming, as being someone he could not cope with. And that's important the night of the murders because his father jerked him out of ROTC, told him he was going to have to leave again, having abandoned him when he was a child, and he began to feel like these people can do anything they want to me. I can't handle it. That was one element in what was going on. And that was the product of these years of abuse and of trying to cope with this demanding, perfectionistic, intermittently explosive father. I don't know whether I've adequately answered your question, but I've told you of the building rage and pain in this man as it came out the night of the murders."

"Let me ask you more specifically, what -- we've heard that on the night that the homicides occurred that Rick's father went to his room and told him, you're ruining my marriage, I can't have you here anymore, you're out of here. What effect would that have had on Rick?"

"Well, in spite of Rick at times wanting to leave, and running away, and not wanting to come to Alaska and things, he never really lost a deep desire to have some kind of relationship with his father. And it did what severe rejection does to children. It just stirred up all the pain and hurt, not just of that night in saying you have to leave, but of the whole experience of having been left, having been abandoned, having felt unloved by his father. That's what it did to him."

"Did you do a psychiatric diagnosis of Rick?"

"Yes."

"When you interviewed him?" said Wally.

"Yes."

"And did you diagnose Rick as having suffered from post-traumatic stress disorder on November 30, 1995?"

"Yes. I felt that was one element in the – in understanding this young man. When you make diagnoses, you attempt to establish -- diagnoses are just words, but they do capture certain sets of symptoms. That was one element in trying to understand this young man's complex history."

"What -- if you can explain for the jury, what is post-traumatic stress disorder?"

"Well, post-traumatic stress disorder is when a person has experienced a significantly stressful situation to have enduring consequences on the individual. It does not have to be an out of ordinary experience. That used to be the case, but that's not the case anymore. So that continuing depression, continuing excessive anxiety. In this case flashbacks which occurred that night as a matter of fact in terms of being flooded not just with the events of that day, but flooded with memories, painful memories especially, about his father. That all -- that flashback and those intrusive memories were also part of this syndrome. There was also a peculiar light color. You know, colors are often used to express emotion. Like he made me see red, or that was the blackest day of my life. With sensory we can experience colors as well as many other kinds of sensory experiences, both good and bad. And when the divorce had occurred, and actually before that, which I won't go into, but there had been a peculiar light, a peculiar color in the room, a kind of rusty -- what he remembers as a kind bluish-rusty color that had actually occurred earlier in his life when he was terribly frightened by something. And that was a color that he experienced that night. That's simply another element of why I believe that he was suffering from elements of post-traumatic stress disorder from the divorce, from the abuse, from being rejected. And it was all coming back to him. It just flooded him."

"What affects, if any, would post-traumatic stress disorder have on Rick's actions on November 30, '95?"

"What it does," said Dr. Smith, "is it focuses back the full impact of the whole long history or memory and pain. In a more dramatic way, it's the same sort of thing if anyone was ever in Vietnam or was in a war, or in Desert Storm. I've seen -- I have seen a number of military people who were in Desert Storm. Where currently something will happen which is not the same as what they experienced at Desert Storm, but the whole impact of having been in Desert Storm will come back to them at one time, and they may have enormous difficulty controlling themselves. That has occurred - certainly a lot of this has been written about the Vietnam experience. Those are more dramatic, out of ordinary experiences. That is the most dramatic kind and most commonly referred to post-traumatic stress disorder. Now abused children and many -- and abused wives, and many other kinds of traumas, the reactions of kids to divorce, all these are now within the purview of -- although it didn't use to be -- of post-traumatic stress disorder. They must have various recurrent symptoms with it also."

"You said that it makes -- post-traumatic stress disorder makes it difficult for a person to control their actions."

"Yeah, because you're overwhelmed by the emotions. It doesn't mean you don't know what you're doing, but it's just that you can't feel and see options. It is -- it's like the boiler that is producing the steam that's down there. It's the previous experiences, the pain, the angers, the memories, that come flooding back to you that make it more difficult for cognition, even though you may know what you're doing, to actually control and manage what you' re doing."

"So, with post-traumatic stress disorder a person becomes so overwhelmed, in layman's terms, that they can't control their actions."

"I would say may become so overwhelmed. If you would say may, then I would agree."

"Okay. In your expert opinion did Rick become so overwhelmed on November 30, 1995, that he could not control his actions?"

"I know he did."

"What leads you to say that?"

"Well, it was -- one -- Rick did something I have never seen in the 25 people, at least, that I've seen who killed a parent. Number one, he's described very well what he felt. But what he did that I've never, ever seen was that he, in his words, killed them twice. The first time he had been down there -- all this had happened that I've been talking about. There are all these memories and painful feelings bubbling up inside him. And then all of a sudden the thought, I'll kill them, flashed into his mind. And he kind of slowly got up from the bed he was lying on and dropped to his knees by a nightstand, took out his favorite pen, or had a pen there, and he wrote what he called an anarchy note. And within that note he described what he was going to do like a plan. And the very peculiar part of that note that I've never seen before, although I have seen adult psychotic people who have killed their mothers who rape them after they kill them, but I've never seen a kid write down I -- rape them. I've never really even seen a note written like that. I've seen other notes that were written, but not of that sort. Not an actual plan. Then after he had done it, he felt relief. And he laid back down, and then he felt very drained, he felt like he was a shell, which is a feeling he's had before and has described to me before, but then his head started filling up again. And it started filling up again with the focus being on his father. Rosemary actually didn't come back to his mind very much at all. His head started feeling up – filling up with memories of his father, the painful times that he had interacted with his father both physically and psychologically, and especially the various times his father had rejected him. That's what began filling up his head again. And after a while he just got up and got his Dad's gun and went up, and tried to stop himself at one point, but didn't. And you could argue that he could, but I don't think he could, understanding adolescent brain development, and understanding what I've seen over the years in terms of the power of emotions, including its physiology, which I won't go into. But -- then he just went ahead and acted out the murders. I've seen several kids who have killed both parents, and this is a rather typical acting out of that reaction. And it gave him a sense of power too. Finally, he was getting some relief over these people who could treat him any damn way they pleased."

"Was he able to -- was Rick able to control his actions when he wrote out the operation anarchy note?

"That was like he was a robot. He just got up out of bed, sat down -- oh, he obviously controlled his actions. He was writing with his fingers. He has a very peculiar finger writing. I mean obviously he was controlling it."

"How about after he wrote the operation anarchy note, and he was laying there on the bed being filled with memories of the divorce, memories of the physical abuse, memories of the emotional abuse? Was he able to control his actions in the events that took place after that?"

"I don't think he could, although he said at one point to me -- Rick's been very honest with me. He said, I don't know, maybe I could have sunk deeper into my pain. But he didn't. And I think there's a limit to what people can tolerate in their head. Some people can tolerate a lot more. Rick really -- Rick is really a vulnerable, rather crippled young man from the standpoint of his personality development."

"You mentioned that there was one instance where he had a second thought, or something like that, before the shooting took place."

"It was upstairs."

"Okay. And that was -- was that before the shootings took place?"

"Yeah. I think he cracked the door a little bit, something came into his mind, he stepped back, went back. Rosemary saw the door open. He swung it open, she saw him there, she screamed, and from that moment on it was just go, go, go."

"Was Rick capable of stopping himself from what was about to happen when he had that thought?"

"I don't think he was. I think he may tell you that perhaps he was. I don't believe he was, based on my knowledge of brain function."

"Well, what is it about your knowledge of brain function that leads you to conclude that he was not able to stop himself?" said Wally.

"Well, once a very powerful discharge occurs, you may think you can control yourself, and you may even say you can control yourself -- there's a certain part of the brain called the amygdala in which enormous -- well, it's the part that discharges whenever we're frightened and it lights up certain parts of the cortex, and it -- once it gets going, it's absolutely outside the control of the person. The discharge is outside the control. Depending on what the cortex is, what the patient's experience has been, what the maturity of the individual is, they may be able to control their actions to some extent, and often do. I mean we all lose our tempers sometimes. But once that gets going in a person as vulnerable as Rick, and under the intense circumstances that were occurring, plus lots of other memories and so forth that he had, I do not think he could stop himself. You can argue that both sides, but in my opinion, knowing how he was functioning, knowing what had happened to him, I do not believe he could stop himself."

"There's been some mention that at some point in time Rick went by the nickname Ghost."

"It's a nickname -- it's a name, a painful name that Rick gave to himself."

"Is there any clinical, psychiatric significance in the fact that he went by Ghost?"

"Well, the significance is the way he experienced himself. It actually came out of when he was much younger and the period following the divorce. Rick went through a very severe depression, which is -- I won't go into the details. But at any rate, he became very depressed. He felt like a ghost. He felt empty. He felt morose. And he began to think of himself as a ghost. Now, later on as an adolescent he nicknamed himself Ghost. But actually that name Ghost is identified with an extremely painful part of his life in which he almost killed himself a couple of times. And it was a very, very bad time for Rick."

"In layman's terms," said Wally, "when you're discussing post-traumatic stress disorder, and a person, in this case Rick, laying there thinking about the years of -- the divorce, his hatred of his dad because of the divorce, his hatred of Rosemary because of the divorce, and the physical abuse, and the emo…"

"Are you talking about the night of the murders?" said Dr. Smith.

"Yes. And the emotional abuse…"

"He wasn't laying there thinking about Rosemary or thinking about his dad."

"Okay," said Wally.

"And he wasn't just think -- he was not just thinking about the abuse. That was part of it. He was thinking about all the pain that be experienced surrounding his relationship with his father. Specific memories kept flashing back into his mind."

"And as a result of those memories, he was overwhelmed?"

"He was overwhelmed. And then he kind of snapped and decided he was going to kill them. And he did."

"What sort of emotions would he be feeling at that point in time?"

"I think when he was doing it, I don't think he felt much of anything. I think by then, as often happens, I think he was just operating on intellect. I don't think he was feeling much of anything at the time he actually killed them. I think he just went through the motions."

"What was the triggering event, if you will, that caused him to go into this state on November 30, '95?"

"The night? Or you mean the whole day?"

"The…"

"The absolute final straw was when they came back fighting with each other. He'd just had that. I mean this was such a hostile home. I mean if you can imagine living in a home in which there's constant fighting. Not just with you, with each other. It is -- and probably some people have. It is a miserable feeling."

"That was the moment…"

"That was really the moment that ended it, in his mind. When they came back fighting."

"Is there a difference between the passion that a person experiences as a result of long-term family dysfunction and the passion that a person feels as a result of a short-term contact with a stranger?"

"It's much more deeply ingrained in the brain in terms of memories. There's actually a lot of work out now on the physiology of abuse and pain, and how it alters brain function. So that -- yes, there is a great deal of difference because of the vulnerability -- it's usually with children. The developmental stages of a child, the long-term nature of it, the extreme dependency that children have on the people that are going through this hostile atmosphere. So, yes, of course, there's a lot more -- a lot more psychological and developmental issues involved in the abuse that goes on in families over a long period of time than in the -- say a dating relationship in which someone hits you or something."

"This state that you were talking about being put in. being overwhelmed by memories, and emotions, and et cetera, was that a state of passion?"

"Well, it's a state of intense emotion, which I believe is defined legally as passion."

"Are you familiar with the phrase, cooling passion?" said Wally.

"Say it again."

"Are you familiar with the phrase, cooling passion?"

"Cooling passion?"

"Yes," said Wally.

"No, I'm not."

"Or the pass -- a person coming out of this state of passion."

"Oh, you mean cooling down?"

"Cooling down."

"Yes, I know that".

"You're familiar with that phrase?"

"Yes. You mean in layman's terms? You're cooling down after an intense passionate experience. Yes."

"How does the ability to cool down after an intense situation and say an argument between strangers? Is the cooling down period different in those two situations?"

"Well, you almost have to be more specific than that. I mean an argument between strangers, you may quickly get over it, it doesn't mean much anyway. That would be one way of looking at it. Or if you happen to have been especially hurt by a stranger, you may harbor a grudge. A cooling down period after these things with families may go on for a long time."

In your expert opinion, did Rick cool down any time between the time that he was overwhelmed by his memories and the time that be killed his parents?

"You mean until the very end of it?"

"Right."

"I think by that time Rick was just on robot. I think that once this was triggered. I think once the cortex was set off like this, I don't think he -- he stopped. He went down, reloaded his gun, and went right back and shot them in a very cold-blooded way. I don't think he ever stopped, in terms of cooling down."

"Would he have ever cooled down after that?"

"What do you mean ever cooled down after that?" said Dr. Smith.

"Would be still – he's not in the same state today, is he that he was in then on November 30, '95?"

"Oh, yeah. I think after this powerful discharge, and then he kind of panicked and ran out in the cold and so forth, yeah, I think he cooled down. I think he was enormously relieved after it was over with. In fact, I know he was."

"What do you mean relieved?"

"He had been in pain so long, he had been in this hostile atmosphere for so long, he had no power to stop it, that it-- and it's -- every kid I've ever seen told me the same thing that their initial reaction was one of relief. It's over with."

"Are you familiar with the term, flat affect?"

"Yes."

"What does that refer to?"

"It means a kind of paucity of feeling and absence of feeling."

"Would Rick have been…"

"I mean usually when we talk, you know, we can tell there's an emotional connection. Flat affect is where the emotions have been cut off and where there's a kind of absence of feeling tone to whatever we're talking about."

"Were you able to review the videotape of the second interview with Rick at trooper headquarters?"

"Where a kind of heavyset detective interviewed Rick?"

"Yes."

"Yes, I saw that."

"In your expert opinion was -- and you see Rick in that video?"

"Did I what?" said Dr. Smith.

"Did you see Rick in the video?"

"Yes. Rick was in the video."

"In your expert opinion, was Rick displaying flat affect during that interview?"

“He was pretty flat.”

“In your expert opinion, Dr. Smith, at the time that the shootings were happening, did Rick love his father at that point in time?”

“He certainly wasn't conscious of it, that's for sure.”

“What about Rosemary?”

“No.”

“No, he did not love her or, no, he was not conscious of it?”

“I don't think he ever loved Rosemary,” said Dr. Smith.

“Was there any point in time on November 30, '95, during the shootings that it was possible for Rick to stop himself and just leave the house or run away?”

“In my opinion, not really. I mean I suppose I could create a scenario in my mind that's theoretical that would say, well, yes, he could because he did this, this or that. Knowing this boy's history, knowing the limitations of his development, knowing once he got started with this, in my opinion, realistically he could not stop it.”

“No further questions,” said Wally. “The defence rests.”[43]

[43] Questions and testimony of Dr. Smith taken from the Court transcripts

CHAPTER FORTY-SIX

Robert Collins gathered his papers, rose from the table and took his place behind the podium. He glanced at the jury, and smiled. He had this case in the bag. He knew it. He could feel it. If the Judge was on his side, the jury had to be right there too. That little teenaged bastard was going to jail for a long time. That was his job, and he was determined to make it happen.

"Thank you, Your Honor. Good morning, ladies and gentlemen. I think you know by now that on November 30th, 1995, Mr. Rick Watkinson executed his parents. He planned these murders. To prove murder in the first degree the state must prove two basic things. First, the event in question occurred at or near Anchorage, on or about November 30th, 1995. There's no dispute about the date. Second, the defendant intentionally caused the death of Robert Watkinson, and Count II, caused the death of Rosemary Watkinson. The real issue in this case is going to focus on the word intent. I'd like to talk to you about that."

"Intent is obvious in this case, ladies and gentlemen. He shot each of these people in the head. He shot each of them multiple times. He shot his father three times. He shot Rosemary twice. Later, if you will recall, in his videotaped confession to Sergeant Marrs you can see that he didn't know that Rosemary had been shot in the chest. When he went back up into that bathroom to find her, you can reasonably infer he thought she was hiding in the tub. This is what he saw when he got up there. He testified -- he told Sergeant Marrs that he thought she was whimpering or crying. He couldn't see the bullet wound in her chest and he shot her in the head."

"You know that this was a planned shooting. You know this was a planned shooting because you have his plan. You know this was a planned shooting because he set his clock. He wanted to wake up at 1:00 a.m. so he could shoot his parents. When questioned by Sergeant Marrs on the video, he said he came up with a plan between 11:30 and 12:00 the night before he did it-- the night of the shooting, November 30th. He wanted to do it at 1:00 a.m…but decided not to wait. Don't forget Sergeant Marrs didn't know about the operation anarchy note or the specifics of the operation anarchy note when he was conducting his interview with Mr. Watkinson."

"Contrary to the story he gave Dr. Smith -- that Rick gave Dr. Smith, if Smith's operation anarchy note version is correct, then why did he set the alarm? Dr. Smith does not have an explanation for that. He intended to kill, you know he intended to kill because when he ran out of ammunition after shooting through the bathroom door, he ran downstairs, ran downstairs, to-reload. If he were in a passionate state -- and I'll talk more about passionate state at length in a little bit - if he were in a passionate state -- you'll recall when he got downstairs, he was analyzing who was on the phone."

"His assumption was Rosemary was on the phone because he knew he had shot his father. But he recognized his father's voice. So, he hurried back upstairs. And another important point is…listen on the video, and go back to the video repeatedly, listen on the video. He tells Marrs what his father was saying on the 911 call. You have the 911 call -- the tape of that call, and you compare that tape with what his father is saying, with what the defendant is telling Sergeant Marrs, and they're the same. He recognized it was his father's voice. He recognized. I've been shot, 11481 Doggie, is what the defendant told Marrs."

"That is extremely good recall. That is not a person in some intense passionate rage who has that ability to recall. Also in a sidelight on this if you'll pay attention to the 911 call, you're not sure -- I don't think anybody can be sure that Robert even knew Rosemary had been shot, much less Rick. On the 911 call Robert says three times, I have been shot, I have been shot, I have been shot. He doesn't say, we've been shot, my wife and I have been shot. He doesn't even say -- actually, he may not even have known -- he probably got a good suspicion, but he may not even have known that Rick was the shooter. It's distinctly possible when he made that all he may not have known."

"The house was dark. Don't forget that. I mean we're all operating in daylight here, but the house was dark. When he went up into the bedroom, they're lying in bed, Rosemary is awake with the night lights on. Now, the room is totally dark. She's back lit here. He's at this door with a little crack in the door that swings open toward the bathroom. Just -- you can use your common sense. You're in a completely -- they -- the parents are in a completely dark room except for the back-lit bed. All this is dark at this point."

"The kitchen light was on when the troopers got there. The bathroom light was on when the troopers got there. You can reasonably infer that somehow the father turned the light on. But all this is dark. If you've ever been in a dark room a bedroom, trying to look out into the hallway, you're not going to see very much. This is where he was when he takes the first shot."

"You know from the physical evidence contrary to the defendant's statements about his dad getting up out of bed and -- he made some reference to it in the videotape with Marrs that he shot his father first. He thought his father would come at him, knew he had the gun. You know from the autopsy, and the photograph, there was blood on the bed, and the bullet hole in the sheet. The bullet hole near the top of the sheet. You'll have a demonstrative aid back in the jury room with you so you won't have to break this open."

"Dr. Thompson told you that bullet came in -- that lower bullet came in at a 45-degree angle. Forty-five-degree angle. You can reasonably infer that his father was lying down when he was standing at the door and fired that first shot. His father hadn't jumped up and was coming at him like he'd like you to believe. I'll get more into that later. Then he tells Marrs -- and this is consistent with the physical evidence, and I invite you to look at the pictures and the various shell casings, and you can reconstruct pretty much what shot happened where, and where he cocked the bullet -- or where he cocked the rifle, using the level action to expel the loaded round, throughout the whole chain."

"He shoots father in bed, and father gets up. He tells Marrs he backs off to the staircase. Father goes down. You'll see the pictures. There's a bigger pool of blood here by the door consistent with father going down there. He shoots father again. The second shot, I submit, comes in at a higher angle, consistent with Dr. Thompson's autopsy. Then father gets up. He comes back in. Father and Rosemary go into the bathroom. He comes back in, stands by the dresser for a few seconds, 10 seconds. And again, this is not a person that's in rage. He's analyzing his options here. Maybe they'd hidden the gun in the bathroom. He's trying to decide whether or not there's going to be any return fire."

"He stands out here, a couple shell casings here, there's another casing here that ejects. He shoots into the door a couple of times. The physical evidence clearly demonstrates that Rosemary was hit by one of those shots. She's hit in the chest. She's standing in some blood. You know that from the blood that's on the sole of her foot. She falls into the bathtub. The gun jams. He runs out of ammu -- it doesn't jam. He runs out of ammunition. He runs downstairs into his bedroom, and his father struggles, bleeds a trail of blood into the kitchen where he gets on the phone. I submit that's probably where the light was turned on when his father was on the phone."

"It must have been because when the defendant comes running back up after reloading the gun and hearing his father on the phone, he sees -- he knows his father's on the phone because he heard him. He sees his father. And this is not a person in a passionate state. According to Dr. Smith he would have shot anybody in the house. He's reacting quickly, he's analyzing, he's assessing the situation. If he were out of control, in this robotic state that Dr. Smith talks about, there's no need to stop here at the foyer."

"He puts the crosshairs on his father's head from down here by the front door, and shoots his father in the head while his father is kneeling on the floor. I think he says his father was sitting or something like that. But again, review the - videotape. And his father collapses immediately. He then goes back up the stairs into Rose -- and coldly, while Rosemary is whimpering -- we'll get into that in a minute -- he says, Rosemary's whimpering or crying. Shoots Rosemary in the head from a distance of a few feet away. That all spells out intent. It screams intent, this entire sequence of events."

"Play the 911 tape and you get a sense of the actual time. We've put the entire tape into evidence so you can get a real timeline. And during that down time after Robert Watkinson stops talking and that snapping sound, and I submit that's when he was shot, then visualize a sequence of events that occurs until the police knock on the door. You can visualize what's taking place. The defendant is scurrying around the house. He's analyzing his options. He knows his dad has gotten to the phone. He tells Marrs that disrupted his plan. That was not part of his plan. Dad getting to the phone was not part of the plan. The assault on his parents and hiding his parents were no longer part of his plan. He had to reassess."

"So what does he do? He goes up to his father's headboard, grabs his wallet. And he turns that over to the police later. And he tells Marrs why he took the wallet. He needed some money. He thought he needed money to just get away. He then goes -- the car keys end up down on his bed downstairs. This is on the hillside, on the upper hillside. You've got a view down below. You can see the lights -- the flashing lights. He knows the car is no longer an option that the police are going to be coming up the hillside, so he's got to get away on foot. Abandons the keys, tosses them onto his bed, comes back up, out the back door, and into the woods and disappears with the gun, with the rifle."

"I submit if he were in a heat of passion, if he was in such an intense passionate robotic state, he would have been sitting on the steps when the police got there. Somebody in a heat of passion cannot turn it off that fast. Now when they realize the police are on their way. He was in a cold, analytical frame of mind, and angry frame of mind, but not a passionate state of mind."

"Talk to you a little bit about serious provocation. One of the elements -- we'll get into this at length later. To justify heat of passion a person has to be led into this intense mental state by serious provocation, due to serious provocation. It means conduct which is sufficient to excite an intense passion in a reasonable person in the defendant's situation under the circumstances as the defendant reasonably believes them to be. Insulting words, insulting gestures, or hearsay reports of conduct engaged in by the intended victim do not alone, or in combination with each other, constitute serious provocation."

"Conduct is not sufficient. Words are not sufficient. Words are insufficient. Let's talk a little bit about Rosemary Watkinson. Among the items admitted into evidence is a letter found in Rosemary Watkinson's nightstand. This is a letter written January 21st, 1995. It was never mailed. It's still stamped. But it tells you her thoughts of January 1995. It's written to an attorney."

Dear Mr. Wheeler,

I want to thank you for taking on the task of helping Bob over the hurdles to obtain legal custody of his son Rick. I would like to know just what happens down the road when Jim, the youngest wants to come here too. Also, Brenda was paid alimony of 500 per month in order to get her into the work force. She has never taken a full-time job, yet could ever - couldn't ever control her kids. Now that Rick is completely out of hand she is willing to let Bob have custody. The problem with this is that I am the one who is having to take on most of the burden. I am going to have to quit a very lucrative job so I can supervise Rick, taking him to his activities and supervise him at home. Since his arrival, he has skipped a week of math class, been insolent to his teachers and has been late to class several times. I have spent several days at his school talking with counselors and teachers. Rick's behavior takes constant monitoring. I left him alone last Monday while I did some tasks, and came home to a puncture in my new sofa, the door to our stereo broken off its hinge. There was no confrontation before I left. Rick was still asleep and. of course, denies that he broke anything.

Rick has a severe temper. In the past, he has broken an antique vase of mine, gouged marks in the table tops, et cetera. We had a counselor for Rick. She has moved away. We are seeking another. The bottom line is I average eleven hundred per month on a part-time basis, 14 hours a week. I had the opportunity to work 35 hours per week, but had to pass it up as Rick arrived. I feel this loss of income needs to be calculated and offset. Since the damage to the furniture this week I have given notice at work. I can't keep up with replacing or repairing what he destroys. It's costing too much. We will put him in weekend activities at our club and with his youth group, and school wrestling and track. Hopefully we can occupy some of his idle time. I do say I resent having to make this change. I just hope it works out. Thank you for taking the time to read this letter. I just wanted to let you know the toll this is taking. Bob and I are seeing a side to each other that we never knew existed, but we shall not let jealousy Rick has for the love we have pull us apart, a most difficult task at times.

Sincerely, Rosemary Watkinson.

"There is no conduct by Rosemary Watkinson -- there is no evidence in this case that Rosemary Watkinson engaged in serious provocation sufficient to excite an intense passion in a reasonable person. There is -- what evidence there is as to Rosemary Watkinson was that she was trying very hard, under very difficult circumstances, to do the right thing for this boy."

"There's been a lot of allegations, several allegations, outrageous allegations, about alleged language Rosemary Watkinson used directed at Rick. It's all hearsay type reports. Even if that's true even if those words are true as a matter of law insulting words aren't enough. Even if she said those things to him every morning when he came down to breakfast – or came up for breakfast, even if she said that, every morning was in his face, insulting words aren't enough as a matter of law. The slap across the mouth a month before the incident is not enough. That's too far removed."

"Dad's -- Robert's last contact -- physical contact with -- Rosemary, by the way, if you'll -- we'll chart out the evidence in a moment -- was about a month, roughly a month, a few weeks, before Rosemary's last contact. That's what the evidence shows. Most of dad's contact that's in evidence occurred a year or better before. That doesn't constitute serious provocation, and I'll talk about that in a moment. Even if dad's contact the month before, let's say in October of '95 ·- the rejection, the words, are not enough. They don't rise to the level of serious provocation. Even if he was somehow provoked in his own mind, it wasn't serious."

"The standard for serious provocation, reasonable person. A reasonable person. The defendant's 16-1/2 years old. A reasonable 16-1/2-year-old adolescent would not be in this situation. A reasonable 16-1/2-year-old male, if in this situation, would have realized plenty -- if the situation was true about all this alleged abuse, would have plenty of opportunity, counselors, teachers, friends, ROTC advisors, Covenant House, even his own mother. If he were being abused, physically abused by his father, as they'd like you to believe, his most logical course of escape or report would be mother. He's good at triangulation, playing one person off against the other. There's a golden opportunity to report to his mother, dad's beating the daylights out of me, help, come get me, rescue me. No report to mother."

"Dr. Smith himself told you this is not a normal young man. I think Dr. Smith's words were abnormal. Don't confuse Mr. Watkinson with a reasonable person. He's an unusually aggressive, abnormal teenager. Angry teenager. The standard is a reasonable person. The legal standard is a reasonable person. Anything less than that would allow people to set their own individual standards of conduct under the law. To recognize this defendant as a reasonable person you would be recognizing any teenager who loses his temper and goes on a rampage, whether it's with a family member or not; says, I was out of control something set me off. The standard is a reasonable person, not a reason -- an angry young man."

"Now, if the defendant were a reasonable person -- say -take a reasonable person and put him in the defendant's situation. A reasonable person would not respond with intense anger. The first time he uses language like eff you and your stupid effing wife, and his father reacts, maybe appropriately, maybe inappropriately, maybe too hard, but takes him down, I submit -- you can reasonably infer that this situation on the Alcan where his father -- after he used those words, and his father threw him in the creek, I think any parent could react -- this is -- cool off. Drag him around in the water. Cool off, kid, you're out of control."

"It's not a beating. It's an attempt, a reasonable, possibly overly aggressive attempt, taking everything in the light most favorable to the defendant, but you can reasonably put yourself in that father's situation, and cool off, drag him around in the water, cool off, kid, you're out of control. A reasonable person would react -- when his father's button --when his father gets pushed to the edge, a reasonable person would not become more defiant, not dig in harder. A reasonable person would go, oops. I really stepped over the line, I've got to back off. A reasonable person would get the message."

"Talk to you a little bit about control. I submit this case really is not about abusive parents. Talk about control and parental guiding -- guidance. The fact that the fa -- that Robert Watkinson allegedly lost his temper and hit him on a couple occasions is not the cause of the defendant's behavior. It might be an excuse, but it's not the cause. I think the real consideration for you to keep in mind is that this defendant did not want to be controlled by anyone. Not just his father, by anyone."

"The best evidence of that, step six, take over Life. What was his purpose in doing all of this? Take over life, regain control. He tells Marrs -- and again, if you have any questions, go back to that video. If you study that video and its content, there is a lot of information in that video. One of the first things he tells Marrs, I didn't want any parental guidance over me anymore. You felt pretty strongly about that? Yes. This is a question about a young man who wants to stay in control. He's been in control. He wants to stay in control."

"I think it's important, when you're considering this whole control scenario -- and we'll start with -- through a chronology. I think it's clear from the evidence that the defendant was in control of his mother. You know, through his mother's testimony, he was in control of his stepfather. His stepfather had asked his mother if he could be involved in the parenting. She told the stepfather to back off, or not to. When she tries to control her son from similar problems he was having up here at school, and she slapped him, similar to what Rosemary did, he slapped her back. He wanted to be -- he was in control and she -- he wasn't going to let her get in control. Rick Watkinson is a very defiant young man."

"When his own mother tells him, obey the house rules or leave, he elects to leave. He's not going to abide by anybody's rules. He's going to stay in control. And if you think about this, his mother actually told you that his stepfather drove him downtown to live on the streets, to get him out of the house. He tells - his mother testified she thought he was living in friends' apartments. He tells Dr. Smith he was living in cars, vans. I submit even the impulsive suicide attempt that he tells Dr. Smith about is an expression of control. He's frustrated with his friends because they run into some - he talks about Crips -- and they back down from the Crips, while he's living on the streets. He's frustrated because they are not in control, I submit. Somebody else is controlling him. He's so frustrated that his friends backed down that he impulsively puts an unloaded gun to his head and pulls the trigger. He's angry. He's intense. He's not in control, he can't take it."

"Now, when -- this leads into the parental guiding phase. When his father -- when Robert learns he's out living on the streets, this bad, evil parent, immediate reaction is go get him. He flies down. There's a nasty scene at home, and that's conceded. But I submit he's so out of control that it took two adult men to drag him from fleeing on the ATV out by the barn, one on each arm, and drag him into the house. This is a young man who is out of control. So, this gives you a sense of what kind of parent Robert Watkinson was. He's very concerned, I submit."

"Going back to this Alcan incident, which pre-dates by a year or so going down to Oregon to get Rick when he was living on the streets. His father knew what kind of son he had, how much out of control he was, but nonetheless he reacts immediately to go get him. There's some evidence, I submit…that this Alcan thing might be exaggerated. Jimmy didn't remember it at all. Rick remembers it in great detail. He remembers Jimmy being scared. Jimmy doesn't remember it. If it's as bad as the defendant says. Jimmy would likely remember."

"So, in spite of the Alcan incident, despite knowledge of his son's temper, his father drops everything, I submit puts his life on hold, of course good parenting, his son needs help, and goes and gets him. This is where it gets very interesting. Rosemary and Bob then try to make a good life for Rick up here. They talk to their friends, what kind of school, what are kids going to need. Jeannie Roth told you that. Want to get him up to speed at school, want him to get -- fit in, so he could get into a happy life up here. He arrives in Anchorage about 10/10/94, and he's quickly into problems."

"You've got the 10/20/94 video clip showing Rosemary very upbeat, you got an A in algebra, she's excited for him, she's trying to generate some enthusiasm for school for him. Shows a very positive parenting approach toward grades, tries to motivate him. That video - the second part of that 10/20/94 video also shows the defendant wanting to stay in control. He's proud of being in control. He even talks about being in kindergarten and being in control. He refused to take a test. His father doesn't even know about that. Nobody's going to tell him what to do. Nobody has ever told him what to do. He's never obeyed anybody all his life."

"The 10/24/94 segment on the video shows Robert Watkinson being a good parent. He's very patient. They're at the dinner table. And that little clip reveals a lot. It also shows a lot about Rosemary's concern and parenting. Even though she didn't have parental authority, she was trying to do the right thing by taking that video. And I'll talk about that in a moment. Robert Watkinson is shown in that short clip exercising patience with somebody who is angry and unreasonable. Robert Watkinson -- you can view that video time and time again, and you can see a lot of the family dynamic in that video. That little segment."

"The fact that Rosemary taped it -- the precise reasons aren't clear. In January she talks about having seen a counselor, having him involved in counseling. I think Dr. Wieger refers to her name. I think it was Angie Drake or something. You can reasonably infer that possibly Rosemary wanted to show the counselor what they were up against. Maybe she wanted to show some school counselors. Maybe she wanted to show Bob. Maybe she showed the defendant, look, this is what you're like. That's - I submit that's good parenting, folks. There's no evidence -- I don't want to suggest there's evidence that any of those things were done, that she showed a counselor, or even showed the defendant. But the mere fact that she did it shows concern on her part."

"The next evidence we have of the defendant's control -- we can jump to that segment on the video of 4/30/95. April 30th of '95, the tennis segment. And in there you can hear the defendant declare his independence. He actually says those words, independence day, on there. You also show -- that little segment shows Bob Watkinson being very patient with a kid that wants to give him a little lip or get a little gruff -- a little grief over getting some water. Shows Bob Watkinson very patient."

"Another important aspect of this control -- controlling behavior by the defendant is just the fights and the arguments. Any parent, any teacher, any cop will tell you once you lose control, lose your temper, control passes to the other person, the person that's confronting you. I submit the defendant, by engaging in this provoking behavior where he was baiting his father, getting his father to react, if any of that is true, in the manner in which he does, by using all that foul language directed at Rosemary, directed at other people, all the school problems, the defendant was exercising control over his father. He gets his father to lose his temper, his father reacts, things calm down. There's some guilt, there's some parental guilt there. I'm sure you can reasonably conclude there's some parental guilt. I hit you too hard, I'm sorry, I shouldn't have acted that way, can't we work this out, let's go on."

"And that brings us to this business with Covenant House and the car, taking the car in 1995. The defendant -- his parents are out. Rick - Jimmy's up for the visit. He takes Rosemary's car. He doesn't have a license. Takes it out for a joyride with a bunch of his friends. You can imagine Robert and Rosemary's concern when they come back and they realize what had happened. Any parent would be terrorized by the risk that took place. The parents of those kids that were in that car that night had to be terrorized at the thought of what could have happened with a bunch of kids who don't know how to drive, flying around town without a -- some kid without a license."

"The defendant knew his father would be angry, so he fled. I submit he wasn't fleeing from abuse. He was fleeing from the consequences. He knew that if he could stall things, dad would calm down, and he could stay in control. He ran when his parents came home a little bit early. He was in the process of drying off the car. He stayed out for a couple of days, got Kristy and her mother to drive him to Covenant House. No report of abuse or fear, no report of abuse to them. Covenant House is a home for runways and abused kids. They're pros. No abuse reported. Golden opportunity. He was there for several days."

"Dr. Smith testified, and I'll paraphrase, it's unheard of for a shelter for runaways, abused people -- abused children, they don't turn abused children back to the abusive parents. You whisper a word of abuse in a shelter, as rightly you should, as rightly those folks should. They're good folks, they work hard. They're very concerned and very sensitive to these situations. You whisper the word, abuse, down there, it's time out. All sorts of people launch into an investigation. Not a hint."

"He goes back. There's an attempt at reconciliation. He and his father take a walk up into the hills. There's another confrontation. He's still pushing dad. Dad loses his temper, gets him down, threatens to hit him, but doesn't, and backs off. Goes back to Covenant House that night. Again, no report. You reasonably infer there was no abuse. He then -- Rick then goes on to a vacation in '95 back down to Oregon for a while. Comes back up to Alaska. Kristy Braman is now out of the picture. And the last best evidence they have of possible physical abuse was through Kristy Braman seeing some bruises. Well, those bruises occurred during the spring of '95, possibly early summer of '95. Kristy Braman's now out of the picture during the fall of '95."

"The cynical side of me wants to say that there's a possibility here that this young man, who is good at manipulating, good at triangulation, good at playing people off one another, has taken advantage of a sensitive, pretty, young girl. He's athletic. It's very possible he picked up those bruises doing things like jumping off the roof. You know he's into sports. Mountain biking, jet skiing. He's a good athlete. I mean you saw the video. He can handle himself on a pair of water skis. That's impressive. It's very possible he picked up those bruises someplace else and he's making a play for this pretty, young girl. She's a sensitive young girl, very nice young girl, and he's making a play for her. He knows what she'll be sensitive to. There's a possibility there, and you can't discount that. He wouldn't be the first guy to lie to a young girl. He really wouldn't."

"Now, she tells you he can't lie to her worth a bean. Maybe -- I mean that might be her perception, but he lied a big one to her on December 1st. She didn't catch it. He told her his parents kicked him out. He told her mother he ran away. He's telling each what they want to hear. What he knows they'll be sensitive to. He's playing on their respective sympathies. He had Kristy fooled. They're joking around at school. He told Marrs he had everybody fooled. He can lie. Incidentally, Mrs. Braman drove Rick to Covenant House. If there -- there's another -- if there's -- possible report. She didn't report abuse either."

"All right. Now we're in the fall of '95. There's possible evidence of another incident with dad in October of '95. That's the last evidence of physical contact, a month -- roughly a month, five, six weeks before the murders, of physical contact. Let's go back to serious provocation. Conduct. Last physical contact there's evidence of. October '95 from dad. We're not sure about when. Push it as close as you want to the end of October."

"Now, let's -- we're in the end of October '95. Let's talk a little bit about Rosemary Watkinson. This lady is very, very much a victim in this case, ladies and gentlemen. She really and truly is. She's put in this situation due to the love for her husband. I submit she loved Rick. He may not have realized it, but she did. His stepfather ignored him. Can you, in your wildest dreams, after sitting through this trial, imagine Rosemary Watkinson driving him down and dumping him off on the street so he can live on the streets?"

"She tried to involve herself with Rick. Jeannie Roth testified about prior to arrival they're trying to get him set up for school, get him involved. 10/24/95, the encouragement on the video. January 1995, the letter to the lawyer. School counseling. She's actively involved with his school, tennis club activities, wrestling. She's trying to get this young man involved."

"Don't forget -- there's a little side note on this. That one reference with Kristy Braman when -- during one of his runaway episodes, Rosemary Watkinson took him back to Kristy's. Kristy was worried about Rick when he was out some night during one of these all-night outings. And Rosemary Watkinson brought him back up to Kristy's house, put him at the door, you owe her an apology, you had her worried sick, and went back to the car. That is not an abusive parent. She's trying to instill a sense of responsibility. Trying to get him to do the right -- what is right. And she did all this without any parental authority support from Bob."

"Summer '95, Rosemary sees things spinning out of control with -- sees Rick spinning out of control. She seeks help from her friends. Vivi Nitteberg. Asks for help. She eventually gets this book. And I'll talk about that in a moment. She's making a very serious effort by the spring of '95 -- by the summer of '95. He hasn't even been up here a year, and she's already seeking semi-professional help, if you will, to try and understand what it's going to take to get to this young man, to get him to turn around. Vivi testifies, she recommended a psychiatrist."

"They eventually get the book. 'Developing Healthy Stepfamilies', 20 families tell their stories. Bob and Rosemary may not have agreed with everything in this book, but you can tell -- it's underlined in passage -- in certain sections. Cynthia Brown, Rosemary's daughter, found it on her bed in her bedroom. Page 32, the term discipline comes from the word disciple, which means to teach, underlined. And there are other significant passages underlined. She was trying. She was trying very, very hard. She was going above and beyond a bitter stepparent that they want you to believe. She was really trying hard, making a sincere effort."

"Meanwhile, the defendant, still in his controlling behavior, really gets into ROTC. He's still in control, and as much as he likes ROTC, he's still exercising control. He starts cutting classes so that he can be more involved in ROTC. He's still maintaining control. It's what he wants to do. Not what the school wants him to do, not what his parents want him to do, it's what he wants to do. He's still in control."

"October 30, 1995, Dr. Wieger enters the picture. The Watkinson's are so concerned they're seeking additional professional help. How can this be a bad parenting case is beyond me. Dr. Wieger meets with the parents, discusses school contracts with them. No abuse reported. We'll talk about Rosemary's slap in a moment. No abuse reported. Abusive parents don't take their people into professional counselors. Dr. Wieger even warned them that if there's any abuse here -- and it's standard sex abuse, physical abuse - I'm mandated by law to report Bob and Rosemary Watkinson were going into counseling. There's no abuse."

"Let's talk about this vacuuming incident for a moment. October 30, 1995, I think you can reasonably infer Bob was out of town or wasn't at home. That incident was very, very upsetting to Rosemary Watkinson. I think that you can reasonably infer that's the first time she's lost -- she's let him get to her. It's the first time she's lost control. She's been living with this kid for a year practically, except when he went down to Oregon, and he hasn't gotten to her yet. He gets in her face. They have this thing about vacuuming. He calls her a bitch, and she reacts and slaps him. That's not a -- that shouldn't be an unexpected parental response."

"She's so upset she reports it to the counselor. She reports it to - she tells her daughter about it down in Boise and she documents it. She's obviously upset with herself for losing control. Document was found in her nightstand, along with that letter that was never mailed to the lawyer. FAO Schwarz stationery.

Me, calm voice, it would be a lot easier if you would just admit you didn't vacuum down here, and that you lied about it. I didn't lie about it, just shut your goddamn mouth and quit being a bitch. Threw sweeper. I said, you don't throw the sweeper. Fuck you, just shut up and let me do it, get out of my face. Then he kicked the sweeper, so I slapped him. Probably mad because I prefaced the fact that he couldn't play the computer."

"He himself says he deserved it. He tells Marrs, he tells the counselor. That's not serious provocation. That is not conduct which leads to an intense passion in a reasonable person. There's minimal evidence. If that's the evidence, ladies and gentlemen, if that's the evidence, it's practically nonexistent. Practically nonexistent as a matter of law. That is not serious provocation to justify the murder of Rosemary Watkinson. All right. With this vacuuming incident - put that aside for a minute."

"Meanwhile, if you take a look at the ongoing chronology, Robert Watkinson is finally figuring out how to gain control. He's finally got a handle on something his son likes. Any parent will tell you, and you know from your own common day -- everyday life experiences, a kid likes something, that's the privilege that's going to alter bad behavior. His father got a handle on the ROTC. Mr. Goodwin told you ROTC is an elective. Some parents use it as a privilege when trying to modify an unruly child's behavior."

"Look at the school contracts. Drag sheets. Drag sheet, you take it around to the classroom every day, parent signs off -- or the teacher signs off to prove to your parents you've been to each and every one of your classes. Any -- I won't read the whole thing. Any new missing assignments are shown on the drag sheet, ROTC drill will be discontinued until they are made up. If they can't be made up, then drill will be discontinued for one day for the first offense, two days for the second, and so on. If drag sheet is forgotten, there will be no drill until it was -- it is produced. If drag sheet is forged, drill will be discontinued for the rest of the year. It should be kept in mind that ROTC and stage band are electives. While I think highly of both classes, they are not core subjects, and as a result, are expendable."

"He goes on. The original agreement regarding the car still stands. Rick's requirements to drive. By this time, the fall of '95, the licensing, I think you can reasonably infer, has been acquired. Now we're trying to use the car as a privilege. Maintain good grades, you can drive. There's another creed here that's got some interesting things relative to raising voices and arguments, being honest, and that sort of thing. I invite you to read these in detail, and compare these with what's said in the video. And compare these to the allegations of bad parenting."

"Let's go back to control. Robert Watkinson finally has a lever. He's got an angle. He's got something that he can use without losing his temper to try and alter Rick's behavior. Grounding hasn't worked. He's ignored that. Stereo, guitar, phone privileges revocations haven't worked. He's learned how to hot wire those things to get around them, how to be defiant. Corporal punishment hasn't worked, whether it's too intense or not. That hasn't worked. He hasn't gotten the message from that. Rick likes ROTC. They've got the contract. It's an elective. He's no longer in control. He's losing control now."

"November 30, 1995, the day of the murders, his father's at school. He'd been skipping some classes earlier in the week. Consequences have been spelled out. He's not in control any more. And all this is happening. Rosemary still doesn't have any support from Bob on this. That's another tragic element of this whole thing. But he wants control. He's losing control. He wants control. He wants to take over his life, so he plans the murders."

"Ladies and gentlemen, he's lied to his parents throughout, I submit he's lied to Dr. Smith, I submit this defense is lying to you, and this defense is trying -- is engaging in an outrageous defense, trying to smear the names of Robert and Rosemary Watkinson. They may not have been perfect. Who is? But they were good people trying to do the right thing. Thank you."[44]

[44] Closing arguments of Mr. Collins (the State) taken from the Court transcripts

CHAPTER FORTY-SEVEN

"Thank you, Your Honor," said Wally placing his papers on the podium. It was time to let it all out. His last shot at convincing the jury not to let a young man rot in prison for two lifetimes. He was prepared. He'd done his homework. Now he just had to deliver.

"Good morning, ladies and gentlemen. I'd like to start out here by thanking you for being so attentive during the last three weeks of this trial because we've really noticed that. It's not usual that jurors are as attentive as you all have been. And I know that this trial has not been a pleasant experience. It is not easy to sit and listen for three weeks about such unpleasant topics as divorce. It's not easy to listen to evidence about a 10-year-old boy who, sensing problems between his parents, asks his dad, when his mom and he are dropping his dad off at the airport, dad, are you going to leave us. And his dad tells him, no, son, I'm not going to leave."

"It's unpleasant to think about that same 10-year-old boy two weeks later when dad comes back from that plane trip and calls that little conference there in the family home in that 10-year-old boy's bedroom. When he comes in and he sets a chair down, and he has the boys sitting there in front of him, and he tells them that he's leaving. It's not pleasant to picture that 10-year-old boy and his eight-year-old brother as they start to cry. It's not pleasant to picture the mom, who is hearing this after 23 years of marriage, and who has asked her husband repeatedly if he was going to leave, and has been told no. It's not easy or pleasant to picture this 10-year-old boy hanging onto his father's legs when his father is walking out the front door, and crying, daddy, please don't leave. It's not pleasant to picture a father pushing his son away and saying, this is the best thing for you."

"It's not pleasant to talk about physical abuse. It's not pleasant to imagine a grown man smashing his forearm into the neck of a child. It's not pleasant to imagine a grown man throwing his child into a wall. It's not pleasant to picture a grown man throwing his son into a river, going in after him and grabbing him by the arm and dragging him through the river, scraping his legs along the stones on the bottom, cutting his legs, causing them to bleed, and then when the father's temper cools, dropping his son in the river like a used rag, and walking away."

"It's not pleasant to think about how that 10-year-old boy suffered in the next few years following the divorce. It's not pleasant to visualize the scene where two weeks after his father tells him he's leaving the family dad comes back and brings his girlfriend. It certainly is not a happy picture to imagine the mother, who has just been left by the man that she has been married to for 23 years, as she watches him come to their house with his girlfriend. She responds hysterically. She's upset, she's angry, she's crying. And Rick is there. And Jimmy is there. And they see all of this happen."

"For any of you who have been involved in a bitter divorce, or who know people who have, you know full well what happened in that household after that visit. Divorces are not normal times, and people do not react the way they typically react during a divorce, especially a bitter divorce, especially where the mother believes that the father has left her for a stewardess. Mom was angry, and mom expressed that anger, and she expressed the anger in front of the kids who were living with her at the time. And the kids came to adopt that anger. The children blamed Rosemary for taking their dad from them, just like their mother did. Those are not pleasant things to think about."

"It's not pleasant to think about what that home must have been like for Rick when he came to Alaska in '94. Rosemary did not want Rick in Alaska, and we'll talk more about that later. He was not welcome in that house. It's not pleasant to think about parents continually referring to their child as asshole, ungrateful little bastard. Those are not terms of endearment. Those are not terms of love. Not to a child. And those are not pleasant things to think about. It's not easy to think about Rick coming home, after his dad pulled him out of drill in front of all the other students, yelling at him the whole way home about skipping school."

"It's not easy to picture him as he's laying there on his bed listening to his parents argue about him, as they always did. Rick is not welcome in the home. I don't want him here. He's ruining our marriage. He's tearing us apart. It's Rick or it's me. And Rosemary storms out the door. Rick's on his bed. Dad is angry and loses his temper just like he had on a number of occasions before. Runs right down to Rick's bedroom and says, you are destroying my marriage, you are out of here, I don't want you here anymore. And chasing Rosemary. Once again, just as in 1989, rejecting the son, in his mind, for Rosemary."

"Rick's laying there on the bed, and all these events are running through his mind. He flashes back to 1989 when his dad walked out the door and left him. Back to the river where his dad dragged him through the river and cut his legs. Back to his dad slamming his forearm into his throat and shoving him against the wall. Back to day after day after day of being belittled, being called asshole and bastard, where every day is a challenge to survive with one iota of self-respect or self-esteem. These emotions overwhelm him as he's laying in the bed."

"He gets out of the bed and he kneels down, and takes his favorite pen and writes out the operation anarchy note. Those are not pleasant things to think about. He lays back down. And Dr. Smith told us about how he felt a flood of relief having written the note. It was a relief for him to write a note about killing his parents. He's laying there. His parents come home, and as soon as their feet hit the floor of the garage, they're still arguing, and they're still arguing about him. He's destroying our marriage. It's the same old song. I don't want him here, you've got to get rid of him, it's him or me, make your choice. And this goes on and on until it's quiet and they go to bed. And it's clear that a resolution has been reached at that point. It's clear to Rick that he's gone."

"The prosecution would have you believe that this was cold and calculated, and that Rick was sitting there, between the time that his parents came home until what followed, thinking about how to do it. That's not the case. Rick laid there in bed, again replaying the divorce, again replaying the physical abuse, again replaying the days and days of name calling and the sense of rejection, and the anger, and the pain, and the fear began to build, and build, and build the entire time that he was laying there until he snapped. He couldn't take it anymore. The rage, and his fear of rejection, and his pain, and his depression overwhelmed him. That's not an easy thing to think about."

"And it's not easy to think about what followed, as Rick went under his bed and got the rifle, and he went upstairs and he killed his parents for the second time. These are not pleasant topics, and they're not easy topics. But Jimmy Watkinson said it best when he testified and he said, this ain't the Brady Bunch. This was Rick's life."

"Rick suffered in silence for six years partly because, as Dr. Smith testified, abused children do not talk about the abuse. It is the norm for abused kids not to talk about it. They don't talk about it because they're ashamed that they are being abused. They're embarrassed that they're being abused. And perhaps the most ironic trait of abused children is that they actually bond with the abusers. Because a part of the abused child very much still loves his father, and wants to love his stepmother, but the other part of the abused child contains all the pain, and all the anger, and all the hatred that slowly builds up over the years of physical and emotional abuse. So, this child who is being abused by a parent actually bonds with the parent and attempts to please the parent as much as the child can."

"But perhaps saddest of all, the reason that Rick suffered in silence is in part due to the way that we are raised and society as a whole. Because there's not a one of us in this courtroom, not in the jury, not the prosecutor table, not in the audience, there's not one person who has been taught as soon as you are capable of learning anything, to respect other people's privacy. Privacy is the golden rule. We're taught not to butt in. We're taught not to intrude. And we're taught not to ask questions. And that played a part several times in Rick's life."

"The person that came closest to finding out what was really going on in the Watkinson house was Kristy Braman. This was Rick's best friend. He confided in her more than he confided in anyone. He was at school. Kristy gave him a hug, and he flinched in pain. Kristy said, Rick, what's the matter. Rick shrugged it off and said, nothing. But Kristy knew better. She knew about Rick's problems at home, and about Rick's fights with his dad, and so she pushed Rick. She grabbed him and dragged him off into a corner and said, Rick, tell me what's wrong. And what does Rick say to the person that he's closest to and confides in? He says, nothing."

"She says, Rick, pull your shirt up. I want to see. He pulls up his shirt, and she sees the bruises that are there. And she asks him, where did the bruises come from. And does he go into a long tirade about the abuse that his father has inflicted on him for the past several years, or the abuse that he's suffering at home? No. He just says. I got in a fight with my dad, and that's it. Kristy hugged him on several occasions after that when he flinched in pain, but never asked any more questions. And I asked her why. And she said. Because I got tired of seeing the bruises. Because the bruises are not pleasant to look at."

"The other people that came close to knowing what was actually going on in the Watkinson house were John Svendsen and Vivi Nitteberg. They were there two days after Thanksgiving and they saw the behavior that caused the concern. They saw Rosemary belittling Rick. They saw Rosemary over-controlling Rick. Rick, go down and put a CD on. Rick goes all the way downstairs, puts on a CD, comes back up. It's too loud, Rick, go back down and turn it down. Rick goes back downstairs to turn down the CD, and comes back up. It's too low, go back down. Rick goes back down and turns it up, comes back up. These are not the acts, as Mr. Collins would have you believe, of a child who resents control."

"Vivi Nitteberg was a psychologist in Norway for many years, and she told you that Rick went out of his way to please Rosemary. And John Svendsen told you the same thing. And they were friends of Rosemary's. So, John and Vivi gave Rosemary a book about step-parenting. Mr. Collins has shown you the book. And Rosemary's response to the book, as we learned a few days later, when John asked her what do you think of the book that I gave you, her response was that's not going to work for me. It's not helping me out."

"And you will see that whoever did the underlining in this book -- on page 32 there's a sentence. The term discipline comes from the word disciple, which means to teach. I feel that is the most important aspect of being a parent. I developed a special relationship with a boy as a teacher and mentor. But there is a difference between discipline and abuse. Calling an adolescent boy asshole to his face, or bastard, is not discipline. That is abuse. Punching an adolescent in the back is not discipline. That is abuse."

"Kristy Braman, John Svendsen and Vivi Nitteberg did as much as they could in this case, and more than most people would have. Because, again, there is a zone of privacy around families. And this zone of privacy and silence is slowly killing hundreds of thousands of abused kids every single year. And it is that zone of silence, and that zone of privacy, that killed Bob and Rosemary Watkinson."

"We have forced you to listen to all these unpleasant topics because the law requires you to consider these when you deliberate on the charges of murder in the first and second degrees in this case. You will see the heat of passion instruction in the packet of jury instructions that you will receive from Judge Sanders. And the jury instruction is that it's a defense to the charge of murder in the first or second degree that the defendant acted in a heat of passion before there had been a reasonable opportunity for the passion to cool, when the heat of passion resulted from a serious provocation by the intended victim."

"Therefore, if you find that the state fails to prove beyond a reasonable doubt that Rick did not act in a heat of passion before there had been an opportunity for the passion to cool and that the heat of passion resulted from a serious provocation by the intended victims, then you must find him not guilty of the charges of murder in the first and second degree. You will then consider whether he is guilty of manslaughter, for which there will be instructions in the packet of instructions you will receive."

"Now, there are several terms of art which are broken down in the heat of passion instruction. First of all, obviously there is the word, passion. The law does not confine the types of passion that are sufficient for heat of passion to one or two types of passion. Passion, under the law, includes humiliation, depression, rejection, fear and anger. And those are the passions that were experienced by Rick Watkinson at the time that he killed his parents on November 30, 1995."

"Reasonable opportunity for passion to cool. The law does not set a time limit on how long it takes someone to cool down when they're in a heat of passion. The standard is the reasonable person in the defendant's situation. So, in this case the reasonable person in Rick's situation, experiencing the things that Rick had experienced since 1989, because -- do not let Mr. Collins mislead you on this point. The law does not confine the events that lead to the heat of passion to the events immediately preceding the killing."

"The law recognizes that you can have events going far back in time that lead a person to kill, just as you did in this case. Because the passion in this case did not simply begin for the first time on November 30. 1995. This passion had been simmering and building, and simmering and building since 1989, since the time of the divorce, since the time Rick's father first rejected him, in his young mind, for Rosemary, which he had to re-live on the night of November 30, 1995 when his father once again rejected him for Rosemary by telling him, you are out of here, you're out of my life, and stormed out the door after her."

"But most importantly, serious provocation. Mr. Collins focused in on two words out of the entire instruction, so you need to consider the entire instruction. Serious provocation means conduct which is sufficient to excite an intense passion in a reasonable person in the defendant's situation, under the circumstances as the defendant reasonably believed them to be. It's not just a reasonable person. It's the reasonable person in Rick's situation, having experienced the things that Rick himself experienced."

"Insulting words alone are not enough for heat of passion. Not words alone. As Mr. Collins indicated to you, it is insulting words. Insulting gestures, or hearsay reports of conduct engaged in by intended victims. Those things, by themselves or in connection with others, in connection with insulting words, in connection with other insulting words, or in connection with insulting gestures, or in connection with hearsay reports of conduct by other people, are not sufficient for serious provocation, but conduct is more than sufficient for serious provocation."

"And in this case the conduct that you have by Bob and Rosemary -- first of all by Bob. The conduct by Bob is not merely the conduct on November 30, '95. The law permits you to consider the conduct of Bob going clear back to 1989. Again, when Bob first rejected Rick for Rosemary. The conduct goes clear back to the time when Bob went back down to Oregon to bring his son up to Alaska to teach him some discipline, and dragged him back into the house in Oregon, and lost his temper, and smashed his forearm into his throat, and threw him against the wall."

"The conduct goes clear back to the river on the Alcan Highway where Rick's dad threw him in the river, dragged him along the rocks on the bottom, and left him there. The conduct includes Bob's conduct on November 30, '95. Going to the school yanking him out of drill team in front of everybody else, berating him about his performance in school the whole way home, and finally telling him that he was no longer welcome in that house, and going after Rosemary."

"What about Rosemary's conduct? Rosemary was in the car when Bob went back to the family home two weeks after he left it, and caused the intense reaction that Rick and his brother observed in their mother. And because of that reaction, and because she was there, and because the mother transferred her hatred of Rosemary to Rick, that was part of Rosemary's conduct. The other portion of Rosemary's conduct was the slap. Now, the state would have you believe that it's perfectly okay to lose your temper and smack your kid. This is not okay. And this is not just an isolated slap."

"You have to remember here that you have to view the circumstances from Rick's point of view. The reasonable person in Rick's situation under the circumstances. This was a woman that Rick blamed for taking his father away from his family. This is a woman who shows up two weeks later with that father. This is the woman who makes it very, very plain to Rick when he arrives in

Anchorage that she does not want him here. This is the woman who on a repeated basis refers to him as asshole and bastard. On top of all that you have the slap. And that is the conduct that is sufficient for serious provocation."

"The state must prove beyond a reasonable doubt that Rick Watkinson did not act in a heat of passion on November 30, '95. But what does proof beyond a reasonable doubt mean? There's a definition in the jury instructions that you will take back with you, and that definition is that proof beyond a reasonable doubt is that you be satisfied -- to be satisfied beyond a reasonable doubt of the defendant's guilt is what is called the burden of proof."

"It is not required that the prosecution prove guilt beyond all possible doubt, for it is rarely possible to prove anything to an absolute certainty. Rather the test is one of reasonable doubt. A reasonable doubt is a doubt based upon reason and common sense. Proof beyond a reasonable doubt must be proof of such a convincing character that after careful consideration, you would be willing to rely and act upon it without hesitation in exercising your own important affairs. The defendant is never to be convicted on mere suspicion or conjecture."

"What does that mean? That's a nice legal definition, and there are a lot of different terms that are bandied about or tossed around when we're talking about burden of proof. Now, after you hear all the evidence in this case and you go back to the jury room and you discuss the evidence with your fellow jurors, and you form an opinion, there are several conclusions that you may come to. You may say to yourself, I don't think -- it's less than likely that he acted in the heat of passion. If that's true, your verdict is not guilty on murder in the first and second degree."

"If you go back there and you say to yourself. I suspect that he was not in a heat of passion when he killed Robert and Rosemary, under the law your verdict is still not guilty on charges of murder in the first and second degree. If you go back there and you strongly believe that he was not in a heat of passion on November 30, '95, your verdict is still, under the law, not guilty of murder in the first and second degree. Because you have to be convinced beyond a reasonable doubt, beyond a reasonable doubt, before you can convict on charges of murder in the first and second degree."

"What does the state offer you to convince you beyond a reasonable doubt that Rick was not in a heat of passion? First of all, the state calls Dr. Rothrock. Dr. Rothrock met with Rick for 90 minutes. He didn't talk to any family members. He didn't talk to any friends. He didn't talk to a single witness. He meets with Rick for 90 minutes, and what is his expert opinion? His expert opinion is that Rick is capable of forming the intent to kill. And the state proposes that to you to convince you that Rick did not act in a heat of passion. But the problem with that legally is that that completely misses the boat."

"The defense is not that Rick did not act intentionally. The defense is that Rick acted in a heat of passion. So, Dr. Rothrock's expert opinion does nothing, nothing at all, to undermine the fact that Rick acted in a heat of passion. Because you can act in a heat of passion and actually intend what you're doing. And I'll give you a couple examples in a minute."

"Dr. Rothrock made clearly an improper diagnosis of Rick when he said that Rick did not suffer from post-traumatic stress disorder. I asked Dr. Rothrock on cross examination, because I wanted to make sure what requirements he was using, or what criteria he was using for post-traumatic stress disorder. And I asked Dr. Rothrock, are you saying that in order to have post-traumatic stress disorder you have to have an event that is outside the normal range of human experience. And Dr. Rothrock said, oh, absolutely. And I said, are you one hundred percent positive of that. And he hemmed and hawed, and said, well, I don't know about a hundred percent positive, but I'm as positive as I can be."

"And then I asked him about the DSM-IV. Because the DSM-IV is what psychiatrists use to diagnose people. This is the manual that is put out by the American Psychiatric Association which contains the criteria that you use in diagnosing a variety of disorders, including post-traumatic stress syndrome. So, after I asked Dr. Rothrock about whether or not you had to have an event which is outside the range of normal human experience, and he said, that he was, I showed him the DSM-IV."

"And the DSM-IV says that the diagnostic criteria for post-traumatic stress disorder are when the person has been exposed to a traumatic event in which both of the following were present. Number 1, the person experienced, witnessed, or was confronted with an event or events that involve actual or threatened death or serious injury, or a threat to the physical integrity of self or others. And number 2, the person's response involved intense fear, helplessness, or horror. Dr. Rothrock said that to have post-traumatic stress disorder you had to have an event outside the normal range of human experience. He also said that it had to be a life-threatening situation, or it had to pose serious threat of physical injury."

"Where did Dr. Rothrock get that definition from if it's not in the DSM-IV? I'll tell you where he got it from. He got it from the DSM-IIIR, which was replaced by the DSM-IV. Because the DSM-IIIR criteria is exactly what Dr. Rothrock said. A person has experienced an event that is outside the range of usual human experience and that would be markedly distressing to almost anyone, e.g. a serious threat to one's life or physical integrity. The problem with that is that the DSM-IIIR is garbage because it was replaced by the DSM-IV, which apparently Dr. Rothrock was not aware of. Dr. Rothrock misdiagnosed Rick because he wasn't even aware of the current criteria for diagnosing post-traumatic stress disorder."

"Secondly, Dr. Rothrock admitted that he was not an expert in adolescent parricide cases. And while acknowledging an entire body of research in that area that clearly indicates that there is a strong connection between family dysfunction -- between physical abuse and emotional abuse there's a very strong connection between family dysfunction and parricide in adolescents. But be completely disregarded that entire line of research in formulating his opinion in this case."

"Even more interesting with Dr. Rothrock, is that I attempted to break down with him the various things that were affecting Rick on November 30, '95. And you will recall that I asked Dr. Rothrock about -- I asked him about divorce. I said, do you think that the divorce bad an affect on what happened on November 30, 1995. And Dr. Rothrock said, well, it probably had some effect, but not an overwhelming effect. Okay. Fair enough. What about the fact that Rosemary in Rick's mind was the cause of the divorce? What about that, Dr. Rothrock? Did that have an affect on November 30, '95? Yeah, it probably had some effect, but again not an overwhelming effect."

"What about the fact that he was forced to live with Rosemary, the person that he blamed for the divorce? What about that, Dr. Rothrock? Do you think that that had an affect on November 30, '95? Maybe some, but not an overwhelming effect. What about the fact, Dr. Rothrock, that Rosemary did not want Rick there? What about that fact? Did that have an impact on November 30, '95? Dr. Rothrock said, it may have had some, but not an overwhelming effect. What about the names? What about calling Rick on a regular basis the names that we've already heard about, over and over again. Did that have any affect on November 30, '95? Dr. Rothrock said, well, maybe, but not an overriding effect."

"What about the slap, I asked Dr. Rothrock. Did that have any affect on November 30, '95? Again, same old story. It may have had some effect, but in my opinion not an overwhelming effect. What about -- let's call these Rosemary names. What about father calling him ungrateful little bastard all the time, would that have an affect on November 30, '95? Same old song and dance. Maybe some, not an overwhelming effect. What about father's rejection of Rick, not only in the divorce, but on November 30, '95, when father said, you can't live here anymore because you're ruining my marriage, did that have any affect? Same thing. Maybe some, not an overwhelming effect."

"What about when father and Rosemary come back and they're still arguing about getting rid of him. We'll call that dad and Rose's rejection. They're still arguing about getting rid of Rick, and about how Rick is not welcome in the home, and about how he's destroying the marriage. What effect did that have on Rick on November 30, 1995? Same old thing. Maybe some effect, not an overwhelming effect. And then finally for the clincher I asked Dr. Rothrock -- I think you're getting the idea where this is going -- that what about if we take everything together, the divorce, plus Rosemary being the cause, plus the fact that he's forced to live with Rosemary, plus the fact that Rosemary does not want him there, plus the fact that Rosemary keeps calling him these derogatory names, plus the slap, plus the father's rejection, and I almost forgot to add the most important part, dad's physical abuse, what about all those things taken together, Doctor, in the mind of a 16-year-old boy on November 30, 1995, do you think that that had any effect at all? Maybe some."

"But it's -- Dr. Rothrock said, it's a judgment call as to whether or not it was an overwhelming effect, and in my opinion, he says, it was not. Well, you know what? Dr. Rothrock's opinion as to whether or not it was an overwhelming effect doesn't matter. It doesn't matter, number one, because his opinion was that Rick was capable for forming the intent. And as I've already indicated, that is not an issue here. Heat of passion is an issue. Number two, it doesn't matter because if anybody makes a judgment call in this case, it is you. That's your job. You make the judgment call."

"But perhaps even scariest of all from Dr. Rothrock, when I started asking Dr. Rothrock questions about physical and emotional abuse, and I asked Dr. Rothrock, Dr. Rothrock, is it physical abuse to slap an adolescent in the face in anger, and Dr. Rothrock said -- shrugged his shoulders and said, depends on the circumstances. Okay. Is it physical abuse to punch your adolescent in the back with your fist and leave bruises? And Dr. Rothrock said -- shrugged his shoulders again, and said, depends on the circumstances. Again, I don't know who raised Dr. Rothrock, but it is not normal to punch an adolescent in the back and leave bruises."

"I asked him about emotional abuse, and I said, is it okay to call your child, in anger, all these nasty names on a continuous basis. He shrugged his shoulders, and said, depends on the circumstances. It doesn't depend on the circumstances. Physical abuse is physical abuse on an adolescent, and emotional abuse is emotional abuse. It is not okay on a continuous basis and in anger to call your kid an asshole or a bastard, or anything like that. And we talked about that in jury selection when we talked about physical abuse and verbal abuse. And we all agreed that that sort of behavior -- actually, as I recall, every single one of you agreed that slapping an adolescent, or punching an adolescent, or calling an adolescent bad names in anger is abuse and is unacceptable."

"And then the state called Cynthia Brown, Rosemary's daughter. And I have to say that it's extremely unusual in criminal cases that the state will call somebody in their rebuttal case that actually helped the defense. And I'm glad that the state called Cynthia Brown. And I want you, when you go back there, to listen to her testimony very carefully, because she shows you a lot about Rosemary Watkinson. She first came in with the video, sixteen minutes of video, sixteen minutes of video out of the fifteen or sixteen full videos that were found in the Watkinson home. Even on this sixteen minutes you still get a glimpse into Rosemary's personality."

"I invite you to watch the video very carefully. Look at the scene where Rick is sitting in the chair, and Rosemary says to Rick, you've been an asshole your whole life, right. Why don't you change the way you dress? And Rick's flip response is, yeah. I've been an asshole and I'll continue to be an asshole. Because that's how kids deal with that sort of abuse. That's how kids cope. And it doesn't matter that she says it in a half joking tone because that is the worst tone to take. You don't joke with your kid -- think about this when you go back into the jury room, and think back in your life and think if you can ever think of a time, any one of you, where you joked with your kid and said, ha-ha, you've been an asshole your whole life. That's not a joke, and that's not funny. That is emotional abuse, and it's captured here on video that Cynthia Brown was kind enough to bring in and show us."

"Think about how the scene between Rick and his dad that's on here played out. That scene was obviously surreptitiously or secretly recorded by Rosemary, which is eerily reminiscent of the audio where Rosemary audiotaped Rick's conversation with his dad and turned that tape over to Dr. Wieger. That's -- I submit that that is bizarre behavior. It shows a me versus him mentality. It's Rosemary against Rick. And that's why she recorded this, and recorded the audio. Not because she wanted to help out the family situation, but because in her mind Rick was tearing Bob and her relationship apart."

"And we see that when Rosemary brings Rick to Dr. Wieger for counseling. Because Dr. Wieger told you that the purpose of his counseling was not to help the whole family get together and figure out everybody's problems. The purpose of counseling in Rosemary's mind with Dr. Wieger was to straighten out Rick. Rick is the problem here. Rick is the problem. Focus on Rick. And that was the focus of the treatment, and that's why Rosemary recorded this and did the audio."

"And you also can't help but notice, when you watch that scene between Rick and his dad that Rosemary is secretly recording that it cuts off right after Rick's comment to Bob. So, we don't get to see what Bob's response was. You know there's more on that video. So, where is it? Why didn't the state bring in the rest of the scene for you to watch? Why did they cut it off right after Rick's comment? Because you know if Rosemary's sitting there, and she's recording this thing as it's happening, she doesn't turn it off after Rick says, I'm not taking this crap, to his dad. It goes on beyond that. And I'll tell you why the state didn't bring that in. Because you know full well what happens after that, because we've seen it before."

"Cynthia also told us some things which tell us a lot about Rosemary Watkinson. We had initially thought that Rosemary and Bob had reached this agreement that we heard about not to have kids in their relationship, we had initially thought that they reached that agreement after they came to Alaska. But Cynthia was kind enough to tell us that that agreement was actually reached back in 1990 before Bob and Rosemary were married. And the agreement was -- Cynthia said that she was there to -- she was there to hear this conversation between Rosemary and Bob."

"And the agreement was that Rosemary said, I don't want any troubled kids in the relationship. This is clear back in 1990. So, at that time Rosemary clearly thinks that Rick and his brother are troubled kids, clear back in 1990. You can imagine what she thought then in 1994 when Bob said. I'm going down to get my son in Oregon and I'm going to bring him back to live with us. And this is after, because of the depression that he was suffering as a result of the divorce, and after missing school, and skipping school because of the divorce and the depression be suffered as a result, which Dr. Smith talked about, that now Bob is going to go down there and bring this runaway kid up to Anchorage. And you know at that point that she knew Rick was a troubled kid in her mind. And she did not want him here."

"We know that from her own letter which was taken from the residence, which is defense exhibit B, which is Rosemary's letter to her attorney which apparently was never sent. Because in this letter Rosemary talks about how she has to quit her lucrative job so she can supervise Rick, talks about how insolent he's been, and about how she's had to go and talk to counselors, and about how he's left - this is very telling. She left him alone last Monday while she did some tasks. She came home to a puncture in the sofa, the stereo door is broken off the hinge, and Rick is sleeping, and Rick denies that he did any of this stuff. But Rosemary is absolutely convinced that he did it."

"She talks about how she had to pass up the job because Rick came. And finally, most importantly, she talks about I just want to let you know the toll this is taking. Bob and I are seeing a side to each other that we never knew existed. Because there were no problems in their relationship before Bob brought Rick back to Anchorage. And they started having fights about Rick. But we shall not let jealousy Rick has for the love we have pull us apart. This is the me versus him mentality that Rosemary had when Rick came to live in Anchorage, and that continued during the year that Rick lived in that house."

"Cynthia talked about how she had a conversation with Rick, and during the conversation she indicated to Rick, good kids get good things, bad kids don't. And so we asked her, where did you get that from? Did you get that from your mother Rosemary? She said, yes, I did get it from her. Good kids get good things, bad kids don't. Cynthia may have been a good kid to Rosemary. Cynthia said she didn't have problems in school she didn't skip school so she got along fine with

Rosemary, because according to Rosemary that's what it takes to make a good kid. So, as a good kid she got good things. She got love and attention."

"Rick was a bad kid, according to Rosemary. According to her own letter. And bad kids don't get good things. While Cynthia's getting love and attention. Rick's getting called asshole and bastard on a daily basis. While Cynthia's getting good things. Rick gets slapped in the face. Rick gets belittled in front of family friends that are over visiting two days after Thanksgiving. Cynthia was a good kid and was wanted in the home. I have no doubt of that. There's also very clear that according to Rosemary, Rick was not a good kid, and was not welcome in the home. Good kids get good things, bad kids don't."

"The state offers you, in addition to Dr. Rothrock and Cynthia, the statements. You have the statement to Marrs at Service High School, and you have the statement to Marrs, which is on video, at trooper headquarters. And the state argues that Sergeant Marrs gave Rick an opportunity to talk about physical and emotional abuse in the interview, but Rick didn't say anything. And the state points out that Rick didn't say anything to his own mother. He didn't say anything to Dr. Wieger. He didn't say anything to anybody about his physical abuse. And Dr. Smith told us that's because that's the norm for abused kids. They do not want to talk about the abuse."

"But what's very interesting about the Marrs' interview, if you go back and you look at the one question where Marrs asks Rick about physical abuse, you'll see that Rick actually indicated that there had been some abuse, but Marrs took it as a negative answer because he wasn't looking for physical abuse. He was not looking for why the events on November 30 happened. He was looking for what happened. And that's very clear from his interviews. Both interviews. Because out of the entire interview he asked very few questions about physical or emotional abuse, and focuses entirely on the what instead of the why."

"I asked Marrs about being trained in questioning children who are physically and sexually abused. And the reason I asked him that is because he has received specific training in questioning children who are -- claimed to have been sexually or physically abused. And common sense will tell you that the last question you want to ask a child who is physically abused is have you been physically abused. Common sense will tell you that if Marrs was actually interested in finding out why this happened when he asked Rick, have you been physically abused, and he said in Marrs' mind he said, no, he would have followed up on that."

"Can you imagine at all a trooper investigating charges of child abuse who calls the child into his office and sits the child down and says, so, Jimmy, have you been physically abused. Jimmy says, no, I haven't. Sergeant Marrs says, thank you very much. Jimmy, see you later, have a good time. Common sense will tell you if you really want to know whether the child has been abused or not, you go into a lot more detail than that. You have to break down what you mean by physical abuse. You have to go into the details. Have you ever been slapped, have you ever been punched in the back, have you ever been dragged through a river. Maybe not that specific, but you need to ask have you been punched, have you been slapped, anybody ever call you names. You have to break it down."

"And Dr. Smith told us why you have to break it down. Because for children who suffer abuse, physical and emotional abuse, and who know nothing else, abuse to them is the norm. They don't even call it abuse. So, you ask a child who is called names on a daily basis, hurtful names, who has been physically abused, who has been punched in the back, who has been bruised, who has been assaulted by his father, you ask this child, have you been physically abused, and because it's the norm for the child, the child says, no, I haven't been physically abused."

"Dr. Smith talked about that phenomenon with abused kids, but that also is true of the abusive parent, because again, this is a norm for the abusive parent. The abusive parent does not see this as abuse. You ask the abusive parent, have you ever abused your child·· I'm sure if you asked Robert Watkinson that, to this day he would say, absolutely not, I would never do anything like that. Because he doesn't consider punching an adolescent in the back abuse. He doesn't consider smashing his forearm into the child's throat abuse. And he doesn't consider rejection a form of abuse, or name calling a form of abuse. That is how an abusive parent comes to be in counseling with the abused child."

"The state asks you to look at the conduct on November 30, '95, and infer from the conduct that Rick was capable of controlling his actions. Do not - that is a shell game. And I ask you when you go back in the jury room do not fall for that shell game, because here's what's happening there. The state is asking you to focus on physical movements, and not on whether or not he was capable of controlling those physical movements. There's a huge difference. And here are some of the examples that I mentioned earlier that we all experience in common, everyday life that show you why there's a huge difference."

"If any of you have ever smashed your thumb with a hammer -- you're out there hammering away, and you hit your thumb with a hammer, and most of us immediately react. And we - maybe we curse. We yell out some really horrible word, and we turn down and look, and there's your five-year-old kid standing next to you who then repeats the word that you just shouted out. When you smash your thumb, you react. Are you physically moving your mouth and fanning words? Sure you are. Are you jumping up and down on one foot or doing whatever it is you're doing with your body? Sure you are. But at that point in time right after you smash your thumb with the hammer, you are completely overwhelmed with pain and with anger at smashing your thumb, and you are unable to stop yourself from what follows immediately after that."

That is what heat of passion is all about. The fact that you cannot stop yourself. It doesn't have to do with physical movements. It's your ability to stop yourself. That's what we're talking about here. And focusing on physical movements is a mistake, and in this case it would be a tragic mistake because it's a shell game, and it's not what heat of passion is about. When you smash your thumb with a hammer, and these words come flying out of your mouth, do you recall what happened after the fact? Can you sit down with somebody and say, I smashed my thumb with a hammer, and I did X, Y and Z, or I said, X, Y and Z. Sure you can. Everybody can. Does that mean that you could control what you were doing at the time? No. Common sense tells you absolutely not."

"And that is just -- the hammer example is just a brief instantaneous provocation with a short loss of control. But what about where you have long-term provocation, as you have in this case. What about where you have a buildup of events that occur over a six-year period, that instead of coping with and letting go, you keep inside, and it builds, and it builds, and it builds, and it builds until finally it spills over. And you end up with exactly the same thing as you do with a person who hits their thumb with a hammer, only it's of longer duration."

"That's what happened to Rick Watkinson on November 30, '95 as he laid there in bed and he relived the pain of the divorce, the physical abuse and the emotional abuse, over and over again in his mind until like a simmering cauldron he boiled over, and his emotions took control of him, and he killed his father and his stepmother. Was he moving his arms and legs? Sure he was. Was he carrying the rifle? Sure he was. Did he walk up the stairs and down the stairs? Sure he did. Did he reload the gun? Sure he did. That does not mean he could stop what he was doing."

"The state makes some other arguments, some direct arguments, some by inference. By inference the state argues that people died here, so somebody has to pay for that. That's not the issue here because the law recognizes that some types of killing that can be charged as murder in the first and second degree are mitigated. And they're mitigated by circumstances surrounding the killings. They're mitigated by heat of passion, by life experiences that overwhelm you and cause you to react in a way that you cannot stop and you cannot control."

"But the law does not say that when there's heat of passion, that the person who did the killing walks free. The law does not say that a person who kills, even in heat of passion, is justified in killing. And we are not saying that. We are not saying that what happened here was justified. We are saying that what happened here was mitigated by heat of passion. And heat of passion merely reduces murder in the first and second degree to manslaughter. That's what happens."

"So don't believe the state's argument that if you find heat of passion, Mr. Watkinson will go free, because that is not going to happen here. The state by inference is arguing – or saying that we, the defense, have said that Bob and Rosemary deserved to die because they were bad parents. That is not the case here. That is not the case. Because we called Dr. Smith to testify, and if you will recall, we called Dr. Wieger to testify. The state didn't call Dr. Wieger. And Dr. Wieger had both good and bad things to say about the Watkinson family. And as Dr. Smith said, abusive parents don't have to be abusive all the time. Abusive parents are capable of doing good things."

"Very few people are cut and dried. People are not full-time monsters or full-time saints. All of us are a little of both. But the bad times in this case happened when the parents lost their temper. And Mr. Collins conceded that in his opening closing statement. He gets to make another closing. But in his original closing he conceded that on a number of occasions Robert and Rosemary lost their temper, lost their control and acted instantaneously without thinking."

"And when Bob acted, he acted physically by hitting, and by punching, and by shoving and pushing. Rosemary reacted by slapping, and by abusive language, and by belittling Rick, and trying to take from Rick, not intentionally, but out of reflex and not thinking, his self-esteem and his self-respect. And the fact that it's out of anger, and it's not done while you're thinking about it, does not make it right. It's still abuse."

"Abusers can go water skiing. Abusers can take the children that they're abusing and put them on a jet ski. That doesn't mean that they're not abusing their kids. And even abusive parents can learn new behavior. And I think the state is exactly right when they say that Bob and Rosemary were attempting to do what was right. They did go to counseling. It was the right thing to do. But it was too little, and it was too late. Because regardless of whether the parents try to do the right thing, that's not the focus here. The focus here is the effects on Rick, because heat of passion is the reasonable person in Rick's situation, as Rick saw things to be."

"And we all need to remember back to when we were kids. We need to remember what it felt like to get slapped by dad. And if any of us have had the unfortunate experience of being punched by dad, we need to remember what that was like. Because to understand what happened here on November 30, 1995, you have to walk six years in Rick's shoes."

"Serious provocation means conduct which is sufficient to excite an intense passion in a reasonable person in Rick's situation. When you think about Rick's situation, the standard, unlike what Mr. Collins said here, is not what the reasonable person sitting in relatively comfortable chairs, in an air conditioned courtroom in Anchorage, would do. That is not the legal standard here. The legal standard is what would a person in Rick's situation do."

"So, when you think about that, do not think about it from a detached viewpoint. Close your eyes and imagine -- remember when you were a kid and when your dad came home. Remember how happy you were to see him. I remember running to see my dad when he came home. Remember what it felt like if you've been the victim of a divorce when you were very young. Remember what it felt like when you realized that your dad was leaving. And remember at that point in time that you don't think he's ever coming back."

"Remember what it felt like to feel the sting of the hand across your face when you were a kid. Remember what it felt like to hear anything negative from your dad or your mom when you were young. I can't imagine that any of you, or any of us were ever called asshole or bastard when we were young. At least I hope not. But imagine what that feels like to a 16-year-old person. Imagine what it feels like to have your dad grab you by the arm and throw you in a river and drag you around. That is the way you need to look at this case, and you need to look at heat of passion because the law requires you to do that. And as I said before, it's not going to be pleasant, and it's not going to be easy, but you took an oath to try this case fairly and truly, and it's something that you have to do.

"But finally, and perhaps most dangerously, the state argues -- or argues by inference that this was normal, that this was nothing. Hey, I suffered worse than this when I was a kid. This is the sort of attitude that you get from Rothrock when he talks about how punching your kid in the back is not physical abuse under certain circumstances. First of all, it's a misleading argument because, again, the standard is not what we would do. The standard is what would a reasonable person in Rick's position do, or how would he respond. That's the issue here."

"And it's a dangerous argument -- and this takes us back to my opening comments. It's a dangerous argument because it implies normality. It implies that it's normal to punch your adolescent in the back, or to throw your young child in a river and drag him around, or to call them names like asshole or bastard, or ungrateful little bastard. That is not normal. Nobody does that to their kids. That's not normal behavior. That attitude is dangerous because abused kids suffer in silence. And if you shrug that sort of behavior off, and you look at that as normal, then child abuse is never going to go away. It's always going to be there until we start recognizing it for what it is, and until we start doing something about it."

"These kids do not have voices of their own. They're too silent, and hurt, and afraid to speak out for themselves. So we have to watch very carefully for this type of thing. We have to be the kind of people who, when we see the bruised child sitting in the classroom, we have to report it. We have to be the kind of people who, when we see one of our friends use foul language to a teenager and throw them on the ground, we step in and we do something about it. We have to be the kind of people that step in when that person in the parking lot slaps their kid out of anger. Because it's time for the apathy to stop. It's time to act and to prevent this kind of thing from happening. And you must act and return a verdict of not guilty in the first – of murder in the first degree, and not guilty of murder in the second degree, but guilty of manslaughter on both counts."[45]

[45] Closing arguments of Wally Tetlow taken from Court transcripts

CHAPTER FORTY-EIGHT

Rick stood as they read the verdict. He should have known what it was going to be. He should have known how this was all going to end.

"In the count of first degree murder in the death Robert Watkinson, how do you find the defendant?"

"We find the defendant guilty."

"In the count of second degree murder in the death Rosemary Watkinson, how do you find the defendant?"

"We find the defendant guilty."

Rick closed his eyes and tried to absorb what had just happened. He expected to be found guilty. He confessed to the crimes. He did not expect to be found guilty of first degree murder and second degree murder. The jury never heard a thing. Never took into consideration anything the defence said or the evidence they presented. They bought into everything the State said, and Judge Sanders promoted. No heat of passion even considered. Rick wasn't a monster. He was a kid, a kid who committed a very horrible act, but a kid none the less.

"We'll appeal it," said Wally putting his hand on Rick's shoulder. "It should have just been manslaughter on both accounts."

"What the fuck does it even matter anymore?" thought Rick. "I killed them. I need to pay."

CHAPTER FORTY-NINE

"Okay, before I get down to sentencing," said Judge Sanders, "it's customary to hear some impact statements from the victim's families. We've already heard from Rosemary Watkinson's sister, so Mr. Collins, who do you have next?"

"Cynthia Brown, your honour. Rosemary's daughter."

"Mrs. Brown," said Judge Sanders, "I remember you from the trial. Please go ahead with your statement."

"Okay, Judge Sanders, my name is Cynthia Ann Brown and I am the daughter of Rosemary Watkinson. I am here today to try and explain what my life has been like since Rick brutally murdered my mother and Bob. Today is June 26th and I have started to think too that maybe time only will stop because it's so painful. My mother was the only one in my life who really knew me. She raised me alone from the age of four, just she and I. I don't know how to put into words the pain I feel, the loss, it hurts. I no longer have anyone to call specifically who can help me with my life. I don't have anyone who really cares. My mom was my best friend. She was always here for me, now I have no one…My mother was my lifeline, and now because of his selfish act, she is gone. My mom was not a quitter. She was a person who believed in right and wrong, she was not going to give up on Rick, she felt she could teach him the difference between right and wrong."

"Judge Sanders, you cannot change the one who does not want to be changed. This got my mom and Bob killed. Again, you cannot save those who do not want to be saved. I wish you could see what I see when I close my eyes at night, let me share with you the visions that I have in my head. I see my mother on a gurney, with a sheet over her body, with only her left part showing. On this left hand is her wedding ring, a symbol of the love she felt for Bob. As the sheet is pulled back, I can see her body but I don't see her face. On the side of her head is a bullet hole with blood. I've seen this vision for one and a half years. I don't think it will ever go away.

"I talked to my mom two days before she was killed. Rick and Bob were outside hanging Christmas lights in the big tree out front. She was laughing, Bob and Rick were having a good time. We were saying only eighteen days until we got to see each other as they were coming to my house for Christmas. Rick with his selfish unjustified actions changed that whole plan. I never saw or talked to my mom again. I don't think you know what it's like to have your whole world turned upside down. To get the phone call saying your mother has been murdered by the selfish uncontrollable person you call your stepbrother. To feel your body hit the floor but not feel the pain because of the shock, to see your children run to you, and they're scared because you're screaming at the top of your lungs."

"To have your sons standing next to you knowing your world is falling apart and yet, this is only the beginning of my pain. I don't think you know what it is like to want so badly to dream about your mom because that is the closest to get to her. To wake up in tears and wish it weren't true. To hope so much that you can go back to sleep, to have that same dream, so that the two of you can be back together. You do not know what it is like to sit your six and three year olds down and try and explain to them that Grandma and Grandpa Bob are in heaven. That they are guardian angels who will always be with them."

"To see your six-year-old break down and cry because he just wants his most favorite grandma. The one who taught him to hit a baseball, or tennis, or took him to fly a kite. To see him look into my face and ask 'How? Please tell me what happened mommy?' I cannot tell him now because I do not want my children knowing that someone in their family is capable of such a horrible, scary disgusting and inhumane actions. I'm afraid that they will not know who to trust, and they both thought Rick was wonderful. How will I ever explain to them the full horror of this incident? Yes, this has in many ways and will always affect my life. If you only knew how many time I have wiped the tears from my babies' eyes because they miss their Grandma and Grandpa Bob so much. If only I know what to do to heal their hearts."

"No more birthdays with them from age six and three, no Christmas together, no Easter baskets, no Valentine's cards, no Halloween goblins. No family reunions. No Grandma and Grandpa, they are gone. So final. For me and my family, all of the parties involved this is difficult. But let me share with you the most difficult of all. My birthday. Every four years my birthday falls on Mother's Day. I used to love this because my mom and I would always plan what to do for our special day. All the fun, it was our girl's days. Last year was the fourth, the great fourth year. I couldn't get out of bed. I cried all day, I was having a case of 'I want Mommy'. 'I want Mommy' was what I used to say when I would call my mom on the phone. It was my way of saying, 'Mom it's been a long time and I miss you'."

"Let me tell you Judge Sanders, my mother couldn't wait for my call. She loved me, my husband, my kids, Bob and his kids. She was a giver. She always wanted everyone to be happy. And happy we were until Rick shot them both in the head. The last time I saw my Mom and Bob, it was when they came to visit us in Boise to help us move into our new house. We didn't have enough for the down payment, overcoming that was easy, with one phone call I just asked, that's all, it was easy. Bob listened and laughed. I think his comment was something like, 'well you'll just cry of you don't get it so we can't have that'. Bob loaned us a thousand dollars for our down, he was such a kind, loving, accepting person. I miss them so much. It was October 1995, the last time I saw both of them. I will never forget that Bob went home four days before my mom, so he could spend some quality time with Rick. We were all sad to see him go but reassured as Christmas was right around the corner, and that he would be back soon. How wrong we were. When I took my mom to the airport to go home to Alaska, we both cried as we always did when we said goodbye. Little did we know we would never see each other again. If I would have known, I'd have never let her go. As I was at the airport to come here, it reminded me of how much I wish I could just fly up to see my mom and Bob or how they would come see me and my family. But what caught my attention more than anything else was seeing a mother and daughter say goodbye. They kept saying, 'I love you mom, I love you'. How I wish I could say that to my mom. How I wish I could hold her and kiss her again. How I wish she could hold and love my kids again. Now we have lost all of that because of Rick's selfish actions."

"Rick, these are some things I would like to say to you. You may have won the battle by killing my mom and Bob, but I will win this war. I will make it my life-long mission to make sure you never get out of prison. I want you to answer for every day of the rest of your pathetic life for what you have done to us. I will make sure you stay caged up like the killer that you are. I will do everything possible to see to it that you never see the light of day, just as my mom and Bob will neither see the sunrise and sunset. Rick, you think you're a tough guy, but really you're a coward. You see, you know, that I know, just as 99.5% of everyone in this courtroom knows, YOU WERE NEVER ABUSED!"

"You see we all know that you are hiding behind your attorney, of what he told you to plead and say. How small minded of you. I guess with two people dead, why not do your best to destroy their character. What a perfect plan. Well Rick, it didn't work. The jury still found you guilty of two counts of first degree murder, and yes, you are totally scum of the earth. However your attorney may lie about that. I know as you know, you killed my mom and Bob because you want all of the control. You did not want to be told to go to school, to get passing grades, to do your homework. You did not want to clean the house or clean your room, you did not want to get in trouble for stealing the car or smoking cigarettes."

"You see Rick, you did not want anyone to care. You were used to walking all over your mother and step-father, and now my mom and Bob weren't going to let that happen. So out of your need for control, you killed them. You have given up so much of your control. Let's see, you are now eighteen, you could be doing anything you wanted, you could drive a car, get into college, or even in the military. You cannot be out to ski or rollerblade, no mountain biking, home cooked meals, fishing…you had so much. But most of all, you had two people who are trying to be good, caring, responsible parents, yes, that is what good parents do. We teach our children right from wrong, and we tell them 'no' when we feel it is best. We don't give up on our kids, we keep trying. If trying gets us killed and is okay, then we as parents are in a lot of trouble."

"One last note Rick. I'm sure if you haven't already, you're going to get up and say you're sorry or you're going to ask for forgiveness. Please keep your hollow, meaningless words to yourself, as we don't want to hear your words, or those of your attorney. Please don't insult as any more than you already have. Judge Sanders, I feel like I can never put to words everything that I have to say. But it was…I just wanted everyone to see. This is a passage…a path…a poem that…

Are any of you wise or sensible? Then show it by living right and by being humble and wise in everything you do. But if your heart is full of bitter jealousy and selfishness, don't brag or lie to cover up the truth. That kind of wisdom doesn't come from above. It is earthly and selfish and comes from the devil himself. Whenever people are jealous or selfish, they cause trouble and do all sorts of cruel things. But the wisdom that comes from above leads us to be pure, friendly, gentle, sensible, kind, helpful, genuine, and sincere. When peacemakers plant seeds of peace, they will harvest justice.[46]

"Judge Sanders, you are a peacemaker, please give us peace of mind by doing the right thing and sentencing Rick Watkinson to two ninety-nine year terms with no parole, to be served in two terms. Two separate lives should hold two separate terms. Please send a message to our youth that we are not going to tolerate this disgraceful violence any longer. We need to hold people responsible for their actions, we need to start now. For me, my family and my children, please keep Rick in prison for the rest of their lives and the rest of his life. But most of all, give him the maximum sentence for my mom and Bob, for they are the ones who have truly lost their lives."[47]

"Okay, thank you Mrs. Brown," said Judge Sanders. "Mr. Tetlow?"

"Robert Watkinson's son, James Watkinson would like to exercise his right to make a victim's impact statement at this time. You can stand right here at the podium if you like."

"I have nightmares," said Jimmy "where I'm reduced to a little lost boy, walking through a field and screaming for his daddy. I don't have a daddy that

[46] James 3:13-18 CEV Bible
[47] Cynthia Brown's victim statement taken from actual Sentencing Transcripts

comes to me. Not even in my dreams. And then there's Rosemary, she has been strict, a perfectionist, which drove me nuts. But she, in a lot of ways was a wonderful person who cared for me. She cared about me. She taught me how to cook. And I miss them both. But I'm not going to call for vengeance! Vengeance is not justice. Vengeance is just to satisfy yourself. I want everyone to look at those pictures right there. Those are of my brother, a little boy who's grown to a big boy, who had a happy life until he moved in with them."

Jimmy couldn't hold back the tears any longer.

"I have looked through those photo albums," Jimmy said pointing to the table, "and I see us wrapped in sleeping bags, playing blanky monster, and doing everything together, dressing up like each other, inseparable. We've been separated. I don't want to be separated from him very long. I get to talk to him through a glass window except for once a week when I can actually touch him." The sobbing continued.

"I HATE WHAT HE DID! But I love him. And human compassion should love him too. But human compassion is something that's been lost among humanity." Jimmy paused and wiped his eyes. "He loved me and he cared for me, and he taught me things, and he always tried to protect me, even if he wasn't…even if he wasn't doing it right, or where in situations where I could protect myself, he always had to protect me. He always had to be the one to be sure that I was alright. A couple of weeks ago, I was sick for two weeks, and he was worried, he was so worried. And he always talked to my mom to find out how I was doing and would see how I was doing on the phone. Because he loved me so much…"

"People only think about themselves. About vengeance but never about the other people whose lives this affects. I'm so sorry that Rosemary is dead because I miss her. I mean, I may have complained about her discipline a lot, but I miss her. I even have a picture of her, my dad and me and Rick, on Christmas of '94, on my wall. And I just stare at it sometimes and cry. Reduced to that little boy in my dreams, curled up all alone."

Watching his little brother sob uncontrollably was killing Rick. All he wanted to do was run up there and give him a hug, tell him it was going to be okay. That somehow, someway, he'd make it all better. But he couldn't. There wasn't a thing he could do to make any of it better.

"We could've lived a happy life," said Jimmy. "Like Cindy said, Rick seemed…he could have had a…life. And Judge Sanders, you could still give him a life. A life where my children don't have to look at him through glass. A life where he can have a wife and his own children maybe…"

"But hey," Jimmy continued. "That's what I want. Doesn't seem to be what anybody else wants. But it's what he deserves. He is sorry for what he did and it's not an insult. He, in a way, loved my dad. They were closest when he was little… And he's beating himself up so much in his head, and then he has all of these other people doing it on the outside too. He doesn't desire to be locked up for ninety-nine years by himself. He desires to have a life with me and the others that he loves. And the girl that he loves, and his friends. He knows he basically screwed that up but he can still have a chance. That's all I have."[48]

Rick smiled as Jimmy walked back to his seat. His brother had given it a shot, and had been honest, and that's all Rick could ask for. Jimmy, the only person who spoke that didn't hate his guts or wish hell on him. He couldn't really blame them. Cindy had been shattered. He knew that, and it broke his heart that he'd caused her so much pain. He'd liked Cindy, always had. She was just standing up for her mom and her family. But still, it cut deep to hear her words, to hear her call him a liar. He wasn't a liar. All those things happened. He didn't make them up. She would never see that though. Why would she? He killed her mother. That was the simple fact. She had a right to be angry. She had a right to hate him. He hated himself for doing what he did. If he could take it all back, he would.

"Okay," said Judge Sanders. "Mr. Watkinson, you have the right to address the Court if you wish to, you don't have to if you don't want. Some defendants want to and some don't. I want to assure you that the Court would not hold it against you if you elected not to speak to the Court, and rely on the attorneys. So whatever you want to do is fine."

"I'd like to speak," said Rick.

"Okay. You can just remain seated there, that's fine," said Judge Sanders.

"Your Honour, I can never justify what I've done. I take full responsibility for what I did. I'll always regret that night. I'll always wish I could take it back and start over. I would like to apologize to Rosemary's family, specifically Cindy, her daughter, her sisters Paula and Nancy, her brother and her parents. I can never apologize enough. I am truly sorry for your loss. I'd also like to apologize to my father's family, his brother, and his mother and father. And I'd like to apologize to my brother and mother for the pain this has caused them too. Your Honour, I have many years ahead of me to think about what I've done, and I'm probably going to end up doing a lot of time and it's up to me for what I do with that time. And I plan to learn from my past and make a better future for myself, and to live my life to the best and fullest, even though I'm in prison. I want to learn from my mistakes and I want to learn what it takes to become someone who is a better person and acceptable to society. Your Honour, I ask that you consider this in your decision today, and I also ask that you give me a chance to go back

[48] Taken from victim impact statement of Jimmy Watkinson in court sentencing documents

out into society someday, to have a future and a life. Again, I would like to apologize everyone affected because of my actions. That's all. Thank you."[49]

Rick closed his eyes. He just wanted this to be over. His life had been forfeit a long time ago. In his heart, he knew that none of this was going to change Judge Sanders' opinion of him. He'd seen the way he looked at him during trial, and all the times that he ruled against the defence, while the State had free rein.

"Mr. Tetlow," said Judge Sanders. "Your sentencing remarks please."

"I wanted to begin my sentencing comments by talking about the offence itself and specifically about child abuse in general. That is to say that it is an unfortunate aspect of child abuse that it often goes, number one, unreported, and number two, undetected and unacknowledged. The problem with child abuse in America is that the child doesn't say anything because the child is trapped in a cage of silence because of embarrassment of reporting to the public the abuse that's going on at home. And because of love of the parent, the same parent that is actually abusing the child. And because of fear of retaliation by the parent whose control of the child he very much remains in, even after the child reports the abuse, and even after multiple attempts to escape the abuse. And because child abuse is a private matter. It's one of those things in our society that remains a veritable secret in the home. Because parents don't beat their kids in public, parents don't call their kids derogatory terms in public when there's other people around to see that happen. Every one of us in society maintains the public image no matter what happens at home, and we've all experienced times in our lives that show exactly that."

"But home lives are often a very different matter than the public image the people project, and I can't say how disappointed I am to hear the Courts comments up to this point because in this case there certainly was evidence of abuse both physical and mental. And I have been…and as a defence attorney, in my time, been accused of a lot of bad things so I'm not surprised to hear that today. But the defence team certainly did not manufacture Kristy Braman's testimony, when Kristy Braman spoke of the incident in high school, where she hugged Rick and Rick flinched in pain, and Kristy asked Rick, 'what's the matter?', and Rick brushed it off and said 'nothings the matter, nothing's happening'. And Kristy being a good friend of Rick's pushed him on the issue, 'I know something's going on here, you need to show me what's going on, life up your shirt'. And he lifted up his shirt and there were bruises on his back. And she pushed him about the bruises on his back, and asked them where they came from. And he said, 'my Dad and I got in a fight'. That's not manufactured evidence. And what's scary and most difficult to deal with in these cases is that oftentimes, that is as close as

[49] Taken from the actual court sentencing transcripts. Statement from Rick Watkinson.

you get to having any sort of corroboration for the real victim's testimony about physical and emotional abuse."

"Again, exactly because it's one of those dirty little secrets that remains in the home and not public. Kristy wasn't the only one who had a glimpse of the abusive relationship that was going on in the Watkinson home. Jimmy Watkinson saw it. He testified about Rosemary and derogatory name calling, which I submit to the Court is not normal – is not normal parenting behaviour. And we also saw it on the video that was introduced by the State, when Rosemary called Rick a derogatory term on the video that was brought in and shown to the jury. And I had thought that the Court had seen the physical and emotional abuse that was occurring here when the Court found that we had established some evidence justifying a Heat of Passion instruction. And then that finding was substantiated by the Court of Appeals when the State asked for a hold to take it off, on Petition for Review and the Court of Appeals rejected that petition."

"Rick Watkinson was a victim of a dysfunctional family. There is no question that his parents divorced when he was age 10 and that life up to age 10 was normal. And that he had no problems before then. And then we heard not only from Rick, but from his Mom and Jimmy about the scene when his dad came home and said, 'I'm leaving you, I don't want to be with you anymore' and then turns around to walk out the door, and Rick, aged ten, grabbed his leg and said, 'don't go'. And what an emotional experience that was for everyone involved, and how Bob said that, that was in Rick's best interest, and pushed him away and left. And then came back a week later with Rosemary."

"It's no surprise that Brenda Jo'e blamed Rosemary for taking Robert Watkinson from the family. It's not abnormal or unexpected that in that situation she would take her anger out on Bob and reflect that upon the kids. And it's not unusual that the kids would draw their own conclusion when they see their father come back a week later after leaving their mother, with Rosemary in tow. When Doctor Smith was interviewing Rick, as Doctor Viccary as well, Rick indicated that he felt like he was dead inside on that day, and I don't think that is that difficult to imagine. We also know from Dr. Smith and Dr. Viccary that as a result of the divorce, Rick suffered from depression for a number of years, and then we start to see the downward spiral that did not exist prior to the divorce. We start seeing his rebellion teenage years, we start seeing slipping grades, we start seeing suicide attempts of which there were two, Dr. Smith testified about those. On one occasion how Rick took a loaded – or a gun that he thought was loaded and put it on his head and pulled the trigger, and about another time that he put a knife on his chest, but did not actually plunge it in. Then we have a song that Rick wrote that his mom submitted for the Court's consideration that talks about the pain and suffering that he felt as a result of the divorce. And he did not have any psychiatrist treatment for that depression at any time."

"So he's rejected by his dad the first time when his dad chooses Rosemary and leaves, but then, his dad decides to leave the state and comes to Alaska and to have a life with Rosemary. Here is the second rejection of Rick by his father. And then we have his father coming back to get Rick because his father feels that his mother is not being strict enough with Rick and that he needs to come down and impose some discipline, which in and of itself it not a bad idea. The problem is that Rosemary and Bob had a new life together, which was a very good life to hear everybody tell it. And Rosemary and Bob had an agreement that the children of prior marriages would not come into the new marriage because they had both raised their kids and it was time to get past that and enjoy the things in life that cone after you've finished raising your children. That all parents talk about while their children are home before they go off to college, all parents talk about, well someday our kids will be grown, they'll be out of the home, we'll be able to go on these trips we wanted to go on and do the things we've always wanted to do, that you cannot do when you're a parent and the children are at home."

"Rosemary told that to Dr. Wieger, Dr. Wieger testified that Rosemary told him that she and Bob had an agreement that they would not take the kids into the marriage. I cannot imagine a worse family scenario than the one that was created in this situation. Because you have a child who blames his father for tearing the family apart, who does not see the father coming down to get him, and dragging him back up to Alaska, not as an act of love, but more an exercise of dominion and control…in an effort to save face, the father's face, and not have his son do something that the father does not approve of. Rick did not see that as an act of love, and he certainly did not see Rosemary's derogatory name calling as an act of love. As often happens in trials, I think that different sides have become polarized, in the eyes of spectators, simply because they're on different sides. And in this case the State presented Bob and Rosemary as excellent parents, and we presented some of the bad things that were done during these relationships. But in fact, it's not black and white and I'm not going to stand here and say that it is. And I think that, Jon Svendsen said more eloquently that I would have in his letter to the Court…when he said, and I'm quote directly from his letter, 'Bob and Rosemary were nice people, but nice people make mistakes too, and sometimes the mistakes are not so nice', and that's exactly what happened in this case."

"Taking your child on vacation and taking them wind surfing, taking them to counseling, when it's much too late…don't make up for the name calling, don't make up for the years of depression suffered as a result of the divorce. They don't make up for the physical abuse, and they certainly do not make up for the fact that the child realizes that he is not welcomed in the home where he is staying…which was made very clear in this case. The physical and emotional abuse was also corroborated by the work that Mr. Mones has done in the hundreds of parricide cases that he has worked on, and he submitted a brief to the Court that basically shows that Mr. Watkinson fits exactly the profile of a psychologically abused child. And the reason we have to rely on these profiles is again exactly because child abuse is a dirty secret and remains in the home. It is not talked about. What happened the night of the killings was testified to you during the trial that Rick was in an argument with his dad about skipping school. Rosemary came home and started in on Rick and then, Rosemary and Bob got into it again over Rick and who would discipline Rick, which Rick had heard many, many, many, many times before. So Rick goes downstairs while Rose is still arguing. Rosemary gets angry and leaves, and Bob is going to go after her…but on the way, Bob stopped by to make sure and tell Rick that Rick is to blame for their failing marriage, and that he is not welcome in the home anymore, and once again in Rick's mind choosing Rosemary over him."

"I do not see how the Court can find that that is not a substantial factor in what happened on the evening in question. One account I heard that I think is most absurd is…there was an account made of…he probably thought he was going to get away with it. But when you look at the facts in the case that clearly is not true because what happens is, Rick is out wandering all night long and goes to school the next morning. As if he somehow thought that the place they're not going to be looking for him and the very first place that they would look for him would be at school. And the police state that they did not expect him to show up at school. Because anybody who's running from the law or running from what they had done, would not have gone to school, and would have been out hiding somewhere but Rick did not do that. Rick went to school the next day fully expecting to be taken into custody. He was taken into custody, he was arrested and confessed to it…the technicalities of what he had actually done. And I'd like to talk about the offender as well. He was 16 years old at the time, he's 18 years old now, no prior record whatsoever, no prior juvenile record, which is typical as Mr. Mones indicated of children in parricide cases who are physically and mentally abused. Above average intelligence is very clear in his writings to this Court, and as Dr. Viccary and Dr. Smith indicated in their psychiatric evaluations, has not been sitting idly in custody, waiting to be sentenced in this case. And during this pending case has obtained his GED, and is enrolled in correspondence college courses, because in spite of the fact he knows he's looking at the possibility of consecutive life sentences in this case, he is not willing to give up on himself, but is working to better himself and to move on from here."

"No drugs in his background, no alcohol in his background. When he did express an interest in something at school, an activity that he in the Reserve

Officers Training Corps, Jon Goodwin testified that he was excellent as a student in that program, he applied himself. He was a leader of the other students, and set and excellent example. So he clearly is someone who has a lot to offer to society. Especially at such an early point in his life, when at only 18 years of age, he very much has his entire life ahead of him, it has not even started. So the Court should consider rehabilitation in fashioning a sentence in this case because assuming that the Court see's Mr. Watkinson being released at some point in his lifetime, the Court needs to look at what he will be like when he is released. And so the Court must balance deterrence and community condemnation against rehabilitation because cases like this where the emphasis is too much on deterrence, and the community condemnation of young men, you do so to the detriment of rehabilitation because we all know that jail is not a good place to put anyone. You don't learn anything while you're in custody and Mr. Watkinson has actually learned the most that he can while he's in custody is more than most offenders that come before the Court ever do."

"I just don't know what the legislature was thinking when they decided that 16-year-old kids, in adult facilities with pedophiles, and put them in open population. And I'm not sure what they had in mind or what they thought they would accomplish by doing that. But that's what's happened in this case. Jail time, this is addressing deterrence, will not deter Mr. Watkinson or anyone else from committing similar offences. And the problem is that these types of offences are not offences where the offender engages in a contested analysis. That's not reality, it don't work that way. In these types of cases what you have is, you have a series of events that finally at some point in time overwhelm the person's ability to cope with those events, until the person loses the ability to rationally perceive what it is that they're doing. And they act out of overwhelming emotion much more so than out of calculation or plan. And I submit that the evidence establishes with clear cause that that is what we had in this case. Addressing deterrence…further jail time is not the only way to address deterrence in many cases. I think that we oftentimes forget that. And I think that what we tend to lose sight of in this case is that Rick Watkinson has suffered a loss incurred by his own hand already. Mr. Watkinson, as Jimmy testified, has beat himself up since day one on this case because he took the life of his own father. And he has suffered a loss at his own hands. He will have to live with that every single day. And he also has to live with the fact that he has taken Rosemary from her family. He is not happy that that happened. He did not take Rosemary from her family as some sort of an act against her family…"

"And he has expressed remorse for his actions in this case. Dr. Viccary and Dr. Smith both indicate that Mr. Watkinson expressed remorse when discussing the offense with them. And he certainly expressed remorse during the trial in this case on numerous occasions. And you can have an opinion either way on his expression of remorse in the Court during the trial, but the Court is the finder of that, the Court can make his conclusion about whether or not Mr. Watkinson's expressions were pitiful or not. So I'll leave that up to the Court."

"And I want to talk about community condemnation…and I ask the Court to consider all the statements of all the victims in this case. In a lot of cases there really is never a division of opinion. I can't recall how many cases I've done where I've come in and the victims come on and make their victim impact statements, and they are all the same. Maximum sentence, maximum sentence, maximum sentence, maximum sentence, and there's no division whatsoever. But look at the impact statements in this case. You have Fay and Barry Watkinson, who were Bob's parents, who expressed compassion and understanding for Rick in spite of the fact that Rick took the life of their own son. Jim Watkinson, Robert's brother, and he expressed the same compassion and the same understanding. Then we have Jimmy Watkinson, who came to the Court and testified, and I think who…put it much more eloquently than I could have on my own, in what he said that vengeance is not justice. And vengeance is not justice in this case. Jon Severdsen and Vivi Nettenberg wrote letters, they were close friends of both Bob and Rose and Mrs. Nittenberg spoke very eloquently about her relationship with Rosemary, and they saw the dysfunctional family dynamic that was going on and they tried to help. But it was too late. And they have expressed an understanding and a compassion for Rick and an understanding of the situation he was in, and they asked the Court for leniency on his behalf."

"The State and society have made an effort to put on blinders and choose to believe what they want to believe, and you can always hate those who bring truth to the light because sometimes the truth is not the most pleasant thing to acknowledge. And as I said before it's not the first time that I've been called names by family members and it won't be the last – exactly because of that, the people would not like to deal with the truth when that situation occurs, and I am not going to apologize for doing my job. But what we're asking this Court to do is balance condemnation, which is not justice, with what the Court acknowledged in this case by giving the Heat of Passion instruction – that what occurred in this case occurred because of family dysfunction, that occurred because of physical and emotional abuse, and it was not discovered because of the same reason that child abuse is not discovered as a general rule, because it's a dirty family secret. We're asking the Court to fashion a sentence in this case that does not create one more victim of an extremely unfortunate dysfunctional family situation. That's all I have left."[50]

[50] Taken from Court Sentencing transcripts. Sentencing remarks of Wally Tetlow.

There it was. In his defense, Wally Tetlow put everything out on the table for Judge Sanders to ponder. No one ever asked that Rick not be punished for his crime. No one even suggested he walk free. All they were asking for was a consideration of all the factors, from the very beginning to the very end. All they wanted was for the Judge to be fair in his sentencing. Rick closed his eyes and took a deep breath as Judge Sanders fiddled with some papers on his desk and adjusted the microphone. The moment of reckoning had arrived.

CHAPTER FIFTY

Judge Sanders cleared his throat, then took a sip of water. It was a powerful thing to hold the fate of a person in your hand. He liked that power. He'd been elected to office on the mandate of getting tough on youth crime, and while this had been a compelling case, and certainly a little out of the ordinary, his views were strong, and his opinion set. They'd been that way since the case first hit his docket.

"Alright," said the judge. "The Court is faced with a situation which is not all that uncommon, and that is, a victim of a crime procuring upon the Court, expressing heart felt emotions and urging the Court to impose the maximum penalty allowed by law. At the same time having a defendant and his or her family pointing out considerations which would justify the minimum penalty allowed by law. And for people who have attended this proceeding, it's apparent that both sides are heartfelt and emotionally charged, and make, from their point of view, very compelling arguments. And it would certainly be easier for a sentencing judge, if they had the option of picking one or the other, and following that so that at least half the people would leave the courtroom satisfied that justice had been done."

"But that does not happen and is not permitted by law. It's also easy or tempting for a Court to make a decision in terms of fashioning a sentence based on emotion, but the Court is directed by law not to consider pleas either for a Defendant for compassion in an emotional setting or by other interests including the victims. The Court, to eliminate decisions, sentencing decisions based on emotion or, based on a particular judge's personal view has given sentencing judges guidelines to follow, and so in fashioning a sentence, this Court will not rely on emotion, as compelling as it is, and will not rely on personal views because those are historations, which are inappropriate and rightfully so. I will, in determining what a just sentence is for Mr. Watkinson, look to guidelines given to the Court by the legislature and by appellate courts. The legislature has directed sentencing judges to look at certain criteria, and those are four broad guidelines."

"One to consider is community condemnation or reaffirmation of societal norms. Two is deterrence of the offender, in this case Mr. Watkinson, and deterrence of others. Three is isolation of a Defendant to prevent criminal conduct during confinement, and finally rehabilitation of the offender into a noncriminal member of society. So in this case, as in every case in which the Court is asked to sentence a Defendant upon conviction of a crime, the Court looks to those guidelines in determining what a just sentence is. There are other guidelines that assist in taking away a judge's discretion in fashioning an appropriate sentence. For example, the legislature has given the Court guidelines and maximums and minimums, and for murder in the first degree, the minimum sentence is twenty years and the maximum sentence is ninety-nine, and the Courts have also given direction to sentencing judges in terms of deciding when a Defendant should receive a concurrent sentence, when he is being sentenced for two crimes, and when he or she should receive consecutive sentences, and this Court will look to those cases which interpret those sentencing criteria in determining what a just sentence is for Mr. Watkinson."

"The sentencing range is from 20 to 99 years for first degree murder. Twenty years is for the most mitigated circumstance. There are oftentimes comments that first degree murder is the ultimate crime and reserves the ultimate punishment, and there are certainly circumstances where that's correct. Obviously, the legislature has recognized that there are men and women who commit first degree murder where it's a mitigated circumstance, and therefore does not justify a maximum penalty, in fact…may justify a minimum penalty of twenty years. And the circumstances which would justify that type of sentence for first degree murder are endless probably, but certainly the Court could appreciate some sort of mental handicap for example, somebody with a mental status of low I.Q. for example…might justify making it much more mitigated that the norm."

"A particularly youthful defendant, complete self-defence, and a variety of other considerations. But the legislature has certainly recognized that there are certain defendants who even though they may have committed the ultimate crime, deserve a sentence of twenty years. The upper range is ninety-nine years, and in the Court's view is not for the norm, it's not for a typical defendant. Ninety-nine years is for the far end of the spectrum, that defendant who is unusual in negative respects."

"For example, somebody who would be a career criminal, somebody who is mature, thoughtful and has planned an execution. Somebody who has tortured a victim before murdering them, there could be a variety of circumstances too endless to go into here but, it would be at that far end of the spectrum which would justify the maximum penalty. So the typical first degree murderer, in this courts view, does not qualify for the low end sentence in the range of twenty to forty years, nor does he or she qualify for the high range, which would be in the neighbourhood of ninety-five to ninety-nine years. Typically, a sentence would be some place between, and the Courts, and Appellate Courts have not given sentencing judges a benchmark that they have for other crimes. For a typical defendant committing second degree murder, a judge is given a benchmark range to look at, which is twenty to thirty years for a second degree murder. The court of appeals and the Supreme Court have not yet given trial judges that sentencing range or a benchmark for first degree murder."

"So to that extent this Court is left on its own but…based on sentencings that other judges have imposed and based on sentences this Court has imposed in the past, a reasonable range for a defendant convicted of first degree murder, a typical defendant being convicted of a typical first degree murder is probably…it's reasonable to assume that they will receive a sentence of fifty to seventy years. There are factors which may increase a sentence beyond that…as I have articulated, there are factors that may increase it, and I would like to go through and articulate what in this instance are factors that the Court would consider in either increasing the sentence beyond the mid-range or…increasing it or decreasing it."

"Factors that would decrease the sentence in this instance would be Mr. Watkinson's youth. The Defendant was sixteen and a half years old at the time he committed these murders. He was not an adult, in fact some people in our society would say that when you're sixteen years old, you're a child. The State recognizes that children are not adults and are not treated as adults, they're not permitted the same privileges and rights as adults. The reason they're not afforded these privileges and rights is because, according to legislature they do not have the judgement or wisdom of adults."

"Children oftentimes do not understand fully the consequences of their acts, and as a result of that we see…selective decisions made concerning people under the age of eighteen. For example, we don't let people under the age of eighteen vote, we don't let people under the age of eighteen serve on a jury. We don't let a person under the age of eighteen get married without their parent's permission, we don't let somebody under the age of eighteen sue or be sued. We don't let people under the age of eighteen even buy cigarettes in this community. So, there is an endless list of things in which our community and our society and our state have said that…that recognize youthful people, people under the age of eighteen, are not adults and do not have the same rights or privileges as adults."

"The Courts treat adults and children differently, the reason in this Court's view is because, youth is often synonymous with poor judgement and immature thought. A failure to recognize the consequences of one's acts. On the other hand, the law recognizes that Mr. Watkinson will be treated as an adult for criminal culpability, at sixteen years old, if a defendant or a person decides to engage in murder, intentional murder without justification, that person will be treated as an adult for purposes of criminal culpability. But the Courts have made it absolutely clear that although age is not a consideration in terms of determining culpability, it is a consideration in sentencing and the Court routinely sentences defendants differently because of their age, either because of their youth, or because of their mature years."

"Therefore, it's this Court's view that the Defendant's youth at the time these crimes were committed would justify a reduction in the normal sentence. The Defendant argues that the sentence should also be reduced below the norm because the Defendant acted at a time when he was under unusual circumstances, specifically that his conduct in engaging these crimes was a result of a long-term pattern of physical and emotional abuse. The Court finds that the primary source of evidence for this is the Defendant Rick Watkinson. This is a circumstance in which the alleged abusers, his father and step-mother, are unable to rebut those assertions. Therefore, the Court looks to other evidence to determine whether or not these claims of abuse are meritorious or not, and the Court is not persuaded that they are correct or true."

"First of all, I would refer to Dr. Wieger. Mr. Watkinson was taken to Dr. Wieger shortly before the murders, and was there for purposes of family counselling. Dr. Wieger testified here at trial, appeared to be confident, he has a good reputation in the community, and spent time alone with Rick Watkinson discussing the family dynamics. And Dr. Wieger first indicated, and I find this credible, first indicated that there are few parents that take their children to a psychologist or a psychiatrist and discuss family dynamics, who are engaged in abuse."

"I find that Mr. and Mrs. Watkinson, the decedents, were certainly average middle class citizens who would understand the consequences of what might happen if their son disclose that they were abusing him at home, on a consistent basis. The Court considers it unlikely that the Watkinson's would have taken their son to Dr. Wieger for independent counselling to improve family dynamics or find out what was going on with Rick if they had been engaged in a consistent pattern of abuse."

"Moreover, the Court is persuaded by the fact that Rick Watkinson had an opportunity, a perfect opportunity to discuss with Dr. Wieger what was going on. He did not disclose any abuse, in fact, and I think this is quite significant, there was a time, this arose at a time, when a meeting with Dr. Wieger had taken place shortly after there had been an argument between the Defendant and Rosemary Watkinson in which he had called her a 'bitch' and she had slapped him, and she on her own, at the next meeting with Dr. Wieger disclosed that…was very forthcoming about that…they had a frank discussion with Dr. Wieger – Dr. Wieger had a frank discussion with Rick Watkinson about what happened, so there did not appear to be any pattern of withholding abuse if it was going on.

The Court finds it unlikely that this would have been raised in a forum like…with Dr. Wieger if they were all alarmed about disclosing ongoing abuse. In any event, during these sessions with Dr. Wieger, the Defendant never indicated that he was abused in any way, in fact at one point, described his idea of the emotional turmoil, at one point was describing a friend of his who had contemplated suicide and his efforts to assist his friend. There was no effort to raise issues with Dr. Wieger about being abused."

"Subsequently, he did talk to Sargent Marrs during the interview and disclosed that he had sessions with Dr. Wieger and at least told Sgt. Marrs that his statements to Dr. Wieger were honest and forthright, so that would confirm that, in the Court's view, that his statements to Dr. Wieger were honest, forthright and no disclosure of abuse. Equally compelling, if not more compelling was the testimony of Brenda Jo'e. Frankly, the Court was taken aback by her testimony."

"In some respects but certainly one comment sticks out, one piece of testimony, and that was the question asked of her whether, during the entire period of time that the Defendant lived with his father and step-mother, there was an exchange, telephone conversations…they routinely called back and forth once a week or so…in which Rick Watkinson would talk to his mother, and discuss what he was doing…sounds like completely normal conversations and the question asked of his mother was…did Rick ever tell you he was being abused by his father or step-mother? And she said no."

"And the Court concludes that a person in Rick Watkinson's situation, somebody who is unhappy with his family situation, desperate to get out of a controlled environment where he's got his father and his step-mother who expect more of him than he is willing to deliver. The easiest solution to his problem would have been to disclose that he was being abused. Certainly would have mentioned it in some fashion, the Court concludes, in some manner for his mother, who he did care about allegedly, and the Court had no reason to disprove or disagree with that. I…the Court finds that Mr. Watkinson has fond feelings for his mother and they allegedly have a close relationship, so I…the Court has no choice but to conclude that, he would have discussed this with his mother at some point. Maybe not in detail, but would have disclosed it, and the fact that he didn't, again confirms to the Court that it wasn't happening."

"Finally…is the statement to Sgt. Marrs, in which Sgt. Marrs was interviewing him the morning of the murders. The conversation was polite, calm. Sgt. Marrs was asking him a series of questions in which Mr. Watkinson, the Defendant was polite, calm, answered the questions, never seemed to be confused about what was being asked, and the question was asked was…because I think what the record clearly reflects from the video tape and from the transcript of that video tape, is that Sgt. Marrs is absolutely baffled about what's happened, and is looking for something that would justify what had happened…and there was inquiry of sexual abuse, because certainly a reasonable suspicion for an experienced police officer would be, were you being sexually abused by your father? Were you being sexually abused by your step-mother? Maybe that would justify what's gone on here…and the answer was 'No'. Were you being abused? You know, were you being beat-up…were the thrust of the questions there…however they were articulated specifically but, the inquiry was…Are you being abused? And his answer was 'No'."

"So there were opportunities in which…if Rick Watkinson was a victim over a period of time of consistent abuse, that there would be some confirmation of that, a more solid fashion, and there was at trial…the testimony, the primary source of information for the Court and the jury to consider in terms of him being abused were his statements that he was being abused. There was…as Mr. Tetlow noticed…noted to the Court, there was other testimony, there was testimony from Mr. Watkinson's friend that she hugged him and he had bruises that was a result of his father, and the Court doesn't disregard that…and the Court is not including that…that the Defendant and his father had a perfect loving relationship. But there is a difference between having problems with your father, and at times even ya know, getting into a physical altercation, which the Court has no basis to conclude it never happened but…the Court does not see sufficient evidence to corroborate the Defendant's statements that there was a pattern of physical abuse."

"Regarding the emotional abuse, I think that, and this is where I think youth plays a role, is that I think Mr. Watkinson, or the Defendant Rick Watkinson, did feel he was being abused by his step-mother and by his father, I think that that Defendant also felt he was being emotionally abused by his mother and his step-father. He thought he was being emotionally abused because they wanted him to go to school, and they wanted him to get good grades, and they wanted him to act in a certain fashion. And I think that the record reflects, that he did not consider that to be necessary from his standpoint."

"So there was a reference to Rosemary Watkinson calling him a name, the Court recalls seeing a videotape, in which, my vague recollection is she referred to him as 'asshole', she was sitting in the living room videotaping Rick at the time. They were engaged in a conversation which the Court viewed…she was friendly…jokingly referred to him in that manner. I don't think it was intended to be a literal statement that was not said in harsh tones, so I certainly, the Court does not seize on that particular statement as evidence that she was verbally abusive to him. The Court, on the other hand, would not conclude that she had never used harsh language at him, that his father may have used harsh language at him."

"On the other hand, the record I think is clear from the Defendant's statement, certainly the statement that was given to Dr. Wieger and there are statements that the Defendant routinely engaged in harsh language, routinely called Rosemary a 'bitch', routinely referred to her in other derogatory terms, and called her names in front of his father. So, certainly the Court would not be surprised by the fact…the Court would conclude that probably there was some harsh words transferred back and forth between Rosemary and the Defendant, the Defendant and his father…not surprising at all under the circumstances. But does it give rise to a situation where the Court concludes that the Defendant was emotionally abused to the point where it would somehow justify an act of violence against his father or step-mother…and the Court cannot reach that conclusion."

"What did happen? The Court finds that, for the record, that the Defendant's parents divorced when he was approximately ten years old. And the Defendant quite clearly seizes upon this moment as the turning point, the pivotal point in his life. And certainly the Court would also note that divorce in this day and age is extremely common. Fifty per cent of marriages, first marriages, end in divorce. So, the idea that a defendant can be so emotionally distraught by divorce that that sets in course all these other things is not particularly persuasive in light of the fact that there are literally millions and millions of people functioning in our society, who have grown up with parents who have gotten divorced, either they have grown up with one parent and the other parent has never seen them. Certainly many people are raised by no parents, they are raised by grandparents, aunts and uncles. There are many people who are raised by a father or mother who may have been married and divorced four or five or even six or seven times."

"So, the Defendant was ten years old when his parents got divorced, the Court recognizes that that would have had a significant impact on him as it would any other young man or woman at the time. To say that the Defendant had a quality of life and was a straight arrow and so forth, up to the age of ten, the Court is not surprised by that. Most people do not have a pattern of juvenile crime prior to the age of ten. But what the Court does reflect is that in the years following that, the Defendant had problems that many young men do, nothing too serious, but at the age of thirteen or fourteen, engaged in a pattern of behaviour around the house, even though it may not have been such that it would draw the attention of law enforcement authorities or resulted in his arrest or anything serious at the age of thirteen or fourteen. He is engaging in a pattern of conduct around his mother's home, who has since remarried and he has a step-father, engaging in a pattern of conduct which is so serious that his mother, who the Court concludes loves him dearly, tells him to hit the road. If you can't live by our rules, leave. And he left."

"So he lives out on the streets, in Oregon for a couple of weeks, and apparently seemed to think that was perfectly acceptable. His mother apparently felt there was no other option but to let him live on the streets, and it wasn't until the Defendant's father called, and asked where he was that it was disclosed he was on the streets. At that point, Mr. Watkinson and his new wife had a couple of options. One, is they could say, that's too bad, and they could have stayed in Alaska and I suppose let the mother deal with it, and let Rick continue to live on the streets. Or, they had a variety of options but the option they took, which is the one that I think any reasonable parent would do, and that is, he jumped on the first airplane, flew down to Oregon, told the mother Rick is coming home with me. Which, she did not object to. She understood that the options were few and that he was not susceptible to control by her, and therefore, it would be in everybody's best interests for the Defendant to return to Alaska with his father. The Defendant didn't want that, the Defendant was resistant to the idea of having to leave home and…not that he was living at home, but leave the home turf, apparently he was happy living on the streets at that time.

"So we have a situation which is ripe for problems, the Defendant, who is fourteen or fifteen years old, has been taken to a state that he has never lived in, put in an environment which is different that he is used to. He is now living with his father who travels a lot and a step-mother who is full-time at home, not working for a period of time. And it's a different environment, it's an environment which is much more controlling, much more demanding, the standards are different, the rules are different. There's no more running around probably at night and staying out late, and probably the environment was much stricter. And school was mandatory. Attend school, get good grades. I think that the Defendant recognized he was capable of getting straight A's if he wanted to, and I think as any responsible parent in that situation would do, they expected good grades out of him."

"So these were the new rules that were set down and there was resistance to these rules. What appears is over a period of time that Mr. Watkinson, the Defendant, was resistant to being told what to do and felt restricted by the rules and regulations set forth by his father and step-mother. So it is certainly no surprise that the Defendant had a difficult relationship with Rosemary, many teenagers in his position would have a difficult relationship. Many step-mothers would have a difficult relationship dealing with Rick Watkinson. There was testimony that she was reluctant to have him come to Alaska, the Court does not find that to be at all troublesome. The idea that she was going to invite this young man into her household with open arms, and be absolutely delighted about it is probably asking too much, so it's not surprising that she took him in with the understanding that she would expect him to follow certain rules of the household. The Defendant was resistant to that. The father and the step-mother had a difficult time dealing with Rick Watkinson."

"There were events such as stealing the car, that stand out in the Courts' mind, this is the one time where he did seek outside assistance, the one time he went to Covenant House that the Court knows of, was precipitated by him stealing or taking the parent's car, driving around with a bunch of friends and coming home and being caught. And then, rather than even dealing with his father or step-mother, left home and was hanging out with friends for a couple days before he was finally taken to Covenant House."

"The Court would not be surprised if Mr. Watkinson and Rosemary Watkinson were distressed about the fact that he did these things, the Court's not the least bit surprised that the father and step-mother were distressed about the fact that the Defendant, despite the fact that he was capable of being an 'A' student, and despite the fact that he is capable of writing like he does that this Court has seen…fully capable of doing very well in school, skipped school and was disinterested in school and was not engaged in performing up to his capacity. I think that any reasonable parent would feel the same frustration that they did. The precipitating event which occurred shortly before the murders were that the Defendant skipped school and his father went down to the school and got him because he was irate."

"They went up, back up to the house, and they had a confrontation, and the Court does not find this to be too surprising under the circumstances. I'm sure that they have had many, many conversations about school, grades, the consequences of skipping school. I'm sure that father made the threat that he probably made many times before which was…I'm going to take away the thing you want and that is if you want to go to ROTC, you're not going to get to go unless you go to school and you get good grades. And so that night, there was the discussion back and forth again. The Court's not a bit surprised by the discussion that took place, and that is between Mr. Watkinson and Rick, and Mr. Watkinson and Rosemary."

"The discussion was, what was he going to do, and the further discussion was, who was going to discipline the Defendant, who was going to discipline Rick Watkinson? And if the Defendant's version is correct it was Rosemary's view was that she should have the right to discipline, and Robert's view was that she shouldn't. And they had a disagreement about that. And under the circumstances of this situation, the fact that they would have a disagreement about that, and the fact that they would have a disagreement about that, and the fact that they would argue about that is not totally surprising. Rosemary Watkinson was primarily in charge of Rick because his father traveled so much, and it would be reasonable that she would want to have some say over what happened in the household when he was gone."

"So we have this confrontation that night and emotions are running high, they have dinner, Rick goes downstairs and lays in bed and listens to his father and step-mother argue. As he lays there, a fit of rage wells up inside him, and he decides to take some action, and the action is that he decides he will kill his father and kill his step-mother. So he gets the gun, gets the ammunition, he lays in bed and thinks about what he's going to do. And then he writes a note in which he discloses what the plan is, and he plans to get the gun, kill his parents, and then be on his own, be free of this parental authority over him. So he sets forth his plan in writing, sets the alarm for one o'clock so he knows they'll be asleep, and he waits. He waits until he thinks his parents have gone to sleep. So then once he's satisfied that the time is right, he gets his gun, it's loaded, he walks upstairs, he opens the door, he looks inside and he's seen by Rosemary. This is his version."

"So this is the version that is told to us by the only witness to the crime. He opens the door and shoots his father. He then…chaos breaks out…and the father and the step-mother flee to the bathroom for protection. He then fires after shooting twice at his father, he fires through the door until he runs out of ammunition. He then goes back downstairs, two flight, reloads, walks back upstairs, and finds his father calling 911. He then, coming up the stairs, focuses on his father's head with the specific intent to shoot his father in the head, to kill him, and he fires. He then goes upstairs and finds Rosemary Watkinson in the bathtub, whimpering…shoots her in the head. He then gets his father's wallet off the nightstand, and departs the scene knowing that 911 has been contacted and the authorities are on their way."

"He walks around for several hours, contemplating why and what he's done, and then at about six o'clock in the morning, he goes to a friend's house because he feels bad about what happened with this girlfriend of his and I don't mean that in a romantic sense, but a woman friend of his, and they've had a falling out. And he feels bad about that, and he wants to set the record straight with her. So within hours after murdering his father and step-mother, he goes over to his girl's house, and he walks in and they have breakfast. And nobody at the breakfast table senses there's anything wrong, he's upset because, as he says he's been thrown out of his house but surely nobody suspects that the Defendant is acting is a clue as to what may have occurred. He then gets a ride to school with the girl's brother and goes to school and according to his statement to Sgt. Marrs."

"Police come to the scene and arrest him. He gives a statement to the police, lengthy video-tape that the Court has viewed several times, I've read the transcripts several times. And the conversation is calm, collected, no real emotion, and if you turn down the sound or turn off the sound so you can't hear what's being discussed, you would get the impression that Sgt. Marrs and Rick

Watkinson are talking about some event like school or sports or something else. There is no apparent emotion in the discourse between the two of them. No suggestion by the way he conducted himself that there was much concern on his part about what happened. I think the way that the Court interviews what Sgt. Marrs said at one point, or at the end of the interview was telling and that is that he said he couldn't figure out what there was…I don't remember the exact words of what it is you're doing here, what it is that's gone on because I think that the explanation of what had occurred and the way it occurred and his description of it, and the tone of voice that he used, was what, the Court can only say completely baffling to an extremely experienced homicide detective for the State of Alaska."

"The Court concludes that based on this, that the murder of Mr. Watkinson and Rosemary Watkinson was planned, thoughtful, deliberate, so the question is, if the Court is not persuaded it was a result of abuse, what was the precipitating factor? And there may not be a clear explanation for that. But the Defendant himself in talking to Sgt. Marrs that morning gives some clues as to what he was thinking at that time, whether or not this is credible or not, we don't know. This is the question that was asked by Sgt. Marrs, okay, how do you feel about your dad? I mean thinking back now, how did you feel about him before you shot him, and how do you feel about him now? And Rick said, 'I've always hated him'. Why? Why do you think that is? Because he divorced my mom and destroyed our family."

"And he goes on at a later point, what was so important that you…what was so important that you had to kill him? I mean was there…? Rick says, 'I was just sick of their fighting, I didn't want to listen to it anymore. I didn't want any parental guidance over me anymore'. Okay this is Sgt. Marrs talking…. 'Okay, do you feel pretty strongly about that?' Answer. 'Yes'. So if you take the Defendant's statement to the police literally… What was the cause of the murders? It was he hated his father, and always had since the divorce. That he didn't want any parental guidance, that there was a rage in him that frankly this Court does not understand. The notion that any rational, logical explanation would justify a child shooting their father. There is none."

"There is certainly no rational reason for the murder of Rosemary. In this Court's view, she was murdered because she was there. The Court concludes that killing a parent under these circumstances, although there may be circumstances which would justify a child in some circumstances doing something like this. These are, I'm sure, many situations in which a child may act out, in fact, the Court has seen them, under appropriate circumstances, but what the Court see here is the killing of parents under circumstances which are inexplicable, and make no sense. The…so that is the background."

"The Court would turn to the Chaney criteria. Community condemnation, we see that in fashioning a sentence if the…if the Courts reasoning is adopted that is, that there was no valid justification for the murder of these two people, certainly the community would expect that a sentence would express the societal norms that would be that this kind of conduct is to be condemned without question. That, this is not a circumstance which has justification under the law and the Court will address the…that in just a moment. The deterrence of the Defendant and others, I…frankly, I agree with Mr. Tetlow on this…that the fashioning of the sentence for a Defendant that the…or somebody in this circumstance, frankly anybody that is able to do this is not going to be deterred by what this Court does probably."

"It's such a baffling, horrendous event or act that deterrence by what this Court does today may not have much impact, but certainly a message needs to be sent to any person that this kind of conduct will be penalized harshly. Isolation. The Court rarely imposes a sentence to isolate a Defendant, but the legislature mandates it in this circumstance. The…without anything else, first degree murder mandates that a defendant is isolated for an extended period of time, and the Court in this situation would conclude that the Defendant needs to be isolated because there is no plausible explanation for what happened here, and that in so many other ways, I think that is so disturbing to so many about this case is that Mr. Watkinson in so many ways…looks, talks, acts…absolutely normal. And there is something going on with him which is not explainable and the Court considers him to be extremely dangerous."

"Rehabilitation, this Court is going to impose a sentence which does not place rehabilitation at the top, simply because the other considerations mandate in this Court's view a sentence which is so lengthy that, assuming your attorney is correct that rehabilitation does not occur in prison, that rehabilitation drops to the bottom of the list here, or near the bottom of the list of Chaney criteria because…you'll be incarcerated so long that it's not a realistic goal in the interim. The high end for a mature adult committing this crime, the Court believes would be justified to sentence a defendant near the ninety-nine-year range."

"In other words, if Mr. Watkinson was an adult, a mature adult, the conduct which he engaged in here is so severe and serious by its act alone that the Court would feel justified in giving a ninety-nine-year sentence. But as I indicated before, the Court does consider it appropriate to sentence the Defendant in view of his age, so the Court would not impose the same sentence it would if he was a mature adult. The Court concludes that I think there is ample evidence that much of the thought process that the Defendant gave to this, or some of it certainly is the result of his youth."

"And in this Court's view what Mr. Watkinson, the Defendant said, taken in context with what his experts said constituted any evidence. It was…there was some evidence. And that's the purpose of the jury instruction. The…the jury considered the evidence and concluded that there was no basis to conclude that…to find that the Defendant acted in heat of passion. In fact, the jury's verdict was, and the Court has no reason to second guess that decision. The jury's verdict is that the State proved beyond a reasonable doubt that the Defendant did not act in heat of passion."

"So, it wasn't kind of a situation where there was kind of a close call about heat of passion. And as I articulated earlier, it was the Court's conclusion that the Defendant was, in order to be convicted of first degree murder, it need not be premeditated or well and carefully planned out. It only needs to be intentional. The Court finds here that it was not only intentional but premeditated. So the question is how should the Court fashion in the youth of the Defendant. And the Court has frankly considered that issue very seriously in trying to determine what a just sentence is. I have sentenced other Defendants for first degree murder that were young and I have reduced from the zone of the norm for youth, and I would be consistent in this situation."

"Based on all the findings that have been previously discussed, the Court sentences the Defendant on Count I to eighty years, on Count II, the defendant would be sentenced eighty years. The question now is whether or not any part of that should be concurrent or consecutive…. The Court sets aside its own personal views of what a Defendant has done or not done and looks at guidelines from the court of appeals and legislature. But the Court makes findings, and this finding is based on the statements I've made and that is, this Court having thought a lot about what's happened, has struggled with the question of what may have been the cause, having rejected the idea that there was a pattern of abuse which would justify first degree murder here."

"And this Court is not a psychologist or a psychiatrist or mind reader, and so what the Court's left with is a record, and the record is that Rick Watkinson has a very calm, passive, placid exterior. And if one had met Rick Watkinson a week before this incident, for example, if somebody had come to their house and had dinner, or somebody had met him in school, or somebody had met him at ROTC, they would probably conclude that he was a fine young man, non-violent, pleasant, and see many good qualities in him. The Court would not be at all surprised, if an average person meeting Rick Watkinson at that time would have reached all those conclusions."

"But the events that occurred on the night in question that resulted in the deaths of these two people indicate to the Court that there is something else inside of Rick Watkinson, and there is a rage that is unexplainable, there is a view of the world which is unimaginable, as I've tried to articulate some of the high points of that. It's one thing completely unimaginable to kill your parents. It's another thing to do that and then go down and talk to your one of your friends to make up with them and have breakfast, and then go to school. And then to describe the events the way it was described on the videotape with Sgt. Marrs. It's extremely chilling stuff."

"And so the Court has no choice but to conclude based on the record as I've articulated it. There is something about Rick Watkinson that makes him unpredictable and extremely violent. And I find that he is a danger to the public. The Court recognizes that there are people that want Rick Watkinson to receive the maximum sentence and if the guidelines articulated by the Court justified that, the Court would impose the maximum penalty. But this Court is following the law as it understands it, and that's why neither the maximum nor the minimum is being imposed."

"Based on the Nelson case then, the total sentence would be one hundred and sixty years. I'm going to run eighty of that…take twenty from one of those, so it will be eighty plus twenty and sixty concurrent, so it will be a composite sentence of one hundred years to serve. And as I indicated the Court articulates that sentence and says the following, 'the sentencing judge is to impose appropriate term of incarceration on the assumption that the entire term may be served'. To conclude, the Court finds that imposing this sentence it recognizes that Rick Watkinson may serve one hundred years in prison."

"Mr. Watkinson, I'm going to advise you that you have the right to appeal my sentence to the higher courts if you think that I may have made a mistake in sentencing you. Of course, you may appeal any part of the trial if you think mistakes were made, and I would…you've got two confident counsel with you and I would review it with them about your rights to appeal. Is there anything else?"

"No, I thank you Judge," said Mr. Collins.

"No," answered Mr. Tetlow.

"All rise," said the Clerk. "The Court stands in recess."[51]

[51] Entire chapter excerpted from Sentencing documents and statements of Judge Eric Sanders.

CHAPTER FIFTY-ONE

That was it. One hundred years. One hundred years. One hundred years spent behind bars. Judge Sanders hadn't heard a word. Didn't give a shit. One hundred years. A nice round number. Easy to remember. Impossible to swallow. Rick would spend the rest of his life behind bars. Rehabilitation? According to Judge Sanders, there was no chance in hell that Rick ever becomes 'rehabilitated'. Society failed him because they deemed him not even worthy of the effort. That's the sad thing. To tell a person, a young person, that they just aren't worth it. It's what he's heard his whole life.

Once a monster, always a monster. A kid cannot kill his parents. It's unthinkable. It's unjustifiable. Never mind all the mitigating factors that went into creating that event. Never mind the number of times the child was beaten down, both physically and emotionally by the parent, the child must never retaliate against the parent.

"You must never go against me!" Bob would say.

"You must never speak to me that way!" Rosemary would say.

The child is at fault. He is a monster. He should have been able to control his emotions. They were just words. He should have been able to recognize that. There was never any abuse they all said. Nothing. Of course, none of this justifies what Rick did. He killed two people. Shot them in cold blood, and he'll be the first to admit that he should be punished. In fact, he's probably harder on himself, than anyone. He takes full blame for what happened, even when the full blame is not his to take. So many people let him down. So many people failed to see the signs. So many people failed to take that extra step, to protect him, to guide him, and to keep him safe.

Was Rick Watkinson born a killer? Did he have an innate propensity to kill? Absolutely not. No child does. There is always something, some sort of trigger, some sort of event that puts the wheels in motion. In Rick's case, the wheels didn't start with the divorce, they started much sooner. They started when his mother forced him to break into the neighbours' house to see if she was a witch. They started with the nightly indoctrination of God and the Devil. One or the other, black or white, no in between. The donning of the armour. Christ's Little Warrior. From an early age, Rick learnt that there were only two paths in life, God or Satan. No matter what, he had to conform. No choices, no leeway.

What is a ten-year-old supposed to think when his mother tells him that his Daddy left them because he was full of a demon, put there by Satan himself. Daddy becomes evil. We're against Daddy now. There's no grey. No in between. Loving Daddy and wanting a relationship with Daddy was against what God wanted. We hate Daddy. At all costs. Robert Watkinson was no angel, and certainly wasn't a model parent. He had severe anger and control issues, but he wasn't evil, and didn't deserve the literal demonization given to him by his ex-wife. He never stood a chance with his boys, especially Rick, God's 'Golden Child'.

The wheels just kept on rolling. One source of angst after another. Nothing was normal in this boys' childhood and adolescent years. Nothing. Running the streets at eleven-years-old. Seeing things he had no business seeing, experiencing things he had no business experiencing. One thing after another. Violence, death, destruction. No one to trust. No one to talk to, so he bottles everything up inside. Rick felt betrayed. It was the major source of his anger, and when the betrayals kept adding up, he couldn't deal with it, and he eventually snapped. But why did he always feel so betrayed? Simple. When you've grown up in such a strict moral environment, without learning any sort of flexibility of thought, anything against that thought, would be seen as a betrayal. If you're not with God, you're against God. If you're not with the family, then you're against the family. If you love her, then you cannot possibly love me.

Black and white, no give or take, no grey areas at all. All or nothing. It was Rick's mantra, and the way he lived his life, and maybe some of that came with his personality, such as his competitiveness, but most of it was learned behaviour.

"Anyone who isn't with me opposes me, and anyone who isn't working with me is actually working against me." Matthew 12:30.

Rick took this mantra and applied it to everything in his life, not necessarily in a Biblical sense every time, but in a literal sense. If you're not with me, then you're against me. That's why he was continuously waging war. He had to have someone to fight, someone to oppose. He didn't know how to live without it. He didn't know how to live in the in between, to find the grey areas, where flexible thought and reasoning lived. No one in his family did. Not Rick, not Bob, and certainly not Brenda. Bob needed Rick to conform to his way of thinking, but Rick had already conformed to his own way of thinking. Neither would give an inch. Neither would even attempt to stick a toe outside their own boxes of rational thinking, and it cost them. Black or white. One way or the other, it could never be both. Compromise was never an option.

But that didn't mean the love wasn't there. There is no question that Robert Watkinson loved his boys, especially Rick. And despite all his professions of hate, deep down inside Rick loved his father, adored him, and wanted to be just like him. If he didn't, then the betrayals wouldn't have hurt so much. All Rick ever wanted was for his father to love him and to accept him; and for him to be able to freely love and accept his father, without punishment or higher moral consequences. It seemed so simple. Just love each other. Have a little give and take. But nothing was ever simple with The Watkinson's.

Life is a complicated road of intricate twists and turns, and sometimes when things go wrong, there's no way of righting the wheels before they spin wickedly out of control, destroying anyone and anything in their path. It didn't have to be this way. Nobody had to die. Nobody had to go to jail. If only someone had stepped up, been an adult, and not let the kid drive the fucking car on his own since he was ten-years-old. Rick will take full blame for what happened, but he shouldn't. As a society, this one is on all of us.

THE FINAL LETTER

The content for "Ghost" was received through a series of approximately 90+ handwritten letters Rick Watkinson wrote from his prison cell over the course of almost three years. The letters covered the periods of his "pre-murder" and "post-murder" life up until the trial and sentencing. This is an excerpt from Letter 78 of the "pre-murder" series. In his own words…

"What did happen?" These were the words Judge Sanders would begin his closing remarks with on July 1st, 1997. He would go on to conclude that my crime was "chilling", that I was "extremely dangerous", and that there "was a rage in him that frankly this Court does not understand." And how could he? How could he have known about any of the sources of my rage, affliction, and sorrow. The only person who had even spoke of any of this was Dr. Smith who had spent a total of two and half days "evaluating" me as a psychiatric expert.

Was the name Ghost even uttered a single time during the trial? How could Sanders even begin to know any of the details of my life or what would cause me to explode. I was silent, too much of a basket-case to take the stand. My mother was silent, there was no testimony or admissions about "demons" or what she had mentally and spiritually put me through. Jackie was silent, Andrew was silent, Creek was silent – their names forgotten, remaining veiled beyond the grave. No one could or would speak up, certainly not me. I was wracked with guilt for taking two lives and believed I deserved death. The very last thing I was going to do was drag everybody else with me.

There were only really two legal conclusions for Sanders, or any judge for that matter, to make. Either the fault of the crime laid with "situational" factors, or it laid solely with the individual. Either, I was an abused and broken child who had simply been put through too much, or, I was a cold, juvenile psychopath who murdered his parents in cold blood. The final reality was that both statements bear truth. I was both. Sanders acknowledged that there was "some evidence" of physical abuse (a legal conclusion), which was why he gave the jury a "heat of passion" instruction. He also later fully concluded that there wasn't a pattern of abuse, and even continued to acknowledge the "physical altercations" my father and I probably had. The bitch of it all was that I fully agreed with him. To my attorneys, friends, family, and loved ones, I called our fights "altercations" and refused to call them "abuse". But was I a product of situational factors that resulted in my being capable of committing the crime? Of course.

My entire life had been the culmination of suffering and strife that led to that single night. I had been "trained" in spiritual warfare and given a very black and white, good vs. evil, God vs. Satan worldview. I had been taught from as early as I can remember that the world and our very souls were a "warzone" and that to survive, I had to learn how to fight. My mind was then subjected to paranormal experiences, and a realm full of spirits, angels, demons, and unspeakable terrors, experiences that would destroy even most adult minds. I don't give a fuck what anyone says, you cannot see or go through the shit I did even as early as age 11, and remain unscathed. The knowledge and burden of knowing what's out there will scar you for life.

Then I was subjected to a series of deaths of friends and loved ones. Many people go their whole lives without losing someone violently or suddenly. I watched three lives be extinguished in a matter of two years. You can't imagine, unless you've been there, how that changes your world view. And through it all, I was dead inside, a Ghost, and the more betrayal and death I encountered, the more hatred, apathy and affliction I took on, burdening my soul, turning it from gold into the drossest lead. And let's speak of betrayal, of the disconnect with society and existence that developed over time.

It had started with the divorce and my father's "betrayal" of our family, of me. I was too young to see it or understand it any other way. These days, I don't fault my father one bit for wanting to get away from my delusional mother and move on to find a happy life. There's no way in hell I was comprehending that at age 10, especially with the spite and "spiritual twist" my mother had put on the whole thing. No one could talk me into believing anything other than the fact that my father had "betrayed us", destroyed my family, killed me inside, was possessed by the Devil, and was nothing more than a selfish bastard. No one could talk me out of my hatred for him.

Then came my betrayal by God. I hadn't asked or enlisted in fighting the war. I had been told I had to fight. Yet, I was forced to choose one side or another. Either I was "with Him" or the same Devil that stole my father was creeping into my own heart. And I certainly didn't ask for the "gift" of the Eyes of the Spirit or how my Christian comrades chose to use that sight. If it had been something I could pluck out and cast away from my own being, I would have. So when I was baptized and specifically asked God to take it away, and He refused, of course I felt damned, forsaken, and lost. It was the ultimate form of tyranny over my entire life – when the Creator, the 'God of Love', denies you and forces you to suffer even when it's eating you alive.

Shortly after that, maybe within a year, I realized that my mother and the entire body of Christianity had betrayed me. They were delusional liars who simply used His "flock" for their agenda, and had no clue what it was they were even talking about. I had been raised in nothing but lies, and now my father, my mother, and every preacher and dogma I had listened to amounted to shit. By the time I was 13, I felt such a disconnect from the world and everything I had known, that I was already completely lost and alone. I believed, and rightly so, that no one would ever understand me, and that I was doomed to suffer alone. So I did the only thing I knew how. I went to war and drug my friends with me. For two long years, I fought the "Angel of Death" until Death itself came and took one of my friends' lives. Regardless of how violent and fucked up it was; I was doing it. I was surviving and making it by.

Then came the next betrayal, when my mother sold me out to my father, tricked me into coming home, and my life in Alaska began. Taking me up to Alaska had its desired effect, it removed me from the volatile environment I was dwelling in, and gave me a fresh start. It also robbed me of my ability to do the one thing I really knew how to do – wage war. So I waged war on the man who had started it all, my father. For thirteen months, we battled for control over my life, which manifested in altercations about grades, school, my future, conduct, appearance, and shit in general, I could not have given a fuck about.

But in that thirteen months, I had also found a new family, fallen in love, and had been given the opportunity to get a head start on my true calling in life, to be a soldier. Those kids, my friends, that Unit, Drill, the Drill Team, the Four Horseman, the uniform, my future in the Navy, that had become my life, and the people I was in it with were my family. I would have fought for them as hard as I had against any demon or drug-dealer. So when my father picked me up the day of November 30th, 1995, and told me that I had to leave them behind, that in itself was a betrayal. "I'm pulling you from the program", were his words. I explained to him during the car ride home that ROTC was my life and that I couldn't abandon my Unit and my friends, my "family", and my pleas fell on deaf ears.

As a general tool of punishment, he took from me whatever I loved and wanted the most. The absolute thing that would hurt me the absolute most was to take me away from ROTC, and he was at his wit's end, he obviously had felt there was no other choice. I was a warrior, and fiercely defensive over those I saw as "mine". I would fight him tooth and nail just for trying to take me away from the one's I saw as my real family. It's not something I would have killed him over, I still had other alternatives. So why did I?

Probably the most critical point of the entire story and case, and undeniably the least understood, was that the murders had nothing to do with power and control over my life. Sanders made it apparent that he believed I murdered my father and my step-mother to take/remove their "parental control" over my life. It was the thrust of the State's entire argument. Yet, my father had given me full control that night when he put me out on my own. The arguments over ROTC that day were devastating to me, and turned my world upon its head, but it was really no different or no more cataclysmic than the hundreds of arguments we had previously.

As I wrote in the originals (both the 34-page Statement and my original letter to you), at least 70% of the arguing that night took place between my father and Rosemary. Parental control, discipline, their marriage, me…to the point that they were slamming doors and cupboards, breaking things, and at one point even getting physical with each other. Then, around 9 that night, as documented in the case, my father came downstairs and told me to get out, I had to leave. I was ruining his marriage and his life with Rosemary and I had to go. "I need you to get out. I need you to leave, you're destroying my marriage". I remember sitting up looking at him and asking, "Well, can I at least get a plane ticket back down to Oregon?" His reply completely blew my mind. "No, just get your things and be gone in the morning." The next time I saw my father I was aiming a rifle at him as he scrambled to get out of bed, shooting him twice before he and Rosemary fled to the bathroom.

But why? Hadn't he just given me what I always wanted? If I wanted complete control over my life, he had just given it to me. No more parents. Kicking me out meant that I was completely, 100% free. My mother didn't have a chance in hell at controlling me, and in that single sentence, "I need you to leave", my father had given up and relinquished his hold on my life. That event was in fact mentioned in Court, even on the day of my sentencing, but its implications were never discussed, not even by Wally and Randall. If my father had just relinquished all control of my life and thrown me out of the house, then why did I need to kill him for parental control?

The very presence of this question abolishes the State's entire argument and most people's conclusions regarding the "why" of my case. I could have left that night. Being on the streets to me wasn't a bad thing, in fact it was where I felt most at home and meant "freedom". I had a million possibilities and options at that point, so why didn't I take them? I could have called Amy, called my mother, or any of my friends down in Oregon. I could have easily packed my shit, grabbed my cigarettes and my vodka and hoofed it down to any one of my friends' houses that night, including Nat's or Kristy's. Shit, I could have broken into the school that night and slept there. When everything was said and done, I probably would have been taken in by Top or Gunner or any one of the numerous families of friends from my Unit. Why didn't I? This was exactly the freedom and sovereignty I had desired over my own life since I was about 12. And that night I had it. I could have gone, done, and been anything I wanted. Instead, I picked up a rifle, went upstairs, and didn't leave the house until my father and stepmother were dead. WHY? One word. Betrayal.

In my young, warped and afflicted mind, my father hadn't given me my freedom, he had betrayed me all over again. He chose someone and something else over me, all over again, just as he had done six years prior. He betrayed his son's love for his own selfish gain – again. But it went even deeper than that. In effect, by throwing in the towel and kicking me out, he also had given up on me, and that was simply too hard for a son's heart to bear. You see, he had set me on a road those six years ago, he had <u>made</u> Ghost. Without the divorce, Ghost would have never become. I would have never been left to my mother's designs and driven to the extent of her spiritual warfare. There would have never been a Jackie, an Andrew or a Creek. There never would have been the death, loss, misery or subsequent betrayals I had suffered. I would never have found my family, the Unit, or had my heart broken by Kristy. None of it.

That single decision he made six years' prior had committed my life to a certain course and path, and in giving up on me, he said, "So what? Who cares about the pain and suffering I have caused you? The path and series of events my decision placed before you? Who cares about the death, loss, and affliction you have endured? I cast you away from me because my life and desires are more important than yours". In the end, the six years that would have been immeasurably different <u>had he not left</u> didn't matter two shits to him. In the end, he simply threw me away. That is why he died that night. That is why, in my subconscious mind, I <u>had</u> to kill him and all he loved. It was like he told me that Jackie, Andrew, and Creek's lives hadn't mattered. Like the demons, the pact, what I could see, and what I had to live with didn't matter. Like the six years worth of hating him because he broke my heart, and I had loved him so much – didn't matter.

So I snapped, lost it, even Ghost couldn't save me, and I killed him and his wife. The "why" should be as tangible as humanly possible to you now, as should the irony, contradictions and truth. I don't believe I need to rehash the details of that night or how incredibly out of my mind I was. The live rounds ejected around the house, the fact that I hadn't waited, planned or executed the crime as I should have – the details speak for themselves. I was not in any manner of cognizant control. Believe me, had I been, things could have been much worse, methodical, efficient, accomplished. When the sub/unconscious mind takes over, when emotion, raw and unbridled, assumes control, it is a phenomenal force of nature that cannot be stopped, only extinguished.

I had front row seats that night, above and behind my body. To this day, there are very few details or images I can recall in "first person" clarity. I watched myself murder my own father and step-mother, powerless to stop the madness, and the event is so far beyond recall, I don't even dream of it. As if the memories belong to the subconscious self, beyond a wall or a veil I cannot pierce, and even my subconscious mind won't allow me to access. The truth is this; I was most certainly afflicted beyond what any human mind should have to endure, but I was also very chilling, extremely dangerous, and full of an indescribable rage.

The only remaining relevant question is that of "blame". Who's to blame? Was it my father? My mother? God? Oblivious counselors? Preachers? My friends? Or did it all fall on me? The truth is, it was all of us. My mother and father were two very stupid people with some serious issues. My mother was weak and delusional, Christ was her crutch, God was her answer for everything, and as most religious fanatics, she was blind, and felt she was "right" every step of the way. My father in fact was a selfish person, stubborn and temperamental, and an absolutely crappy parent. He honestly believed that being a parent gave him the divine right to tell his children what to do. That they "belonged" to him. That he never had to get to know them, understand them, or treat them like people. Combined, they took their own petty differences and completely botched a relatively "normal" thing like a divorce. My father turned it into a competition for our possession, and my mother into a win for Satan in His war against us. The result was two very distraught children that were <u>both</u> sent into a tailspin. But Sanders was right, divorces are relatively common, so who else was there to blame?

I won't even waste my time railing against all the "holy men" and preachers who filled my mind with garbage. There were plenty of teachers, school counselors, parents of friends, and even a psychologist (Dr. Wieger) who missed the mark and should have seen the writing on the wall. Even my friends, especially the ones I was close to. How could you stomach having this awesome "Refuge" in your life, who solves all of your problems, yet you don't reach out and make sure you save <u>him</u>? Would I have let them? Most certainly not. My suffering was mine alone, and no one got to share in that burden.

Was Rosemary to blame? Of course. You can't marry a man and pretend that his past baggage doesn't matter, like he doesn't have sons that should not be neglected. For them to even make a deal where "no previous children from previous marriages" were allowed into their lives was just plain dumb. It was easy for her, her children were both grown. To demand that out of a father who truly loved his sons was wrong. Her snide, disrespectful treatment of me didn't help, and she made sure she dumped plenty of fuel on the fire of our household strife. But while everyone shared some blame and played their part, was it all worth the cost of two lives? Did two people really deserve to die that night? Of course not. There's a finality to death that transcends all conceptions of "right" or "wrong" or what anyone may "feel". So that leaves me. The one who pulled the trigger.

Over the years, even now, various people have argued over the "weight" of blame and how much should be assigned to others versus myself. We could argue this until we were blue in the face, and <u>everyone</u> will have a different opinion and point of view. Did my parents fail me? Did God and the Church? Did the school system? The court system? In the end, "blame" and pointing fingers matters not one bit. Even the excuse of my youth is superfluous to the reality of the crime. The only thing that matters is those things which can't be done without consequence. You can't abandon your wife and kids without expecting some hard feelings. You can't tell yourself as a ten-year-old that you're "dead inside" and shut off all your emotions for the next ten years. You can't brainwash your son into believing there's only two alternatives – God or the Devil – in everything he does. You can't. You can't. You can't. Ad nauseam. You can't do these things and not expect there to be repercussions, consequences that would eventually accumulate and end in disaster.

Even understanding all of this, no one can take away from me the shouldering of all the blame. Until you have taken a life and know how that feels, there's no way to understand the guilt, shame, and blame involved. What happened shouldn't have, it wasn't necessary, and it is irreversible. I understand fully why I did the things I did, my reasons for the decisions I made, and the paths I took. And because I have a perfect understanding of my own mistakes and errors, it will always be my fault. The biggest problem, mistake or flaw was that I refused to let anybody in. That disconnect that had formed over religion, and only deepened as the years went by, literally became that internal fortress of black ice from which none could enter, and none could leave.

Out of survival, I had forged my own psycho-spiritual prison – within myself – and banished anyone and everyone from ever gaining entrance. That prison, the failure and absolute refusal to let anyone in, or even share my suffering and torment, that was the single greatest contributing factor that led up to the night of the murders. I had no choice and knew no other way. I was trapped. No one was going to understand the demons, the moment Jackie died in my arms, watching Andrew lay there cradled in tubes and wires, watching my brothers' brains splatter on the side of a moving truck. The death, betrayal, terror and sorrow. I was wrapped in leaden chains, sinking to the bottom of Samsara, and couldn't cry out for help. I didn't even know how. I couldn't even begin to describe or understand all of this as a 16-year-old boy, let alone stop it.

Even after it happened, I couldn't explain it to attorneys, counselors or psychologists. Not even to save my life. Can I fault Sanders for his conclusion? Only partially. Someone should have been able to make two plus two equal four, and see that killing my parents for control over my life made no sense, not in the same night that I was given that very control. But no one twenty years ago had all the information in front of them, and I either couldn't or wouldn't remedy this deficiency.

A huge part of my silence was wanting to protect my own mother – for I still fiercely loved her and shielded her then. Yet, her own silence in all of this has been deafening. Why would you fail to mention to his attorneys or the Court that you trained your own son to see, hunt, and wage war against demons? Why would you neglect to mention all the hatred and bitterness you <u>well know</u> that you instilled in your son against his father? How you made the divorce a spiritual battle instead of simply a marital one? At one point, my attorneys even told me in private that they wanted to explore how much my mother may have projected her own anger on to me and "programmed you to kill your father". I went ballistic. I refused to even entertain that line of defence and threatened to throw the case over it, <u>even though it was not so far from (part of) the truth</u>. Yet through it all, she remained silent, scared of how it would make her look, of being attacked and made to feel an inkling of responsibility.

Three years ago, when I told her of the book, she again expressed this fear. "I'm worried about how the world will see me? What if my friends from church or those who know me read it?" A better question. Why would a mother have anything to fear if she didn't know that she bore some of the responsibility? Even more damning, what mother would allow her son to do two life sentences in prison and be the sacrificial lamb merely for the sake of her precious reputation? What's strange is that I bear my mother no malice, she is old, and I wish her naught but a happy end to her life. But I would be lying if I didn't say that her delusional weakness didn't disgust me.

Yet, the greatest irony of all is this; I spent six years of my life voluntarily imprisoning myself in the name of survival, and the result was my physical imprisonment for most of the rest of my natural life. I sit here, twenty years later, writing these letters as an act of purification, in hopes that in releasing Ghost, in giving the world a tour of my black ice fortress, that somehow, someway, I will be partially freed of my burden in this life. That through understanding, through dispelling some of the ignorance, the world will become less prone to repeating the same mistakes. A feeble hope I know.

We are fairly stupid creatures who are far too often trapped in our own subjective understanding, and our collective ignorance will rise and fall, and rise again. We think we know, and understand, "got it figured out", when really we don't know shit. We continue on in our lives with our self-righteous, selfish agendas, and are silly enough to believe that our conceptions of "right and wrong" matter to the rest of the universe. Is it "right" that I spend the rest of my life in prison? I've always felt I've deserved far worse, but who the fuck am I to judge? I asked for the death penalty, and instead spend my days in these petty places with some of the most disgusting creatures mankind could contrive.

My one solace is that in breath there is potentiality, and I have proven to myself that I have the capability of transmuting the darkness into light. I make people happy, heal the sick, help the "blind" to "see", and in general, help my loved ones make their lives a better place. There are not many I find worthy of caring for, but even among the "lost", I attempt to show them the path of self-evolution and enlightenment. For regardless of what I or anyone else may think I'm deserving of, that is all I have left, to evolve – to fulfill that final and most solemn promise I made twenty years before, that when I die, I will be able to look into my father's eyes, and see not sorrow, anger, or regret – but to see love, and most importantly pride.

In loving memory of Robert George and Rosemary Jo Watkinson
~Rick Watkinson ~

ABOUT THE AUTHOR

Trish Faber was born in Markham Ontario, Canada, the youngest of five children. She began to write at the age of five, using her family as characters in her first epic novel, "The Rabbit Family". Although never formally published, the single, handwritten, and self-illustrated copy of "The Rabbit Family" did make appearances at the local school, grocery store, bowling alley and bridge club meetings, courtesy of an enthusiastic mother and her large purse.

Trish is grateful to her family for allowing her to develop her imagination and creative flair without ever passing judgment. She realizes that at times this must have been difficult. Trish holds an Honours Degree in English and History from the University of Western Ontario, and a life degree in the trials and tribulations of being a restaurant owner, an academic tutor and life skills coach, as well as a business owner. She likes music, sports, tomato soup, and has secret aspirations of one day becoming a rock star. Most of all, she loves spending quality time with her friends and family.

TITLES
"Songs About Life" (1st Edition 2006, 2nd Edition 2016)
"I Was, I Am, I Will Be" (2010)
"Pierre's Story" (2013)
"Ghost – The Rick Watkinson Story" (2016)

Connect with Trish Online:
Website: www.trishfaber.com
Facebook: www.facebook.com/pages/Trish-Faber-Writer
Twitter: @trishfaber
Wonder Voice Press: www.wondervoicepress.com

www.ingramcontent.com/pod-product-compliance
Lightning Source LLC
Chambersburg PA
CBHW061043110426
42740CB00049B/1268